^{the}Un... Guide® to Skiing in the West

3rd Edition

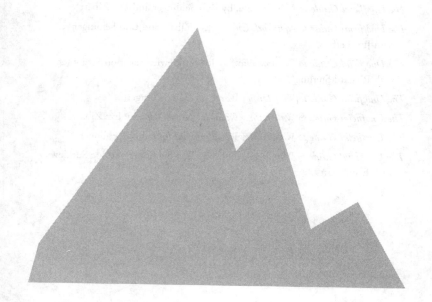

Also available from **MACMILLAN TRAVEL**

the Unofficial Guide® to Skiing in the West

3rd Edition

Lito Tejada-Flores

Peter Shelton

Seth Masia

Bob Sehlinger

Ed Chauner

Macmillan • USA

In addition to the authors, some of the best ski instructors in the country assisted in developing the mountain ratings found in this guide. Demonstrating great sensitivity to the needs of skiers of all skill levels, the project group was assembled by Snowbird staff trainer and senior instructor Ed Chauner and consisted of PSIA Demo Team members Dave Merriam (Stowe), Dave and Tabby Mannetter (Mammoth Mountain), Craig Webb (Vail), and Scott Mathers (Alta).

Special thanks also to Geni King of Snowmass and Shirley Gutke of Salt Lake City, who contributed to the chapter on lodging.

Finally, high fives for the production team of Barbara Williams, Julie Allred, Holly Cross, Georgia Goff, Brian Taylor, Sarah Nawrocki, and Ann Cassar, who turned all of this effort into a finished book.

Every effort has been made to ensure the accuracy of information throughout this book. Bear in mind, however, that prices, schedules, etc., are constantly changing and some ski areas may have made mountain improvements after the manuscript was finalized. Readers should always verify information before making final plans.

MACMILLAN TRAVEL
Macmillan General Reference USA, Inc.
1633 Broadway
New York, New York 10019-6785

Produced by Menasha Ridge Press
Design by Barbara E. Williams

MACMILLAN is a registered trademark of Macmillan General Reference USA, Inc.

UNOFFICIAL GUIDE is a registered trademark of Macmillan General Reference USA, Inc.

ISBN 0-02-863278-8
ISSN 1083-1479

Manufactured in the United States of America

10 9 8 7 6 5 4 3 2 1

Third edition

Contents

List of Illustrations

the Unofficial Guide® to Skiing in the West

3rd Edition

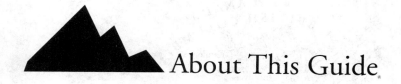# About This Guide

Why "Unofficial"?

The material in this guide originated with the authors and researchers and has not been reviewed, edited, or in any way approved by the ski resorts and the ski areas profiled. In this "unofficial" guide we have elected to represent and serve the *skier*. If a resort is plagued with congested slopes, awful food, or intolerable lift queues, we can say so. We are also free to highlight everything we love best about a ski resort, even if it doesn't fit the official image. In this way, we hope we can make your ski experience more fun, efficient, and economical.

Westward Ho

Look at a 3-D relief map of North America, and if you love mountains, your gaze will automatically swing left to the West. The western side of the map—and the continent—is full of mountains, more mountains, bigger mountains, long chains of mountains. There are the Rockies, not one range but a confabulation of many ranges and subranges. Taken together, in their intricate braided complexity, they define the backbone of the continent and here in the United States span six states. West of the Rockies it doesn't stop. There are still more mountains—Sawtooth, Wasatch, Tetons, Sierra Nevada, Cascade, Carson—interior ranges, coastal ranges, snowy ranges blanketed with crystallized moisture from the Pacific. Snow is why we care about these mountains. We're skiers. We're in love with snowy mountains, and the West is our mecca.

Let's be fair. American skiing began in Norwegian farming and mining towns in the Midwest—places like Ishpeming, Michigan, and Red Wing, Minnesota. But western ski snobs like to point out that what passes for a mountain in the East is more like a big rounded hill (ancient mountain ranges do wear down through the ages into rounded hills). And you don't have to be a chauvinist to admit that there are not just more mountains and more snow out west, but more ski areas and ski resorts, more skiing, and more great skiing.

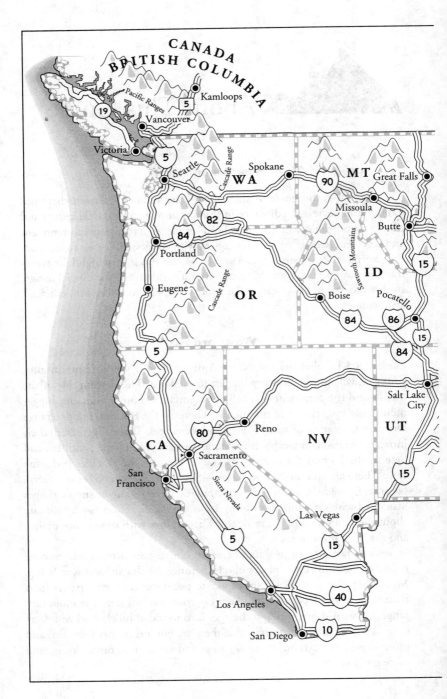

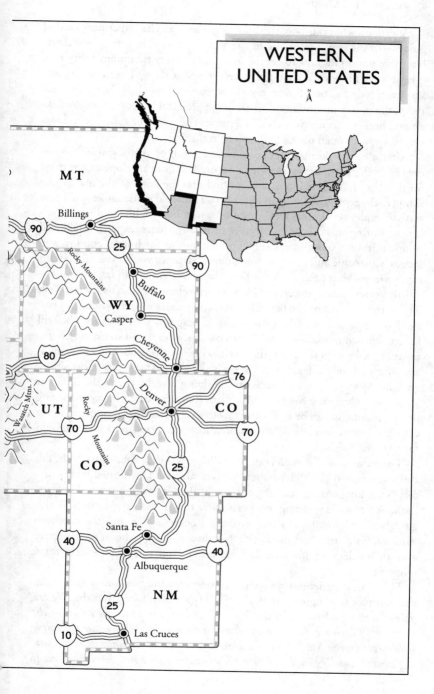

WESTERN
UNITED STATES
N

And that's what this book is about: a guide—an altogether new kind of guide—to the very best skiing in the West. Where it is, how to get there, but more important how to get the most out of every mountain, every run, every turn. This book is, first and foremost, about *skiing*. I mean *skiing*, not ski-resort lodging, not dining, not ski-town shopping, but *skiing*. The real thing, the poetry in motion underneath the predictable prose of airline tickets and hotel reservations and dollars spent. The magic of movement down surreal snow-covered peaks. Skiing. The real thing.

After a life of skiing, my bookshelves are full of skiers' guidebooks—dozens of them promising the lowdown on American ski slopes, even more for the Alps. But when I look closer, I find that the heart of the matter, the skiing itself, generally gets short shrift. In all these ski guidebooks you'll find statistics aplenty: vertical feet; elevations; numbers of lifts and trails; percentages of terrain devoted to beginners, intermediates, experts. You'll find phone numbers and addresses; recommendations for hotels, condos, and lodges, either chic and pricey or low-budget bargains; you'll even find restaurant reviews—but precious little about the skiing. And I can tell you why—a little secret, just between us: Most ski travel writers can't ski very well. There, the cat's out of the bag. I know travel writers whose bylines and stories have appeared in leading American ski magazines for decades who still haven't learned to make a parallel turn on skis, who spend weeks on assignment at the best ski resorts in the Rockies or in Europe but somehow manage to spend only a few hours on their skis. And that's why most skiing guidebooks scarcely talk about what the skiing is really like at the different areas and resorts they cover; seldom paint a clear picture of why the skiing on one mountain can be so different from that on another mountain; never offer the sort of insider's tips that can unlock the secrets of a ski mountain for any level of skier.

The authors of this guidebook are a different breed. Four of us, Seth, Ed, Peter, and myself (Lito), have spent years as successful, dedicated ski instructors—working, skiing, teaching at some of the biggest important ski resorts in the West—and we bring that perspective to our respective sections in this guidebook: Colorado and the southern Rockies, Utah and the northern Rockies, California and the Pacific Northwest. An instructor's perspective and an insider's perspective. Let me expand on this double idea for a moment.

When an experienced ski instructor starts teaching on a new mountain, the first task is to figure out all the basic types of information that we are going to share with you in this book: *The best runs to warm up on in the morning. Which are the best ways down in the evenings? Where are the traffic bottlenecks and how to avoid them? How to find the best ski lunch without wasting time or standing in line. Above all, what slopes offer just the right blend of challenge and comfort for each student—that is to say, for each level of skier.* It's a real art to figure all this out in a day or two, in order to give your students the absolute best experience possible from the very first day of the season. But that's exactly what good ski instructors do, what we've all done for years, and exactly what we've tried to do in this book.

And what about the role of the skiing insider? Who are we talking about? Someone who lives the ski life daily, someone who has explored a mountain year after year, from the first autumn snowfalls to the last corn-snow day of spring. Someone who has spent years ferreting out a mountain's secrets and who's willing to share them. Someone who sets the alarm clock for 5 A.M. to go up with the patrol on a powder morning; and who still knows where to find the last untracked stash, two days after a storm. Someone who can find the warmest, sunniest run on the coldest day of winter, the best-shaped moguls, the most interesting groomed runs. Someone who knows the best boot fitter, or the best ski tuner in town, and wants to tell you about them. The sort of skier you'd like to meet when you first visit a new ski area.

Peter, Seth, Ed, and I have lived this life—we've called more than one ski resort *home.* And we are ready to take you on an insider's tour of *our* favorite ski mountains. Sure, it's a tall order to give you the inside scoop on the fifty major western ski areas and resorts visited in this guide. We have lived for years at some, taught skiing at others, and visited still others so often they feel like second homes. No, we can't claim total, intimate, in-depth "insider's" knowledge of every one of these amazing ski areas, although— to answer an obvious question—yes, we really have skied every area we've written about. So our solution is to offer a multiple look at things, to give our own impressions, naturally very personal and very opinionated views, of skiing in our respective regions of the West. But we've also gone out of our way to round up and consult local insiders in virtually all these ski resorts in order to ask them for the sort of information that we could only know about our own "home" mountains.

Bob Sehlinger, the creator of the *Unofficial Guide* series and the fifth author of this guide, is known for his detailed, consumer-oriented travel journalism. While Seth, Peter, Ed, and I flexed our legs over the bumps, cruised the bowls, and tracked up the fresh powder, Bob was unraveling the mysteries of finding the perfect condo, shopping for ski vacation packages, and getting discounts on lift tickets. Equally important, Bob brought to this collaboration the singular perspective of a not overly skilled yet avid inter- mediate skier. His sensitivity to the aspirations and fears of beginner, novice, and intermediate skiers is central to our focus throughout the guide.

This combination of an instructor's perspective and practical consumer tips, we know, really works. This *Unofficial Guide* to the best skiing across the West grew out of several earlier volumes that focused on Colorado and on Utah, that quickly became the most trusted and most useful skiers' guides to those states. This more comprehensive guide has expanded the concept, the geographic range, and the number of ski areas and resorts covered. It will take you a skier's lifetime to explore and enjoy every ski mountain covered here. It won't be a wasted lifetime.

—*Lito Tejada-Flores*

Skiing the West: An Overview

OKAY, we confess. It was somewhat arbitrary to divide this guidebook to western skiing, as we have, into three sections. It could have been two: the Rockies and the coastal mountains. Or we could have taken a state-by-state approach. But there's a certain logic, and a lot of practicality in the way we divided our coverage of the western ski scene.

To begin with, Rocky Mountain skiing differs from West Coast skiing because Rocky Mountain snow is so different from the denser, moister snow that falls near the Pacific. Snow is lighter and drier throughout the entire Rocky Mountain region than anywhere else in the country. And while Colorado and its Rocky Mountain neighbors can't really dispute Utah's claim to the lightest, driest snow of all, to visitors it all seems feather-light.

Why is this snow so light, so dry, so fine? It's because the Rockies enjoy (and occasionally suffer from) an altogether different climate—a so-called "continental" rather than a "maritime" climate. All other ski regions in the United States are close to the coasts or the Great Lakes. And water means wet: wet sand at the beach, wet snow at Tahoe, at Sugarbush in Vermont, at White Pass in Washington. But when storms travel a thousand miles or so, over intervening ranges and rain-shadowed desert basins, losing moisture all the way, what they finally drop on mountain ranges in the center of the continent is light, dry fluff. The name's the same (only Eskimos, we're told, have over thirty separate words for different types of snow) and so is the color, white on white on white, but there the similarity ends. Rocky Mountain snow is drier, lighter, fluffier than can possibly be described or imagined if you haven't already skied it.

And why is light snow important? Light, dry "continental" snow versus wetter, heavier "maritime" snow? Simple: People tend to ski better—much better—on light, dry snow. That's a promise. You'll ski better in the Rockies than you do at home (unless the Rockies are your home). This is the real reason skiers from all over tend to get hooked on Rocky Mountain skiing and return, year after year after year. This promise—that you'll actually ski better—is not clearly articulated on the cover of any of the hundreds of thousands of ski/tourist brochures that tout the virtues of the Rocky Mountain ski experience. But an enormous segment of the tourist economy of

Colorado and Utah depends on this particular promise being legitimate. It is.

In the Rocky Mountain ski region Colorado and Utah often get the lion's share of attention. Not, we hasten to add, because their ski resorts are that much better than those in nearby states, but simply because there are more major resorts in those two states than in the rest of the Rockies put together. That's why we've divided our Rocky Mountain ski coverage into two sections. Colorado and New Mexico form a natural pairing. In terms of climate, skiing in the southern Rockies is a sort of luxury experience, in part because of the abundant sunshine and the seldom bitter winter temperatures. By contrast, winter in Utah and the northern Rockies states of Wyoming, Montana, and Idaho is perhaps a harsher, more hard-core experience. This is not to say that ski areas in these states aren't blessed with sunny days too; they are, but maybe fewer of them. And these states are also blessed with the same phenomenal, light Rocky Mountain snow. And since Utah's mountains intercept eastward-moving storms long before they hit Colorado, their powder dumps are often larger and deeper. In the last analysis, storms, not sunshine, define a skier's experience, a skier's memories. But when contrasting skiing in the northern and southern Rockies, the best one can come up with is a difference of degree, not of kind. Sharper differences emerge when one looks at California and West Coast skiing.

West Coast snow has its own pluses, its own charms, its fanatical aficionados too. But it's different. The maritime climate of the coastal states makes this snow wetter (relatively speaking) and denser; but the snow makes up in depth and in abundance what it lacks in lightness. Ski resorts out West don't generally have to invest millions in snowmaking systems to guarantee early openings before Christmas. And surprise: West Coast snow actually lets you ski more terrain, since it fills in rocky shapes (even cliffs) with something more than light fluffy powder. As the season progresses, more and more unlikely spots become skiable. At areas like Squaw Valley, Mammoth Mountain, and Whistler-Blackcomb, this deep, dense snow allows bold skiers to leave their tracks on slopes that would be suicidal in the Rockies. And the not-so-bold, or the rest of us, can enjoy a far longer ski season in California's High Sierra or in the Pacific Northwest than anywhere else in the country. Late spring skiing is the norm, not the exception, in this region.

There is another subtle and rather intriguing difference between skiing in the far West and skiing in the Rockies. In general, you'll find more ski *resorts* in the Rocky Mountain states and more ski *areas* along the West Coast. This is not a facetious or merely semantic distinction. By ski *resort* we mean a skiing destination where the village beneath the ski mountain is part and parcel of the skier's experience. A ski *area*, by contrast, need be nothing more than a mountain, a lift system, and a parking lot. Generally a ski resort invites you for at least a week-long ski vacation or longer, while a ski area tempts you only for the day or maybe a weekend. Now that's a very broad generalization, as is the claim that there are more resorts in the Rockies. Generalizations invite exceptions, and there are many.

And you'll notice immediately that we've been very inclusive, describing both major ski resorts and smaller ski areas. But not all of them. Our goal was simple: write an insider's guide to the *very best skiing in the West*. We've looked for the best skiing across our vast region, and described it in detail. And we have left out ski areas, ski resorts, ski mountains, ski places that were not exciting enough to really capture and captivate distant skiers. (It's always reasonable to visit and enjoy your local ski area, no matter how small or limited—as thousands of dedicated midwestern skiers prove every weekend of the winter on ski hills only a couple of hundred feet high.)

Typically, Rocky Mountain ski resorts draw skiers from both coasts, from all over the country, and from abroad, while for the most part, West Coast skiing attracts residents of California, Oregon, and Washington. High Sierra ski resorts, for example, have been hard put to convince East Coast skiers to fly over the Rockies to visit Lake Tahoe. However, they attract Europeans and Japanese by the thousands. Nevertheless, we'd encourage skiers from any corner of the country to explore this whole region—including California and the Pacific Northwest—where you'll find great resorts and legendary skiing. Where will you find your favorite skiing? Where will you live your most memorable days on skis? That's impossible to say, but we can promise you this: In another twenty ski seasons you are not going to run out of exciting ski destinations or snowy surprises here in the West.

Although we've focused our eyes, our hearts, and our word processors primarily on the skiing itself—describing how skiers of every level, beginner, novice, intermediate, advanced or expert, can enjoy a peak experience on each mountain—we haven't really neglected the resort life below the slopes. Our favorite lodges, restaurants, and local hangouts are spotlighted, even though we didn't think it necessary, or appropriate, to turn this skiing guidebook into an encyclopedia of travel details.

How to Use This Guidebook

This book is designed for browsing, for reference, for fun. But above all, it's designed to encourage you to visit new and different ski destinations across the West. And to get the most out of each mountain once you get there. If you were the kind of skier who was content to visit the same local ski area forever, you probably would never have picked up this book. But now that you've been touched by a winter wanderlust, where to start? And how to choose?

To help you navigate your way through the in-depth chapters covering each ski destination (the heart of the book), we've put together mini-descriptions of each ski mountain that summarize what differentiates the skiing and vacation experience there. You'll find an innovative rating comparison of ski area statistics in the section on planning your trip. And of course, you'll probably want to browse through the different chapters in your own particular order of interest. You can read summaries of ski resorts that friends have told you about or ski destinations that have been written up in the national ski press to see whether we agreed or disagreed with *Skiing, Snow Country, Ski,* or *Powder* magazines. Eventually you may read every chapter in this book—but please, not straight through, not from beginning to end.

Yet when the time comes to make plans for next season's ski vacation, don't trust statistics, don't take out a pencil and make a list of pluses and minuses. Instead, listen to that little voice inside you that whispers: "Wouldn't it be neat to go out to Utah and see if the snow's as good as they say," or, "Why don't we visit one of those little unknown places this time," or, "I've never skied in California, wonder what it's like," or, "Let's go somewhere really hard and see if we're up to it." In short, choose your ski vacation destination for the same, inexplicable, unjustifiable sort of reasons that made you a skier in the first place. For romance. For adventure. For the hell of it. The West, as they say, is a big place. You'll find all the snow, all the adventure, all the romance you can handle out here. And more.

Tech Tips

Because three of us are ski instructors, we would feel remiss if we didn't encourage you a little to improve your technique. To this end we have sandwiched some instructional tips between our profiles of the resorts. We call these tips "Tech Tips."

There's no way to become an accomplished skier without paying your dues. Frustrations, falls, occasional failure, lots of days, and lots of miles on skis are part of the recipe. But there are also shortcuts, learning strategies that will make your practice time pass more quickly and will get you where you want to go faster. Here's our list of suggestions for faster, more efficient progress on skis.

Terrain will be your best teacher. It's humbling for a ski instructor to admit this, but it's true. You should learn to distinguish between three types of ski terrain: practice/learning slopes, pleasure/performance slopes, and challenging slopes. Basically "learning terrain" is ski terrain that's a little *too* easy for you: slopes so easy there is absolutely no doubt in your mind that you can make every mistake in the book and still recover. This is essential if you are going to concentrate 100 percent on new, hence psychologically risky, moves. It's even true in bumps. You will master medium-size bumps by practicing in trivial mini-bumps, learn to ski giant man-eating moguls by practicing the moves in comfy medium-size ones. Always pick practice-learning terrain that's too easy; it frees your mind.

At the other end of the scale you'll find "adventure" or "challenge" terrain: slopes that are honestly too hard, where you're scrambling just to survive. It's okay to ski over your head from time to time, which can be a confidence builder of a sort. But don't let friends, or your own ego, push you over your head too often. It will permanently retard your progress as a skier by reinforcing awkward survival moves to the point of ingrained habits. Your best bet for rapid progress is to spend about two-thirds to three-quarters of your skiing day on performance slopes (slopes in your comfort range) and the rest of the time really concentrating on repeating key moves on easier learning terrain. But don't practice anything all day long, or even for hours on end; you'll burn out. Better to ski three runs for the hell of it, and then slow down and focus your attention on skiing form for just one good run. A good instructor will automatically strive for this sort of balance between concentrated focused practice and relaxed pleasure skiing where you can slowly "ski in" the new habits.

But while constant attempts to practice new skiing skills, hour after hour, are usually counterproductive, it is still a good idea to devote a week of time to achieving some sort of major goal or breakthrough in your skiing. Whether a simple week of group lessons, or a more focused program, the effect of such commitment is cumulative and dramatic. On the other hand, one- or two-hour lessons are a waste of time for most skiers. And half-day lessons or three-hour "clinics" are about as successful as any other quick-fix remedies and not effective at all in terms of changing your basic skiing habits. Change takes time. And the advantage of longer lessons (all day at a minimum or week-long if possible) is that your instructor will have sufficient time to guide and adjust the alternation of focused practice periods with spontaneous skiing mileage in such a way as to achieve the greatest results and the longest-lasting ones.

Finally, focus on one thing at a time: one movement, one skill, one skiing pattern. No one can do more. Don't let your concentration get fragmented by half a dozen well-intentioned tips. A good instructor may express the same point in a variety of ways, but he or she will continue to guide you toward one goal at a time.

Good skiing!

Letters, Comments, and Questions from Readers

Many of those who use the *Unofficial Guides* write to us asking questions, making comments, or sharing their own strategies for planning and enjoying a trip. We appreciate all such input, both positive and critical, and encourage our readers to continue writing. Readers' comments and observations are frequently incorporated into revised editions of the *Unofficial Guides* and have contributed immeasurably to their improvement. Please write to:

Lito, Peter, Seth, Ed, and Bob
The Unofficial Guide to Skiing in the West
P.O. Box 43673
Birmingham, AL 35243

When you write, be sure to put a return address on your letter as well as on the envelope; sometimes envelopes and letters get separated. It's also a good idea to include your phone number. And remember, our work often requires that we be out of the office for long periods of time, so forgive us if our response is a little slow.

PART I

Planning Your Ski Trip

BOB SEHLINGER

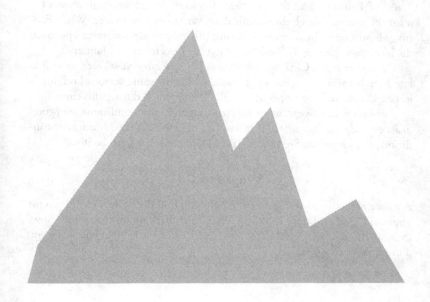

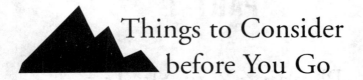

Things to Consider before You Go

Tʜɪs guide has a double function: first, to help you select the right ski destination for your specific skill level, preferences, and enthusiasm; and second, to help you get the very most out of your visit to any skiing resort in the West. However, before you leave home, in the early stages of planning your perfect ski trip, there are a number of issues that also must be considered.

When to Go

The resorts are busiest, the slopes most crowded, and the lodging at capacity during the Christmas/New Year's week and over the Presidents' Day holiday weekend in February. When there is early snow, the Thanksgiving holiday period is also very busy. If you are crowd-averse, these are times to avoid.

All of February and the first three weeks of March are high season for most ski resorts, though the specific dates vary from area to area. While February is still quite busy, crowds during this month almost never approach the levels seen during the holiday periods in December and January.

December *before* Christmas week and January *after* New Year's, as well as late March and early April, are considered low or value season. Lodging is less expensive and the slopes are usually less crowded during this time.

The best time of year for sparse crowds, good snow conditions, *and* good deals on lodging and airfare is in January after New Year's. Mountain conditions in November, December, late March, and April can be iffy.

Where to Go

A major objective of this guide is to help you find the perfect mountain for your skill level and taste in skiing. Prior to embarking on that quest, however, we thought we would share some insider knowledge that will make you a more savvy shopper.

Special Events

In addition to snowfall, holidays, and high and low seasons, you also need to consider special events. The Sundance Film Festival, for example, held during the latter half of January in Park City, Utah, puts quite a strain on lodging and restaurants and also adds significant numbers of skiers to nearby slopes. Spring break brings increased business to ski mountains, as do ski races, music festivals, and conventions.

Local Skier Impact

If skiing conditions are good and a resort is located within two hours of a large city, you can expect to be joined on the mountain by an army of locals. This is particularly true on weekends. If you truly hate crowds, you might consider going to a more isolated resort like Telluride, Steamboat, Crested Butte, Jackson Hole, Big Sky, or Sun Valley. While isolation does not guarantee that you'll have the mountain to yourself, you will avoid the throngs of day skiers pouring out of the large cities.

If you choose a resort region accessible to locals, head for the least difficult mountains on weekends. Beaver Creek, for example, will be less crowded than Vail on weekends. Likewise, Buttermilk will be less populated than Aspen Mountain or Snowmass. In the Salt Lake City area, avoid Alta, Snowbird, and Park City on weekends. Instead try Brighton, Snowbasin, and the Canyons. You get the idea.

Games Ski Mountains Play

Ski mountains are like politicians: They want to be all things to all people. Forget the limitations of the mountain; the marketing department will make things right. Every mountain, for example, represents itself as providing a complete skiing experience. This means, of course, that there *must* be beginner terrain, intermediate terrain, and advanced/expert terrain. Even if the whole mountain consists of three runs drooping off a 200-foot moraine, you can bet that one of the trails will be rated green, one blue, and one black.

The grand result of this denial and wishful thinking is a ski trail rating system that has its origins in Fantasyland and lacks any hint of objective rating criteria. If you can handle the black diamonds at Ober Gatlinburg in Tennessee, does that mean you are ready to ski advanced terrain at Telluride? Hardly. In fact, you would be much better off preparing for Telluride by skiing the green runs at Snowbird!

The more benign manifestation of marketing-driven ratings is seen in the easier mountains that tend to overrate their trails. Skiing black-marked trails that are really blue, and blue-marked trails that should be rated green, makes the skier feel more skilled than he actually is. This builds confidence, reinforces the ego, and enhances enjoyment of the day. Regardless of the objective validity of the trail ratings, this skier is skiing within his skill level and probably will not get into anything seriously over his head unless, of course, he decides to go to another mountain.

While those who ski over-graded mountains might form an exaggerated opinion of their ability, skiers skiing under-graded mountains have the potential for getting into real trouble. Mountains that do not offer much, if any, easy terrain owe it to the skier to acknowledge this fact. Aspen Mountain, for example, states forthrightly that there is no easy terrain. Read my lips, "no green runs." Most mountains, unfortunately, are less forthcoming. In our mountain profiles, therefore, we have taken pains to identify mountains where trail difficulty is over- or under-graded. Take this into consideration when choosing a resort.

Another deceptive, though less dangerous, marketing trick is the skiable acreage exaggeration game. Skiable acreage is the statistic resorts use to describe size. Supposedly, the more skiable acreage, the larger the resort. Skiable acreage at many resorts, however, has little to do with the number or length of maintained trails. Instead, it is the total number of acres within the resort boundaries where skiing is allowed. Some resorts count all of their acreage, including those acres occupied by roads, parking lots, buildings, unskiable cliffs, and streams. Others count parts of the ski area not serviced by lifts. In the final analysis, because every resort uses a different calculation, it is impossible to compare resorts on the basis of skiable acreage.

Ski mountains are also notorious for exaggerating their vertical—the difference in altitude from the top of the resort to the base. The most common prevarication here is to measure from the top of the highest peak, even though the lifts don't go up that high. Additionally, on many mountains, you cannot ski all the way from the top (whatever that may be) to the bottom. Instead, you must interrupt your descent with a lift ride to reposition yourself for the continuation of the run to the bottom. Then there is the "longest trail" ruse. While resort promotional literature could boast a trail three and a half miles long, the run in reality often may be either a catwalk or three or four different trails somehow tenuously connected.

Lift capacity—the number of skiers the lift system can move up the mountain in an hour—is another misleading descriptor. For most resorts, the number is derived by adding the hourly capacity of all lifts. This bears little resemblance to actual conditions on the mountain because it assumes an optimal distribution of skiers to all of the lifts. In reality, some lifts are inundated with skiers, while other lifts dispatch chair after empty chair up the mountain. Quite a few resorts have lifts that are not even opened unless the mountain is really swamped with business. In any event, lift capacity and mountain design are vastly different animals. A resort can have an impressive lift capacity on paper but function inefficiently as a result of poorly designed and badly placed lifts.

A Word about Grooming

Many American skiers love smooth, manicured, machine-groomed slopes. Some skiers even choose a ski mountain on the basis of the resort's reputation for grooming. As long as the sun shines, life is good for the well groomed. When it snows, however, it usually takes the cat operators a day or two to get the new snow smoothed and packed down. If you are a skier who by preference or skill limitations demands groomed runs, here are a few things you should know.

Although some mountains groom more than others, every mountain has a basic grooming plan, and most are similar in several respects. Grooming usually begins as soon as the mountain shuts down for the night. Advanced/expert runs scheduled for grooming are tackled first, followed by intermediate runs. Lower intermediate and beginner runs are groomed last, often in the early morning just before the mountain reopens.

If new snowfall stops by midnight, many blue and almost all green trails will be groomed before morning. When the snow continues past midnight into the wee hours, new snow will fall on many runs where grooming has been completed. While some resorts take a second crack at popular green runs just before opening, there's generally not much that can be done until the next evening's crews go out. If you are looking for the best-groomed mountain around after a new snow, odds are it will be the mountain that caters more to beginners and intermediates.

Special Considerations

When determining where to go, there are some situations that require special consideration. If you are not in as good physical condition as you would like to be, you might give some thought to looking at mountains less than 10,000 feet high. There are more of them than you might expect. Also look at resorts where there is good skiing of the type you prefer (cruising, bumps, whatever) lower on the mountain. Conversely, if you are skiing in November, late March, or April, higher mountains provide the greatest assurance of good skiing conditions.

If you are a party animal and like to stay out late, or if you just enjoy sleeping in mornings, you might be happier skiing in Utah, Montana, or

Idaho. Because these states are situated in the westernmost part of the mountain time zone, it stays light later in the day, and some of the resorts remain open an hour or so longer than many Colorado resorts.

If you want to ski in the West, but have a limited number of days available, you can increase your time on the mountain by skiing on your travel days. If you are flying, travel-day skiing is most easily accomplished at one of the nine resorts within 45 minutes of Salt Lake City. An early flight from most cities will get you to Salt Lake City before noon, even with a connecting flight. If you have your own equipment, you can be on the slopes by 1 P.M. Most Utah resorts keep lifts running until 4 or 4:30 P.M. On your return, you can ski until 2 P.M. or so and still make it to the airport in plenty of time to catch a flight home.

If you are flying from the Pacific Coast states, you can also enjoy travel-day skiing by flying into Reno, Nevada, and hitting the slopes at one of the Lake Tahoe resorts, or flying into Vancouver, British Columbia, and skiing Whistler or Blackcomb. Travel-day skiing in Colorado is difficult, even if you take a commuter flight to the resort area. If you fly into Denver International Airport and rent a car, you are really at a disadvantage. You must drive from one and a half to four hours to reach the resorts. If you are really avid, however, and if you can get an early direct flight to Denver, it is possible to arrive, rent a car, and drive to Loveland, Keystone, or Breckenridge in time for a half day of skiing. When the mountain closes, you can continue on to your final resort destination.

Comparing Ski Mountains

The essence of this guide can be found in the comprehensive profiles of the ski mountains. It is here that we take you on a detailed tour of each mountain, pointing out all the characteristics that make that mountain special. By reading the ski mountain profiles, you will discover the particular features, style, and atmosphere of the resorts, and you will be able to confidently select a resort that fits your skiing and vacation preferences. At the same time, we understand that you may want to narrow your range of choices before you dig into the profiles. Thus we have attempted to rate the ski mountains in a number of areas that are of interest to skiers of all skill levels. The ratings are presented specifically to facilitate a quick comparison of the ski mountains. It should be stressed that many important aspects of a ski vacation, such as restaurants, nightlife, and the character of the overall resort community, are not included in the ratings.

Because the *Unofficial Guides* are known for their strong consumer orientation, we are accustomed to being direct, evaluative, and critical. Thus it is our preference to compare, rate, and rank according to measurable and verifiable objective standards. When we initiated the process of comparing ski mountains, however, we encountered strongly held personal differences within our research/author team. One point of view is that a ski mountain, by virtue of changes in season, temperature, visibility, weather, slope grooming, and the number of skiers on the mountain, provides a totally different experience every day. This immense variability of conditions, it follows, precludes drawing conclusions from ratings that compare different mountains. Moreover, mountains with very similar statistics and physical characteristics can have a very different feel.

The counterargument is that every ski area starts with a mountain, a unique physical presence that is designed and arranged in a definite way. Trails can be measured in terms of top-to-bottom elevation differential and length of run. Mountain design and lift placement likewise can be analyzed and rated for adequacy, convenience, and efficiency. According to this counterargument, there is, for any ski area, a baseline measurement that represents that mountain's design and physical characteristics.

After much discussion, we agreed to rate all of the major western ski mountains (as well as a sampling of the smaller mountains) and allow the reader to determine whether or not the rating comparisons are useful. Variables such as inclement weather, poor visibility, changing surface conditions, unusually light or heavy skier traffic, seasonal thawing or freezing, and/or inadequate snowbase are not considered. Instead, the mountain is evaluated on a mythical average day when the snowbase permits operation of the entire mountain, when visibility is perfect, when normal slope-grooming schedules are followed, and when skier traffic is average. Rating each mountain's characteristics, serviceability, and design sometimes calls for a physical measurement, sometimes for a personal opinion, and sometimes for both.

Mountain Size

Maintained Trails The relative size of the resort in terms of developed and maintained (but not necessarily frequently groomed) trails—trails depicted as green, blue, and black on the resort trail map.

Size ratings run along a continuum and are scored as follows:

Very Large	Large	Medium	Small	Very Small
▲▲▲▲▲	▲▲▲▲	▲▲▲	▲▲	▲

Off-Trail Skiable Terrain This is a rating primarily of interest to advanced and expert skiers. Using the same rating scale as above, the area is rated in terms of the size of its off-trail skiable terrain. This rating wholly *excludes* all developed trails, but includes bowls.

Skiable Vertical Top-to-bottom skiable vertical served by lifts. This excludes any vertical where the skier must climb to a higher elevation from the lift exit.

3,100 feet & higher	2,600–3,099	2,100–2,599	1,600–2,099	1,599 & less
▲▲▲▲▲	▲▲▲▲	▲▲▲	▲▲	▲

Average Length of Run Excludes catwalks and nearly flat run-outs at the end of runs. On average, the designated runs/trails are:

Very Long	Long	Average	Short	Very Short
▲▲▲▲▲	▲▲▲▲	▲▲▲	▲▲	▲

Mountain Size			
Maintained Trails	Off-Trail Skiable Terrain	Skiable Vertical	Average Length of Run
Alpine Meadows ▲▲▲▲	▲▲▲	▲▲	▲▲▲
Alta ▲▲▲	▲▲▲▲▲	▲▲▲	▲▲▲
Arapahoe Basin ▲▲	▲▲	▲▲▲	▲▲▲
Aspen Highlands ▲▲▲	▲	▲▲▲▲▲	▲▲▲
Aspen Mountain ▲▲▲	▲▲	▲▲▲▲▲	▲▲▲
Beaver Creek ▲▲▲	▲▲	▲▲▲▲▲	▲▲▲▲
Big Mountain ▲▲▲▲	▲▲▲▲	▲▲▲	▲▲▲▲
Big Sky ▲▲▲▲	▲▲▲▲▲	▲▲▲▲▲	▲▲▲▲
Blackcomb ▲▲▲▲▲	▲▲▲▲▲	▲▲▲▲▲	▲▲▲▲▲
Breckenridge ▲▲▲▲	▲▲▲	▲▲▲▲	▲▲▲
Brian Head ▲▲▲	▲	▲	▲▲▲
Bridger Bowl ▲▲	▲▲▲▲	▲▲	▲▲▲
Brighton ▲▲▲	▲▲▲	▲▲	▲▲▲
Buttermilk ▲▲	▲	▲▲	▲▲▲
The Canyons ▲▲▲	▲▲▲	▲▲▲▲	▲▲▲
Copper Mountain ▲▲▲▲	▲▲▲	▲▲▲▲	▲▲▲
Crested Butte ▲▲▲	▲▲▲▲	▲▲▲	▲▲▲
Crystal Mountain ▲▲▲▲	▲▲▲▲▲	▲▲▲▲▲	▲▲▲

Mountain Size (continued)

	Maintained Trails	Off-Trail Skiable Terrain	Skiable Vertical	Average Length of Run
Deer Valley	▲▲▲▲	▲▲▲	▲▲▲	▲▲▲
Grand Targhee	▲▲▲	▲▲▲▲	▲▲▲	▲▲▲▲
Heavenly	▲▲▲▲	▲▲▲▲	▲▲▲▲	▲▲▲▲
Jackson Hole	▲▲▲▲	▲▲▲▲▲	▲▲▲▲▲	▲▲▲▲▲
June Mountain	▲▲▲	▲▲	▲▲▲	▲▲▲
Keystone	▲▲▲▲	▲	▲▲▲	▲▲▲▲
Kirkwood	▲▲▲	▲▲▲▲	▲▲	▲▲▲▲
Loveland	▲▲	▲▲▲	▲▲	▲▲▲
Mammoth	▲▲▲▲▲	▲▲▲▲	▲▲▲▲▲	▲▲▲
Mission Ridge	▲▲▲	▲▲▲▲	▲▲▲	▲▲▲
Mount Bachelor	▲▲▲▲▲	▲▲▲▲	▲▲▲▲▲	▲▲▲▲
Northstar	▲▲▲	▲▲	▲▲▲	▲▲▲▲
Park City	▲▲▲▲	▲▲▲▲	▲▲▲▲▲	▲▲▲
Powder Mountain	▲▲▲	▲▲▲	▲	▲▲▲
Purgatory	▲▲▲	▲	▲▲	▲▲▲
Santa Fe	▲▲▲	▲▲	▲▲▲	▲▲▲
Schweitzer Mountain	▲▲▲	▲▲▲▲	▲▲▲	▲▲▲▲
Sierra-at-Tahoe	▲▲▲	▲▲	▲▲▲	▲▲▲▲
Snowbasin	▲▲▲	▲▲▲	▲▲▲	▲▲▲
Snowbird	▲▲▲	▲▲▲▲▲	▲▲▲▲▲	▲▲▲▲
Snowmass	▲▲▲▲▲	▲▲▲▲	▲▲▲▲	▲▲▲▲
Solitude	▲▲▲	▲▲▲▲	▲▲	▲▲▲▲
Squaw Valley	▲▲▲▲▲	▲▲▲▲▲	▲▲▲▲	▲▲▲
Steamboat	▲▲▲▲▲	▲▲▲	▲▲▲▲▲	▲▲▲▲
Stevens Pass	▲▲▲	▲▲▲▲	▲▲	▲▲▲
Sugar Bowl	▲▲▲	▲▲	▲	▲▲▲
Sundance	▲▲	▲	▲▲▲	▲▲▲
Sun Valley	▲▲▲▲	▲▲▲	▲▲▲▲▲	▲▲▲▲
Taos	▲▲▲▲	▲▲▲▲	▲▲▲▲	▲▲▲▲
Telluride	▲▲▲	▲▲	▲▲▲▲▲	▲▲▲▲
Vail	▲▲▲▲▲	▲▲▲▲▲	▲▲▲▲▲	▲▲▲▲
Whistler	▲▲▲▲▲	▲▲▲▲▲	▲▲▲▲▲	▲▲▲▲▲
Winter Park	▲▲▲	▲▲	▲▲▲	▲▲▲▲

Skiable Terrain Available for Specific Skill Levels

This rating is designed to allow you to make comparisons between ski mountains of different sizes concerning the availability of a particular type of terrain.

The rating has nothing to do with a resort's percentage breakdown of terrain (i.e, 25 percent beginner, 50 percent intermediate, 25 percent expert). A small resort may have 90 percent intermediate terrain, but still not have enough runs to keep an intermediate skier happy for half a day. A high rating (5) for intermediate terrain availability would indicate that an intermediate skier would have a large and varied selection of suitable terrain, so much, in fact, that it would take two days or more to explore it all. Conversely, a resort where the intermediate terrain could be exhausted in a morning would receive a low score.

Extensive Availability		Moderate Availability		Limited Availability
▲▲▲▲▲	▲▲▲▲	▲▲▲	▲▲	▲

Available Skiable Terrain				
	Beginner	Novice	Inter-mediate	Advanced	Expert
---	---	---	---	---	---
Alpine Meadows	▲▲▲	▲▲▲	▲▲▲▲	▲▲▲▲	▲▲▲▲
Alta	▲▲	▲▲▲	▲▲▲	▲▲▲	▲▲▲▲▲
Arapahoe Basin	▲▲	▲▲	▲▲▲	▲▲▲	▲▲▲
Aspen Highlands	▲▲	▲	▲▲▲▲	▲▲▲	▲▲▲
Aspen Mountain	none	none	▲▲▲▲	▲▲▲▲▲	▲▲▲▲
Beaver Creek	▲▲	▲▲▲	▲▲▲▲	▲▲▲	▲▲▲▲
Big Mountain	▲▲▲	▲▲▲▲	▲▲▲▲	▲▲▲▲	▲▲
Big Sky	▲▲▲▲	▲▲▲▲	▲▲▲▲	▲▲▲▲	▲▲▲▲▲
Blackcomb	▲▲▲▲	▲▲▲	▲▲▲▲▲	▲▲▲▲▲	▲▲▲▲▲
Breckenridge	▲▲▲▲	▲▲▲▲	▲▲▲▲	▲▲▲	▲▲▲
Brian Head	▲▲▲	▲▲▲	▲▲▲▲	▲▲▲	▲
Bridger Bowl	▲▲▲	▲▲▲▲	▲▲▲	▲▲	▲▲▲▲
Brighton	▲▲	▲▲▲	▲▲▲▲	▲▲▲	▲▲
Buttermilk	▲▲	▲▲▲	▲▲▲▲▲	▲	none
The Canyons	▲▲▲	▲▲▲	▲▲▲	▲▲▲	▲▲▲
Copper Mountain	▲▲▲	▲▲▲▲	▲▲▲▲▲	▲▲▲	▲
Crested Butte	▲▲▲	▲▲	▲▲▲▲	▲▲▲▲▲	▲▲▲▲▲
Crystal Mountain	▲▲▲▲	▲▲▲	▲▲▲▲	▲▲▲▲▲	▲▲▲▲▲
Deer Valley	▲▲	▲▲	▲▲▲	▲▲▲▲▲	▲▲▲
Grand Targhee	▲▲	▲▲	▲▲▲▲	▲▲▲▲	▲▲
Heavenly	▲▲▲	▲▲▲	▲▲▲▲▲	▲▲▲▲▲	▲▲▲▲
Jackson Hole	▲▲	▲▲▲	▲▲▲▲	▲▲▲▲	▲▲▲▲▲
June Mountain	▲▲▲▲▲	▲▲▲▲▲	▲▲▲▲▲	▲▲▲▲	▲▲

Available Skiable Terrain (continued)

	Beginner	Novice	Intermediate	Advanced	Expert
Keystone	▲▲	▲▲	▲▲▲▲▲	▲▲	▲
Kirkwood	▲▲▲	▲▲▲▲	▲▲▲▲▲	▲▲▲▲	▲▲▲▲
Loveland	▲▲	▲▲▲	▲▲▲	▲▲	▲▲
Mammoth	▲▲▲	▲▲▲▲	▲▲▲▲▲	▲▲▲▲▲	▲▲▲▲▲
Mission Ridge	▲▲	▲▲▲	▲▲▲	▲▲▲	▲▲▲
Mount Bachelor	▲▲▲▲	▲▲▲▲	▲▲▲▲▲	▲▲▲▲	▲▲▲
Northstar	▲▲▲▲	▲▲▲▲▲	▲▲▲▲▲	▲▲▲▲	▲▲
Park City	▲▲▲	▲▲▲	▲▲▲▲▲	▲▲▲▲	▲▲▲
Powder Mountain	▲▲	▲▲▲▲	▲▲▲	▲▲	▲▲▲
Purgatory	▲▲	▲▲	▲▲▲▲	▲▲	▲
Santa Fe	▲▲▲	▲▲▲	▲▲▲	▲▲	▲▲
Schweitzer Mtn.	▲▲▲	▲▲▲	▲▲▲▲	▲▲▲	▲▲
Sierra-at-Tahoe	▲▲▲▲	▲▲▲	▲▲▲▲▲	▲▲▲▲	▲▲▲▲
Snowbasin	▲▲▲	▲▲	▲▲▲▲	▲▲▲	▲▲▲
Snowbird	▲▲	▲▲	▲▲▲▲	▲▲▲	▲▲▲▲▲
Snowmass	▲▲▲	▲▲▲	▲▲▲▲▲	▲▲▲▲	▲▲
Solitude	▲▲▲▲	▲▲▲	▲▲▲	▲▲▲	▲▲▲
Squaw Valley	▲▲▲	▲▲▲	▲▲▲▲	▲▲▲	▲▲▲
Steamboat	▲▲▲	▲▲	▲▲▲▲▲	▲▲▲▲▲	▲▲▲▲▲
Stevens Pass	▲▲▲	▲▲▲▲	▲▲▲▲	▲▲▲▲	▲▲▲▲
Sugar Bowl	▲▲▲▲	▲▲▲▲	▲▲▲▲	▲▲▲▲	▲▲▲
Sundance	▲▲	▲▲▲	▲▲	▲	▲▲
Sun Valley	▲▲▲▲	▲▲▲	▲▲▲	▲▲▲	▲▲▲
Taos	▲▲	▲▲	▲▲▲	▲▲▲▲	▲▲▲▲▲
Telluride	▲▲▲	▲▲▲	▲▲▲	▲▲▲▲	▲▲▲▲▲
Vail	▲	▲▲	▲▲▲▲▲	▲▲▲▲	▲▲▲▲
Whistler	▲▲▲▲	▲▲▲	▲▲▲▲▲	▲▲▲▲▲	▲▲▲▲
Winter Park	▲▲	▲▲	▲▲▲▲	▲▲▲▲	▲▲▲▲▲

Mountain Characteristics and Design

The following categories rate how well the mountain is designed, taking into consideration design elements that are particularly vexing to beginner and intermediate skiers. All categories are rated on 0–5 scale, with 5 stars considered best and 0 considered worst.

Ease of Orientation How easy is it to find your way around the mountain? This considers quality of resort maps and signage. An easy mountain to navigate will score 5 stars.

Forgivingness Can a beginner or intermediate really get into a bind by taking a wrong turn, or is there usually an escape route? A very forgiving mountain will score 5 stars.

True Fall Lines This is the natural line of travel down the slope. A mountain with all or almost all true fall lines will score 5 stars. We realize that some more experienced skiers may prefer irregular fall lines, but as mentioned, the scoring is in accordance with the preferences of less skilled skiers.

Run Width A mountain with a high percentage of wide runs will score 5 stars. For most beginners and intermediates, wider is better.

Line of Sight This relates to the skier's ability in clear weather to see what is coming up during the run. Areas with a lot of blind drops and sharp turns score low in this category.

Intersections This relates to the crossing of trails and the potential for collision. The fewer intersections the better, and the higher the score.

Confluence This relates to some or many trails feeding into a single, congested trail or runout. A ski area where most of the mountain feeds into a primary trail to the resort center will score low.

Cat Tracks or Difficult Traverses An area where skiers (beginner and intermediate, especially) must use cat tracks and/or difficult traverses to get down the mountain will score low.

Visual Intimidation This psychological dimension relates to how intimidating the run appears from the top. A ski area with a number of visually frightening runs will score low.

Interesting All the Way Down This rating characterizes whether, on average, runs maintain interest and challenge to the skier from beginning to end. Mountains where many runs traverse long flat sections and/or feed into long, uninteresting runouts will score low.

Mountain Characteristics and Design Table I

	Ease of Orientation	Forgiv-ingness	True Fall Lines	Run Width	Line of Sight
Alpine Meadows	▲▲▲	▲▲▲▲	▲▲▲	▲▲▲	▲▲▲
Alta	▲▲▲▲	▲▲▲	▲▲▲▲▲	▲▲▲▲	▲▲▲▲
Arapahoe Basin	▲▲▲▲	▲▲▲	▲▲▲▲	▲▲▲▲▲	▲▲▲▲▲
Aspen Highlands	▲▲	▲▲	▲▲	▲▲▲	▲▲▲
Aspen Mountain	▲▲▲▲	▲▲▲▲	▲▲▲▲	▲▲▲	▲▲▲▲
Beaver Creek	▲▲▲▲▲	▲▲▲	▲▲▲▲▲	▲▲▲▲	▲▲▲▲
Big Mountain	▲▲▲	▲▲▲▲	▲▲	▲▲▲▲▲	▲▲▲▲
Big Sky	▲▲▲▲	▲▲▲▲	▲▲▲	▲▲▲▲	▲▲▲
Blackcomb	▲▲▲	▲▲	▲▲	▲▲▲▲	▲▲▲
Breckenridge	▲	▲▲▲▲	▲▲▲	▲▲▲▲	▲▲▲▲
Brian Head	▲▲	▲▲▲▲	▲▲▲	▲▲▲▲	▲▲▲
Bridger Bowl	▲▲▲▲	▲▲▲▲	▲▲▲▲	▲▲▲▲	▲▲▲▲
Brighton	▲▲▲▲	▲▲▲	▲▲▲▲	▲▲▲	▲▲▲
Buttermilk	▲▲▲▲▲	▲▲▲▲▲	▲▲▲	▲▲▲▲	▲▲▲▲
The Canyons	▲▲▲	▲▲▲▲	▲▲▲	▲▲▲▲	▲▲▲
Copper Mountain	▲▲▲	▲▲▲▲	▲▲▲▲	▲▲▲▲	▲▲▲▲
Crested Butte	▲▲▲	▲▲	▲▲▲▲	▲▲▲	▲▲▲
Crystal Mountain	▲▲▲▲	▲▲▲	▲▲▲▲	▲▲▲▲	▲▲▲▲
Deer Valley	▲▲▲	▲▲▲▲	▲▲▲▲	▲▲▲▲	▲▲▲▲
Grand Targhee	▲▲▲▲▲	▲▲▲▲	▲▲▲▲▲	▲▲▲▲▲	▲▲▲▲▲
Heavenly	▲▲	▲▲▲▲	▲▲	▲▲▲	▲▲▲
Jackson Hole	▲▲	▲▲▲	▲▲▲▲▲	▲▲▲▲	▲▲▲
June Mountain	▲▲▲▲	▲▲▲▲▲	▲▲▲	▲▲▲▲	▲▲▲▲
Keystone	▲▲▲▲	▲▲▲▲	▲▲▲▲▲	▲▲▲▲	▲▲▲▲
Kirkwood	▲▲▲▲	▲▲▲	▲▲▲▲	▲▲▲	▲▲▲▲
Loveland	▲▲	▲▲▲	▲▲▲	▲▲▲	▲▲▲▲
Mammoth	▲▲	▲▲▲▲	▲▲▲	▲▲▲▲	▲▲▲
Mission Ridge	▲▲▲▲	▲▲▲▲	▲▲▲	▲▲▲	▲▲▲
Mount Bachelor	▲▲▲▲▲	▲▲▲▲	▲▲▲	▲▲▲	▲▲▲▲
Northstar	▲▲▲▲	▲▲▲▲▲	▲▲▲	▲▲▲	▲▲▲▲▲
Park City	▲▲▲	▲▲▲▲	▲▲	▲▲▲▲	▲▲▲▲
Powder Mountain	▲▲	▲▲▲	▲▲▲▲	▲▲▲	▲▲▲▲
Purgatory	▲▲	▲▲▲	▲▲▲▲	▲	▲
Santa Fe	▲▲▲▲	▲▲▲▲	▲▲▲	▲▲▲	▲▲▲
Schweitzer Mtn.	▲▲▲▲▲	▲▲▲▲	▲▲▲▲▲	▲▲▲▲▲	▲▲▲▲▲
Sierra-at-Tahoe	▲▲▲	▲▲▲▲	▲▲▲▲	▲▲▲	▲▲▲▲
Snowbasin	▲▲▲▲▲	▲▲▲	▲▲▲▲	▲▲▲▲	▲▲▲▲
Snowbird	▲▲▲▲	▲	▲▲▲▲	▲▲▲▲	▲▲▲▲
Snowmass	▲▲▲	▲▲▲▲	▲▲▲▲	▲▲▲▲▲	▲▲▲▲▲
Solitude	▲▲▲▲	▲▲	▲▲▲▲	▲▲▲▲	▲▲▲

Mountain Characteristics and Design Table I (continued)

	Ease of Orientation	Forgivingness	True Fall Lines	Run Width	Line of Sight
Squaw Valley	▲▲▲	▲▲	▲▲▲▲	▲▲▲	▲▲▲
Steamboat	▲▲▲	▲▲▲	▲▲▲▲	▲▲▲	▲▲▲▲
Stevens Pass	▲▲▲▲	▲▲▲▲	▲▲▲▲	▲▲▲▲	▲▲▲▲
Sugar Bowl	▲▲▲▲	▲▲▲▲	▲▲▲▲	▲▲	▲▲▲
Sundance	▲▲▲	▲▲▲	▲▲▲	▲▲▲	▲▲▲
Sun Valley	▲▲▲	▲▲▲▲	▲▲▲▲▲	▲▲▲▲	▲▲▲▲▲
Taos	▲▲▲▲	▲▲	▲▲▲▲	▲▲▲	▲▲▲
Telluride	▲▲▲	▲▲▲	▲▲▲▲	▲▲▲	▲▲▲
Vail	▲▲▲▲	▲▲▲▲▲	▲▲▲▲	▲▲▲▲▲	▲▲▲▲
Whistler	▲▲▲	▲▲	▲▲	▲▲▲	▲▲▲
Winter Park	▲▲	▲▲	▲▲▲▲▲	▲▲▲	▲▲▲

Mountain Characteristics and Design Table II

	Intersections	Confluence	Cat Tracks/ Traverses	Visual Intimidation	Interesting All the Way Down
Alpine Meadows	▲▲▲	▲▲▲	▲▲▲▲	▲▲▲▲	▲▲▲
Alta	▲▲▲	▲▲▲▲	▲▲▲	▲▲▲	▲▲▲▲
Arapahoe Basin	▲▲▲	▲▲▲	▲▲▲▲	▲▲▲	▲▲▲▲
Aspen Highlands	▲▲▲▲	▲▲▲	▲▲	▲▲▲	▲▲
Aspen Mountain	▲▲▲	▲	▲▲▲▲	▲▲▲	▲▲▲▲
Beaver Creek	▲▲▲	▲▲▲	▲▲▲▲	▲▲▲▲▲	▲▲▲▲
Big Mountain	▲▲▲	▲▲▲	▲▲▲▲	▲▲▲▲	▲▲▲▲
Big Sky	▲▲▲▲▲	▲▲▲▲▲	▲▲▲▲	▲▲	▲▲▲
Blackcomb	▲▲▲	▲▲▲▲	▲▲▲	▲▲	▲▲▲▲▲
Breckenridge	▲▲	▲▲▲	▲	▲▲▲▲	▲
Brian Head	▲▲▲▲▲	▲▲▲▲	▲▲▲▲▲	▲▲▲▲▲	▲▲▲
Bridger Bowl	▲▲▲▲	▲▲▲	▲▲▲▲	▲▲▲▲	▲▲
Brighton	▲▲▲▲	▲▲▲	▲▲▲▲	▲▲▲▲	▲▲▲▲
Buttermilk	▲▲▲▲▲	▲▲▲▲▲	▲▲▲▲	▲▲▲▲▲	▲▲▲▲
The Canyons	▲▲▲	▲▲	▲▲	▲▲▲	▲▲▲
Copper Mountain	▲▲	▲▲▲▲	▲▲▲	▲▲▲▲▲	▲▲▲
Crested Butte	▲▲▲▲	▲▲▲	▲▲▲	▲▲	▲▲▲▲
Crystal Mountain	▲▲▲▲	▲▲▲▲	▲▲▲▲	▲▲▲▲	▲▲▲▲
Deer Valley	▲▲▲▲	▲▲▲▲	▲▲▲▲▲	▲▲▲▲▲	▲▲▲▲
Grand Targhee	▲▲▲▲	▲▲▲▲	▲▲▲▲	▲▲▲▲▲	▲▲▲▲

Mountain Characteristics and Design Table II (continued)

	Inter-sections	Confluence	Cat Tracks/ Traverses	Visual Intimi-dation	Interesting All the Way Down
Heavenly	▲▲	▲▲	▲	▲▲▲▲	▲▲▲
Jackson Hole	▲▲▲▲▲	▲▲▲▲	▲▲	▲	▲▲▲▲▲
June Mountain	▲▲▲▲	▲▲▲▲	▲▲▲▲	▲▲▲▲▲	▲▲
Keystone	▲▲▲	▲▲▲	▲▲▲▲	▲▲▲▲	▲▲▲
Kirkwood	▲▲▲▲	▲▲▲▲	▲▲▲▲	▲▲▲	▲▲▲▲
Loveland	▲▲▲	▲▲▲	▲▲▲▲	▲▲▲▲	▲▲
Mammoth	▲▲▲	▲▲	▲▲▲▲	▲▲▲▲	▲▲▲▲
Mission Ridge	▲▲▲	▲▲▲	▲▲▲▲	▲▲▲▲▲	▲▲▲
Mount Bachelor	▲▲▲▲▲	▲▲▲▲▲	▲▲▲▲	▲▲▲	▲▲▲▲
Northstar	▲▲▲▲	▲▲▲	▲▲▲▲	▲▲▲▲	▲▲
Park City	▲▲	▲▲	▲▲▲	▲▲▲▲	▲▲▲
Powder Mountain	▲▲▲▲	▲▲▲	▲▲	▲▲▲▲▲	▲▲▲▲
Purgatory	▲▲▲	▲▲▲▲	▲▲	▲▲▲▲▲	▲▲
Santa Fe	▲▲▲	▲▲▲	▲▲	▲▲▲	▲▲▲
Schweitzer Mtn.	▲▲▲▲	▲▲▲	▲▲▲▲	▲▲▲	▲▲▲▲
Sierra-at-Tahoe	▲▲▲▲	▲▲▲▲	▲▲▲	▲▲▲▲	▲▲▲▲
Snowbasin	▲▲▲▲	▲▲▲	▲▲▲	▲▲▲	▲▲▲▲▲
Snowbird	▲▲▲	▲▲▲▲	▲▲	▲	▲▲▲▲▲
Snowmass	▲▲▲▲	▲▲▲	▲▲▲▲	▲▲▲▲	▲▲▲
Solitude	▲▲▲	▲▲▲▲	▲▲▲	▲▲	▲▲▲▲
Squaw Valley	▲▲▲▲	▲▲	▲▲▲	▲▲▲▲	▲▲▲▲
Steamboat	▲▲▲	▲▲▲	▲▲▲▲	▲▲▲▲	▲▲▲▲
Stevens Pass	▲▲▲▲	▲▲▲	▲▲▲▲	▲▲▲▲	▲▲▲▲
Sugar Bowl	▲▲▲▲	▲▲▲	▲▲▲▲	▲▲▲▲	▲▲▲▲
Sundance	▲▲▲▲	▲▲▲	▲▲▲▲	▲▲▲	▲▲▲
Sun Valley	▲▲▲▲	▲▲	▲▲▲▲	▲▲▲▲	▲▲▲
Taos	▲▲	▲▲▲	▲▲▲	▲	▲▲▲▲
Telluride	▲▲▲	▲▲	▲▲	▲▲	▲▲▲▲
Vail	▲▲	▲▲▲	▲▲	▲▲▲▲▲	▲▲▲
Whistler	▲▲▲▲▲	▲▲▲▲	▲▲	▲▲	▲▲▲▲
Winter Park	▲▲▲▲	▲▲▲	▲▲▲	▲▲▲	▲▲▲

Crowd Conditions and Skier Traffic Control

These items rate how well the mountain handles skier traffic on an average high season weekday. If a mountain scores low, assume that the congestion will be significantly worse on weekends and holidays.

Lift Design, Adequacy, Placement This relates to the number of lifts, the types of lifts, and the extent to which the lift system distributes skiers effectively around the mountain. The more efficient the system, the higher the score.

Lift Line Crowding Can the lift system accommodate the average number of skiers on the mountain with little or no wait? This item is scored in terms of the more popular lifts and parts of the mountain, as opposed to averaging all of the lifts. A resort where skiers wait less than five minutes to board a lift that services a popular part of the mountain will rate high.

Beginner/Novice Area Congestion Is there enough beginner/novice terrain on the mountain relative to the average number of beginner/novice skiers? The less congestion, the higher the score.

Intermediate Run Congestion Is there enough intermediate terrain on the mountain relative to the average number of intermediate skiers? The less congestion, the higher the score.

Crowd Conditions and Skier Traffic Control			
Lift Design, Adequacy, Placement	Lift Line Crowding	Beginner / Novice Area Congestion	Intermediate Run Congestion
Alpine Meadows ▲▲▲▲	▲▲▲	▲▲▲▲	▲▲▲
Alta ▲▲▲▲	▲▲▲	▲▲▲▲	▲▲▲▲
Arapahoe Basin ▲▲▲	▲▲▲	▲▲▲▲	▲▲▲
Aspen Highlands ▲▲▲▲	▲▲▲▲▲	▲▲▲	▲▲▲
Aspen Mountain ▲▲▲▲	▲▲▲▲▲	n/a	▲▲▲
Beaver Creek ▲▲▲▲	▲▲▲▲	▲▲▲▲	▲▲▲▲
Big Mountain ▲▲▲	▲▲▲▲	▲▲▲▲	▲▲▲▲▲
Big Sky ▲▲▲▲▲	▲▲▲▲	▲▲▲▲▲	▲▲▲▲
Blackcomb ▲▲▲▲	▲▲▲	▲▲▲▲▲	▲▲▲
Breckenridge ▲▲	▲▲	▲▲▲▲	▲▲
Brian Head ▲▲▲	▲▲▲	▲▲▲	▲▲▲▲

Crowd Conditions and Skier Traffic Control (continued)

	Lift Design, Adequacy, Placement	Lift Line Crowding	Beginner / Novice Area Congestion	Intermediate Run Congestion
Bridger Bowl	▲▲▲	▲▲▲	▲▲▲▲	▲▲▲▲
Brighton	▲▲▲▲	▲▲▲▲	▲▲▲	▲▲▲
Buttermilk	▲▲▲▲	▲▲▲▲▲	▲▲▲▲▲	▲▲▲▲
The Canyons	▲▲▲▲	▲▲▲▲	▲▲▲▲	▲▲▲▲
Copper Mountain	▲▲▲	▲▲	▲▲▲▲	▲▲▲▲
Crested Butte	▲▲▲	▲▲▲▲	▲▲▲	▲▲▲▲
Crystal Mountain	▲▲▲	▲▲▲▲	▲▲▲▲	▲▲▲▲
Deer Valley	▲▲▲▲	▲▲▲▲	▲▲▲	▲▲▲
Grand Targhee	▲▲▲▲▲	▲▲▲▲	▲▲▲	▲▲▲▲▲
Heavenly	▲▲▲	▲▲	▲▲▲	▲▲▲▲
Jackson Hole	▲▲▲▲	▲▲▲▲	▲▲▲▲	▲▲▲▲
June Mountain	▲▲▲	▲▲▲▲	▲▲▲▲▲	▲▲▲▲
Keystone	▲▲▲▲	▲▲▲	▲▲	▲▲
Kirkwood	▲▲▲	▲▲▲	▲▲▲▲	▲▲▲
Loveland	▲▲▲	▲▲▲	▲▲▲	▲▲▲
Mammoth	▲▲▲▲▲	▲▲	▲▲▲	▲▲
Mission Ridge	▲	▲▲▲	▲▲▲	▲▲▲
Mount Bachelor	▲▲▲▲▲	▲▲▲	▲▲	▲▲
Northstar	▲▲▲	▲▲▲	▲▲▲▲▲	▲▲▲
Park City	▲▲▲▲▲	▲▲▲	▲▲▲	▲▲
Powder Mountain	▲▲	▲▲▲▲	▲▲▲	▲▲▲▲▲
Purgatory	▲▲	▲▲▲▲	▲▲▲▲	▲▲▲
Santa Fe	▲▲▲▲	▲▲▲	▲▲▲▲	▲▲▲▲
Schweitzer Mtn.	▲▲▲▲	▲▲▲	▲▲▲▲	▲▲▲▲
Sierra-at-Tahoe	▲▲▲▲	▲▲▲▲	▲▲▲▲	▲▲▲
Snowbasin	▲▲▲▲	▲▲▲▲	▲▲▲▲	▲▲▲▲
Snowbird	▲▲▲▲▲	▲▲	▲▲▲	▲▲▲
Snowmass	▲▲▲▲	▲▲▲▲	▲▲▲	▲▲▲
Solitude	▲▲▲▲	▲▲▲▲	▲▲▲▲	▲▲▲▲
Squaw Valley	▲▲▲▲	▲▲▲	▲▲▲	▲▲
Steamboat	▲▲▲	▲▲▲	▲▲▲	▲▲▲▲
Stevens Pass	▲▲▲	▲▲▲	▲▲▲▲	▲▲▲
Sugar Bowl	▲▲▲	▲▲▲	▲▲▲	▲▲▲
Sundance	▲▲▲	▲▲▲▲	▲▲▲	▲▲▲▲
Sun Valley	▲▲▲▲▲	▲▲▲	▲▲▲▲	▲▲▲
Taos	▲▲▲	▲▲▲	▲▲▲	▲▲▲
Telluride	▲▲▲	▲▲▲▲	▲▲	▲▲▲
Vail	▲▲▲▲	▲▲▲▲▲	▲▲▲	▲▲▲▲
Whistler	▲▲▲▲	▲▲▲	▲▲▲▲▲	▲▲▲
Winter Park	▲▲▲	▲▲▲	▲▲▲	▲▲▲

Beginning Skier Considerations

These ratings take into account two items of interest to beginner and novice skiers.

Nonbeginner Traffic in Beginner/Novice Areas   Relates to the amount of nonbeginner traffic passing through beginner trails or practice areas. Ski areas where a lot of nonbeginner traffic is present on beginner trails will score low. "Beginner trails" in this context refers to the first-timer area(s) and to those green trails that first-timers would logically graduate to after a few days.

Beginner Terrain Transition   Relates to the availability of trails of incrementally increasing difficulty, thus allowing first-timers and novices to transition gradually to more challenging terrain. A ski area with good transitional terrain will score high.

Beginning Skier Considerations		
	Nonbeginner Traffic in Beginner/ Novice Areas	Beginner Terrain Transition
Alpine Meadows	▲▲▲▲	▲▲▲▲
Alta	▲▲▲▲▲	▲▲▲
Arapahoe Basin	▲▲▲	▲▲
Aspen Highlands	▲▲	▲▲
Aspen Mountain	n/a	none
Beaver Creek	▲▲▲	▲▲▲▲▲
Big Mountain	▲▲▲▲	▲▲▲▲
Big Sky	▲▲▲▲	▲▲▲
Blackcomb	▲▲▲	▲▲▲▲▲
Breckenridge	▲▲▲▲	▲▲▲▲
Brian Head	▲▲▲	▲▲▲▲
Bridger Bowl	▲▲▲	▲▲▲▲
Brighton	▲▲	▲▲▲▲
Buttermilk	▲▲▲▲▲	▲▲▲▲▲
The Canyons	▲▲▲▲	▲▲▲
Copper Mountain	▲▲▲▲▲	▲▲▲▲
Crested Butte	▲▲▲▲	▲▲▲
Crystal Mountain	▲▲▲▲	▲▲▲▲
Deer Valley	▲▲▲▲▲	▲▲
Grand Targhee	▲▲▲▲	▲▲▲
Heavenly	▲▲	▲▲▲

Beginning Skier Considerations (continued)

	Nonbeginner Traffic in Beginner/ Novice Areas	Beginner Terrain Transition
Jackson Hole	▲▲▲	▲
June Mountain	▲▲▲▲	▲▲▲▲
Keystone	▲▲▲▲▲	▲▲▲
Kirkwood	▲▲▲▲	▲▲▲▲
Loveland	▲▲▲	▲▲▲▲
Mammoth	▲▲▲▲	▲▲▲▲
Mission Ridge	▲▲▲▲	▲▲▲
Mount Bachelor	▲▲	▲▲▲▲▲
Northstar	▲▲	▲▲▲▲
Park City	▲▲▲	▲▲▲
Powder Mountain	▲▲▲	▲▲▲▲
Purgatory	▲▲▲▲	▲▲▲
Santa Fe	▲▲	▲▲▲
Schweitzer Mountain	▲▲▲▲	▲▲▲▲▲
Sierra-at-Tahoe	▲▲▲	▲▲▲▲
Snowbasin	▲▲▲▲	▲▲▲▲
Snowbird	▲▲▲▲	▲▲
Snowmass	▲▲▲	▲▲▲▲▲
Solitude	▲▲▲	▲▲▲▲
Squaw Valley	▲▲▲	▲▲
Steamboat	▲▲	▲▲
Stevens Pass	▲▲▲▲	▲▲▲▲
Sugar Bowl	▲▲▲	▲▲▲▲
Sundance	▲▲▲	▲▲▲
Sun Valley	▲▲▲▲▲	▲▲
Taos	▲▲▲▲	▲▲
Telluride	▲▲▲▲	▲▲▲
Vail	▲▲▲▲▲	▲▲▲
Whistler	▲▲▲	▲▲▲▲▲
Winter Park	▲▲▲	▲▲▲

Groomed Cruising Terrain and Bumps

These categories rate the availability and plentifulness of groomed cruising as well as entry-level moguls. All three categories assume normal grooming operations. The higher the number of stars, the more this type of skiing is available.

Groomed, Friendly Angle Cruising Relates to the availability and abundance of mellow, "friendly angle," groomed cruising runs.

Groomed Steeps Relates to the availability and plentifulness of steep groomed runs.

Entry-Level Bumps Relates to the availability of entry-level bumps. An ideal situation offers smaller bumps adjacent to a groomed run, thus allowing the learning skier to enter and exit the bumps easily (without committing to an entire bump run).

Groomed Cruising Terrain and Bumps		
Groomed, Friendly Angle Cruising	Groomed Steeps	Entry-Level Bumps
Alpine Meadows ▲▲▲▲	▲▲	▲▲▲
Alta ▲▲▲	▲▲	▲▲▲▲▲
Arapahoe Basin ▲▲▲	▲▲▲	▲▲
Aspen Highlands ▲▲▲	▲	▲▲▲
Aspen Mountain ▲▲▲	▲▲▲▲	▲
Beaver Creek ▲▲▲▲	▲▲	▲▲▲
Big Mountain ▲▲▲▲	▲▲▲▲	▲▲▲▲
Big Sky ▲▲▲▲▲	▲▲▲	▲▲▲▲▲
Blackcomb ▲▲▲	▲▲▲▲▲	▲▲
Breckenridge ▲▲▲▲	▲▲▲	▲▲▲
Brian Head ▲▲▲	▲▲▲	▲▲▲▲
Bridger Bowl ▲▲▲▲	▲▲	▲▲
Brighton ▲▲▲▲	▲▲▲	▲▲
Buttermilk ▲▲▲▲▲	▲	▲▲
The Canyons ▲▲▲▲	▲▲▲	▲▲▲
Copper Mountain ▲▲▲▲▲	▲▲▲	▲▲▲▲
Crested Butte ▲▲▲	▲▲	▲▲
Crystal Mountain ▲▲▲	▲▲▲▲	▲▲▲▲
Deer Valley ▲▲▲▲	▲▲▲▲▲	▲▲
Grand Targhee ▲▲▲	▲▲▲▲	▲▲▲▲
Heavenly ▲▲▲▲▲	▲▲▲	▲▲
Jackson Hole ▲▲	▲▲▲▲	▲▲
June Mountain ▲▲▲▲▲	▲▲	▲▲▲
Keystone ▲▲▲▲	▲▲▲	▲▲▲▲▲
Kirkwood ▲▲▲	▲▲▲▲	▲▲▲▲
Loveland ▲▲▲	▲	▲▲▲
Mammoth ▲▲▲▲▲	▲▲▲▲	▲▲
Mission Ridge ▲▲▲▲	▲▲	▲▲▲
Mount Bachelor ▲▲▲▲▲	▲▲▲▲▲	▲
Northstar ▲▲▲▲▲	▲▲	▲▲▲▲▲

Groomed Cruising Terrain and Bumps (continued)

	Groomed, Friendly Angle Cruising	Groomed Steeps	Entry-Level Bumps
Park City	▲▲▲▲	▲▲▲	▲▲▲▲
Powder Mountain	▲▲▲▲	▲▲	▲▲
Purgatory	▲▲▲	▲▲	▲▲▲
Santa Fe	▲▲▲▲	▲▲	▲▲
Schweitzer Mountain	▲▲▲	▲▲▲▲	▲▲▲▲
Sierra-at-Tahoe	▲▲▲▲	▲▲▲	▲▲▲
Snowbasin	▲▲▲▲	▲▲▲	▲▲▲
Snowbird	▲▲▲	▲▲▲	▲▲▲▲
Snowmass	▲▲▲▲▲	▲▲▲	▲▲▲▲▲
Solitude	▲▲▲	▲▲▲▲	▲▲▲▲
Squaw Valley	▲▲▲▲	▲▲▲	▲▲▲
Steamboat	▲▲▲▲	▲▲	▲▲▲
Stevens Pass	▲▲▲	▲▲	▲▲▲
Sugar Bowl	▲▲▲▲	▲▲	▲▲▲
Sundance	▲▲▲	▲▲▲	▲▲▲
Sun Valley	▲▲▲▲	▲▲▲▲▲	▲▲
Taos	▲▲	▲▲	▲▲
Telluride	▲▲	▲▲▲▲	▲▲
Vail	▲▲▲▲	▲▲▲	▲▲▲
Whistler	▲▲▲▲	▲▲▲▲▲	▲▲
Winter Park	▲▲▲	▲▲	▲▲

Weather

While just about any kind of weather can be encountered on any mountain, the fact is that certain conditions are experienced more frequently on some mountains than on others.

Ice Relates to the probability and extent of ice forming on ski runs during the heart of the season—late December through the third week in March. The more pronounced the tendency to ice, the lower the score.

Wind Relates to the probability of high winds. Areas with frequent high winds score low.

Cold If the mountain, for whatever reason, is unusually cold, the score will be low.

Weather		
	Ice	Wind	Cold
Alpine Meadows	▲▲▲	▲▲▲	▲▲▲▲
Alta	▲▲▲▲▲	▲▲▲▲	▲▲▲▲
Arapahoe Basin	▲▲▲▲	▲▲	▲▲
Aspen Highlands	▲▲▲	▲▲▲	▲▲▲
Aspen Mountain	▲▲▲	▲▲▲	▲▲▲
Beaver Creek	▲▲▲	▲▲▲	▲▲▲
Big Mountain	▲▲▲▲	▲▲▲	▲
Big Sky	▲▲▲▲	▲▲	▲
Blackcomb	▲▲	▲▲	▲▲
Breckenridge	▲▲	▲	▲▲
Brian Head	▲▲▲	▲▲▲▲	▲▲▲▲
Bridger Bowl	▲▲▲▲	▲▲▲	▲▲
Brighton	▲▲▲▲	▲▲▲	▲▲▲▲
Buttermilk	▲▲▲	▲▲▲▲	▲▲▲
The Canyons	▲▲▲	▲▲▲▲	▲▲▲
Copper Mountain	▲▲▲	▲▲	▲▲▲
Crested Butte	▲▲	▲▲▲	▲▲▲
Crystal Mountain	▲▲▲	▲▲▲	▲▲▲▲
Deer Valley	▲▲	▲▲▲	▲▲▲
Grand Targhee	▲▲▲▲	▲▲	▲▲
Heavenly	▲▲▲	▲▲	▲▲▲▲
Jackson Hole	▲▲▲	▲▲	▲▲
June Mountain	▲▲▲	▲▲▲▲	▲▲▲▲▲
Keystone	▲▲▲	▲▲▲	▲▲
Kirkwood	▲▲▲▲	▲▲▲	▲▲▲▲
Loveland	▲▲▲▲	▲▲▲	▲▲▲
Mammoth	▲▲▲▲	▲▲	▲▲▲▲
Mission Ridge	▲▲▲	▲▲▲	▲▲▲▲
Mount Bachelor	▲▲▲	▲	▲▲▲
Northstar	▲▲▲	▲▲▲▲	▲▲▲▲
Park City	▲▲▲	▲▲▲▲	▲▲▲
Powder Mountain	▲▲▲▲▲	▲▲▲▲	▲▲▲
Purgatory	▲▲▲▲▲	▲▲▲▲▲	▲▲▲
Santa Fe	▲▲▲▲	▲▲▲▲	▲▲▲▲
Schweitzer Mountain	▲▲▲	▲▲	▲▲
Sierra-at-Tahoe	▲▲▲	▲▲▲	▲▲▲
Snowbasin	▲▲▲▲	▲▲	▲▲▲
Snowbird	▲▲▲▲	▲▲▲	▲▲▲
Snowmass	▲▲▲	▲▲▲	▲▲
Solitude	▲▲▲	▲▲▲	▲▲▲
Squaw Valley	▲▲	▲▲	▲▲▲▲
Steamboat	▲▲	▲▲▲	▲▲

Weather (continued)

	Ice	Wind	Cold
Stevens Pass	▲▲	▲▲▲	▲▲▲▲
Sugar Bowl	▲▲▲▲	▲▲▲	▲▲▲▲
Sundance	▲▲▲	▲▲▲	▲▲▲▲
Sun Valley	▲▲	▲▲▲▲	▲▲
Taos	▲▲▲▲	▲▲▲▲	▲▲▲▲▲
Telluride	▲▲▲	▲▲▲	▲▲▲▲▲
Vail	▲▲	▲▲▲▲	▲▲▲
Whistler	▲▲	▲▲	▲▲
Winter Park	▲▲▲	▲▲▲	▲▲▲

Getting There

Flights are cheaper and more readily available if you can come and go on a weekday. Tuesday is generally the slowest day of the week for airlines, followed by Thursday and Wednesday. Book the earliest flight possible even if it means setting off before the sun rises. According to the department of transportation, flights that leave before 9 A.M. are 33% more likely to arrive on time than flights departing after 9 A.M. Also, taking an early morning flight makes for an easier day. Even if you do not intend to ski on your arrival day, the early start will ensure that you have plenty of time to drive to your final destination (if you rent a car), check in, buy groceries, rent equipment, and get settled in.

If you want to use frequent flyer miles, start calling in July for major air destinations like Salt Lake City, Reno, San Francisco, Vancouver, and Denver. For smaller mountain destinations like Aspen, Gunnison, Steamboat, Bozeman, and the like, don't call until the seasonal air service is downloaded into the system in September. If you can't find a seat on a weekend, try for a Tuesday, Thursday, or Wednesday.

Most airlines review their bookings for January and February in December. If business is soft you can expect a big cut-rate fare sale to ensue around December 7th for travel in January and February. We recommend hedging your bet by buying tickets at the best rate you can obtain in mid September. If a sale occurs in December, some airlines will credit the difference between the price you paid and the sale price, while others will allow you to switch to the lower fare after deducting a change fee. Each airline is a little bit different, so ask, "What are my options if I buy now and you run a fare sale later?"

Because flying is always problematic during the winter months, try to keep your itinerary as simple as possible. Let's say you live in Louisville and want to fly to Bozeman, Montana (for Big Sky). The airline will try to sell you an itinerary where you fly from Louisville to Cincinnatti, connecting to Salt Lake, with a second connection from Salt Lake to Bozeman. In the winter this is one connection too many. You're better off eliminating one connection by driving from Louisville to Cincinnati and initiating your flight itinerary there. If you live in a city served by two or more airports, you can bet that one of the airports is better designed and equipped to handle winter weather than others. In the New York area, for example, Newark and Kennedy airports are better winter alternatives than LaGuardia.

Before you head to the airport, check the weather channel for winter storm advisories affecting your hub city. If the weather is iffy, see if your carrier will reroute you through a another hub. Returning to Atlanta from Whistler out of Vancouver, we discovered that our hub airport, Chicago O'Hare, was experiencing major weather delays. On request, our airline gladly rerouted us through Phoenix. If a reroute is not possible, we advise booking a hotel room at the hub city in case you get stuck. If you don't need it you can always cancel the reservation. Incidentally, in the event of weather delays or weather related flight cancellations, the airlines will not arrange or pay for a hotel.

If you can afford it, commuter flights from a major airport to the resorts make life a lot easier, providing the weather is good. When the weather is bad, the smaller airports in the mountains are sometimes forced to suspend operations. If you are en route to the mountains, you may be seriously delayed or, alternatively, be forced to drive from the nearest major airport. On your return trip, weather delays and flight cancellations at the smaller airports also may cause you to miss your connecting flights.

Five major airports serve most of the ski mountains described in this guide. From these five you can either continue on to your resort destination by rental car, resort shuttle service, or, in some cases, by commuter flight. The big five are Denver International Airport (Colorado), Salt Lake International Airport (Utah), Vancouver International Airport (British Columbia), Reno-Tahoe International Airport (Nevada), and Albuquerque International Airport (New Mexico).

The Reno and Albuquerque airports are small and efficient. Baggage handling is expeditious, it's easy to rent a car, and the airports are convenient to town. Vancouver International is undergoing a major renovation that will occasion delays, hassles, and additional expense for the foreseeable future. The really big players in the ski market, however, are Denver International and Salt Lake International airports.

The Denver International Airport (DIA) opened in the spring of 1995. Technologically state-of-the-art, the new airport is designed to minimize the kind of traffic and weather delays that plagued Stapleton Airport (the old

Denver airport). DIA for pilots is a dream come true. DIA for passengers, however, is sometimes a nightmare. For starters, the airport is in the middle of nowhere, 30 miles from Denver on the desolate prairie. For skiers, the location of DIA adds about 30 minutes to the commute to the mountains.

Much of the cost burden of the $5 billion airport is passed along to user airlines, which (surprise!) pass it along to their customers. The cost of doing business at DIA was so great that Continental Airlines abandoned Denver as a hub and cut departures by 80 percent. Continental's bailout left United with more than 68 percent of the market and not much in the way of competition. Bottom line for skiers: inconvenient location, less service, and higher ticket prices.

All of the rental car agencies except U.S. Rent-a-Car, Affinity, and All America have processing counters on the fifth level (baggage claim) of the terminal. We recommend that you complete your paperwork while you are waiting for your skis and luggage. Be prepared to pay more for your rental car than you were quoted by your travel agent. You will be hit with a $3-a-day surcharge for the privilege of using this wonderful airport in addition to 11 percent taxes.

Paperwork, luggage, and skis in hand, head out the level 5 doors to catch a van or bus to the rental agency lots where you will pick up your car. To save time at the car lot, designate one of your party to sprint to the counter as soon as the bus arrives, while the remainder of the group handles the luggage and skis. If you have completed your rental agreement at the airport and want to pick up your car while the rest of your group waits for the luggage and skis, proceed through the level 5 door to the courtesy shuttles and from there to the car lots. After picking up your rental car, return to the airport via Pena Boulevard. Follow the Passenger Pickup sign to the fourth level, where you can meet your group and load at the curb.

We have every hope that conditions will improve at DIA. If they do not, however, anticipate burning 1.5–2 hours from the time you get off the plane to the time you drive away in your rental car.

On the return trip, be sure to fill your rental car with gas before you leave Denver, or at the new gas station just inside the DIA grounds, near the toll booth on Pena Boulevard. Assume a 45-minute commute (longer during rush hours) from Denver to the airport, 15 minutes to turn in your car and catch the courtesy bus, 5–10 minutes to get to the terminal, 30 minutes to check in, and 25 minutes to reach your departure gate. All told, about two hours and some change. Rental car courtesy vehicles, incidentally, will drop you off on the fifth level. To reach the ticket counters and baggage check, you must haul your luggage and skis up the escalator to the sixth level.

Compared to DIA, western skiing's other major hub, the Salt Lake International Airport, is a breeze. The airport is almost never shut down due to inclement weather, luggage and skis are delivered expeditiously, and best of all, the facility is only 10 minutes from downtown Salt Lake City and 45–60 minutes from ten different ski resorts.

A Word About Checked Luggage

Twice in the past three years, our ski gear has missed an air connection and was missing in action for a day or two. Now we pack ski boots, goggles, long underwear, ski socks, parka, and gloves in a carry on bag along with such necessities as prescription medication. Everything else needed to ski can be rented, so there's no worry about missing the first day of skiing because of lost luggage.

Rental Cars

If a rental car is part of your ski vacation plans, remember that you might have to drive through mountainous terrain in less than optimal driving conditions. At the very least, rent a vehicle with front-wheel drive. If conditions warrant, upgrade to a four-wheel-drive vehicle. If you rent your car in a desert or Pacific Coast city that doesn't see much snow, make sure that the car has tires suitable for driving in snow. Also check the windshield wiper cleaning fluid and look to see if a windshield scraper is provided.

Take into consideration that you will require luggage space on arrival and departure days. Be certain you rent a car large enough to comfortably accommodate your entire party as well as your luggage and skiing equipment. For convenience and maximum space utilization, rent ski racks (most hold five pairs of skis), and have members of your group pack their belongings in soft luggage.

Try to avoid itineraries that involve long drives into the mountains after dark. If you are contemplating such a drive and the weather is bad, seriously consider getting a hotel for the night and starting fresh in the morning.

Lift Tickets

Except in unusual situations, you should not have to pay full price for lift tickets. For starters, ski mountains compete for local skiers by discounting tickets in major urban areas within driving distance of the resort. In Denver, King Soopers (a supermarket chain) sells discounted tickets to Keystone, Copper Mountain, Winter Park, Eldora, and Breckenridge. Discounts average $5–9 per day depending on the resort. If you are driving to the mountains from Denver International Airport, the most convenient King Sooper is on Youngfield Street, 300 yards from the West 32nd Avenue exit off I-70. Call (303) 238-6486 for information. In Salt Lake City, try Dan's Foodstores, Harmon's, and Smith's (supermarkets) for discounted lift tickets.

Dan's (phone (801) 943-7601) sells only Solitude lift tickets; Smith's (phone (801) 328-1683) sells Snowbird and sometimes Deer Valley tickets; and Harmon's (phone (801) 967-9213) sells only Brighton tickets.

For discounts on lift tickets, as well as on ski equipment rentals, ski lessons, lodging, and even dining, order a World Skier Membership Discount Kit from the World Ski Association, (303) 629-7669. The first kit is $19.95; second and subsequent kits are $14.95 each. The kit includes a services directory and a membership card, among other things. To obtain discount lift tickets and other services, present the card at participating resorts' lift ticket offices. For certain mountains like Aspen, Buttermilk, Snowmass, and Aspen Highlands, lift tickets can be purchased in advance. Not all ski mountains participate in the program, and some who do offer only nominal savings, such as $5 off on night skiing. In general, the discount program is strongest in Colorado. WSA members are limited to purchasing discounted lift tickets once each day and only for their own use. Members, in other words, cannot buy discounted ski passes for others in their family or group. Each person seeking to obtain the discount must have his or her own membership card.

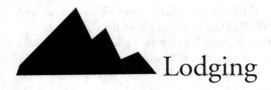 # Lodging

Ski resort lodging is unique in the tourism and hospitality industry. Because skiing is social, it has great appeal to parties, families, and groups of various sizes. This translates into a tremendous demand for lodging that not only furnishes sleeping accommodations, but also provides space where members of the group can come together to dine and socialize. In ski resort communities, the accommodation of choice is increasingly the condominium or rental home. While hotels continue to serve solo travelers and couples, most of the lodging growth in western ski venues is in condos and homes.

The resort towns at the base of most ski mountains are more than a service infrastructure for tourists. In the main, these towns are well-established communities with strong identities and sizable year-round populations. The beauty of the mountains in conjunction with civic pride, a largely affluent population, and cultural resources seldom found outside of major cities make ski resort towns very desirable places to live any time of year.

Ski resort communities usually have more in common with real estate developments than with tourist destinations. The ski mountain is a recreational centerpiece used to attract buyers in the market for a primary or vacation residence and serves the same function as golf courses in real estate developments elsewhere in the country. In most ski resorts, condos and homes have eclipsed hotels as the most prevalent form of lodging. For example, in Aspen, Colorado, arguably the capital of American skiing, there is only one chain hotel.

From a consumer point of view, the explosion of condominiums and rental homes has resulted in a very decentralized lodging inventory. Whereas a central reservations service or convention authority in Chicago or Miami might be expected to know what is available and which hotels have vacancies, it doesn't work like that in ski venues. There is usually a central reservations service in a ski resort community, but owing to the diverse private ownership of most of the accommodations, it is practically impossible for that service to keep track of what is available.

Because demand for accommodations in the mountains is very predictable, rates are established and remain fairly stable. Hotel and condo owners in popular ski destinations know that, barring a bad snow year, they can pretty much charge full rack rate. There is, in fact, little discounting of ski resort accommodations. Half-price clubs and room consolidators are conspicuously absent in the ski vacation industry. There is less emphasis on negotiating price than on matching specific skiers with accommodations that meet their physical and budgetary requirements. When deals are made, they are usually promoted through high-volume tour operators who sell ski vacation packages.

An exception is lodging discounts offered to members of the World Ski Association (mentioned on page 38). The WSA publishes a directory for its members that lists participating hotels and condos in almost all western U.S. and Canadian ski areas. Discounts range from 5 to 20 percent off, depending on when during the ski season you want to book. All discounts are subject to availability. Members must contact the hotel or management agency directly and make the reservations themselves. Callers must identify themselves up front as members of the WSA and quote the specific offer described in the directory. Accommodations available include hotel rooms and suites, condos, and homes. Some accommodations are ski-in/ski-out. For additional information, call the World Ski Association at (303) 629-7669.

The Sellers

There are a lot of different players selling lodging to skiers—so many, in fact, that sometimes the market is very confusing. The trick is to differentiate the "order takers" from the really knowledgeable agents who can provide valuable information and dig up the best deals.

Ski Vacation Tour Operators. Also called packagers, these are companies that sell complete ski vacations including airfare, lodging, lift tickets, rental car or airport transfers, and, if needed, ski equipment. Most packagers offer both condo and hotel accommodations. Large tour operators offer ski packages to most major western resorts. Later in this section we will tell you how to evaluate ski vacation packages and how to elicit the best deals from tour operators.

Central Reservations Services. Most large resorts have one, and they are usually operated by the resort management company, the local chamber of commerce, or the tourist bureau. Central reservations services book both hotels and condos and attempt to function as a lodging clearinghouse. Though many central reservations services are very good, very few are able to keep track of all the lodging inventory available in their area. If you can specifically define your budget and lodging requirements, a well-organized central reservations service can be very helpful in locating accommodations. Seldom, however, will central reservations services be aware of available discounts or other special deals. Usually the central reservations service represents the resort management as well as various local realtors and property management enterprises that have private condos and homes to rent. Central reservations operates in a passive, responsive mode, and you must be able to ask the right questions in order to obtain useful information. Most central reservations agents are order takers. Furthermore, central reservations agents do not usually have the authority to negotiate rates or make special arrangements. Central reservations services will deal directly with you or work with your travel agent.

Receptive Operators. These are local, independent lodging agents who intimately know the local hotel and condo scene. Receptives often come from, or are involved in, the local real estate market and have physically inspected the properties they suggest. Best of all, most are aware of condos and homes not listed with the local central reservations service. A good receptive operator will work hard to find that perfect place that fits both your budget and your lodging requirements. Though receptives work directly with consumers the majority of the time, most are willing to assist travel agents. When this occurs, the receptive and the travel agent usually split the available commission. To locate a receptive, call the tourist bureau (or its equivalent) in the resort town of your choice and ask for the names of some good receptive operators. Sometimes the tourist bureau will even assist in sorting out which receptive can best help you. Occasionally you may reach someone unfamiliar with the term "receptive operator." When this occurs, explain that you are looking for a local independent reservations service.

Local Realtors and Management Agencies. These are companies that maintain, manage, and rent privately owned condos and homes for absentee owners. While most realtor and management agency rentals are arranged by the central reservations service or by receptive operators, the realtors and property managers will rent to you or your travel agent if you contact them directly. Sometimes they have nice properties that have recently become available and have not been listed or publicized. Unlike central reservations services and receptive operators, most realtors and management agencies do not work on sales commissions. Instead, they are paid a monthly fee by the owners of the properties they represent. Properties they rent, however, are usually commissionable to your travel agent. The local tourist bureau or association of realtors will put you in touch with management agencies and realtors that rent the type of condo or home you are looking for. As you might guess, the rental condo or home inventory of a particular realtor or management agency will be much more limited than that offered by a good receptive or even central reservations. On the other side of the coin, you might unearth some special property that is never available in the general market.

Individual Property Owners. Some property owners, for a variety of reasons, elect to manage the rental of their own condo or home. Their properties are advertised in the classified ad sections of major skiing specialty magazines, and sometimes in the travel sections of newspapers. While you can occasionally save some money dealing directly with property owners, you may not be able to resolve maintenance or other problems that arise once you have arrived. Properties booked through central reservations, receptives, realtors, or management agencies usually have people on call 24 hours a day to attend to problems in rental units. Likewise, individual owners can be more elusive when it comes to issuing confirmations, arranging for the transfer of keys, and getting back your damage deposit.

A Word about Ski-In/Ski-Out Accommodations

Believe us, there is nothing more wonderful and liberating than being able to walk out your door and commence skiing. Unfortunately, only a fraction of the accommodations billed as ski-in/ski-out provide this convenience. Usually, either coming or going, you will have to shoulder your skis and take a hike. What ski-in/ski-out really means is that you will not have to use your car or catch a shuttle. It does not necessarily mean that you can access the slopes or the lifts right outside your door.

If you are thinking about ski-in/ski-out lodging in a large hotel, consider that you might have a long walk to the elevator from your room and another long walk to the slope or lift access. Also, most hotels require that guests check their skis as opposed to taking them to their rooms. If the ski-check room is run efficiently, it's a labor-saving service; if improperly manned, however, it can be a bottleneck.

Ski-in/ski-out condos and homes are frequently connected to the slopes by cat tracks, sidewalks, or roads. Although it's possible to access the slopes and lifts, access is neither direct nor easy. In the final analysis, if you are willing to bear the additional expense of a ski-in/ski-out hotel, condo, or home, make sure you qualify what ski-in/ski-out actually means before you book.

Condos and Rental Homes vs. Hotels

Now that you know who the sellers are, let's examine the differences among rental homes, condos, and hotels. Hotels, of course, provide public areas like lobbies, lounges, restaurants, swimming pools, and exercise rooms, as well as daily maid and other services. Hotels in most resorts are not any more likely to be closer to the slopes than condos or rental homes.

Rental homes are freestanding, while condominiums are usually part of a large development and almost always share a common wall with adjoining units on either side. Many condos offer the same features as rental homes. While rental homes do not usually offer swimming pools, condominium complexes frequently do. Very, very few condominium complexes, however, include restaurants or lounges or the type of services usually associated with a hotel. There is no daily maid service in most condominiums, though a mid-week tidying up and change of linens on a weekly rental is not uncommon.

If you are considering a multi-mountain resort area such as Vail/Beaver Creek, Aspen/Snowmass, the Lake Tahoe area, or Park City, Utah, there will usually be some part of the overall area where lodging is less expensive. Snowmass, for example, is usually less expensive than Aspen, which is nine miles down the road. At Park City, you can get a better deal on rooms and condos at the Canyons than at Park City Ski Resort or at Deer Valley (the other two nearby ski mountains). Some of the best deals on accommodations in the West are at stand-alone mountains like Big Sky in Montana, or at smaller ski venues such as Powder Mountain or Snowbasin in Utah, or Monarch in Colorado.

Condos and Rental Homes

If there are three or more adults in your party, you will usually be better off in terms of both accommodations and cost to go for a condo or home as opposed to a hotel. In addition to being roomier, the condo (or home) will have a living area where you can be together with the others in your group, and a kitchen and dining area. Eating in your condo instead of in restaurants can save hundreds of dollars.

In addition, although there are some extraordinary hotels at ski resorts, many motels and hotels in the mountains offer not-so-beautiful views of highways, parking lots, and the backs of other buildings. While, of course, there are exceptions, we nevertheless recommend a condo or a rental home as the best way to enjoy the mountains. Many private homes and condos can be had for less than the price of a hotel room and include such amenities as decks, fireplaces, and even hot tubs. Most important, in our estimation, however, is that the condos and rental homes provide exactly the kind of quiet, solitude, and remote beauty that most folks come to the mountains to experience.

The way to go about renting a condo or home is to make a list of features that are important to you. How many beds, bedrooms, and baths do you require? Do you need a full kitchen? When you get your list together, call (or have your travel agent call) a receptive operator and order your home or condo like you would order a pizza. We phoned a receptive in Aspen/Snowmass, Colorado, and said, "We want a two-bedroom, two-bath condo for two adult couples. We prefer to be high on the mountain, with a good view, in a remote quiet area. We don't care about a hot tub, but we do want a fireplace and a nice big deck."

Whether you get what you want depends on how far in advance you make your reservation, when during the ski season you want to visit, what you are willing to spend, and how close you want to be to the lifts, the resort center, or the main shopping and restaurant district. Regarding proximity to the lifts, you can usually get a much nicer condo or home for the money if you are willing to lodge a little farther from the lifts. All large and most medium-size ski resorts have efficient free shuttle service to the slopes. If you have a car, feel free to use it. Even at large resorts like Vail and Snowmass, parking is no problem except on very busy weekends.

When you have figured out what features you want, where you want to be, and when you want to go, then you can start shopping. Initiate your search by calling the local chamber of commerce or tourist information office at your chosen destination. Information specialists will provide you with the names and phone numbers of local area receptive operators, realtors, and management companies that rent the kind of accommodations you are looking for.

The better homes and condos are reserved well in advance. Some renters sign up for next year during this year's stay. The earlier you plan, therefore, the better your chances of getting what you want. If you are picky, or are looking for something special, start your shopping early. If there is a ski area you visit every year, take a day off skiing and go look at some possible rental properties for next year's trip.

When you talk with a receptive or rental agent about a particular home or condo, ask how old the property is. If it's older than five or six years, ask if it has been recently renovated. If the property sounds appealing, request that you be mailed photos of both the exterior and interior. Color is better than black and white, but either will do. Some agents have only one set of color photos. If this is the case, suggest that the agent send photocopies in black and white or color. Write off any agent that will not supply some sort of photograph or copy. Never reserve a property strictly on the basis of a rendering, sketch, or line drawing. Insist on a photograph. As an aside, be aware that many homes and condos, while beautiful outside, offer interiors that range from truly tasteless to absolutely bewildering. Mining Town Bordello, Decorator Tepee, and Longhorn Anatomy are but three of the major decorating styles alive and well in western mountain rental properties.

Particularly during the busier times of year, some agencies require a five- or seven-day minimum rental. We were able to work around the minimum, however, by finding properties with two-, three-, and four-day gaps between renters. We found a three-bedroom condo, for example, that was reserved from January 11 through January 17, and from January 21 to January 27. The agency was more than happy to rent us the condo for the short intervening period (January 18, 19, and 20). Reservation gaps, as well as cancellations, are common but unpredictable. You have to call around and ask the right questions to uncover the deals. For weekly rentals, check-in and check-out are usually on Saturday, though sometimes other arrangements are possible.

Once you have found a suitable property, you will usually have to prepay with a credit card or check. Some agencies will mail you a rental contract to sign and return, while others will process the whole deal over the phone. Cancellation policies vary, so be sure to inquire. Some agencies charge a set price for the rental property, while others charge on a per-head basis for the number of persons accommodated. If you are asked for a damage deposit, make sure it's refundable and that you understand your obligations. For most rentals, check-out is essentially the same as at a hotel. Some rental agencies, however, request that you strip the beds, take out the garbage, and clean up the kitchen. A few demand that you sweep and vacuum. The easiest way to preclude being unpleasantly surprised is to nail this kind of stuff down before you book.

Once the reservation is made, most agents will provide written confirmation. If written confirmation is not routinely provided, ask for it. Along with your confirmation, the agent will also provide directions to the rental office. Most rental offices operate seven days a week during ski season. Here, you will register, pick up your keys, and be given directions to your rental unit. Once in your home or condo, check to make sure that everything is in order. If there is a problem, most agencies offer 24-hour maintenance service.

If you plan to cook a lot of your meals, as opposed to going to restaurants, be aware that grocery markets in resort communities are often expensive and sometimes may not offer the variety that you're accustomed to at home.

Hotels and Lodges

Hotels in ski resorts run the gamut from large chain hotels to small, cozy, privately owned inns. We recommended hotels for couples or solo travelers, for folks who intend to eat their meals in restaurants, and for skiers who require such amenities as swimming pools, lounges, nightclubs, and daily maid service.

During ski season, except for lodging sold by packagers, there are few discounts offered. For each property, by and large, there is an established rate for each month of the ski season. That is the rate that is quoted and that is the rate you will pay. Chain hotels, to a degree, constitute an exception. Because they are part of a chain, they usually must offer the same discounts as their sister hotels across the country. These include corporate discounts, preferred rates, and other specials. Most hotels in ski venues are listed in the *Hotel & Travel Index*, an industry reference work that your travel agent has.

If you are considering a hotel, you can check its quality as reported by a reliable independent rating system such as those offered by the *AAA Directories*, *Mobil Guides*, or *Frommer's America on Wheels*. Checking two or three independent sources is better than depending on one. If the hotel is not listed in these sources, it may be because it is a privately owned hotel with a loyal repeat clientele.

Before you book, ask how old the hotel is and when the guest rooms were last refurbished. Locate the hotel on a local street map to verify its proximity to the lifts, restaurants, and shops. If you will not have a car, make sure that there is bus or shuttle service that satisfies your needs.

To protect yourself, always guarantee your first night with a major credit card (even if you do not plan to arrive late), send a deposit if required, and insist on a written confirmation of your reservation. When you arrive and check in, have your written confirmation handy.

Getting a Good Deal on a Hotel

The benchmark for making cost comparisons is always the hotel's standard rate, or rack rate. This is what you would pay if, space available, you just walked in off the street and rented a room. In a way, the rack rate is analogous to an airline's standard coach fare. It represents a straight, nondiscounted room rate. In the mountains, you assume the rack rate is the most you should have to pay.

To learn the standard room rate, call room reservations at the hotel(s) of your choice. Do not be surprised if there are several standard rates, one for each type of room in the hotel. Have the reservationist explain the differences in the types of rooms available in each price bracket. Also ask the hotel which of the described class of rooms you would get if you came on a ski vacation package sold by a tour operator or travel agent. This information will allow you to make meaningful comparisons among various packages and rates.

Tour Operator/Packager Deals

Recognizing that an empty hotel room is a liability, various travel entrepreneurs have stepped into the breach, volunteering to sell rooms for the hotels. These entrepreneurs, who call themselves tour operators and travel packagers, reserve or "block" at a discounted rate, a certain number of rooms that they in turn resell at a profit. As this arrangement extends the sales outreach of the hotels, the hotels are only too happy to cooperate with this group of independent sales agents. Although a variety of programs have been developed to sell the rooms, most are marketed as part of ski vacation packages.

This development has been beneficial to both the skier and the hotel. Predicated on volume, some of the room discount is generally passed along to consumers as an incentive to book. By purchasing your room through a tour operator or packager, you may be able to obtain a room at the hotel of your choice for considerably less than if you went through the hotel's reservations department. The hotel commits rooms to the wholesaler or tour operator at a specific deep discount, usually 18–30 percent or more off the standard quoted rate, but makes no effort to control the price the wholesaler offers to his customers.

Packagers and tour operators holding space at a hotel for a specific block of time must surrender that space back to the hotel if the rooms are not sold by a certain date, usually 30 days in advance. Since the wholesaler's or tour operator's performance and credibility are determined by the number of rooms filled in a given hotel, they are always reluctant to give rooms back. The situation is similar to when a particular department at a university approaches the end of the year without having spent all of its allocated budget. The department head reasons that if the remaining funds are not spent (and the surplus is returned to the university), the university might reduce the department budget for the forthcoming year. Tour operators and packagers depend on the hotels for their inventory. The more rooms the hotels allocate, the more inventory they have to sell. If a packager or tour operator keeps returning rooms unsold, it is logical to predict that the hotel will respond by making fewer rooms available in the future. Therefore, the packager would rather sell rooms at a bargain price than give them back to the hotel unsold.

Incidentally, the relationship also works in the other direction. If the hotel is sitting on a goodly number of unsold rooms, it will contact the tour operator and ask for his or her help in selling them. When this happens, it is usually under "fire sale" conditions, and the skier can sometimes score a truly remarkable deal.

You and your travel agent do not have to buy an entire package from a tour operator to get a good rate on a hotel room (some packages offered by airline travel companies are an exception). Also, be aware that some of the really hot deals become available at the last minute, one to four weeks before the dates in question. If you have your heart set on getting a bargain, make your reservations through a tour operator about two weeks or so before your departure date. Could you get stuck without a room? It's possible, but not likely, particularly if your party consists of just two people. If your party is larger than two and there is no room at the inn, you always have the option of going the condo route.

Casino Hotels

If you plan to ski one or more of the Lake Tahoe, California/Nevada mountains, consider rooming at a casino hotel on the Nevada side of the lake. You may be a little farther from the slopes and the ambience will resemble Las Vegas more than Aspen, but the price of your hotel room will be a bargain. Likewise, food and après-ski entertainment will be plentiful and affordable.

For even greater savings, try one of the ski deals offered by Reno casinos. Last year Circus Circus and the Biltmore, among others, featured room rates as low as $45 a night. Some casinos threw in buffets, welcome cocktails, and transportation to Squaw Valley (about 50 minutes west). A brochure describing Reno casino deals for skiers can be obtained by calling (800) 367-7366.

Hotel-Sponsored Deals

In addition to selling rooms through tour operators, most hotels periodically offer deals or packages of their own. Sometimes the deals are specialized or the packages are only offered at certain times of the year, for instance only in November and December. Promotion of hotel specials tends to be limited to the resort area's primary markets. If you live in other parts of the country, you can take advantage of the packages, but you probably will not see them advertised in your local newspaper.

An important point regarding hotel specials is that the hotel reservationists do not usually inform you of existing specials or offer them to you. In other words, you have to ask. Finally, if you are doing your own legwork and are considering a hotel that is part of a national chain, always call the hotel instead of using the chain's national 800 number. Quite frequently, the national reservations service is unaware of local specials.

AAA and AARP

Members of the American Automobile Association and the American Association of Retired Persons are eligible for discounts at many ski area hotels. Call your local AAA office or check the AARP monthly magazine for additional information.

Special Weekend Rates in Big Cities

Hotels in Denver, Sante Fe, and Salt Lake City—all within easy driving distance of the slopes—are good prospects for weekend lodging deals. Most downtown hotels that cater to business, government, and convention travelers offer special weekend discount rates that range from 15 to 40 percent below normal weekday rates. You can find out about weekend specials by calling the hotel or by consulting your travel agent.

Getting Corporate Rates

Many hotels offer discounted corporate rates (5–20 percent off rack). Usually you do not need to work for a large company or have a special relationship with the hotel to obtain these rates. Simply call the hotel of your choice and ask for their corporate rates. Many hotels will guarantee you the discounted rate on the phone when you make your reservation. Others may make the rate conditional on your providing some sort of *bona fides*, for instance a fax on your company's letterhead requesting the rate or a company credit card or business card upon check-in. Generally, the screening is not rigorous.

Preferred Rates

If you cannot book the hotel of your choice through a half-price program, you and your travel agent may have to search for a lesser discount, often called a preferred rate. A preferred rate could be a discount made available to travel agents to stimulate their booking activity or a discount initiated to attract a certain class of traveler. Most preferred rates are promoted through travel industry publications and are often accessible only through an agent.

We recommend sounding out your travel agent about possible deals. Be aware, however, that the rates shown on travel agents' computerized reservations systems are not always the lowest rates obtainable. Zero in on a couple of hotels that fill your needs in terms of location and quality of accommodations, and then have your travel agent call for the latest rates and specials. Hotel reps are almost always more responsive to travel agents because travel agents represent a source of additional business. As discussed earlier, there are certain specials that hotel reps will disclose only to travel agents. Travel agents also come in handy when the hotel you want is supposedly booked. A personal appeal from your agent to the hotel's director of sales and marketing will get you a room more than 50 percent of the time.

Ski Vacation Packages

Hundreds of ski packages are offered to the public each year. Some are created by members of the National Ski Tour Operators Association, a consortium of packagers that combines the buying power of its members to negotiate bulk discounts on lodging (both condos and hotels), airfare, rental cars, and lift tickets. Other packages are offered by airline touring companies, independent travel agents and wholesalers, the resorts themselves, and local or regional ski clubs. Big ski clubs are usually nonprofit social organizations that negotiate lodging and lift ticket packages directly with ski resorts and secure group air discounts with the carriers. By our observation, the big ski clubs strike some of the best deals going because they normally are able to bypass all the middlemen. It is probably worth your while to join a good ski club just to take advantage of their ski packages.

While most ski packages include airfare, lodging, and lift tickets, it is usually possible to buy the "land only" part of the package. When you purchase land only, you must make your own air transportation arrangements. This is a good strategy if you can take advantage of an airfare price war or if your city usually enjoys below average rates for air travel. Be aware that November, December, and January, except for the holiday periods, are usually low-volume months for the airlines. It is not unusual to see discounted airfares and other promotions during this period.

On the other side of the coin, package airfare prices are locked in. If you get an urge to go skiing but are too late to buy a 7-, 14-, or 21-day advance purchase ticket from the airlines, a tour operator can almost always find you an affordable fare. Likewise, when the airlines are sold out, tour operators frequently have seats available. You may not be able to fly on your favorite airline, and you may not be eligible for frequent flyer mileage, but you will be able to go skiing.

Ski package prices vary seasonally, with the Christmas/New Year holiday period and Presidents' Day weekend being the most expensive. Next most expensive is early February through the third week of March. Least expensive are November (excluding Thanksgiving), the first three weeks of December, January, and late March through the end of the ski season.

If you are flexible and can book at the last minute, you might be able to get a highly discounted package even in high season. Here's how it works: If a lodging property has a group cancellation or advance bookings are slow for certain dates, management will get on the phone with high-volume ski packagers and cut a special deal to sell the rooms. The packager in turn will promote the deal to customers who call in. It's a win/win situation all around. The hotel fills the rooms, the packager sells packages, and the skier gets an amazing deal. On March 3, as an example, we called Any Mountain Tours, a large packager that handles 24 different resorts, and asked for their best Colorado deal for March 11 through 18. We indicated that we wanted hotel accommodations for two nonsmoking adults traveling from Chicago. In response, Any Mountain Tours suggested the Pines at Beaver Creek Resort (just west of Vail), a plush ski-in/ski-out lodge. The price quoted was $573 per person, or $1,146 altogether for the couple. When we called Vail/Beaver Creek Resort Management (the central reservations service that handles bookings for Vail Associates lodging properties), we were quoted $2,293 for the same room and dates!

Almost all package ads feature a headline stating "Vail for Three Days from $498" or "Five Days at Crested Butte from $705" (or some such). The prices quoted are per person, and the key word in the ads is "from." The rock-bottom package price connotes the least desirable hotel accommodations. If you want better or more conveniently located digs, you'll have to pay more, often much more.

Most packages offer a selection of four or more hotels and several condos at each featured resort. Though some properties are very good, others run the quality gamut.

Packages should be a win/win proposition for both the buyer and the seller. The buyer only has to make one phone call and deal with a single salesperson to set up the whole vacation: transportation, rental car, lift tickets, lodging, and even equipment rentals. The seller, likewise, only has to deal with the buyer once, eliminating the need for separate sales, confirmations, and billing. In addition to streamlining selling, processing, and administration, many packagers also buy airfares in bulk on contract like a broker playing the commodities market. Buying a large number of airfares in advance allows the packager to buy them at a significant savings from posted fares. The same practice is applied also to lodging, lift tickets, and rental cars. Because selling ski vacation packages is an efficient way of doing business, and because the packager can often buy in bulk individual package components (airfare, lodging, etc.) at discount, savings in operating expenses realized by the seller are sometimes passed on to the buyer so that, in addition to convenience, the package is also an exceptional value. In any event, that is the way it is supposed to work.

All too often, in practice, the seller realizes all of the economies and passes nothing in the way of savings on to the buyer. In some instances, packages are loaded additionally with extras that cost the packager next to nothing but run the retail price of the package sky-high. As you might expect, the savings to be passed along to customers are still somewhere in Fantasyland.

When considering a package, choose one that includes features you are sure to use. Whether you use all the features or not, you will most certainly pay for them. Second, if cost is of greater concern than convenience, make a few phone calls and see what the package would cost if you booked its individual components (airfare, rental car, lodging, etc.) on your own. If the package price is less than the a la carte cost, the package is a good deal. If the costs are about the same, the package is probably worth it for the convenience.

Listed below are airlines and tour operators that offer ski vacation packages:

Any Mountain Tours, (800) 296-2000 or www.anymtn.com is a large tour operator that sells nothing but ski packages. A good source of discounts and last-minute deals, Any Mountain sells packages and land-only to 24 U.S. and Canadian resorts.

Central Holidays sells ski packages through travel agents to Italy, Austria, France, and Switzerland, as well as to the U.S. and Canadian Rockies. In addition to competitive prices, Central Holidays features a deal where a sixth person receives free accommodations with five paid packages.

Daman-Nelson Travel is a full-service travel retailer specializing in packages to Sun Valley, Jackson Hole, Banff, Whistler, and most major Colorado and Utah ski areas. For a free newsletter, call (619) 235-6454 or check out www.skirun.com on the Web. Clients include both individual skiers and travel agents.

Delta Airlines, (800) 872-7786 or www.deltavacations.com. Delta Dream Vacations offers ski packages to the western United States and to the Alps. Delta's package prices for American resorts are reasonable but do not represent a great bargain. From the eastern United States, Delta has some of the best routes to Salt Lake City, Utah, as well as to Montana.

K+M Tours, (800) 233-2300 or www.kmvacations.com, has been packaging ski vacations for over 30 years. Headquartered in Pittsburgh, K+M sells discounted packages to most major U.S. and Canadian ski resorts. All air reservations are booked on regularly scheduled flights. Clients include both individual skiers and travel agents.

Mountain Vacations, Inc., sells through travel agents and offers competitive packages to 21 western U.S. and Canadian ski resorts. Mountain Vacation packages feature many upscale properties.

Northwest Airlines, (800) 800-1504 or www.nwa.com, features packages to some of the more remote western resorts, including Big Sky in Montana. Package prices are very competitive for resorts in Northwest's service area.

Rocky Mountain Tours is a New Jersey packager that sells ski vacations to the U.S. and Canadian Rockies. Clients include both individual skiers and travel agents. For a catalog, call (800) 525-SKIS or check out www. skithewest.com.

Southwest Airlines, (800) 423-5683 or www.swavacations.com, runs affordable packages to Taos, the Salt Lake City area resorts, and the Lake Tahoe area resorts.

Aspen Ski Tours, (800) 525-2052 or www.skitours.com, focuses on the American and Canadian West. Its packages have been fairly competitive, especially its ski vacations to Whistler/Blackcomb in British Columbia.

Helping Your Travel Agent to Help You

Most travel agents do not ski and consequently have only a limited knowledge of the major ski areas. This lack of information translates into travelers not getting reservations at the more interesting hotels, paying more than is necessary, or being placed in out-of-the-way or otherwise undesirable lodging.

When you call your travel agent, ask if he or she has been to the ski area you wish to visit. Firsthand experience means a lot. If the answer is no, be prepared to give your travel agent a lot of direction. Do not accept any recommendations at face value. Check out the location and rates of any suggested hotel or condo and make certain that the hotel or condo is suited to your needs.

Because travel agents are often unfamiliar with ski venue alternatives, your agent may try to plug you into an airline travel company ski vacation or some other preset package. This essentially allows the travel agent to set up your whole trip with a single phone call and still collect an 8–10 percent commission. The problem with this scenario is that most agents will place 90 percent of their ski business with only one or two tour operators. In other words, it is the path of least resistance for them and not much choice for you.

To help your travel agent get you the best possible deal, do the following:

1. Determine which ski areas you are interested in. Decide whether you prefer a hotel, condo, or rental home.

2. Check out the skiing travel ads in the Sunday travel section of your local newspaper and compare them to ads running in the newspapers of your preferred destination's key markets. A key market for the Lake Tahoe area resorts, by way of example, is San

Francisco. Dallas, Houston, Los Angeles, Chicago, and New York are key markets for most Colorado resorts. Mammoth and June Mountain resorts heavily target Los Angeles. Because the competition among resorts and tour operators in key market cities is great, you will often find deals that beat the socks off anything offered in other parts of the country. Scan the ads in the papers of these primary market cities and see if you can find some hotel discounts or packages in the ads that sound good.

3. Call the packagers, hotels, or resorts whose ads you have collected. Ask any questions you might have, but do not book your trip with them directly.

4. Tell your travel agent about what you found and ask if he or she can get you something better. The packages in the paper will serve as a benchmark against which to compare alternatives proposed by your travel agent.

5. Choose from among the options uncovered by you and your travel agent. No matter which option you select, have your travel agent book it. Even if you go with one of the packages in the newspaper, it will probably be commissionable (at no additional cost to you) and will provide the agent some return on the time invested on your behalf. Also, as a travel professional, your agent should be able to verify the quality and integrity of the package.

PART 2

Colorado and
the Southern Rockies

LITO TEJADA-FLORES

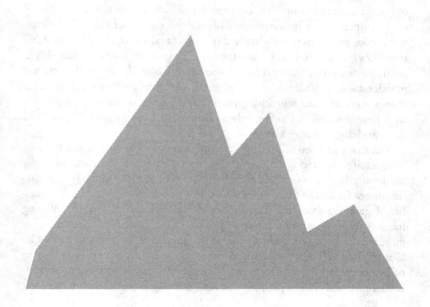

WHY ski Colorado? I live here, so I'm prejudiced—spoiled, too. But my life as a ski writer takes me away from these mountains, my adopted home mountains, for weeks and months at a time every winter. And still I'm always excited to get home and get out on these slopes again. In over 20 years of living here, I haven't run out of reasons to love Colorado skiing.

Of course, it starts with the snow, but we've already sung the praises of light, dry, Rocky Mountain snow in the introduction to this book. And I'm the first to admit that Colorado holds no monopoly on light, dry, white stuff. Partisans of Utah claim their snow is deeper, drier; aficionados of New Mexican *nieve* swear it's the lightest of all; locals in the northern Rockies claim that their dry snow falls more frequently and piles up higher. And so it goes. But if Colorado snow is not absolutely unique here in the Rockies, it is still a small miracle—the stuff of which skiers' dreams are made. Not only does Colorado snow fall from the sky as fluff, as true powder, but lowering temperatures after a storm will often dry it out even further. Snow here sometimes gets lighter and drier a day after it's fallen. In skiers' terms, this translates into less resistance, less friction, less work to turn and slide. It's as though one's skis are always better waxed on Colorado slopes. Untracked powder snow in Colorado is for play not penance, an invitation with no strings attached; and when it's groomed and packed down into pistes, this stuff becomes a sort of Teflon velvet where skis can perform to 110 percent of their design potential.

But that's just the beginning. As important as its snow, but surely more unique, are Colorado's ski towns. The resort flavor of Colorado skiing is unlike anything you can find elsewhere. One could easily say that what distinguishes Colorado from other ski regions in our country is not the number of great ski areas, but the number of great ski resorts. I'm not splitting hairs. A ski area is a mountain equipped for skiing, period. A ski resort offers far more than just skiing ideally; life at the bottom of the mountain must be as intriguing and as intoxicating as turns on the hill. A real ski resort has to offer more than strip development, motel-style or minimalist condo accommodations, and endless parking lots. And the majority of Colorado ski areas are real "resorts" in this sense. The very best ski resorts of all are actually true villages, towns, communities where the whole rhythm and fabric of life, the atmosphere in the streets, the focus and passion of locals as well as visitors, are inextricably tied to skiing. Where everyone, visitor and local, in some way or another lives the ski life. Great ski villages are easy to find in the Alps; they are all too rare in the States, and most of those we have are in Colorado.

But I'm taking you on a tour of the *best skiing* in Colorado, not just the best resorts, so we'll also be visiting a couple of areas that don't qualify as proper resorts but do offer dynamite skiing. Still I've been very choosy. There are more than 30 ski areas in Colorado. In this section, we're going to visit only 16. The 16 best plus 2 great ski destinations in New Mexico. It was easy to slip New Mexico skiing into a section primarily devoted to Colorado. Colorado, after all, lies in the southern Rockies, and that means slightly warmer winter temperatures, more sunshine, and blue skies. It is the high altitude as much as or more than winter cold that keeps our snow so light and dry—as is the case in New Mexico. Three Colorado ski resorts, Telluride, Crested Butte, and Purgatory, are hidden away in the southwest corner of the state, closer to the New Mexico border than to Denver—so it was easy to cross that border and add two of my very favorite ski destinations, Taos and Santa Fe, to this mostly Colorado collection.

It's also easy for me to promise you, in general terms, a tour of Colorado's "best skiing," but some readers may already be wondering where they'll find *the* best skiing, *the* best ski mountain, *the* best ski town. I've lived in one Colorado ski town, Telluride—a place I fell in love with 21 years ago and still adore, but which I wouldn't dare claim was the best. Every good ski resort is somebody's favorite. The special quality of light, snow, friends you're skiing with, your own state of mind and body—all this makes one day, one place, one memory the best. With any luck you'll have numerous "best days" on Colorado slopes. So I'll leave ultimate judgments to each reader.

But there is still a pecking order. If Colorado can be called the capital of American skiing, then it must be said that the twin capitals of Colorado skiing are Vail and Aspen. And this is where we'll start our insider's tour of the southern Rockies—with these two ski towns that set the standards by which other ski resorts are judged. Two leaders in a wave of change that is altering the nature and quality of Colorado skiing. I call it a white revolution.

There are so many skiers now in Colorado, both locals and out-of-state vacationers, and the competition between resorts to attract these skiers is so fierce, that the average level of skier service and amenities—what you get for your skiing dollar—seems higher here than anywhere else in the country. Just as important, however, you're getting something *new* for that dollar.

For generations, lift lines have been the bane of downhill skiers' existences. Lift lines haven't disappeared in Colorado, but they're on the way

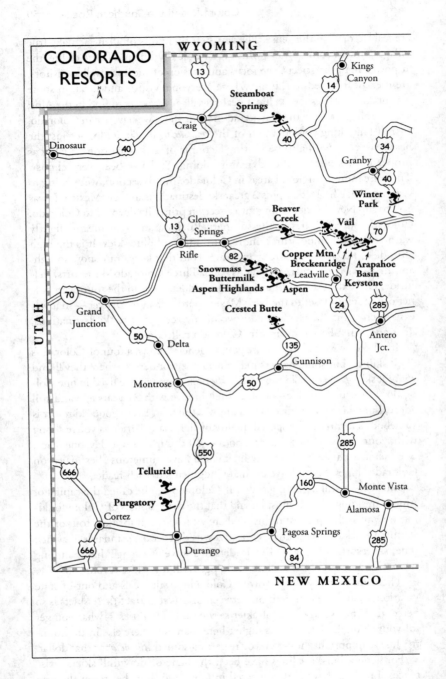

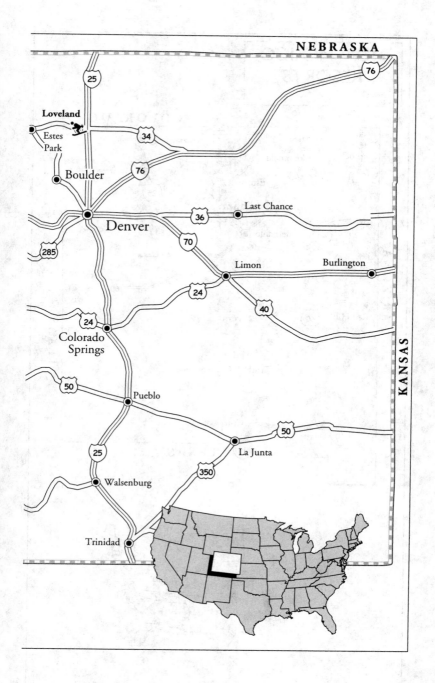

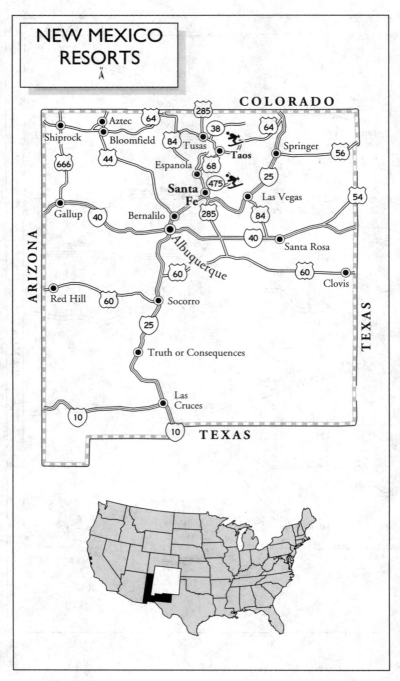

NEW MEXICO RESORTS

N

COLORADO

Shiprock
Aztec
64
285
38
64
Bloomfield
84
Tusas
Springer
56
666
44
Espanola
68
Taos
666
44
475
25
Santa Fe
Las Vegas
54
Gallup
40
Bernalilo
285
84
Albuquerque
40
Santa Rosa
60
60
60
Clovis
Red Hill
60
Socorro
25
Truth or Consequences
Las Cruces
10
10
TEXAS

ARIZONA

TEXAS

out. The solution, like the problem itself, comes from technology. New lifts with higher capacity and dramatically faster uphill speeds are not only eliminating lift lines, but cutting the total time you spend going uphill almost in half. The cunning machines responsible for this white revolution are high-speed, detachable, four-person chairlifts, also known as express lifts or super chairs. They work the way gondolas do, moving at slower speeds through the loading and unloading stations, then accelerating down a ramp to gather speed and hook on to a fast-moving cable. By now, all American skiers have at least heard of, if not ridden on, detachable quad chairs. But the super-high price tag for these super-fast lifts (well over $1 million each) means that you're not likely to see them at small, weekend ski areas. Of course, high-speed lifts are not a Colorado monopoly; they're found everywhere today. But there are more of them in Colorado. It's been years since I spent more than five minutes in a Colorado lift line.

While it's true that lift ticket prices have risen here in recent years largely as a result of these new high-speed lifts, the cost of quality skiing has actually come down—if you think in terms of dollars per vertical feet. It's a brave new world, and skiers who never even managed to get enough runs in one day now find themselves quitting at 2:30 in the afternoon because they've skied so much, so fast, that their legs are tired. A nice feeling. And a new feeling in American skiing.

The radical revamping of lift infrastructure is only the most obvious change in the Colorado ski scene. On closer inspection, the new lifts are just part of a generalized upgrading of all mountain facilities. Many areas have greatly extended their snowmaking—already nearly universal as a form of pre-Christmas, early-season insurance. Some have recently opened large, steep, formerly out-of-bounds zones to adventurous skiers willing to hike for their adrenaline. Many areas have completely remodeled their base facilities and on-mountain eateries in recent years. On-mountain, sit-down restaurants are proliferating as alternatives to the usual dreadful cafeteria fare. All told, Colorado ski corporations have just lived through a cycle of investment in the future of a magnitude never before seen. And in the base villages below the lifts, skier services have become more sophisticated than ever. Like I said, it's a white revolution.

A new form of "skiing" has appeared as well. By this, I mean snowboarding, a controversial rarity a decade ago, now quite common at all but one Colorado ski resort. Snowboarding is challenging and graceful, but above all it's new. And that is exactly why it's so attractive to youngsters who, on the slopes as in everyday life, delight in anything that sets them apart from their parents' generation. Far from being a subversive threat to the integrity of our sport, as some over-reacting ski area managers initially perceived it to be, snowboarding has actually brought more families to the slopes together; it has given more kids a reason to accompany their parents willingly rather than grudgingly on annual Colorado ski jaunts.

The latest wave of change in Colorado skiing has been a spate of mergers and acquisitions. Vail has recently acquired both Keystone and Breckenridge, and Intrawest, the extremely sophisticated outfit that already owns or manages some of the biggest and most sophisticated ski resorts in North America (like Blackcomb at Whistler, Mont Tremblant, and Stratton Mountain), is merging with (read taking over) Copper Mountain. Despite a certain amount of predictable grumbling about Colorado ski resorts becoming homogenized corporate amusement parks, I am betting that this consolidation of ski resort ownership in some very capable hands will only result in continued and perhaps accelerated upgrading of skier services, although nothing I can imagine will improve Colorado skiing more than high-speed lifts already have.

The white revolution, first in Colorado skiing and today across the country, is the final and perfect justification for this guidebook. The new super lifts have changed more than just uphill access times. They've changed the way we think about our ski mountains, the best way to ski them, the best way to plan your day for maximum enjoyment. What this book is all about. . . .

Enough introductions. We have 16 major ski mountains to visit, a lot of glorious white miles to cover together. Needless to say, doing the "research" for this guide—skiing and re-skiing all these Colorado and New Mexico areas—has been fantastic. A ski writer's fantasy. One that's waiting for you, too, on Colorado ski slopes.

 # The Vail Valley

Vail The original American megaresort, Vail is an enormous ski mountain with the most advanced lift system (and the largest number of high-speed detachables) in Colorado; groomed trails plus ungroomed back bowls, but a little shy on true beginner terrain; and a great kids' program. The town of Vail is a large, diverse, Alpine-style, pedestrian village whose twin centers are seamlessly linked with swift, free buses.

Beaver Creek Vail's smaller sister resort offers better novice terrain and really splendid not-too-steep, introductory bump skiing and, of course, fewer skiers on a mountain that is a good deal smaller than Vail, although still of respectable size. The village is handsome but rather small, upscale, and exclusive; more modest accommodations can be found down the hill, in nearby Avon.

VAIL

I've always thought of Vail and Aspen as the twin capitals, not only of Colorado skiing, but of American skiing. This said, I should underline the differences between them: Aspen is older and richer in history and community, but its slopes—quite diverse and never crowded—are spread out across four separate ski mountains. Vail, on the other hand, is a newer and brasher resort, but Vail has it all, all together, all at once. Closer to Denver, Vail sometimes seems crowded with skiers, but never as packed as its Summit County neighbors, and its mountain is big enough to absorb crowds without feeling crowded. Vail is the most complete all-around ski mountain and seamlessly polished vacation-resort machine you can imagine. It's probably the easiest place I know where a skier, any skier, can have a perfect day any day.

It's no accident that Vail is the first ski resort we're visiting in the Colorado section of this guidebook. Or that Vail comes in first by most terms with which the ski world measures success: number of visitors, size of ski

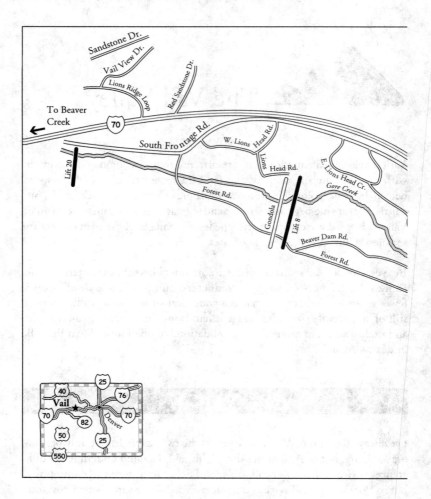

school, the sheer boggling sums that vacationing skiers leave in this jewel of a ski-resort town, and above all in the size of its skiable terrain. Vail's mountain is enormous. In 1989, when Vail doubled its total skiable acreage by opening five new Back Bowls, it could boast that it had more skiable acreage than its neighboring Summit County resorts—Keystone, Arapahoe, Breckenridge, and Copper Mountain—put together. Of course, since then, those nearby resorts have added new terrain of their own, but the comparison gives you an idea of just how big Vail really is.

But Vail is no zoo. The town and mountain "work" in ways that other ski

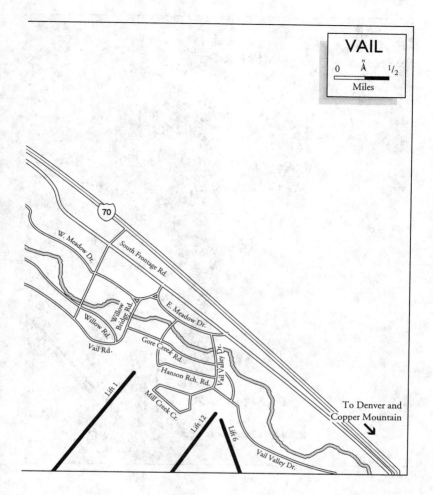

areas only dream about. To serve its vast ski terrain, Vail boasts more high-speed detachable lifts than any other mountain in Colorado. Also, Vail Village is the first true pedestrian ski town in North America—a lesson that resort planners everywhere should have learned from and unfortunately haven't.

Virtually every one of the 16 major Colorado ski areas we visit in this guidebook can boast one or two special facets of the skiing experience in which it absolutely excels: the grandest views, the best beginner area, the finest glades. Vail, too; its multiple Back Bowls are easily the best powder

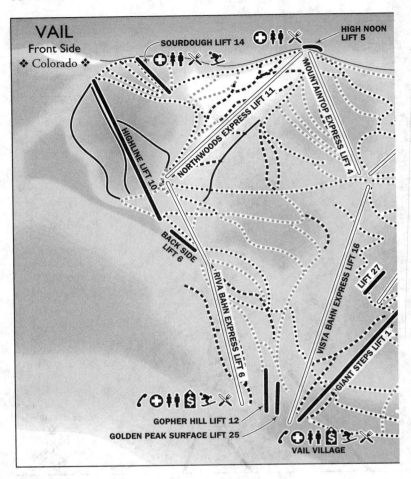

preserve in the whole state. But—an important but—no other American resort offers as complete a spectrum of ski options on one mountain for every level of skiing. A family group spanning three generations and twice that many skiing styles and ability levels can ski Vail Mountain, meet for lunch, separate, and meet again in the evening with no frustrations. Each individual, like the proverbial blind men describing an elephant, will be skiing his or her own version of Vail Mountain. This kind of all-around ski mountain, where no one need be bored, frustrated, or over-challenged, is a rarity.

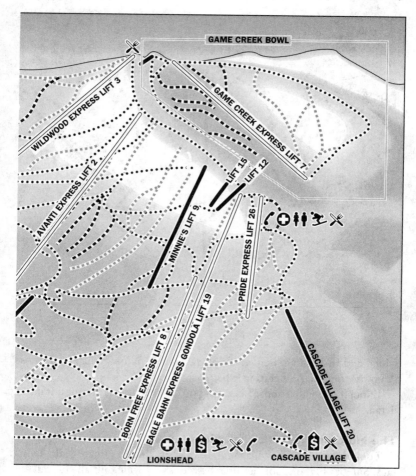

In addition, Vail is probably the most ego-building ski mountain I know. For a curious reason: Vail's first trails and runs were cut by early-day ski fanatics, veterans of the 10th Mountain Division, armed only with chain saws and visions of the wide-open skiing they'd enjoyed in the Alps after World War II. Unencumbered by university degrees in ski-area design, computer-generated mountain models, and environmental impact statements, they just went and cut themselves exceptionally wide runs. Wide runs have a subconscious but critical effect on a skier's frame of mind: With no potential obstacles looming up on either side, all skiers ski better. Vail's runs are

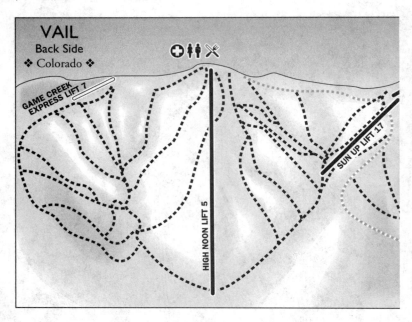

wider, and thus, in a purely artificial way, more "natural" than what most skiers are used to. A liberating experience.

Enough generalizations. Let's look at this beauty of a ski mountain in detail.

The Multiple Worlds of Vail Mountain

Looking up from the village, one can easily underestimate Vail Mountain. Sure it's big, or, more accurately, wide, very wide, but all you can see from below is a friendly forest cut here and there by white ribbon runs, rising gently, then sloping back out of sight. Most of the mountain, in fact, is out of sight. From Vail Village, the original town center, you catch a couple of tantalizing glimpses of steep ridge runs high up. From Lionshead, the second resort center to the west, the upper mountain is totally invisible. But it's up there, waiting.

Vail is a wide mountain, not a tall or narrow one, defined by a long ridge running roughly east to west. The whole ski area measures over seven miles across, east to west. It's also a two-faced ski mountain, not merely in the sense that it faces both north and south, but that it exhibits a totally different character on each side. Both faces, luckily, are lovable. Dropping down toward the twin resort centers of Vail Village and Lionshead, the front or

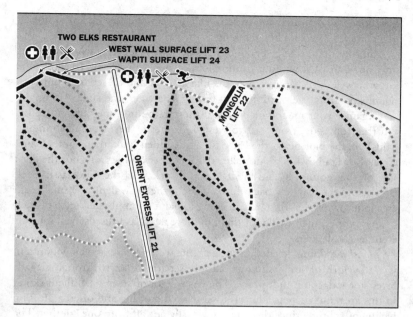

north face is classic Colorado ski country: dark green mountainsides of dense forest that only ingenuity and chain saws could have transformed into a big ski area. (Colorado, I should explain, has a remarkably high tree line compared to most other mountain regions in America, with evergreen forests growing right up to 12,000 feet.) The front side offers mostly trail skiing, with only a few wide-open clearings and small bowls high up.

The back side of Vail Mountain is another story. Forest fires in the late nineteenth century stripped the slopes of timber, and the intense solar radiation and evaporation on these high, south-facing slopes kept the forest from reestablishing itself. Hence the Back Bowls, Vail's not-so-secret advantage. Not just one back bowl, but a whole series one after the other, mile after mile.

From Vail's opening in 1962 until 1988, only two of these bowls, *Sun Down* and *Sun Up,* were part of the ski area, and they literally made Vail's reputation as a ski mecca. These two bowls are, in fact, huge. But they've been dwarfed in area, if not in reputation, by the five new bowls—*China, Teacup, Siberia,* and *Inner* and *Outer Mongolia Bowls*—that were opened up to skiers by a major expansion project in the summer of 1988. The good news for most Vail fans is that these new bowls are somewhat easier angled, hence more accessible to average skiers, than *Sun Down* and *Sun Up.* The

new bowls are definitely not experts-only terrain, but they're just as imposing, empty, white, and breathtaking as the two classic bowls.

Vail Mountain is large enough that skiers often spend whole days skiing
only one part of it without running out of new runs to try. To those who
know it well, Vail Mountain seems like a collection of separate but contiguous ski areas, each with its own feeling, character, and style of skiing.

Organize your mental map of Vail Mountain into nine different zones.
On the front side, from east to west: Lionshead, the Middle Mountain,
Mid-Vail, the Northeast, the Far East, and Golden Peak; then comes Game
Creek Bowl, a bowl in a side valley that's neither on the front nor the back
side of the mountain; and finally, on the back side, the two classic Back
Bowls, and the five new Back Bowls. Each is the equivalent of a smaller ski
area in its own right. To start, I'm going to paint a thumbnail sketch of each
of these zones, then we'll visit them in more detail as I discuss Vail for different levels of skiers.

Lionshead skiing, located at the extreme western side of Vail Mountain,
is a labyrinth of long, sinuous, cleanly separated paths through elegant
forests of lodgepole and spruce. There isn't a lot of steep or difficult skiing
in this area, but there is a lot of good relaxed cruising and often a pleasing
feeling of solitude since the runs are visually cut off from one another. The
Lionshead side of Vail Mountain is also well served with three high-speed
lifts, a new gondola, and two detachable quad chairs. The real good news
here is that most of the lifts on this far western end of Vail Mountain have
been upgraded in recent years. A high-speed quad, Lift 26, the Pride
Express, completed the all-quad chair trip up to Eagle's Nest Ridge. But the
best news is the replacement of the old Lionshead gondola with a stunning
new 12-passenger version; this new gondola has all but eliminated the morning bottleneck of skiers trying to get up on the mountain from Lionshead
village. Eagle's Nest, at the top end of the gondola, has also been turned into
a sort of nighttime amusement park with an ice skating rink, a snowboard
terrain park, a tubing area, and a novice skier area, all under the lights—a
short ride in a heated gondola from the valley floor. But for skiers, the net
result of all these upgraded lifts in the Lionshead area is to invite one to
spend more time than ever before cruising lovely sinuous trails like *Pride,
Bwana,* and upper *Simba.* These trails are never crowded, even on big weekends, and they offer the sort of high-speed cruising that would be impru-
dent on the more peopled slopes above Mid-Vail.

The Middle Mountain is a nebulous zone that is somewhat underskied
and underappreciated. I'm talking about the runs dropping below *Eagle's
Nest Ridge* from *Avanti* across to *Columbine* and their lower extensions,
dropping all the way down into Vail Village. Because it doesn't have a real
name, a unique geographical identity or mystique, this center region of the

front face is skied less than it deserves, usually only as a way home at the end of the day. But World Cup Giant Slalom (GS) and downhill races are held on the Middle Mountain. These are very long, very interesting runs. Don't forget them. In recent years, a high-speed detachable quad lift, the Avanti Express, has replaced two fixed-grip chairs (former Lifts 2 and 17) on the upper half of the Middle Mountain. Skiing in this zone has become a more enjoyable experience as this is often a cold part of Vail Mountain, and the Avanti Express lift also makes life easier for skiers who want to cross the front face from Vail Village to Lionshead or vice versa.

Mid-Vail, of course, is the classic mid-mountain restaurant, remodeled endlessly into today's giant hub. But I also use the name Mid-Vail for the wide basins above this restaurant. This Mid-Vail area is not quite a bowl in the pure sense; instead it is two open alpine valleys served by two lifts and two fast quads, and it's chock-full of runs—a great variety of runs that are interesting but short and usually a trifle crowded. I'm not sure if "crowded" is the right word, but if any zone on Vail Mountain seems crowded, this is the one. Why? Because the fanciest lift out of Vail Village, the Vista Bahn Express quad, arrives smack at Mid-Vail with an endless stream of skiers, many of whom, through some sort of gregarious herd instinct, tend to just stay right there. Don't fall into this trap. Mid-Vail skiing is like a visit to a lovely but small ski area within a giant ski area; if you spend all day on the slopes above Mid-Vail you will be enjoying only a fraction of what Vail has to offer.

From Mid-Vail itself, Lift 4 carries skiers up to the top of Vail Mountain. Calling it a summit would give too much dignity to what is little more than the highest bump on a system of ridgelines, but it's still the top. Locals call it "PHQ" for Patrol Headquarters. PHQ is also the key crossroads on the mountain where Lift 5 comes out of the classic bowls and Lift 11 arrives from the Northeast side.

The Northeast side of Vail lies just around the corner, east of the Mid-Vail basin. This is an area of steep forests, lots of steep runs, and lots of hard skiing. In fact, the most challenging skiing in Vail—if not the most beautiful—and the greatest concentration of black diamond runs on the front side are all on the Northeast. There are rolling, swooping, "easy" black trails, there are steep and moguled ridgelines, there is even a kind of bump skiers' ghetto—Lift 10, with its demanding double blacks. The Northeast is where serious Vail skiers head, at least once a day, for a real workout.

The Far East is a small area at the east end of the upper mountain, a long, long way from where we began in Lionshead. There's only one lift up here, Lift 14, which is a triple. This is a novice skier's paradise of gentle, friendly, low-angle runs where inexperienced skiers can cut loose and soon transcend their novice limits. It is also the obvious gateway into the new bowls. The Far East can be reached by taking Lifts 6 and 10 to 14, but it's often faster to take the Vista Bahn Express and Lift 4, then cut across to Lift 14 on *Timberline Catwalk.* From the top of Lift 14, one is only a stone's throw from Elk Restaurant, a new, giant, log-and-glass structure with the best views on Vail Mountain.

Golden Peak is also at the far eastern end of Vail Mountain, but low down, and right out of the village. It's actually a separate subpeak, or detached ridge, named for the fiery autumn colors in its dense aspen stands. Although there are a few comfortable intermediate runs down here, Golden Peak has always been primarily a ski-racing and race-training enclave, plus a beautifully arranged children's skiing area (which I will describe later). But that's changing. Old Lift 6 has just been replaced by Vail's newest high-speed quad, its tenth, the Riva Bahn. Starting from a totally rebuilt base lodge complex, the Riva Bahn climbs, or zips, up Golden Peak, dropping some skiers at an intermediate unloading point, and then continues on, above Golden Peak, to the foot of Chair 11, the Northwoods Express. This new lift allows skiers who start their day at Golden Peak to access the Back Bowls in two quick express-quad rides.

And then there are the bowls. Vail simply wouldn't be Vail without these white spots on the map; in skiers' minds, these are empty, delicious, open arenas of white-on-white.

Game Creek Bowl lies over the ridge from Mid-Vail via Lift 3. Game Creek used to be a smaller place altogether, but with the cutting of a number of new runs on its left or north-facing flank and the upgrading of Lift 7 to full detachable status, Game Creek has become one of the most complete intermediate ski zones on the mountain.

The classic Back Bowls and the new Back Bowls are the frosting on Vail's cake, and we'll visit them in more detail in the following sections. But to complete your bird's-eye overview, remember that the two classic Back Bowls, Sun Down and Sun Up, lie just behind PHQ. You dive into them from the top of the mountain and come back out to PHQ via Lift 5. Although the main entrance to these two bowls is from PHQ, you can also enter Sun Down from the top of Lifts 3 and 7, and even sneak into the far side of Sun Up from Lift 14. A recent addition to the lift system, Lift 17 serves the formerly hard-to-reach glades of *Yonder* and *Over Yonder* on the east flank of Sun Up Bowl and gives skiers access to the west end of the new bowls.

The five new Back Bowls are strung like pearls along Vail's main ridge, to the east of the two classic bowls, and together they boast a skiing acreage equal to the rest of Vail Mountain! As we'll see, the new Back Bowls have truly changed the feel and flavor of Vail skiing. They are most easily entered from Lift 14 and the Far East but can also be reached from PHQ via *Sleepy-time Catwalk*. From west to east, you'll encounter Tea Cup Bowl, China Bowl, Siberia Bowl, and Inner and Outer Mongolia bowls. They are served by the Orient Express high-speed quad, out of the bottom of China Bowl, and by three short surface lifts (two of which simply pull skiers along flat ridges back toward the site of Two Elk Restaurant).

And that's Vail, a totally diverse mountain, a world of subworlds, the biggest of the big ones. The common denominator at Vail Mountain is its user-friendly character. Most runs lie square in the fall line, most steeps offer a way around for skiers who suddenly realize they don't belong there, and most runs are steady and continuous. Vail is perhaps more of a cruiser's mountain than an adventurer mountain. But Vail cruising is sensational, and there are still enough challenges on this monster to keep hyperactive hot-shots happy for a long time. Let's get more specific. I want to tell you about my favorite runs, the best runs for different level skiers.

Vail for Good Skiers

The term "good skiers" sounds pretty vague, but what I have in mind are skiers who feel at home on their skis, who have probably been skiing for quite a few seasons, who spend most of their time on blue slopes and look pretty spiffy on moderate terrain. These are skiers who can definitely get down a black diamond slope, or two, or three, but don't hang out all day on these steep, moguled runs. Skiers who can cope with fresh snow and powder, but who don't exactly dance through it. Skiers who ski the whole mountain, but don't yet "own" it. Skiers who don't make heads turn with admiration as they flash by, but who flash by nonetheless and enjoy skiing at a pretty good clip when the slopes are comfortable. Sound like you? You're in luck. Vail is a paradise, a Valhalla for good skiers.

This is exactly the sort of skier that the Mid-Vail runs are designed for. But as I've already said, although popular, Mid-Vail is both limited and limiting if you ski there too much. The finest run here is *Cappuccino*. The relatively obscure and narrow entrance from *Swingsville* hides a real gem. *Cappuccino* is more varied in pitch than the runs on either side, and there are wonderful stands of widely spaced trees that invite you into a kind of natural, giant-slalom game. The widest run in this area is *Ramshorn,* which is marked green but is actually indistinguishable from a lot of the blue runs around it. (Someone apparently felt the need to show green runs on the map from the top of the mountain down to Mid-Vail, which is why *Ramshorn,* *Swingsville,* and *Christmas* are colored green in defiance of common sense.) For me, the extra space on *Ramshorn* is a real incentive to fast big turns. You can indulge in a few extra miles per hour here without disturbing (or even coming close to) other skiers.

If you start your day on the Vail Village side of the resort (as opposed to the Lionshead side), you'll probably hop the Vista Bahn Express and warm up with a couple of runs on the slopes above Mid-Vail. But then I'd recommend a couple of early-morning cruises down *Northwoods* and *Northstar* on the Northeast side. The charm of *Northwoods* is its length and the fact that you are skiing down continuously changing mountain shapes: rolls, dips, short flats, and inviting drops. *Northstar,* which is half-hidden in the forest to the left of *Northwoods,* is the same sort of run, only more so: The steeps are somewhat steeper and the rolls and drop-aways are more inviting. Although marked black on the trail map, *Northstar* isn't really very hard; but unlike *Northwoods* there is no way around the steeper pitches. Return to the top is rapid via Lift 11—the Northwoods Express quad—which can also bring you back from *Riva Ridge* (another "easy" black slope), provided you turn right onto *Trans Montane Catwalk* at the bottom of the actual ridge of *Riva Ridge.* Before this handy catwalk leading back to Lift 11 was cut, *Riva Ridge* was only used for skiing home at the end of the day or skiing down to the Village for lunch. Now skiers can also take advantage of the high-speed return offered by the Vista Bahn Express and Lift 4 to ski full mountain runs here: *Riva Ridge* to *Tourist Trap* to the Village via *Mill Creek Road.*

Good skiers who begin their day on the Lionshead side of Vail will follow a different path. Instead of heading for Mid-Vail and *Northwoods,* I'd recommend several warm-up runs on Lift 26, the Pride Express. Let your skis run over the big roller-coaster humps and hollows of *Bwana* and *Safari,* where there are no obstacles, no sudden surprises. Then after an hour or so here, you'll be ready to drop over the back side of *Eagle's Nest Ridge* into Game Creek Bowl.

Game Creek Bowl is another paradise for good skiers, where the black runs feel almost "bluish," or friendly, and the blue runs are continuous enough to feel "blue-black," dramatic if not difficult. Lift 7, another high-speed quad, keeps you circulating at a brisk clip. My favorite run here is *Dealer's Choice,* a masterpiece of trail cutting. Looking downward, the runs on the right side of Game Creek Bowl are all marked black. However, they are short and very wide, offering good skiers lots of options rather than only one or two forced paths through bumpy obstacles as black slopes so often do. These runs, *Deuces Wild, Faro,* and *Ouzo,* are almost treeless, which makes them into friendly, nonthreatening powder lines after a storm. A good place to practice and develop your deep-snow skills.

What about the Back Bowls for good skiers? Sure, why not? But please, not every run back there. Until the opening of Vail's new Back Bowls, your choices in the back were much more limited. In fact, the new bowls are generally less steep and hence more inviting to average skiers than Sun Down and Sun Up bowls ever were. So start out in China Bowl.

What's it like back there, aside from big? The new bowls are so vast that you can actually find almost every kind of skiing there, but the eastern sides of both China and Siberia bowls (on your left looking down) are wide and fairly low-angle slopes. These are ideal terrain for your first Back Bowl adventure. In addition, Vail manages to keep the two main routes into China Bowl groomed; these are *East* and *West Poppyfields,* the only runs marked blue in all seven miles of Vail's Back Bowls. Next door in Siberia Bowl, the easiest skiing is found on the west-facing, eastern flank known as *Bolshoi Ballroom* and right down the center on *Gorky Park.* These are all stress-free runs—Back Bowl skiing for everyone.

On the east side of China Bowl you'll find *Shangri-La,* an area of sparse trees that offers skiers multiple gladelike paths, none of which are hard. You can ski run after run here and never dive through the same grove of trees twice. These *Shangri-La* trees are an important exception in the middle of this wide-open treeless terrain, for they allow, and even encourage, Back Bowl skiing on stormy days by providing extra visibility and shelter from wind.

The western sides (on your right when looking down) of China and Siberia bowls are fairly steep and for the most part should be considered legitimate black expert terrain. They also receive a good deal more wind-blown snow than the two classic Back Bowls, so that when the patrol records 6 or 7 inches of new snow at PHQ, lines like *Jade Glade, Bamboo Chute,* and *Genghis Kahn* on the west side of China Bowl can be filled in with 18 to 24 inches. I owe you one more caveat here: *Rasputin's Revenge,* the steep face directly beneath the western ridge of Siberia Bowl, is another great Back Bowl powder shot; however, it is also the single steepest pitch in the back—so leave it for experts.

Teacup Bowl, at the lower west end of the new bowls, is a special case. It's likely to be best in springtime, corn-snow conditions and isn't really steep enough for good deep-powder skiing. At the eastern end of the new bowls, Inner and Outer Mongolia bowls (known to locals as "Innie" and "Outie") are big and friendly but perhaps too low-angle to attract a lot of skiers. They are also a bit out of the main traffic pattern here, since you must reach them by traversing across Siberia Bowl and then riding the Mongolia Surface Lift. The farther east you go in Mongolia Bowl, the gentler the terrain. This area is a virtual mecca for telemark skiers on their more delicate, three-pin Nordic gear.

Once you've explored the less-demanding lines in China and Siberia bowls and want to venture into Vail's two classic Back Bowls, I'd recommend skiing the *Slot* into Sun Up Bowl first. Despite their names, Sun Up Bowl has no monopoly on early morning light, and Sun Down does not get great sunsets. Like the new bowls, there aren't any traditional runs back here at all, only generalized lines that have been given separate names. Although all these lines are marked black on the Vail trail map, some are much blacker than others. The *Slot* is the only run in the classic bowls that's ever machine groomed. Since both Sun Down and Sun Up are more suitable for expert and near expert skiers, I'll describe them in more detail in the next section.

I've already suggested that your day will have a different feel if you start out on the Lionshead side of the mountain. One look at the trail map shows you that the runs on the western end of Vail Mountain are quite long and that there is hardly any black showing over here. The finest runs in Lionshead are the longest and most continuous ones on the far western edge of the mountain, especially *Simba,* with its branches and variants, *Safari, Pride,* and *Cheetah.* The continuous nonstop quality of skiing over here gives these runs a special feeling that shorter runs of the same difficulty lack. This is Vail cruising at its finest.

After Vail's first massive infusion of high-speed quad lifts during the 1985–1986 season, skiers rapidly became spoiled by the no-lift-line conditions on the middle and upper sections of Vail Mountain. Transportation bottlenecks on the Lionshead side seemed so frustrating that knowledgeable skiers just didn't bother to ski over there much. This state of affairs has now changed completely with the Born Free Express, the Pride Express, and the new high-speed, high-capacity gondola. Still, these westside runs don't seem to get the skier traffic they merit. If you're in reasonably good shape, you can try to ski these long Lionshead runs nonstop, top to bottom, or at least in longer sections than normal. Pure exhilaration.

Cruising is a sport, or addiction, best practiced on newly groomed runs—"virgin corduroy," as some call it, referring to the patterns made in the snow by the grooming vehicles' big rollers. At Vail you can lift any mountain telephone and dial 4018 to get a prerecorded report telling you which slopes were groomed the night before. Vail also posts a highly visible grooming symbol at the top of any run that's been groomed in the last 24 hours. A nice touch.

Vail for Experts

There is still a certain lingering snobbishness in Colorado ski circles that insists that while Vail is a great cruising mountain for average skiers, real experts will sooner or later get bored there. Nonsense! Vail is not one of those mountains whose trail map looks like a forbidding grill of black bars. With its enormous size, Vail still has more serious expert runs than most other mountains in Colorado. This expert skiing comes in two flavors: steep, fierce bump skiing and ungroomed, all-terrain, all-snow skiing primarily on the back side. A day in the Back Bowls in fresh powder is the finest experience Vail has to offer.

Bump skiing isn't everyone's cup of tea, but moguled runs are a daily challenge that few expert skiers can resist. At Vail, you'll encounter the challenge of the steep and lumpy in two main areas: Lift 10 and *Prima*.

Lift 10 is bump city. Its three main runs, *Blue Ox, Highline,* and *Roger's,* deserve their double black diamond designation. *Blue Ox* is the easiest of the lot and the first one to try if you're hesitating. *Highline,* right under the lift, is the steepest and most continuous—the best long, pure bump run in Vail. That's where you'll see the hot young bumpers with their 20-year-old knees pounding the fall line. This is straightforward, clean bump skiing on big, well-shaped moguls down an obvious fall line, with plenty of width and options for changing lines. In short, it's a beaut, unlike the third run, *Roger's* (pronounced Roh-jhay's after early Vail Ski School director Roger Staub), which leads you leftward to the bottom of Lift 11 and is very narrow at the start and generally messy. This run could be greatly improved by discreet widening and the elimination of a couple of obnoxious tree islands.

Skiing down from the very top of Vail Mountain along the wide boulevard of *Swingsville Ridge,* one eventually comes to a fork: On the left are the friendly steeps of Riva, and on the right is *Prima,* Vail's classic bump run. Such a classic, in fact, that for years the ski school awarded Prima Pins to students who manage to ski it with a bit of grace and composure. The first major steep on *Prima* is called Brown's Face. The left side of Brown's Face lies back at a slightly gentler angle, attracting the majority of skiers, but I find the skiing much better on the far right, where the bumps are bigger, smoother, and above all more rounded. Below Brown's Face you can take a short cut back to Lift 11 by taking the *Pronto* cutoff. (Bump specialists, on their way from the top of Vail Mountain over to Lift 10 and *Highline,* ski what they call "PPL," a killer combination of *Prima, Pronto,* and *Logchute.*) But I don't recommend *Pronto* for mere mortals. The bumps (or more accurately the troughs and gullies) on this short steep face are gnarly and gouged beyond belief. Although only marked black, not double black, I find *Pronto* to be the meanest, most technically difficult skiing at Vail. Most skiers, even most experts, would do better to follow *Trans Montane Catwalk* back around to Lift 11. *Prima Cornice,* an extremely steep exit near the top of *Prima,* is surely the most scary, adventurous, and serious run at Vail; in low snow years it often remains closed because its cliff bands aren't sufficiently covered. Don't even consider *Prima Cornice* unless a steep pitch like *South Rim Run* seems easy to you.

But for true experts, much of the magic of Vail Mountain is found in the classic Back Bowls. Other Colorado areas like Winter Park's Mary Jane, Aspen Mountain, and Telluride also have terrific bumps, but there are simply no other Back Bowls. I've skied the Back Bowls in every condition, every season. If you're good, they're always good. But there is nonetheless a sort of hierarchy of adventures back here; lines to ski first, lines for later. And on stormy whiteout days, forget the Back Bowls; you might as well ski where you can see.

Sun Down and Sun Up bowls are separated by a massive central ridge. The lines on either side ultimately lead you down to roads that take you back to Lift 5. The action is all over when you reach these catwalks, so be sure to look around and enjoy the view. *Sun Up Catwalk,* in particular, brings you around a corner to a sudden splendid view of the peaks of the Holy Cross Wilderness framed between two snowy ridges; this is Vail's most dramatic alpine view.

If you enter the classic bowls through the first gate east of the Lift 5 lift line, you'll find yourself skiing along the flat top of the central ridge, *High Noon Ridge,* for a few hundred yards. (All of Vail's bowls, by the way, are separately controlled areas that one enters through marked gates in roped-off control fences; generally they close earlier than the front side of the mountain to give skiers a chance to get back up and down to the Village by a reasonable hour.) The slopes leading down and left from this central ridge are the first ones to hit on a powder morning; they're steep, direct and delicious, and easy to get to, and they get tracked up quickly. You arrive first at *Milt's Face* (which pretty much represents the whole side or flank of this ridge) and then at *Cow's Face* (the obvious nose at the end of this ridge). There is no correct or best place to drop off this ridge. Simply turn and dive off where there are few or no tracks. Skiing here is so wide and free that it's quite vague where one named zone stops and the next starts (trail maps, for example, indicate an area between *Milt's* and *Cow's Faces* called *Campbells,* but most longtime Vail skiers won't recognize the name or the spot). There's room for at least a hundred sets of nonoverlapping tracks out here. Make one or two sets and head for less popular areas in the back.

Next in ease of access, less steep but just as broad and even longer, is the left side of Sun Down Bowl immediately west of the Lift 5 lift line. Close to the central ridge this line is called *Forever,* and farther right into the bowl you'll be skiing *Wow.* Both are best reached by a gate just west of the Lift 5 top station, which seems to usher you into a narrow tree slot rather than a proper bowl. Not to worry; the trees quickly thin out into a few hundred yards of beautiful glades before disappearing altogether at the top of *Forever.*

Because most skiers in the two classic bowls seem to circulate in the central area that can be easily reached from Lift 5, the many lovely lines on the extreme sides of Sun Up and Sun Down don't get skied as much or tracked out as fast, and often yield great powder late in the day or even a day or two after a snowstorm.

From the ridge between the Sun Up and Teacup bowls you can access

Yonder Gully, Yonder, and *Over Yonder,* which offer wonderful, obscure skiing on the far west-facing flank of Sun Up Bowl. This area has a feeling all its own with patchy, widely spaced trees—after *Shangri-La,* these are my favorite Back Bowl lines on a stormy day.

On the opposite, extreme western side of Sun Down Bowl, two other remote zones known as *Seldom* and *Never* provide that same, away-from-it-all feeling. Here, there are a few rock bands and mini-cliffs to look out for but nothing extreme. You reach *Seldom* and *Never* by entering Sun Down Bowl from the top of Lift 7 and then traversing all the way right. Other lines on this side, like *Morningside Ridge* and *Ricky's Ridge,* which are also reached from Lift 7, provide pretty good skiing but lack the wild character of the classic bowls at their best.

Finally, there are some mysterious lines in the two classic bowls that few skiers ever seem to find. *Windows* is a nonstarter; in the four years I spent teaching skiing at Vail, I skied it only a few times and never managed to have a great run. You have to ski down Minturn Mile from the top, turn left at the *Windows* gate, and bushwhack through a dense, unpleasant forest, and when you come out in the open, you wind up with a much abbreviated version of *Wow.* It's not worth it.

Quite the opposite are two of the finest lines in the Back Bowls: *Après Vous* and *Chicken Yard.* To find *Après Vous,* head for *Cow's Face* and hug the right-side control fence, which takes you around the corner to a hidden face. This is *Après Vous,* a triangular face that often has a gentle cornice wave at its crest and typically receives deeper wind-drifted snow than the rest of Sun Up Bowl. The beauty of *Après Vous* is not so much the skiing, which is splendid, but the sensation of being out of sight of everything and everyone else in the back. Eventually this hidden face narrows into a gully that cuts through sparse aspen forests down to the *Sun Up Catwalk.* Even wilder and more isolated is *Chicken Yard,* a second hidden slope that you reach by once again hugging the right side of the *Après Vous* control fence and ducking through a marked gate in the ropes. This gate existed for many years before Vail finally put *Chicken Yard* on its trail maps. At the top of this run one has the peculiar sensation of being suspended high above the valley floor that only convex, fall-away terrain conveys. Despite this suspended-in-the-sky feeling, *Chicken Yard* isn't really very steep; the hardest moment comes in the exit gully, which is barred by small cliffs. When there isn't enough snow to negotiate the cliffs, the patrol simply closes the *Chicken Yard* gate.

Another great bit of expert-only terrain that many skiers never find is the *Ouzo Glade* (or the *Ouzo Trees*), located in Game Creek Bowl. Use the *Eagle's Nest Ridge* entrance to *Ouzo* and then traverse right for a hundred yards or so on a grooming road before peeling down into the forest. There are many lines here, with continual surprise openings in the trees. In winter the snow is fantastic in these trees, but on spring afternoons it turns heavy because of its direct western exposure.

Vail Mountain is a more intriguing playground for expert skiers than many believe. This is true not only because of its hard runs and Back Bowls, but because of the sheer amount of nonstop skiing available. There is enough terrain here—both obvious and hidden—to keep your sense of discovery and surprise alive for many seasons. The only reason for one Vail ski day to resemble another is a lack of imagination.

Vail for Less-Experienced Skiers

Inexperienced skiers, emerging novices, subintermediates—skiers who lack either mileage or confidence or both—can still have a great time on this mountain. But in all honesty, Vail's choices for this level of skier are somewhat limited. You can wind up spending a lot of time on fairly boring catwalks. Novices and "emerging intermediates" will probably enjoy themselves more, and certainly make more progress, if they spend a few days skiing at Vail's sister ski area, Beaver Creek, where they'll find more ideal terrain.

If you're somewhat better than an emerging novice but still not a very experienced skier, cheer up, you won't feel out of it for long. While you're working on new skills, remember the following lifts and runs: The very best, gentle skiing at Vail is served by Lifts 3, 7, and 14—although you'll have to take some other lifts (and ski down some other runs) to take full advantage of these hyper-friendly zones.

In my opinion, the finest run for inexperienced skiers on Vail Mountain is *Lost Boy*, the left-hand ridge run of Game Creek Bowl. It's long and somewhat flat but still feels like a big-mountain experience. Cruise *Lost Boy* to your heart's content—but remember, it's the only run in Game Creek that's really suitable for inexperienced skiers. Afterward, when leaving Lift 7, be sure to turn left down *Eagle's Nest Ridge.* Then you can either return to Mid-Vail via *The Meadows, Jake's Jaunt,* or *Over Easy,* or continue on down *Eagle's Nest Ridge* to the Lionshead side of the mountain. From Mid-Vail, less-experienced skiers should start down the mountain on *Lion's Way,* a gentle packed road. When this road ends, a series of broad open slopes (where runs like *Pickeroon* and *Berries* dead end in flats) will steer you down toward the top of Lift 1 and the loading maze of Lift 2. From here, follow *Gitalong Road* back to Vail Village (ski sections of Bear Tree when you cross them—if they look groomed and inviting). Another option, if you're heading home to Lionshead, is to continue traversing across the mountain when you pass *Bear Tree* and you will wind up on *Born Free,* the main drag down into Lionshead. Hesitant skiers should avoid the one steep spot here by following a trail marked *Village Catwalk* into the forest and back in a long zigzag that takes them around the last steep pitch on lower *Born Free.*

I've already said that the Far East is also a real novice skier's paradise. All the runs on Lift 14 are optimal for inexperienced and learning skiers. The only flaw here is the trip home, which necessitates taking *Flapjack* all the way to the bottom of Lift 11 (*Flapjack* is easy if it's been groomed recently but daunting if it hasn't been—so ask an instructor). From the bottom of Lift 11, you'll slide down *Skid Road* to the backside loading station of Lift 6, and from the top of Lift 6, ski an easy blue, *Ruder's Run,* back to the Village.

Already, you may have spotted Vail Mountain's only real weakness. Extremely inexperienced skiers tend to spend a lot of time on roads and catwalks. The reverse side of the coin is that you won't stay inexperienced for long on such a friendly mountain.

Suppose, however, that without being a very strong skier, you are pretty good at coping with average blue runs—even though you don't "bomb" them the way I assume good skiers do. In that case, you have a lot more choices. Around Mid-Vail, start with *Swingsville,* its neighbor *Christmas,* and *Ramshorn* (they are all marked green but are actually easy blue in difficulty). I'd also recommend several beautiful cruising runs on the Middle Mountain: *Avanti* and *Pickeroon.* Each has one steep black face, but you can go around these steep pitches on conveniently provided escape paths. Farther west, you should try *Columbine* and *Ledges.* Finally, the westernmost run on the whole mountain, *Simba,* is easy, wide, and inviting for most of the way down until you reach *Post Road.* When you hit *Post Road,* follow it right to *Born Free* and you'll be home free.

Vail for Beginners

Vail has two separate beginner areas on different sides of the mountain. There is a difference between them, and you should take this into account when deciding where you or your friends will start learning how to ski on Vail Mountain.

On the Vail Village side, first-time and beginner classes meet at Golden Peak, and students will soon be riding Lift 12. This chair serves an area that's nicely roped off from traffic but is still, for beginners, a bit steep. Yet as a result of this robust practice environment, beginners who learn at Golden Peak are better prepared for what is called at Vail the "first-day mountain" experience—skiing the whole mountain from top to bottom.

Lionshead beginners, by contrast, are taken right to the top on the gondola and make their first moves on the wonderful, gentle slopes of Lift 15. A nearly effortless experience. The rub is that Lift 15 is too easy; beginners who learn up there are often not well prepared for their first full-mountain experience. Lionshead instructors therefore have cunningly put together the absolutely easiest way down their side of the mountain, combining bits and pieces of various runs into what they call the "teaching trail." If you're looking for an extremely gentle way down the mountain from *Eagle's Nest,* here it is. At the bottom of Lift 15, turn right onto *Owl's Roost.* Follow this catwalk straight across several steeper bluish runs like upper *Ledges* and *Lodgepole,* until it turns a sharp corner and zigs back left across the same runs, leading you into the middle green section of *Ledges.* This series of gentle pitches around small tree islands leads you to another road, *Cub's Way,* which you'll follow to the right to the top of Lift 1. From there, *Gitalong Road* takes you home to the bottom of the mountain. It's a mighty roundabout journey, but it works, even for those who can barely stand up on skis. The upper part of this teaching trail and the top sections of *Ledges* and *Lodgepole* have been designated as a practice park so that learners won't be distracted or scared by stronger skiers whooshing by.

Special Programs, Special Tips

Vail boasts the largest ski school in the country and certainly one of the best. I was quite proud to instruct there for a number of years wearing the blue uniform with the black-and-white, diagonal stripes that Roger Staub made famous. But all ski school programs are not created equal, even at Vail. Here are a few recommendations.

Vail's children's ski school is incredible; I still think it's the best I've seen anywhere. In fact, within it there are a number of kids' ski schools and special programs. Starting with *Small World,* a nursery for youngsters from two months to two and a half years old, kids graduate into Mogul Mice and then to Super Stars. There are splendid child-care facilities at both Golden Peak and Lionshead, from which the littlest ones can forge out for short introductions to skiing or travel in more experienced groups when they're ready. The Children's Ski Center at Golden Peak is a modern, two-story kids' palace. The "regular" kids' ski school teaches children from six years old and up, and teenagers are grouped together in their own classes. In recent years the children's ski school has been the most creative branch of this giant ski school and has developed an amazing Children's Adventure Program on Vail Mountain. A unique kids' trail map outlines a multitude of special children's activities and ski programs and points the way to mysterious mine shafts designed for young skiers to explore, Indian villages and burial grounds, a mountain lion's den, and more. The children's program on this mountain has been as much a contribution to the future of skiing as all of Vail's quad chairs, and it has been widely and successfully copied at other Colorado ski resorts.

What about adults? I'm less sanguine about the quality of grown-up instruction here for a curious reason. Vail has the largest and most affluent private lesson clientele of any North American ski mountain. (Of three ski school base locations, one in the heart of Vail Village specializes only in private lessons.) Since instructors make a far better living teaching private than group lessons, all the hot instructor talent at Vail winds up booked for the season with private lessons. That's all well and good, if you can afford the tab, which is upwards from $100 per hour, and upwards from $400 for an all-day private lesson. But an unfortunate side effect of this is that instructors teaching group lessons on Vail Mountain are apt to be less experienced, less motivated, and less skilled, and the chances of getting a great group lesson are correspondingly low.

While bottlenecks and crowding are, generally speaking, not problems during a day's skiing on Vail Mountain, the same can't be said of the typical traffic jams as skiers return to the valley in the evening by the most obvious trails. Mountain Hostesses and Hosts are pressed into service to direct homeward traffic and help keep skier speed down. You'll wish there was another way to get down in the evening. There is. In fact there are several. In Lionshead, most skiers ski home via *Born Free,* but instead I'd recommend *The Glade,* one of the most delightful, semihidden spots on Vail Mountain. *The Glade* is a series of openings in a beautiful aspen forest that's usually half-deserted when *Born Free* is choked with bodies. If you're a strong skier, there are short black pitches into Lionshead that avoid the evening congestion; it's also more pleasant to ski home on the western side of the gondola line, following lower *Simba,* than on *Born Free.*

To return to the Vail Village side of the resort in the evening, sans crowds, I recommend the same route. Head for the Lionshead side, ski *The Glade,* and when you emerge on the last shoulder of *Born Free,* take *Village Catwalk* all the way back across to the Village.

And one final skiing tip: In stormy weather forget the Back Bowls without trees; visibility is so marginal that it just isn't worth it. In fact, the lower mountain is much better than the upper ridges. The Lionshead side of the mountain really comes into its own in storms. For one thing, you can ride the gondola and really stay warm and dry; for another, the timber on this side of the mountain is denser, so the runs not only feel more sheltered, but your visibility will be at a maximum. The basic strategy for a stormy day, anywhere, is to ski right next to the trees and avoid the featureless center sections of wider slopes.

Lunchtime

I've already given Vail Mountain enough sincere, well-deserved praise that I don't feel the least bit negative when I tell you the best lunches on Vail Mountain are actually in the Village or in Lionshead down below.

Food service on the mountain is certainly adequate. But the food is resolutely institutional—that is to say, mediocre. And Vail's mountain restaurants, whether cafeteria style or sit-down, simply lack charm. Two Elk

Restaurant on the ridge above China Bowl was a step forward architecturally (unfortunately destroyed by arson in the fall of 1998), but it's still just another ski area cafeteria. When a ski resort is as exceptional as Vail is, you have to compare it with the best around, and for my money that means European mountain food service, which is in a whole different league.

However, there's an easy alternative to mass-produced mountain grub. Ski down and eat lunch in any of the fine eateries off the mountain. Before the days of high-speed quad lifts, this was never an option for serious skiers because getting back up the mountain after lunch wasted too much time. The new lifts have changed that. Long middle mountain runs like *Avanti* or *Lodgepole* are totally empty around noon, as are lower *Prima* and *Riva*. You'll be downtown in a flash. You can enjoy a far better lunch at better prices in the Village and be back up on top of the mountain in plenty of time to wear your legs to a frazzle long before the lifts close.

If you're in the mood for a really romantic lunch up on the mountain and the weather looks good, I'd recommend picking up a classic French *pique-nique* (in a small backpack) from Les Délices de France in Lionshead and enjoying it with a bottle of Beaujolais on one of the many mountain picnic decks that are marked on the trail map. My favorite picnic deck used to be at the Wildwood Shelter, overlooking Sun Down Bowl. But Wildwood has now been enlarged into a good-size (260-seat) restaurant; though still not large by Vail standards, it is no longer the intimate, almost deserted little hideaway it once was.

Around Town, Vail Ambience

The town of Vail has grown up in little more than 25 years from less than modest beginnings (a single homestead in a green and grassy valley) to an alpine urban center with three (count them!) exits from the I-70 freeway that runs through the valley linking Denver with Grand Junction and various points west. It's really a small mountain city more than a town or a village, and despite its size and bustle it's still a remarkable place to spend a ski vacation.

For one thing, unlike many ski resorts (to which Gertrude Stein's classic comment about Oakland, "There's no there, there," applies all too well) Vail has a real center—two centers actually—that gives a human and commercial hub to town life. Vail-bashing is a popular activity at other Colorado ski towns, where folks complain about Vail's ticky-tacky, instant atmosphere and its imitation Tyrolian architecture. I'd say they're all wet. Such comments come more from jealousy than judgment. The architecture does have alpine overtones, ranging from subtle woodwork and rounded chimney-cap details to cartoonlike pastiche. But in fact it's a good deal more tasteful and more authentic in the sense of being true to itself than a lot of recently built ski villages I've visited in the Alps. In a word, I like it. You will too.

Vail Village is more intriguing than Lionshead, which is understandable since the Village is roughly ten years older. Both town centers are true pedestrian zones, where life and living people—not cars and exhaust—fill the streets. I've already said that Vail is the only true pedestrian ski village in North America, and this is an enormous part of its ongoing success. Vail has banished America's worst urban plague, the automobile, to the outskirts of town and to the outer reaches of vacationing visitors' consciousness. If you bring your car to Vail (which certainly isn't necessary), you're going to park it and forget it for the rest of the week and love living without it.

Both Vail Village and Lionshead are so crammed full of shops, boutiques, galleries, eateries, and lodges, you'll need a week to explore the place—and you'll need a lot of money to take advantage of it all too. The price of success, this much success, is price. And Vail is as pricey as they come with nouveau riche overtones that are so up-front they don't really offend. The flow of people and commerce in Vail Village sweeps you along Bridge Street, which runs from a totally hidden, three-story, underground parking structure, over the landmark Covered Bridge, and on uphill to the Vista Bahn Express. Bridge Street is the axis of social life in Vail Village. Within half a block you'll find the two most chic sports/fashion stores, Gorsuch and Pepi's, a few too many designer fur shops, and all the ritz and glitz of a big-time resort. But Vail Village isn't a one-block shopping stop either. There are back streets, arcades, tucked-away courtyards, and shops that will take you more than one or two evenings to find.

The après-ski scene on this side of town is a little more intense than it is in Lionshead. And you'll soon discover the basic Vail Village pub crawl, known around town as the Bridge Street Shuffle. Los Amigos is the slopeside center of the nachos-and-Margarita set, and its deck is wall-to-wall tanned bodies on spring afternoons. In fact, the finest après-ski show in town is the view of the Gore Range high over town turning rose and purple in the late-evening alpenglow.

To get from Vail Village to Lionshead or vice versa, and indeed to get around town, you'll want to use Vail's free shuttle-bus system. It'll take you only one ride to get oriented. The town loop is continuous and obvious and even very young kids use these buses to navigate Vail on their own. Between the Village and Lionshead, there is a key bus stop for the Dobson Ice Arena (public skating at various hours as well as fierce, local hockey action). The trip from one side of Vail to the other is only about five minutes.

Lionshead is a more free-form resort center with open plazas and stairways rather than an actual grid of streets defining its spaces and circulation. There is more lodging (more condos and condotels) than over in Vail Village, so it's never empty even though, as I mentioned, the Village side seems to offer more in the way of shopping and après-ski. A new addition to the Lionshead après-ski scene is noteworthy: the top floor of the old gondola building has been converted into a 100 percent authentic German brewery and beer hall, a perfect replica of the Musicians' Hall in the Neuschwanstein castle in Bavaria. Its Kaltenberg Pils is one of the best beers available in Colorado and Kaltenberg Weiss (or wheat) beer is the ultimate après-ski drink on a warm spring afternoon. . . .

Dining and Lodging in Vail

In several of the Colorado ski resorts covered in this guide one really has to search to get a fine meal. This is not exactly the problem in either of Colorado's two premier resorts, Vail and Aspen. Here the problem is one of an embarrassment of riches.

For the past ten years my absolute number-one choice for dinner in Vail has been Sweet Basil, a tastefully decorated, low-key sort of "California nouveau" restaurant that is definitely neither the most expensive nor the most elegant place to eat. Sweet Basil simply serves the most consistently interesting cooking in town, which is quite a compliment considering the competition!

There are a number of fairly classic French and Frenchified restaurants at Vail, of which the Left Bank is the best known. But I find these restaurants too predictable—the service slightly too elegant, the prices slightly too expensive, the menus slightly too familiar—rather than wonderful culinary surprises.

If the prices, and pretensions, of some Vail restaurants start to get you down, consider an evening in nearby Minturn. A scruffy, true-grit sort of town, Minturn lies ten minutes from Vail, tucked away in a side canyon under the rocky crag that gave Lionshead its name. The town owes both its existence and half its population to its railroad yards. Here you'll want to visit the Minturn Country Club, a funky, cook-your-own-steak emporium, and the Saloon, a giant, barnlike Mexican restaurant. Both are longtime local favorites and both provide a lively counterpart to the more formal Vail dining.

I hope you'll forgive me for being even less exhaustive about Vail accommodations than about its restaurants. Your choice of good lodging is, if anything, greater and broader than that of good food. Naturally Vail has a reservation system to lodge its guests (see the Vail Data section) in anything from very posh, full-service hotels to luxury apartments to quite basic, ski resort condos.

But I have a couple of personal favorites to pass along, chosen for—what else—atmosphere, architecture, and charm: the Sonnenalp's Bavaria House and the Christiania Lodge. The Christiania is definitely "old Vail"; it stands at the foot of the slopes in Vail Village, and its old-fashioned bar/lounge is surely the least trendy après-ski rendezvous in Vail. The Sonnenalp's Bavaria

House seems more old world than old Vail. This magical building was remodeled from a formerly boring block of 1960s apartments into an authentic Austro-alpine, wood-and-plaster masterpiece. Whenever I'm in Vail on a Sunday, I try to have brunch at the Sonnenalp—unforgettable!

Lodging a bit out of town, say on the other side of the I-70 freeway that bisects the valley or slightly west in the direction of the adjoining bedroom community of Eagle-Vail, will cost somewhat less than staying right in Lionshead or Vail Village. But I must say, despite its outrageously deluxe reputation—and its outrageously deluxe reality—most of Vail lodging is comparably priced with similar lodging in other Colorado ski areas. Many of the outlying lodging complexes offer their own shuttle-van transport to and from the center so you can still enjoy the pedestrian quality of a Vail vacation. Skiers staying at or near the Westin Hotel way out in West Vail even get to use a special lift, Lift 20 (the Cascade Village Lift), which was built exclusively to connect this outlying district with *Simba* and the Lionshead trail system. A comeback catwalk, *Westin Ho!,* brings Westin Hotel guests home when the lifts have closed.

VAIL DATA

Mountain Statistics

Vertical feet	3,330 feet
Base elevation	8,120 feet
Summit elevation	11,450 feet
Longest run	4.5 miles
Average annual snowfall	335 inches
Number of lifts	31, including 10 high-speed quads and 1 12-passenger gondola
Skiable terrain	4,112 acres
Opening date	mid-November
Closing date	mid-April
Snowboarding	Yes!

Vail shares a common lift ticket with Beaver Creek

Transportation

By car Two hours (in good road and weather conditions) from Denver, approximately 100 miles east on I-70.

By bus or limo Two hours from the Denver International Airport.

By plane Many direct flights land at the Eagle County Airport just 35 miles from Vail.

Key Phone Numbers

Ski Area Information
   (970) 476-5601
Snow Report (970) 476-4888
Reservations (800) 525-2257
www.snow.com

A Powder Primer

Powder skiing is a great liberation from gravity, effort, and worldly cares. But you have to defeat the powder paradox first. The paradox is this: Once you know how to ski in deep snow, it seems much easier than skiing on the packed snow; but learning to ski powder is always harder than learning to turn on packed slopes. Here's a simplified approach to get you past the frustrations of learning to ski powder as quickly as possible.

Balance first. Or as I used to tell my students, stability before mobility. You'll need a new sort of balance in deep snow—standing two-footed, weight roughly equal on both skis. If you stand on one ski, which is the normal mode for hardpack, that weighted ski will dive down while the other one floats up, and whoops! To develop two-footed powder balance, be sure you do a bit of straight running and traversing before you start turning downhill in deep snow. Bounce and flex up and down on both skis as you descend in a straight line, and adapt your stance for better balance by spreading your arms wider than normal.

Slow-motion speed control. Everything takes longer to accomplish in deep snow: Skis don't just whip around, they come about slowly and gently.

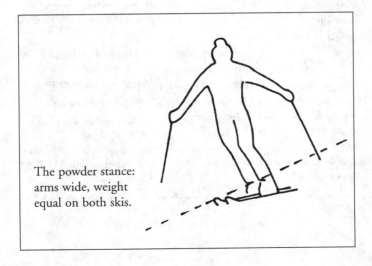

The powder stance: arms wide, weight equal on both skis.

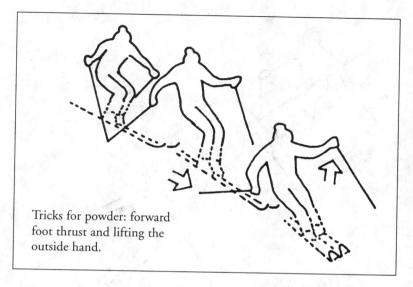

Tricks for powder: forward foot thrust and lifting the outside hand.

You'll feel as if you are skiing in slow motion. This is normal and is due to the extra resistance from your skis being buried inside the snow rather than just sliding over the top of it. Get used to finishing turns gently and pulling smoothly out of the fall line much slower than normal. A jerky attempt to pivot your skis sideways in powder will inevitably produce a fall. From a steep traverse, sink down and then slowly, smoothly twist your skis uphill while extending your legs and pushing and grinding your heels sideways. Twisting extension is the key to a strong finish for a powder turn.

Launching your turns down the hill. Here we have another powder paradox: For experienced powder skiers, short-linked turns are easiest, but newcomers will find that individual medium- to long-radius turns result in more success. Launch these turns by using a couple of "powder tricks," either separately or together. The first trick is to vigorously lift your outside hand as you start your turn. This will help to unweight the fronts of your skis and bank you neatly in the direction of the turn—a real secret weapon in extremely deep snow and a big help when you're learning. The other trick is more subtle. If it works for you, great; if not, don't give it a second thought. I'm talking about pushing both feet forward as you start your turn. This is a hard-to-observe move, but believe me, good powder skiers do it a lot and often subconsciously. By thrusting both feet forward in the direction of the new turn down the hill, you will be guaranteeing equal weight on both skis, and once again, helping to lighten the fronts of the skis.

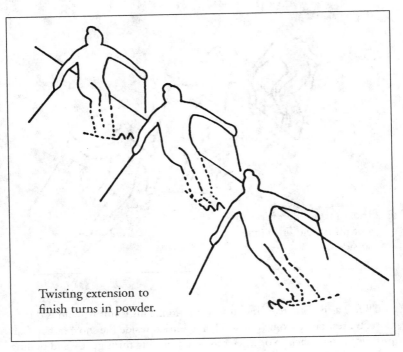

Twisting extension to
finish turns in powder.

And please, don't be too demanding or too judgmental about your own
performance on your first few excursions into powder snow. Falling is
inevitable and with the right attitude almost fun. At first, surviving turns in
the deep and just staying on your feet is more important than doing them
right. After you've proved to yourself that you can make it down a slope covered with a foot and a half of fluff, it's easier to find the confidence to work
out the details and ski the same slope better, more smoothly, and more
gracefully. Like everything else on skis, powder skiing is a progression.
Remember the sequence: First develop a new type of balance on two feet
and two skis, then work on a slow-motion finish to your turns, and finally
master a powerful "lifting" start to launch them. And I have one more tip.

A secret weapon: fat skis. In recent years, the introduction of extra-wide
and slightly shorter powder skis has thrown the door to deep-snow performance wide open. These skis have so much flotation that they never seem
to get stuck or "railed" in the powder snow. Skiers who have never really had
the time to go out and practice in deep snow will find these wide skis sim-
plify the whole problem of developing deep-snow balance. You very nearly
can't make a mistake on them, and if you do make a mistake, you almost
can't fall. Known affectionately as "fat boys" or "powder pigs," these extra-

wide skis have become ubiquitous in just a few seasons. Rent a pair the next time you find yourself looking at a foot or more of new snow. You will be amazed and delighted.

And that's the powder story. Soon you'll be connecting medium-radius turns through knee-deep powder that used to psych you out. At first, you shouldn't try to link turns too closely—that will be your final step. Initially, you'll want to use the space between turns to catch your breath, smile in amazement that you made it, and get yourself together for that next turn. After your first few successes, you'll know why skiers rave about powder. It really is the ultimate. It is very close to flying.

BEAVER CREEK

Years ago when I first started skiing at Beaver Creek, I thought of it as Vail's little sister. Beaver Creek was created and is still owned and managed by Vail Associates (today known as Vail Resorts), one of the most sophisticated ski companies in North America. It was to be expected that they would do a good job, and they did. My only reservations were about the mountain itself. It didn't seem interesting enough to hold my full skier's attention, no matter how well designed the lifts, how efficient the snowmaking system, or how attractive the new village at its base. Well, I was wrong. Vail's little sister has grown up and today she is quite a beauty. Maybe all new ski resorts (and nowadays there are almost none) have to go through the same awkward years before everything clicks into place and the sophisticated skier can finally say, "Wow, that's quite a mountain!"

In skiing terms, what made all the difference was the opening up of a whole new peak several seasons ago. Grouse Mountain, a separate and well-defined ridge rising at the head of a side valley located between the main ski mountain and Larkspur Bowl to the west, has provided lots of the playful yet not stressful advanced terrain that Beaver Creek always lacked. Today, Beaver Creek is a complete, well-balanced ski mountain. It would be disingenuous to complain that there aren't any Back Bowls; none of Colorado's other great ski resorts, aside from Vail, is blessed in this regard.

At the same time, I'm delighted to say that the base village at Beaver Creek has grown up too. Those noisy years when this base area was more of a permanent construction zone than a mountain village are over. The finished architecture is rather distinctive (a little monumental for my taste) with a handsome mix of stucco, stone, and tile. It is less of an alpine look-alike and has more of its own personality than nearby Vail. And best of all, this base village really works well as a pedestrian space. A handsome network

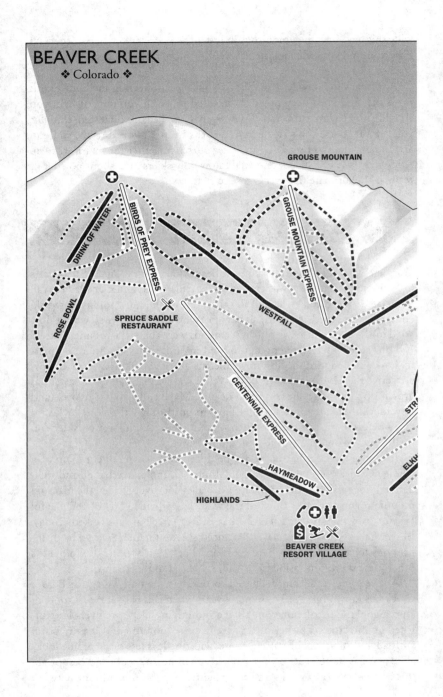

BEAVER CREEK
❖ Colorado ❖

GROUSE MOUNTAIN

DRINK OF WATER

BIRDS OF PREY EXPRESS

GROUSE MOUNTAIN EXPRESS

ROSE BOWL

SPRUCE SADDLE
RESTAURANT

WESTFALL

CENTENNIAL EXPRESS

STR

ELKH

HAYMEADOW

HIGHLANDS

BEAVER CREEK
RESORT VILLAGE

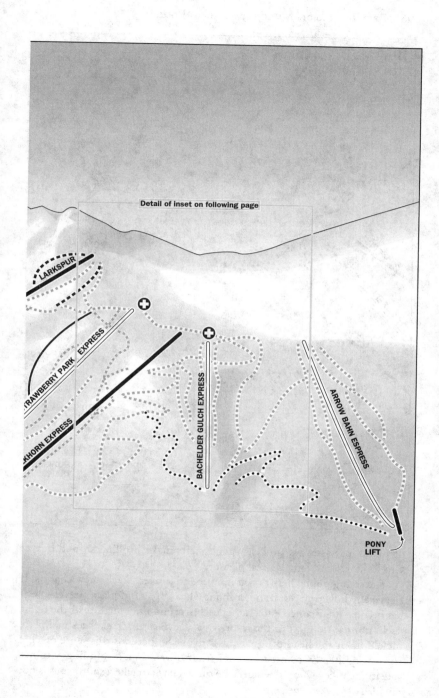

Detail of inset on following page

LARKSPUR

STRAWBERRY PARK EXPRESS

ELKHORN EXPRESS

BACHELDER GULCH EXPRESS

ARROW BAHN EXPRESS

PONY LIFT

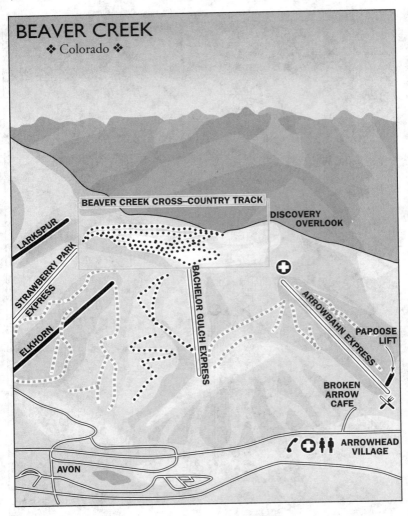

of plazas, passageways, and easy-angle stairs make strolling around Beaver Creek's stores and lodges a real pleasure.

The skiing public hasn't been immune to Beaver Creek's new charms. If I have any lingering reservations about what a splendid place Beaver Creek has become, they concern the rather exclusive and pricey nature of the resort itself, not the skiing. But the resort village at Beaver Creek is a small place tucked up at the head of a narrow canyon. So perhaps this sense of chic exclusivity literally comes with the terrain. Even so, a forbidding entrance gate to the valley where day skiers are turned back to take a shuttle bus is not my idea of a warm welcome.

As we'll see in this chapter, there are a couple of skiing dimensions in which Beaver Creek not only rivals but surpasses its older sister Vail. Even though Beaver Creek is now a successful destination resort in its own right, its closeness to Vail makes it easy for many skiers to split their Vail Valley experience by skiing at both Vail and Beaver Creek during a week-long holiday.

And finally, before we start our detailed exploration of Beaver Creek, I should add that Vail's little sister now has a couple of little sisters of her own. Just west of Beaver Creek, a small ski area named Arrowhead was created a few years ago as a kind of owners-only adjunct to a new golf-course community of the same name. Vail Resorts has now taken over Arrowhead and created another small but intriguing ski zone and resort/second-home development called Bachelor Gulch between Arrowhead and Beaver Creek. Then they linked up all this add-on skiing with a couple of new lifts. This new expansion of Beaver Creek's terrain is served by three lifts, including two high-speed quads, the Arrowbahn from the Arrowhead base and the Bachelor Gulch Express from Bachelor Gulch village. The skiing in the westward expansion of Beaver Creek is fun but not spectacular, mostly blue runs through mixed aspen forests, with quite a few of the trails cut simply as real estate amenities. No matter—more space to ski and new runs to cruise are always welcome, and a ski jaunt from Beaver Creek over to Arrowhead for lunch and back is a worthy project. But most of the excitement on Beaver Creek's mountain lies directly above the main village. Let's look closer.

The Lay of the Land, Valley, and Mountain

You don't just drive up to Beaver Creek and go skiing. The area is located at the upper end of a steep side valley that enters the larger Eagle River Valley by the new town of Avon, which is a few miles west of Vail on I-70.

Avon and Beaver Creek are as different as night and day. Avon provides lots of affordable and low-cost housing near two super ski areas, especially for Vail Valley locals—and in this respect reminds me of Dillon and Silverthorne in Summit County, more of a sprawling suburban shopping center than a resort village—while Beaver Creek's base village provides a compact assortment of resort amenities, elegant mountain architecture, and luxury accommodations.

Unless you're staying at Beaver Creek or riding the bus from Vail, you'll have to park in a large lot at the mouth of the canyon and take a shuttle bus up to the area. The shuttles leave every few minutes and the ride is quite short. Up at the base you'll find yourself looking in two directions. There's the main mountain straight ahead of you, a spacious beginner pasture at the bottom, and a quad chair charging right up the center of a massive rounded peak where ribbon runs alternate with dark evergreen forests. On your right, another chair rises through open aspen trees up what looks like a different mountain altogether, which it is. And what you can't yet see is a third mountain, Grouse Mountain, way in the background, rising between these two. The new Bachelor Gulch/Arrowhead expansion area is well out of sight behind the right-hand mountain you see from Beaver Creek village.

That's Beaver Creek in a nutshell. The main mountain is a massive central ridge, essentially two lifts high. The Centennial Express quad carries you most of the way up to the large mid-mountain restaurant at *Spruce Saddle,* and from there the Birds of Prey Express quad takes you on to the top. The top of the mountain is as gentle as can be, and another chair slanting up from the east serves a fantastic network of easy and forgiving novice trails. Farther down the same east side of this big ridge, the recently added Lift 4 serves a slanting side drainage called Rose Bowl. On the opposite, or western, side of the main ridge, Lift 9 serves Beaver Creek's most serious and celebrated terrain, the three Birds of Prey runs, *Golden Eagle, Peregrine,* and *Goshawk.*

Directly west of all this, across a small creek-bed drainage, lies a second smaller mountain that for the moment is served by only two lifts, 12 and 11. (On top of this side of the mountain is a surprise: Colorado's most unusual cross-country ski area, about which I'll tell you more later.) But this side mountain is now linked to Bachelor Gulch and Arrowhead, occupying the next valleys farther west, making this side of Beaver Creek much more attractive. Already, the replacement of Lift 12, the Strawberry Park Lift with a high-speed quad, had brought more skiers over to this side of the mountain, and this popularity will grow. These westside slopes are bathed in early morning light and have a very different feel from those on the main side of the mountain—light and airy like the pale aspen forests around them. Farther west, Bachelor Gulch and Arrowhead together add 30 percent more skiable terrain to Beaver Creek, mostly unchallenging intermediate cruising (and a few ski-in/ski-out real estate routes that you do not want to take by accident).

The small canyon separating the main mass of Beaver Creek from this "side mountain" to the west dead ends in a sort of cul-de-sac. Here Lift 9 rises up and left toward the Birds of Prey, Lift 11 rises up and right into Larkspur Bowl, and at the dead-end back of this small valley, Lift 10, a high-speed quad, climbs straight up Grouse Mountain, the "third" mountain that has completed Beaver Creek's skiing picture.

Beaver Creek for Beginners and Less-Experienced Skiers

This is one class of skiers that will absolutely go crazy over this area. There's much more suitable and intriguing skiing terrain for novices, and more of it, here at Beaver Creek than at Vail. That famous first-day mountain experience—where skiers leave the cradle, forgo the comfort of the beginner slope, and go on up the mountain like everyone else—is a snap at Beaver Creek. Novices here get to go to the very top and ski on runs like *Red Buffalo, Booth Gardens,* and *Powell* all morning long; these are gentle, barely inclined rivers of snow. And then they can take *Cinch* or *Dally* back to the bottom, all without a traumatic moment.

This is not to say that the whole mountain is flat; quite the contrary. There is simply so much gentle skiing at the very top, and this novice paradise is connected to the base by easy descent roads that are well designed and well groomed. *Cinch* is just that, a big road that doesn't have a cramped, narrow "catwalk" feel. Beaver Creek is a novice skier's dream. Also, my guess is that a beginning skier can get a better group lesson here than at Vail. This is because the Beaver Creek ski school (which, like the rest of the mountain staff here, is really an extension of the Vail original) hasn't yet developed the amazing private lesson clientele that Vail has, so you are more likely to find top instructors teaching group lessons.

I should add that while it's the easy upper-mountain terrain that makes Beaver Creek such a standout for novice and learning skiers, first-timers here are well served too. The Haymeadow beginners' area at the base, with its slow user-friendly East Haymeadow Lift, is all one needs for a successful first day on skis.

Beaver Creek for Good Skiers

What does Beaver Creek offer good skiers? A very straightforward gradation of terrain, steady pitches and excellent grooming, no nasty surprises, no blue runs suddenly turning black and ugly, and, for the most part, uncrowded and reasonably wide slopes. I'm hesitating on this last point because not all the slopes at Beaver Creek are as wide as I'd like to see them, or as wide as most slopes at Vail. Particularly the runs underneath *Cinch* on the lower mountain like *Assay, Fool's Gold,* and *Latigo,* which are all a little harder than the slope would lead you to think simply because they're narrow. Others, like *Centennial* (Beaver Creek's longest run from top to bottom) and especially *Red Tail,* are absolutely perfect, wide-open sheets of snow where intermediate skiers can stretch their wings and fly. *Red Tail* (despite the name, this is not one of the infamous double diamond Birds of Prey runs) takes you down to Red Tail Camp, a wonderfully intimate luncheon hut that reminds one more of the Alps than of an American ski area cafeteria, and the bases of Lifts 10 and 11. Red Tail Camp lies at the head of the small side valley that separates the main mountain from that "second mountain" to the west that I talked about earlier and the new "third mountain," Grouse Mountain, just above.

Up on Grouse Mountain, which is served by Lift 10, all the runs but one are black, and that lone blue run is only marginally gentler than the others.

But I'll put off a discussion of this newest Beaver Creek ski terrain until we reach the section on expert skiing, except for one thing: Grouse Mountain is one of the best places in Colorado to begin to master moguls. The bumps on this mountain are so round and friendly and the slopes so wide and inviting (for bump runs, that is) that they may be a perfect transition for good skiers who want to tackle something more serious. No doubt about it, bump skiing is the single biggest challenge at most modern ski resorts. But Grouse Mountain bump slopes are more friendly than challenging. Good skiers wanting to experience these deliciously formed bumps should start on *Raven Ridge*. If all goes well, then try *Ptarmigan* or *Ruffled Grouse*.

Directly across the valley from *Red Tail*, Lift 11 climbs up to the top of Larkspur Bowl. Along with *Red Tail* and *Centennial*, this is the other "perfect" upper-intermediate run on the mountain—very wide, very free, a true bowl leading into wide aspen-lined avenues at the bottom; it's the sort of run on which everyone skis just a little bit better than normal.

The same is not quite true of the other "opposite-side" runs served by the new Strawberry Park Express quad, Lift 12, which is lower down on Beaver Creek's westside mountain. Here the combination of lower altitude and direct sun exposure works against the snow conditions, and runs like *Pitchfork* and *Stacker* often turn icy late in the season.

By the way, if you think you've missed a few lifts in my thumbnail descriptions of how the mountain works, don't worry. The numbering system is based on some eventually-to-be-completed master plan; although there is a Lift 12, there are only 10 lifts in total. Patience.

Beaver Creek for Experts

There are several steep black pitches on the right bank of Larkspur Bowl, some short steep slots dropping into Rose Bowl, and a couple of short black stretches on the lower main mountain. But really, there are two main areas that will delight expert skiers at Beaver Creek: Grouse Mountain and the Birds of Prey.

I've already praised Grouse Mountain as a zone of friendly, easy-to-learn-on bump runs. Why is it so attractive to dyed-in-the-wool expert skiers? The runs to the left of the chair looking up are indeed some of the most graceful and relaxing bumped-out slopes I've ever skied. What an expert skier does with these bumps is ski them faster than usual. It's a place for dash and style, for getting a little air between bumps, and for something between cruising and bumping. Delicious. On the right side of the lift, again, looking up, the runs are a bit steeper, demand more concentration, and they're appropriately labeled with double diamonds. But the best adventure on this side in *Royal Elk Glades,* a steep flank just beyond all the cut runs that is really more dense forest than open glades. Although a boundary rope will keep you from straying too far, this is skiing that demands cunning route-finding, quick feet, and powerful turns. It's never groomed, of course, seldom packed out, and always interesting.

Before Grouse Mountain was opened, expert skiing at Beaver Creek was synonymous with the Birds of Prey, and the Birds of Prey were synonymous with steep, demanding moguls. Still are. A lot of skiers find the three Birds of Prey runs daunting; they can seem harder, or at least more awkward, than Vail's classic Lift 10 bump runs like *Highline* and *Blue Ox.* They're really not; but they seem more hemmed in by trees, a factor that can inhibit even expert skiers. They also tend to get a bit wind scoured, which can create some sudden, rocky surprises early in the season. *Goshawk* is the shortest of the three and a good run to test yourself on first if you have any doubts. I always thought *Golden Eagle* was the most enjoyable, and nowadays it is even better since it has been widened and somewhat recontoured to make it an international-class downhill course and site of the downhill at the 1999 FIS World Championships. Golden Eagle now starts from the very top of the mountain, and it's still a real thrill. Despite the steepness of these runs, I have to tell you that the bumps you'll find on the Birds of Prey are really good. They don't get skied as hard or as often as similar bump runs at Vail, so the gullies around individual moguls don't get pounded into narrow grooves. Even on the Birds of Prey, you can almost always find good, rounded exit lines from every bump.

Après-Ski and Extra-Ski in Beaver Creek

For après-ski, Beaver-style, let me suggest a whole evening. A trip to Beano's Cabin. The word "cabin" is a misnomer. Beano's is a large, handsome building (call it "designer rustic" for its stone and logs, but a cabin it ain't) that is a members-only, on-mountain luncheon club by day and an open-to-all dinner restaurant in the evenings. If you can combine dinner at Beano's, good weather, and a full moon night, then you've really got something. In the same vein—only more so—would be an overnight stay at Trapper's Cabin. This beautiful lodge (a cabin grown up and gone to heaven) in the forests of McCoy Park above Beaver Creek, is surely Colorado's most exclusive B&B, and your overnight stay includes dinner too. Trapper's Cabin is designed and priced to make you feel like a featured guest on *Lifestyles of the Rich and Famous.* If you happen to be rich or famous or just want to splurge, this is the place.

The "extra" I want to tell you about is the Nordic trail park on top of Lift 12. I realize that not many downhill skiers share my passion for cross-country skiing, and that in the minds of most downhillers, Nordic or cross-country skiing is equated with jogging or with the shuffling timid strides of people who have a pathological fear of sliding and hide in the valley bottoms while their spouses and friends fly off the summits. This is not necessarily true. For starters, at Beaver Creek the Nordic area is located on top, where the great views live. It's a real delight just to be there, and even more so to ski there. And second, cross-country skiing today is a brand new ball game. Skating, something that Alpine skiers are generally very good at, has changed the complexion of cross-country forever. It has become a high-speed, gliding, flowing sport; it's a ball. And there's no better or more beautiful place to see what modern cross-country skiing is all about than on the McCoy Park cross-country tracks, high above Beaver Creek. Take a "skating" lesson up there, and you'll be blown away.

BEAVER CREEK DATA

Mountain Statistics

Vertical feet	4,040 feet
Base elevation	7,400 feet
Summit elevation	11,440 feet
Longest run	3.5 miles
Average annual snowfall	331 inches
Number of lifts	14, including 6 high-speed quads
Skiable terrain	1,529 acres
Opening date	mid-November
Closing date	mid-April
Snowboarding	Yes!

Beaver Creek shares a common lift ticket with Vail.

Transportation

By car Two and a half hours (in good road and weather conditions) from Denver, east on I-70 to the Avon exit, then south 1 mile. Beaver Creek is located about 10 miles west of Vail.

By bus or limo Two and a half hours from the Denver International Airport.

By plane Many direct flights land at the Eagle County Airport only 25 miles from Beaver Creek.

Key Phone Numbers

Ski Area Information
  (970) 845-9090
Snow Report (970) 476-4888
Reservations (800) 934-2485
www.snow.com

Polishing Parallel

This is the age of parallel skiing, but it might be more accurate to call it the age of "sloppy parallel" skiing. Nowadays it's easier than ever to make turns with your skis parallel. In fact, two out of three skiers on the slopes don't do anything special to turn their skis, they just twist 'em around in the direction they want to go. By twisting both skis more or less together, they pull off more or less parallel turns.

Most intermediate skiers know what I'm talking about. They turn their skis together, but the result is a kind of sloppy, ill-defined, wide-track skid rather than a graceful carving arc where the two skis slice around in a narrow, elegant track. Parallel turns of a sort, but not the sort that instructors and experts make. Let's do something about it. The secrets of a polished parallel turn are fewer than you think and relatively easy to master. The first, critical step is learning to ride the arc of the turn.

This one is easy, if I can convince you to stand exclusively, 100 percent, on your outside ski. That's right. Average skiers who make rough-and-ready, hit-or-miss parallel skids, skis wide apart, always stand almost equally on both skis. What's the difference? Modern skis are softer in flex than earlier skis; this allows them to bend under the skier's weight (so-called reverse camber), and this bent ski is what "carves" a pure round arc in the snow. But in order to make your skis bend, you really have to load them up with maximum weight. Suppose you weigh 150 pounds and stand equally on both skis; then each ski only supports 75 pounds. But if you stand completely over one foot, it's like dropping an additional 75-pound sandbag onto that ski. You've doubled the weight on that ski, and it will bend and carve for you. It's that simple. Modern skis are designed to turn best with the full weight of your body pressing down on only one ski, the outside ski of the turn. (By the way, the reverse bend, or reverse camber, in the ski is hard to observe—you can see it best in still photos—but it's always there in a good turn.)

So your first step in mastering modern parallel is to develop the balance needed to put all your weight on one foot. Practice one-footed skiing on gentle flats and catwalks. Lift the light foot up off the snow just to check whether or not you're cheating. Play with the idea, make it a habit. Your turns will improve immediately, and, believe it or not, your legs will be less tired at the end of the day. In actual skiing you don't want to lift that light inside ski up off the snow—that's too much work. Just let the light inside

Skiing with all your weight on the outside ski.

ski float along on the snow next to the loaded outside ski that's doing all the work. Skiing this way is like walking in slow motion: first one foot . . . then the other . . . one complete turn on one foot . . . then another on the opposite foot. . . .

You'll discover an interesting bonus. Not only are your turns rounder, more carved, and more efficient, but your skis will stay closer together. Say good-bye to that old wide track. It's very easy to change the position of the light inside ski in relation to the weighted outside ski. If you stand on both skis equally, trying to move one closer to the other is as impossible as lifting yourself off the ground by your bootstraps.

Nothing else can change your skiing as much as learning to stand exclusively over that outside ski. I call this the best-kept secret in modern skiing because it's so hard to observe that great skiers are really standing exclusively on one foot—first on one foot, then on the other. But they are, and you can too. Naturally, that's not all there is to polishing your parallel turns, but it is the most important step.

Greater Aspen

Aspen and Aspen Mountain Aspen is the most sophisticated ski town in the Rockies, with more good coffeehouses, bookstores, galleries, and restaurants than any other Colorado resort. Aspen Mountain is only one of four Aspen-area ski mountains, just the tip of the iceberg. But a very impressive tip. No green beginner slopes at all here. Instead, friendly, inviting steeps, modest rather limited cruising, and a high-speed gondola to maximize slope time and vertical.

Buttermilk This is the second mountain in the Aspen constellation. It's a perfect learning and practice hill just outside Aspen's city limits with a dynamite ski school and mostly lazy, laid-back terrain. A few steeps but virtually no bumps. Buttermilk is an underappreciated, uncrowded, and truly splendid ski area.

Aspen Highlands The polar opposite of Buttermilk, also on the outskirts of town, this mountain is an often gnarly performance arena for skilled and athletic skiers. Good bumps, steeps, and trees, but an awkward mountain layout for cruisers. New high-speed lifts have made Highlands an attractive alternative for strong skiers.

Snowmass This is the cruising capital of the Aspen ski region. Snowmass is an immense ski mountain with a modern lift system serving long, wide-open runs. Aspen's best all-around, all-skier mountain. The most famous slope: the Big Burn—sparsely treed with ski-everywhere terrain. And there's just enough ungroomed steeps to keep experts from getting bored. Snowmass Village is more about lodging than resort life; it's still just a suburb of Aspen.

ASPEN AND ITS MOUNTAIN

Aspen is the quintessential Colorado ski town in exactly the same way that Vail is the quintessential Colorado ski mountain. Aspen is the one every other ski town gets compared with. The one that's got it all: history and

tradition, money and chic, Victorian architecture and postmodern boutiques, culture and clout, narrow streets and tall views, remarkable sophistication and unquenchable enthusiasm. And . . . oh, yes, good skiing too.

The town of Aspen, like a good-hearted, sporting girl from its rowdy
mining past, has lived through it all—discovery, abuse and prostitution,
good and bad years—has sold or pawned everything it ever held dear, and
somehow continues to enchant. For years people have been bemoaning the
premature demise of this dynamite town. "Where are all the old locals?
Whatever happened to off-season? Remember when Aspen was so small you
knew everybody at the post office? The old Aspen we used to know is gone,
a victim of its own success, dead . . ." Believe me, that hasn't happened.
Aspen is hipper, trendier, and more expensive than ever. But it's also just as
exciting, just as real a place. I'd say that, paradoxically, the secret of Aspen's
enduring fascination as a resort is that, despite everything, it's still more of
a community than a resort. Real people, unusual and creative people, have
put down deep roots here, have made this town different and, in a non-
superficial way, more sophisticated than any other ski town or mountain
town in America.

A decade ago I wasn't so crazy about the skiing in Aspen; it was okay,
sure, but . . . That's changed now. With the new gondola and a radical revamping of lifts and services, Aspen Mountain has become one of the best
treats advanced skiers can offer themselves. The mountain has always been
interesting, but now the bottlenecks and frustrations are gone, and you can
ski yourself silly any day. And that's just on the first of Aspen's four ski
mountains. For skiers, the Aspen area works more like a large European ski
region than like a single resort; its four separate mountains offer a range of
skiing choices and diverse terrain. (We'll visit Aspen's other three mountains
in the next two chapters—I couldn't fit this amazing destination into just
one section.)

To set the record straight, I should quickly add that while a week in
Aspen is a stunning resort experience for anyone, skiing above town on
Aspen Mountain is not for everyone. This mountain is simply too hard for
a lot of skiers—there are no green or novice runs here at all, and the blue
runs require a certain degree of skiing experience if not outright talent. Yet
Aspen's other three ski mountains—Buttermilk and Aspen Highlands right
on the outskirts of town and Snowmass only a short drive away—take up
the slack and offer a much wider spectrum of slopes than the mountain
above town, including fabulous terrain for beginners and novices. All four
of these Aspen ski mountains are a well-integrated part of the Aspen experience. You can have your cake and ski it too by visiting all four ski areas or
finding your own favorite Aspen ski mountain.

I'm lucky that I get to visit Aspen several times every season. Even though

I look forward to skiing on Aspen Mountain with something akin to glee, I look forward even more to just plain being in Aspen. Invariably, when I get home, I remember the conversations, the people I've met, the museum shows and galleries I've taken in, the pulse and panache of Aspen just as vividly as powder mornings on the face of Bell Mountain. You will too.

Because I've promised myself that my contribution to this guidebook will, first and foremost, take the form of a skier's guide and not a shopping/lodging/dining directory, I want to take you on a guided tour of Aspen Mountain before exploring the town in more detail.

Aspen's Own Mountain: An Introduction

Ajax, which almost nobody calls Ajax anymore but rather Aspen Mountain, has come a long way since its discovery and launching as a ski area just after World War II. There's an inescapable snob appeal, a built-in cachet, to a ski area that doesn't have a single green run! Aspen Mountain deserves this reputation. The skiing is not formidably difficult; it's merely serious— exciting, continuous, sometimes but not always quite challenging. This is skiing for confirmed, even accomplished skiers, not for beginners or novices. Good skiers will find Aspen Mountain as good as they are. And my observation, these last few years, is that there are more strong skiers on this mountain than on any other in Colorado. And not just in numbers. I'm also talking about the average level of skill on these slopes. The average skier on Aspen Mountain skis better than the average skier elsewhere in the state.

Aspen Mountain is not a wide ski area like Vail, Copper, or Breckenridge, but instead a long narrow ski area extending back from the valley floor along the flanks and tops of a couple of long ridges that run down perpendicular to the Roaring Fork Valley. You look up from anywhere in town and the ski mountain looks damn serious but not very big. Don't be fooled. It goes back and back and back. What you see from town is only the tip, or actually the foot, of the iceberg.

Two parallel mountain shapes define Aspen's ski area. On the right side looking up from town, you'll see the slopes of the World Cup downhill course peeling down the front face. These steep slopes drop off a long ridge that for most of its length is called *Ruthie's Run* and runs clear back to the top of the ski mountain. This ridge marks one edge of the ski area. The parallel valley below and east of *Ruthie's* more or less represents the middle of the ski area and finishes in a classic Aspen run, *Spar Gulch*—the path most skiers take off the mountain. (In the evening, however, *Spar* can be too crowded for comfort and a last run down *Ruthie's* is a better bet.) The side of *Spar Gulch* opposite from *Ruthie's* is formed by the flank of Bell Mountain, a second, long, ridgelike shape. Bell Mountain has its own mystique and absolutely no easy-angle runs. There are also a number of runs on the

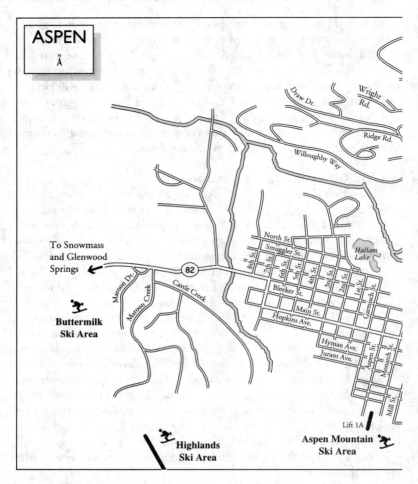

far, or eastern, side of Bell Mountain, but they all seem to belong to the Bell Mountain half of the ski area. These last runs finish in a second rounded gully called *Copper Bowl. Copper Bowl* is analogous to *Spar Gulch* although less long and wide, and it brings skiers back around the bulk of Bell Mountain to join the down-mountain traffic flow in *Spar.*

In short, if you're skiing continuous runs down the mountain, you'll either be skiing somewhere on the *Ruthie's* side or somewhere on the Bell Mountain side or in the valley between them. Simple, right? With this general picture in mind, you can find your way around Aspen Mountain like an

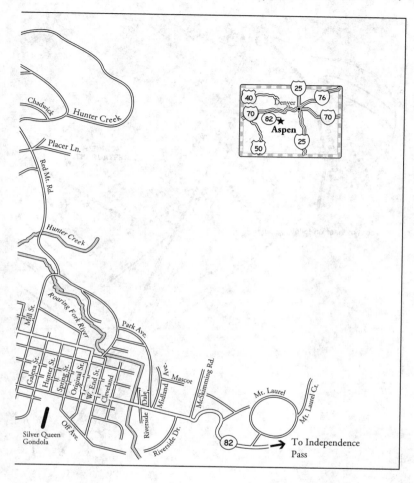

old hand. And long continuous runs are definitely what's happening here—a key strategy. But it wasn't always so.

I've already hinted at the major lift changes in recent years that have altered skiing on Aspen Mountain dramatically. The most important change was the installation of the Silver Queen gondola, a six-passenger beauty that takes skiers from the base to the top of the mountain, a 3,267-vertical-foot hop, in 13 minutes. This lift makes me nostalgic for the Alps because it is of a design seldom seen in America. The Silver Queen was built by the French company Poma, and the cars are spherical in shape and without doors. Pas-

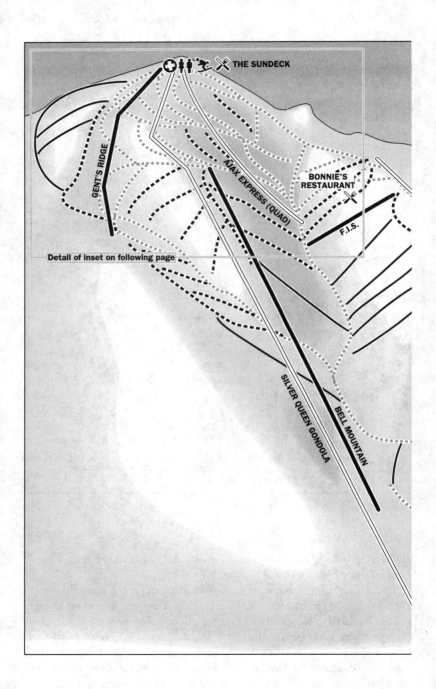

THE SUNDECK

GENT'S RIDGE

AJAX EXPRESS (QUAD)

BONNIE'S
RESTAURANT

F.I.S.

Detail of inset on following page

SILVER QUEEN GONDOLA

BELL MOUNTAIN

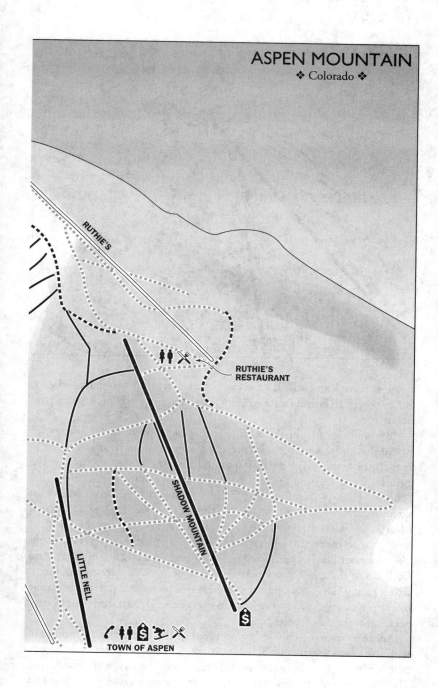

ASPEN MOUNTAIN
❖ Colorado ❖

RUTHIE'S

RUTHIE'S
RESTAURANT

SHADOW MOUNTAIN

LITTLE NELL

TOWN OF ASPEN

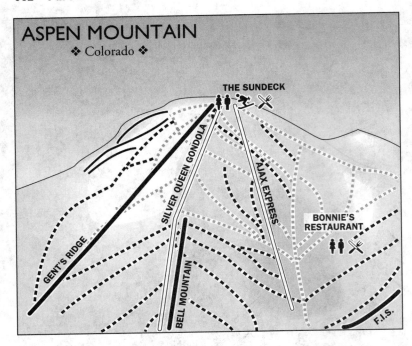

ASPEN MOUNTAIN
❖ Colorado ❖

THE SUNDECK

SILVER QUEEN GONDOLA

AJAX EXPRESS

GENT'S RIDGE

BELL MOUNTAIN

BONNIE'S
RESTAURANT

F.I.S.

sengers sit back to back and the car hinges apart into two halves when it enters the top or bottom station. French skiers have aptly baptized such gondolas "eggs."

It was obvious from the start that this high-speed, high-capacity lift would alter the way people skied on Aspen Mountain, and it has, totally. I've spent memorable days on this mountain, skiing myself right into the ground, skiing only top-to-bottom runs, and never riding any lift except the gondola. There is a natural tendency, or a routine that makes sense at most ski areas, to ride lifts up to the top and then stay on the upper slopes all day. Most Aspen skiers seem to do this too. But this pattern ensures that the gondola never seems to get really crowded. It moves so fast that even what looks like a monster line in the morning gets one on board in a few minutes. And finally, even though the very bottom slopes aren't very interesting in themselves, strong skiers can shoot across them in a hurry and actually save time by simply skiing down to the bottom every run. This strategy would have been unthinkable a few years ago.

Another dramatic change has occurred in the upper middle mountain with the upgrading of Lift 3, which is now a high-speed detachable quad that serves the not-very-steep or difficult central basin above *Spar Gulch*. This lift, plus the "eggs," has provided a kind of access to Aspen Mountain for skiers who previously wouldn't have dared ski there. It's now possible to ride the Silver Queen to the top and then just yo-yo around on the easier blue runs served by Lift 3, runs like *Pussyfoot, Silver Bell,* and *1 & 2 Leaf,* and even take the gondola down in the evening if you don't feel comfortable on *Spar Gulch.* A lot of weaker skiers have figured this out, which has inevitably led to some serious overcrowding on these easy, top-of-the-mountain, Lift 3 runs.

Why do they bother? Status, I guess. It doesn't take long to figure out that Aspen Mountain has the big reputation in these parts, and it is where the local heroes ski. Some skiers try to buy into this mystique before they're ready for it. My recommendation: Unless you're truly comfortable on Aspen Mountain (which means, at a minimum, short turns on steeper blue slopes), you should spend most of your Aspen vacation skiing Snowmass and Buttermilk. No, you certainly won't be bored, and yes, you will make phenomenal progress as a skier. Progress that I guarantee is just about impossible if you start hanging out on Aspen Mountain before you're ready. As you'll see in the next two chapters, these other Aspen areas are in no way also-rans or second-bests; in many ways they can provide average skiers with a richer, more satisfying experience.

But if you belong on Aspen Mountain, you'll be in hog heaven. And to speed your exploration of this expert's stash, here are a few of my favorite runs.

Aspen Mountain: Hot Tips and Favorite Spots

A quality Aspen Mountain experience divides neatly into steep giant-slalom-style cruising and even steeper bump skiing. If you hate moguls, you just won't get all this mountain can offer, but you don't need to spend all day abusing your knees either.

Usually, Aspen hosts world cup races, downhill or Super-G, in December. But any time during the season, you can enjoy the sequence of slopes that together constituted one of the most exciting downhill courses in North America. This run begins at the lower end of *Ruthie's* and strings together a number of separately named runs: *Aztec, Spring Pitch, Strawpile*—steep, exciting, and remarkably continuous.

In fact, you'll find the best nonmogul skiing on and around and over toward *Ruthie's*—the left-hand side of the area as you ski down. There are a lot of variations and detours on this big ridge to delight the cruising skier: *Roch Run* and *International* both fit this category, as does *Buckhorn,* the best way to start in this direction off the top. The Ruthie's Ridge Lift, a very slow double, has been a good reason not to spend too much time on this side of Aspen Mountain, but it's now to be replaced by a high-speed chair—a high-speed double chair, not a quad—the only high-speed, detachable, double chairlift I know of. The idea is to eliminate the long ride but still preserve some of the tête-à-tête, conversational intimacy of riding a double chair, which has become an unintended casualty of the white revolution. This new lift is a nice demonstration of the Aspen Skiing Company's decision not to expand the size of its skiing area, only the quality.

A quick glance at the trail map shows you that there are still three marked levels of difficulty on this mountain: Green runs are missing, but double black diamonds have been added at the top of the scale. Anything marked double black is not merely steep and moguled, but the moguls themselves will be of the extra-demanding sort rather than garden variety. Let's start with some friendlier bumpy lines.

First off, the *Face of Bell*—this is a beaut. Ski down *1 & 2 Leaf* and cut left just under the top of Bell Mountain, traversing out on its flank to arrive at the first of a series of open moguled faces separated by long hedgerow lines of evergreens. Bumps on the *Face of Bell* are usually large and round with more than enough space beneath each one to complete your turn and control your speed. These are welcoming and enticing bumps. There's a special way to ski the *Face of Bell:* Start anywhere and ski most of the way down, but before you actually reach *Spar Gulch* turn right in a long horizontal traverse that will take you across to the next open face. Locals refer to this as "going back up." Since *Spar Gulch* (which is the "floor" beneath the *Face of Bell*) keeps dropping away, each traverse brings you back up to the top of another bump slope. You can repeat the process again and again for one of the most satisfying bump runs around.

Bell Mountain has other less-than-fierce bump lines to check out on its far, or eastern, side: *Christmas Tree* and a generalized area called *Back of Bell.* But on this side the trees are denser—although the skiing company has done a wonderful job of thinning out the best tree lines. Very quickly you'll find that this mountain pushes you onto steeper, more challenging, double black runs. It's not the steepness that creates the difficulty, but usually the fact that the bumps are tighter, less rhythmic, and the gullies between them sharper and narrower. This gives you less space to finish turns and slow down and fewer choices. Even so, Aspen's most difficult bumps are merely tight and almost never ugly—probably because the technical level of the skiers making them is higher than that at many other resorts. For experts in search of a workout, the *Ridge of Bell,* a long steep nose facing straight down toward Aspen, offers the most challenging skiing on this side of the mountain.

There are a lot of exciting, double black gullies, steep and rather narrow, on the front face above town. But there's not always enough snow this low on the mountain to cover all the rocks on such steep slopes, so I only ski these runs on really big snow years. *Corkscrew* and *Corkscrew Gully* are the best of these lower bump slots.

Aspen's toughest bump runs are found in two separate zones: the Mine Dumps and *Walsh's Gulch*. The Mine Dumps are a series of thrilling, half-open gashes through the steep aspen forest on the west bank of *Spar Gulch* —*Bear Paw* through *Last Dollar*. The Dumps were originally created when miners pushed the slag and rubble from their "holes" down the mountainside. Unless you can successfully launch a turn, anytime, on any bump, no matter how weird, don't tempt fate over here. . . . Try to ski the Mine Dumps early in the morning, since they catch the first sun beautifully.

Walsh's Gulch used to be the most infamous, out-of-bounds skiing at Aspen (along with nearby *Difficult Gulch,* which is still out of bounds). These two renegade powder paths lead down steep, cliff-cut slopes into the Roaring Fork Valley miles upstream from Aspen; over the years they have claimed a respectable number of avalanche victims. The ski area has now avalanche controlled it and opened the best of it, which consists of the upper slopes of *Walsh's* and a couple of parallel lines next door on *Hyrup's* and *Kristi*. These are short but fierce runs, steep enough to make even brilliant skiers pay attention. A must if you want to say you've skied the most serious slopes on Aspen Mountain.

But don't make the mistake of taking Lift 7 back to the top when you come out of *Walsh's*. This must be the world's slowest quad, and it spoils a thrilling run with a boring aftermath. Better to head on down the eastern border of the ski area and enjoy the most obscure skiing on Aspen Mountain: *Gentleman's Ridge* and the gladed trees below it (*Jackpot*, just below *Gentleman's Ridge,* used to be out of bounds). These runs are so far off the beaten path they don't see much traffic, but they don't get groomed either, which means more bumps. They also catch the afternoon sun so there's no hurry to get there early.

Actually, given the number of bumps, Aspen Mountain is not the greatest powder skiing venue, even after a serious dump. You're more likely to ski powder-covered moguls than real powder, except on the *Ruthie's* side. The very best powder days at Aspen are always during heavy storms— fair-weather skiers stay home, there's almost no one on the mountain, and you can ride the "eggs" back up after each run, warm and dry.

Lunchtime

Lunch, on mountain and off, is better around Aspen than in most ski resorts. The Aspen Skiing Company has begun to take over and operate the restaurants that were formerly leased to individual owner operators. But wisely, they have kept the individual style and flavor of each restaurant rather than subjecting them all to corporate homogenization. This is true at all four of the mountains now run by the Aspen Skiing Company— Aspen Mountain, Buttermilk, Aspen Highlands, and Snowmass—and skiers benefit enormously. Aspen Mountain has three lunch spots. The Sundeck on top has always offered better views than food—the view off the backside of the mountain into the heart of the Elk Range features 14,000-foot summits lined up like a special effect for a Spielberg film. Now under the care of chefs from the Little Nell restaurant in town, the food is slowly catching up to the panorama. Bonnie's at Tourtelotte Park is the most traditional Aspen Mountain lunch stop. Bonnie is a real woman, not just a legend, and has been behind the counter of her "old Aspen" Mountain restaurant as long as I've been skiing here. She serves German-inspired food, and I've had friends argue seriously that a trip to Aspen is wasted unless one samples Bonnie's Bavarian Apple Strudel at least once. Ruthie's, a much newer, on-slope eatery near the bottom of *Ruthie's Run,* between Lifts 1-A and 8, has both a cafeteria and an extraordinary sit-down lunch restaurant that, in many Colorado ski resorts, would be the best restaurant in town. Down below, in-town lunch options are plentiful and easy to enjoy without sacrificing any ski time now that the gondola tends to lure good skiers to the bottom so often.

Aspen Ambience, Aspen Style

Did I talk about skiing yourself silly? The Silver Queen gondola gives you so much vertical so quickly that you can really hurt yourself. Lots of skiers, strong skiers, hang it up before the lifts close because their legs are saying, "Please!" In Aspen it's okay to quit early; there's more than enough to do off the slopes.

For years and years, Aspen après-ski began regular as ritual at Little Nell's, the funky, old-fashioned, rundown, crowded, and wonderful slope-side bar at the bottom of *Little Nell,* which is the last and lowest slope into town below *Spar Gulch.* But Little Nell's is dead—long live Little Nell's! The bar was sacrificed on the altar of a massive base redevelopment project, and Little Nell's is now a very chic hotel beside the gondola terminal (but its bar does boast good jazz). So where do the ski patrollers and instructors, debutantes and demimonde stop for a drink after skiing? There will always be a number-one locals', après-ski bar. In Aspen today, it's probably Little Annie's, which is a few blocks from the base of the mountain. It's a draught beer kind of place, so don't bother to order a champagne Kir.

Not exactly classic après-ski, but my own favorite activity after a long day on Aspen Mountain is a cappuccino at the upstairs café in the Explore Bookstore across from the Jerome Hotel. An Aspen treasure, this wonderful Victorian house/bookstore/café is one of the last things you'd ever expect to find at a ski resort. But then Aspen is different.

It's the most complex, intriguing, and hard-to-pin-down ski town I know: arty, design-conscious, too sophisticated for its Levi's britches, and still just right. If Vail represents nouveau riche ski society, then Aspen could be characterized as old money. (Like Vail, but in a completely different way, Aspen is a great vacation spot even if you don't ski.) Aspen's real secret isn't money at all, but the large underground of writers, artists, and other creative refugees from the so-called real world who have gravitated to the Roaring Fork Valley over the last 30 years and have given this town an unexpected and disarming sophistication. Aspen's sophistication somehow transcends the normal ski-world reality of development pressures, scheming real estate villains, and tourist-dollar feeding frenzies that all successful ski resorts fall prey to. Even the newly arrived visitor, who obviously doesn't have a circle of fascinating Aspen friends and fringe types, can feel this sophistication in the streets. Galleries here show serious art by nationally known artists, not just cowboy art and fun prints; Aspen fashions are real fashions, not just fun furs. *Aspen Magazine* is the most polished and ambitious resort magazine in the country, showcasing writing and cultural reporting you'd expect to find in New York, L.A., or Santa Fe. The Aspen public, local and transient, is tuned into the arts in a way that no other ski town can imagine, much less equal.

No other ski town has anything like the Aspen Museum of Art. It's an old, brick powerhouse transformed into a postmodern palazzo located a few blocks from downtown just across the Roaring Fork River. Shows here generally tour L.A., Chicago, and New York museums as well. It's a must visit if you're into contemporary art. Shopping as art, albeit wacky pop art, got a curious boost a few years ago with the opening of Boogies Diner, a two-story pastiche of avant-garde and retro trends and trendiness. Some Aspenites swore it was the end of the world, but I guess they had no sense of humor.

And eating out: There are too many good choices for serious reviewing in this short chapter. Suffice it to say that you can find almost anything, and spend any size fortune in Aspen's restaurants. One restaurant where you won't spend a fortune and which is intimate, unpretentious, and delicious to boot is Cache Cache. Aspen boasts two—count 'em—superb sushi houses, Kenichi and Takah Sushi, with fresh fish flown in from far-off coasts. And I have to end with my new favorite Aspen restaurant, the Ajax Tavern at the foot of the slopes. These guys are upsetting Aspen's long-established restaurateurs with astonishing San Francisco Italian food and style, at very attractive prices that are distinctly *un*-Aspen: understated trattoria decor, white tablecloths, and wild mushrooms—heaven.

So how do you find things, places, and addresses in Aspen? Although Aspen is the largest ski town in Colorado, its downtown core is compact and intimate. Two one-block pedestrian malls define the center of the grid; when you ask directions, the reply will probably be in terms of a number of blocks north or south or up or down from the malls. Still, these pedestrian streets are the "too little" that came "too late." Aspen doesn't function very well as a true pedestrian village, and parking downtown is a nightmare of meters and 90-minute-only signs. Still, from the transportation center downtown (two blocks from the gondola) you can board free shuttle buses every few minutes that will take you to Aspen's other mountains and to Snowmass Village. In-town transportation remains somewhat awkward. However, once you've made your way downtown you can walk everywhere.

So naturally the two hotels I'm going to recommend are within walking distance of everything. Recommend? Well, not for everyone, because both the Jerome Hotel and the Hotel Lenado are rather expensive—actually very expensive; but they're also very wonderful. The Jerome is Aspen's pearl. A classic historical structure from the glory days of Aspen's silver mining, it has been totally renovated and the new addition behind the hotel surprised almost everybody—a perfect complement to the old grande dame of a hotel. It's a classic. If you can't afford to stay at the Jerome, as most of us can't, at least raise a glass in its dark, warm fin-de-siècle bar. The Hotel Lenado, diagonally across from Paepcke Park, is a different story altogether. A modern pocket hotel designed by Aspen architectural wizard Harry Teague, the Lenado is an intimate, low-key, postmodern masterpiece in pale wood and Buddhist prayer flag colors. It is simply the best new hotel in the Rockies. Of course, Aspen has the whole spectrum of skier accommodations. Other addresses, like the Little Nell, are definitely in the running for most expensive and most luxurious; but even in Aspen money isn't everything. For me, the Jerome and the Hotel Lenado come close to some Platonic ideal of perfect ski resort lodging.

What more can I add except: Enjoy. At the end of a week-long stay, you'll have the impression that you're just beginning to get the hang of this remarkable ski town. You'll be back.

ASPEN MOUNTAIN DATA

Mountain Statistics

Vertical feet	3,267 feet
Base elevation	7,945 feet
Summit elevation	11,212 feet
Longest run	3 miles
Average annual snowfall	300 inches
Number of lifts	8
	1 gondola
	1 high-speed quad
	1 high-speed double
	1 fixed-grip quad
	4 double chairs
Uphill capacity	10,755 skiers per hour
Skiable terrain	631 acres
Opening date	Thanksgiving weekend
Closing date	early April
Snowboarding	No!

Aspen Mountain shares a lift ticket with Buttermilk, Aspen Highlands, and Snowmass.

Transportation

By car Four-and-a-half-hour drive from Denver, east on I-70 to Glenwood Springs, then south on Highway 82 to Aspen.

By bus or limo From the Denver International Airport.

By plane Some direct flights and many connecting commuter flights from the Denver International Airport land at the Aspen Airport just outside of town. (On Sundays, the Aspen Airport is the busiest airport in Colorado after Denver.)

Key Phone Numbers

Ski Area Information (970) 925-1220 or (800) 525-6200

Snow Report (970) 925-1221 or (888) 277-3676

Reservations (800) 262-7736

www.skiaspen.com

LITO'S TECH TIP

Short Turns—The Key to Black Slopes

What is it that keeps some skiers off steep slopes while others can't get enough steep black skiing? Short turns—not just short, but smoothly, crisply linked short turns right down the fall line, tick-tock, side-to-side, as inevitable and rhythmic as a pendulum. Short swing, as it's often called, is the key that unlocks steep, narrow, and challenging terrain. (Medium and long turns build up too much speed too fast.) And as usual, there's a trick to it. I call this trick, or technique, dynamic anticipation. This is how it works.

Suppose, before turning your skis down the hill, your whole upper body—hips, shoulders, head, and arms—was already turned and aimed downhill. Then your skis would turn faster and easier, pivoting rapidly around to line up beneath your body, which was already in the fall line. Less mass to turn means less effort needed, which in turn means faster, snappier results—the very essence of short-linked turns. In skiing this pretwisting of the upper body in the direction of the coming turn has always been called anticipation. But we can do better.

Our goal is not to turn the body first and then let the skis catch up, but instead to let our bodies move straight down the slope while legs and skis pivot back and forth beneath us. That's where the action is, down below the stable quiet mass of the upper body. And it's this back-and-forth, wind-up and release, preturn and return sort of action that I call dynamic anticipation. Everyone has seen and admired this type of skiing, but how do you learn it?

It isn't so very easy. Dynamic anticipation is the watershed skill that divides average good skiers from extremely good skiers. But here's a simple game plan.

First, be sure you're skiing in a loose upright stance with a very relaxed lower back. This is the region that acts as a pivot point, or hinge, letting your legs and skis turn beneath you without the body itself turning. If you're bent forward with a hollow, tight lower back, nothing will work.

Next, try a few hockey stops. Slide straight down the hill and twist your legs and skis sideways to a stop beneath you. They turn, you don't. After you get the hang of it, smooth out your hockey stops into round uphill curves that work the same way: skis turning up the hill but body floating along motionless above them, still facing down the fall line. We call these uphill curves with anticipation (that uninvolved, motionless upper body) *preturns*.

Then use your preturns to launch new turns down the hill. Just add a pole plant while shifting your weight to the top ski and, wham, the skis will (or should) turn back downhill almost on their own. That's the reaction from the action of the preturn. And of course, you'll want to capture this feeling and prolong it in a continuous series of turns—the end of each turn becoming the preturn—or wind up for the next turn.

What I've just given you is only the bare outline of a game plan to develop dynamic anticipation (for the details, see Chapter 4 of my book *Breakthrough on Skis* from Random House or my videotape of the same title) but it should give you a sense of what's involved in developing short turns. The more natural your anticipation becomes—that is, the more your upper body relaxes and floats instead of actively turning from side to side with your skis—the easier it will be for you to link short turns.

One last tip. The trigger, the signal that launches one turn right after another down the fall line, is always a pole plant. By reaching straight down the hill with your pole, rather than letting it swing around and across the hill with your skis, you will help to keep your body lined up in that going-down-the-mountain direction. Short turns in a nutshell: You keep going down the mountain while your skis twist back and forth beneath you.

ASPEN'S OUTSKIRTS: BUTTERMILK AND ASPEN HIGHLANDS

The two Aspen ski areas we're going to visit in this chapter, Buttermilk and Aspen Highlands, don't quite loom dramatically over town—but almost. Considering how Aspen has grown, it would be no exaggeration to say that these two areas are in the suburbs or outskirts of Aspen. Close enough to belong. And, more important, different enough from Aspen Mountain itself to balance and complete the town's ski offering. Both these areas have changed dramatically in recent years; both are better than ever. Let me explain.

Buttermilk has undergone a merry-go-round of name changes in recent years. For a while it was called Buttermilk/Tiehack (Tiehack was the steeper, eastern side of the area), then just plain Tiehack, and in 1995–96 it became Buttermilk once again in honor of Friedl Pfeifer, who founded and named the ski area in the 1950s. What's in a name? Tiehack refers to the forest stands where loggers used to cut trees for railroad ties. In early-day Aspen, the Sterner family had a homestead and dairy farm right about where the ski area base lies today. When the Sterner daughters, so the story goes, took fresh milk up the mountain to the loggers hacking ties from the forest, the jolting of their buckboard on the rough track turned the milk into buttermilk. Buttermilk, in any case, became synonymous with Aspen's beginner area, and when the Aspen Skiing Company decided it was time for a major upgrade and facelift, they changed the name to Tiehack, and then they thought better of it.

But you shouldn't think of Buttermilk as a beginner area; quite the contrary. It is, however, an ideal learning and teaching mountain for virtually every level of skier. There's no question that Buttermilk is certainly the most underrated ski experience in Aspen. I really love this little mountain.

There's a lot more to Buttermilk than beginner- or novice-level skiing. Sure, skiing here is fairly easy for the most part: no heroes, no hotdoggers, *ni trompettes, ni tambours,* no guts, no glory associated with skiing on this mountain. But what about charm? The runs are beautifully cut. The terrain is mostly medium- and low-angle, seldom steep, with lots of variation, and lots of character. You'll find extremely aesthetic, reasonably steep, upper-intermediate runs on the East Tiehack side of this mountain. And yes, it is also a great place for beginners and a wide spectrum of learning skiers. For my money, this is the very best teaching/learning terrain in Colorado with one of the very best ski schools. Buttermilk may welcome novice skiers, but it also produces real experts. I'm hoping that after reading my review of Buttermilk you won't underestimate it.

Aspen Highlands has always been the maverick of the Aspen ski scene—run by its own independent ski corp, clinging stubbornly to its archaic lift layout and its eccentric, rather old-fashioned ski school method. Aspen Highlands was always proud, too, of its low-priced lift ticket and of being the first of the Aspen ski areas to actually welcome freestyle bump skiers and snowboarders—but nowadays everything has changed. It's a brand-new mountain, although "mountain" may be stretching it. Aspen Highlands is really more of a ridge that rises up toward Highland Peak between the Castle Creek and Maroon Creek valleys just outside the town of Aspen. I'd say it's not a natural ski mountain since all the natural fall lines take you down one side or the other of the ridge, and, inevitably, there's a certain amount of traversing to get "back to center" which makes the ski terrain feel smaller than it really is. But for the 1994–95 season, something terrific happened. The Aspen Skiing Company took over the management of this little country cousin and immediately upgraded the lift system. Now two new high-speed quads whisk you to the top in a fraction of the time it used to take. Runs have been widened, and skier services vastly upgraded. In one day you can ski more than twice the vertical you could with the old lifts. It's about time. And that's not all; an actual base village is under construction at the bottom of Highlands, replacing acres of muddy parking lots. The outlines of this new village will be visible for the 1999–2000 season, but while the temporary construction buildings will be gone, like all such projects, we won't see the final result for years.

The most exciting novelty on this mountain hasn't happened yet, but it may before long. Highlands Bowl might finally be opened to skiers. This immense, treeless bowl, dropping from the summit of Highland Peak just beyond the current ski-area boundary ropes, has haunted skiers' imaginations for years. It's been widely assumed that this giant bowl, the scene of at least one major avalanche tragedy that killed a group of patrollers, was simply too dangerous to ever become part of the ski area. But now the Aspen Skiing Company has begun a study to discover how avalanche hazard in Highlands Bowl can be controlled, and this exquisite, high-alpine terrain opened to skiers. I'm betting it will happen in a few years, and when it does, Aspen Highlands will become overnight the most exciting ski destination in the state.

Until then, I don't recommend your spending most of your Aspen sojourn here—a day or two days maximum as you explore and enjoy the diverse offerings of Aspen's four mountains. But now, let's zoom in on suburban Aspen skiing.

Buttermilk: The Biggest Little Ski Area in Aspen

Buttermilk is an easy mountain to understand; it's a three-pronged area with three major, branchlike skiing zones that slant down from its summit ridge. The front side, or Main Buttermilk, is a tongue of interlaced blue and green runs that drop northward in two steps toward the main base. The main lift at Main Buttermilk is the high-speed Summit Express quad that whisks you from base to top in around eight minutes; this lift has totally changed skiing on this mountain by doubling downhill time and cutting in half lift-riding time on an average day. There's also a short double chair that serves the upper third of the mountain for skiers who don't want to circulate back to the base on every run. This upper area is a fanlike bowl of beautiful wide blue runs: *Savio's, Friedl's, No Problem,* and the top of *Buckskin.* Then there's an awkward gap in the mountain's downhill flow that one has to get around either on the *Homestead Road Catwalk* or *Lover's Lane,* a wide, flat, roadlike gully. Below this gap, the runs to the bottom are less direct and more round-about and winding than the upper slopes but still quite aesthetic. There's a tendency to stay on the main drag to the bottom, *Midway Avenue.* But excursions to the left and right, to the long snaking grooves of *Jacob's Ladder* and *Bear,* are well worth it.

The second branch of the area is East Tiehack, which slants down from the top in the direction of town—east, naturally. East Tiehack, with one long chairlift back to the top and a short one to nowhere right at the bottom, is considerably steeper than Main Tiehack and full of blue and black runs (although the blacks feel more blue-black and are not too demanding). The two most continuous runs here are *Sterner* and *Tiehack Parkway*—on the very edge of the crest overlooking Maroon Creek—which turn into *Racer's Edge* and *Javelin.*

Finally, slanting down diagonally to the other side is the third branch of the mountain, West Buttermilk, which is another gentle area of blue and green runs. Although at a lower angle than the runs of Main Tiehack, the runs of West Buttermilk are no less esthetic, with long sweeping views. (Both the western and eastern branches of Tiehack, by the way, have their own bases with small parking lots.) Again there's an obvious main-drag way down, *Westward Ho,* an inviting green highway until the last broad blue face. But there's more to explore. Check out *Red's Rover* and two short, surprise black pitches, *Little Teaser* and *Lower Larkspur,* which along with *Sterner* have the only moguls to be found at Tiehack. Café West, at the bottom of

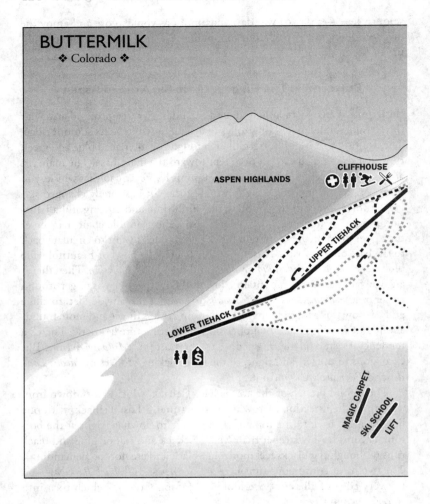

this Buttermilk West zone, also serves the only on-mountain luncheon crêpes at any Aspen ski restaurant and a killer artichoke soup. Café West is tiny and intimate with the flavor of a lunch chalet or *stube* lost high in the Alps.

The West Buttermilk Lift, Lift 3, takes you back up to a slightly higher summit than those reached by the Summit Express Lift. From here you can begin one of the loveliest runs at the area: a ridge run all the way down to the bottom of East Tiehack via *Tom's Thumb*, *Tiehack Parkway*, and *Racer's Edge*. This edge of the ski area is particularly impressive because it overlooks Maroon Creek, the deep alpine valley separating Tiehack from Highlands.

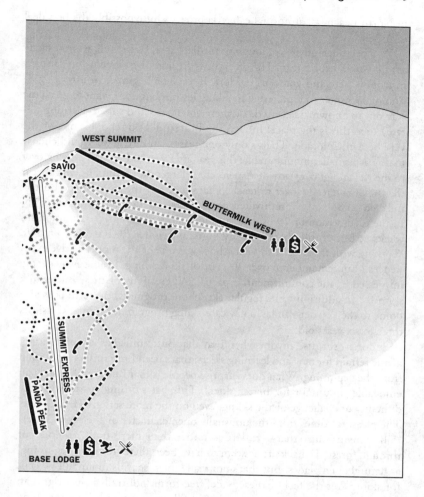

The view from the Cliff House terrace at the top of the Summit Express Lift, looking out over Maroon Creek with Pyramid Peak looming up like the Matterhorn at the end of the canyon, is one of the grandest at Aspen. Unfortunately, the grub doesn't match the view. So enjoy the Cliff House terrace on sunny spring afternoons, and for the best ski-area cafeteria meal in the whole country (I'm not kidding!) ski all the way to the bottom and eat lunch at Bumps. This remarkable example of lowly ski-area cafeteria elevated to another level is run by the folks who own and operate the famous Fog City Diner in San Francisco, and it shows. Fresh-baked foccacia accompanies made-to-order Caesar salads and pasta dishes that would pass muster in North Beach, all at normal cafeteria prices. Quite possibly the best deal in Aspen.

As a beginner, novice, or low-intermediate area, Buttermilk works exactly as you would expect it to. The green runs are an honest green; you can't get in trouble here and you can't get lost. If you're a beginner or novice vacationing in Aspen and interested in taking lessons but don't want to go all the way out to Snowmass every day (where you'll also find superb learning terrain) then this is the place! In fact, the Buttermilk ski school is one of the very best in Colorado. There's only one reason an instructor would choose to stay at a smaller mountain like this year after year rather than moving over to the ritz and glitz of any of Aspen's three larger ski mountains, and that is that he or she really loves to teach. That's precisely the story of the Buttermilk ski school: gifted, motivated ski teachers and ideal terrain to work on. In the early season of 1994, I organized a series of intensive saturation ski weeks at Buttermilk, based on my book and video *Breakthrough on Skis*. Working with the pros at this ski school was one of the most positive experiences I can remember in over 20 years of ski teaching. I came away deeply impressed by the commitment, capacity, and creativity of these Buttermilk ski pros. In addition to its regular ski school programs, Buttermilk is also home to the Powder Pandas, a day care/skiing program for mini–ski visitors three to six years old.

It doesn't surprise anyone when I say that Buttermilk has lots of inviting, gentle terrain for new and learning skiers; that's been Buttermilk's reputation from the beginning. What does surprise people is that Buttermilk is such an enjoyable mountain for better skiers. This has nothing to do with the difficulty or challenge of the skiing, even on the more serious Tiehack side. The pleasure comes from the unusually open character of the runs. Buttermilk runs are just that—real runs rather than mere trails or slots cut through forest. Tiehack's runs seem to have been there from the beginning, as natural open glades. But that's not really the case; this mountain was cut for skiing. Yet the feel of these wide, free-form, nontrails is just right: an invitation to swoop, move around, and fill up space with long sweeping curves rather than heading right down the groove in a businesslike, no-nonsense way. I love this sort of skiing. That's also what makes Tiehack such a favorite for snowboarders on European-style "carving boards." Big turns on this constantly undulating terrain are an ideal expression of what these boards can do.

It's true that Buttermilk just isn't big enough or varied enough to keep good skiers stimulated day after day. Like Highlands, this is not a place to spend a whole week, but do give it at least a day! It is a parenthesis in time and space, an escape from the bigger-is-better school of thought that most serious skiers fall into—an escape that substitutes relaxation and good humor for raw challenge.

And did you know that East Tiehack is one of the better spots at Aspen to ski powder after a big dump? So few skiers head over to this "unfashionable" mountain that powder here lasts a good deal longer than it does on Aspen Mountain. East Tiehack is so compact and served by one main lift that you don't waste a lot of time getting over to your powder slopes or traversing back from them either. The slopes are wide and constantly varying in pitch and respectably inclined but never steep enough to give you pause. Tiehack has also become an active ski racing site in recent years; there are new electronic timing facilities for the National Standard Race (NASTAR) and self-timer courses, and lots of junior and amateur races are run on the eastern flank of the mountain. A natural, giant-slalom flavor to East Tiehack terrain makes you want to ski it in big fast turns as well, even if you haven't worn a racing bib for years.

Finally, there's another Buttermilk that exists as a sort of parallel universe to the one we know. This is Buttermilk for kids. A special kids' trail map (for both Buttermilk and Snowmass) points out mountain highlights like *Toad's Road,* the *Wall of Death,* and the *Black Hole.* Aside from the log palisades of Fort Frog, adult skiers seem quite unaware of this other mountain—perhaps because most Buttermilk kids' runs are secret mini-trails snaking through dense trees beside the regular runs.

BUTTERMILK DATA

Mountain Statistics

Vertical feet	2,030 feet
Base elevation	7,870 feet
Summit elevation	9,900 feet
Longest run	3 miles
Average annual snowfall	200 inches
Number of lifts	7
	1 high-speed quad
	5 double chairs
	1 handle-tow surface lift
Uphill capacity	7,500 skiers per hour
Skiable terrain	410 acres
Opening date	Thanksgiving weekend
Closing date	early April
Snowboarding	Yes!

All Aspen ski areas share a common lift ticket.

Key Phone Numbers

Ski Area Information
(800) 525-6200 or
  (970) 925-1220
Snow Report (970) 925-5300 or
  (888) 277-3676
Reservations (800) 262-7736 or
  (970) 925-9000
www.skiaspen.com

Aspen Highlands: Maverick No More

Nature hasn't exactly favored Highlands, except perhaps in terms of spectacular views. It's a difficult mountain to ski well or to serve well. Like Aspen Mountain, Highlands is a long, thin area extending back from the base on a north-south axis. But where Aspen Mountain has several ridges and valleys for a pleasing variety of terrain, Aspen Highlands is really only one long ridge—a crest from which the terrain drops off steeply on both sides. This means that there's a serious lack of natural fall-line skiing. Straight descents to one side or the other of the central ridge line often exact a toll in tiresome come-back traverses. And even though it boasts one of the longest vertical drops in Colorado (some 3,635 vertical feet), Highlands doesn't really have as much ski terrain as this statistic might suggest. Out of necessity, most runs are crowded in to the crest of Highland's long ridge. But by sticking close to this crest and utilizing the new fast lifts, skiers can enjoy longer-than-average continuous runs, up to three and a half miles' worth.

Highlands has also marked its runs accurately and honestly. This is rarer than you might think. Areas that don't have much hard skiing often jack up the ratings to make their trail maps look a little more serious. Other ski areas that are shy on good intermediate terrain consistently underrate the difficulty of their runs to make average skiers think they have more terrain to play on than they really do. Not so with Highlands. Here the double diamond runs on *Steeplechase* and *Olympic Bowl* are legitimate experts-only terrain. The blacks are honestly hard, and so on.

How does this mountain work? Right at the base is a large open bowl; strangely, its east side is known as *Powder Bowl* and the west side as *Thunderbowl*—a real visual landmark. But this bowl looks more inviting than it actually is because the sun hammers the snow on this exposure, especially in spring, and because, despite the name, powder doesn't stay powder here for long. But *Powder Bowl* is a kind of detour; the main route up the mountain starts with Lift 1, Exhibition, a new high-speed detachable quad rising through steep forests and following the easier angle crest of the middle mountain to the Merry-Go-Round Restaurant at midway. "Midway" is what the trail map calls it, but here you are already two-thirds of the way up the mountain.

Lift 3, a conventional double, runs parallel and to the right of the new Exhibition quad and serves the easier-angled area I mentioned above. This Lift 3 zone is the novice, low-intermediate area for Highlands—a braid of friendly, mostly green runs. Inexperienced skiers can spend most of their day up here, eat at the Merry-Go-Round, and ski back to the base via *Park Avenue,* the only easy trail down the lower third of the mountain. Unless you're a pretty secure parallel skier, I wouldn't recommend venturing

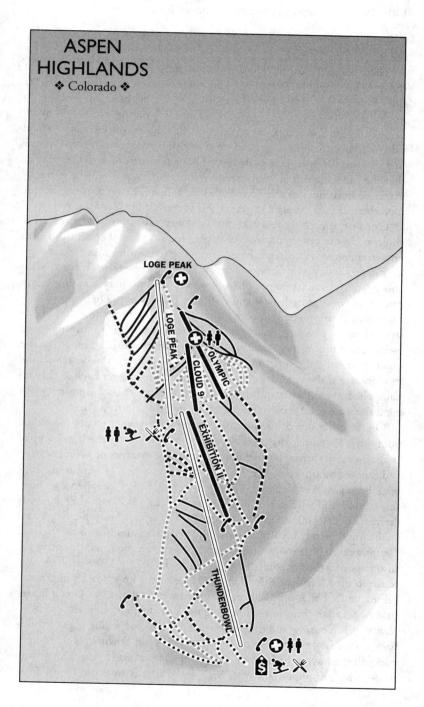

above the Merry-Go-Round Restaurant—from there up there's no easy skiing.

There is, on the contrary, quite a bit of steep and challenging skiing at the uppermost end of Highlands' long ridge or, more accurately, on either side of this upper ridge. Everything up here is blue, black, or blacker. To reach the top from the Merry-Go-Round, just hop on the second new quad, Loge Peak Lift, spectacular because it rises right above the crest of the final ridge with breathtaking drops and views to either side. I skied Highlands the first day this lift opened in early December a few seasons ago. I remember that the hill was packed with curious locals, but even when the entrance mazes on both sides of the Loge Peak Lift were full to overflowing, it only took three or four minutes to get on this super-fast lift. Bravo.

Once on top of Loge Peak, strong skiers have two very stimulating choices. On the eastern or town-of-Aspen side is a zone of small steep faces known collectively as Steeplechase—from top to bottom: *Kessler Bowl, Snyder's Ridge, Soddbuster, Garmisch,* and *St. Moritz. Kessler Bowl* is barely wide enough to deserve its name. The others all turn into fiery, exciting bump pitches as soon as each new snowfall gets packed out. Their top-of-the-mountain location guarantees the sort of cold, dry, firm snow that makes steep skiing a pleasure, and they are all bathed in lovely morning light. Steeplechase is now more exciting than ever with the installation of the top quad. Formerly, the long and boring traverse back to the center of the mountain and the complex chair-hopping required to get back to the top dampened my enthusiasm for repeating this experience. No more; when conditions are good, experts may want to spend all morning here.

On the other side of the summit ridge is a pitch that gets my adrenaline pumping a lot harder than Steeplechase. Olympic Bowl, which isn't a bowl at all, no matter what the trail map says, instead consists of one very steep and exposed bump face—Deception—and a collection of semitreed, semi-open lines like *Aces & Eights, Aerobie, Why,* and *Why Not.* The views here, across steep and wild out-of-bounds country toward Pyramid Peak, are as dramatic as any you can find in Aspen. And *Deception* is steep enough that a fall would be terribly unpleasant. The various glades just to the right of *Deception* are a little more forgiving and a lot more varied, and they have the advantage of a shorter come-back traverse to the base of Lift 5 or all the way across to the Merry-Go-Round and the base of the upper quad. In general, I think you're better off to cut right at the base of all of these Olympic area runs rather than continuing down the flank of the mountain via *Robinson's Run,* which is narrow and uninviting and will cost you a long poma-lift ride back up to the Merry-Go-Round. If you do head down *Robinson's,* keep going all the way to the bottom and hop the lower quad again. The general strategy for any mountain with high-speed lifts is this: use them. They almost always guarantee more skiing time even if you have to ski farther than normal to board them.

Before we leave Highlands, a couple of final tips: The runs around Lift 4, just above the Merry-Go-Round, are certainly the most conventional, in the sense that they are direct, no-nonsense, fall-line runs with no long traverses. This is a dense zone of good upper-intermediate skiing, but I still wouldn't take Lift 4 to access them. It's faster to go to the top of Loge Peak on the quad and then sail down the crest of the ridge on *Broadway.*

On their way down the mountain, strong skiers should be sure to check out *Bob's Glade* — my own favorite run at Highlands; it's seldom packed out, never bumped out. This is a wonderful slope of wide-open trees (take a left off *Golden Horn*) that gets very little traffic and after a good storm offers some of the most intriguing powder skiing at Highlands. Although marked double diamond, *Bob's Glade* is nowhere near as steep as the Steeplechase or Olympic Bowl areas, and there's plenty of room to maneuver between the trees. It's a gem.

Actually, the whole area has become a real gem with the simple addition of two high-speed lifts. Lots of serious intense skiing, for the first time, without the frustrating "forever" lift rides that used to make me gnash my teeth with impatience at Highlands. If Aspen Skiing Company's plans to open Highlands Bowl come to fruition in a few years, look out; Highlands could easily become the most adventurous and aesthetic ski area in the state.

ASPEN HIGHLANDS DATA

Mountain Statistics		**Key Phone Numbers**
Vertical feet	3,635 feet	Ski Area Information
Base elevation	8,040 feet	(970) 925-5300 or
Summit elevation	11,675 feet	(800) 525-6200
Longest run	3.5 miles	Snow Report (970) 925-1221
Average annual	300 inches	Reservations (970) 925-9000 or
snowfall		(800) 262-7736
Number of lifts	9	www.skiaspen.com
	2 high-speed quads	
	3 double chairs	
	1 triple chair	
Uphill capacity	9,145 skiers per hour	
Skiable terrain	not available	
Opening date	early December	
Closing date	April	
Snowboarding	Yes	

Collision Avoidance

Mountain maps always seem to incorporate some version of the Skier Responsibility Code. Among other things, the code admonishes skiers to "ski under control so you can stop or avoid other skiers or objects" and to "avoid skiers who are ahead of you—they have the right of way."

Some of the worst injuries on the slopes result from skiers colliding; collisions that are not only avoidable, but also predictable. Most ski wrecks involve one or more of the following:

Icy slopes. Two of the most attractive characteristics of western skiing are good snow and (compared to the East) very little ice, both of which translate into an added measure of control for all skiers. In the West, icy conditions are generally localized and easy to avoid.

Poor visibility. Poor visibility can affect any mountain. When the mountain is weathered in, stay on trails that are familiar and preferably tree-lined. Cut back on your speed and anticipate unexpected stops. Ski tight, controlled turns, avoiding wide cross-slope traverses. If you stop for a breather, stop on the far side of the trail.

Crowded slope conditions. A mountain or trail with fewer skiers provides fewer opportunities for a collision. You cannot, after all, run into people who are not there. If you are a beginner or intermediate skier who sometimes struggles with control, try to ski on weekdays on mountains with less traffic. If you are skiing on a popular mountain, ask the ski patrol or ski school which runs have fewer crowds.

Marginal to gross lack of control. The Skier Responsibility Code aside, all skiers lose control from time to time. While occasional loss of control is part of the learning process, there are things you can do to avoid collision. First, rein yourself in quickly and deliberately when you feel your control slipping. Stop if necessary and collect yourself. There is no excuse for flailing and careening down the mountain. If you find yourself on a trail that is more challenging than you expected, and your control is marginal or worse, stop and wait to proceed until there is a gap in the traffic.

Skiing too fast relative to other skiers. In the main, your skiing speed should be roughly compatible with that of the other skiers on the slope. If you are blowing past other skiers, or alternatively, if they are zipping by you left and right, you need to find another trail. This goes double when visibility is bad.

Erratic, unpredictable movements and stops. Remember that skiing is a rhythmic pattern of linked turns. The path of a good skier down a mountain is as predictable as a road map. Beginners and even intermediates, however, ski more erratically, sometimes stopping suddenly or breaking out of their turn pattern. If you are still learning, remember that your unanticipated movements can wreak havoc on skiers behind you. Check out the traffic uphill every time you turn and try to keep your skiing as predictable as possible. If you are more advanced, expect that less-experienced skiers in your path will do truly weird things. Spot struggling skiers while you are considerably upslope and give them a wide berth.

Stopping where not visible from above. Stopping below dips and rises is a no-brainer. Do it and you will probably get creamed.

Stopping in a place that obstructs the trail. Obstructing or partially obstructing a trail is asking for trouble as well as being inconsiderate. Find someplace else to stop.

Failing to yield the right of way. Skiers downhill of you have the right of way. Period. They may be staggering beginners or timid intermediates traversing back and forth across the trail like a turkey in a shooting gallery. Either way, it's your responsibility to watch out for them. When merging, entering a trail, or starting downhill, skiers already on the trail, both above and below you, have the right of way.

Skiing while intoxicated. Dumb and dangerous. Don't do it.

SNOWMASS

Snowmass is, hands down, the best all-around ski area in Aspen, yet it's only a part of Aspen. If Snowmass were somewhere else, all by itself, it would still be one of the big three in Colorado along with Vail and Steamboat. But interestingly enough, Snowmass isn't, never has been, and perhaps never will be a stand-alone type of ski resort. Snowmass has been working hard to develop an independent resort identity ever since its first lifts opened, trying to persuade skiers to love it for itself and not as part of greater Aspen. But hey, Aspen is bigger than itself, larger than life. Snowmass today is just one more reason to love Aspen.

True, there is a village in a lovely rolling side valley above the Roaring

Fork, only a 20-minute drive from Aspen. There's an amazing variety of attractive condominium lodging in Snowmass too. Snowmass is a fine place to stay, not just to ski—especially with a family—but . . . The "but" in this case is that beds alone don't make a resort, much less a ski town. Snowmass Mall, the central plaza that is the shopping area and heart of this resort, is little more than a block long. Even so, one modest mall and a big convention center simply don't add up to an exciting ski town. As soon as they've kicked off their ski boots, savvy Snowmass skiers head for Aspen. And a very efficient bus system run by RAFTA (the Roaring Fork Transit Authority) makes it easy to commute between Snowmass and Aspen or vice versa. In fact, no matter where you stay, there's no reason not to ski all four Aspen mountains during your Aspen-area vacation, as more and more skiers are discovering.

Judging it as a ski mountain, I give Snowmass only rave reviews. You will, too. I've found it to be a pretty effortless trip up from Aspen, either by the free shuttle bus or by car, so there's no reason for winter visitors staying anywhere in the Aspen area not to ski Snowmass to their hearts' content. Like Vail, this is an all-around mountain for every family member and every skill level, with separate zones that feel like separate ski mountains in their own right. As at all the other Aspen Skiing Company mountains, the level of skier service at Snowmass is very slick, polished, and gracious. The white revolution in high-speed lifts has transformed this mountain that, even at today's prices, is an absolute bargain for your lift dollar. And the revolution isn't over. A brand-new base facility called Two Creeks and a new high-speed quad of the same name provide skiers who aren't staying in Snowmass Village with rapid access to the Elk Camp or east side of the mountain. And the Aspen Skiing Company has redesigned and greatly expanded the Snowmass snowmaking system as a form of early season insurance.

The Shape and Feel of the Mountain

Wide-open spaces—that's how I'd start out telling a friend about Snowmass. The most celebrated ski terrain here is the Big Burn, a large mountainside half denuded of trees by an ancient fire. While the Big Burn is only a tiny section of modern Snowmass, it is still an effective symbol of the flavor and feel of this mountain—room to move.

Snowmass is a very wide, spread-out mountain, and the only problem with having so much room is that without a clear mental picture of the whole area you can wind up wasting a lot of time just getting from one place to another. (Trail condition reports at the bottom of lifts make your early morning decisions about where to ski easier.) For example, if you're skiing in the higher zones, it is not a good idea to ski back to the village for lunch.

If you start your skiing day on one side of the mountain and discover that you really want to be on the other side, it may take you a couple of hours to get there. This is not really a disadvantage, just a fact of life on a really big ski mountain. And Snowmass is that. So I'll try to paint a quick picture of how the mountain is laid out and then offer some strategies for different levels of skiers in search of differing experiences on this friendly giant.

Snowmass divides more or less naturally into five skiing areas. Look straight uphill from Snowmass Village and you'll see the lifts and runs of Sam's Knob, not a very poetic name but an apt one for what is essentially just a big bump on a long high ridge. This is a high-traffic area full of skiers heading out into the back of Snowmass beyond. But thanks to a couple of high-speed quads, it's not a bottleneck. The upper slopes of Sam's Knob are wide blue freeways. The very bottom of this front hillside turns into *Fanny Hill,* a gentle beginners' slope that laps up against Snowmass Village. The staggered tiers of lodging units rising uphill past the village provide the most convenient ski-in/ski-out situation you'll find anywhere in Colorado. I should also tell you that the restaurant on top of Sam's Knob has the best views on the mountain; you eat looking directly out over the bare white summits of the Snowmass wilderness.

Dropping down to the right, or north, from the top of Sam's Knob is the Campground area, a very important part of the Snowmass skiing spectrum. These long elegant runs are marked black on the map although they would be dark blue almost anywhere else. Runs like *Slot, Campground,* and *Wildcat* are the finest sustained upper-intermediate skiing on the whole mountain—pure fall lines, continuous pitches, runs that go on and on and on. This is perhaps the time to say that all Snowmass runs are a little overgraded. A lot of blues should be greens, a lot of blacks should be blues, and some of the double diamond blacks could be normal black slopes. But I think they've done this on purpose. It's far better than the opposite, underranking of runs that can get skiers into real trouble. The Snowmass approach tends to make you feel like a better skier than you really are. But isn't that what we all want? And isn't that what all great ski mountains do one way or another?

On the southeastern side of Sam's Knob is the Big Burn area. It starts with the *Burn* itself and extends across eastward until it reaches a great scooped-out hollow in the middle of Snowmass Mountain, the *Cirque,* a romantic windswept alpine basin that sits (almost unskied) like a parenthesis in the center of an otherwise continuous ridge line interrupting the smooth succession of runs across the upper face.

The *Big Burn* itself has a number of named lines indicating regular ski runs on the trail map: *Wineskin, Dallas Freeway, Timberline,* etc. To me these names seem artificial. The beauty of this terrain, which is not steep but simply vast, is that you can ski anywhere and everywhere without once

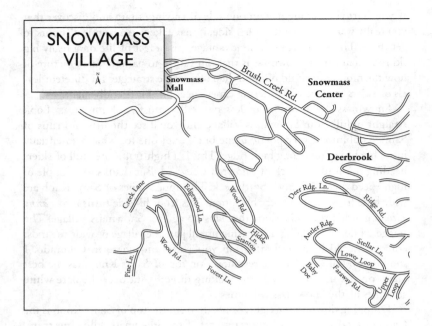

encountering the sort of obstacles, natural or man-made, that so often delimit the edges of a run or trail. Even more remarkable is the terrain just east of the *Burn* itself, served by the Sheer Bliss Lift. *Coyote Hollow* and *Sheer Bliss* are not the result of a long-ago forest fire but instead represent the finest job of man-made glading I think I've ever seen. Given enough money, man-power, and Forest Service permission, it's relatively easy to create wide-open treeless slopes. It's a lot harder to create slopes that still have a forested feel to them but that ski as if they were wide-open treeless slopes. That's exactly what you'll find on both sides of the Sheer Bliss Lift! It's also a good deal harder to groom such gladed mountainsides, but they do it at Snowmass after the first fresh blanket of powder has been tracked up, and typically they do it well.

Next door, to the east, the *Cirque* scoops out a big gap in the mountain (and the mountain's development). A platter-pull lift now takes skiers from the top of the Sheer Bliss Lift up to the very top of Snowmass, above the *Cirque*—a wide treeless expanse of relatively low-angle snow rising clear up to 12,510 feet! And although high winds or insufficient snow can keep this uppermost extension of the Big Burn zone closed for weeks and weeks, it's nonetheless a wonderful addition to Snowmass, not so much for the skiing as for the endless views.

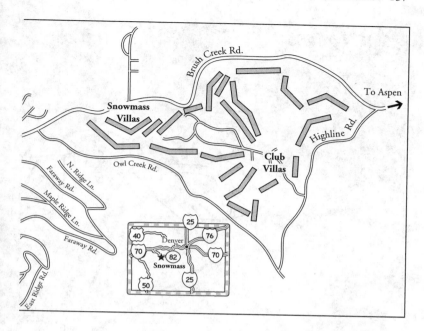

Beyond the Cirque, to the east, we reach the High Alpine pod. At High Alpine you already feel as though you are a long, long way from the village, and there's still one more skiing zone to go: Elk Camp, a low-angle novice paradise still farther east. High Alpine has two personalities: a lower section served by the Alpine Springs and Naked Lady lifts with a lot of fairly ordinary ho-hum sort of blue runs—lots of mileage but not much charm or character; and an upper section, served by the High Alpine Lift, which is terrific. This upper zone contains some moderately steep and very pleasant bump skiing, one long and roundabout "blue" adventure (ironically named *Green Cabin*) that winds its way into and down the side of the Cirque. The High Alpine Lift is also the gateway to the most exciting terrain at Snowmass, the Hanging Valley. Although you ride the High Alpine Lift to get there, Hanging Valley is a separate world that we'll look at in more detail a little later.

Elk Camp is the last stop on our west-to-east trip across the mountain. It's strictly a one-shot deal: one lift; one type of skier; comfortable, moderate-to-easy practice runs that are marked blue but wouldn't have produced a single lifted eyebrow if they had been graded green. Elk Camp is connected down to the Village via a long, diagonal boulevard of a run called the *Funnel* and connected in the opposite sense by the very long Funnel chair-

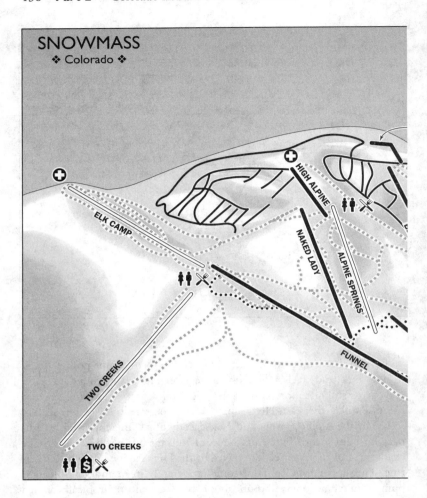

lift—a fun route only to coast home on in the evening (too long and too cold in midwinter). Far quicker, and more fun, is to reach Elk Camp by traversing eastward from High Alpine. Elk Camp, of course, is also accessed by the Two Creek quad from the new Two Creek base area, but the return run is a winding blue-green road that seems more of a ski-in/ski-out amenity than a full-blown ski experience.

Now that I've given you a hint of this mountain's size and a way of breaking it into submountains, let's look at some special places and special strategies for different sorts of skiers.

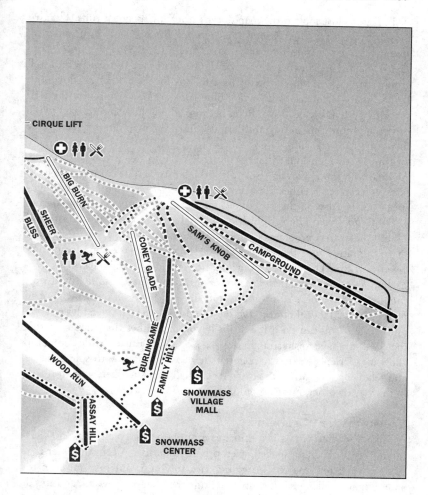

Snowmass for Learning Skiers

It's not fair to say that Snowmass has better learning terrain than Buttermilk; it just has a lot more of it. Newcomers will be initiated into the friendly mysteries of snow sliding on *Fanny Hill,* doubtless in a ski school context, which is always the best way to go. But once skiers have acquired even a modest repertoire of basic moves, they can move around far easier on Snowmass Mountain than at most other big Colorado areas where novices are often confined to small ghettos near the base and have trouble skiing the "whole mountain." Snowmass is actually a better mountain for novices than the trail map seems to indicate.

In fact, a close look at the map doesn't reveal many green runs. The two most obvious are the *Funnel* (via *Funnel Bypass*) and a meandering green route down from the top of Sam's Knob (*Max Park* to *Lunchline* to *Dawdler*). But at Snowmass many of the blue runs are so friendly and well groomed that skiers who normally have to look for the easiest way down can handle them with ease. But which blue runs are they? In a way the trail marking system breaks down here, because some blue runs are easy while others are more demanding and serious. Since the map doesn't make these fine distinctions, I will.

I've already mentioned that the entire Elk Camp area is very, very gentle. Anyone who can make some sort of skidded turn will be comfortable here. Now you can reach either Elk Camp or the *Funnel* via two brand-new high-speed quads. Also on the eastern side of the mountain, *Adams Avenue* and *Green Cabin* (from High Alpine down!) are barely in the blue category and should present no problems to unskilled skiers. Back on the main flank of the mountain above the village, novice skiers can also escape from their green-only world by making a big loop from the top of Sam's Knob via *Trestle* (a short, friendly road) and the lower portion of *Green Cabin*. But novices should avoid the blue runs on the front face of Sam's Knob, which are all rather serious. How about the *Big Burn* for inexperienced skiers? It's not recommended. You can do it for thrills if you remember that there's no rule that says you have to ski straight down a slope. The Burn is wide enough to allow inexperienced skiers to negotiate it via very long side-to-side traverses and relatively few turns. It's also wide enough that such behavior won't get in the way of other, more accomplished skiers.

Snowmass for "Cruisers"

Like Vail, Snowmass is a cruising mountain par excellence. In skiers' lingo, "cruising" has a special, even privileged, sense. A cruising skier is at one with the terrain, not struggling, not solving problems, not even responding to challenges but simply savoring the rush of snow, air, and speed. A cruiser prefers the natural lines that the mountain offers, takes them, and flows. Cruising is not showing off, not carving your initials on the snow, not going for big air in the bumps under the lift. The cruiser instinctively dials in big turns and long, smoothly blended curves, heads for open spaces, and prefers a steady nonstop pace down the mountain. Does it sound like fun? It would be easy to argue that cruising is the most fun you can have on skis; and Snowmass is a good place for you to find out if that's true.

Where will the cruiser find true happiness on this mountain? The Big Burn and Sheer Bliss lifts are cruising headquarters. It's easy to spot the most popular lines here and easy to consciously ski away from them so that a touch of extra speed won't disturb other skiers—elementary cruising courtesy. There's no reason a creative skier couldn't cruise these two lifts all day without ever repeating exactly the same line. Next to the Burn I'll nominate *Slot* and *Wildcat* over on the Campground side as cruisers' heaven. A lot of skiers are hesitant to let their skis run on the somewhat steeper pitches of the Campground runs. But by drawing out the end of each turn into an arc across, rather than down the hill, one can turn even a steeply tilted slope into a cruiser's delight, provided there's enough room, and room is no problem on any of the Campground runs. (For more cruising tips, see the next Tech Tip section.) Unfortunately, Sam's Knob introduces a short uphill stretch into the otherwise continuous slope between the Big Burn and Campground. But by schussing the last slopes of *Sneaky's,* keeping your speed up, and cutting south around the knob itself, you can put together a truly enormous and memorable cruising run and continue to the bottom of the Campground lift in one fell, thigh-burning swoop.

The blue runs of the Alpine Springs area are less interesting, less open, and less exciting for serious cruising than the western side of the mountain (but often they're also less crowded). But since these runs are cut through a dense forest, on stormy days you'll find both better visibility and more sheltered conditions over here. There's nothing wrong with the "front" terrain on Sam's Knob for cruising except that this is typically a high-traffic area, and fast skiing and crowds don't mix.

Snowmass for Adventure

Don't get the idea that I've called Snowmass a cruising mountain simply because it lacks steeper, harder slopes. It doesn't. You can find pitches here that will wake you up, make you concentrate, and leave you feeling proud of yourself after a successful run. But there isn't a great deal of hard skiing at Snowmass, which is fine on such a balanced mountain because only a minority of skiers are looking for that kind of excitement. Still, there's enough to keep that minority happy.

The biggest thrills at Snowmass are in the high alpine terrain of the *Cirque* and Hanging Valley. From the top of the Sheer Bliss Lift (Lift 9), you can ski down along the edge of the Cirque, the large central amphitheater that looks like it was scooped out of the Snowmass ridge with a giant ice-cream scooper. The left, western bank of this hole in the mountain is formed by a long series of cliffs, but there are a couple of ways through—gaps in the wall—and they're intensely exciting. Signs and ropes will lead you to *KT Gully* and *Rock Island,* which deserve their double black diamond designations. Once you have performed your obligatory short swing dance down these steep gullies, the skiing mellows out as you slide down to *Green Cabin.* Even more stimulating is *AMF,* a steep alpine gully dropping into the very top of the Cirque. *AMF* is a local tag that has found its way onto the trail map, and that may (or may not) stand for *adiós, my friend.* The best route back up to *AMF* is to ski all the way down to the Cony Glade quad and take it and the Burn quad back up. (These new lifts are so rapid that it's often better to ski farther down the mountain in order to ride faster lifts back up.) Next door to *AMF* is an even steeper gully, *Goudy's,* sometimes called *80/20* because 80 percent of the skiers who look over the edge chicken out.

Even finer, even longer, and much more remote are the "runs" from the top of the High Alpine Lift into Hanging Valley. I put the word "runs" in quotes because these aren't the usual trails through trees but instead just named zones on a big alpine mountainside. Hanging Valley is marked on the map with double black diamonds; while all the terrain back here isn't terribly difficult, this area is so remote and dramatic that such a rating is certainly fair. It was an enlightened move to open Hanging Valley to the skiing public; for many years the Snowmass ski patrol kept it to themselves as a kind of insiders' powder preserve. It's a difficult and remote area to control, patrol, and sweep—a sort of "inbounds" outback situation. Hanging Valley gives Snowmass a dimension it would otherwise totally lack. You can see them up there—these beautiful steep alpine slopes—overhanging the gentle cruising trails of Elk Camp like a perpetual dare, telling Snowmass skiers, No matter how good you become, there'll always be a challenge waiting for you. Nice.

The *Hanging Valley Wall* is a longer, more intriguing route than the *Hanging Valley Glades* that branch to the right off a normal black bump slope, the *Edge,* on the High Alpine Lift. The extra ten minutes you'll spend walking east from the top of the High Alpine Lift to the *Wall* is well worth it. The *Wall* is a two-step affair. The first pitch is a steep but short face that drops you from a high, bare ridge down onto a timbered bench in the middle of nowhere. There seem to be a lot of choices, and at first one has the impression that there is more vertical and more powder to be had by trending right down the second, longer step. In fact, you're better off to head left, dropping down along the left edge of the final high wall until you spot your perfect line. The pitches on this lower face are known as *Wall 1, Wall 2, Strawberry Patch, Cassidy's,* and *Union 1 & 2.* (It's nice to talk the same language as the locals.) Hanging Valley is real adventure terrain; there are no trail signs, warning signs, or other ski-area information back here. If you're hesitating, the ski school also offers guided tours back here. Check at the ski school desk at the High Alpine Restaurant.

Even in the wilds of Hanging Valley, the ski area has been worked. The reason it's so easy to reach the best lines on the *Wall* is because the forest along its edge has been discreetly thinned. Even when you fly out across the rolling flats where the *Wall* joins *Sandy Park,* you will owe your last dozen turns to the efficient, almost invisible glading that the ski area has done in summer. Good work, guys!

There are numerous control ropes in this area as well as beneath the big Cirque. At first they don't seem to make sense, since you can sometimes spot runs coming in on both sides of the ropes. These are not really closure ropes but rather control ropes that separate different areas, which the patrol has to check and sweep at different times—so it's important to respect them. They're not put there just to irritate you.

How about powder days at Snowmass? While strong intermediate and advanced skiers will tend to head for the *Big Burn* on a powder morning, expert skiers should strike out for the *Wall* right away. The quickest way to get there from the village is to take the Wood Run, Alpine Springs, and High Alpine lifts in succession. If you head for the *Wall* via the super quads up the front, it may be tracked up by the time you get there. Check the double black diamond status boards at the bottoms of the Sheer Bliss and High Alpine lifts to see what's open.

Snowmass and the Future

As good a mountain as Snowmass is, it's still not perfect; that is to say, in my opinion, it's not yet finished. I hope we'll eventually see new lifts and runs on the eastern (Elk Camp and Hanging Valley) end of the mountain.

Even more exciting—but currently stalled in a limbo of environmental and political bickering—is the possibility of linking Snowmass to Buttermilk via Burnt Mountain, a kind of miniature Snowmass lying between the two. With new super-fast quad lifts, this linkup is no longer merely a pipe dream. It would create an awesome mega-area with one base in the Roaring Fork Valley just outside Aspen, adding the possibility of European-style, village-to-village skiing to the Aspen ski scene. Aspen and the upper Roaring Fork have been so buffeted by the pressures of resort development and outside money that today there is an understandable tendency for local voters to greet each new project with a chorus of no's. So the future of this Burnt Mountain linkup is anything but assured. I think we'll see skiing in Highland Bowl first, but who knows?

SNOWMASS DATA

Mountain Statistics

Vertical feet	4,406 feet
Base elevation	8,222 feet
Summit elevation	12,510 feet
Longest run	5 miles
Average annual snowfall	270 inches
Number of lifts	20, including 7 high-speed quads
Uphill capacity	6,200 skiers per hour
Skiable terrain	2,500 acres
Opening date	Thanksgiving weekend
Closing date	early April
Snowboarding	Yes!

Transportation

By car A four-hour drive from Denver on I-70 to Glenwood Springs, then south on Highway 82 (in good road and weather conditions).

By bus or limo From Denver's International Airport.

By plane Numerous commuter flights from Denver International Airport. Direct flights from other cities may vary from one season to the next.

Free shuttle bus from downtown Aspen.

Key Phone Numbers

Ski Area Information
 (970) 923-1220 or
 (800) 525-6200
Snow Report (970) 923-1221
Reservations (800) 598-2004 or
 (800) 332-3245
www.skiaspen.com

LITO'S TECH TIP

Cruising—Big Turns for Big Mountains

The cruiser's secret weapon is an effortless, energy-saving, long-radius turn—more elegant and more efficient than the way most intermediate skiers hack their way down the slope. To ski this way, you'll need two skills: a smoother beginning to your turn and a means of controlling your speed that doesn't depend on skidding or digging your edges into the snow.

A smoother start to the turn Having polished up the arc or trajectory of your turn by learning to ride that outside ski exclusively, your next step is to start into the turn with less oomph and less effort. If you just twist,

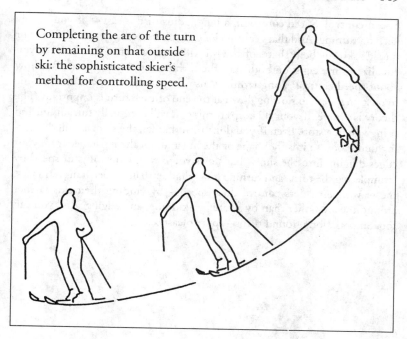

Completing the arc of the turn by remaining on that outside ski: the sophisticated skier's method for controlling speed.

swing, or throw your skis around sideways, you're not only wearing yourself out, but you make it harder for the ski to follow its own bent curve in the snow. You'll skid down the mountain in short bursts of motion rather than cruising it in big effortless arcs. The ideal cruising turn starts slowly, progressively, with the skis peeling gradually off into an arc and not jammed quickly around the corner. How does it work?

The pure, smooth start to your parallel turn depends on an early weight shift. Most skiers try to turn their skis and feet before they shift weight to the outside ski. I'm going to ask you to try a very curious thing: Stand on your new outside foot before you twist it into the turn. At first, you won't be able to do this on a steep or impressive slope. Play with this idea on wide-open, gentle green runs just to see what it's like. Shift your weight first, then turn. Surprise—the start of the turn will take more time. And because you're already standing on the top, soon-to-be-outside ski of the turn, you won't be able to twist it as much. The turn itself will slow down, and you'll find yourself carving a cleaner, longer arc. As the habit develops, you will notice that even when you get in trouble, even on steep slopes, even in bumps, as long as you shift your weight onto the new ski before turning then both skis will always pivot smoothly together into the new turn. (That's right, it really is the top ski I want you to step on before turning downhill.)

Speed control Speed control in a long radius turn is easy—if you simply keep on turning. And that's easy. As long as you keep all your weight on your outside ski, the bent shape of the ski will keep it turning. As soon as you equalize your weight on both skis, the turning action disappears. But how about speed control? Long-radius turns give you more time in the fall line to pick up speed, so slowing down at the end of each turn is important. The theory is simple: If your ski keeps turning, it will eventually turn uphill and bring you to a stop. Even if you don't turn that far, the slope is still decreasing underfoot, so it is the shape of the hill and not the resistance from your edges digging into the snow that slows you down. Control your speed by "completing the turn" and turning longer rather than harder. This is, in fact, the way expert skiers control their speed—by guiding their skis farther around the arc rather than by scraping, skidding, and edging. And you can too. Smooth, long, round turns—pure pleasure.

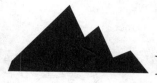# North from Denver

Steamboat One of Colorado's big three (along with Vail and Snowmass), Steamboat is very nearly a perfectly balanced mountain with elegant tree skiing taking the place of open bowls at the upper end of the spectrum. It's an easy mountain to move around on, with great fall lines, great valley views, and efficient lifts. A sort of informal skiers' village is evolving (or sprawling) at the base of the ski mountain, but the real Steamboat Springs, an authentic ranching town with deep roots, is a few miles away, still close enough to enjoy.

Winter Park Strong on skiing and weak on resort and vacation atmosphere, Winter Park is a young, athletic, gutsy sort of mountain that doesn't pamper its guests with too many luxuries. Mary Jane, heaven for serious bump skiers, seems almost like a separate ski area, but it's just another side of this big, varied ski complex. Popular with Denver locals.

Loveland A charming, and charmingly old-fashioned, day ski area near Denver (actually it's the nearest skiing to Denver)—just skiing, no resort, no condos, no glitz. Interesting terrain right under the continental divide and the highest lift in Colorado. Loveland is more impressive than it looks from the interstate.

STEAMBOAT

I rank Steamboat right next to Vail and Aspen in quality, size, and importance as a Colorado ski resort—one of the big three for sure. But no clone. While Vail adopted the style of a European Alpine village and Aspen has always clung to its gold-mining roots, Steamboat has an altogether different image, actually a misleading image.

Steamboat has worked awfully hard to craft an old-time western ranching image for itself composed of cowboy hats and chaps, horses belly deep in snow, and soulful old barns, a kind of daguerreotype frozen on the pages

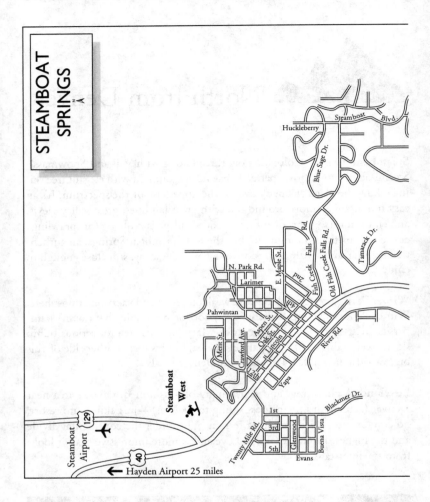

of ski magazines and in skiers' minds—but this is an image that doesn't have much to do with Steamboat skiing. Steamboat skiing is thoroughly modern and simply outrageous.

Steamboat is a giant of a ski mountain, and its advertising never led me to suspect how big it was and how much skiing it offered. Finally, many years after I moved to Colorado, I visited Steamboat. My only excuse for waiting so long was that I had settled in the southwest corner of the state, and Steamboat is the most northeastern of Colorado resorts. A poor excuse, I know. But what a wonderful surprise it was. Steamboat is a far better ski

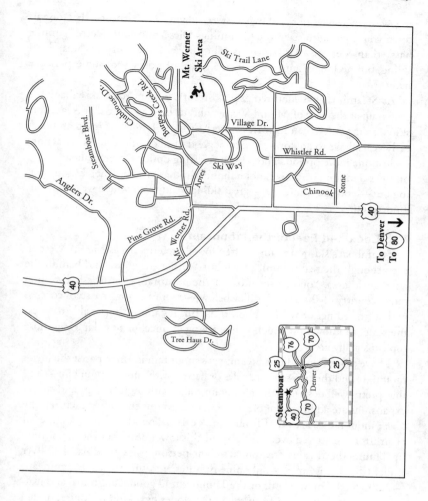

resort than any of its ad campaigns, or indeed anything I've ever seen written about it, would lead you to believe.

The western metaphor, I suppose, is a natural one because the town of Steamboat Springs (a few miles from the ski area) really is a regional ranching center and a market town for cattle raisers up and down the wide Yampa Valley. But a Wild West theme park it ain't. Steamboat Springs is a traditional western strip town with a long main street; there are few historical touches, no cutesy false fronts and, thank god, no staged shootouts for tourists on the main drag. Steamboat Springs is an everyday working western town, not a show western town, which means that down-town you're going to see more Cummings Diesel and John Deere "gimmie hats" than Stetsons. This town is a big part of the story of Steamboat skiing, but no longer automatically a big part of skiers' vacation experience here.

As Steamboat has matured as a ski resort, a brand-new ski village has grown up at the base of Mount Werner and its lifts, a village that is far more ski-contemporary than historic-western. You no longer, as in Steamboat's early years, have to go downtown for a good meal or a little après-ski action; it's just one more option. The most interesting options at Steamboat are up on the ski mountain. This is not a mountain that provides merely good ski-ing but—you can quote me—great skiing. And that's where we'll start our guided tour.

The Look and Feel of the Mountain

Steamboat's ski mountain is often loosely referred to as Mount Werner, even though the real summit of Mount Werner sits above and behind the current ski area. You can see most of the mountain from the flat, rolling ranch country of the Yampa Valley below—a series of massive steps covered with a frosted net of white ribbon runs. But it's almost impossible to guess the scale, to know how much you're seeing at once, or how far away those top runs really are.

I have always thought of Steamboat's mountain in three parts: the lower mountain and the two separate sides or halves of the upper mountain—and that pretty well describes the mountain today, although current and future expansions are adding a couple of new zones to this simplified picture. The lower mountain is a kind of frontal peak called Thunderhead. A number of chairlifts are scattered over the slopes of this lower peak, but the main route up Thunderhead is via Steamboat's eight-person Swiss gondola, the Silver Bullet (the ride is rapid—only nine minutes; and the vertical is significant —2,200 feet). You walk out of the Thunderhead gondola terminal and real-ize you are still separated from the upper slopes by a kind of long rounded saddle. Instead of going right on up, you must ski down a ways into one of the basins on either side of this high Thunderhead saddle and only then continue on up to the crest of either of the two upper peaks.

Decisions, decisions: right or left? If you ski down to the left, you'll reach chairlifts that take you up on the slopes of *Storm Peak,* the left-hand or northernmost region of Steamboat's twin upper summits. If you ski down to the right side, you'll reach lifts that take you up the right-hand or south-ern summit of the upper mountain, *Sunshine Peak.* So far, so good: one large lower mountain, sitting out in front of two broad upper peaks. Each of these different "mountains" functions as a separate ski domain with its own character, its own views, its own type of skiing; and each feels about as big as many respectable-sized ski areas in their entirety.

It's possible to ski across from the Storm Peak side to the Sunshine Peak side, and vice versa, once you're up there. But the natural tendency is to ski on one side or the other, and then take a comeback chairlift back up to Thunderhead Saddle. Then it's decision time again: Visit the opposite side of the upper mountain, ski on the lower slopes, or maybe lunch in one of the various restaurants in the massive Thunderhead gondola building.

The mountain below Thunderhead has an enormous amount of good skiing on it, and if there weren't something about human nature that makes us all want to head for the summits, this lower mountain could hold your attention all day. At first you'll probably just ski down it in the evening. But it's worth some serious exploration during your week at Steamboat. And, of course, we'll go on to explore all three zones of the mountain in more detail in the next sections, focusing on different levels of skiers.

I mentioned "your week" at Steamboat because this is definitely a vacation resort, not a weekend ski resort. Even though the drive from Denver to Steamboat is not really that much longer than the drive to Summit County resorts like Breckenridge, Copper, and Keystone, it is widely perceived as both much longer and tougher. As a result weekend skiers don't flock here in great numbers as they do in Summit County. This is a big plus for Steamboat. It means there are no big ugly parking lots scattered around the base of the mountain to absorb waves of weekend visitors and undermine both the resort's architecture and the mountain views. (There are a couple of discreet and quite adequate parking structures, and of course, most lodging units have their own self-contained parking.) And it means that when the mountain is "full," it doesn't feel crowded.

That's also the result of a very intelligent lift layout. Steamboat was one of the last big Colorado resorts to install high-speed detachable quad chairlifts, preferring instead to double up their conventional chairs with fixed triple chairs running parallel to the earlier ones. It worked very well for a while. But Steamboat, too, finally joined the white revolution of high-speed lifts, initially installing two express quads right where they would do the most good—up the center of the two upper mountains, Storm Peak and Sunshine Peak. Two more high-speed detachables followed soon after. Even the conventional fixed-grip lifts (doubles, triples, and a fixed quad) tend to be placed in strategic spots, to give skiers the option of several ways back up. Steamboat has mostly eliminated those natural bottlenecks where everybody skis down into a cul-de-sac from which there's only one direction and one chairlift out. But I have to say that I'm one of those skiers who loves to use high-speed lifts almost to the exclusion of all others—when available. I generally go out of my way to ski farther down the mountain than I normally

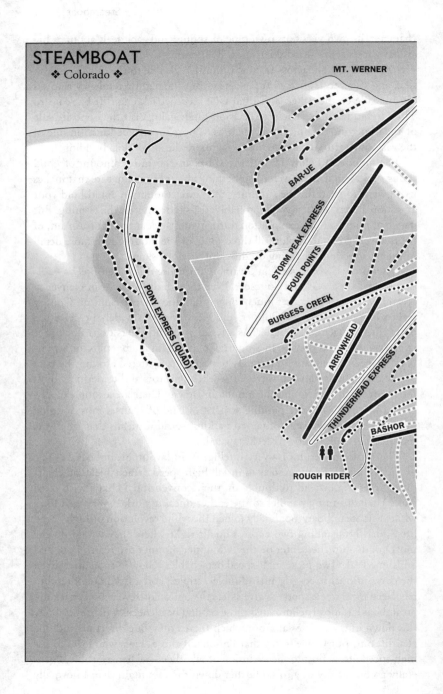

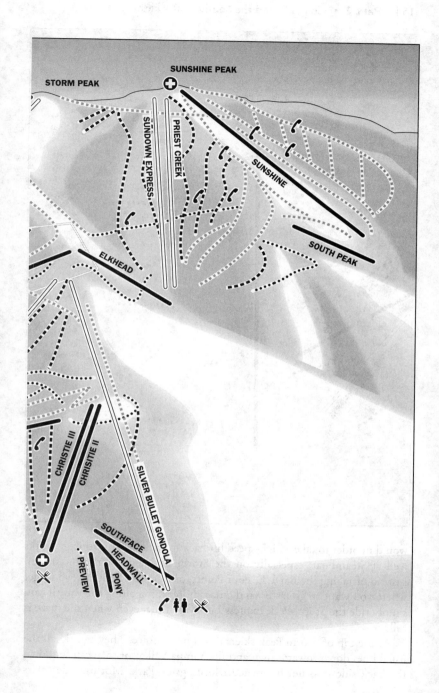

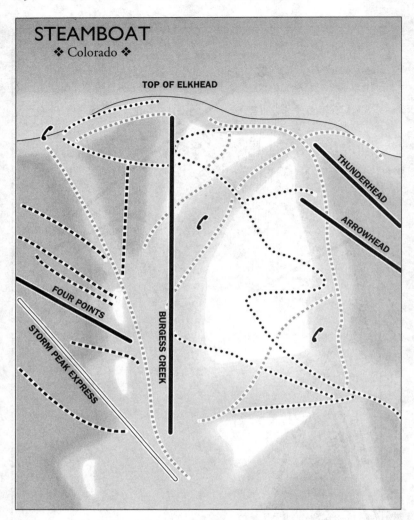

would in order to take a high-speed lift back to the top. This strategy works well at Steamboat, especially on the Storm Peak side of the mountain. Instead of taking the Bar-UE, Four Points, or Burgess Creek lifts, you'll get where you want to go faster, and enjoy more skiing along the way, if you simply ride the Storm Peak Express Lift every time, even when the maze is full.

At the top of Storm Peak skiers face a new choice. They can ski all the usual lines down toward town and the Yampa Valley, or they can ski down the back side into newly opened Morningside Park. Morningside offers more intermediate and advanced terrain and is served by its own new lift, a fixed triple chair that brings you back up to Storm Peak. This area, which opened to skiers for the 1996–97 season, is just the first fruit of a five-year expansion plan that has recently led to the opening of Pioneer Ridge (to the north of the existing ski area). With the opening of 12 new trails in this Pioneer Ridge zone, served by the Pony Express quad, Steamboat became the second largest ski mountain in Colorado (8 vertical feet and 2,939 acres of terrain).

The intelligence of Steamboat's lift layout makes the beautifully designed electronic lift status boards almost redundant, but they're a good example of efficient, modern ski-area signage. Before finally leaving the subject of lifts, I'll add that somebody should be praised for deciding to paint Steamboat's lift towers a deep, rich midnight blue that seems to come right out of the dark north Colorado sky.

Dramatic color and its corollary, dramatic light, are part of the everyday Steamboat ski experience because of a natural fluke. This mountain faces west! Most ski areas are laid out facing primarily north, which guarantees cold, dry snow conditions but also keeps many slopes gray and somber. On a primarily west-facing peak like Steamboat, the afternoon light is more intense and golden, and even the morning shadows seem deeper and more dramatic. Yet Steamboat is high enough and far enough north that its snow conditions don't seem to suffer from this western orientation. And the view from the mountain—a wide westerly panorama of broad white valleys and rolling, receding, snow-crusted foothills that stretches on and on because there are no high peaks to the west—is actually enhanced since there are no bare south-facing slopes in sight. This stunning view, by the way, seems to be built into just about every run on the mountain.

This brings me to a final observation before we look in detail at particular runs for particular skiers. Every ski mountain has its own feel, its own flavor, its own atmosphere—the result of a hard-to-analyze combination of snow conditions, terrain, scenery, trail design, and even the attitudes of skier service personnel like lift operators, ticket punchers, and patrollers. Two mountains with the same statistics, vertical drop, uphill capacity, etc., can have a completely different feel. What I want to say is that Steamboat has a wonderful feel. When I try to pin it down, remembering great days at Steamboat, I come up with two or three special qualities: the steady continuous nature of most runs, which go on and on in long uninterrupted pitches, not in fits and starts, not in flats and drops, not in sudden constrictions and sudden widenings; the wide, plunging views that I've already mentioned—that suspended-in-the-sky feeling that makes skiers feel like privileged characters (which they certainly are); and finally, the aspen trees. Steamboat is not as high as resorts farther south, so its magnificent aspen stands grow right to the top of Sunshine Peak (10,385 feet). These aspen groves, we'll see, are incredible to ski through, but they're also fabulous to look at. Taller, whiter, and straighter than aspens on other Colorado ski mountains, they have lacy, fringy tops that seem to glow against the deep winter sky. Aspens are everywhere on this mountain like no trees you've ever seen.

Steamboat for Less-Experienced Skiers

Steamboat is not a mountain with a lot of green on its trail map; in fact, there are almost no green runs at all on the upper mountains. Not to worry. There is a wonderful area on top of the mountain that's only nominally blue and is very, very friendly to less-experienced skiers. I refer to the runs on the far side of the Sunshine Lift, especially *Tomahawk* and *Quickdraw* and the short connecting runs between them. These runs are so low-key and friendly that locals call this zone "Wally World." I wouldn't hesitate to recommend these slopes to inexperienced skiers who normally stick to green runs but who still want to experience the whole mountain. These runs are long, gentle, and extremely wide, and I don't see how anyone who can make some kind of sloppy, skidded christy can get into trouble up there—provided you take the right route back down the mountain. To exit Wally World in one piece, novices should be sure to take *Duster,* a cross-mountain catwalk, from near the Rendezvous Saddle House (Ragnar's Restaurant). This catwalk cuts across the mountain behind Thunderhead peak, eventually turning into a greenish run called *Park Lane* that connects with several easy ways down the lower mountain (all green slopes).

There are a lot more green practice runs on the lower mountain, especially from the top of the Christie lifts. Two long green trails, *B C Ski Way* and the more interesting *Why Not,* which wind their way completely around the lower mountain, can be reached from the top of the Silver Bullet gondola. There's also a super beginner area at the base of the mountain that is served by both a double and a triple chair plus a tiny, mitey-mite drag lift, which is where the ski school starts their first-time beginners.

Steamboat for Good Skiers

Somewhere past parallel, when cruising fever takes hold, Steamboat skiing really starts to get exciting. *Buddy's Run* from the top of Storm Peak is a favorite: lots of room and lots of variations. No pressure to turn here, there, or any particular spot. No reason not to accept a bit more speed. This classic cruiser, along with runs like *High Noon* on the Sunshine Peak side and *Heavenly Daze* on the front face of the lower mountain, spells bliss for strong skiers who just don't want to bother with short turns, putting on the brakes, or, above all, with bumps.

There are also a lot of black runs at Steamboat that are just plain inviting for average good skiers, black runs that scarcely require expert skiing
skills at all. I'm thinking of runs like *The Ridge* and *Crowtrack* on Storm
Peak and *Valley View* below Thunderhead that require short turns and fall-
line skiing but never seem to throw any awkwardly shaped bumps in your
way. And if it's friendly bumps you're searching for, you'll often find them
on *Twilight, One o'Clock,* and *Two o'Clock,* slightly steeper lines that drop
down and right from the *High Noon* ridge run on the Sunshine Peak side.

A good strategy for good skiers is to explore one area of the mountain in
depth on any given day, working lunch into your plans. For example, spend
a morning on Sunshine Peak exploring the blues and the easy blacks that
lead past Rendezvous Saddle and back to the Sundown Express quad, and
then treat yourself to a real Norwegian lunch at Ragnar's on Rendezvous
Saddle. Or spend a morning cruising both sides of the Storm Peak Express
Lift, letting *Rainbow* and *Buddy's Run* and all their variations funnel you into
the bottom of the Burgess Creek drainage and stopping at the Four Points
Hut for lunch. This is a tiny, low-key eatery with an immense nonstop view
of the Yampa Valley spread out like a tabletop beneath the ski mountain.
This miniature mountain restaurant has fewer choices than you'll find in the
multistory, multirestaurant Thunderhead building, but it reminds me of the
fabulous little lunch huts I've always stopped at in the Alps smack in the
middle of a long ski run. After lunch at the Four Points Hut, you can pump
yourself up again by exploring the latest additions to Steamboat skiing, the
blue runs and black tree glades (shading into expert country) on both sides
of the Pony Express quad, a distinct zone with its own distinct flavor

Or, as a final option, after spending a morning on the lower mountain
skiing the pleasant runs on both sides of the Arrowhead chair, leave your skis
at the gondola and enjoy an uncrowded lunch off the slopes while the
Thunderhead mountain eateries are packed. The Silver Bullet will get you
back up the mountain in no time after lunch.

Steamboat for Experts

A great ski mountain should get better as skiers get better. Steamboat
qualifies. If you're an expert or near-expert skier, you'll go nuts here. I don't
necessarily mean a hero, a hotshot with rubber knees and thunder thighs,
but simply a very strong skier, a skier who's at home on moderately steep
bumps, comfortable in powder, and capable of turning not just where you
want to but where you need to. A lot of skiers fit this description. It's a reasonable, practical goal that I really believe most skiers can achieve with
enough patience and practice. (In fact, my book *Breakthrough on Skis* and
my videos of the same title are based on this premise, and they both outline

out a pretty straightforward path to expert skiing.) So just what does Steamboat reserve for expert skiers? Powder. Trees. And often both together. The combination is dynamite.

There are a fair number of exciting black runs, steep and moguled, on both the upper and lower mountain. But Steamboat's most exciting skiing is found among its aspen trees. For some reason, the slender white aspen trunks on this mountain are almost perfectly spaced, and there's enough room between them for good skiers to weave through these forests without you feeling pinched, pressured, or wondering if you're going to make it. These classic, open aspen lines abound in the Priest Creek area on the Sunshine Peak side of the upper mountain. Priest Creek used to be a kind of locals' preserve, but then a second lift was put in, and several open lines to the right of the new lift, as well as the lift lines themselves, were actually widened into proper, treeless runs. Paradise lost, wailed a few diehards, but it's not true. There is still an enormous amount of lovely, exciting tree skiing up here, right in the heart of the open aspen forest. The angle steepens a bit, and skiing is more exciting to the north of Sundown Express and Priest Creek lifts (to the left of the lifts as you ride up) where the two main lines you'll see on the trail map, *Shadows* and *Closet,* are only generalized areas, not clearly defined runs.

Good short turns are a must. In periods between storms, you'll even encounter moguls, not mean moguls but still moguls, among these trees. But I repeat: Steamboat tree skiing is not just for heroes; these are actually the easiest forests to ski in Colorado. For a strong skier, the experience involves far more pleasure than challenge.

I talked about trees and powder. Steamboat tends to catch northern storms out of Wyoming that sometimes miss central and southern Colorado resorts. A lot of skiers think that, next to Vail's Back Bowls, Steamboat offers the best powder skiing in the state, and I agree. The combination of trees and powder creates an experience that's greater than the sum of its parts. Steamboat's western orientation and the typical westerly winds that accompany big storms transform the aspen forests into fairy groves of white trees whose delicate bare branches are festooned with white hoarfrost lace— incredible!

For unusual tree skiing, and perhaps some stashes of late powder long after Priest Creek is tracked out, explore the forest zones in between the zigzags of *Why Not,* an easy green comeback trail on the lower mountain— some of the best hidden tree skiing at Steamboat.

Mountain Eating

Most days, it makes more sense to eat lunch up on the mountain than to ski down to the base village for lunch. There are three mountain restaurant locations but considerably more than three restaurants to choose from. At Rendezvous Saddle below the Sunshine chair you'll find a regular mountain cafeteria, barbecue on the deck, and the mountain's most popular sit-down lunch restaurant, Ragnar's. The wild Norwegian names on the menu are equaled by the good Norwegian cooking (not an oxymoron). Try the *fyldt pandekager* (shrimp crêpes) or the *stekt rødspaette trondheim* (sautéed sole with asparagus and leeks). I've already sung the praises of the tiny but cool Four Points Hut at the top of Four Points Lift, halfway up Storm Peak. Then there's Thunderhead, the massive mid-mountain crossroads at the top of the Silver Bullet gondola. Last time I counted, there were at least four separate restaurant/cafeteria facilities in this large building, where the fare includes Mexican, Italian, midland American, country and western, pizza, barbecue, etc.

Hazie's, the fancier of the two sit-down restaurants at Thunderhead, competes head-to-head with Ragnar's with a menu full of gourmet touches. But Hazie's (named for Steamboat ski champion Buddy Werner's mom, Hazie Werner) is an even better place to spend an evening. You can ride the Silver Bullet gondola up in the early evening, when the lower edge of the winter sky is still a band of pale orange, and enjoy a knockout dinner with one of the best wine lists in town at a table by a panoramic window that almost lets you reach out and touch the lights of Steamboat Springs sparkling below. Reserve at least one Steamboat evening for this treat!

Steamboat Extras

Not all of Steamboat's winter adventures are found up on the ski mountain. I can think of at least three of these, of which the best, surely, is a day of deep-powder skiing above Buffalo Pass just north of town. Jupiter Jones (that's his real name) and his wife, Barbara, run Steamboat Powder Cats, probably the best snowcat skiing operation in Colorado—not just because their price for a day of snowcat skiing is a bargain, not just because they and their guides are fun to ski with, but above all because they have more terrain to choose from than any other snowcat operation. With Jupiter, you'll sometimes be making tracks in virgin snow a week to ten days after the last storm has blown through. This expansive, wide-open terrain plus fresh snow equals poetry in motion.

There's also a unique winter driving school run by French rally champion Jean Paul Luc. On safe courses of watered ice, you'll learn all the tricks of keeping yourself and your car on the road in the most treacherous conditions. I took this one-day course to write a story for *Skiing* magazine some years ago, and what I learned has saved me much grief on treacherous mountain roads more than once.

Finally, if you have any extra time at all—a big *if* at Steamboat—you may want to consider a hot-air balloon ride. The wide Yampa River Valley beneath the ski mountain is ideal for ballooning, and several different balloon companies offer a variety of silent, over-Steamboat excursions in their multicolored *montgolfiers*.

Down below the Mountain

Shall I be honest? Why not. Steamboat is definitely a mountain to fall in love with, but there is not much about the base—either the newish ski village at the base of Mt. Werner or old-town Steamboat a few miles away—to make you lose your head. In fact, the base village is a pretty likable place: good facilities, hotels, lodges, and condo-style units; good selection of eateries, sport stores, conventional and even offbeat shops; good service with a good attitude. In short, it has all the amenities you'd expect at a first-class Rocky Mountain ski resort, which Steamboat definitely is. But you won't find a lot of character, the kind of character that could make Steamboat the resort feel as different from other Colorado resorts as Steamboat the mountain feels different from other Colorado ski mountains. Don't be discouraged; every great ski mountain can't have a great village at its base (and vice versa), and a good one is quite sufficient.

I like the ski village (officially Steamboat Village) because it functions as a pedestrian environment. Cars are out of sight and unneeded. The main centers at the base of the ski mountain, Gondola Square and Ski Time Square, are integrated multilevel plazas and arcades. You can easily stroll from one cluster of activity to another in minutes, and it will probably be several nights before you've explored the ski village thoroughly enough to be tempted by the ten-minute drive to downtown Steamboat Springs.

Lodging at the base of the mountain is mainly in stylish modern condo/apartment blocks that are all within easy walking distance of the slopes. There is even a newish Sheraton Hotel, a full-service extravaganza. Of course, one advantage of having an honestly working-class, western ranch town nearby is that one can organize a week's lodging at almost any price range imaginable, from slopeside deluxe to a modest downtown motel. And that's the positive side of my comment about Steamboat's town and village not having as much unique character as its mountain does. No one can call Steamboat pretentious or precious, nor is it self-consciously pricey. The town of Steamboat may not be easy to fall in love with, but it's damn easy to enjoy.

STEAMBOAT DATA

Mountain Statistics

Vertical feet	3,668 feet
Base elevation	6,900 feet
Summit elevation	10,568 feet
Longest run	3+ miles
Average annual snowfall	300+ inches
Number of lifts	25, including the Silver Bullet gondola (8-passenger) and 4 high-speed quads
Uphill capacity	30,081 skiers per hour
Skiable terrain	2,939 acres
Opening date	Thanksgiving weekend
Closing date	mid-April
Snowboarding	Yes

Transportation

By car About 160 miles northwest of Denver. Take I-70 west through the Eisenhower Tunnel to the Silverthorne exit, then go north on Colorado Highway 9 to Kremmling and west on U.S. 40 to Steamboat Springs.

By plane From Denver via small commuter planes to the Steamboat Airport; plus direct flights from major cities to the Yampa Valley Regional Airport.

Key Phone Numbers

Ski Area Information
  (800) 922-2722 or
  (970) 879-6111
Snow Report (970) 879-7300
Reservations (970) 879-0740 or
  (800) 922-2722
www.steamboat-ski.com

LITO'S TECH TIP

Trees without Fear

For much of this last section I've been raving about the beauty of Steamboat's trees, aspen glades that are universally considered to offer the finest tree skiing in Colorado. But I know that not everyone feels at home among these tall, slender, white trunks. When compared with the middle of a large, well-groomed run, tree skiing—even friendly, Steamboat-style tree skiing —can seem cramped, restrictive, and, with so many arboreal obstacles, downright intimidating. Here are a few tips to help you make peace with these noble trees.

True, you need good short turns to ski among trees. You also need an anticipated style, a quiet upper body aimed more or less down the hill while legs and skis turn from side to side beneath you and, above all, a rapid decisive pole plant. Your pole plant is the trigger that launches a good short turn, and if you hesitate with your pole, you'll probably hesitate to turn your skis too, and, whoops! Here comes that big tree trunk.

To ski well among trees, whether tight trees or widely spaced Steamboat trees, you have to plan ahead and you have to get rid of that "what if" anxiety. What if I don't make the next turn? What if I hit a tree? You won't. Because if you're about to hit a tree you can just sit down in the snow. Not very elegant to be sure, but very safe. You certainly won't be skiing at high speeds among trees, so you can always "save yourself" from disaster by just bailing out and sitting down. Once you realize this, and maybe do it once or twice, you just won't worry about hitting trees anymore. As I've said, Steamboat has some of the friendliest, most widely spaced aspen groves in the West. Tree skiing is almost too easy.

Like a chess player, you'll want to plot your strategy several moves or turns in advance. Look up, look ahead, and keep adjusting your line to take you toward the widest gaps between tree trunks. If you look at your ski tips, you're lost.

Any time you're skiing through or near trees, you should also make a point of taking the straps of your ski poles off your wrists. If you snag a pole on a twig or branch, this will keep you from spraining your wrist, or worse.

Finally, at an area where tree skiing is as popular as it is at Steamboat, you'll often find moguls between the trees. What then? No big deal; simply use these moguls—incipient or fully formed—to ski with less effort than you might otherwise. By always initiating your turns on the high spot or crest of the bump, which serves as a free pivot point for your skis, you can turn with far less speed than you usually use. While you're getting used to navigating through trees, less speed is definitely a blessing. It gives you that much more time to look ahead and plan your route through these giant, inviting, but inflexible slalom poles.

WINTER PARK

In Colorado skiing, Winter Park is an exception to the norm in more ways than one. It's a very big ski mountain (two mountains really) but neither a big nor a well-known ski-vacation destination. Winter Park is a publicly owned ski area (in this age of privatization, it is owned by the city of Denver) with a wonderful management philosophy, focused exclusively on delivering the best ski experience for the best price rather than playing a real estate game in parallel with ski-area operations, as is so often the case. Winter Park is a mecca for expert skiers in search of a challenge, but also quite possibly Winter Park introduces more beginners to the sport than any other Rocky Mountain area. It has also developed the finest handicapped skier program in the country and may be the last ski area in the West you can ride a ski train to!

Winter Park lies just on the north side of Berthoud Pass, a 11,315-foot gap in the ranks of high, rounded mountains lining both sides of I-70, Colorado's main auto route across the Rockies. You branch off this freeway about halfway between Denver and the continental divide, turn north, and zigzag up and over Berthoud Pass through steep, densely timbered slopes. This is classic Colorado front range country: dark green mountains, narrow shadowy valleys, and, for the motorist, slow and twisting roads. You wind down the far side of the pass, and just before exiting the mountains onto the open rolling parklands that lead on north toward Steamboat, you stumble onto Winter Park.

It's a novel approach: driving downhill to a ski area, alerted only by a few big signs and a couple of ski runs barely seen through the trees, and turning off a small highway onto an even smaller "way" in search of the area's base facilities and parking lots. Nothing about your arrival at Winter Park will make you think that it's really a big ski area. But let's look closer.

The Shape and Feel of the Mountain

Most of Winter Park is out of sight from the bottom—from either bottom. There are two bases and two distinct, although interconnected, mountains. The main base area serves the original ski mountain, Winter Park proper. The other base, back up the canyon a mile or so and reached by a small road that winds quite a distance in from the highway, is known as Mary Jane, like the mountain it serves. In all fairness, I have to say that one can also think of Winter Park as being composed of three mountains, since the Vasquez Ridge area on the Winter Park side seems to qualify as a separate peak. But for me the division of Winter Park into two ski areas —Winter Park and Mary Jane—makes more sense.

Mary Jane is not just the new half of Winter Park; it is also the challenging half, where the easiest runs are serious blues, where the big bumps live. Mary Jane is almost entirely responsible for Winter Park's reputation among serious, hot, young skiers. It is a two-sided mountain whose summit can be accessed by any of the three long chairs that run parallel up its front face. The middle one, Summit Express, is a high-speed detachable quad that gets most of the traffic, unless weekend skiers start filling its maze and forcing skiers onto the Challenger and Iron Horse lifts, which are slower, traditional double chairs. Both sides of Mary Jane are equally steep, fierce, or "interesting," depending on your point of view. What the trail map labels as *Mary Jane's Backside* is more the left flank of the mountain (looking up) than

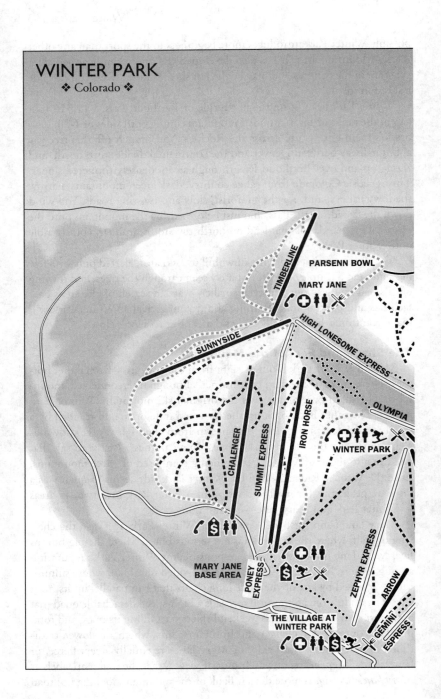

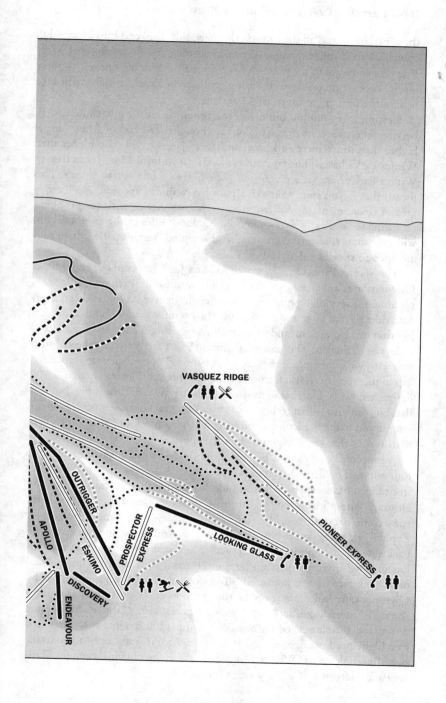

the actual back, and all the runs on this back side dead end into a long, dull comeback road called *Corona Way,* whereas the runs on the front of Mary Jane take you right to the bottom. Recently, a new chair has opened up some lovely, above-timberline-style skiing in Parsenn Bowl, a high open area behind the former "summit" of Mary Jane.

Getting from one mountain to the other, or crossing back and forth between the two, demands a bit of forethought. The top of Mary Jane is higher than the Winter Park side, and Mary Jane's base is also higher than Winter Park's base. Thus you can easily ski down from Mary Jane's base to Winter Park's base via a green trail, *The Corridor,* but not vice versa. This means that if you start your ski day on the Winter Park side, you'll enjoy greater freedom of movement around the mountain, with no problems returning to your car in late afternoon. (On both sides of the mountain you will find some interesting groomed and sculpted "terrain parks"; here they are open to snowboarders and skiers alike!)

The Winter Park side, as opposed to Mary Jane, is spread out and diffuse. Orientation is a challenge on this complex, multisummited, multiridged ski mountain. Every high point seems to offer alternative ski routes down alternate sides so that after a while you lose the notion of front and back, realizing that this ski area meanders over numerous ridges and down numerous valleys or drainages. The task of orientation isn't facilitated by the enthusiasm with which the mountain crew has baptized every single slot, opening, gap in the trees, or shortcut from one run to another. The trail map lists 100 designated trails. Don't take this too seriously; Winter Park is big, but not that big! Still, it's worth trying to absorb an accurate overview of the mountain; if you make the wrong choices, you can waste a lot of time on endless flattish runs that seem to go nowhere slowly.

A simplified overview of Winter Park (*sans* Mary Jane) would divide into four zones. The first, directly above the base (I suppose that makes it the front face), has steeper black and blue-black runs that are fairly serious— although one notices, looking up from the base, that a number of easier runs come back in from the right side—somewhere around the corner. Zephyr Lift takes you to the summit of this front zone and opens up the back side of the mountain, an altogether different sort of ski domain with lots of long, inviting, easy blue and green runs. Half the runs on this second, back face of the mountain drop down into a long valley served by Olympia Lift, and the rest of the runs tend to curve down and around to the right, funneling skiers into a wide, flat area with a large warming hut/restaurant complex called the Snoasis. Olympia Lift has just been upgraded to a high-speed quad, a very positive move since it is not only a key transportation link on the Winter Park side but also the obvious route for Winter Park skiers to access Mary Jane's runs.

Behind Snoasis rises a sort of overgrown hill (or mini-mountain) served by two short lifts from opposite sides and offering short runs of every difficulty. You can ski here or cross over this mini-summit to reach the last skiing zone, Vasquez Ridge. (In fact, you can reach Vasquez Ridge by skiing down below Olympia Lift too.) Vasquez is a long, low-angle ridge that offers mainly easy blue runs and is served by a monster detachable quad, the Pioneer Express Lift. The skiing on Vasquez Ridge is friendly, unchallenging, and uncrowded, but it's a major undertaking to get back to the main Winter Park areas via the long Olympia Lift.

Obviously, learners and less-experienced skiers will find the backside of Winter Park more to their liking; dyed-in-the-wool experts will head right for Mary Jane, and skiers in between (the majority) can find some runs to their liking almost everywhere on this twin mountain. Let's consider all these options in more detail.

Winter Park for Inexperienced Skiers

You'll definitely want to avoid Mary Jane your first day at Winter Park. Once you start finding your way around the mountain and you're sure you feel comfortable on all the green runs and some of the easier blue trails, there is one Mary Jane adventure I can recommend. But for starters, try this sequence. Take any of the three lower, shorter lifts from the main base (Arrow, Hughes, or Gemini lifts). Not all of them will be running unless it's a crowded weekend. They arrive at roughly the same spot (don't ask me why they installed three lifts, almost side by side, going to the same place). Then warm up on a friendly green trail, *Parkway*, just to get your ski legs back. Avoid *Interstate*, which is marked on the trail map as the "easiest way down." It's altogether too roundabout and too flat to enjoy unless you're a rank beginner. If your first run seems comfortable, take right off for the top via the left-hand base lift, the Zephyr Lift. Don't get psyched out by the steeper runs you'll ride over in this chair. All your skiing will take place on the very friendly back side.

From the top of this lift—a rendezvous known as *Sunspot* where several other lifts also arrive—head straight back a hundred yards or so and turn right down a blue run called *Cramer* or go a little farther, past a line of trees separating these runs, and take the next run, which is a green trail called *Allan Phipps*. At first, everything on this side of the mountain seems almost the same. As you head down, the runs on the right steepen and those on your left remain flatter. Take your choice. You can also choose whether or not to contour right around the mountain by following *Allan Phipps* or to continue to go more or less straight down to Olympia Lift on *March Hare* or *Mad Tea Party*. Olympia Lift generally offers the best skiing at Winter Park for strong novices or weaker, less-experienced intermediates, so you'll soon get to know it pretty well.

Two other options will help inexperienced skiers stave off the boredom of always remaining on one part of the mountain. You can ski down to the Pioneer Express quad, and from its top ski on Vasquez Ridge by sticking to *Gunbarrel* and *Lonesome Whistle*. But remember that the blue runs on Vasquez Ridge tend to be more difficult and demanding than the blue runs on Olympia Lift. There's also the Mary Jane adventure I promised: From the top of Mary Jane (reached either by the Summit Express Lift from the Mary Jane base or by the High Lonesome Lift) you'll find several very long, very easy, and very scenic green routes to take you back down to the Winter Park side. (The best of these is *Switchyard*.) There's definitely enough easy skiing, enough green and easy blue runs at Winter Park to give even timid skiers the sense of exploring a big mountain.

Winter Park for Average Skiers

You're a good solid intermediate. What to expect? Where to go? There are so many runs, aimed in so many different directions, that it's all too easy to waste hours of your skiing day zigzagging around the mountain with no game plan, getting stuck on a lot of the boring, roadlike connectors that abound at Winter Park. My recommendation to strong but not overly bold or ambitious skiers (skiers who don't want to spend all day boogying and bashing in the bumps) is this: You'll find the most enjoyable upper-intermediate skiing on the two opposite sides of the mountain—that is to say, on the far side of Vasquez Ridge and on the farther backside slopes of Mary Jane. Generally, you can ignore the blue slopes of the main or middle section of Winter Park because, frankly, they lack character and interest. Don't worry, you'll get to see this part of the mountain anyway, cruising down *Jabberwocky* or *White Rabbit* on your way from *Lunch Rock* (the name of the Mary Jane summit) back down to the Vasquez side; it's just not worth tarrying here.

The blue runs on Vasquez Ridge, like *Stagecoach, Sundance,* and *Quickdraw,* have plenty of character. They twist and turn; their pitch and contour change often; their steeps flatten out before they can psych you out; and when moguls appear, they do so in inviting patches rather than forbidding phalanxes. The only flaw with skiing over here—as on any long ridge—is that when runs follow a natural fall line down the flank of the ridge, they always bottom out too soon. So you'll wind up with a few boring minutes of flat skiing along *Big Valley* or *Wagon Train* at the end of every good run on Vasquez Ridge.

In fact, it may strike you that the bottom terminal of the quad lift that serves Vasquez Ridge has been placed a few hundred yards too low, because these last few hundred yards seem to be pointless, flat, skating terrain. Rest assured, there was a reason. The bottom of the Pioneer Express Lift is placed in this unlikely spot in order to render it accessible to skiers returning from the upper Vasquez drainage, those high white corniced bowls you can see in the distance.

The back side of Mary Jane has pleasant surprises in store for good skiers: real open-glade skiing through a naturally thinned-out, high-altitude forest in *Wildwood Glade* and *Belmont Bowl,* and even more open skiing in *Parsenn Bowl.* This is a special treat at Winter Park because most of the forests on the mountain are so dense and dark that they're almost oppressive. This open top area on the back side of Mary Jane also offers the best views on the mountain—sweeping panorama up to the big peaks on the continental divide rather than the endless succession of green timbered slopes one gazes at (and soon comes to ignore) on the front side. Although they are not at all challenging, I find these runs, along with *Roundhouse,* to be among the most esthetic experiences at Winter Park. The installation of Sunnyside triple chair, up the back side of Mary Jane, has made these runs even more attractive by sparing skiers a long, slow comeback trail.

Winter Park is also a good place for intermediate skiers to push their skills and comfort levels upward one notch at a time, without risking any unpleasant surprises. If you're a pretty fair skier who wants to start challenging steeper and bumpier slopes, you should take advantage of several trails marked with an alternating blue-and-black line on the trail map. These are perfect transition runs to test yourself on before attacking the real black diamonds. On the Mary Jane side, ski *Sleeper* before trying any of the black runs. On the main front face at Winter Park try *Hughes* or *Bradley's Bash* (a smidgen harder) before tackling any blacks.

Winter Park is definitely not one of those obvious-to-ski areas like Copper Mountain, where a trail map seems almost redundant and skiers couldn't get lost if they tried. But one of the advantages of skiing a complicated mountain is that, if you keep your wits about you, you can find slopes of virtually any difficulty on any exposure. My hints should keep you on the right track until you've found your own favorites.

Winter Park for Very Strong Skiers

There are ski mountains in Colorado where the three-color, national trail-marking system has been skewed so far in one direction or the other that skiers can look at a blue square or black diamond sign and still not have a clue as to what sort of experiences, terrors, or delights await them. When I skied and reskied every area in Colorado, gathering information for this guide, I found one area calling a slope blue that could have been double black anywhere else, and other areas where the black slopes were ridiculously easy. I tell you this so you'll know what a compliment it is when I say that Winter Park's rating system is extremely honest. If a trail is marked black, it is black; that means two things. It's steep and there'll be plenty of bumps. Winter Park's black runs are not wimpy, but they're not ugly either. I find the bumps on Mary Jane unusually well formed, big and rhythmic, with rounded exit gullies. Seemingly these bumps don't get hacked up and chopped off because skiers here avoid such runs if they are not ready for them. But if you are ready, the gullies and short, clifflike faces of the upper section of Mary Jane, around *Sluice Box* and *Pine Cliffs,* are good warm-ups for tackling the harder bump lines to your right (looking down). The dividing line between the front and back sides of Mary Jane is a long bumped-out ridge run called *Derailer,* and the hardest, best bump runs branch off *Derailer* on both sides. I find the backside runs like *Cannonball* and *Long* and *Short Haul* to be straighter, steeper, and more continuous than the bump runs on the other side—more fun too, once you're into it.

The most difficult and certainly the most exciting runs in all of Winter Park are the three chutes—*Awe Chute, Baldy's Chute,* and *Jeff's Chute*—that drop off the back side of the *Derailer* ridge. They are reached via a special gate on the side of *Derailer,* furnished with a special and very sobering warning sign. If the conditions aren't adequate, that is to say if there isn't enough snow or the snow is too hard or icy, the patrol closes this gate. Take these runs very seriously. They are very steep, narrow, twisty, and rocky, and a fall could be dangerous. It's a tribute to the spirit of Winter Park management that these runs are marked and often open. As long as skiers can continue to find challenges like this at ski areas, downhill skiing still qualifies as an adventure sport.

Of course, there's more to expert skiing than the pursuit, and mastery, of pure difficulty—there's the aesthetic side as well. Experts willing to hike a bit will find a wonderful combination of high-alpine aesthetics plus steep chutes and mixed open trees in the wilds of upper Vasquez Cirque, a remote drainage behind Parsenn Bowl. These lines (indicated on the trail map) are accessed from the Timberline chair, and once you've left your tracks in upper Vasquez Cirque, you'll ski out a long canyon to the Pioneer Express lift.

Base Facilities and Village

The trail map tells you that the big base facility at the bottom of the main mountain is called the Village at Winter Park. Why not? It's a big interesting place, full of shops and eateries, and it is actually more interesting than the town of Winter Park, which is a few miles down the road. There's the rub. Calling this nearby agglomeration of shops, services, and lodging a town is not sufficient to make it feel like one. The village certainly doesn't feel like a Colorado ski town, and this town, or absence of town, is the big flaw in Winter Park's offering.

The town of Winter Park is an unplanned, underdeveloped strip of a town, a loose collection of random-access parking lots and shopping, eating, and lodging facilities thrown up in the woods on either side of U.S. 40 that runs for a couple of miles—one of those less-than-urban assemblies where the individual elements may work (for example, there are a couple of wonderful 1940s-style, dark wooden lodges, and a couple of really handsome contemporary condo castles) but where nothing is tied to anything else, where there's no center, no circulation, and no local character. It reminds me of Mammoth Lakes, California, another nonstarter in the mountain village sweepstakes where uncontrolled strip development provided a lot of lodging units but knocked out any chance of real resort-town life. Enough said.

Is it too late? I don't know. It's easy enough to see why a proper town didn't develop here. For years and years Winter Park was the classic popular weekend destination for Denver skiers and little else. After a remarkable period of ski area expansion, Winter Park's mountain facilities are now on a par with Colorado's other destination resorts. Maybe a hot ski town can grow out of the chaos down the road. I hope so.

The ski-area base itself is an interesting hodgepodge of architecture, skier services, and good vibes. The entrance buildings, ticket windows, etc., are intact monuments to ski history with a building style that could be called early Forest Service Tyrolian. Just beyond rises an impressive cubist building structure of corrugated metal and glass—an integrated mini-mall of retail, rental, eating, and drinking spots that really works. Sun decks everywhere face the mountain, and a classic, timeless après-ski scene with collegiate overtones of beer drinking and girl watching is under way here long before the lifts close.

WINTER PARK DATA

Winter Park Statistics

Total vertical feet	3,060 feet
Base elevation	9,000 feet
Summit elevation	12,060 feet
Longest run	5.1 miles
Average annual snowfall	370 inches
Number of lifts	20, including 8 high-speed quads
Uphill capacity	27,884 skiers per hour
Skiable terrain	1,105 acres
Opening date	November 6
Closing date	April 18
Snowboarding	Yes

Mary Jane Statistics

Vertical feet	2,610 feet
Base elevation	9,450 feet
Summit elevation	12,060 feet

Vasquez Ridge Statistics

Vertical feet	1,214 feet
Base elevation	9,486 feet
Summit elevation	10,770 feet

Transportation

By car A 90-minute drive (in good road and weather conditions) from Denver. Take I-70 west to exit 232 (7 miles west of Idaho Springs) and drive west on U.S. 40.

By bus From the Denver International Airport, also by Gray Line bus service daily from Denver. Free shuttle buses from the nearby town of Fraser and also between Winter Park and Mary Jane.

By train Daily scheduled service from San Francisco east and Chicago west on the California Zephyr; also Rio Grande Ski Train weekend service from Denver (leaves Denver's Union Station at 7:30 A.M. direct to Winter Park; leaves Winter Park to return to Denver at 4 P.M.). For more information call Amtrak at (800) USA-RAIL.

Key Phone Numbers

Ski Area Information
   (970) 726-5514
Snow Report (970) 726-5514
Reservations (800) 453-2525 or
   (970) 726-5587
www.skiwinterpark.com

Basic Bumps

Bumps (or "moguls") on a ski slope can delight or frustrate. Personally, I love them, but I know that most skiers don't, which is natural because they have a hard time skiing them. They don't have a hard time turning, but they do have a hard time feeling and staying poised and comfortable from turn to turn.

The reason bumps exist at all is because any little high spot or lump on the slope, serving as a natural pivot point, facilitates turning your skis. Skiers figure this out early and use bumps (whether they enjoy bump skiing or not) to trigger or launch their turns. The real problem comes in putting it all together, staying in balance on a moguled slope, controlling your speed in the limited space available, and arriving at the end of one bump turn poised, comfortable, and ready for the next. In a word, finishing a bump turn well is harder than starting that turn. Here's a basic plan that should improve your mogul skiing manyfold.

Start your bump turns the way you always do—only less so. By this I mean that when you cross over the top of a bump don't pivot your skis as hard as you normally do. Trust in the fact that your skis will follow the scraped-out hollow of the bump's trough. That's right, the round shape of the turn is already there in the rounded shape of the bump's gully; all you need to do is let your skis drift. They will follow the curved gully in an arc that brings you around under the bump.

Most skiers who have trouble with bumps simply overpivot their skis on the very top. They complete the entire turning action in the first foot or two and find themselves out of balance, with their skis jammed sideways or crosswise to the gully at its narrowest point. One reason skiers seem to have a hard time just letting their skis drift on down through the gully is an anxiety about picking up too much speed. It's true, you will go a little faster right in the middle of each turn as you're coming around the side of the bump. But you will finish each turn underneath the bump, where you'll have more room to turn your skis sideways without getting them caught in the gully.

So this should be your basic pattern for comfortable bump skiing: a slow start, pivoting your skis just enough to get them into the turn; a relaxed middle phase drifting around the bump, letting your skis follow the rounded gully; and finally, an active finish below the bump where you actually turn your skis as far across the slope as you want to slow down. Remember, slow down beneath the bump, not in the middle.

Loveland is the closest ski area to Denver. I blush to tell you how many times I drove by this small ski area, nestled under and spreading out above the East Portal of the Eisenhower Tunnel on I-70 above Denver, without pausing— dozens, if not hundreds, of times since I moved to Colorado in 1976. Seems like I was just too snobbish to stop and ski there—until recently. Better just drive on through the tunnel, I always thought, into Summit County, or if the roads were clear, turn off I-70 and drive over Loveland Pass to Arapahoe Basin, another small area but one that always seemed more imposing, more alpine. How, I thought to myself, could an area as small as Loveland offer good, serious, exciting skiing? I was dead wrong. I admit it.

Loveland is tiny, certainly the smallest ski area in the Colorado section of this guidebook. I believe it may be the oldest; at any rate, Loveland celebrated its 60th anniversary as a ski area in 1997. But since 1937, it has remained precisely that, a ski area, a day area, not a full-blown ski resort in the usual Colorado sense of the term. It's still a real gem, an area that offers some stunning skiing and, even better, a ski experience that's hard to find elsewhere. Loveland doesn't seem to be a great financial success story as a ski area, and one has the feeling that it's been left behind in the white revolution of high-speed lifts that's been transforming Colorado skiing into something resembling a brand-new sport. Loveland seems half deserted on weekdays, and even on weekends, when the parking lot finally fills up mostly with Denver skiers, Loveland still doesn't seem full or crowded. Today there are a couple of fixed grip quad chairs and two triple chairs; the rest are old double chairs that have always been painted a shade of powder blue that somehow makes them look even older than they are. Even recent upgrades of its base facilities haven't eliminated the wonderful old-fashioned feeling of this area. The whole Loveland experience seems to come straight out of another place and time. For one thing, the daily skiing ticket is cheap by Colorado standards. For another, in this age of heightened ski-area liability concerns and general corporate uptightness, there are places at Loveland where the ski-area boundary is left vague and almost undefined, where the distinction between tamed ski area and wild mountainscape is no longer clear. This is exactly what I like most about Loveland skiing.

The Layout and Feel of the Mountain

Strike that word "mountain." Loveland is a bowl or high alpine basin rather than a peak. It's set among mountains, to be sure—the high summits and ridges of the Continental Divide. Its main base area is only a stone's throw from the twin tunnels where I-70 plunges under these peaks en route from Denver to Dillon, to Vail, and ultimately to Grand Junction and points west. Even from the highway you can see that just above this base—above the tunnel—everything changes.

Timberline is only a few hundred feet above the parking lot; the dense, front-range forest thins out quickly and disappears altogether in a last scattering of sparse and stunted dwarf trees. The world turns white or almost white; snowy basins and distant corniced ridges alternate with windswept rocky, patchy cliffs. In its openness, Loveland is the exact antithesis of Winter Park, which has been literally chopped out of deep, dense, forested slopes, and where every run is bounded by curtains of dark green. Here the eye ranges unchecked across wide and wide-open snow basins: an alpine rather than subalpine world. An unmistakable, high-mountain feeling informs Loveland skiing.

For the most part, Loveland skiing isn't very hard. The ski area has two parts. Loveland Basin, the first part, spreads out above the freeway tunnel and is, for me, the real ski area. A mysterious appendage, the second part, about a mile down the road called Loveland Valley, has a tiny beginners' chair and a medium-size double chair serving a couple of blue runs. The two halves of the area are linked by a long horizontal chairlift (Lift 5) that exists only to shuttle skiers back and forth. Despite the recent upgrade of Loveland Valley's chair to a fixed-grip quad, the skiing down the road is not so memorable. Most skiers still prefer to stay up on top. But it is a plus for beginners to have their own area, Loveland Valley, well away from more advanced traffic.

The main (or upper) area has six chairlifts and one poma that fan out in a semicircle into all sides of the basin above the highway. The leftmost chair (looking up) is the steepest and serves respectable, even fierce, black bump runs as well as a number of interesting blues, which sweep around into the center of the basin rather than descending the steep face above the lodge. While this triple chair (Lift 1) serves the most technically demanding runs at Loveland, this is not necessarily where you'll find the most beautiful skiing. In fact, this side of the basin is densely treed, so it doesn't share in that high, above-timberline atmosphere I mentioned earlier, although a new, legitimately black run, *Over the Rainbow,* dives down through some steep trees.

To get right into the Loveland feeling, take Lift 2, another triple, up to Ptarmigan Roost and you'll find yourself in the middle of an expansive bowl that seems to invite you to ski in all directions at once, which is just what you do. . . . What I meant is that, although the named "runs" or "lines" indicated on the trail map up here are all easy-angled blues with a few greens, there are no boundaries between them. Or anywhere up here. You are

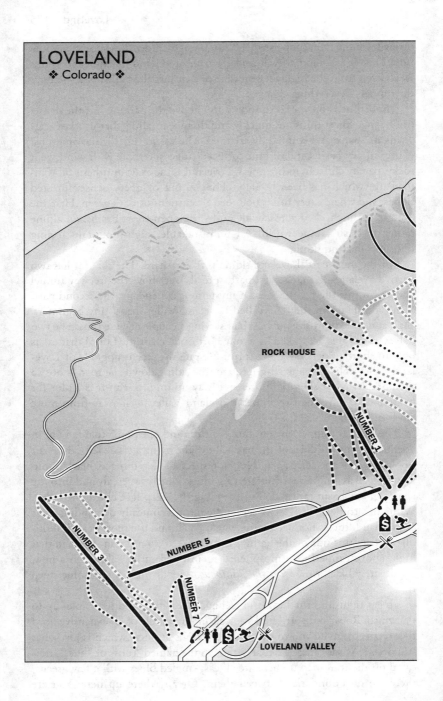

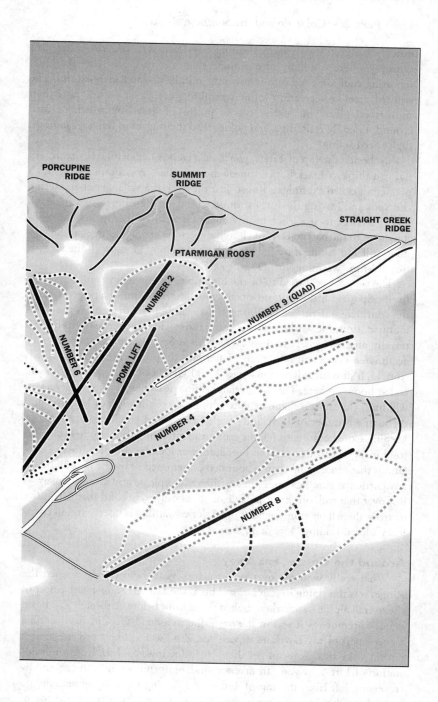

quickly tempted into a more dashing free-form style of skiing: big-turn cruising, where you look for mountain shapes to turn on rather than just repeating your same old moves down the middle of a well-defined run. The stunted, treelike vegetation (often resembling evergreen bushes more than mini-trees) gives you widely spaced points of green by which to turn around. Friendly rolls, dips, and gullies lend themselves to flowing, smooth, high-speed skiing.

Just beside the top of Lift 2, you'll see a wooden chaletlike structure. Ah ha, you think, a snack bar or top-of-the-mountain restaurant. Nope, it's a picnic hut called Ptarmigan Roost. Just the idea of a ski area not exploiting this spot and leaving the hut for those who pack their lunch in a rucksack takes you back to an earlier, more romantic era. I love it. You feel like dashing down to the base to buy lunch in the cafeteria or a hamburger at the outdoor grill and taking it up the lift with you to enjoy, along with the view, at this old-time warming hut. Do it.

The top of Lift 2 used to be the high point of the lift system, but a new fixed-grip quad lift, Lift 9, now takes you all the way up to a ridge marking the continental divide at 12,700 feet. Loveland boasts that this is the highest quad lift in the world, and it accesses more wide-open, above-timberline terrain, an area loosely known as *The Ridge*. Strong, ambitious, and well-acclimated skiers can hike even higher and drop into the topmost bowls from high summit ridges at just over 13,000 feet. But average skiers too will feel at home up here. This is Loveland skiing at its best. From up here, you will find you can travel and explore a long way to the right or left, into and through a number of Loveland's high basins. And you'll explore without keeping score because, to tell the truth, the different "runs" up here all tend to blur together, but not from boredom. For me, the real pleasure at Loveland is that sense of not being bounded or hemmed in by the boundaries of any particular run. I can head in any direction I please and know it's okay— just over that roll, on the other side of that boulder, beyond that tiny grove of trees, there'll be more friendly, open slopes waiting. It doesn't feel like typical Colorado skiing. *Vive la différence!*

Around the Corner, Far Away

What really won me over to Loveland, years before they opened the Ridge, was the skiing in *Zip Basin*. This is the farthest right-hand aspect of the overall alpine basin when looked up at from below. Although Zip Basin is not as remote as it was in the past, due to a quad lift, Lift 8, it is still a favorite part of my Loveland experience. Zip Basin is like a private ski area within a ski area. You can get there by following *Zip Trail* from the mid-station of Lift 4, or you can take a roundabout (but more scenic) route by traversing left from the top of Lift 4 and staying high—you actually go around the shoulder of a peak, turn the corner, and come out at the top of a long series of open treeless slopes that constitute Zip Basin. These slopes drop away leftward into a sort of gully or natural drain way down below you. The surprise is that you've skied clear out of sight of the ski area behind you, although you can still look across the basin to the tiny bumps over on Lift 1. Even though the new lift has made Zip Basin much more accessible —and above all, invites you to stay there, around the corner for a number of runs—this zone still doesn't seem to get nearly as much traffic as the main slopes above the day lodge. Skiing here is very much like skiing in a miniature version of Vail's Back Bowls, a very alpine experience.

These slopes are continuous, never very steep, and always inviting. It's not always clear where the ski area stops in Zip Basin, and it doesn't seem to matter because any line you ski will funnel you down into the natural drainage of a side valley that slants back to the bottom of Lift 8.

There are two alternatives for getting back to the main ski area over there, on the other side of a four-lane interstate highway! From the top of Lift 8 follow *Zippity Split* back to Lift 4—an easy but roundabout route. A much faster route is to simply follow the trail that snakes down the creek-bed drainage below the loading area for Lift 8 and finishes above the highway on a steep shoulder, the Face, which is usually moguled. A small pedestrian/skier tunnel crosses under the freeway and brings you back to the Loveland base lodge. I shake my head when I think of all the times I drove over this spot, unaware that accommodating highway engineers had constructed a comeback route for skiers who had just enjoyed one of the best hidden runs in Colorado!

LOVELAND DATA

Mountain Statistics

Vertical feet	2,100 feet
Base elevation	10,600 feet
Summit elevation	12,700 feet
Longest run	2 miles
Average annual snowfall	392 inches
Number of lifts	11
	9 chairlifts
	2 surface lifts
Uphill capacity	12,437 skiers per hour
Skiable terrain	1,265 acres
Opening date	mid-October
Closing date	mid-May
Snowboarding	Yes

Transportation

By car A 45-minute drive (in good road and weather conditions) from Denver, east on I-70 to exit 216, which is just before the Eisenhower Tunnel.

Key Phone Numbers

Ski Area Information
(303) 571-5580 or
(303) 569-3203
Snow Report (800) 225-LOVE
Reservations (800) 225-5683
www.skiloveland.com

Stepping Out: Skiing Off-Piste

Off-piste is a wonderful expression and a wonderful feeling. European skiers call their ski runs "pistes" and use this expression to describe skiing away from prepared runs. This doesn't refer to just powder skiing but skiing in a mixed bag of variable, natural snow conditions. Skiing off-piste demands an adaptable and secure technique to cope with anything from wind-ruffled powder to breakable crust. The high treeless basins at Loveland, exposed to sun and wind, are perfect places to experience the delights and frustrations of ungroomed, variable snow. Here are a few general tips and strategies to use whenever you ski in tricky variable snow conditions.

Security first. Maybe the surface will support you, maybe it won't; if you have doubts, ski it slowly—high-speed tumbles are much riskier. Ski it on two feet with both skis equally weighted. This is the opposite of normal packed-slope technique, where you want to be exclusively balanced over your outside ski. But in unknown snow conditions, equal weighting gives you several advantages. If the snow surface has a light unstable crust, you're less likely to break through with only half the weight on each ski, and if one ski does break through to become trapped inside or under the crust, then you've still got your other ski for support and turning while you try to get it—or them—back together.

For similar reasons, I suggest medium-radius turns in variable and tricky snow conditions.

If the snow seems extremely variable and catchy, you'll probably want to use a smooth, powerful up motion to start your turns. Add that snappy lifting of your outside hand and arm that I mentioned in connection with powder to punctuate this up movement. But don't simply jump in the air and turn your skis and come down hard; a hard landing can trap your skis again in deep crusty snow. Instead, try to follow your smooth upward extension with an equally smooth progressive sinking to absorb some of the extra pressure of this landing.

In difficult variable snow I make an effort to lean or bank into my turns. This tilts your skis up in the snow and reduces the likelihood of catching an outside edge in the crust. This is not something I'd ever recommend on a packed slope, but it's helpful in heavy, difficult snow.

# Summit County

Keystone The closest of the four Summit County ski areas to Denver, Keystone has greatly expanded its ski offerings in recent years. It has three separate mountains to ski, long fall-line slopes, a superb snowmaking system, and efficient lifts. Keystone is mostly a cruiser's mountain. There is a small and tasteful base village, and a new village center, River Run, is nearing completion. A wide choice of additional lodging is near the base or in the nearby Summit County area.

Arapahoe Basin The highest ski area in Colorado, and always the last to close in spring, "A-Basin" is a day area, not a full resort. It's renowned for late-spring skiing in an alpine, above-timberline setting. A-Basin is always worth a day when you're in the area.

Breckenridge A former mining town that has now been totally transformed into a popular destination resort, Breckenridge is the only true ski town in Summit County. The ski area is spread out over three-plus mountains and, like the town at its base, can absorb a lot of skiers. Breckenridge skiing offers a little of everything, especially fine beginner and novice learning terrain; some open-bowl skiing if you're willing to hike; short steeps; and lots of basic blue. Close to Denver and the rest of Summit County.

Copper Mountain The full spectrum of Colorado-style, groomed trail skiing, plus a series of intriguing high, open bowls, on a logically laid-out mountain that seems wider than it is tall. The resort village at the base has always been a little short on charm, but in the hands of its new developers, Intrawest, Copper is poised to become a real ski village at last. Easy access from Denver and to and from the rest of Summit County.

KEYSTONE

If there were such a thing as a prize for the most improved ski resort in Colorado, Keystone would win it time and again. Once more, during the several seasons leading up to the publication of this guidebook, Keystone has reinvented itself, adding a whole new mountain called the Outback to its already considerable offering and polishing its already polished skier services to a new level.

Keystone is an unlikely success story in Colorado skiing; it's the little ski area that could. It's hardly little any more, and it has been beautifully organized, developed, and expanded to a degree no one but the visionaries who did it would have believed possible. It's tempting to say that Bob Maynard and his team, who took over Keystone's destiny when the Ralston Purina Corporation bought the original wee ski area, made a silk purse out of a sow's ear. That's not exactly fair. It is fair, however, to say that Keystone is not a great "natural" ski mountain, being a bit short on both natural snowfall and ideal skiing terrain, especially open terrain. Like Winter Park, this is a densely forested dark green mountain. Even the Keystone trail map, which after all is only an artist's idealized conception, looks a good deal greener than that of other mountains (and I'm talking green forests, not green runs). But Keystone has been cut, carved, groomed, and honed into one of the biggest, most successful ski areas in the state. It has consistently broken new ground in skier service, starting with Colorado's first giant, modern snowmaking system. And it's paid off because Keystone has become a perennial favorite with Denver skiers, who have the opportunity in one winter to sample more Colorado resorts than most out-of-state skiers can visit in five years.

Keystone today is three areas in one and maybe more if you want to count the artificially lit night-skiing runs separately. And that's exactly what Keystone would like you to do because they have gone overboard to create a separate identity complete with a separate graphic logo for each section, each aspect of their mountain: Keystone Mountain, North Peak, the Outback, and Keystone by night (or "Night-Ski Keystone" as the starburst-and-K logo has it).

First comes Keystone Mountain, the main mountain: a big, broad flank of forest-lined fairways, groomed sweeps that flow rather than drop toward the valley with smooth, fast, and relaxed trail skiing. This is the original mountain, now much improved with two high-speed quads and a high-speed, high-capacity gondola. Most runs here tend to be of the green and blue variety.

Next comes North Peak, the mountain behind the mountain, Keystone's first major expansion with new lifts, new exposures, new views, and generally more difficult and challenging skiing than that on the front side. Despite its own lightning-bolt logo, North Peak doesn't feel like a *separate* ski mountain but simply a terrific *addition* to a mountain that was previously too heavily weighted toward novice and low-intermediate skiers. North Peak, with its preponderance of black runs and very inviting bump skiing, balances the spectrum at the upper end. Initially, the North Peak expansion was served by two chairlifts, one on the slopes of North Peak and one to bring skiers back up to the summit of Keystone itself. Now there is also a new gondola connecting the top of Keystone's mountain with the top of North Peak and the remarkable Outpost Lodge there.

The Outback is the most recent addition to the Keystone complex. Think of the Outback as the mountain behind the mountain behind the mountain; in other words, you must cross over North Peak to get there. The Outback is well served by a single high-speed quad. There's another quad, too, but not of the speedy, detachable variety, which takes skiers back up to the top of North Peak on their way home. The Outback is a very elegant and satisfying addition to Keystone skiing, with its long runs and true fall lines. Many of its wide runs are groomed on one side only. Thus they offer skiers two choices: on one side, dynamite cruising on a sustained pitch or more of the same forgiving, inviting bumps that make North Peak so special.

All this expansion, one mountain after another, tends to put skiers farther and farther from the base. But luckily, the mountain layout doesn't oblige one to take boring roads and catwalks to get from one peak to the next. The "get-there" runs linking the different peaks provide attractive and sustained skiing. So if you're heading over to North Peak or on to the Outback, getting there can indeed be half the fun. Naturally, you'll need a few important strategies to find yourself at the right place at the right time of day on such a big ski complex, and we'll cover them in more detail a little later.

Keystone, of course, also has a village—a small, but very attractive, modern resort village that is, like Keystone's mountain, more a triumph of hard work and try-harder management than of natural advantages. The problem is simply that Keystone's resort village isn't exactly at the base of the ski mountain; it's a couple of miles down the road. By the time serious resort planning began at Keystone, most of the land at the base of the mountain was lost in a hodgepodge of individual ownership and speculation. But as Keystone's ski mountain has expanded, new terrain, east toward the continental divide, became available for a second chance to create a perfectly sited base village. The jury is still out because construction only began in

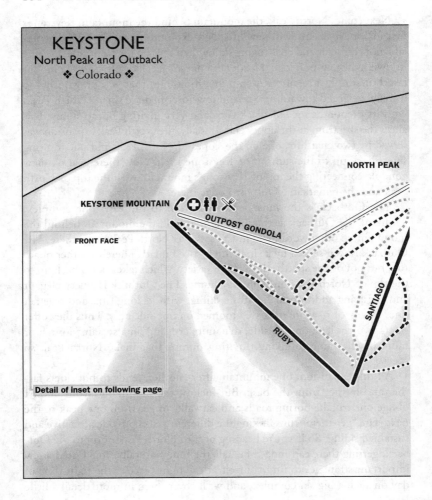

1996–97, but River Run village, near the base of Keystone's gondola, now has a chance to make up for lost opportunities. The major partner in this new village development, which will take years and countless millions of dollars, is Intrawest, a Canadian resort company with deep pockets and deep vision. I'm very optimistic for the long run.

But today, just down the road from the ski mountain itself, Keystone village is aesthetically pleasing, tightly integrated, and altogether successful— without any ski-in/ski-out cachet. It's a true pedestrian precinct that spreads (but doesn't sprawl) around an artificial lake that in winter turns into Col-

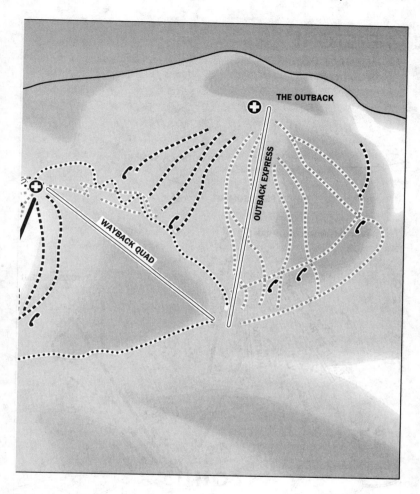

orado's finest outdoor skating spot. It's nicely done. We'll take a second look at the village after our tour of this big mountain.

Understanding Keystone's Front Mountain

Keystone itself—I'm now talking about Keystone's first or "front" mountain—is as wide or wider from side to side as it is tall. This impression is reinforced by the fact that the mountain has two base locations. On the western side, closer to Keystone Village, the original base is focused around an attractive day lodge called the Mountain House. Farther up the canyon,

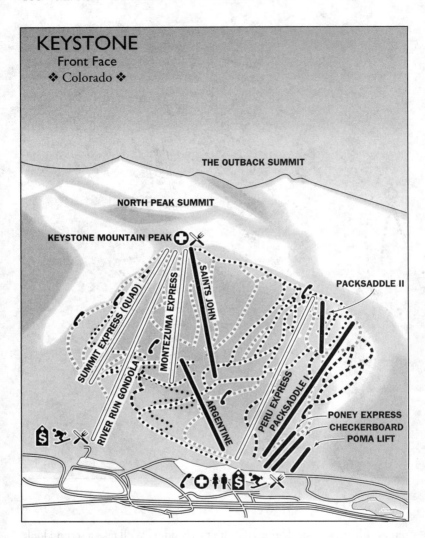

is a separate parking complex (big lots checkerboarded among trees) that serves Keystone's high-speed Skyway gondola. The gondola takes you from the River Run Plaza to the Summit House in one straight shot.

Despite its twin base areas, Keystone divides neatly in thirds. The gondola and the Erickson Lift define and serve the east side. Then there's what I think of as the center or middle mountain, which is served by the Argentine Lift from the Mountain House base and three higher chairs—the Montezuma Express quad, and two conventional doubles, the Saints John and Ida Belle lifts. Finally there's the western side of Keystone Mountain, served by the Peru Express quad and the two Packsaddle Lifts. (All the lifts here, you may already have guessed, are named after historic mine sites.)

I find this far western side to have more character than the rest of the front face. Not that it necessarily has better skiing, but it has more distinctive skiing because on a big forested mountain like Keystone runs can begin to resemble one another, and there's a remarkable similarity among the long blue runs on the center mountain. It's sometimes hard for nonlocals to tell runs like *Flying Dutchman, Frenchman,* and *Paymaster* apart, whereas on the western side one starts with *Packsaddle Bowl,* Keystone mountain's only real open-slope skiing and a delightful contrast to its tree-lined roller coasters. This is a great place to head early in the morning because *Packsaddle Bowl* is tilted somewhat east and catches the early sun. Proceeding on down this far western flank you encounter a few serious black slopes, the hardest skiing on the front mountain—and suddenly you know you're not just cruising another Keystone ski boulevard. But don't let me give the impression that these ski boulevards aren't worth cruising; they are. The best thing about the green and blue runs that snake down the front mountain at Keystone is their length. There are relatively few trail intersections and cross-traffic is seldom a problem.

While it may seem tempting to ski the center of Keystone's front mountain top to bottom, I think you can actually log more miles of skiing by using the Montezuma Express quad to circulate on runs like *Flying Dutchman* and *Bachelor.* If you're dead set on skiing long top-to-bottom runs, focus on trails east of the gondola like *Spring Dipper* with its variants, *Santa Fe, Swandyke,* and *Whipsaw.* Then pass the bottom of the Erikson triple chair and continue down to River Run Plaza via the *Missouri* trail and ride the gondola again. As usual, whenever you have a choice between a traditional fixed-grip chair and a high-speed detachable (chair or gondola), my advice is to take the high-speed lift.

Keystone Style, Keystone Snow

Keystone is a fine cruising mountain, and on a mountain this friendly, speed adds excitement. The average Keystone skier is nowhere near as skilled as Aspen skiers and nowhere near as well dressed as Vail skiers, but I'm always struck by how gutsy skiers here are. There's a go-for-it attitude in the air, and Keystone skiers, even less-experienced novices, are simply not timid. I find that there's also an intriguing relationship between skiing style and snow surface.

Keystone is both the pioneer and acknowledged leader among Colorado resorts when it comes to artificial snow. Today the whole front face of the mountain is covered 100 percent by the snowmaking system. This is not to say that Colorado snow is unpredictable or sparse, but the truth is, no ski area in the world can guarantee good skiing conditions in November and

December every year. Snowmaking alters the toss-of-the-coin uncertainty in early-season vacation planning, and at Keystone the early season (sometimes from mid-October on) is always safe. They not only make a lot of early snow, they groom the daylights out of it, which is crucial because if left untended artificial snow turns to ice. At its best, it's still a hard surface, and the only way to make such hard snow agreeable is to throw a lot of money, man-power, and machinery at it: tilling, raking, scraping, texturing, churning up the surface with "powder makers" and other hydraulic gizmos that sprout from modern snowcats.

This constant grooming and care of Keystone's artificial snow means that you can just forget about moguls on the front face—there aren't any; this is one reason skiers like to move fast. Also, the snowfall in this part of Summit County is steady, but it comes in small doses rather than big dumps; fast-skiing, intermediate skiers, who typically skid most of their turns, are forever scraping the new snow off to the sides of the runs. In short, the smooth, hard snow encourages a fast, skidded style of skiing, and this style in turn helps keep the snow smooth, scraped, and hard. At Keystone, especially on the front face of the mountain, this rather hard, artificial-snow surface tends to persist all season. It's a rarity in Colorado.

Such snow would be a definite drawback for front-face Keystone skiing if this mountain weren't so accommodating, gracious, and well managed. Of course, it's a trade-off. In return for this harder snow surface, skiers have a longer and earlier season, and, on occasional dry years, a better one. But this is only the front of the mountain. Let's look at the other side.

North Peak

To reach North Peak, part two of the Keystone experience, you ski down one of three trails from the top (the Summit House at 11,640 feet) of Keystone mountain and enter a different world. North Peak is really another separate, forested peak behind the main mountain. Here, too, trails have been cut through the trees, but they are a good deal steeper and more stimulating for advanced skiers. A number of runs are also equipped with snow-making, but the snow never has that scraped feeling of the front mountain, due in large part to the fact that the style of skiing changes back here. Turns shorten, and the terrain demands a more conscious, more curvy, less straight-ahead style.

Diamond Back and *Mineshaft*, the two black runs that take you down to North Peak, are usually rivers of black bumps. *Mineshaft* is shorter, but both runs have a curious sun exposure, which means there's seldom good skiing until the bumps soften during the afternoon. The main way down to North Peak, a blue beauty called *Mozart*, may well be the finest run at Keystone. It is spacious, inviting, and extremely varied: Random tree islands block and then reveal views; the terrain is constantly folding and rippling into small microgullies, drops, and momentary sidehills. An irresistible invitation to playful skiing, *Mozart* is a great name for a great run.

On the front side of North Peak, served by the Santiago triple chair, you have your choice of mostly bumped-out black and blue runs. Surprise: For those skiers who don't yet feel at home in bumps, these are the friendliest mogul runs in Colorado (well, actually there are a couple of similar runs at Steamboat, but you'll find more user-friendly bumps here). What makes these bumps so easy to ski? Steady, sustained pitches rather than drops and flats. And perhaps also the fact that two categories of skiers are conspicuously absent: inexperienced skiers who wander onto bump runs by accident and chop off the back sides of bumps with panic pivots; and, equally destructive, the real hot shots who ski straighter, faster lines and hammer rounded gullies into narrow slots with the tails of their skis. As an instructor, my eyes light up when I ski North Peak runs. This is just the sort of inviting bump terrain I would choose to introduce good skiers to the esoteric pleasures of mogul skiing. You'll usually find one or two bumpless runs that have been recently groomed, but generally the front side of North Peak is all bump skiing of a pleasant, almost relaxing, variety. Don't miss it.

Like Keystone's main mountain, North Peak has a backside too, but it's more of a skiers' bridge to the next mountain than a skiing zone in its own right. Two parallel blue runs, *Anticipation* and *Spillway*, take skiers down to the Outback, and a single green trail, *Fox Trot*, provides an easy, roundabout, low-angle path back to the base of the North Peak's front side.

But North Peak still has a couple of other treats. On its summit, which is only 20 feet higher than the summit of Keystone mountain at 11,660 feet, you'll find one of the most handsome mountain restaurants of any Colorado resort: a beautiful log structure called the Outpost. The main eating hall in the Outpost is so attractive that you want to rush right into the cafeteria and fill your tray. But hold on. Next door in the same building is something even better, a sit-down restaurant called the Alpenglow Stube. Nowadays, there are quite a few other sit-down restaurants at Colorado ski resorts: the Cookshack at Vail, Spruce Saddle at Beaver Creek, Hazie's and Ragnar's at Steamboat, and La Baita on Aspen Mountain. But the Alpenglow Stube on Keystone's North Peak wins the sweepstakes. And I'm not just talking about the rather charming old-world decor. The food is a cut above. Like most fancy on-mountain restaurants, lunch reservations are needed. But at the Stube you can usually be even more spontaneous, walk in without reservations and still sit at the counter just on the other side of the open kitchen, and talk with the cooks while they perform their culinary magic for you. After a long morning blasting down the Outback, a gourmet lunch at the Alpenglow is hardly sinful.

The Outback, the next mountain we're going to visit, is the farthest from Keystone's base. So how do you get there early enough to ski yourself silly and still get back to the top of North Peak for lunch? Keystone's second gondola is the answer. Its cables are strung between the main peak and the Outpost on top of North Peak, and the ride is a short one. Now I'm going to let the cat out of the bag. My favorite strategy for a perfect day at Keystone is to ride the Skyway Gondola to the top of Keystone Mountain, take the Outpost Gondola over to North Peak, put on your skis, and dive down *Anticipation* to the Outback and ski there till around 11 A.M.; only then start working your way slowly back to the front. You'll be skiing the Outback, North Peak, and Keystone in that order while most Keystone visitors are busy skiing the reverse order. In this way, you'll find yourself moving against the natural flow of skier traffic, and you'll generally avoid lift lines and bottlenecks even on the busiest weekends. Now that the Outback is firmly in our sights, let's take a closer look.

The Outback: Keystone's Third Mountain

In Colorado, the runs on Keystone's Outback are comparable only to those on the Campground side of Snowmass. Long, beautifully cut lines drop straight down the fall line. No distracting or boring flats. No nasty surprises of any sort. The pitch is predictable and sustained. The grooming is impeccable. In short, this is probably the best skiing at Keystone.

For a change, the finest run over here may be the one right under the Outback Express Lift. *Elk Run* is very wide, and the feeling of skiing down a natural crest is delicious. The runs next door are all blue, but they are the least boring blue runs I can think of because of their splendid, but never too steep, pitch. Even dyed-in-the-wool experts will probably prefer these long runs to the shorter black ones farther to the left of the quad (when looking up) simply because cruising at this pitch is so rare. In our Keystone overview, I've already mentioned that these long blue runs are often groomed on one side only. This enables you to dip in and out of moguls as often or as much as you like. A short athletic workout and then, before your legs are too tired, cut out to the groomed side and carve some big 100-foot turns.

The farther you go from the Outback quad, the narrower the runs and the more they begin to resemble glades. On tough runs like *Timberwolf* and *Bushwacker* or easier ones like *Wolverine* and *Wildfire* you can dance through trees along both edges of the Outback, and the only price you'll pay is a rather longish traverse back to the quad. On the trail map, two black diamond bowls, *North Bowl* and *South Bowl,* are shown above and behind the top of the Outback Express quad. Obviously these are meant as hike-to terrain, open only when the patrol judges them to be safe. I've never skied the Outback when these bowls were open, so it's best not to count on them.

Keystone by Night

Night skiing is well known in some parts of the country (in the East and Midwest it's an accepted way for urban ski hordes to get maximum benefit from small nearby areas), but Keystone is the only major area in Colorado to offer night skiing, and, like everything else they've done, they've done it well. The gondola is the main route up at night, although the Argentine and Montezuma lifts or the Peru Express run at night, providing beginners access to some gentler green trails like *Schoolmarm*. Some 13 runs are well lit. If you're spending a week in Summit County, this is definitely worth a night just for the change of scenery. Long eerie runs in the iridescent purple shadows cast by vapor lamps, a tent of high-altitude stars, a carpet of moon-gray snow—all the ingredients of a truly surrealistic evening.

Keystone Village Tips

Skating on the frozen lake is a must. It too is lit up at night, and rental skates are available. Probably the best Keystone dinner is at The Ranch, a refurbished log cabin on the nearby golf course. But an even more romantic place to dine is not in Keystone itself but a ten-minute drive up Montezuma Road toward the old ghost town of Montezuma. I mean Ski Tip Ranch, a wood-and-plaster, Austro-alpine hideaway that was hand-built by Max Dercum, the man who started Keystone. The Dercum family has sold Ski Tip, but the romance lives on; it's a lovely inn too, but you don't have to stay at Ski Tip to dine there.

To tell the truth, as attractive as I find the village development at Keystone—clean, unpretentious architecture terraced down the hillside from a wonderfully bold concrete-and-glass main lodge, with a series of pedestrian walks and plazas, and dramatic views over the skating lake toward the ski mountain—this village just isn't big enough, active enough, or diverse enough to keep you stimulated for a whole week. A second village center, River Run, is growing up around the base of the River Run gondola. But much of what I've just said about Keystone's original village center applies here too. Handsome condos and a few attractive shops don't add up to a real mountain town.

Of course, in Summit County that isn't a tragedy. From Keystone you're only a short drive from three other serious ski mountains, two of which have their own base-area/village complexes. Even nearer is the Dillon/Silverthorne area, the rambling, high-altitude suburbs around Lake Dillon, just off I-70 (you drive through this area en route to Keystone). Even though Keystone Village is the nicest place to stay in the east end of Summit County, a lot of Keystone skiers stay in and around Dillon and save money.

There are also several good restaurants in the Dillon area. There is at least one all-time classic: a barnlike Mexican restaurant and honky-tonk, the Old

Dillon Inn, just a block or two the other side of I-70 when you follow the main drag in from Keystone. Generations of ski bums, instructors, and lift operators have found happiness in the dark, dense atmosphere of the Dillon Inn. Maybe you will too.

KEYSTONE DATA

Keystone Statistics

Total vertical feet	2,900 feet
Base elevation	9,300 feet
Summit elevation	11,640 feet
Longest run	3 miles
Average annual snowfall	320 inches
Number of lifts	15
	1 high-speed gondola; 2 high-speed quad chairs; 2 triple chairs; 6 double chairs; 4 surface lifts
Uphill capacity	19,582 skiers per hour
Skiable terrain	599 acres
Opening date	late October
Closing date	May
Snowboarding	No!

North Peak Statistics

Vertical feet	1,620 feet
Base elevation	10,040 feet
Summit elevation	11,660 feet
Longest run	2.5 miles
Number of lifts	3
	1 gondola 1 quad (fixed-grip) 1 chair 1 triple chair
Uphill capacity	5,200 skiers per hour
Skiable terrain	249 acres

The Outback Statistics

Vertical feet	1,740 feet
Base elevation	10,460 feet
Summit elevation	12,200 feet
Longest run	2.5 miles
Number of lifts	1 high-speed quad
Uphill capacity	1,800 skiers per hour
Skiable terrain	889 acres

Transportation

By car A 90-minute drive (in good road and weather conditions) from Denver. Take I-70 west through the Eisenhower Tunnel to the Dillon exit, #205, then 6 miles east on U.S. 6.

By bus or limo From the Denver International Airport.

Key Phone Numbers

Ski Area Information
   (970) 468-2316
Snow Report (970) 496-4111
Reservations for Keystone
   Condos and Keystone Lodge
   (888) 222-9298
www.snow.com

Hard, Icy Snow

It's a matter of regional pride to assert that there are never icy conditions in the Rockies. Of course, it isn't true. But it's certainly fair to say that there is much, much less ice in the Rockies than skiers from both coasts are used to. All mountains experience very "firm" conditions whenever and wherever artificial snowmaking systems have been used. Sometimes, as in the case of a World Cup race course, this hard surface is a real advantage; most of the time it's a pain simply because everyone skis better on perfect packed powder. Here are a few techniques and tips to help you fight back.

The two main problems that plague skiers on very hard snow are overturning and overedging. The first, overturning, is a natural occurrence because on a slick, hard surface, there is much less friction between skis and snow. That means that once you twist your skis sideways into a turn, they just keep on turning. Nothing slows down or inhibits this turning, pivoting action, and before you know it you are skidding sideways in a straight line rather than carving a clean arc. At this point, most skiers compound the problem by trying to "dig in" or edge their skis harder to stop such skidding. It doesn't work; in fact, the harder, or icier, the slope is, the less good it does to strongly edge your skis. Real masters on hard, icy snow try to edge their skis just barely enough to hold, knowing that if they overdo it, their skis will immediately start to chatter and slip. So what to do?

Your first step will be to quiet down all your movements, and try to make what I call the minimum start to your turns. That is, simply shift onto the new ski and wait. . . . It takes a second for something to happen but this is exactly what you want: a slow, progressive start to the turn, in which your weighted ski will carve slowly around. If you get impulsive and give one or both skis a powerful twist, then it's all over—you will have initiated a skid, rather than a turn. As long as your skis are primarily slicing forward rather than moving sideways, relatively little edging is required to keep them "on track." Once they've begun to skid out on a very hard, scraped surface, however, no amount of edging will produce a good turn.

Since the edge of your turning ski doesn't bite or grip this "firm" snow very well, the distribution of weight along the edge of that ski becomes critical. If you put too much weight on the front or on the back of your ski, the tail will break loose in a skid. So it is important to distribute your weight evenly along the whole edge of the carving ski, or, to put it another way, to stand evenly on the whole edge of that foot, neither on the ball nor on the

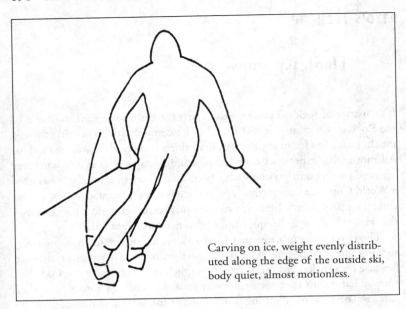

Carving on ice, weight evenly distributed along the edge of the outside ski,
body quiet, almost motionless.

heel. One way to maintain this even, unvarying weight distribution is to
calm down any upper-body activity, especially arm movement. Spread your
arms in a poised, balanced position and keep them there. On icy snow, any
sudden arm-hand-pole movement is enough to make your skis skid right out
from under you.

And that's your basic strategy for very hard, icy snow. Calm, almost
motionless skiing—as though you were skiing over acres of delicate, white
eggs, careful not to break a single one with a sudden movement. Try it; it
works.

ARAPAHOE BASIN

Arapahoe Basin, or "A-Basin" to natives, with a summit elevation of 13,050
feet, is usually thought of as the highest ski area in Colorado—although
Loveland is really in the same league. It is certainly one of the oldest, and its
season is the longest by several months. Like Loveland, Arapahoe is one of
those small ski areas that feels much larger, precisely because it's set at a high
altitude, among large and dramatic mountains.

A-Basin is tucked into a kind of fold in the Continental Divide, just over the western side of the actual divide, and a few hairpin turns down from the summit of Loveland Pass on what used to be the main road west from Denver. Since the construction of the Eisenhower Tunnel, I-70 speeds motorists under the Continental Divide into Summit County, and nowadays most skiers get to Arapahoe by driving up the canyon from Keystone (or taking a shuttle bus from Keystone). For a long time I thought of Arapahoe as Keystone's older brother (it is older) or sometimes as Keystone's little brother (it's certainly much smaller), because A-Basin was owned and managed by Keystone. But when Vail Resorts bought both Keystone and Breckenridge a few years ago they cut this little brother loose. In fact, the high-alpine flavor of A-Basin skiing is so different than anything else in Summit County that it certainly merits a chapter of its own. This is genuine, white-on-white, above-timberline skiing in a splendid remote setting.

Quick Tour of an Alpine Area

There are only four full-size chairlifts at A-Basin (plus one wee beginners' chair), but despite this, the mountain offers a lot of variety. The main chair up from the base lodge is the Exhibition triple, and both this lift and the runs it serves are still in the forested zone. Above Exhibition Lift, the scene changes. The trees thin and rapidly disappear. Skiers can enjoy every square meter of several wide-open, rolling bowls. This upper area is served by two more lifts, the Norway and Lenawee double chairs; skiing up here is marked a sort of generic blue (with the exception of one easier angled hollow known as *Dercum's Gulch,* named after the same Max Dercum who built Ski Tip Ranch and started both the Keystone and A-Basin ski areas). None of these slopes is really steep, but they are constantly varied and have so much character that no one could be bored. When you ski this sort of treeless terrain, it's always possible to dive into beautiful short steep faces right in the middle of an otherwise easy stretch of mountain, pitches that most skiers might avoid but that you can take advantage of if you wish, because everything, literally, is skiable. However, if you're looking for more adrenaline, A-Basin can provide it.

Arapahoe Adventures

There are two sorts of adventurous skiing here: untracked off-piste lines on the East Wall and breathtakingly pure, steep bump skiing in and around Pallavicini.

The East Wall is more or less the whole steep mountain flank that you see off to your right when you look down from the top of the Lenawee Lift. It's pretty obvious where the skiing stops and the steeper rocky mountainside continues on toward high craggy ridges that overhang the whole area.

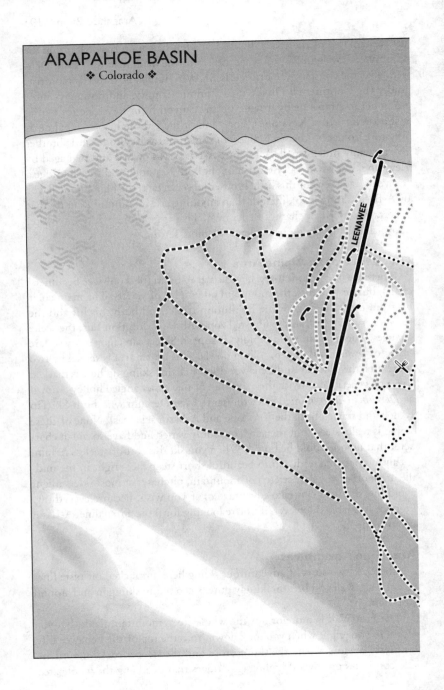

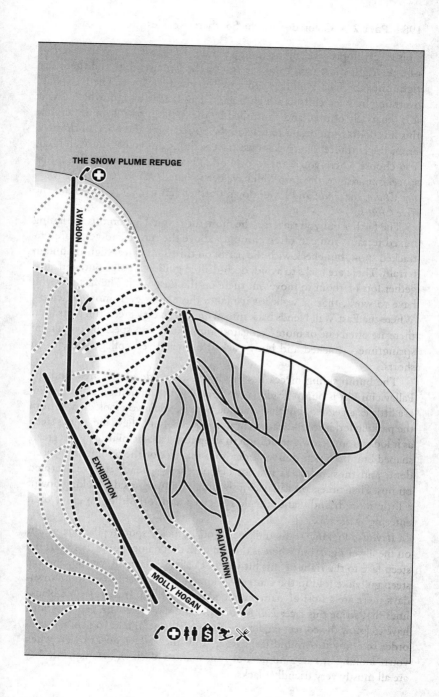

This is very impressive, alpine-feeling terrain. To ski the East Wall, take *Falcon*, the right-most run, from the top of the Lenawee Lift and then turn right onto the East Wall through a well-marked entrance. The East Wall, overhung by steep cliffs, is a high-potential avalanche hazard, which is why it is separately opened and controlled by the A-Basin patrol. In terrain like this it is doubly important to read all the posted signs and obey all closures. From the entrance a long ski-track traverse leads out across the Wall itself. You choose where you want to peel off. There are no runs out here, just space, but areas of the East Wall have been named: *North Pole Plunge, Corner Chute*, the *Falls*, and lower down (farther across), *T.J. Cornice* and the *Tree Chutes*.

The farther out you traverse, the more turns you'll log on this intriguing mixed terrain. You can often climb up above the traverse to get more untracked snow, but check with the patrol on this. This is real high-mountain terrain. There are rocks to avoid, deep-drifted gullies to scope out, and altogether lots of room to move out there on the East Wall. The fact that you have to work, that is, walk for it makes these lines even more delicious. Where the East Wall blends back into *Wrangler*, an easy green run at its foot, there are often one or more "kangaroo jumps" that are especially popular in springtime—tracked and body-packed by wild-eyed college students in shorts.

The bump skiing mecca lies on the western side of the area, and the Pallavicini Lift is bump headquarters. Possibly the reputation of Pallavicini is a little exaggerated, but that's natural because when you look up at it from the parking lot, it seems dead vertical. It is steep, but believe me, not as steep as it looks from below. In addition to steepness, Pallavicini usually has great-shaped bumps. Skiers don't wander onto this face of the mountain by accident, and those who ski it a lot belong there—hence the well-formed bumps. First-timers on Pallavicini should find the right side, looking down, a little more friendly and a little less steep and forbidding to enter than entering at the top.

If you're looking at the trail map, you'll quickly spot the Pallavicini Lift on the lower right, but where is the run with that name? Gone. For years the steep face to the right of this lift was just called Pallavicini, period, and the steep gullylike fold in the center was known as Pallavicini Couloir. Nowadays there are a host of names attached to the black (really double black) lines that stripe this face: *Pali Main St., The Spine, Pali Face*, etc. You don't have to know the correct tag for the part of Pallavicini that you are skiing in order to enjoy it. Around the corner from the Pallavicini Lift (left when you're looking up) are a number of runs marked black on the map, but they are all mostly very friendly blacks.

Seasonal Tips, Extra Dimensions

I haven't yet told you the most important thing about A-Basin. Ski there in spring! Yes, the area is indeed open for the whole season, from mid-November on, but in winter it can be deadly cold and windy; skiing on tree-sheltered runs at Keystone is usually a better bet unless a big snowstorm has just passed through. In that case, Arapahoe will have more powder to track up than Keystone, which is not only lower, but always more crowded.

A-Basin really comes into its own in springtime. The high-altitude sun bouncing off the reflector-oven walls of its high alpine bowls quickly transforms the snow into the most consistent corn in Colorado. When other areas are closing in early April, the scene at A-Basin is just warming up, literally and figuratively. All the good Colorado skiers I know treat themselves to an after-the-season ski season at Arapahoe. It's part of the normal ritual and tradition of skiing in this state. Of course, you have to change your strategy a bit. No one wants to ski icy moguls in the early morning (see the following Ski Tech pages for more spring-snow strategies). In spring there is an optimum time slot for almost every exposure.

You'll also want to eat at the outdoor barbecue at the warming hut on top of Exhibition Lift, or bring a picnic and find a flat, dry rock somewhere under the East Wall. On an average-to-good snow year the lifts keep running until June. But as May wears on and the snow, even at 12,000 feet, starts to thin out, Arapahoe skiers often drive up to Loveland Pass, and with a little hiking along gentle ridge tops, they can usually find beautiful untracked corn-snow lines leading back down to the highway on either side of the pass. One of the most famous (or infamous) out-of-bounds runs is a steep, smooth face called *The Professor* that drops down across the road from the A-Basin parking lot. *The Professor* is completely outside and separate from the ski area; it's uncontrolled and can be (and has been) a death trap in winter. Don't take foolish risks for a few powder turns; it's far better to wait until the late spring weather has solidified all the out-of-area slopes around Loveland Pass before hiking out there for an adventure. If the springtime corn snow up on the pass is still fairly solid and not mushy in late morning, then it's most likely safe.

ARAPAHOE BASIN DATA

Mountain Statistics

Vertical feet	2,250 feet
Base elevation	10,800 feet
Summit elevation	13,050 feet
Longest run	1.5 miles
Average annual snowfall	360 inches
Number of lifts	5
	1 triple chair
	4 double chairs
	(1 is a beginner lift)
Uphill capacity	6,200 skiers per hour
Skiable terrain	490 acres
Opening date	mid-November
Closing date	mid-June
Snowboarding	Yes

Transportation

By car A 15-minute drive up the canyon from Keystone; or over Loveland Pass on the Highway 6 cutoff from I-70 just before the Eisenhower Tunnel.

Key Phone Numbers

Ski Area Information
  (970) 468-2316
Snow Report (970) 496-4111

LITO'S TECH TIP

Corn Snow and Springtime Strategies

Spring snow conditions can be both the best and the worst surfaces a skier ever gets to play on or curse all on the same day. Variable, challenging, and sublime, spring snow is the result of repeated daily melting and nightly freezing. During the day this snow goes through three distinct stages.

Early in the morning, spring snow is simply ice; it's not the smooth polished ice that racers love to hone their carving skills on. Morning ice in spring is lumpy brutal stuff with every rut, every track, and every glob of slush thrown up the previous evening turned into a rock-hard obstacle. Icy slopes on a spring morning have no redeeming qualities.

As the snow surface melts toward midday, it mellows into a condition skiers call "corn." Corn snow is to skiers what sweet corn is to the inhabitants of Garrison Keillor's Lake Wobegon, a delight that banishes all the trials of their existence. This is the ultimate snow surface, on which a good skier can do anything. Skis bite cleanly, hold effortlessly, slide smoothly, and come alive.

Alas, perfect corn conditions only last from about 10:30 A.M. to 1 P.M. Then, as the thawing penetrates deeper into the snowpack, corn turns to slush that is challenging, annoying, and occasionally dangerous to ski in. As usual, there are tricks to tame it.

Early in the morning you have two choices: sleep in or head directly for the eastern-facing slopes that have already been thawing in the sun for a couple of hours. Lumpy spring ice can't be tamed and shouldn't be skied. In fact, the idea of watching the sun and choosing your slopes accordingly works all day long. If eastern-facing slopes are the first to "corn up," they are also the first to turn slushy by early afternoon. At that time you should have already moved around to the opposite, western exposures that are just starting to get good.

Unlike lumpy morning ice, afternoon slush can be skied well. The problem is just the opposite of a smooth icy slope where there often isn't enough friction. Here there is too much resistance to your skis' movement. If you twist your skis violently, they won't skid; they'll simply catch or stick in the gluelike snow, knocking you off balance or worse. The remedy is simple: minimum twisting action and longer turns, allowing your skis to slice forward much more than they move sideways.

On late spring afternoons, moguls can become dangerously soft. The danger, in fact, lies in burying the front of your skis in a soft bump.

At that point only perfectly functioning bindings stand between you and an injury. To avoid this, try to slide diagonally into slushy moguls so that your ski tips never hit the backside of the bump directly. Or better yet, quit early and go swimming. After three hours of sweet corn, why fight it?

BRECKENRIDGE

Breckenridge is the princess of Summit County ski areas. Like its neighbors, Breckenridge offers a lot of skiing on an up-to-date modern mountain, but unlike Keystone and Copper, Breckenridge is a genuine Colorado ski town.

So many of Colorado's ski towns were mining towns, yet they're all different. Even today, with T-shirt shops fast becoming the universal common denominator of the American resort landscape, their differing architecture tells a very different story. Aspen was a silver mining center, Crested Butte a proletarian coal mining community, and Telluride a remote gold camp, while Breckenridge was a famous placer mining district. Surreal gravel bars and placer gravel mounds greet you as you drive in from Lake Dillon. In winter these ghostly white lumps might be the leftover moguls from a vanished race of giant skiers. The Ten Mile Range above town echoes these same domelike shapes in large white rolls that make skiers drool. No need to drool. Peaks 8 and 9 are spider-webbed with lifts, Peak 10 has recently come on line, and now the high summit bowls of both Peak 7 and Peak 8 are open (and, maybe more important, avalanche controlled) for skiers willing to walk uphill for their adventures.

Take your choice: an above-timberline bowl, relaxed and mellow trail cruising, the largest, longest novice slopes, or some of the narrowest and gnarliest bump runs in the state. All in all, Breckenridge is a very well-balanced ski mountain—lots of terrain for the "rest of us," plus some unusually inviting first-timer and beginner runs. And there's the added plus of downtown Breckenridge, a multicolored, Victorian main-street strip running like the border stripe of a hand-woven rug beneath mixed layers of condos and forest.

A Breckenridge Overview

Coincidentally, the Ten Mile Range has ten major summits, logically although prosaically named Peaks 1 through 10, like a row of giant windswept milemarkers. The town of Breckenridge lies under the slopes of Peak 9 at one end of the range. And while the ski area doesn't reach all the way to the top of this imposing series of peaks, the rounded frontal ridges and the deep-cleft valleys between Peaks 8, 9, and 10 define the playing field at Breckenridge and divide the area into distinct zones to directly shape your skiing day.

On the north end of the ski area, Peak 8 offers steeper skiing, open bowls, and a graceful mixture of sparse timberline trees with open slopes for serious skiers.

Even though it isn't lift-served, Peak 7 is the northward extension of this open-bowl terrain. It is big and exciting, and since one must hike uphill a long way (at high altitude) to ski it, I should probably add that it's for even more serious skiers.

Moving south from the high bowls of Peaks 7 and 8, we encounter the valley or gully between Peaks 8 and 9. This area is intense: steep, "rad," and thoroughly bumped out. On both sides of this drainage, but especially on the so-called North Face of Peak 9, young bump specialists find the tightest, most challenging moguls at Breckenridge. Most of the 108 acres of skiable terrain added to the resort in 1997 lie in this area, mostly steep and intriguing chutes.

Peak 9 itself is a mountain for the masses. Its front side is all user-friendly, nonchallenging skiing. The lower half is strictly for beginners. The upper half of Peak 9 is low-key, low-intermediate-level skiing.

Moving southward one more mountain, Peak 10, which was opened by a new quad lift a few years ago, completes the Breckenridge spectrum with what I'd call classic upper-intermediate skiing: blue and black runs that aren't too demanding but still keep your attention.

Once you understand this zone-by-zone overview of what can otherwise be a very spread-out and confusing ski mountain, it's duck soup to tailor your Breckenridge experience to your own level of skill and your own desire for challenge or ease. We'll look at each zone in more detail, starting with the friendliest skiing Breckenridge has to offer.

Peak 9: A Perfect Warm-Up Mountain

Peak 9 is the middle mountain at Breckenridge and offers pretty much middle-of-the-road, or middle-of-the-piste, skiing. It's also the mountain you will reach if you take a lift directly up from town. The lower slopes are served by Colorado's very first high-speed super chair, the Quicksilver quad, and they are a pleasant maze of extremely gentle green beginners' runs. This is Breckenridge's main novice ski zone, and it's just too flat for experienced skiers to do anything more than schuss on through. This is also where I would recommend that beginners take lessons at Breckenridge, even though there is a second ski school location at the base of Peak 8 that also has a small zone of easy green practice runs. There's much, much more easy terrain over here at the base of Peak 9, and what beginners need most, in addition to a patient instructor, is lots and lots of inviting suitable terrain.

The Beaver Run high-speed quad that starts just a little uphill from the Quicksilver quad can take you right to the top of Peak 9 in one shot. The upper half of Peak 9 is laced with attractive, meandering blue runs—the sort of intermediate skiing that doesn't pose any special challenges or offer any special rewards, just basic wandering trails steep enough to slide along at a good clip but never steep enough to make you want to put on the brakes. For me these runs don't have much charm, but I recognize that they are exactly what an enormous number of skiers need in order to develop early parallel skills and confidence. Peak 9 is a great learning mountain, and even for better skiers it's a good place to warm up and get back on your ski legs the first day of a Summit County vacation.

Peak 8: The Peak Experience at Breckenridge

Peak 8 has a good deal more character. It lies north of Peak 9 (to the right looking up from town) and is set back from and above the village. Its higher altitude partly explains its alpine feeling. You reach Peak 8 by a winding ten-minute drive up Ski Hill Road from town or by skiing across from Peak 9, which can be daunting for nonbumpers unless they follow an easy green catwalk called *Union*.

Stronger skiers in search of excitement and intriguing terrain will prob-

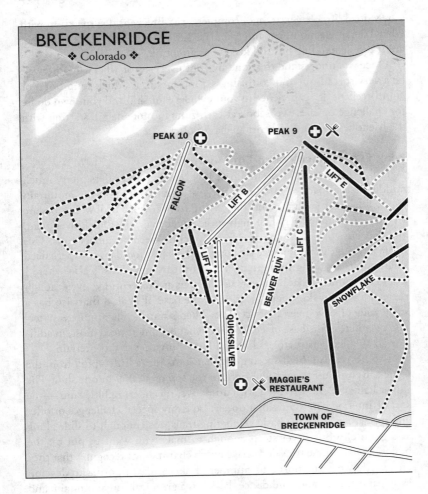

ably spend most of their Breckenridge ski time on Peak 8. The lower half of this mountain is striped with steeper blue and moderate black runs whose most characteristic features are big swooping rolls and dips (very different from the more uniform pitch of Peak 9 runs). Although these are all trails cut through thick forest, they don't seem as closed-in as many forested trails do.

Just above the forest on the far left side of Peak 8 (looking up), half into and half out of the white world above the timberline, is a collection of ten runs, from *Quandry* across to *Psychopath,* that are collectively known as the

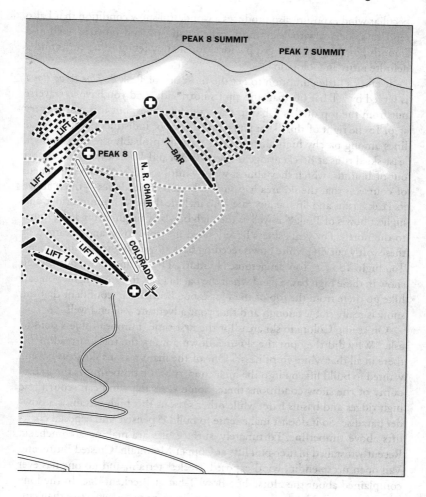

back bowls of Peak 8. These are more designated lines than real runs, fanning out and down from Lift 6, the Snowbird Lift. This is an ideal area for creative skiing: threading new paths through partly timbered, partly open, reasonably steep, but never scary, terrain. It's an area to explore as well as just ski.

But the real magic lives on the upper slopes of Peak 8, where the ski area emerges into wide-open, treeless terrain. *Contest Bowl* and *Horseshoe Bowl* are the centerpieces: smooth, steep, white basins that remind me a lot of the high open bowls at Mammoth Mountain in California's High Sierra. Their peculiar wind exposure also produces a wonderful snow condition that I also tend to associate with Mammoth called wind-packed powder: cold and smooth powder, hard but grippy, ideal for snappy rebounding turns and a definite rarity in Colorado.

It takes a little gumption to get the most out of Peak 8. *Horseshoe Bowl* is served by a T-bar lift that runs up its north side, and you have to traverse out from the top of this T-bar to reach the best lines, but it is worth every step. To the right of this T-bar you'll find a zone of indistinct black and blue lines among patchy high-altitude trees that are probably the least-known, least-skied runs at Breckenridge. *Forget-Me-Not* and *White Crown* feel almost out of bounds, which they almost were—until recently. What's happened, of course, is that the ski area has pushed back its boundaries—those above its Peak 8 runs and lifts, at any rate—to include the actual summit ridge and highest bowls of Peak 8 as well as the high bowls of neighboring Peak 7, just to the north. For years skiers have looked up from town and dreamed of these softly curving white bowls receding back toward higher, farther ridges. Too high. Too far. Too dangerous. No more. The ski area now controls the snow in these high basins, and when the patrol gives the green light, you can hike up there from the top of the Horseshoe Bowl T-bar, confident that the snow is really stable enough and that your adventure will end well.

On seeing Colorado ski areas for the first time, European skiers tend to ask, "Why did they put the ski area down among the trees instead of up there in all that white emptiness?" One of the main reasons ski areas haven't wanted to build lifts up into the high country above timberline is the uncertainty of the snow conditions there. Some years the wind can scour these high ridges and basins bare, while other seasons this high terrain is a powder paradise. So it doesn't make sense to build expensive and exposed chairlifts above timberline. Fortunately, surface lifts are making a comeback. Recently installed platter-pull lifts at Copper Mountain, Crested Butte, and Vail open up splendid, wind-exposed, treeless terrain, and no one has ever complained about the Horseshoe Bowl T-bar at Breckenridge. In the long run, opening up high basins with surface lifts is more cost-effective than cutting new runs in dense forest; and it provides a perfect counterpoint to the sort of trail skiing usually served by modern high-speed quads.

So I'm hoping that the recent opening of Peak 7 and the top of Peak 8 to hiking skiers is not the end of the story. Allowing skiers to climb above the highest lifts is not quite the same as really making those upper slopes a part of the ski area. Breckenridge has had a series of different owners in recent years, but today it's run by Vail Resorts, which has added both Breckenridge and Keystone to its home-base resorts of Vail and Beaver Creek. It shouldn't be too hard for a ski company with this depth of experience to figure out how to provide lift access to these magical upper slopes. In the Alps it would have been done long ago, so why not here?

Bumpety, Bumpety, Bump

Bump skiers tend to hang out on the steep sides of the valley or gulch that separates Peak 8 from Peak 9, where you'll find the most demanding technical skiing at Breckenridge. I know that most Colorado skiers and most of the readers of this guidebook are not wild about bump skiing. But I think this zone is worth a special mention because of the importance of freestyle and mogul competition in the Breckenridge story. Breckenridge began to host international freestyle competitions — moguls, ballet, and aerials — years ago, fostering the development of this exciting, gymnastic branch of ski competition in a period when it was generally misunderstood and ignored. Naturally, with this freestyle background, Breckenridge was one of the first mountains in Colorado to encourage snowboarding. Bravo!

The difficult bump runs I mentioned are concentrated in two pods on either side of the gulch between Peaks 8 and 9. The runs on the north face of Peak 9 are the wildest, meanest, and the most fun when you survive them. Runs like *Mine Shaft* and *Devil's Crotch* are extremely narrow, sometimes only two or three moguls wide, and absolutely unrelenting. No flats, no rest spots. You just get in the groove and go. By comparison, the four double black diamond runs on the opposite south-facing Peak 8 side of the gulch, from *Southern Cross* to *Mach 1,* seem positively forgiving. They are almost as steep and every bit as moguled, but there's so much more room to maneuver that you are almost overwhelmed with choices. This whole zone provides a serious workout for strong skiers.

Peak 10: New Kid on the Block

Peak 10 is the newest lift-served addition at Breckenridge, opened up in one fell swoop by one new lift, naturally a super quad. You reach Peak 10 by skiing across from the upper slopes of Peak 9, or from town take the Quicksilver quad and cut a sharp left at the top. This is not nearly as big an area as the other two peaks, but it's a perfect complement to the rest of Breckenridge skiing. Peak 10 saves the southern end of Breckenridge from the dreaded epithet of "boring" because it adds precisely what the central slopes lack: stimulating, upper-intermediate skiing and even some seriously advanced pitches. On the left of the lift, looking up, you'll find the most popular Peak 10 skiing — easy blacks and solid blues. Personally, I find these runs, like so many recently cut trails in the West, a little too narrow. I don't know whether it's a case of ecological consciousness vis-à-vis tree cutting, timidity, or laziness, but ski areas today don't seem to be cutting runs as wide as they used to.

The surprise treats on Peak 10 are the harder runs to the north of the lift (that is, on the right side as you're riding up). *Spitfire* and *Corsair* are narrow, steep, and serious. But best of all is *The Burn,* a mountain flank where lightning and a forest fire did the sort of radical tree clearing that ski areas can't.

For years, skiers coasting down *Upper Lehman*, the gully run dividing Peaks 9 and 10, have looked up and thought of this steep open burn. Sometimes they would hike and traverse up into it to enjoy one perfect set of tracks. Now it's lift-served. In lighter snow years this steep flank of Peak 10 may not be open, but it still gives a lot of character and drama to this end of the mountain.

Breckenridge: Townscapes and Town Tips

Breckenridge is an honest, no-nonsense ski town with just enough history on Main Street to let you know it's been here for a long time; enough modern lodging blocks stacked up the hill behind Main Street to pamper an enormous number of skiers; enough garishly painted false fronts to suggest that someone is trying to turn this town into a cutesy little theme park for skiers; and enough locals who still care to make you hope it won't happen. One friend of mine calls Breckenridge a "middle-class Aspen." But I don't think that quite captures it, even though Breckenridge prices aren't nearly as alarming as Aspen's or Vail's.

You won't exactly need a map to orient yourself in Breckenridge, since Main Street is where everything is, where everything happens. It's a real walking street: human in scale, full of goodies, and a scene that will certainly take you more than one evening to explore.

My village favorites include the Terrace, the finest restaurant in town; and for variety and a different sort of atmosphere altogether, the Briar Rose, which has to qualify as Breckenridge's most traditional good restaurant; breakfasts and Mexican food at the Gold Pan; and, for when you tire of run-of-the-mill ski town shopping, visit the Hibberd-McGrath Gallery at the corner of Main Street and Ski Hill Road—no paintings or prints here, but museum quality "craftwork"—ceramics, weaving, assemblage, jewelry and metalwork, pieces of work by some of the country's top artisan/craftspeople—and shows that would not be out of place in New York or San Francisco.

BRECKENRIDGE DATA

Mountain Statistics

Vertical feet	3,398 feet
Base elevation	9,600 feet
Summit elevation	12,998 feet
Longest run	3.5 miles
Average annual snowfall	255 inches
Number of lifts	23
	6 high-speed quads
	1 triple chair
	7 double chairs
	9 surface lifts
Uphill capacity	30,625 skiers per hour
Skiable terrain	2,043 acres
Opening date	mid-November
Closing date	early May
Snowboarding	Yes

Transportation

By car A 90-minute drive in good weather and road conditions from Denver on I-70, west to the Breckenridge exit, #203, then south on Colorado Highway 9.

By bus or van From the Denver International Airport.

Key Phone Numbers

Ski Area Information
 (970) 453-5000
Snow Report (970) 453-6118
Reservations (970) 453-2918 or
 (800) 221-1091
www.snow.com

LITO'S TECH TIP

A Snowboarding Primer

Few things are as humbling or as stimulating to a good skier as abandoning the security of a sport already mastered to become, once again, an awkward beginner. This is true on cross-country skating skis, on telemark skis, on monoskis, and especially on snowboards. Recently, I strapped on one of these amazing contraptions for the first time and loved it. Here's a little of what I learned.

Which foot forward? Snowboarding, like surfing and skateboarding, is a sideways-standing sport. To discover your natural stance find an icy stretch of pavement or a frozen puddle, run a few feet, and let yourself slide across it. Which foot do you instinctively stretch forward? That's your front foot on a snowboard.

To get started, pick an easy hill with soft snow. What precisely does one do with a snowboard? There are several competing approaches in snowboarding instruction, but this is what worked for me. Go across the hill first.

You will gain more confidence and control, more quickly, if you develop a traversing/sideslipping/braking pattern first, before heading straight down the fall line. Unlike skiing, traversing across a slope on a snowboard is quite different depending on which way you're heading. You will have a backside traverse (back to the mountain) and a frontside traverse (facing the mountain). The backside traverse is a stronger, easier maneuver because the high plastic spoilers of most snowboard bindings give you more support in this direction—you can lean back against them to increase edging. On the frontside traverse you feel like you're standing on your toes, and it takes more strength to control the board. Experienced skiers seem to react differently to snowboards than those whose only experience of sliding over snow has been on a board. Instinctively, the skilled skier who tries snowboarding wants to develop strong edge control. The shortest route to this end is to use hard plastic snowboarding boots rather than soft Sorel-type, felt-lined boots and wraparound bindings. Hard boots greatly strengthen your frontside edging.

While you traverse the slope, flatten and sideslip your board from time to time; to stop, push the board away from you, twisting it up the hill, while you let it slip. And—very important—when you get in trouble, sit down! In fact, you can sit down and flip your board around between traverses until you're ready to turn downhill. As in skiing, the downhill turn is the soul of the sport, but don't try it until you feel comfortable just sliding sideways and across the hill. When you're ready, start your downhill turn by committing your body in the direction you want to go—leading with your front hand —and then swivel the board with your feet to catch up to where your body already is. The feeling is almost like falling into a turn, insecure but very effective.

This thumbnail sketch doesn't take the place of lessons, and nowadays most ski schools have become ski and snowboard schools, so it won't be hard to find good snowboarding lessons at most ski areas. Five years ago it would have been a challenge, ten years ago impossible. Good riding!

COPPER MOUNTAIN

Copper Mountain is a great place to ski, yet I have always felt frustrated that it wasn't as great a place for a complete winter vacation. That's about to change. I give Copper's mountain top marks for snow quality and for the natural skier's logic of its layout. But the resort facilities at its base never added up to a successful ski village. Copper has been an underachiever. As good as it is, it could, and should, be even better. And now it will be. This change in Copper Mountain's fortunes is due to its merger with Intrawest, the remarkable Canadian ski resort developer. Intrawest has done an extraordinary job of revitalizing the base village at Quebec's Mont Tremblant and has created a fabulous base village at Whistler in British Columbia. Already, they have completed a master plan for the sort of attractive, integrated, human-scale resort village that should have been planned and built from the beginning (instead of the characterless and chaotic collection of parking lots that Copper skiers have put up with for years). Generally, in this guide I've tried to describe only what already exists and I've avoided passing on the bright promises of resort PR material. But Intrawest has such a great track record and has already made such a major commitment to its plans for Copper Mountain that I have no hesitation in saying that this resort's time is about to come. A long-term $450 million expansion and redevelopment effort, guided by Eldon Beck, a brilliant mountain-resort planner, should do the trick (Intrawest spent $66 million to get started in the summer of 1998).

Imagine a mountain, a grand mountain, whose main axis seems to be horizontal rather than vertical, stretching sideways around the fork of an alpine valley rather than up toward the sky, and you'll get a sense of Copper's paradoxical topography. It sounds weird, but it skis great. Copper must have been designed by the great forest ranger in the sky just to keep different levels of skiers from getting in each other's hair. Looking up from the base you see a beginners' mountain on the far right, a steep bumped-out experts' mountain on the far left, and the smoothest gradation of ski terrain imaginable in between. From wherever you find yourself, you can move one run to the east and the skiing will be a fraction harder, one run farther west and the slope will be a tad gentler and easier. I don't know any other mountain in Colorado where average skiers can fine-tune the degree of challenge they'll face, or satisfaction they'll receive, on each run quite this easily.

Some Pluses on the Mountain

Copper Mountain was one of the first Colorado areas in recent years to make a serious effort to open up some of that tantalizing treeless skiing that's always been just out of reach above the timberline, and it's been a grand success. They've done it in a logical, step-by-step way: First they added a surface lift to open up *Spaulding* and *Hallelujah Bowls,* the handsome, treeless faces below the summit ridge of 12,441-foot Copper Peak. Then they built Lift S, opening some serious, even magical skiing in *Union Bowl* and on the slopes of Union Peak, the second summit on the long ridge that defines the front side of Copper's ski terrain. Most recently, they opened Copper Bowl, a large, mostly above-timberline cirque on the back sides of Union and Cop-

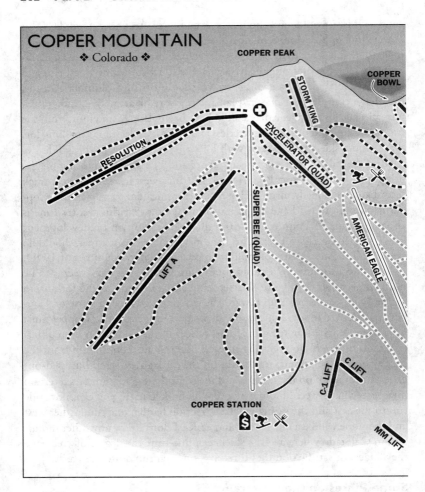

per peaks—a stunning "back bowls" experience, with over 700 acres and 1,200 feet of vertical in an alpine setting. And there are still more of these high back bowls waiting to be opened up by new lifts on the flanks of Tucker Mountain, Union Peak, and farther back on Jacque Peak. Let's keep our fingers crossed.

The conventional wisdom in Colorado used to be that skiers would find such above-timberline slopes too exposed to sun and wind, too difficult to enjoy, that only tree-sheltered powder was really any good, that lifts would be hard to run up there above timberline—in short, that it wouldn't work.

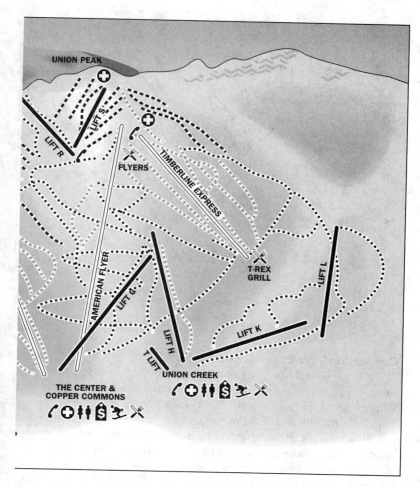

Copper has proven otherwise in the last few years. And Copper today is a far more exciting mountain to ski on than it was a decade ago.

Finally, Copper deserves kudos for its early-season slope preparation. They have a lot of snowmaking and use it well, generally opening a limited number of runs with very good cover long before Thanksgiving. The U.S. ski team has traditionally used Copper Mountain for early-season training, as do a lot of my friends, ski instructors, and ski fanatics. There's no doubt that Copper Mountain, along with Keystone, offers the best early-season skiing in Colorado.

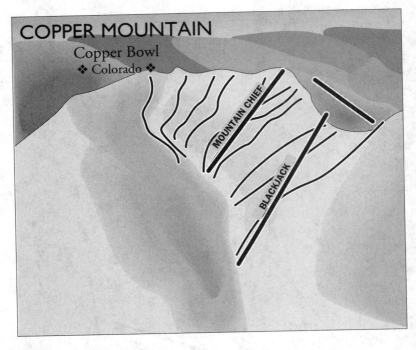

Copper for Less-Experienced Skiers

There are several base clusters at Copper. At the far left side (left when looking up, that is) the new Super Bee six-seat detachable rises from the East Village (part of the base redevelopment) and serves an area of steep, mostly moguled runs. This end of the mountain is really for strong skiers only, but less-skilled skiers can take the new six-pack lift and then traverse west to more moderate skiing on the center of the mountain. The Copper Commons base is the heart of the new village redevelopment project, right beneath the center of this wide mountain flank. This is where most skiers start their day, and from here two high-speed super quads will get you high on the mountain in a hurry. The American Eagle quad slants up and left, depositing skiers at a halfway point and mountain cafeteria called Solitude, in the heart of a zone with upper-intermediate runs. The other quad, the American Flyer, and a conventional chairlift, Lift G, both slant up and right toward more modest lower-intermediate and novice ski terrain. The final base pod, Union Creek, is still farther right along the base of the mountain, and its lifts serve very easy terrain. True novice skiers should start their day from Union Creek.

Such novices get short-changed at many Colorado ski areas, where you have to be a pretty fair intermediate-level skier to ski and enjoy the whole mountain, or "ski it from the top." But at Copper, very weak or inexperienced skiers can still have a major mountain adventure by riding the American Flyer quad and then circling around to the extreme far right or western side of the area on a gentle green run called *Soliloquy*. You can continue this far-west circle tour by skiing *Roundabout* or *West Ten Mile* over by Lift L, a very quiet, gentle backwater on the mountain. This makes an enormously long run, but the final return to Union Creek is almost painfully flat, with nature taking care of the slow-skiing injunction. For a better finish, cut right on *Soliloquy* where *Roundabout* branches off and follow *Woodwinds* to the bottom.

For another novice "mountain adventure"—still on all-green slopes but somewhat more demanding—ski down from the top of Lift R into *Copper Tone* and then follow it or *Care Free* to the bottom. Your two choices off the top of Lift R, *Union Park* or *Wheeler Creek,* are unusually attractive greens and have a totally different, upper-mountain feel than all the other easy skiing on the western side of Copper Mountain.

Copper for Strong Skiers

Very strong skiers will find happiness clear across the mountain on Lifts A and B, which rise from the valley floor, and the Resolution Lift higher up, as well as on the above-timberline zones I've mentioned: the slopes off the Storm King platter lift, *Union Bowl,* and, of course, *Copper Bowl.* The only consistent disappointment for strong skiers is *Enchanted Forest,* a mouthwatering area of half-open bowls and thin sparse trees descending from the shoulder of *Hallelujah Bowl* to the middle-mountain drainage of *Wheeler Creek* and *Copper Tone. Enchanted Forest* has almost never been open while I've visited Copper Mountain and seems to be especially exposed to wind, which scours its ridgelike upper slopes into veritable rock gardens.

The runs on Lifts A and B (now the new Super Bee) are medium-steep bump slopes that are straight and straightforward. Lift A (around the corner) gets less traffic, so its bumps often seem better shaped. But the best skiing of all for strong skiers is in the high bowls above timberline that I talked about earlier. This is the real thing. A nice linkup is to ski Spaulding Bowl from the top of the Storm King platter lift and continue down *Highline,* my favorite among the four black runs served by the Resolution Lift. It's obvious that the exciting new runs on Union Peak are an exception to my sweeping generalization about the skiing getting easier and easier as you move west across this mountain. That's okay; all generalizations have exceptions, and the east-west spectrum of decreasing difficulty is still a good overview of how Copper Mountain functions, especially on the front side. (And Copper Bowl on the back side is a world unto itself: wide, empty, delicious, almost treeless, an expert's playground . . .)

Copper for Intermediate Skiers

The only class of skier who may feel a little cheated on this mountain is the gung-ho, go-for-it intermediate skier who loves to ski hard and fast but doesn't really ski well enough to handle black slopes with ease. There aren't that many attractive blue runs in the center of the mountain that haven't been designated as slow-skiing zones, and this may become frustrating. Indeed, such skiers may feel more at home at Keystone.

Calmer intermediate skiers who are looking for friendly runs rather than speed will find lots of choice on what I call the middle mountain, around and above the Solitude Restaurant at the top of the American Eagle quad. *Copperopolis* and *Ptarmigan* off Lift E (recently upgraded to detachable quad status and now called the *Excelerator* lift) are delightful, and, to tell the truth, the black runs between these two are not very black. The two best intermediate cruisers back down the center of the mountain are *Collage* and *Bouncer*. The best would have been *Main Vein* under the American Eagle quad, but its slow-skiing designation tends to dampen one's spirits.

There is also good, fairly low-angle intermediate cruising on the Timberline Express, the high-speed quad that has replaced Lifts I and J. You can get there in a hurry by taking the American Flyer quad and dropping right down *I-Beam* or *Copperfield*. The blue skiing on Timberline will take you several hours to explore, and it's worth it.

Resort Design Revisited—Pros and Cons

In earlier editions of this guide, I ended my Copper Mountain chapter with a fairly tough critique of the successes and failures of its resort village design, or lack thereof, and I concluded that although the skiing at Copper Mountain was great, there just wasn't enough resort there to keep visitors stimulated for a week. Given the recent infusion of money and ideas from Intrawest, I have to say that as a resort, Copper Mountain today is a work in progress. I'm looking forward to writing an in-depth review of the "new" village that will appear here in the next few seasons. Given Eldon Beck's successes in creating wonderful pedestrian villages at Whistler and Mont Tremblant, I'm betting that in a few years, the Copper Mountain base resort will be a beauty. Stay tuned.

A lot of vacationing skiers prefer to sample a broad cross-section of Summit County skiing in the course of a week, skiing a couple of days at Copper Mountain, a few days at Keystone, and a couple of days at Breckenridge for a really diverse ski experience. Breckenridge is only a half-hour away, and Keystone is maybe a 45-minute drive from Copper. There's a wide choice of lodging, dining, and shopping in the different Summit County communities dotting the mountain valleys between these three ski resorts: Frisco, Dillon, and Silverthorne. For skiers taking this smorgasbord approach, the current lack of a lively village atmosphere at Copper Mountain isn't such a minus.

COPPER MOUNTAIN DATA

Mountain Statistics

Vertical feet	2,601 feet
Base elevation	9,712 feet
Summit elevation	12,313 feet (summit of Union Peak)
Longest run	2.8 miles
Average annual snowfall	280 inches
Number of lifts	20
	1 high-speed 6-place chair
	4 high-speed quads
	5 triple chairs
	6 double chairs
	4 surface lifts
Skiable terrain	2,433 acres
Opening date	mid-November
Closing date	late April
Snowboarding	Yes!

Transportation

By car A 1-hour-and-45-minute drive in good weather and road conditions from Denver, west on I-70 to the Copper Mountain exit, #195.

By bus or limo From Denver International Airport.

Key Phone Numbers

Ski Area Information
  (970) 968-2882
Snow Report (970) 968-2100
Reservations (800) 458-8386 or
  (970) 968-2882 ext.7881
www.ski-copper.com

LITO'S TECH TIP

Improving Your NASTAR Handicap

Copper Mountain has been associated with the United States Ski Team and with the Alpine National Championships for so many years that I thought it would be appropriate to talk about ski racing in this Tech Tip section. For most skiers, racing is synonymous with NASTAR, the national standard race held at hundreds of ski areas across the country: an open, single-flag, giant slalom type race where skiers compete against a base time established by a designated pacesetter. Almost every skier has run a NASTAR race or two, but very few have achieved their full potential between the gates. Here are two simple but vital tips to improve your NASTAR handicap.

Turn early. This is the key advice, and it's so simple I'm amazed more skiers haven't figured it out. Don't wait until you reach the flag that you have to turn around before starting that turn. If you start your turn at the flag itself, you will invariably turn too hard (to aim back at the next flag) and, in so doing, you will find yourself skidding down below the optimum fastest line between the two flags. Instead, start your turn well before you reach the flag, curving around in a wider, longer arc, so that when you actually pass the flag, your turn is complete and you are already aimed for the next flag! This way you will be making a rounder longer turn, but you won't skid down below the optimum line—which is where most skiers lose precious seconds.

Step your turns. This one is simple too. Instead of turning both skis, step dynamically to the side on the ski that is going to become the outside ski of your turn—for example: step laterally onto your right ski in order to turn left—and then make your turn completely on that ski. Why? By stepping to the side you can gain a foot or more of extra distance away from the pole, which gives you more room to complete your turn early, without waiting to get by the pole before making your move.

The final result: a smoother run, no sudden jerky turns, no skidding low in your turns, and a better NASTAR handicap. Maybe a gold this year. Five, four, three, two, one . . . Go!

The Soulful Southwest and Northern New Mexico

Crested Butte A gem! This intimate ski mountain welcomes skiers of all abilities but scores highest with experts looking for all-terrain, ungroomed snow adventures—simply the best steep adventure terrain in Colorado. Crested Butte has two villages, a modern condo complex for ski-in, ski-out convenience at the base of the ski mountain, and a wonderful, well-preserved mining town (that hasn't been turned into a theme park) only a few miles away. Great snow conditions are the norm here. Remote and well worth the trip.

Telluride Staggeringly beautiful mountainscapes surround this "happening" ski resort. The old mining town of Telluride provides historic funk and charm; the newer Mountain Village on the other side of the ski mountain has deluxe modern accommodations. Skiing is more balanced than the Telluride legend of steep bumps would have you believe, although the resort is a bit shy on sustained upper-intermediate cruising. Telluride is relatively hard to reach. Ace card: the unreal backdrop of the San Juan mountains.

Purgatory A rather small but easy-to-ski, easy-to-get-around mountain near the attractive western town of Durango in the heart of Louis L'Amour country. The skiing is mostly middle-of-the-road intermediate blue on relatively narrow runs cut through the forest. Purgatory is a favorite drive-to destination for Arizona skiers, with limited lodging at the base of the mountain and an abundance of choices in Durango.

Taos Adventure skiing on a richly complex mountain, justly famous for its steeps. An intimate base village gives a Taos ski vacation an old-time European flavor, but for something completely different, dining and lodging in the nearby town of Taos changes your vacation atmosphere from alpine to Hispanic and historic Southwest. This mountain is less appropriate for beginner and novice skiers.

Santa Fe A compact but satisfying day ski area with breathtaking views. There's a good kids' program that makes Santa Fe family-friendly. Above all, the ski area is only a short drive from one of the most romantic cities and popular vacation destinations in America, old Santa Fe—an opportunity to mix art, as well as southwestern culture and cuisine, with skiing.

CRESTED BUTTE

In Colorado, Crested Butte is only a medium-size ski resort, but in much of the rest of the country it would be a giant. But it is a "beaut" any way you spell it. The mountain, the resort at its base, and the old town of Crested Butte a couple of miles away all nestle together on the southern side of the Elk Range—just a few miles and an overnight ski tour away from Aspen, but seemingly a world away. Indeed, this is another world. Driving from Aspen to Crested Butte, one would have to circumnavigate three sides of a massive mountain range, a long day's drive. And when you got there . . .

Like all of Colorado's most romantic ski towns, Crested Butte was originally a mining settlement. But here men mined coal, not gold, and there's an earthiness and a funky down-home simplicity about the Butte today that must have its roots in this particular past. As a coal-mining town Crested Butte couldn't put on airs, and as a ski town it doesn't choose to. Charm yes, glitz no.

How can I introduce you in a few words to Crested Butte's very special character? There's the countryside: a broad open ranching valley that reminds me of long, lonesome Wyoming ranch country. There's the old town of Crested Butte, a few miles away from the base of the ski mountain. Here you find one of the most vital small towns in the Rockies. It's a town that pulled together to defeat a giant, Molybdenum Corporation's big-buck plans to turn the southern Elk Mountains into a slag-heap strip mine; a town living its own life behind old-time wooden false fronts, sharing its Main Street with winter tourists instead of simply turning it over to them. And there's the new town of Mount Crested Butte up at the base of the ski area. Mount Crested Butte is fundamentally a tourist lodging community whose modern condos and lodges are in no small measure responsible for preserving the charm of old Crested Butte from ski-development pressures that would have altered it irrevocably and not for the better. And finally, there's the mountain. The mountain itself is a curious and handsomely shaped plug of a peak, or "butte," that really is named Crested Butte, and there is the ski mountain grafted onto it. The ski mountain has a very good if not an ultra-modern, high-tech lift system. But it boasts some amazing advantages. First, Crested Butte is blessed with the best weather pattern in the state, lying at the overlapping intersection of southerly and northerly storm tracks—this is Snow City, Colorado. On average the Butte receives more snow, more often, than other major Colorado resorts. Second, an experts' mountain, the North Face, right beside the regular ski mountain, offers, in my opinion, the finest "adventure skiing" in Colorado. Have I whetted your appetite? Let's look closer.

The Way the Mountain Works

Unlike so many ski mountains, Crested Butte doesn't exactly have a front side or a back side. It does have a front, but also a side valley; an upper "around-the-corner" side, which is the North Face area that I'm so in love with; a lower "around-the-corner" area called East River; and—just to confuse matters—a small subsidiary area of easy skiing that is quite detached from the rest of the mountain across a sort of low pass. Complicated, but I want to give you at least a general impression of the rich topography of this area.

The new town of Mount Crested Butte sits in a sunny, almost treeless saddle underneath the Butte itself. And, as is the case with Steamboat, the wide, white, treeless lower slopes coming down into town remind me a lot of the Alps. Crested Butte is a very distinctive-looking peak, a sharp, pointed, art director's conception of a mountain. But the summit that you can admire from the valley floor is as rocky as it is snowy, so the ski area is located just beside the sharp peak of the Butte itself. The peak and its rocky ribs loom off to your right, as you ride one of several lifts out of the village of Mount Crested Butte. The Silver Queen, Crested Butte's first high-speed quad, takes you up as close as you can get to that pointed summit and opens up a steep front face full of classic black runs. A second chair, the Keystone lift, recently upgraded to high-speed quad status, slants up and left, crossing and serving a much gentler area of the front face with a host of meandering green runs. But wait a minute. Where are the blue runs? Not to worry—from the top of both of these frontside lifts you can drop over a kind of ridge into *Paradise,* a parallel valley running sideways and down to the left, which is the heart of the intermediate or blue skiing on this mountain.

Paradise is also the name of Crested Butte's third detachable quad lift. The lift takes you up into *Paradise Bowl,* a large open arena up at the head of this side drainage, and the first area on your right as you ski down from Paradise Lift. But you can call the whole shooting match back here Paradise and everyone will know what you're talking about. Runs are all honest blues, longish, with some flatter sections near the bottom, and they are very pleasant indeed. The Paradise Lift serves every run back here, and it's longer with a lot more vertical than the parallel Teocalli Lift. The only reason for riding the Teocalli Lift is to get back to the point on the front ridge from which all the easy ways down the front fan out.

Continuing on below the bottoms of Paradise and Teocalli lifts and trending rightward around the corner, you come to a separate, one-lift ski area, East River. The triple chair here serves runs that are a little steeper and more continuous than those in Paradise, but these black East River runs are very friendly indeed. *Resurrection* is the best of them, a tilted boulevard of steep rolling steps. All these runs dead-end near the bottom of a wide river valley. On the opposite, south-facing slopes, long treeless ridges will make you drool as you stand in line, waiting to come back up the East River Lift. The slopes on this "next-door" mountain have been pretty much stashed away behind a wilderness designation, so all skiers can do is daydream or break out their touring skis.

But to me the most interesting part of Crested Butte is the long and rugged mountain face that rises in bold, clifflike steps above Paradise and looms high above East River—the North Face. This is experts-only country of a kind found at no other Colorado ski resort. The ski company here deserves a lot of credit for opening up this terrain on a regular basis to the skiing public, and they did it in a brilliant, cost-effective way. A short, two-minute platter-pull ride from *Paradise Bowl* was all that was needed to replace the strenuous half-hour climb that used to be skiers' only option to reach the North Face. This ridiculously small and inexpensive lift added 260 acres of the most dramatic, serious, ungroomed double black diamond skiing imaginable to the ski area, and in my book raised it into a whole different league! Crested Butte calls this wonderful expert mountain face its "extreme limits" terrain; but most skiers just refer to this whole side of the mountain as the North Face, even though there are many separately named areas within it, including a zone called, appropriately enough, *North Face.*

The ski area received such kudos and admiration for opening this sensational terrain that it didn't stop there. Several seasons after the North Face had become a legend among Colorado's expert skiers, the High Lift T-bar was put up above the top of the Paradise Lift. This T-bar gives access to the *Headwall* and *Teocalli Bowl* and facilitates access to another zone of extreme terrain on the front side of the mountain, suspended just below the horn like the summit of the Butte, the *Banana Funnel,* the *Peel,* etc.

Did I mention the snow? Crested Butte lies at the snowy crossroads of Colorado's two major winter weather patterns. It gets hit by the southerly storms that sweep up across Arizona over Taos and Telluride, and it also receives northern dumps roaring down from Canada that hit resorts like Steamboat and Winter Park. I've always encountered remarkable snow conditions here.

Crested Butte for Nonexpert Skiers

If my enthusiasm for the North Face has got you worried, relax. Learners or inexperienced skiers and cautious, conservative intermediates can have a great time at the Butte. Down in Mount Crested Butte, off to the right, is a small practice lift called Peachtree with wide green slopes completely out of the mountain's traffic pattern. I've already mentioned that all the runs underneath Keystone Lift are friendly, low-angle greens, and I want to tell you about a zone that bolder skiers never seem to find at Crested Butte but which is tailor-made for cautious and inexperienced skiers. I think of it as the North Pass area, and it's comprised of two lifts that stick out in the opposite direction to everything else on the mountain. Painter Boy and Gold Link lifts are short chairs that serve flat, open, and sparsely timbered slopes on both sides of a low, round side peak to the north of the Keystone runs. *Little Lizzie, Splain's Gulch,* and *Topsy,* the gentle green runs that come down the Painter Boy side, are the only runs at Crested Butte that take one right through aspen groves, always a very esthetic experience. The runs on the Gold Link side of this extra little mountain are all harder, but none are very hard, and they're never crowded. This is a lovely area to build mileage and confidence.

Inexperienced skiers that want to graduate to the blue cruising runs in Paradise should first ski *Bushwhacker* down to the Teocalli Lift. Then, if that seems easy, take the Paradise Lift up into upper *Paradise Bowl,* which is considerably steeper. Think of Paradise Bowl as middle-of-the-road intermediate skiing; the blue runs on East River as slightly more challenging, upper-intermediate terrain for more experienced skiers; and the blue runs on the Teocalli and Gold Link lifts as friendlier and more suitable for emerging and low-intermediate skiers.

Crested Butte for Strong and Adventurous Skiers

While good skiers at the Butte spend most of their time in the large Paradise area and on the East River runs—which, as the name hints, receive wonderful morning sunlight—very good skiers in search of adventure will tend to ski these two zones only for a warm-up and maybe for a little R&R after particularly harrowing runs on the North Face.

Aside from the North Face, which we'll cover in a minute, there is one other zone of challenging advanced skiing near the top of the front face that is served by the Twister Lift. It's all relative, though. These demanding, well-banked runs are perfect racing trails and have been used for the Downhill and Super G courses at the U.S. National Championships. But they are simply steep trails with nice fallaways, a sustained pitch, sweeping turns, and sweeping views back over the valley toward old Crested Butte. Nice, but nothing to get excited about. Farther west (to the right as you ride up the Twister or Silver Queen lifts) are some more unusual sections of the mountain marked with telltale double black diamonds, a sure sign of excitement at the Butte. I use the term "sections" advisedly because these are not cut runs but rather zones to explore. Yet *Peel* and *Upper Peel* and the lines

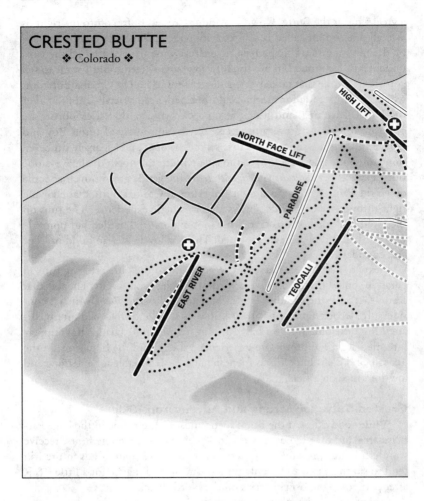

around them under the big *Banana Funnel* are seldom in good shape, and they're often closed by the patrol because wind sweeping around the peak tends to scour out their snow cover. This is the terrain used for the U.S. Extreme Skiing Championships. But the North Face is generally a safer bet for snow and a much bigger playing field for ski adventure.

What do I mean by adventure skiing? Naturally I'm talking about skiing in an ungroomed and wild mountain setting, but I also mean skiing that demands judgment and imagination as well as technique. Skiing that's not obvious. That challenges you to think clearly as well as to move well. The

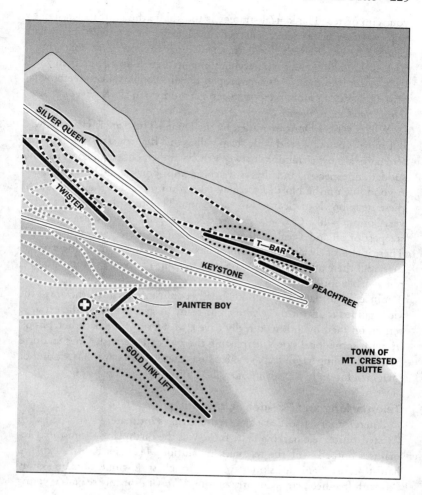

North Face fits this description perfectly. If you ski in here carelessly or fool-ishly, you'll go right over a cliff. No, the North Face is certainly not a death trap, but it is very serious. You could easily get into trouble back here. You can have the time of your life back here, too.

A good way of seeing whether you're up to it is to ski the *Tower 11 Chutes* first. Instead of taking the North Face Lift, just follow the right side of *Paradise Bowl* until you reach a marked gate in the boundary rope, and then traverse right to the chutes. These are openings in steep forest right under the Paradise Lift line, and if you feel at home here, then the North Face will be your cup of tea. The logical strategy is to explore the North Face step by step, by skiing farther across it at each run. The first lines lead through what's called *The Glades;* next you'll traverse across to *High Life,* following a packed-out hiking trail that everybody else up there follows, and then you'll drop down into the *North Face* proper. Finally, you'll want to see how far across this vast mountain face you can get, and you'll ski *Spellbound Bowl, Third Bowl,* and *Phoenix Bowl.*

What's it like? Don't be misled by the names. These aren't classic bowls, but rather open faces and wide steep gullies in a rugged, stair-step face that alternates almost at random between thick timber, cliffs and couloirs, and sudden, unexpected, and always welcome mini-bowls and chutes of snow. A good line on the North Face may take you into and through several of these steep bowls or clearings in succession. The steep slotlike faces at the very bottom—like *Cesspool, Last Steep, Staircase,* and *Phoenix Steps*—are the steepest of all and a real challenge to ski well when you are getting tired. There is almost always a best, or most obvious, line down any of these openings, and there are numerous variants. On some of these variants falling is not a viable option.

Since this is daunting and potentially confusing territory, the area provides guided tours for those who aren't ready to start exploring the extreme terrain on their own. But to really have a wonderful time back here, hook up with some local skiers. Exploring the North Face with Crested Butte friends doubling as guides, I've skied lines that I could never have found or imagined for myself, at least not easily. This is high-energy skiing.

Telemarking and Powder at the Butte

There's another sort of ski adventure that's intimately associated with Crested Butte: telemarking. The Butte was the birthplace—and today remains a hotbed—of the telemark revolution. This is a hard-to-explain, hard-to-resist mania for skiing even the toughest downhill runs on skinny skis with free-heel, cross-country bindings. You'll probably see more young telemark heroes at Crested Butte than anywhere else in Colorado.

The telemark is a rediscovered artifact from the dark ages of skiing and Nordic history that is done in a semikneeling position with one foot and ski advanced and the other foot and ski trailing. It's a singularly graceful and very athletic variant of skiing, but it's definitely not for everyone. In fact, its main attraction, at least at ski areas, is its difficulty; its main converts are gifted young alpine skiers who have literally run out of challenges and are looking for something newer and harder. Let me be a little more precise: telemarking per se is not so hard—it is in fact an easy way to maneuver skinny cross-country skis in soft backcountry snow; and doubtless, the reason that telemark skiing took off in Crested Butte is the amazing amount of soft powder that falls there. But telemarking down steep runs at a ski area can be quite an exciting challenge. If you're curious, consider taking an introductory telemark lesson while you're at Crested Butte.

Speaking of soft snow in the backcountry, you might also want to consider a day of snowcat skiing at Irwin Lodge, which is located only a few hours by snowcat in the mountains behind the old town. The terrain is fabulous, the atmosphere congenial, and the cost fairly reasonable for so much guaranteed powder snow.

Atmosphere, Après, Victuals, and Lodging

If you've gotten the idea that I love Crested Butte, you're absolutely right. This place is a gem of a ski resort. Although it's hardly unknown, the Butte has nowhere near the reputation of the big guys across the range, so one always has a certain feeling of discovery when skiing here for the first time.

I enjoy the town as much as the mountain. The old town of Crested Butte, that is. While the new town of Mount Crested Butte plays a vital service role (this is where most of the guest accommodations are located, and it's hard to beat the slopeside convenience), it is just not a place I can get attached to. You'll find every sort of lodging up there, including a full-service hotel, the Grand Butte. But when you feel like a night on the town, you'll probably take the shuttle bus or drive a few miles down the hill into old Crested Butte.

Life in town pulses up and down Elk Avenue, which is the narrowest main street in any Colorado mining town I know, something that gives it an especially intimate character. (The railroad was already here when the town was founded, and that meant the first town fathers didn't have to plan extra width on Elk Avenue for long wagon teams and mule trains to swing around.)

A classic western ski town has to have a classic locals' bar, and Crested Butte has two. The Wooden Nickel is the hangout of choice for ski-area types, patrollers, and instructors, whereas the down-valley locals prefer Kochevars (pronounced *Ka-chivers*) for serious drinking and pool playing; it's still owned by the Kochevar family, who built it in 1900, which makes it the oldest bar in town.

Crested Butte is full of restaurants with great atmosphere, but it's a little shy on restaurants with great cuisine. After a lot of testing, I've concluded that the best restaurant in town is Soupçon, a historic, miniature log cabin in a back alley where you (and only a handful of others) are likely to enjoy some very imaginative and refined French dishes. Le Bosquet is a runner-up but far more conventional. Altogether unconventional is the Powerhouse Bar y Grill, a Mexican restaurant in the town's old powerhouse that serves real cabrito on butcher-paper-covered tables.

Lodging in old Crested Butte is scarce—only a couple of hundred pillows at most—compared to the wide gamut at Mount Crested Butte. But the insider's best bet is the Elk Mountain Lodge, once an in-town boarding-house for miners. The Elk Mountain Lodge was formerly owned by the town's biggest employer, CF&I (Colorado Fuel and Iron), and today has been totally refurbished into a delightful inn.

CRESTED BUTTE DATA

Mountain Statistics

Vertical feet	2,775 feet (lift-served); 3,062 feet (requires a hike to the peak)
Base elevation	9,100 feet
Top of lifts elevation	11,875 feet
Longest run	2.6 miles
Average annual snowfall	270 inches
Number of lifts	14
	3 high-speed quads
	3 triple chairs
	3 double chairs
	4 surface lifts
	1 magic carpet
Uphill capacity	16,560 skiers per hour
Skiable terrain	1,160 acres
Opening date	mid-November
Closing date	April
Snowboarding	Yes

Transportation

By car A 30-minute drive from Gunnison on Highway 135.

By limo From the Gunnison Airport.

By plane Via connecting commuter flights from Denver International Airport.

Key Phone Numbers

Ski Area Information (970) 349-2333
Snow Report (970) 349-2323
Reservations (800) 544-8448 or (970) 349-2222
www.visitcrestedbutte.com

LITO'S TECH TIP

Telemark Skiing

A lot of skiers have seen young telemarkers flashing by in their curious but elegant kneeling position. And a lot of downhill skiers have tried cross-country skiing in a track and may even own their own cross-country gear. But even most serious cross-country enthusiasts have never tried telemark turns. Telemarking well in all conditions is a real challenge, but merely learning the turn is easy. If you have a pair of cross-country skis (you don't need special teleskis to learn the basics) and want to try, do it like this.

First, get used to the telemark stance in a straight run down a very gentle slope. Slide your skis apart, fore and aft, as you drop into a semikneeling position: the rear knee almost touching the ski, the front knee bent at 90 degrees. Then rise and slide the rear ski forward as you drop into the opposite kneeling position, front and back legs reversed. Now repeat this kneeling/sliding position a couple of times.

Next, do a couple of fast, smooth wedge turns with your feet pretty close together in a small, narrow wedge. Then, halfway through one of these wedge turns, drop into the telemark position you practiced earlier, outside ski ahead, inside ski trailing (that is to say, if you're turning right, you'll slide your left ski ahead and let your right ski drop back as you kneel). This wedge-into-telemark works just like a stem christie to sneak you into a beautiful sliding finish, only this time it's a telemark finish to your turn rather than a christie skid. Believe me, it's easy . . . if you try it from a narrow wedge.

Next, do a few more of these wedge telemarks to both sides—fairly long turns, please—letting your skis come around on their own in the telemark position rather than forcing them around quickly. Progressively narrow your wedge more and more while skiing somewhat faster, and in about 15 minutes you'll be guiding a pure telemark turn down your gentle practice hill. A packed-out beginner slope at a downhill ski area is the ideal spot for this eye-opening experiment.

TELLURIDE

It will be obvious after reading a few lines that Telluride is one of my favorite places, and it should be. Telluride was my adopted home for years, and I moved here for the simplest of reasons: I fell in love with the place. Not, I should add, because it has the best skiing in Colorado, much less the slickest amenities, or the liveliest ski-resort atmosphere, but simply because the Telluride Valley was the most beautiful alpine valley I'd ever seen in the Rockies, or in any other range, for that matter. This steep-sided box canyon is a mind-boggling setting for a lovely medium-size ski area that nonetheless reserves some fierce challenges for expert skiers. At the end of the canyon nestles a tiny town that's still struggling to make a graceful transition from a hard-rock mining community to a polished, nationally known resort. When I moved to Telluride in 1976, the ski area was four years old and the local mine still employed 300 miners. The tunnels are closed now, the mill padlocked, and the miners gone. Skiers, tourists, T-shirt merchants, and real estate developers in nearly equal numbers have discovered this enchanted valley. Telluride has changed dramatically, is still changing, and I'm still in love with the place.

Why? Maybe it's the 13,000- and 14,000-foot peaks of the San Juan Mountains ringing the valley and the ski area, or the waterfalls that turn into giant crystal organ pipes in winter, or the sunsets that slant through this east-west canyon like flash floods of liquid gold, or the cockeyed Victorian houses self-consciously spiffy in their new paint. Telluride is outrageously beautiful every day of the year, even more so in winter.

Today Telluride is a happening resort, home of Hollywood stars, and quite possibly the most romantic ski destination in Colorado. But its ski mountain suffers from the same experts-only bad rep as Taos. From the town it looks radically steep (and it is), but actually most of the reasonable or everyday skiing is found on the other, much larger side of the mountain, which faces west and has a hundred-mile view all the way to the Utah border. True, Telluride almost certainly boasts the longest, steepest bump runs in America, but there are plenty of alternatives for every level of skier.

The Shape and Layout of Telluride's Mountain

Telluride is a two-sided ski mountain with three bases. The front face rises dramatically above town and has two bases and two separate lift access routes. The Coonskin Lift is located at the entrance to town and rises up to a midpoint on the long ridgelike crest of the mountain. The Oak Street Lift, from the center of town, with its continuation, the Plunge triple chair, takes skiers over 3,000 vertical feet up to the very top. All the skiing on this front side is serious except for one zigzag road, the *Telluride Trail,* that provides a comfortable come-home route for weaker skiers who are too self-conscious to ride the Coonskin Lift back down into town. The rest of the runs on the front are marked blue and black, but skiers should beware: A blue run on Telluride's face would be black at most ski areas, and a black run here could be double black elsewhere.

The back side, which is really the main side because that's where most of the skiing is located, is large, spread out, and far friendlier for mere mortals. I've called Telluride a medium-small ski area, but it is a medium-size ski area draped in separate pods over an amazingly large mountain. The skiing zones are fragmented into these separate pods by a host of natural obstacles: cliff bands, creek beds, and secondary hilllike summits. When you actually total up the amount of skiing available, it's less than one would expect for such a massive mountain. Curiously, this doesn't matter very much because Telluride's mountain capacity is still bigger than its bed base. In all the years since the ski area first opened, no one here has ever seen the kind of lift lines that are routine at most ski areas. This means you can get in as much skiing as your legs can take. There are seven lifts on the back side of the mountain (including a poma on the race hill). We'll look at them in more detail when I recommend runs for different levels of skiers.

There is also a second base to the ski area on this other side. Not just a base lodge, but a second village. A short drive around the mountain from town, the ski corporation has constructed a brand-new resort called Mountain Village at Telluride; it is a handsome project with lots of elegant stonework, southwestern tile roofs, and above all, a genuinely spectacular setting in a wide meadow at the foot of Lifts 3 and 4, the main intermediate skiing zone. Such projects take years, but finally, just as it happened at Beaver Creek, the construction phase is virtually over and a very handsome resort village has appeared. A new high-tech gondola opened in 1996–97 connecting the town of Telluride with Mountain Village. The gondola ride is free and the gondola runs late into the evening, making this one of the most innovative people-moving systems at any Colorado resort and tying the town and Mountain Village closer together than ever before. Although the new gondola doesn't open up any new ski terrain, it offers another route from town up onto the mountain, and its speed, views, and comfort have made it quite popular with skiers too. But we'll visit Mountain Village and Telluride proper in more depth after we've toured the mountain.

Telluride for Mere Mortals

From town, most skiers will want to take the Coonskin Lift and immediately head down the other side, at least for a warm-up run or two. If, instead, you decide to take Lifts 7 and 8, the Oak Street and Plunge lifts, to the very top, you will find that there is only one comfortable, nonblack run off the top. This is *See Forever,* a long ridge-line cruiser that doesn't have quite as good a view as the name suggests because it is lined with dense trees for most of its length: "Ski Forever" would be more accurate. *See Forever* takes you back down to the top of the Coonskin Lift anyway, so it's faster to begin your day on Coonskin and head up to the top of the mountain around noon to enjoy lunch with a view—the most spectacular view of any Colorado ski area—at the tiny summit café.

Standing at the top of the Coonskin Lift, looking west, you will find yourself on the rim of a large forested bowl that contains Telluride's greatest concentration of intermediate trails. The runs to your left are easier (and *Village Bypass* is absolutely the easiest way down this side of the mountain). The two runs straight below you, *Hermit* and *Smuggler,* are short and rather steep and occasionally lightly moguled. To your right, several more runs stretch out—longer and smoother, wide boulevards with sustained pitch but no sudden drops. *Butterfly* drops directly down to the big mid-

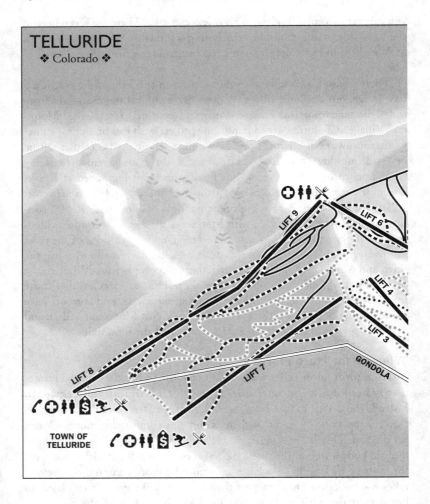

mountain restaurant at Gorono Park, and *Lower See Forever* bears right all the way down to the lift. Or should I say lifts?

You run out of slope at the edge of Mountain Village and coast up to Lifts 3 and 4, a double and a triple that together serve over 50 percent of the good intermediate skiing on the mountain. Lift 3 takes you back to the ridge near the Coonskin Lift terminus, while Lift 4 is longer and accesses some additional runs. The least-skied run off Lift 4 is *Humbolt Draw,* a lovely half-hidden valley that twists like an outsize toboggan run and is well worth checking out.

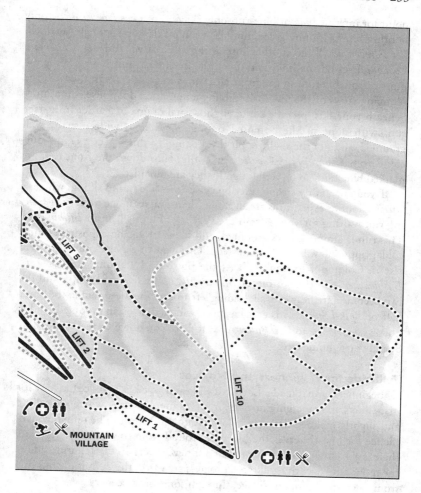

From the top of Lift 4 you can also traverse around the corner on a road to Lift 5, which once again feels like a separate ski area. It's an important one, though, because it features the only consistently easy bump run at Telluride, which is *Palmyra*. If you have ambitions to ski *The Plunge* or other hard black runs, polishing your bump turns on *Palmyra* first is a very good idea. From the top of Lift 5 you can also traverse down and right to Lift 6, which serves another distinct skiing pod or section and takes you right up to the top of the ski mountain.

As I mentioned before, the top of the mountain is a zero option take-off point for intermediate or blue-run-only skiers, since *See Forever* is the only nonthreatening, nonmoguled, nonblack run off the top. But halfway down *See Forever,* you'll see another interesting alternative, and that's *Lookout.* *Lookout* dives off the ridge and down the front face, and it is certainly the most reasonable run on the front face for average skiers. On *Lookout,* the plunging views of the town, resembling a miniature dollhouse community beneath your skis, provide some of the visual drama of harder front-face runs with none of the potential trauma. *Lookout* is wide, usually well groomed, and not the slightest bit threatening. In this aspect it's quite different from *Coonskin* or *Woozleys,* two other runs down the front that are marked blue but can be very tough if they are moguled.

If you are a fairly strong skier but just don't like bump skiing, which is what Telluride's expert runs are all about, there is at least one more very exciting run waiting for you—from the very top. By this I mean *Bushwacker.* This run is almost always groomed, and its north-facing exposure ensures cold, grippy snow. But it's damn steep. This would be a black run anywhere else in Colorado, so don't fall. At the bottom of its long, steep sweep, *Bushwacker* joins the bottom of *Mammoth Slide,* a river of bumps, and the two become a friendly catwalk leading left around the mountain to the lower half of *Spiral Stairs.* This area has been widened, is often groomed, and is not as steep as the top of *Bushwacker.* It takes you down to the base of Lift 8, and you're home free.

Telluride for Beginners and Novices

Beginners have it made. Lift 1 is a wide and gracious practice universe for first-timers and emerging novices. It serves the *Meadows,* which are rolling and slightly inclined flats just below Mountain Village. The only inconvenience for first-timers is the bus ride around from town, but believe me, there is absolutely no learning terrain for never-evers on the Telluride side of the mountain. Security and rapid progress are worth the 20-minute bus ride from town to Mountain Village, through some great scenery.

Almost as soon as they've mastered a solid wedge and some kind of sloppy, basic christy, novice skiers will be able take the Coonskin Lift up from town and make it safely to the beginner area by following *Village Bypass* all the way left and down. Almost more of a ski tour than a run, this trail brings one down to the *Meadows,* avoiding all traffic and all steeps, even mini-steeps, through a lovely aspen forest.

And finally there's Lift 10, slanting up into thick forest from the old base lodge at the bottom of Lift 1. As your christies, your skidded turns, begin to improve, you'll find the long runs on Lift 10 very suitable and almost ideal for the sort of mileage that makes progress inevitable. But I want to add that for better skiers, Lift 10 is one of the most pointless pieces of lift engineering ever dreamed up. Yes, it is a state-of-the-art, high-speed detachable quad. But hard-skiing Telluride locals have nicknamed it "the lift to nowhere." In actuality, it's more a real estate lift than a ski lift and is designed to provide ski-in/ski-out access to high-ticket homesites adjoining Mountain Village. Stronger skiers should certainly venture over to Lift 10 anyway just to see what's what and enjoy the views, which at Telluride are all great, but skilled skiers won't spend much time here.

Telluride for Experts

Despite all its intermediate skiing, Telluride has been stereotyped in the folklore of Colorado skiing as an experts' mountain. Fair or unfair? A bit of both. The bell-shaped curve operates here too, and on any given day you'll find more intermediates enjoying themselves on Telluride slopes than experts. But it's also true that the better you are, the better you'll like this mountain. To ski every run well at Telluride demands much more skill than it does at Steamboat or Snowmass. But if this is, in some sense, an experts' mountain, it's also a mountain for a particular breed of expert skier. Telluride is bumper heaven. Its black slopes are very steep and always densely moguled. These bumps are really wild. It's not that they're badly formed; they're simply big, awesomely big and deep. To use the appropriate bump skiers' vernacular, Telluride bumps are gnarly.

There are two main mogul skiing zones. The first, short and sweet, is Lift 6, sometimes just called Apex after *Apex Glade,* the large, half-open area to the north of the lift. The skiing here is just as interesting as on the front face, but the runs are much, much shorter. *Zulu Queen,* a narrow slot through the woods, is the hardest line; *Silver Glade* and *Apex Glade* are the most fun; and *Allais Alley,* under the lift line, is strictly for showoffs. On Lift 6 even the forest between the mogul runs gets moguled!

The second, legendary bump zone comprises the long black runs coming right off the top and tumbling down the front in a 2,500-vertical-foot, nonstop cascade. The best-shaped moguls on the front are found on *Mammoth Slide,* the worst on *Kant-Mak-M,* but both these runs eventually feed into the middle of the *Stairs.*

The *Spiral Stairs* is the granddaddy of all mean mogul runs. It starts innocently enough, branching off from *See Forever* ridge at *Joint Point.* A quarter-mile later it simply drops out from under you. The start is breathtaking, and the rest—once you recover from the sudden visual impact of coming over a lip and looking straight down almost 3,000 feet—is just as hard. I rank the *Stairs,* along with the top pitch of Mont Fort at Verbier and the West Face of KT22 at Squaw, among the steepest, hardest bump runs anywhere. Don't ski it your first morning in Telluride. Just left of the *Stairs* is *The Plunge,* a run of a different color, so to speak. It's still black (or should be, even though the ski area inexplicably colored it blue on the trail map, which gets a lot of innocent skiers into trouble), but it's far, far easier than the *Stairs*. And just as famous. In all fairness, I should add that the ski area has done wonders to groom *The Plunge*, or rather the left half of it, by using the new winch-cat technology, where one snowcat pulls another one up a slope that would ordinarily be too steep to groom. *The Plunge* very nearly deserves its blue designation now—but remember, that's a special shade of Telluride blue.

Telluride's final treat for expert skiers is Gold Hill. This is an area of steep chutes above the top of the ski area that are now controlled and, as often as possible, opened by the patrol. Skiers hike uphill for 10 to 20 minutes to reach lines like *Killer, Electra,* and *Little Rose,* which are several hundred vertical feet of mixed snow and cut-up powder that bottoms out in a long traverse back to Lift 5. This has all the thrill of out-of-bounds skiing, only now it's legal and the snow is safe when the patrol opens the gate. Although the Gold Hill "powder preserve" is marked double black on the trail map, it isn't nearly as serious as the big bump runs on the face that are marked as mere single black diamonds.

A Tiny Town and Its Treasures

Telluride (including its box canyon) is scarcely more than four blocks wide. It's a miniature mining town, not another Aspen. Despite its trendy reputation, Telluride is still rough around the edges, good-natured, and warm-hearted. A place where volunteer firefighters coexist uneasily with Lear Jets parking at the new airport outside town. Cars are unnecessary, and if you need to go clear to the other end of town, say with a bag of groceries over one shoulder and skis on the other, you can always take the free town bus. Just what do you do in Telluride when you're not standing around with a crick in your neck admiring the 13,000-foot peaks that ring the town? Leimgruber's is a popular post-Plunge pub with a vast collection of imported German beers. The Sheridan Bar is pure unretouched, unadulterated turn-of-the-century mining town chic. Actually, Telluride is still too small and too down-home to compete in big-league après-ski, although there are always a couple of bars and clubs with live music and recently a lot of live jazz. If any sort of show is playing in the old Sheridan Opera House—movie, amateur theatrical, or concert—don't miss it. The Sheridan is one of the most beautiful gold-rush opera houses left in Colorado, and it's perfectly restored. For the last word in antislickness, you can rent a pair of skates and walk over to the town park to skate on an outdoor oval under the giant cliffs of Bear Creek.

Eating out is easy. Telluride has better restaurants than one would guess, or perhaps than it deserves. The finest is La Marmotte, a French restaurant that fits beautifully into a historic, brick ice house located two blocks below Main Street. Friends of mine from Vail and Aspen who eat at La Marmotte each time they visit come back raving, "We don't have anything this good back home." This is a kind of ultimate food review in a Colorado ski resort. Less of a gourmet adventure, but still a knockout, is 231 (the address of an old Victorian house on South Oak Street), which has refined food in a refined atmosphere at prices even locals can afford. At the other end of the spectrum, Baked in Telluride, the local bakery, produces the best bagels this side of Katz's delicatessen.

All the normal ski lodging options are found here too, plus a couple of gems. The New Sheridan Hotel (which was already called the New Sheridan when William Jennings Bryan gave his celebrated "cross of gold" speech in front of it) is Telluride's equivalent of the Ritz and used to boast the only elevator in San Miguel County. In recent years, we've seen the beginning of a trend toward intimate bed-and-breakfast inns rather than more and more condo blocks. The most interesting of these B&Bs is the San Sophia. If you want to break the usual vacation mold you should consider staying at Sky-line Ranch, an incredibly beautiful and romantic old-time guest ranch just a few miles outside town.

How about Mountain Village? Lodging up there is first class. A grand, or perhaps grandiose, spa hotel called the Peaks is as luxurious as any grand hotel in the Rockies. There are lots of other, only slightly more modest choices. The dinning selection in Mountain Village is still rather thin—though a southwestern restaurant, Cazwella's, is getting rave reviews—and interesting shopping is almost nonexistent. Most skiers staying in Mountain Village still prefer to spend their evenings in downtown Telluride, on the other side of the mountain. This is a lot easier now that the new gondola connecting the town to Mountain Village has opened. It was designed more as a transportation link than a ski lift and operates late into the night. One has to applaud any resort transportation solution that reduces the use of cars and buses, and this gondola is a bold move that will help keep Telluride an intimate and unspoiled destination a little longer.

TELLURIDE DATA

Mountain Statistics

Vertical feet	3,155 feet
Base elevation	8,735 feet
Summit elevation	11,890 feet
Longest run	2.85 miles
Average annual snowfall	300 inches
Number of lifts	11
	1 gondola
	1 high-speed quad
	1 fixed-grip quad
	1 triple chair
	6 double chairs
	1 surface lift
Uphill capacity	10,836 skiers per hour
Skiable terrain	735 acres
Opening date	Thanksgiving weekend
Closing date	early April
Snowboarding	Yes

Transportation

By car A 1½-hour drive south from Montrose, Colorado, or a 1-hour-and-45-minute drive north from Cortez.

By van From the Telluride or Montrose airports.

By plane Via connecting commuter flights from Denver International Airport.

Key Phone Numbers

Ski Area Information
   (970) 728-3856
Snow Report (970) 728-3856
Reservations (800) 525-3455 or
   (970) 728-4431
www.telski.com

LITO'S TECH TIP

Skiing Super Bumps

Skiing bumps is one thing; skiing extra-big, extra-steep bumps is quite another. As usual, there are a few tricks to it, and, as with an advanced graduate course at a university, there are prerequisites. Unless you can ski medium and small bumps smoothly and efficiently, you'll be floundering on serious bump runs. But given the basics, here's how to adapt to tougher stuff.

On mega-bumps the slope changes so radically from one moment to the next that you're always playing catch-up with your skis, which tend to drop out from under you in the steep gullies. The solution is faster, more dynamic pole action. By the time your skis have pivoted into the fall line, you should already be reaching straight down the hill with your pole for the next bump.

In effect, this pulls your body forward so you can keep up with your skis and, of course, gets you ready for the next turn.

But often in big hard bumps there isn't much room to finish your turn between one bump and the next, so once again speed control becomes an issue. The solution is simply to accept a little more speed and then, periodically, wherever there's room to do so, complete your turn by curving up and over the shoulder of the next bump. This extra uphill hook will cut your speed way back from time to time.

As you ski faster, in bigger bumps, you will often feel yourself compressed, your legs pushed up beneath you, by the force with which you contact the bump. This compression is a natural form of shock absorption, but it only works once. To use your legs as shock absorbers again, on the next bump and the next, you need to make a continual effort to extend your feet and legs back down into the trough as you come over the lip of the bump, stretching out to fill up the available space, and getting tall to absorb the next compression.

Of course, that's not the whole story of super bumps, but it's a good start. You'll find more information, more detail, more help with this and other skiing challenges in my book *Breakthrough on Skis,* a Vintage paperback from Random House.

PURGATORY

Purgatory, the most southwestern of Colorado ski areas, is small, remote, and charming. Its charm, however, is a fragmented one. Purgatory is located in the southern San Juan mountains, not far from Telluride as the crow flies but a helluva long way around by road. It's blessed with typically stunning San Juan Mountain scenery—panoramic views of granite peaks and deep gorges. Despite some ambitious base development in recent years, there's no real resort life at Purgatory; it has remained just a ski area. The town that naturally goes with Purgatory, Durango, isn't at the foot of the slopes, as it certainly would be if this were really the best of all possible worlds. Instead, Durango lies a half-hour drive to the south, where the Animas River flows out of the mountains into the first high, red mesas of Anasazi country. If fate had only put these two together.

Durango is a great western town, more a small city than a town, actually, with an old historic main street, a state college, and enough good shops, restaurants, and lodging to make most ski towns jealous. But you don't get to walk home at night watching the moonlight painting milky brushstrokes down runs you've just schussed that afternoon. Pity.

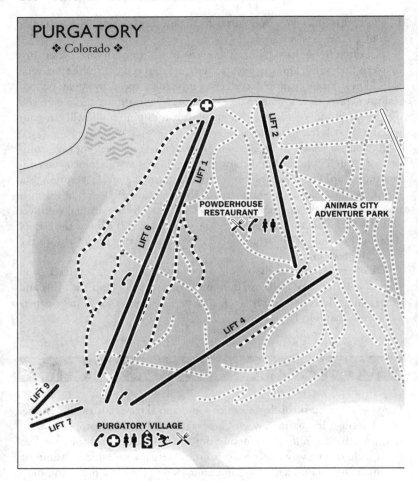

The Purgatory-Durango combination still works well, and it's been a longtime favorite with skiers from Albuquerque, Phoenix, and elsewhere in the Southwest. The ski experience at Purgatory is intimate and low-key rather than challenging and grand, but the skier service level is high and the natives are friendly. It's hard not to like Purgatory.

How the Mountain Works

The mountain you see when you arrive at the base faces due east, across the great hollowed-out gorge of the Animas River, with a stunning view of a rugged subrange appropriately called the Twilight Peaks, on the other side

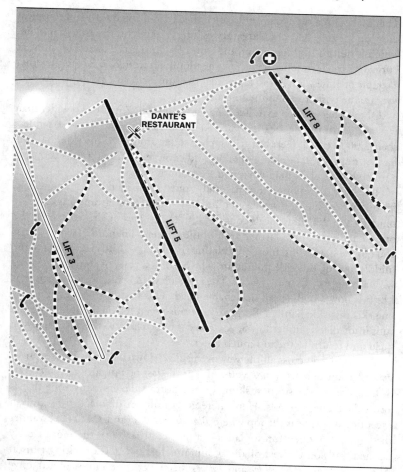

of the canyon. Lifts 6 and 1 march right up the front face, which looks, and is, respectably steep. Lift 4 slants off to the right, opening up an area of friendly green runs where novices will spend most of their time. (Purgatory's chairs, by the way, are numbered in the order in which they were built.) The best time of day to ski the front face is early to mid-morning in order to take advantage of the direct early light. By late afternoon one is liable to find crusty or scraped conditions.

As soon as you tire of the front side, you'll discover that this mountain folds or wraps around the corner to the right into a side valley. The runs on this side mountain (served by Lifts 2, 3, 5, and 8) face almost due north.

That makes for a pretty fair trade-off: either great views on the front or great snow on the side. Most of Purgatory's skiing is found on this side mountain, which is quite a bit bigger than the front. So during the course of a day at Purgatory you'll wind up traversing the mountain from one side to the other a couple of times. It helps to know that the runs marked *Parkway* or *Expressway* are the best cross-mountain trails.

I should tell you too that, like Copper Mountain, Purgatory is wider than it is tall. Most of the area is what you could call "one lift high," a tad less than 2,000 vertical feet; but it stretches so far around to the side that one has the impression of skiing on a big and complex mountain. It is certainly a much bigger place than what you see from the road.

The large side mountain is naturally zoned or divided into skiing terrain for different abilities. It starts out quite easy with a lot of green runs and easy blues on Lift 2. (Many locals consider Lift 2 to be part of the front since the other chairs are much farther around the corner.) Then, the farther across you go, the harder and more stimulating the skiing is. Lifts 3 and 5 serve the middle area of this side mountain, which holds a zone of longer blue runs with a couple of friendly blacks. The good news for Purgatory skiers is that Lift 3 is now a high-speed detachable quad. This basically changes the way one skis this side flank of Purgatory, because even if you are following the runs immediately under Lift 5, you can cut back across to the bottom of the quad and return to the top much faster.

Finally, if you cross all the way over, skiing down an uninspired expressway of a run called *Legends,* you arrive at the last of Purgatory's chairs, Lift 8. Lift 8 serves the steepest skiing on the north side, an entire zone that is also called The Legends. Here there are a number of black runs and an exceptional area near the top where *Blackburn's Bash* and *Paul's Park* wander through steep, open forest glades—a nice contrast with the more clearly defined trails on the rest of the mountain. The two most exciting runs at The Legends are *Ray's Ridge* and *Elliot's:* steep, varied terrain with attractive banked sides to play on.

Purgatory runs, gentle or tough, share a common flavor, a special character that makes skiing intriguing but not effortless. Purgatory is a roller coaster where the pitch of the slope is seldom continuous. There are numerous breakaways in almost every trail and a roller-coaster sequence of steeps and flats with abrupt, sometimes exciting transitions. These transitions aren't so abrupt that they'll get you into trouble, but they do keep you on your toes, then heels, then toes, etc. Personally I love this sort of skiing, where you are constantly forced to adapt and adjust to changing terrain—skiing a real and variable mountain shape rather than slopes of man-made smoothness. But you have to be careful not to "blind jump" any of these sudden lips where the slope changes angle, or, conversely, not to stop beneath any of these breaks in pitch where a flying skier might nail you.

I'm less enthusiastic about the other characteristic of Purgatory's trails. I find them all a bit narrow for my taste—the one exception being *Dead Spike,* located right in the middle of the northern side of the mountain. Everything else being equal, skiers, even expert skiers, always ski better and feel freer on wider runs. If most of the runs at Purgatory could be widened by 50 percent, they'd have a remarkable mountain.

There are, however, remarkable mountains all around Purgatory, and the easy way to ski them is to sign up for a day's powder tour with the San Juan Powder Cats. Dave Rule, the guiding spirit behind this new snow-cat operation, has worked out a cooperative arrangement for booking tours at the Purgatory ski-area ticket office. He has a vast area under permit from the Forest Service, with above-timberline terrain for sunny days and handsome steep-treed slopes for gray and stormy weather. This snow-cat option has definitely added an element of big-mountain adventure to the Purgatory experience.

Drinking, Dining, and Dancing in Durango

Despite some really good-looking development at the base of the ski mountain, including a pedestrian plaza that has a great feel to it and great views too, there just isn't much to do at Purgatory except ski. Most Purgatory skiers will head for Durango immediately after the last run.

Durango is an easy town to find one's way around in since it's organized around a traditional, western main street axis. The south end of Main Street is the old section of town, with the last two or three blocks qualifying as a historic district. One of the most imposing buildings on lower Main Street is also the fanciest place in town to stay, the elegant, historic Strater Hotel. This grand, four-story, red-brick building is both a treat and a bargain. In Aspen, the Strater's rooms, with their all-antique furnishings, would go for three or four times the price. The Strater also houses two other Durango musts: the Diamond Belle Saloon, an old-time bar that's still a marvel despite bartenders in corny period costumes; and the Diamond Circle Theatre, a classic melodrama and vaudeville stage where the same corny, old-time costumes are, in fact, just right.

The best food in Durango, however, is not in the Strater but a few blocks away at a wonderfully unpretentious but very sophisticated restaurant called Ken & Sue's, or simply 937 (after its address, 937 Main Street). This is a real find, a knockout combination of creative cooking and modest prices. Mysteriously, neither 937 nor any other restaurant in town seems to take reservations. So dine early or plan to spend some time nursing drinks while you wait for a table.

Unfortunately, the one longtime Durango tradition that winter ski guests can't enjoy is the weekly rodeo at the fairgrounds, which is a summer-only event. No matter, you'll be back.

PURGATORY DATA		
Mountain Statistics		**Transportation**
Vertical feet	2,029 feet	**By car** A 30-minute drive north from Durango on U.S. 550.
Base elevation	8,793 feet	
Summit elevation	10,822 feet	**By plane** Commuter flights to Durango at the La Plata County Airport, 44 miles south of Purgatory.
Longest run	2 miles	
Average annual snowfall	240 inches	
Number of lifts	9	**Key Phone Numbers**
Uphill capacity	12,700 skiers per hour	Ski Area Information (970) 247-9000
Skiable terrain	630 acres	
Opening date	November 27, 1997	Snow Report (970) 247-9000
Closing date	April 12, 1998	Reservations (800) 525-0892
Snowboarding	Yes	

LITO'S TECH TIP

Skiing against All Odds

This is not one of my how-to "ski tech" sections but, instead, a note of appreciation, admiration, and genuine awe for the handicapped skiers you'll see on the slopes of Purgatory and other Colorado ski resorts. Calling these skiers blind skiers, one-legged skiers, paraplegic skiers, "physically challenged" skiers, or "adaptive" skiers, as we do nowadays, doesn't do justice to the hurdles they have overcome or properly recognize their determination and their very real athletic gifts. The wonderful thing is that so many have become, simply, skiers.

Purgatory, like Winter Park, has a terrific reputation for teaching the handicapped to ski. And if you have a friend in a wheelchair or on crutches, who you think might love to try skiing, these are the two resorts to consider. Specially trained instructors, using amazing ski-seat contraptions as well as the more usual outriggers for one-legged skiers, can do wonders with people whom common sense tends—wrongly—to classify as permanently excluded from the skiing experience.

There is a very effective program for blind skiers, called the Bold Skier program, at many Colorado ski areas. Blind skiers ski with guides who give them verbal information about where to turn and what's coming up on the slope ahead of them. Both the blind skier and the volunteer guide are identified by bright orange bibs.

But there are relatively few serious ski-teaching programs oriented especially to the needs of variously and seriously disabled skiers. Purgatory and Winter Park, and nowadays Snowmass, are exceptions. Both Winter Park and Purgatory have been pioneers in this area. Bravo! My hat's off to these skiers and to all who have helped them to ski.

For more information on this remarkable program, you can contact the Adaptive Sports Association. ASA runs their Purgatory ski program from a small wood building just below the base-area plaza, and their phone number is (970) 247-9000, ext. 3217. Or you can phone the DPASA Durango office at (970) 259-0374.

TAOS

Taos is one of those rare ski areas of which you can truly say that they don't make 'em like that any more. And indeed, they never did. The conventional wisdom of today's ski industry says that you just can't build a ski area where 51 percent of the terrain is expert level. But lucky for us, Ernie Blake, who founded the area in 1955, made a habit of never heeding conventional wisdom. An expatriate Swiss war hero, aviator, and a great skier in his own right, Ernie was a living legend until his death in 1989. Now he's simply a legend, but everything about this ski mountain bears his stamp and expresses his vision of skiing. Ernie isn't here to contradict me, but I'd say his vision was that of skiing as adventure, not just winter recreation. Today when you ski Taos, you're going to have an adventure.

The resort is really called Taos Ski Valley—in New Mexico they have a thing about calling ski mountains "ski valleys." Indeed, the highest, snowiest peak in the Sangre de Cristo Mountains that one gazes up at from the town of Taos is called Vallecito Peak, or "little valley" peak. Go figure. And this Taos ski valley is not only the finest skiing in New Mexico, but one of the handful of really great ski resorts in the country. It's an unlikely venue. Ernie Blake initially spotted this area from a plane; you certainly can't see it from the town of Taos. But this town is part of the surreal charm of Taos skiing. A Spanish colonial settlement, Taos has been a refuge for artists and writers since D. H. Lawrence and his friends wandered into the place in the 1930s. Its adobe architecture, like its indigenous Spanish and Indian culture, is still largely intact, and to most visitors Taos feels more foreign, more exotic than France, Austria, or Switzerland. From town, one drives half an hour up a narrow, steep-sided, densely forested canyon before arriving suddenly at the

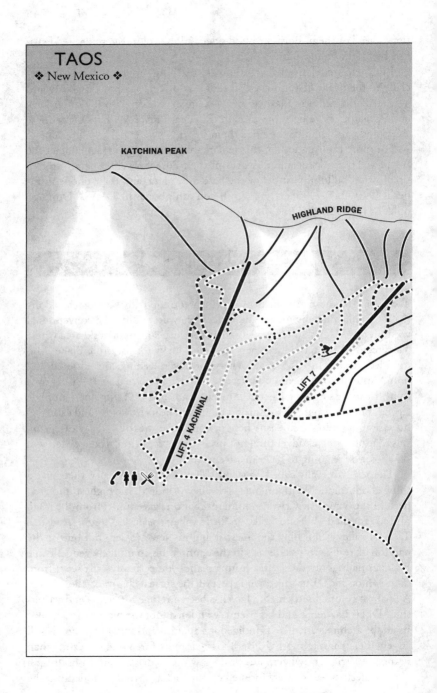

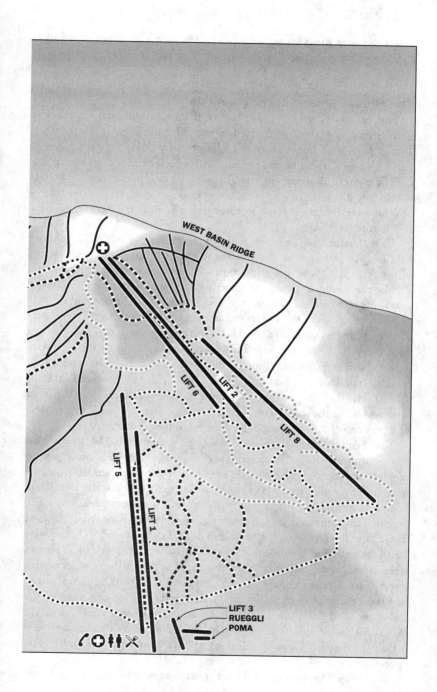

parking area of the compact alpine-village base of a ski area that seems to consist of only a couple of steep runs. Wrong. Taos is full of surprises. Get ready.

The Hidden Shapes of the Mountain

For years skiers arriving at the base of this unconventional ski area have been greeted by a large sign that tells them: Don't panic, what you see is just a small portion of our runs; there's a lot of easier skiing farther up, out of sight. It's a good thing because mostly what you see is *Al's Run,* a steep cascade of big moguls, dropping straight and relentless to the base of two lifts —the only lifts in sight except for a tiny beginner chair and a faint tracery of other steep bump runs curving through the forest to the right of *Al's Run.* It's an impressive introduction.

To understand the shape of the ski mountain that's out of sight above you, imagine *Al's Run* and the lifts that run up it as the spine or central axis of the ski area. This central spine continues upward until it runs into a high skyline ridge, and it divides the mostly north-facing area into two halves consisting of a west side and an east side, that is, the right side and left side as you look up. Both these sides contain large rolling basins, the two intermediate skiing zones at Taos. And both these basins steepen as they rise in a final sweep to the skyline ridge I mentioned earlier. Most of the legendary expert and expert-plus runs drop off this skyline ridge. At its far eastern end, far left as you look at the trail map, this summit ridge rises to a real summit, 12,481-foot Kachina Peak, whose immense treeless face provides the most aesthetic, if not the scariest, of Taos's adventures. But that is just an overview of a very complex mountain, full of secrets, full of discoveries.

Your first lift ride up the mountain will get your attention because it takes you right up *Al's Run,* that steep river of bumps, before depositing you on much friendlier terrain high above the valley. You look around and see, off to your right, a different kind of mountain altogether. This is the *West Basin,* a large friendly bowl full of curvy, interesting blue runs and even a few greens. This is the first of two very attractive intermediate skiing zones at Taos. It's well served by a new fixed-grip quad, Lift 8. Above Lift 8, the West Basin steepens and climbs toward the dramatic skyline ridge in a series of steep chutes and gullies that form the upper and right-hand sides of this basin. These upper sides are all high-drama, expert skiing, and to reach it, one takes either of two parallel lifts, Lifts 2 and 6, which climb out of the top of the West Basin toward ski patrol headquarters—fairly high up on the ski valley's central spine but still well below the topmost ridge. Here there is a fork in the path—expert skiers go one way, intermediate and merely "good" skiers another.

When the ridge is open, this is where experts start hiking. Ten or fifteen steep, hard-breathing minutes bring you to the crest of the *West Basin Ridge,* where you can start traversing down and right in search of your perfect chute, or traverse left, eastward, along what is called *Highline Ridge,* from which the runs are generally less wild but still very steep. If the ridge isn't open, experts slide right from the top of Lift 2 across the *High Traverse,* a thin and thrilling traverse line that cuts across most of the expert runs off the West Basin Ridge. Not to worry, there's still lots of vertical and lots of thrills below the *High Traverse* line.

From Patrol Headquarters, intermediate skiers have only two choices. They can return to the West Basin via *Bambi,* which snakes down the crest of what I've called the ski area's spine—everything else is too steep—or they can head east, along a gentle traversing green trail called *Honeysuckle,* to access the fabulous long green and blue runs served by the Kachina quad. This is the other intermediate skiing zone at Taos: as good as or better than the West Basin but a little harder to get to.

Taos for the Rest of Us

I want to describe the skiing that Taos offers to good skiers first so you don't get the impression that unless you eat black moguls for breakfast, this is no mountain for you. Taos really does offer some superb intermediate skiing but not lazy, laid-back skiing. There's a plethora of stimulating, upper-intermediate skiing here and very little low-intermediate or novice cruising. This is a mountain (excuse me, a ski valley) that challenges you at every turn. Even if you are skiing beautifully down a blue run like *Upper Powderhorn* (that's even designated a slow-skiing zone), you can look up out of the corner of your eye and see the hot shots shredding the black bumps of *Castor* and *Pollux* just above you. That's the way it is everywhere. Clifflike black runs seem to loom above the friendlier blues and greens, reminding you that however skilled a skier you are, you could always be better. At Snowmass or Vail, by contrast, one can ski for days on green and blue runs and forget that such a thing as a steep black face exists. What I mean to say is that your skier's ego is not entirely safe at Taos. This is a ski resort for people who relish the idea of challenge.

But let's start in the West Basin. As soon as you get off Lift 1 from the bottom, turn right and take *Porcupine* (then a small section of *White Feather*) down to the Lift 8 quad. *Porcupine* is a blue highway that sweeps down and left on a small crest with beautiful plunging views and terrific sustained pitch. From the top of Lift 8, the most attractive runs are *Lower Stauffenberg* and its several variants that blend a succession of rolls, drops, and short flats just left of the lift line. There are many alternate lines on the skier's left side of this basin and usually less traffic as you avoid the black-run skiers heading for Lift 2 as well as skiers heading to the Whistlestop Café near the bottom of Lift 6. Once you've got your bearings on this complex mountain, it doesn't take long to ski down to the bottom for lunch. The choices are good. In the early years at Taos, Ernie Blake stopped the lifts at noon so skiers would return to their lodges for lunch, so I guess skiing all the way down for lunch has a bit of tradition behind it. To return home from the West Basin, ski down below Lift 8 where three or four runs funnel into *White Feather,* which in turn becomes a roadlike catwalk that brings skiers around to the front mountain under the last bumps of *Edelweiss* and *Snakedance.* Most skiers follow *Powderhorn* out of the bottom of the West Basin, but it's worth zigging left into *Bambi Glade,* a green gem, or banking off the sides of *Whitefeather Gully.*

On the other side of the mountain, in what I think of as *Kachina Basin,* under the high, white backdrop of Kachina Peak, the skiing varies from green to blue to black. All you need to remember is that the farther right you ski, the harder the slopes get. *Honeysuckle,* the main access route from Patrol Headquarters to Lift 4, the Kachina quad, can be a little boring, so I recommend you drop left off *Honeysuckle* into *Totemoff* (blue or green depending on how you ski it). This takes you to the base of Lift 7, which is definitely worth a couple of blue runs before you move on east to ski on Lift 4. The best thing about the runs on the Kachina Lift is probably the open high-alpine feeling of the first few hundred yards below the top of the lift: stunning views and lots of room to move. The comeback trail from the bottom of the Kachina Lift to the area base is another green road, *Rubezahl,* longer and flatter than *Whitefeather* on the other side. No sweat if your skis are waxed. And they should be. Loony Tunes in the base village is probably the best ski-tuning shop in the Rockies.

Taos for Gutsy Experts

This is it. Mecca. There are only a small handful of American ski areas that offer the kind of steep, high-alpine, high-drama adventure skiing that Taos does. I'm thinking of Squaw Valley, Jackson Hole, and Crested Butte. But no area offers as high a percentage of adventure skiing, and no one else's trail map is this black. In fact, there are more dotted black lines (the code for double diamond runs) than simple black lines on the Taos Ski Valley map.

What to look for? What to ski first? If it snowed overnight (20 inches of feather-light powder at Taos is one of my best skiing memories), you'll find that it takes the patrol quite a while to complete their avalanche control work on the steep chutes off the *High Traverse* and longer still off the ridge. While you're waiting, let me suggest another kind of treat: powder in the trees. A number of runs drop right off the long spine of *Bambi* and aren't runs at all, just places with names: *Walkyries Chute, Sir Arnold Lunn,* and the

Lorelei Trees. A few yards past the entrance you'll be looking for your own line around reasonably spaced trees and always finding it! There's room for hundreds of sets of tracks here. These "runs" bottom out at Lift 7; take it and the short 7th Heaven Lift back to Patrol Headquarters and do it again. I should tell you, at this point, that Taos snow is amazingly dry and light. Logic tells me that snow here can't be any drier or lighter than it is in Colorado, but it seems so. And these are, after all, the southern Rockies, seldom bitterly cold, often sunny. . . .

When you're ready to test yourself against Taos steeps, I recommend you take it step by step. Start with a mere black like *Reforma* or *Blitz* off the *High Traverse.* These runs are steep slots in a steep forest rather than slots through cliffs. If all goes well, you can ski a little farther across the *High Traverse* each run (the return via Lift 2 is rapid and scenic). Somewhere beyond the *West Blitz Trees* and *Spitfire,* the traverse itself starts to get serious: You sidestep gingerly above real cliffs and look down into steep chutes where missing, or blowing, your first turn would be unthinkable. Many of these lines are only one turn wide. Still, the snow in these ultra-steep gullies is usually fantastic—hard, cold, packed powder. It's a good thing, too, because no one could talk me onto the *High Traverse* if conditions were icy. By now you're no longer warming up for Taos steeps, you're skiing them. If you can handle lines like *Oster* and *Stauffenberg,* you're ready for the longer but not any harder lines off the Ridge when the patrol opens it. Actually, I'm talking about the West Basin Ridge here.

If you want both the views and the cachet of skiing the ridge but runs like *Stauffenberg* give you butterflies, no disgrace, you are not out of luck. When you reach the ridge, turn left in the direction of Kachina Peak, and you'll find that the lines off this side (the ridge here is called *Highline Ridge*) are merely exciting, not terrifying. Sometimes it seems as though Ernie Blake was writing a history quiz when he named his favorite runs. (Ask a local who Stauffenberger was. A clue: not an Austrian ski instructor but a tragic figure in World War II.) And how about my favorite Highline Ridge run, *Niños Heroes?* Unlike the martyred Mexican military cadets, the "child heroes" this run is named for, you will not be doomed as you dive off the edge onto this steep but welcoming pitch. A piece of cake compared with a lot of Taos's double blacks.

The finest adventure an expert can have at Taos is walking all the way up the ridge to Kachina Peak and leaving a trail of tiny miniature esses down the center of this vast alpine face. It's not always, or even often, open, so if it is, grab a candy bar for energy and start walking. This is one of the most extraordinary inbounds ski runs in North America.

Perhaps the silliest thing an expert can do here is to spend all day pounding the bumps on Al's Run. But hey, *de gustibus non disputandum*—no accounting for tastes! In fact, expert skiing at Taos is mostly of the high-alpine, ski-what-the-mountain-has-to-offer variety: Narrow chutes, cliffs and couloirs, rocks and trees, deep snow, provide the spice instead of the skier-made bumps. But the lower front face and the black runs under Kachina Peak have all the moguls you could want, as many as you want, and as mean as you want. *Al's Run* in particular is continuous, unrelenting, and famous. If you're skilled enough to handle it, don't leave Taos without skiing it at least once just to say you did. Even if your heart is up there on the ridge.

Taos for Learning Skiers

A ski resort can hardly exist without a learning area for first-timers and novices, and Taos has one too. A ski school likewise has to offer beginner and novice lessons, and the Taos ski school does. But why bother? What Taos lacks are long inviting flats where novice skiers can log lots of mileage and progress without stress. The terrain just isn't there. So the only reason for very inexperienced skiers to pick Taos is if they happen to be accompanying friends who are very experienced skiers. Don't worry if that's you; you'll still have a good time and still learn a lot about skiing. But it won't be like flying. Better, if you can, let your experienced friends ski at Taos Ski Valley while you drive a half hour over Palo Verde Pass to practice your novice skills at Angel Fire. Angel Fire is not my idea of a magical ski resort, but it does have lots of wide-open, low-angle cruising and practice terrain. A big plus for less-experienced skiers.

I've implied that Taos is for good skiers who want to become even better skiers. And there's a ski school here that can help you do it. This is one of the few ski schools in the West where a package of five continuous days of lessons is standard (actually it's five continuous half-days), and the continuity of instruction works wonders. It was inevitable that a ski school on a mountain this challenging would specialize in helping people come to terms with steep and challenging skiing. And why not? I've taken pains to point out that Taos skiing is not just for experts. But the fact remains: The better a skier you are, the more you'll love Taos skiing.

Taos Atmosphere

Up in the ski valley the rather minimalist base facilities have grown into a very attractive, somewhat European flavored mini-village. It's not a real village because there just isn't enough flat land in this high canyon to build one. But there's a lot more up here than just a base lodge. The new resort center complex gives this mini-village a crossroads, and the medieval murals painted on the sides of buildings reinforce the Swiss connection.

There are lodges too, wonderful old-style, full-service lodges where you can sleep, eat, and be merry rather than just condos where you just crash after skiing. The classic Taos Ski Valley lodge is the Hotel St. Bernard, an oasis of dark wood and French hospitality. And speaking of dogs, my favorite lunch spot is the Stray Dog Cantina, a Mexican saloon with great food and equally great locally brewed beer. Don't pass up Eske's green-chile beer if it's on tap the week you're there.

But as honestly cool—and convenient—as this tiny community up at the head of the canyon is, the old town of Taos, only a half-hour away, is a lot more interesting. It should be; it was founded in 1540. Driving down out of the canyon, one enters another world. Adobe buildings, flat roofs, strings of red chilies hanging from protruding timbers, vigas, a sleepy central plaza, and the most photographed and painted adobe church in the West. Taos is a southwestern fantasy, still more or less intact.

Lodging in town is more varied, from B&Bs in 100-year-old adobes to the Taos Inn, a bastion of old New Mexico luxury where every room has its own beehive fireplace. As good as the lodging is, the food is even more unusual. Almost anything you order elicits the query, "Red or green?" Referring to chile, of course. For gourmet meals in Taos try Doc Martin's and Casa Cordova. But for family-recipe versions of traditional northern New Mexico dishes like *carne adovada,* visit Roberto's, only a block from the plaza.

Finally, if you're staying in old Taos, grant yourself the luxury of completely forgetting about skiing from time to time and tuning into the pulse of this remarkable place. What other town of only 4,500 souls has so many great bookstores, so many art galleries, and such frequent concerts? Taos and Santa Fe are the twin cultural epicenters of northern New Mexico, and, of the two, tiny Taos is more unlikely and more special. You can find every sort of art in Taos's dozens of galleries and six museums. But the most sophisticated environmental sculpture in the region is on display at Philip Bareiss Contemporary Exhibitions near the Ski Valley Road turnoff. If, by chance, your ski vacation plans bring you to Taos during Christmas week, stop skiing early on Christmas Day and watch the ceremonial dances at Taos Pueblo just outside of town—a trip through time to an earlier America and every bit as special as a perfect run off the ridge.

TAOS DATA		

Mountain Statistics		**Transportation**
Vertical feet	2,612 feet	**By car** A 30-minute drive from Taos; Taos itself is about a 2½-hour drive north of Albuquerque via Santa Fe and Española.
Base elevation	9,207 feet	
Summit elevation	11,819 feet	
Longest run	4+ miles	
Average annual snowfall	320 inches	**By plane** To Albuquerque Airport, then drive to Taos and the Ski Valley.
Number of lifts	11	
	3 quad chairs	**Key Phone Numbers**
	1 triple chair	Ski Area Information (505) 776-2291
	6 double chairs	Snow Report (505) 776-2916
	1 surface lift	Ski Valley Reservations (800) 776-1111 or (505) 776-2233 or (800) 992-7669
Uphill capacity	14,000+ skiers per hour	
Skiable terrain	1,100 acres	
Opening date	mid-November	www.taoswebb.com or www.skinewmexico.com
Closing date	mid-April	
Snowboarding	No!	

LITO'S TECH TIP

Safety on the Steeps

So few American ski resorts offer truly steep skiing that the skills involved are anything but widespread. Here are a few tips that should help already strong skiers adapt their technique to the sort of steeper-than-usual slopes they'll find at places like Taos Ski Valley.

First, get used to the angle before starting to turn. Do this by sideslipping in a very anticipated position, hips and shoulders turned straight down the mountain, downhill pole extended and ready, just as if you were about to turn. Sideslip straight down a few feet, then set your edges with a quick flick of your knees into the hill. Repeat this a couple of times on the very top of the steep slope you are about to ski. By doing so, your body, and your mind too, will adjust to the angle of the slope before the real action starts. When you do turn, you will have had a foretaste of the all-important control phase at the end of each turn.

Second, make your turns short, quick, and powerful. On very steep slopes you want to bring your skis rapidly from one almost horizontal position to another one, facing the opposite way without spending a lot of time in the middle or fall-line phase of the turn. Lingering in the fall-line on steep slopes, you'll pick up too much speed too fast. Start your turns with a snappy, positive up motion (either bouncing up from quick edge set or actually projecting yourself upward with a strong extension of the legs), and then you'll be able to turn your skis into the fall line very rapidly, virtually in the air. When you "land" from this rapid, initial pivoting, try to land softly; don't jam your edges into the steep snow; instead let the skis skid or sideslip. (Over-edged skis tend to accelerate!) Then sink and steer your sideslipping skis (especially your outside ski) quickly around to the horizontal. Spend as little time as possible in the middle or "belly" of the turn.

And finally, once you start turning, keep turning. Things get out of hand only when you freeze or hesitate between turns. Continuous short turns are the recipe for control on very steep slopes. To eliminate any hesitation, keep reaching your outside/downhill pole straight down the hill—even a little farther down than you usually do, to help balance your body over the downhill ski. Plant that pole without hesitation and you'll find that triggers the next turn without hesitation. Just as with super bumps, if your hand and pole are late, then you'll be late.

One last piece of advice: Find a practice slope that is very steep but neither long nor dangerous (i.e., no obstacles to fall into) on which to practice these extra-quick, extra-short turns. The top of *Stauffenberg* is no place to start trying to shorten your turns. You don't need much vertical to practice on: Three or four turns will do. Take a deep breath, and go.

SANTA FE

New Mexico skiing has a lot going for it: dry snow conditions that seem to depend more on dry southwestern air than on bitter cold temperatures, lots of sunshine, and the special flavor of traditional, Hispanic hospitality. The only problem is that there's only one New Mexico ski area that feels like a true Rocky Mountain resort to me, and that is Taos Ski Valley. The other ski areas are either day ski areas rather than destination areas, or their ski offering is too limited to deserve a chapter in this guidebook. Colorado, too, has a number of very small ski areas that were not included in this guidebook because I'd promised myself I was only going to write about the very best skiing in Colorado and the southern Rockies. A few exceptional day areas (as opposed to full resorts) have already slipped in, such as Loveland and Purgatory, and now we're about to visit another: Santa Fe.

If this small ski area—formerly known as Santa Fe Ski Basin and now known simply as Ski Santa Fe—is not a real vacation destination, the same

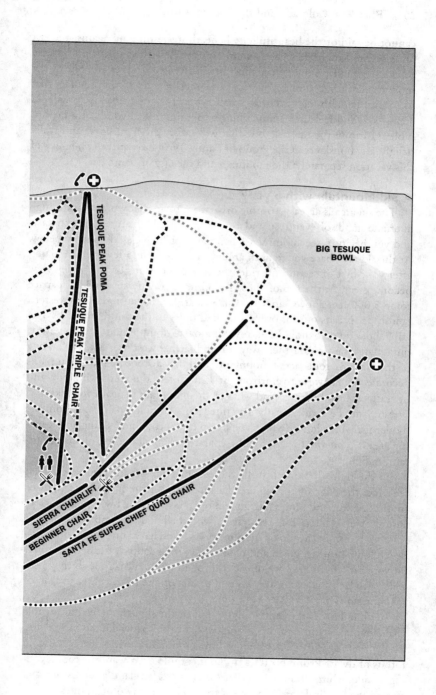

TESUQUE PEAK POMA

TESUQUE PEAK TRIPLE CHAIR

BIG TESUQUE BOWL

SIERRA CHAIRLIFT

BEGINNER CHAIR

SANTA FE SUPER CHIEF QUAD CHAIR

cannot be said of the beautiful city beneath it, nestling up against the last folds of the Sangre de Cristo Mountains at the very southern end of the Rockies. Santa Fe is one of the most beautiful historic cities and one of the most romantic vacation destinations in America. Add to that the fact that Ski Santa Fe, although a rather small ski area—a very *friendly* small ski area—skis and feels like a much bigger mountain, and you have a memorable ski trip in the making, one that will satisfy die-hard skiers and really delight any nonskiers in the group or family. We'll look at the two halves of this vacation separately: the mountain and the city of Santa Fe.

A Ski Mountain with a View

The ski area is an easy 16-mile drive from town that winds you through alternate stands of evergreen and aspen. Periodically the forest curtain parts and you begin to see an immense panorama of high desert country below. At the ski area base you're back among the trees, but a few minutes later, after your first or second lift ride, the true dimensions of this valley view become clear. At the top of the ski mountain you are suspended in space some 5,000 feet above Santa Fe. On a clear day, the austere southwestern landscape spreads out for over a hundred miles to the south and west. The tall silhouette of Sandia Peak, towering over Albuquerque 70 miles away, punctuates the view; farther away still and farther west rises Mt. Taylor, one of the Navajos' four sacred mountains, and the sawtooth Jemez Mountains decorate the far western horizon. At 12,000 feet the view is literally and figuratively breathtaking. And what of the mountain beneath your skis?

Ski Santa Fe divides neatly into three parts fanning up and out from the modernistic base lodge (where you'll also find a cool kids' skiing and learning area, *Chipmunk Corner*, totally separated from all the rest of the mountain traffic).

To the right (looking up) the Super Chief quad takes you up to what feels like the edge of the ski area basin. Just over the hill, to the right or south, one sees and senses a large semiopen bowl, dotted with sparse widespread trees. This is Big Tesuque Bowl, which I'll talk more about in a minute. But from the top of the Super Chief you have your choice of a half-dozen long, flowing, green and blue runs (with a couple of moguled blacks on your far left). These are runs cut through trees, and although they flow well, they lack the expansiveness and drama of the next, center section of the mountain.

Tesuque Peak is the central high point of the ski area, served by a triple chair that takes you right up a long crest, and this is where the fun begins. To the right of this lift (looking up) the mountain is wide-open. Scattered forests of dwarf krumholz trees thin out completely toward the top, revealing a wide, white alpine world that turns into a fairyland after a storm has frosted the last, isolated, windswept trees. There are two main lines on this side, *Parachute* and *Gayway*, wide-cut and groomed paths. But the beauty is that you can ski almost anywhere down here. It's unusual to experience this sort of back bowl, ski-anywhere-you-want terrain at such a small ski area. But as I said earlier, Santa Fe feels, and skis, bigger than it really is. *Parachute* dives right down the convex flank of the mountain—steepening progressively to a very respectable pitch—while *Gayway* and its variations meander out to the left and back for a much lower-angle run.

On the other side of the Tesuque Peak triple chair, the left side as you ride up, you'll see slopes of dense timber. A different flavor of skiing altogether. This forested face is accessed from a catwalk called *Sunset*, and although there are several runs cut down through the steep trees—*Burro Alley, Wizard,* and *Columbine*—once again you'll find that you can ski anywhere in here. *Tequila Sunrise* is the name of a large partially gladed and very inviting forest zone, not an actual run, where you can and should do just that—ski anywhere. That is, if you're a strong enough skier, since this whole forested face is very legitimately marked black. This steep skiing all funnels down into an open side valley, *Alpine Bowl,* that slants back to the base of the Tesuque Peak triple chair and is full of friendly blue and green runs.

And, finally, I should say that beginners have a zone and a chairlift of their own, the Easy Street beginner chair, which stretches right above the base lodge.

Getting the Most out of Santa Fe Skiing

Santa Fe is a small enough ski area that you won't have any trouble figuring it out—at least not compared to some of the giants like Vail and Snowmass. But here are a few tips anyway. Inexperienced and learning skiers and novices will spend most of their time on the long friendly flats just above the base lodge. This area is served by two lifts: the tiny Pine Flats surface lift, and the longer Easy Street beginner chair. Don't stay on the bottom flats; take the chair right away. Lots of mileage is even more important for beginners and novices than lots of instruction. While there is no easy green way down from the top of Tesuque Peak, there are a number of friendly green routes down from the top of both the Super Chief quad and the Sierra Lift. These involve roundabout traverses to the right or left, so don't just head straight down or you'll be skiing blue runs before you're ready.

Good skiers will spend much of their time higher on the mountain, circulating on the Tesuque Peak Lift. Take either the Sierra or Super Chief lifts for one warm-up run—they both serve almost the same runs—before heading to the top, and then start on *Gayway*. When you get bored with this wide-open cruising, try the other side of the peak, following *Sunset* in a long zig and a short zag all the way around the steep forested runs I mentioned earlier, in order to access the pleasant blue-green terrain in *Alpine Bowl*.

Strong skiers in search of a challenge should start exploring the forest right next to the Tesuque Peak Lift line. There's a long platter-pull lift in the woods, parallel to the triple chair, that is a favorite with Santa Fe skiers because it is actually faster than the chair. It's hard to know where you are in this forested zone unless you're skiing with a local. Run designations like *First Tracks, Avalanche,* and *Desperado* seem to apply equally to a large, steep zone of trees. The snow is protected from wind by the trees and is usually quite good even though nothing in this area is really ever groomed.

But as exciting as these tree runs are, I'm always glad to emerge back into the world of light and space which I think is the aesthetic edge of Santa Fe skiing. And you'll find that in spades along the boundary between the ski area and Big Tesuque Bowl. This immense open draw funnels down to the highway a few miles below the ski-area base. So you don't want to just hike out there and go. But in fact, the boundary between the ski area and Big Tesuque has never been too perfectly defined or too rigidly marked, so strong skiers have always allowed themselves fleeting excursions into and back out of this sublime bowl. In the past the ski area sometimes aided and abetted this out-of-area skiing by arranging shuttles down the highway to pick up skiers who followed Big Tesuque all the way down; but nowadays, if a Big-T excursion tempts you, it's best to organize your own shuttle by leaving a car at the Forest Service's Big Tesuque picnic area on the access road several miles below the ski area. I do know that the ski area has been patiently jumping through all the environmental hoops needed to put a lift in Big Tesuque and make it an official part of the Ski Santa Fe experience. When this happens, it will double the size and quality of Santa Fe skiing overnight.

Santa Fe, the City below the Mountain

Après-ski, Santa Fe–style, is limited by only two factors: your imagination and your pocketbook. The readers of *Condé Nast Traveler* voted Santa Fe "the top travel destination in the world," and while the citizens of Paris or Rio might disagree, that's still some kind of recommendation. My own recommendation for a perfect vacation is to split a week between skiing and exploring Santa Fe. In several days one barely scratches the surface of this arty, adobe city.

Consider staying at one of the great inns, La Fonda, the Inn at Loretto, or the newer but lovely Inn of the Anasazi, all within easy walking distance of the plaza. This large central square was the hub of life in colonial Santa Fe 400 years ago, and it's still the hub today. On the plaza check out the Palace of the Governors and the Art Museum next door, and if you're look-ing for a small slice of authentic New Mexico pop culture, treat yourself to a Frito pie at Woolworth's across the plaza. For more serious eating adven-tures, don't miss Pasquale's, a block from the plaza, gourmet New Mexico cooking without pretensions. For southwestern cuisine *with* pretensions, but delicious nonetheless, the Coyote Café lives up to its reputation.

Art is found all over town; the small streets around the plaza are chock-full of galleries and innovative boutiques that would appear to be galleries in any other city. There's Canyon Road, a narrow, one-lane street winding up into the hills, and lined with the oldest galleries in Santa Fe, in beautiful, crooked, one-story adobes that have inspired generations of painters. Just a short drive north of town, in the neighboring village of Tesuque, you can visit Shidoni, a large outdoor sculpture park and a working bronze sculpture foundry that keeps the lost, wax-casting tradition alive. On the south edge of Santa Fe you'll find a whole district of stunning museums: ethnography, art, and folklore. Even a museum devoted to toys from around the world. Have I told you enough? Not really, because Santa Fe is worth a guidebook of its own. But our subject is skiing. If I've tempted you to spend a few days in Santa Fe on your way to and from some southwestern powder, that's well and good. You won't be disappointed.

SANTA FE DATA

Mountain Statistics

Vertical feet	1,650 feet
Base elevation	10,350 feet
Summit elevation	12,000 feet
Longest run	3 miles
Average annual snowfall	225 inches
Number of lifts	7
	1 quad chair
	1 triple chair
	2 double chairs
	3 surface lifts
Uphill capacity	7,800 skiers per hour
Skiable terrain	550 acres
Opening date	Thanksgiving
Closing date	mid-April
Snowboarding	Yes

Transportation

By car Less than a half-hour drive from downtown Santa Fe (16 miles) on NM Highway 475. The city of Santa Fe itself is approximately 1 hour by car from the Albuquerque Airport on I-25. Convenient service from the Albuquerque Airport to Santa Fe by ShuttleJack bus.

By plane Direct flights from major cities to the Albuquerque Airport; no commercial flights to Santa Fe itself.

Key Phone Numbers

Ski Area Information
    (505) 982-4429
Snow Report (505) 983-9155 or
    (800) 982-SNOW
Santa Fe Central Reservations
    (800) 776-SNOW
www.skisantafe.com or
www.skinewmexico.com

Protection from the Elements vs. Style

Actually there's no conflict here, or there shouldn't be, since skiers who are warm and comfortable move well and look good—and what else is style about? There are a lot of tricks to staying comfortable on the slopes, in all weather, that experienced skiers take for granted. Tricks I thought I'd share with you.

Start with your skin. Time was when ski instructors were stereotyped as the bronzed gods of the slopes. Nowadays a skier's tan is no longer something to be desired. High-altitude sun (remember, even at Santa Fe, you're skiing at 12,000 feet) can do more than sunburn you. There's a very real risk of skin cancer from too much high-altitude sun. So take a tip from today's instructors and use sunscreen with the highest sunblock rating you can find (25 is not too high).

The knit "neck gaiter" is another secret weapon in the fight for comfort on the slopes. It is nothing more than the large turtleneck of a turtleneck sweater—without the sweater. In other words a tube, knitted wool or a less scratchy synthetic. These are so small and light you can keep one in an inside parka pocket and only put it on when the wind comes up or the sun goes down. Skiers hide in their neck gaiters on cold days or when they're skiing in clouds of boiling powder, pulling them up to cover mouth and nose as needed.

In the worst stormy conditions, with the wind howling and snow driving horizontally into your face, the combination of neck gaiter, goggles, and a knit hat is still all you need to stay snug from the shoulders up. There is a good reason why expert skiers almost never pull up the hood of a parka and secure it around their face. A hood tends to interfere with the free-floating motion of a skier's head, and it's precisely your ability to keep your head level as you ski that gives you a trustworthy, level horizon line for better balance. With the hood of your ski jacket pulled up, you definitely lose some of that balance.

At least half the skiers I know suffer from cold fingers from time to time. If that's you, trade your ski gloves in for a pair of mittens. In mittens, your fingers can warm each other. Don't worry; it is not uncool to wear mittens even if World Cup ski racers don't. Skiers with particularly cold-sensitive hands can also carry small chemical heat packs in their pockets. Sold under different brand names in almost all sporting goods stores, these cunning plastic packages come to life when you squeeze them and put out lots of heat for several hours. You can slip them inside your mittens on long lift rides.

Most skiers today know to dress in layers, as many as possible. You'll be more comfortable and warmer when you need to be if you are wearing lots of layers that trap air between them rather than just putting on your heaviest down jacket for a cold winter day on the slopes. Did you know that on very cold days your feet will stay warmer if you wear an extra-thin pair of socks? Heavier socks make you colder by cutting off circulation. And there's no real reason to buckle the front or toe buckle of conventionally designed boots on very cold days either. Give your toes as much room to move as possible.

Finally, while we're on the subject of boots, no matter what the fashion pages of the ski magazines say, resist the idea of in-the-boot ski pants. Snow always packs in there between pants leg and boot, and of course your feet eventually get wet and cold. In-the-boot stretch pants finger you as a "snow bunny" who never skis deep snow; it is a better look for the base-lodge bar than for the slopes. Look for ski pants with an effective snow cuff that slides easily over the top of your boots and seals them against flying snow. Remember, the ultimate fashion statement on skis is a perfect turn, not a perfect ski suit.

PART 3

Utah and the
Northern Rockies

PETER SHELTON
ED CHAUNER

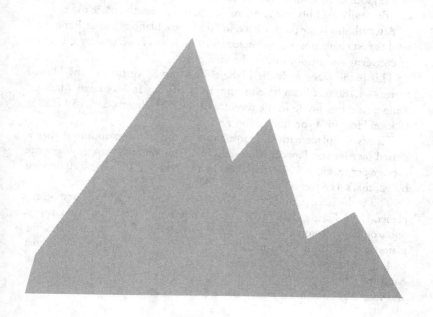

IMAGINE Brigham Young in the summer of 1847, sick with fever after a six-month journey across the plains and over the Rocky Mountains of Wyoming and Utah, peering down on the Great Salt Lake from high up in Emigration Canyon (not far from where I-80 today whisks skiers from the Salt Lake Airport to Park City and Deer Valley). He raises himself up on an elbow and utters the immortal words, "This is the place." For nineteenth-century Mormons it was the place—the place nobody else wanted—where they could build their Kingdom of Deseret by turning the abundant snows of the Rockies out of their creek beds and onto lush valley farms.

For mountain men, from Lewis and Clark to Jim Bridger, the ranges of the northern Rockies were the land of beaver, whose pelts made the finest and most fashionable top hats. For prospectors the Rockies were the place, from Alta to Coeur d'Alene, where 90 percent of American silver came out of the ground. And for skiers the Rockies are the big draw, the snow magnet, the really big hills, the really romantic ski towns: the place to ski.

After all, this is the place where, in Sun Valley, Idaho's Pioneer Range, the world's first chairlift was constructed in 1936. It was conceived by a designer of conveyor systems for loading banana boats.

This is the place with the highest lift—served vertical in the United States—4,180 feet from base to summit at Big Sky in Montana's Madison Range. And it is home to the recently deposed ex-champ, at 4,139 feet, at Jackson Hole in Wyoming's Teton Range.

This is the place with the most snow in the country, an honor that is shared by Alta and Powder Mountain in Utah's Wasatch Range, where the average per season is 500 inches, year in and year out. Let's see: 500 divided by 12; that's 41½ feet of snow, and my house is 23 feet high, and . . .

This is the place with the best snow in the country, maybe the best on the planet. Utah's license plates used to spell it out in no uncertain terms: Greatest Snow on Earth (before the state switched to more colorful, but less interesting, plates on the theme of Canyonlands rock). Utah's snow is regularly on the order of 4 to 5 percent water. Melt a quart of it and you get a sip. Scoop it up in your hand and it blows away like dandelion feathers. Pack it down on a ski mountain and your edges slice it like butter: silent, forgiving, effortless.

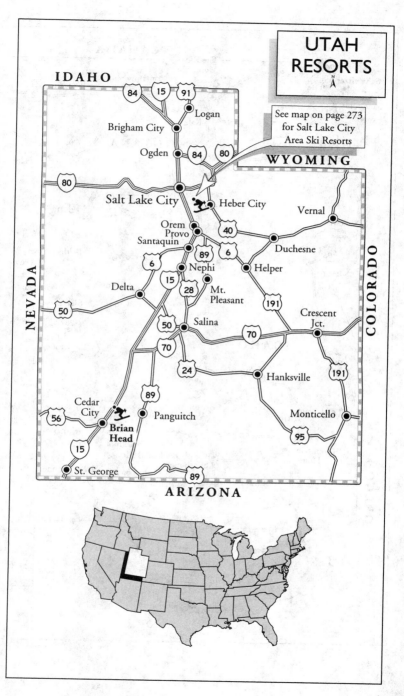

UTAH
RESORTS

IDAHO

84 15 91
Logan
Brigham City
Ogden 84 80

See map on page 273
for Salt Lake City
Area Ski Resorts

WYOMING

80
80
Salt Lake City
Heber City
Vernal
Orem
Provo 40
Santaquin 89 6 Duchesne
6
Nephi Helper
Delta 15
28 Mt.
Pleasant 191
50
50 Salina
70
70 Crescent
Jct.
24 Hanksville 191

Cedar 89
City Panguitch Monticello
56
Brian 95
Head
15
St. George 89

ARIZONA

NEVADA

COLORADO

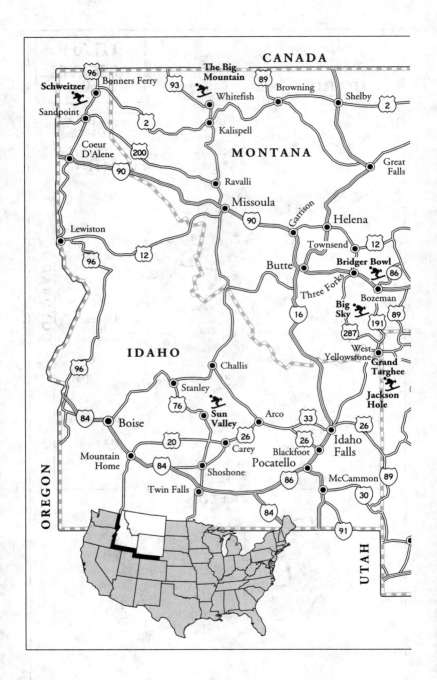

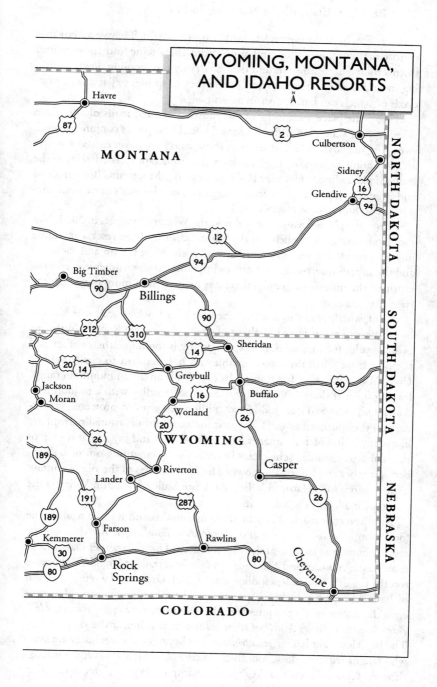

WYOMING, MONTANA, AND IDAHO RESORTS

N

MONTANA

Havre

87

2

Culbertson

Sidney

Glendive

16

94

NORTH DAKOTA

12

94

Big Timber

90

Billings

90

212

310

94

14

Sheridan

20 14

Greybull

90

Jackson

Moran

16

Buffalo

26

Worland

20

WYOMING

Casper

SOUTH DAKOTA

26

Riverton

Lander

189

191

287

189

Farson

Rawlins

Kemmerer

30

80

Rock
Springs

80

Cheyenne

NEBRASKA

COLORADO

Utah gets it, as do the resorts farther up the chain. They've all got that continental climate a thousand miles from the Pacific and those winter storms rolling across the western deserts: drying out, cooling down, climbing toward the continental divide, where they drop big, stellar flakes, hundreds of which can balance on an aspen twig.

This is the place with some of the most-recognized icons of American skiing—Sun Valley, Snowbird, Jackson Hole. These places conjure graceful, swooping magic in the minds even of those who have never carved a winter arc. It is home to some of the least-known or underappreciated gems in the lexicon, places like Schweitzer Basin and the Big Mountain, Bridger Bowl and Brighton—places where the skiing is so good the locals don't want anyone else to know those places exist.

This is the place, finally, that will host the Winter Olympics in 2002. Not that Utah needs the publicity or the business. Most of the resorts are doing just fine, thank you very much. It's just that given the terrain and the snow and the superb transportation links and the fine ski-town amenities and the esprit of the mountain people, there has never been a more perfect site to stage the games.

All of which is not to say that the northern Rockies are some kind of homogeneous extension of Utah, or of the better-known Rocky Mountains of Colorado, for that matter. The geography is too huge, the weather and the people who live there too variable and independent to classify glibly. Utah's Wasatch Range, for example, is practically an urban mountain range, leaping up as it does 7,000 vertical feet out of a valley with a million residents, and Jackson Hole, hidden by millions of acres of protected wilderness on the southern edge of Yellowstone and Teton National parks, feels like a tiny island of human energy in a sea of rock and sky. Up at the tip of the Idaho panhandle, Schweitzer Basin is slowly emerging out of a slumbering timber and railroading town. The same applies to the Big Mountain high in Montana's Flathead Valley. And Sun Valley, well, Sun Valley is the queen of it all, and she knows it.

Read the trail maps at any of these mountains and it's like reading the local history. *Sublette Ridge* and *Rendezvous Bowl* recall the days of the mountain men at Jackson Hole, which is named for the trapper Davey Jackson. Ski the *Bannock* and *Shoshone* and *Blackfoot* trails at Grand Targhee and feel the tug of a wilder, less spoiled time. Chief Targhee led a renegade band of Bannocks against the U.S. Army in one of the last Indian wars. Alta's runs echo the names of silver mines from her boom years: *Emma, Rustler, Hellgate, Peruvian, Patsey Marley.* Other ski mountains honor the ski pioneers. The Big Mountain has its *Toni Matt* trail in honor of the legendary Austrian who taught with the ski school there. Jackson Hole has *Pepi's Run* for long-time ski school director and Olympic champion Pepi Steigler. Sun Valley likes to name trails after its famous racing alumni, including, most recently, Picabo Street, the Olympic downhill racer with the flying ponytail and effervescent smile; you can schuss *Picabo's Street* just off the Warm Springs side of the mountain.

From beaver to silver to cattle dotting the big empty expanse, the northern Rockies have followed the classic western cycle of boom-and-bust. Now it is boom again as the beauty of the mountains and the thrill of the skiing attract stars like Jane Fonda and Ted Turner, Peter Fonda, Glenn Close, Tom Cruise, and the "downhill racer" himself, Robert Redford. Actually, Redford has lived at his Sundance hideaway for 30 years, which qualifies him, almost, for native status. As a skier, he has known for decades what many in America are just discovering: The combination of high elevation, big mountains, and cold snow born on consistent storm tracks makes the skiing in the northern Rockies second to none.

Choose one, any one. In short order, you will proclaim it, indeed, *the Place.*

# Little Cottonwood Canyon

Alta A classic in every sense of the word: huge quantities of soft Utah powder; wide-open, European-style terrain; intimate lodges sandwiched between avalanche run-out zones; tickets priced for the people; and a history that reads like a who's who of American skiing. Some will be put off by the lack of high-speed lifts and the preponderance of ungroomed slopes, but that's the way Alta likes it: Ski the wild snow, and keep the crowds on the lifts rather than on the trails.

Snowbird Alta's younger, slicker sister is located one mile down the canyon. It has similar snow and superb terrain—especially for very good skiers— and the notable addition of a swift, Swiss 125-passenger tram to the summit. There is limited beginner terrain, but what they do have is first class. The village is dense and high-rise with a lot of concrete and glass; it is extremely efficient but emotionally cold compared to Alta's historic lodges.

ALTA

A is for Alta, and Alta *means* Utah skiing to a lot of people.

These people feel about Alta the way a good Moslem feels about Mecca: No skier should die without having made at least one pilgrimage. Those who can will scrape together as many return trips as possible in a skiing life. Every skier with dreams of deep powder dancing in his head owes himself a trip. At Alta the snow falls deeper and lighter than anywhere else, including Alta's similarly, but not quite so profoundly, blessed Utah neighbors. Anyone with a yen for the truly steep, for chutes and open faces where a pole plant feels like reaching off the edge of the roof, needs to find his way to Alta. Anyone with an appreciation for European-style, above-timberline skiing will recognize a classic in Alta. Anyone with a sense of history who wants to ski the trails where powder pioneers Dick Durrance and Alf Engen and Junior Bounous skied will eventually find his way to Alta, a ski resort as timeless and free of fashion as any in the land.

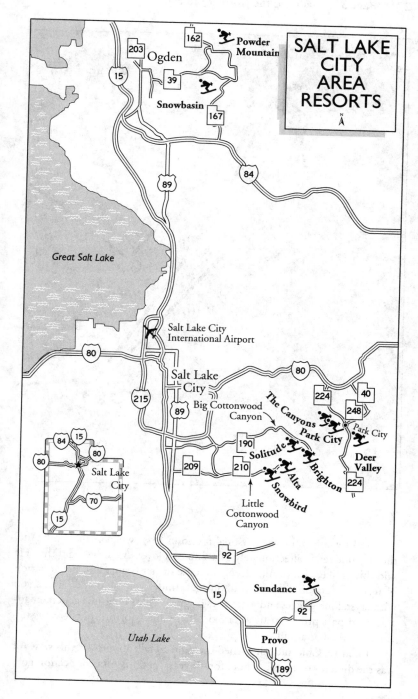

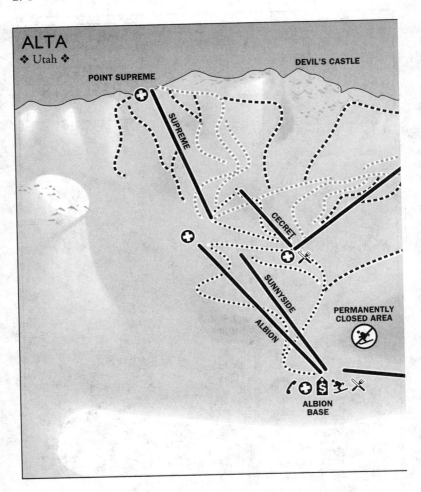

I find I want to use the personal pronoun "she" when I talk about Alta, the way one refers affectionately to a ship or a lover. Alf Engen did this. He said things like, "I love Alta deeply because of her beauty and her variation of terrain." Alta does this to you. She gets under your skin and haunts you with crystalline images and memories of grace. Alta's longtime general manager, and past president of Alta Ski Lifts, Chic Morton, put it very succinctly: "Alta has a soul."

Of course, Chic and Alf earned the right to talk about Alta this way. Alf was the director of the ski school for 40 years, and his Alta connection goes

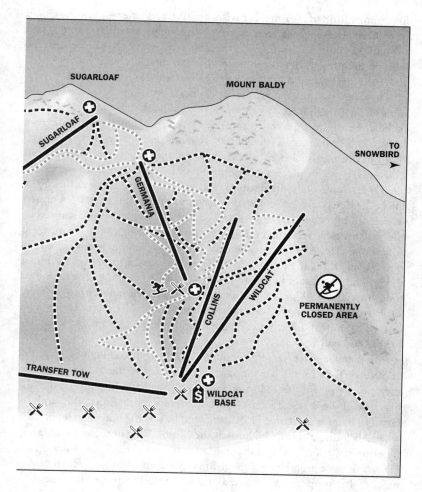

back even further than that. It was Alf, out exploring on skis from his CCC post near Brighton in Big Cottonwood Canyon in 1935, who "discovered" Alta and first harbored the thought of turning her delightful, snowy curves into ski runs.

Like many of the first, and best, ski areas in the West—Aspen, Park City, Telluride—Alta was born a nineteenth-century mining camp.

Legend has it that a party of soldiers and their wives were picnicking in Little Cottonwood Canyon in 1864 when one of the women picked up an unusual rock. It was extremely high-grade silver ore. The mines, with names like Emma, Rustler, Hellgate, Peruvian, and Patsey Marley—now the names of some of Alta's most famous ski runs—sprang up overnight along with a town of 5,000 men and women at the cramped head of the canyon near the base of the present-day Albion Lift. (Today there are barely 1,000 beds above the creekside at 8,500 feet of elevation, and it seems like plenty.)

They were raucous, dangerous days in the silver camp. Alta had 7 restaurants, 2 boardinghouses, 3 general stores, a school, a blacksmith, 2 shoemakers, 2 drugstores, a confectionery, 2 assayers, 4 doctors, a minister, a lawyer, 3 breweries, and 26 saloons. Records show there were over 100 shootings in the Bucket of Blood Saloon alone. The miners literally cut down every tree in the canyon for mine timbers and framing lumber. An already fearsome avalanche problem was worsened, and slides rained down unchecked. According to newspaper accounts of the time at least 74 miners were killed in snowslides between 1872 and 1911. What wasn't destroyed by the avalanches was finished off by a devastating fire in 1878. The town of Alta was leveled. All that remained was "here and there the stump of an old tree . . . only this and nothing more." The old town site was never rebuilt, as the ore had played out in the mid-1880s. A second boom briefly rekindled fevers in 1906–1907, when new technologies allowed the recovery of more silver from old tailings. But that, too, soon died. The Great Depression seemed to snuff all life from the region. Until, that is, Alf Engen skied over the hill and had a vision.

Another character figures prominently in the reawakening of Alta in the 1930s. You'll see his felt hat with a jaunty pheasant feather swept back from the brim along with his old wooden skis and bear-trap bindings in the display case in the Wildcat Ticket Office commemorating Alta's 50th anniversary. His name was George H. Watson, and he was the only man left in Alta when Alf found it. He called himself the Mayor. Why not? He was a majority of one. Watson lived in a shack near the base of the current Wildcat Lift. He was the sole proprietor of the defunct Alta United Mines, which owned most of the property Alf coveted as a ski area. The mayor became Alf's staunch ally in the plan. He was more than happy to deed his 700 acres (as well as nearly 1,000 acres that apparently didn't belong to him) along with his substantial tax bill to the Forest Service, to be developed for winter recreation. Watson stayed on as mayor until he died, in bed, during a snow-storm in the winter of 1952.

From Watson's generosity and the simultaneous formation of the Salt Lake Winter Recreation Association in 1938, Alta was reborn. The nation's second chairlift—actually a converted mine tram near the site of the current Collins Lift—opened for business in the winter of 1938–39. An all-day lift ticket cost a buck and a half.

Things haven't changed all that much in nearly 60 years. Alta's ticket prices have always been about 15 years behind the industry standard. Joe Quinney, one of the guiding lights of the SLWRA, is reputed to have told his successors, "What you do for Alta, you do for me. Take what you need to make a living, *but keep the price down.*" This is still Alta's guiding philosophy. The area is run as a family business: Pay for improvements when you have the cash, don't go into debt, sell skiing not real estate, and keep the price down.

Utah skiers are spoiled by the low price of Alta skiing. (Brighton and Solitude, the Big Cottonwood Canyon areas to the north, are forced to stay competitive with Alta for the local business, which is to the benefit of skiers everywhere.) Out-of-state visitors are pleasantly shocked. Yet Alta makes a profit every year.

Atop the Wasatch Front, at the head of the canyon, at the top of the heap of American skiing, Alta doesn't feel the need to advertise. So they don't. They don't discount tickets—even for children. Area assistant general manager Peter Lawson, grandson of Joe Quinney, says, "We don't sell a children's ticket because everybody pays children's prices."

Amen. Alta's clientele feel themselves to be part of the family. Locals come up from the city on the weekends. Destination skiers, repeat customers most likely, from the far corners of the United States and abroad fill Alta's five lodges during the week. Generations have been returning every winter for decades. Alf is now giving lessons to the grandchildren of people he taught to ski in the early days.

The draw of the place is hard to define, but it surely has to do with the combination of intimacy and grandeur, the hominess of the lodges, and the unquenchable challenge of the mountain, along with the palpable feel of history, the snow, and, of course, the people. An Alta ski patrolman hit the nail on the head when he told me, "At least when you ski at Alta you know you're dealing with real people and not clones manufactured by the marketing department with pasted-on smiles." Alta is a throwback to simpler times. It is about skiing, real skiing.

Alta's Mountain: An Introduction

Alta occupies two distinct basins, like a big W, with the steep Rustler Ridge in the center. The right-hand spike of the W (looking south) is crowned by 11,068-foot Mount Baldy. The left-hand peak is 10,595-foot Point Supreme. Both basins more or less face north, thus preserving that exquisite dry snow, though there are variations of exposure from east around to west. The only thing Alta doesn't have, inbounds, is a true south-facing slope, but there are plenty to be found across the highway. After every storm local backcountry skiers and snowboarders can be seen hiking the naked white slopes of Flagstaff and Superior for a single run down.

Think of the basins as open books. At the bottom of the spine of the right-hand book is the Wildcat/Collins base area. A half-mile farther up the canyon, at the foot of the other book's spine, is the Albion base. Both have parking, tickets, rentals, cafeterias, etc. The Wildcat/Collins base is the original ski terrain at Alta. It is generally steeper and bumpier and has more trees than Albion Basin. Albion is far broader, more spread out, and holds the majority of the beginner and intermediate terrain. The two bases are connected by the Transfer Rope Tow, which traverses the almost flat valley floor where the cabins and tent shacks of Alta's boomtown once stood.

Alta *feels* like a huge area even though it has, by western standards, only a medium-size, 2,100-foot vertical. The reason it skis big has to do with the quality of the choices one faces on the mountain. Every lift ride requires delicious decision-making. For example: I'm at the top of Germania. Do I want to fly down the polished expanse of *Ballroom,* drop down the backside to Sugarloaf, hike to the languid snowfields below Devil's Castle, or slide out the *High Traverse* to the still, steep trees of *North Rustler?* Variety is what keeps Alta's employees around for 20 years and more. It's what keeps Alta perennially young—the constant sense of possibility and discovery that are, I believe, at the very core of skiing.

The area's 2,200 acres (no small fiefdom by anybody's standards) are efficiently served by just eight chairlifts: three on the Collins side and five in Albion Basin. It's an effective layout requiring only two lift rides to reach any of the three high points. Alta purposefully doesn't put too many skiers up the hill. "*Roooons* the skiing," Alf once said in his lilting Norwegian accent. Alta refuses to consider installing high-speed quad chairs as a means of eliminating the sometimes long weekend lift lines, although several lifts have been upgraded to triple chairs in recent years. "We'd just as soon have them in a lift line if it will mean better skiing on the mountain," said Alf. By and large Alta skiers agree. The swooping freedom of an unfettered line on the hill is worth a few extra minutes in line at the bottom. A sign at the base of the Albion lift on busy days says, "Be mellow; we are." And that's the way it is.

Stubborn? Yes. Anachronistic? Perhaps. Mainly Alta is content. And quite sure of its priorities. The downhill experience is number one.

Alta's Justly Famous Steep and Deep

Powder and Alta are practically synonymous. Hardly a week goes by in a normal year that it doesn't snow. The area averages 500 inches a season. Forty-one feet of snow, and most of it is that eiderdown stuff that Utahans rightly call the greatest snow on earth.

The two or three seminal developments in the history of powder skiing were forged here in the 1940s and 1950s. Alf and his brothers Sverre and Corey and America's first ski Olympian, Dick Durrance, together invented a deep-snow technique called the Dipsy Doodle. Actually, there was a Dipsy I and a Dipsy II. Both involved stepping from one ski to the other in order to change directions. One used a closed, snowplow-like stance, the other an open-skating stance. They sound awkward today, but they worked. Parallel turns on the long, stiff, wooden skis of the day required fearsome speeds to get the skis to plane and eventually turn. Then in 1948, after coaching the U.S. Olympic team in St. Moritz, Alf came home and thought, why not ski the powder with both feet equally weighted on a stable, balanced platform? Modern powder skiing was born. In the 1950s Howard Head supplied all the Alta regulars with his revolutionary flexy, metal skis. Engen disciples like Junior Bounous, now the Director of Skiing at Snowbird, refined the movements, quieted the upper body (which no longer needed to rotate strongly to power the skis around), and—voilà! The efficient and elegant powder style of today. Sometimes when I ski *Alf's High Rustler,* the showpiece powder run from the peak of the ridge right down to the Alta Lodge, I can feel the evolution of this technique.

So where do you go if you are a good skier, and it has just snowed 18 inches last night, and you're standing in line with butterflies of excitement in your stomach? First of all, there is no way to ski it all in one day, or two, or ten. But here is one strategy for a new-snow day.

Start on the Collins side. This is the area the patrol opens first. Sugarloaf and Supreme follow in that order. At first glance it looks like the Collins and Wildcat lifts rise to pretty much the same place. But in fact, Wildcat opens up a huge area of expert skiing along the western edge of the resort that can't be reached from the top of Collins. If you like your powder with bumps underneath, stick with Wildcat for a few runs in the morning. *Warmup, Punchbowl,* and *Bear Paw* are humdingers that will keep you bopping and the snow flying.

Most powderhounds head straight for Germania. Even if the *High Traverse* out to *Rustler* is open, I like to make a run or two on Germania before it gets crowded. Some of the best lines are right under and on either side of the lift. The trees to the skier's left are quite steep and spaced just so for powder turns. Right of the lift line, the terrain is more open (out toward the spacious glades of *Race Course*), while the region around *Lower Sunspot* harbors dozens of delightful little shots.

When the patrol opens the gates to *High Traverse,* the real Alta experience begins. Double back to the north from the top of Germania and follow the patrol's traverse tracks out along the ridge. My problem is deciding where to peel off: right away into *Sun Spot's* wide acres, or a little farther out to *West Rustler* or *Stone Crusher* or *Lone Pine* or all the way out to *Alf's?* Or any of the myriad unnamed lines in between? (Alta has so much skiable terrain, even the patrol doesn't have names for everything. I recently skied a run off

Supreme that the patrol called simply "the chute to the skier's right of the little piney ridge"!) Each one looks a little more inviting than the last. The steepest and longest are out near the end. *Stone Crusher* and *Lone Pine* are personal favorites; they are never bumped up, and the pitch stays at a constant, heart-pounding 35 degrees for over 1,000 vertical feet. *Alf's* is *the* classic, of course. It sweeps to the valley floor like the bell of a horn, starting as a rocky pin point and ending at least 200 yards wide at the creek. Because it's such an icon, it is almost impossible, once the season is well under way, to catch it without moguls underneath, a fact that delights mogul lovers to no end.

By this time the Albion side of the Rustler Ridge, known as the Greeley area, is probably open. If you can tear yourself away from another trip down *Rustler,* you will be rewarded with more untracked skiing and some of Alta's longest drops. *Yellow Trail* and *East Greeley* are reached by hiking five minutes from the top of Germania over to the east-facing (morning sun!) side of the ridge. Two of the most exciting runs at Alta, *Gunsight* and *Eddie's High Nowhere,* require a trip out on *High Traverse* about halfway to *Rustler* and then a hike up and over the ridge. The farther out on the ridge you go, the more likely you are to find trackless snow. *Eddie's* soars an uninterrupted 1,800 vertical feet to the bottom of Albion Basin. It takes a little effort to get there—you usually walk the final 100 feet to the notch with skis off—but it's worth every step.

By now you've probably got the idea that hiking, traversing, walking on skis is a big part of the Alta experience. There is plenty of skiing for folks who want never to lift a ski boot out beyond the groomed trails. But for the skier who wants the wild snow and is willing to work just a little for it, Alta is a kind of paradise. In the days following a storm, as the patrol gets around to them, the other areas open up: the huge *Devil's Castle* zone with its undulating convex shapes; the sunny, nearly treeless *Wolverine Peak* area; and so on. When things are really stable, the genuinely extreme *Baldy Chutes* are open to the public, as are the exciting routes off Wildcat Ridge into Snowbird's territory.

Hardly a day goes by in a winter that you can't find some powder or one of its slightly less romantic derivatives to sink your skis into. The search is aided and abetted by Alta's front office philosophy of opening as much terrain as possible as often as possible. It's a kind of throwback to skiing's simpler, less litigious days, and it pervades all of Alta with a warm, adventurous glow.

Oh, yes. I almost forgot Supreme. That's what happens to a lot of Alta skiers, too. With all the other great steeps, it's easy to overlook this area. (Alta patrolmen who are assigned to Supreme good-naturedly consider themselves an autonomous sovereignty, independent of the rest of the area.) In fact, Supreme has a wealth of fascinating glades, gullies, chutes, cliffs, and trees, and because it is the last area to open on a new-snow morning (sometimes not until 11 A.M. if control work is heavy on other parts of the mountain) the powder stays and stays.

The lift passes right over some exquisitely steep terrain: the yellow rock cliffs above *White Squaw,* the tubular confines of *Supreme Challenge,* and the gnarled limber pines of *Piney Glade.* The latter two lead into *Sidewinder,* probably the longest and most interestingly serpentine gully run at Alta. All four can be reached without walking a step. Put on your sidesteppin' shoes, however, and you're in for more treats out on the northern ridge line. *Spiney Ridge* reminds me of steep Squaw Valley or Bear Valley in California's High Sierra: riblike runs through semidesert rocks and wizened old trees.

Supreme faces mostly west. The light is gorgeous late in the day. The sun may already have set in the Salt Lake Valley, but it is still beaming in low and golden on *Sunset.* All of the Albion side lifts close at 4 P.M. It is possible to catch the last chair on Supreme, ski down, grab the Transfer rope tow, and still catch a late ride on Wildcat, which closes at 4:30 P.M. Time it perfectly and you might even make it up Germania one last time. In the last rays, the *High Traverse* takes on magical qualities.

Lunch on the Hill

There aren't many people still out at 4:30 P.M. A full day at Alta is a full day. One strategy to help you make it through to last run time is to wait on lunch and come back fresh for the final two hours or so. Despite repeated, good-natured chastisement from ski writers, most people still take lunch on the hill at noon. Alta's oldest mid-mountain restaurant, Watson Shelter, is long on hearty, moderately priced skier fare but decidedly short on space. The new Alf's Restaurant, in the heart of Albion Basin, offers plenty of indoor and outdoor seating. But from noon to about 1:30, they can be zooey. I usually pack a granola bar or some dried fruit in a pocket, munch on them at noon and ski through while the lines are short and the slopes practically empty. Then I go in for lunch. (Watson's chili with cheese, onions, and salsa is particularly satisfying.) Then I go back out rested and ready to close the place down. If you would like a nice, three-course, sit-down meal around a cozy fire try Collins Grill, located upstairs in the Watson Shelter. Be sure to make reservations because Collins Grill often fills up with those pesky Snowbird instructors skiing their guests from Snowbird over the Baldy Shoulder for a lunch break at Alta.

Alta for Better Skiers

Intermediates of every kind will find freedom of choice the likes of which is rare this side of the Alps. The reason is the open, sparsely treed terrain. Nearly all the blue trails named and numbered on the map actually include many more mini-routes, so your choices multiply. Take the *Devil's*

Elbow trail off Sugarloaf. The line on the map moseys down a delightful succession of bumps, dips, hollows, and soft ridge lines in quintessential Albion Basin style. The number of ways to ski the trail itself, given the inherent playfulness of its path, is practically infinite; this is the polar opposite of bulldozed, the-best-surprise-is-no-surprise intermediate skiing. The options off either side of *Devil's Elbow,* poking around corners and taking the path less traveled, can add up to a whole day's worth of exploratory fun.

The whole Sugarloaf area is characterized by surprise. In the summer, the land beneath the snow beneath your skis is rock: rock slides, rock chutes, rock bowls, rock gullies. When the prodigious snows fill in the shapes—and Alta, like Bear Valley in California and Arapahoe Basin in Colorado, needs more snow than many areas do to operate—the ski surface becomes a complex, surprising, and fluid sea.

The terrain begs to be explored. Try the whalelike rolls to the right (skier's right) of *Devil's Elbow* just below *Cecret Saddle* (Cecret is pronounced "secret"). Or poke around on the *Glory Hole* side of the lift. *Glory Hole* itself is rated black diamond, but that is primarily because of the big bumps that form in its narrow gully. You can escape the bumps if you want to (you can always escape the bumps at Alta with a move to one side or the other) by staying to the left on the gentler, higher ground. The best run for flat-out cruising in this Sugarloaf zone is the aptly named *Roller Coaster.*

On the Collins side of the mountain the intermediate options appear slightly more limited, but only because they are surrounded by so many black diamonds. In fact, in good snow conditions quite a few black runs can be enjoyed by improving skiers. Among these are *Warmup* off the top of Wildcat Lift, *Lower Sunspot,* and the top section of *Bear Paw* before it breaks over the Wildcat face. On one of my first trips to Alta in the late 1960s, I spent a whole morning, run after run, in the spoonlike swales of upper *Bear Paw* and then cut right under the Collins Lift to *Meadow,* the always-groomed intermediate thoroughfare in the center of the gulch.

The classic cruiser on this side is the *Mambo/Main Street* combination off Germania. Some people repeat this one all day long. It's a yin/yang kind of run, convex, exposed *Mambo* turning into concave, sheltered *Main Street.* To this I would add *Ballroom,* one of the most awesome settings for a ski run I've seen. From the top of the Germania Lift you traverse out onto the face of Mount Baldy. The peak rears up like an impossibly huge wave 600 feet above. The *Baldy Chutes,* almost always in their own blue shade and once described by Alta snow ranger Binx Sandahl as "steep as a cow's face," look practically vertical. (When conditions are just right, the chutes are opened and skied by local daredevils.) Below the traverse, the *Ballroom* bowl swoops down in an even, unobstructed curve, like the side of a frozen sand dune, all the way to *Main Street.* It's an exhilarating ride.

Should Germania and Sugarloaf get busy—and they are the two most popular lifts with intermediate skiers—make the pilgrimage over to the far eastern edge of the area and the Supreme Lift. Supreme is almost never crowded and has some of the least-known and most interesting intermediate and advanced skiing at Alta. There's a whole different feel over here. Ancient limber pines, yellowed and twisted by the elements, haunt the rocky ridge lines. The trees are sparser. There are a few aspens on the sunnier exposures, and parts of the area have the feel of the desert ranges of Nevada or eastern California.

From the top of the Supreme Lift you can look east down the backside of the Wasatch Front into the Heber Valley, a region of small farms and cattle ranches surrounding staunchly Mormon Heber City. The skiing off this backside looks pretty tempting, and, indeed, it is skied periodically by telemarkers and alpine tourers, but the walk out is long and arduous.

Coming back west, directly off the Supreme top terminal is the *Challenger* blue run. It's one of the few blues that develops and keeps bumps for most of the year. The pitch is unthreatening, so the moguls take on the character of frisky whitecaps at sea rather than the man-eaters you'll sometimes find on *Collins Face,* for example.

Traverse out south of the summit and you'll find two lovely, Colorado-style intermediate cruisers called *Big Dipper* and *Rock 'n' Roll.* This is great teaching/learning terrain, quiet, smooth, and roll-y. Alf loves to take nascent parallelers out here where the big fallaway shapes make turning easy. In between *Challenger* and *Big Dipper* is a marvelous zone of glades and gentle gullies known as *Sleepy Hollow.* When there is new powder, this is a paradise for intermediates who may not be ready to tackle Alta's famous steeps but who nevertheless want to play with the feathery sensations of deep snow. Gentler yet is the terrain on both sides of the Albion Lift. This is near perfect, first-timer powder land. I once watched a young family—Mom, Dad, and two kids—frolicking in the vicinity of *Patsey Marley* the day after a ten-inch storm. No groomed runs for them. They bounced from one unskied patch to another, slipping by baby evergreens, bobbing, floating, shrieking with delight, not worrying much about turning or looking good, but having the time of their lives.

Alta for Beginner Skiers

The Albion Base is the hub for beginner and novice skiers. This is where you can find day care facilities, the ski school, and the children's ski school. Alf is justifiably proud of the children's center, with its playroom upstairs in the Albion Ticket building and a special dry-land practice room downstairs. Kids who are skiing for the first time have a chance to take skis on and off, practice left and right, learn to walk and sidestep, all on a specially designed carpet with fun instructional graphics built in. They can do this all before ever having to try it outside on the slippery snow.

First-time beginners—"never evers" in ski school parlance—should always start out with a lesson. There's a handy surface lift reserved for classes just down the hill from the ski school meeting place. Groomed each morning and sheltered from skier traffic, it is an ideal practice slope.

Once rudimentary braking and turning skills are mastered, you have a choice: Take either the Albion or the Sunnyside double chairs up into the soft, round shapes of lower Albion Basin. The Albion is almost a mile long, the Sunnyside a little shorter. Both provide access to the three main novice runs. The farthest east, and also the most beautiful, to my mind, is *Patsey Marley*. It takes off at the top of Albion and meanders northwest right down the creek bed at the base of Wolverine Peak, in and out of small stands of evergreens, following the natural roller coasters of the land. *Crooked Mile* zigs back and forth across this gentle, lightly treed terrain. And *Sunnyside,* the farthest west, sweeps over treeless wide humps toward the Alpenglow restaurant and the base of the Sugarloaf Lift before turning north again and joining the other two for the final run home. *Sunnyside* is my least favorite; it has a long flat spot in the middle requiring poling or skating or both, and it's bedeviled by higher-speed traffic from above.

Sunnyside is one of the few traffic problems at Alta. Virtually all of the skiers in the upper basin must exit via the same wide but sometimes congested *Sunnyside* freeway. It's not just the skiers who have ridden up into Albion. A fair number of expert skiers cross over Rustler Ridge, the center of the W, from the Collins side to the powder-rich *Greeley* area, and they too must descend onto *Sunnyside* for the ride out. This means that the whole soup of skiers, some hell bent for the Collins base and others just testing the waters with their first wedge turns, are thrown together in sometimes frightening combinations. Be alert. Watch for faster traffic from above. When I'm skiing with my children in this situation, I keep to one side or the other, herd them in front of me, and play the role of rear guard.

If conditions get crazy on Albion and Sunnyside—and they can in good weather on the big weekends—try the Cecret chair up in the bosom of the basin. Pronounced "secret" (nobody seems to know why the funny spelling; there is a small lake of the same name up near the head of the basin), it was put in primarily as access to the intermediate and expert terrain off the Supreme Lift, Alta's newest territory. But Cecret is also a well-kept secret for slower skiers seeking a quiet ride through the woods. Two runs, *Sweet 'n' Easy* and *Rabbit,* wander through some of the lushest forests in the area (an area that is making a comeback 65 years after the mountain was denuded in the mining frenzy). *Rabbit* in particular has a fine, deep-forest feel; you might even see the tracks of the snowshoe hare, chocolate brown in summer and pure white (but for the tips of the ears) in winter, with overlarge hind feet for easy movement over snow.

True "learning" skiers should not be tempted to try the Collins Gulch side of Alta. Low intermediates with a sense of adventure, however, should try one blue route off the Germania summit, from the top ease down *Mambo* beneath the glowering face of Baldy into the great cupped palm of the mountain known as *Main Street*. From here bear right through *Meadow* to *Cat Track*, which sweeps back and forth, broomlike, across the face of *Alf's High Rustler*, bringing you gently back to the Collins base. There is nothing very steep on this route, though there are certainly steep, slashing runs all around you. The views—down the canyon to the Salt Lake Valley and across to Sugarloaf and the Devil's Castle—and the huge scope of the terrain make it worth the trip.

Alta after Hours

When the day is done and the last powder shredded, long lines of cars form to go down the canyon (this happens on the weekends only; if it's mid-week, this is not a problem). If you're staying down in the valley, this traffic can be a hassle, an unwelcome reminder of the Bay Bridge or the Lincoln Tunnel. Various plans have been put forth to help relieve the weekend traffic on the tiny, two-lane canyon road, including monorails and tunnels through the mountains, but none is likely to be realized soon, if ever. There is a decent bus system connecting the airport, downtown Salt Lake City, and the resorts in Big and Little Cottonwood canyons—decent but not great. Check a UTA (Utah Transit Authority) schedule for routes and times.

If you are driving down, settle in for a slow drive on a busy or very snowy day; it can take one hour to cover what is normally a 15-minute drive. The only other option is to settle in at the lounge at the Goldminer's Daughter (yes, you can get a drink in Utah; see the "Inside Story" on Utah's liquor laws, page 355) and wait for the traffic to subside.

Neither is as good an option as staying in Alta in the first place. Space is limited, so you should reserve as far in advance as possible with Alta Reservation Service or the individual lodges and condominiums. There are only five lodges, each with a character and history of its own. The Peruvian and the Goldminer's Daughter are the least fancy and least pricey. The Alta Lodge, hard by the ghost of old Mayor Watson's shack, and the Rustler Lodge are more expensive and elegant. The Snowpine, Alta's first ski lodge, built by the WPA in 1938–39, is a rustic, stone jewel. All rooms come with breakfast and dinner included.

My own favorite is the Rustler Lodge. The food is exquisite (a choice of European-style entrees each evening; breakfast buffet with fresh fruits and homemade baked breads and muffins). The view down the canyon in the evening (blue mountain silhouettes against a mauve horizon) is almost enough to supplant hunger. The atmosphere is homey, as if everybody there were part of the same big family, as if we all dropped in to visit the Mother Mountain, and we're always welcome. Signs on the outside doors request that you please not let Cec (short for Cecret), the house golden retriever, out during the day.

If you want to go out and sample the dinners at the other lodges, you can do that too. You just have to tell Shawna or Tom in the morning before you go skiing. The only other place to eat in Alta proper in the evening (besides the lodges) is the Shallow Shaft. Try their delicious homemade pizzas with pitchers of Wasatch Ale, which is brewed over the hill in Park City.

If you have a car (which is not at all necessary within Alta), you may want to drive the mile down to Snowbird one evening to sample the fare at one of their fine restaurants. When I'm skiing and staying in Alta, however, I find it exceedingly difficult to rouse myself past the fireplace at the Rustler. After dinner there are always a few knots of friendly conversation around the lounge, buzzing softly about the day's exploits. Then it's off to sleep. Alta is a simple place. Ski hard. Eat well. Sleep well. Ski again. As Chic Morton used to say, "Alta is for skiers."

Amen.

Note: At the time of the printing of this book snowboards were still not allowed at Alta. Call Alta for current policies.

ALTA DATA

Mountain Statistics

Vertical feet	2,100 feet
Base elevation	8,550 feet
Summit elevation	10,650 feet
Longest run	3.5 miles
Average annual snowfall	500 inches
Number of lifts	6 double chairs
	2 triple chairs
	1 connecting rope tow
Uphill capacity	9,100 skiers per hour
Skiable terrain	2,200 acres
Opening date	mid-November
Closing date	late April
Snowboarding	No!

Transportation

By car About 45 minutes from Salt Lake International Airport via I-80 and Wasatch Boulevard south to State 210, Little Cottonwood Canyon. Alta is 9 miles up the road at the head of the canyon.

By bus, limo, or taxi From Salt Lake International Airport.

By plane Via major carriers to Salt Lake International Airport.

Key Phone Numbers

Ski Area Information
(801) 742-3333 and
(801) 359-1078
Snow Report (801) 572-3939
Reservations (801) 942-0404
www.altaskiarea.com

PETER'S TECH TIP

Skiing the Deep

I am convinced that the main reason powder skiing is so delightfully addictive is that it slows things down. Powder just naturally creates the kind of situation that tennis players talk about when they're in "the zone" and everything slows down for them. Baseball players speak of being able to watch the seams of a spinning ball. Almost any athlete in the groove sees or feels himself performing in slow motion. In powder skiing, the resistance from all that snow—on skis, boots, legs, and sometimes (especially in Utah) even thighs and bellies—counters the pull of gravity, holds you up, and slows you down.

Have you noticed how powder skiers seem to have a different relationship with the fall line? Without skiing faster, they can ski noticeably closer to the fall line, closer to "the path of water," as Alf would say. The deeper the snow, the more the skier can give in to gravity. Thus all the talk about floating and free-falling, about pillows and cushions and clouds.

The surest obstacle to achieving this state of bliss is our own hurry. Initiate a turn on a packed slope and you can expect near-instant response from your skis. We not only expect it; we are so accustomed to it that our bodies are prepared to balance only so long over that turning ski. Start a turn the same way in deep snow and you will likely fall over before your skis have completed half the arc. The skis have slowed down but you have not. My first suggestion, then, is to cultivate a kind of extreme patience. Practice making long radius turns on gentle, groomed terrain, at slow speeds. This is important because at slow speeds you are forced to stand in balance over your feet. At high speeds you can lean in, bank onto your edges, and get away with it.

Next, find an ungroomed powder slope. Not steep—you're trying to learn to let go, not hold on. Although it may seem heretical, ski in a straight line down the slope and bounce. Bounce your skis up and down in the snow, first with your weight on one ski, then the other, then with your weight equally on both skis. One weighted ski sinks, creating an awkward split. Two skis weighted more or less equally react as one.

Feel the platform that you create down in the snow when you bounce on both skis. In powder, skis don't turn on their edges the way they do on a packed slope; they turn against this platform they create. Push down into the snow; the snow pushes back against the bottom of the ski. Push a ski that's already beginning to turn into deep snow; the snow pushes back, bends it, turns it (and you).

The other basics of turning still apply. You need to unweight (bouncing is one way to do it), so that you can then steer your feet and skis into the turn. This is the part that takes the patience and balance; things take longer to happen in powder. Finally, you need to weight those skis, both of them, through the arc (more patience) to the finish.

Start with one turn at a time: gliding, steering, pressing up to a stop. Start from a shallow traverse, then make subsequent turns closer to the fall line. When this feels comfortable, try linking a few together. Hands and poles— very important—come into play here. Alf used to teach a technique he called the "quickhand" or the "readyhand." At the moment of pole plant, vigorously raise the outside hand and pole in almost an uppercut. The action lightens the skis for easy entry into the turn and positions the hand for the new pole plant to come.

A solid pole plant also helps stabilize the upper body. Shoulders should be square to the fall line. A good powder skier looks very much like a good mogul skier: The upper body is quiet, and the legs and skis move from side to side beneath the trunk. Where a bump skier finishes each turn on the flat spot at the base of each mogul, the powder skier uses the platform of compressed snow at the bottom of his turning motion.

A final word about rhythm. It doesn't make sense on a languid, rolling pitch to impose the jackrabbit rhythm you might have seen employed on *Gunsight*. "Choose the rhythm to fit the hill," says Junior Bounous, an Engen protégé and the first ski school director Snowbird had. Let the mountain dictate. Balance on both skis. Begin with a strong up motion of the outside hand. Float. Wait. Sink into the soft resistance, and repeat. Soon you too will approximate the feeling Bounous has: "Sometimes I find myself yelling or singing a little because powder is the most exciting, exhilarating skiing there is."

SNOWBIRD

Snowbird is to Alta as a Cuisinart is to a good, sharp knife. Alta's sister resort in Little Cottonwood Canyon is a modern, efficient, high-tech, concrete-steel-and-glass counterpoint to Alta's historic, funky, efficient wood, steel, and stone. The differences are largely a matter of style and tone.

Snowbird has the greater vertical, 3,240 feet worth of it, due to both a lower base and a higher top terminal, and perhaps a few more acres of terrain. Snowbird attracts a completely different clientele with its elegant ten-story Cliff Lodge Hotel & Spa, its 125-passenger Swiss tram, and its pricier lift ticket. But Snowbird is not really out to compete with Alta. Snowbird set out to be (and has largely succeeded in becoming) a classy, upscale, European-style resort that is just a mile down the road from what may be the quintessential western American ski experience.

Whereas Alta grew out of the visions of many men—Alf Engen, Mayor Watson, Salt Lake Winter Recreation Association's Joe Quinney, Monty Atwater, and the men who formed America's first avalanche school (see the "Inside Story," Avalanche Hunters, page 362)—Snowbird is largely the vision of just two men: Alta regular Ted Johnson and Richard D. Bass, the youngest son of Oklahoma oil magnate H. G. Bass. Johnson advanced the idea, and Bass was the answer to Ted's search for "someone with lots of money and a skier at heart."

Bass made some money in the oil business, had a hand in Vail's early development, then turned his sights on Snowbird, which has been his consuming passion ever since. (Well, perhaps not all-consuming. Between 1983 and 1985, Bass and his friend Frank Wells, who was then president of Warner Brothers, attempted to be the first humans to scale the highest peak on each of the seven continents. It took a tremendous amount of planning, effort, and money. Wells struggled and ultimately failed to reach the highest summit of all, Everest. But Bass prevailed, and in so doing also became the oldest man to have climbed Everest at the time; he was 56. You can read about their adventures in *Seven Summits,* written by Bass and Wells with their friend Rick Ridgeway; a copy of the book graces the nightstand in every room at Snowbird.)

Snowbird sprang into existence, like Venus, more or less full grown during the winter of 1971–72. The centerpiece was, and still is, the tram, a magnificent piece of steel and cable architecture that connects the Snowbird Center at 8,100 feet with the summit of Hidden Peak at exactly 11,000 feet. There is almost no flat ground here, so the lodges were built into the hillside between Little Cottonwood Creek and the canyon road. They are spacious and sumptuously appointed and remarkably unobtrusive for their mass. The food is prepared by European chefs. The service is impeccable. Bass says, "My underlying dream for Snowbird is the creation of a year-round resort that respects and complements the beauty and inspiration of this natural setting—a place dedicated to increasing human understanding through the enhancement of body, mind, and spirit."

Yes, Dick Bass actually says things like that. And he means every word of it. He's a lover of mountains and what they can do for the "body, mind, and spirit." He's a dreamer. Lucky for us he's practical enough to have turned this particular dream into reality.

Snowbird: How the Mountain Works

Snowbird occupies two side valleys directly down canyon of Alta's ski terrain. Like Alta, the horizon line appears as a huge W. Mount Baldy crowns the left-hand point (looking up) at the top of the Alta/Snowbird boundary ridge. Hidden Peak is the center spike (Gad/Peruvian Ridge), and the Twin Peaks (at 11,434 and 11,491 feet, two of the highest points in the Wasatch Range) tower over the Gad/White Pine Ridge, the area's western boundary. The western valley is called Gad Valley, and the eastern valley is Peruvian Gulch. The gentlest terrain fills the broad, alluvial mouth of Gad Valley. Up and over on the Peruvian side intermediate, advanced, and super-expert runs coexist in a melange of forest trails and uncut natural shapes.

The Gad base at 7,900 feet (Entry 1 off the Canyon Road) has a parking lot but little else. The real base of the resort is the Snowbird Center, or Tram Plaza as it is sometimes known, accessed from Entry 2. (Entry 3 goes to the Lodge and the Inn at Snowbird, and Entry 4 serves the Cliff Lodge.) At the Tram Plaza you'll find everything on three levels and all under one roof: tickets, ski school, restaurants, deli, ice cream shop, real estate sales, photography services, medical clinic, post office, sport shops, boutiques, grocery store, state liquor store, pharmacy, and bookstore. This, by the way, is one of the hottest little (three-rack!) paperback bookstores on the planet. They've got Mark Twain, Anne Tyler, Kurt Vonnegut, Jr., and Fyodor Dostoevsky.

So if you forget your current reading, stop in; it's a browser's treat. My only complaint about the Tram Plaza, and it's a minor one, is that with all the interesting angles and multiple levels, it can sometimes be hard to find your way out to the skiing.

All of the lodging is clustered near the Tram Plaza; everything is within easy walking distance. Drive in and leave your car parked for the duration. There's even a handy shuttle if you want to go up and ski grizzled old Alta for a day.

In general Snowbird grades its slopes more conservatively than does Alta. They have added a fourth category of difficulty to the familiar green, blue, and black system. Double black diamonds designate runs off the Gad/Peruvian Ridge that are, at times, subject to avalanche activity. (The trail map includes the caution: "Check with the Ski Patrol for current conditions.") These runs are not necessarily steeper than the black diamonds (though some, like *Great Scott* at the upper end of the Cirque, are very steep indeed), but they do tend to be wilder, less visited, more apt to show the extremes of snow, wind, and exposure.

By the same token, I find some of the black diamonds to be eminently skiable—depending on the snow quality—for solid intermediates. Runs like *Primrose Path, Regulator Johnson,* and *Harper's Ferry East* (more on all of these places to come) might not be considered most difficult at Alta, say, or Aspen Mountain. Snowbird has simply chosen to take a conservative overview.

The qualifier "depending on snow quality" looms huge at any area, especially one with large tracts of above-timberline terrain that are exposed to sun and wind. Snowbird enjoys the same superior quality snowfall that blankets most of Utah, but there are days and storms that conspire against certain areas of the mountain while favoring others. *Regulator Johnson,* for example, a classic upper-mountain run, faces the afternoon sun and faces directly into the prevailing winds. On some days it is a bowl of earthly delights, enjoyed by most skiers from intermediate on up; on other days it can be like skiing a giant slab of frozen cod and definitely recommended for experts only.

There are seven double chairlifts, one high-speed quad, and the world-famous Aerial Tram at Snowbird. The tram provides access to almost all of the skiable terrain. The chairs complement the tram by serving each of the five distinct skiing regions. The Chickadee Lift rises a brief 142 vertical feet behind the Tram Plaza. It is strictly a beginners' lift and used mostly for ski lessons. Three lifts serve the vast, easy, lower Gad Valley terrain: Wilbere, Gadzoom, and Mid Gad. Virtually all of the novice and a good portion of the groomed intermediate terrain is here. Baby Thunder opens more novice/intermediate terrain at the area's far western edge.

From both the Gadzoom and Mid Gad lifts there are connecting routes

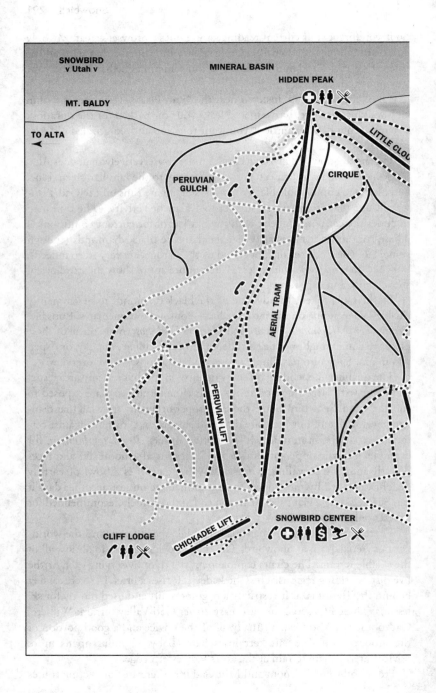

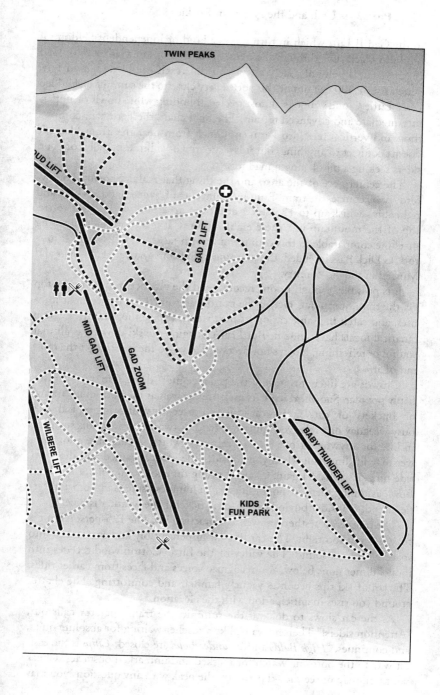

to the Gad II Lift, which in turn serves a kind of independent fiefdom of blue and black runs through the trees. From the tops of Gadzoom or Gad II (the central belly of Gad Valley) you can reach the Little Cloud Lift, which rises 1,300 feet out of this vortex very close to the summit of Hidden Peak. Little Cloud's zone is almost treeless, blinding white bowls of upper-intermediate and advanced terrain. The final chair, the Peruvian, climbs a thousand vertical feet into Peruvian Gulch from near the Tram Plaza. It doesn't connect to anything, but it is a superb yo-yo lift, especially for good skiers seeking a bit of mogul madness.

The centerpiece of the area, and the thing that makes Snowbird Snowbird, is, of course, the tram. Built by Garaventa of Switzerland, its blue and red cabins whisk up to 125 skiers at a time up 2,900 vertical feet to the top of the mountain in a mere eight minutes. It is a monumental skiing machine comparable in this country only with Jackson Hole's tram. It mirrors, as Dick Bass intended, the stunning uphill conveyances of Zermatt and Mürren in the old country.

It is possible, though I don't recommend the practice, to ride to the top via the tram, jump out, race to the bottom in something under eight minutes, and catch the same car on its next return trip to the summit. Certain fanatical locals have done it. But I can't imagine the ski down was all that soulful or refreshing. No, it's not necessary to yo-yo the tram to get the most out of it.

Crowds are likely to prevent the practice most days. The tram is justifiably popular. Snowbird regulars measure the wait at the bottom in "trams" or "buckets" or "cars," a two-car wait or a three-car wait being typical for a busy weekday or a relatively quiet weekend. A two-car wait means standing in line for anywhere from 8 to 16 minutes, which sounds like a lot for a weekday lift line. But when you consider the vertical gained and the short ride time, it's still a bargain. Chairlift riding time to the top of Little Cloud Bowl, assuming there are no lift lines, is 15 minutes using Gadzoom and Little Cloud. Consider buying a chair-only ticket if the weather is nice.

The tram is an aesthetic as well as a practical joy. The 125-person limit is cozy but not too tight. The car lifts off imperceptibly and accelerates into space without a sound. The valley of the Little Cottonwood recedes into model dimensions below. You recognize voices and faces from earlier rides. The sea of ski tips becomes vaguely familiar and comforting. The chatter around you rises in anticipation with the elevation.

As the car slows to dock at the summit, the tram operator calls out, "Attention skiers!" Then he waits, like a teacher waiting for absolute quiet, and continues, "*High Baldy* and *Thunder Bowl* are closed. *Chips* is the easiest way to the bottom. Watch for marked and unmarked obstacles. Check your trail map or see the ski patrol on the peak with any questions you may have. Ski with caution. Have a nice run." The doors open. The noise and energy return, and another wave of skiers clanks down the metal stairs to the summit snows.

The fact that only 125 people leave the top every eight minutes is another reason that endears the tram to Bounous. "I like that it dumps a limited number of people on the terrain. *Chips* (on the Peruvian Gulch side) is my favorite teaching and free skiing terrain because it's a very pleasant experience. No chair can get you there. A wave of people goes by, then it becomes totally silent. I have undisturbed teaching time. *Regulator Johnson* used to be like *Chips* before the Little Cloud Chair went in."

Snowbird for Novice Skiers

Beginning and novice skiers are the only ones who shouldn't ride Snowbird's tram. (*Chips* is the easiest route off the summit, wandering a leisurely 3.3 miles through Peruvian Gulch; it's so gentle, even timid intermediates should have no qualms.) But this is not to say that novices are given short shrift. The lower Gad Valley has some of the friendliest learning turf anywhere.

Big Emma is the star here. Flowing the full 1,300-foot vertical of Mid Gad Lift, *Big Emma* swings beneath the *Gad Chutes* and out onto what I imagine is the jolly, opulent midriff of the mountain. She is as broad as two freeways and as smooth as talc. The lower half, also accessible from the midway unloading station, is gentler still and a lot less crowded. *Upper Emma,* in addition to being prime learning terrain, is also the main highway for better skiers moving around the nose of the mountain to the tram. Pay attention. The slope is so broad and free, it's easy to forget to look over your shoulder.

West Second South is a nice alternative if *Big Emma* gets too zooey. The name refers to the historic red-light district in Salt Lake City, where pleasure came "easy," like the skiing here. (All streets in Salt Lake City are laid out on a grid: east or west of State Street and north or south of Temple. While the system is initially confusing to some newcomers, it is in fact quite orderly.) *West Second South* is really a secluded glade; various fingers dart in and out of little tree clusters, the snow stays soft because of the light traffic, and there is the delicious sense of exploration. Follow *West Second South Long* to *Tiny Tiger* and on down to *Baby Thunder Chair.* The thickly wooded Baby Thunder area is quiet, relaxed, and detached from the main flow of skiers and boarders.

Mid Gad Lift serves both *Big Emma* and *West Second South.* If the lift line there seems to be growing, move over to the Wilbere Lift, which rarely has any kind of wait at all. Junior Bounous loves the variety off the Wilbere, including the *Miners Road* novice area.

Big Mountain Choices for Intermediates

In fact, if Bounous has only one hour in which to teach a private lesson, he usually heads for *Wilbere,* a 660-vertical-foot, mini-ski area unto itself. Shoot off to the right of Wilbere's top ramp and you can ski either *Big Emma* or sunny, gladed *Wilbere Ridge,* a nice intermediate warm-up. Get off to the left and you're aimed toward the progressively more aggressive bumps of *Harper's Ferry, Harper's Ferry East,* and *Lower Mach Schnell.* The lower third of the area is devoted to easy, smooth pitches—perfect learning slopes.

But Snowbird's wonders are way too enticing to spend much of your time on Wilbere, as nice as it is. Up above, the big shapes and the alpine splendor calls. Gad II and the tram beckon.

I am a big fan of the tram, as you have certainly surmised, but I'd like to talk about Gad II for a moment. The lift gains a nifty 1,200 feet in nine minutes, and there's a lot of skiing waiting when you unload. (Peruvian is the only other chair with this much bang for the buck, but it is primarily expert.) Three of Gad II's runs, draped like white necklaces around this semiautonomous peak, are prize-winning blues. *Bassackwards* and *Election* both take off toward the center of the big cupped hand that is the upper Gad Valley. *Bassackwards* is the more scenically splendid, coursing out into the open below the yellow rock cliffs of the Twin Peaks. Both runs suffer a bit from their own popularity and are therefore designated as slow skiing areas. The sleeper here is *Bananas.* Sweeping under the boundary ridge along the area's west edge, *Bananas* tumbles down a delightful combination of draws and rolls, then zigs and zags alongside, but effectively out of the way of *Gadzooks,* the wonderfully named bump run.

Gad II is a cold lift ride. Locals call it "the Fridge." It faces directly north, and its proximity to the Twin Peaks keeps it in the shade during the low sun days of early winter. But that same chilly exposure keeps the snow cold and crisp and guarantees some of the softest snow on the mountain.

To reach the Peruvian side of the mountain from Gad Valley, simply find your way to the Mid Gad Restaurant (all blue roads except *Bananas* lead there), then take *Big Emma* to *Bass Highway,* a broad, comfy catwalk named for the boss. To get from Peruvian Gulch back to Gad Valley, take the blue highway known as *Rothman Way.* The cutoffs run roughly parallel, one on top of the other like arms crossed over the chest of the mountain. The trail map doesn't make it clear, but it is not possible to ride the Little Cloud Lift and then a blue route to the Peruvian side. The Little Cloud stops about 100 vertical feet short and about a quarter of a mile southwest of the Hidden Peak summit. Experts can traverse the top of *Regulator Johnson* to the double diamond *Cirque.* But intermediates are best advised to ride the tram to *Chips.*

The tram. Ah, the tram. In my estimation, the tram is the reason to ski

Snowbird. Take a minute at the top, walk over to the backside rim, and peer over. Huge, naked slopes plunge toward Mineral Basin, which will be developed for skiing and boarding in the year 2000 with a high-speed detachable quad chair. The Heber Valley and Deer Creek Reservoir (a popular wind surfing spot in summer) lie somnolent to the southeast. Fifteen miles directly south you can make out the Sundance ski area on the shoulder of Mount Timpanogos. Back north across the sharp V of Little Cottonwood Canyon, Mount Superior dominates a craggy ridgeline. Superior's half-dozen slide paths are among those most likely to close the highway in a big avalanche cycle. They look practically vertical from here, and yet there are tracks made by backcountry skiers and snowboarders who make the walk as a kind of pilgrimage to a steep, untracked Valhalla.

Now that the crowd has gone, you have *Chips* to yourself. No one else will be starting down for at least another five minutes. Ski north down the Gad/Peruvian ridge 100 yards or so until you can make a right turn. This is *Chips,* a brief road into the pocket below the ridge, then 2.9 miles of open, wheeling, free-flowing terrain to the bottom. It's reminiscent of Alta's Albion Basin; a line on the map indicates the general route, but choices are actually infinite. Poke around, scamper through and around the hundreds of tiny tree islands. One particularly nice whale hump in the upper basin is named *Nacho's Knoll* after a Snowbird rescue dog. A little lower down you'll find yourself in a sunny glade called *Lower Palm Springs,* or so the ski patrol call it; the names are nowhere to be found on the mountain or on the map. You can make up your own names; that's the prerogative of the explorer, isn't it?

Snowbird is grooming more and more of Peruvian Gulch these days, which is good news for intermediates. You may find yourself, for instance, following a nicely pitched, groomed path off *Chips* and discover that it is *Silver Fox,* a black diamond on the map. No matter. The same thing may happen on the lower mountain where some or all of *Chip's Face,* another blackie, may be cut and smooth. Rejoice! Snowbird is one of the rare places where you can find steep, smooth runs, the better to cut loose and feel the weightlessness that experts find here in abundance.

Snowbird for Experts

Snowbird rates 45 percent of its terrain as most difficult. (The mythical industry ideal, a kind of inverse "perfect" figure, is 25 percent beginner/novice, 50 percent intermediate, and 25 percent expert.) While I think some of that may be slightly overrated, we're still talking about one giant playground for the experts. Let's start with the tram and the skiing it serves and then move on to some separate areas.

The most obvious and inviting steep terrain off the top is found in the Cirque on the Peruvian side of the Gad/Peruvian Ridge. (In fact, the traverse down the ridge—similar in feeling and utility to Alta's High Traverse—is known as the *Cirque Traverse*.) It's a vast bald area, like the inside surface of a teacup, with room for perhaps 200 or 300 clear lines into the gulch. The steepest are near the top, where *Great Scott, Elevator Shaft,* and *Upper Cirque* begin their plunges through a rocky cliff band. *Lower Cirque* is beamier if not quite as steep. For such a large space there are few descriptive names—the patrol refers to specific locations by route numbers. On powder mornings, teams of patrolmen follow prescribed routes around the mountain tossing hand charges into spots (called "shots") known to be prone to sliding. Ergot, one of my favorite runs in Lower Cirque, is known as *Route 2, Shots 11* and *12*. I find it by judging my proximity to *Hotfoot Gully*, a colorful moniker, but one that, again, you won't find on the trail map.

Suffice it to say a strong skier could spend all day blissfully playing in the Cirque. But you wouldn't want to. Not when you can drop off the other side of the ridge into the *Gad Chutes* 1 through 13. This is where a good many of Snowbird's promo pictures are taken; it's a spectacular perch. Twin Peaks hovers like the Breithorn in the background. Down the canyon, the Salt Lake Valley (these days most often under its blanket of smog) stretches away toward the lake of the same name. When a storm has just passed through, the gnarly little survivor trees up here are plastered with rime ice. To ski among them is to weave in and out among so many frozen gnomes.

A little farther down the ridge one comes to *Barry Barry Steep,* and that it is, and *Wilbere Bowl*, the longest continuous powder line on the mountain by the time you get all the way down to the Bass Highway. Out at the very nose of the ridge is *Upper Mach Schnell*, a pure north-facing triangle of trees that, because of its distance from the summit, is one of the secret stashes and one of the last places on the mountain to retain powder after a storm. All of the runs from the *Gad Chutes* on down are rated double black diamond, so check with the ski patrol before jumping in.

Little Cloud is another expert area, though, as I have said before, there are a good many days when some runs here could be rated high intermediate: *Regulator Johnson* when the snow is soft, and *Little Cloud* itself, especially early in the season when the bumps are small or nonexistent. This is a mammoth zone, probably a mile wide and 1,300 feet high with very few trees to get in the way; it's a genuine timberline bowl. There are some good bump lines, *Mark Malu Fork* for one, but there are always bump-free lines as well. In the late afternoon with the sun beaming directly on the slopes, I feel lilliputian here amid the bulging, glacial forms—small, but also possessed of the skier's secret joy at mastering these same massive shapes.

Gad II and the Peruvian lift offer the real challenges for mogul masters. To ski moguls well, you have to be able to yo-yo them, up and down and up and down again over the exact same lines until you know their rhythms in your sleep. Peruvian's are the best, if only because the fall lines are truer and longer than the ones on *Gadzooks* and *S.T.H.* (you figure out what it stands for). *Adager* and *Silver Fox,* Peruvian's test pieces, rank with the best bump runs anywhere. The terrain is serpentine, interesting, and fiercely steep. *Primrose Path,* right under the chair, gets more high-intermediate traffic because the gradient is less severe, and the moguls suffer accordingly. Panicky turns make for sharp, squared-off bumps. (The best "trainer moguls" are on *Harper's Ferry* and *Regulator Johnson.*)

Two of the best expert areas aren't even on the map. When they are open —and they are the last places the patrol opens, usually two or more days after a storm—*Baldy Face* and *Thunder Bowl* are sublime chunks of powderland. Baldy, of course, is the peak on the border with Alta. When the northwest face of this mountain has been favored with new snow and not much wind, it is a jewel. Long, fingerlike chutes cut through spare vegetation and deposit you gently, we hope, in upper Peruvian Gulch near *Chips.*

Thunder Bowl is on the opposite boundary, just off the ridge that separates Gad Valley from White Pine Valley to the west. *Thunder* is a kind of Shangri-la; it's barely visible from the rest of the ski area, and none but the heartiest powderhounds make the trek out from *Boundary Bowl.* Steep meadows and stairstep benches cut through the forest for 1,000 vertical feet before you have to cut back east, across the appropriately named *Pearly Gates,* to the Gad base. To ski it again requires two lift rides, back to the top of Gad II, but if there is powder in the trees, it's worth every minute.

You don't have a lot of time to explore on your own? You want to go directly to the best snow? Sign up for the Mountain Experience, a popular Snowbird program open to advanced and expert skiers. You ski with a ski school guide and get a quick line to the powder or other off-trail skiing.

Expansion Snowbird

One of Dick Bass's dreams is to put a revolving restaurant on the top of Twin Peaks, with a tram gliding up into the basement, like the one on the Schilthorn in Mürren, Switzerland. Snowbird currently has plans for expansion off the back side of Hidden Peak into Mineral Creek Basin, a sunny south-facing drainage. The first chair lift is planned for the 1999–2000 season. Plans for a second lift into Mineral Basin are on the drawing board. Snowbird is rarely crowded. Holidays and the sunny weekends following new snow, when local Utah skiers come out of the woodwork, are the exceptions.

As it is, many aficionados consider Snowbird to be nearly perfect— blessed with Utah snow and complex, inviting terrain, as well as the tram, and seated at the top of the world right next to Alta. They'll get no argument from me.

Snowbird Lodging and Dining

Snowbird operates all of the lodging at the resort. You have some basic choices: the condos at the Lodge at Snowbird, the Inn, and the Iron Blosam Lodge or the magnificent Cliff Lodge. The condos are similarly appointed and identically priced. The Cliff is Snowbird's centerpiece hotel. Some say its $60+ million remodel job to over 500 rooms a few years ago almost broke Dick Bass. It's a glass palace, modern and severe on the outside, spacious and airy on the inside. A nine-story atrium with full-size trees looks up the slopes of Peruvian Gulch on the building's south side. It's expensive but commensurately luxurious, with a huge staff and service reminiscent of a European grand hotel. The western third of the Cliff has been modified into the "Cliff Club" condominiums with private hot tubs and sumptuous mission-style furnishings.

The absolute best thing at the Cliff is the rooftop pool and hot tub. After a day on the slopes, there's nothing like it. The hot tub holds 20 people, the pool (which is almost as warm) holds 60. Waitresses glide by bringing trays of drinks, and the setting sun turns the Wildcat Cliffs to gold. You forget you are in the bottom of the sharp canyon, and you feel suspended in a power center between the walls, bathed in ethereal light, just floating.

The Cliff is like a small city. It has three restaurants, two lounges, two swimming pools, four hot tubs, an ice skating rink, and a large modern game room. Check out the Aerie and the Keyhole for dinner.

The Aerie is on the Cliff's top floor, California Deco, with fresh seafood specials and live piano in the lounge. The southwestern food at the Keyhole is legit: locally made chips, fresh salsas (ask for hot and you get hot), a good selection of Mexican beers, and generous hot plates of southwestern favorites.

Two of the condo lodges feature fine restaurants as well. The Lodge Club at the Lodge at Snowbird is a popular après-ski bar with the local crowd, and then it turns into a restaurant featuring fine American cuisine. The Wildflower Restaurant at the Iron Blosam Lodge specializes in Italian dinners.

My favorite dinner spot is the Steak Pit on Level 1 of the Snowbird Center. Great steaks, fish, or chicken served up by very experienced service people that can answer almost any question you have about Snowbird and the history of the canyon. Next door to the Steak Pit is the Tram Club, which is a must for après ski.

Lunch I find problematical at Snowbird. The cafeteria fare at the Mid Gad Restaurant, the only on-mountain food area, is passable but uninspired. Mid Gad Restaurant does have a large south-facing sundeck which is a hot spot on those warm spring days. Most people congregate on the big deck of the Tram Plaza—you can ski right up to it—where you can munch, indoors or out, then hop back in line for the tram. (Be sure to check out the 200-pound chunk of the Matterhorn displayed on a concrete pedestal near the skiers' bridge. Snowbird and Zermatt are sister resorts, and the Swiss brought a piece of their signal peak for Americans to ponder. Odd but worth a touch.)

The Birdfeeder is your basic Coney Island hot dog/french fries/frozen yogurt stand. I like it. If you want to sit down, the Forklift around the corner has good burgers and sandwiches. If the weather is gorgeous and the skiing fine, I will sometimes grab a deli sandwich from the grocery known as General Gritts on one of my tram stops and carry it with me for lunch at the top of the mountain. One end of the ski patrol shack—and it's a real shack by Snowbird's architectural standards—is reserved for brown baggers. Just some benches and big windows, but the view is edge-of-the-planet spectacular, eye-to-eye with the Twins across the way.

SNOWBIRD DATA

Mountain Statistics

Vertical feet	3,240 feet
Base elevation	7,760 feet
Summit elevation	11,000 feet
Longest run	3.3 miles
Average annual snowfall	500 inches
Number of lifts	7 double chairs, 1 high-speed Quad 1 125-passenger tram
Uphill capacity	11,000 skiers per hour
Skiable terrain	2,500+ acres
Opening date	mid-November
Closing date	sometime in June
Spring season	Yes, usually until June 15
Snowboarding	Yes

Transportation

By car About 45 minutes from Salt Lake International Airport (40 minutes from downtown) via I-80 and Wasatch Boulevard south to State 210, Little Cottonwood Canyon. Snowbird is 8 miles up the road, 1 mile short of Alta.

By bus, limo, or taxi From Salt Lake International Airport.

By plane Via major carriers to Salt Lake International Airport.

Key Phone Numbers

Ski Area Information
  (801) 742-2222
Snow Report (801) 565-5944
Reservations (800) 453-3000
www.snowbird.com

Powderbird Heli-Skiing

(Call for availability during the 1999–2000 season)

Is it redundant to have a helicopter skiing service at an area that receives over 500 inches of powder a year? No. Even at Snowbird, those 500 inches get skied out pretty quickly. If you know where to look, you can find soft snow two or three days after a storm by poking around in the trees and rocks. But what about that unimpeded, open-slope experience you see in the pictures? What about skiing untracked powder all day? The only place to live out this dream is in the backcountry, and the easiest way to get there is with the Powderbird Guides.

Wasatch Powderbird Guides offers daily helicopter skiing to those trackless, inviting realms out beyond the ski area boundaries. It's expensive, yes, and chancy. Bad weather might mean postponement or cancellation of your prereserved heli day. (For this reason, they also have a complex but workable and flexible reservations system.) But if you hit even an average good day, say a five or a six on a scale of ten, you will likely come back bubbling over.

Here's how the day goes. A Powderbird person calls you the night before to confirm. Then that person calls again the next morning; cofounder and chief guide Greg Smith will have checked the weather and snow conditions and determined that it's a go for 9 A.M. You find your way to Powderbird's heliport just east of the Cliff Lodge. Inside, it smells of fresh coffee, fruit, and pastries. You are too nervous to eat, but it looks too good not to. Smith lightens the mood with tales of how some of Snowbird's "easy" runs got their names. *West Second South* was Salt Lake City's erstwhile red-light district, and *Big Emma* was one of the best-known madams.

The day's skiers are divided into compatible groups. You are issued a rescue beacon and special straps for tying your skis and poles securely together. Outside, pilot and guide go over the safety procedures regarding the Bell Jet Ranger. The $4 million machine revs into action. The roar would seem to blot out the world. You clamber aboard and buckle your seat belt.

Without your noticing, the pilot lifts the bird off. Gently, as if guided by a giant hand, the helicopter climbs to the ridge north of Snowbird and dives over the other side. It banks and stirs the air and sets down on a tiny ridge line without a bump. Greg Smith throws his pack to one side, then begins unloading skis. You jump down and crouch around the pack, kneeling in the snow, gloved hands on each other's shoulders like worshipers. Greg gives the pilot the thumbs up. The bird rises and then bolts toward the canyon floor, prop-washed snow blasting over you like a wave.

Then it's utterly still, jarringly quiet. At your feet, a run called *Meadows Chutes,* a morning run facing the sun, 2,000 vertical feet sparkling, a few aspen trees, shadows down in the creek bottom where the pilot waits, not another skier or ski track in sight. You click into bindings. Breathe twice, deeply. The snow feels like cream . . .

On a typical day you'll ski seven runs like this. Most often they will be in the side canyons of Big Cottonwood, north of Snowbird, west of Solitude, though you may fly as far north as Mill Creek Canyon or as far south as Provo. You may ski runs called *Fat City, Two Guys* (an Italian restaurant downtown in Salt Lake City), *Cardiac Ridge* (120 turns without stopping, if you want), *Holy Toledo,* and my favorite, *The Hall of the Giants,* with its spiraled, spreading, 400-year-old limber pines.

At the end of the day there is cold beer, soup, and sandwiches at the heliport. Voices hum with the day's triumphs and foibles already legend. Nobody seems to want to leave.

Big Cottonwood Canyon

Brighton Kids, families, church groups, lessons, night skiing—Brighton is "where Salt Lake City learns to ski." Recent expansion and redesign have catapulted this small area into the big time, with big snows, big terrain variety—especially strong on winding forest cruisers—plus a couple of big new quad chairs. Brighton is owned by Big Sky's parent company, Boyne USA. There is *limited* lodging, but it's only 40 minutes from downtown Salt Lake City.

Solitude Next door to Brighton and once linked via the eponymously named Solbright Trail, Solitude has completed the first phase of what will be the only destination village in the canyon. The mountain itself remains an exquisite, moderate-size day area with long, sunny novice and intermediate trails, gently pitched bowls, and secret steep trees for the wily experts who know to avoid Alta on big weekend days.

BRIGHTON

Brighton likes to call itself "the place where Salt Lake City learns to ski." There'll be 150 first-timers on the broad, gentle base of Mount Majestic every Saturday of the season. At night (Monday to Saturday from 4 to 9 P.M.) more beginners, school kids, novices, and working people in need of an after-hours ski fix can be seen ghosting in and out of the lights, swishing big christies in the cold, flour-fine snow.

But Brighton is a good deal more than just a learners' hill. It's a kind of mini-Alta (it also reminds me of Colorado's Arapahoe Basin) with largely underutilized intermediate and advanced terrain, Alta-like snow, big views, and nobody but nobody there on weekdays, or on weekends, for that matter, if the weather is snowy, cloudy, cold, windy—anything short of perfection, in other words. Utah locals, you will learn if you are a visitor, tend to be very picky about their ski days. They can't help it; they're spoiled.

Out-of-state skiers rarely venture up Big Cottonwood Canyon because there are almost no overnight accommodations up here. (With Alta and Snowbird just over the ridge line, why bother?) Summer cabins dot the sunny, aspen-studded hillsides on the north side of the canyon, but Brighton itself has only one small lodge and a few rental "chalets." The reasons for this lack of development are threefold: There is a paucity of private land, but there are limited water rights in the canyon to serve development (Big Cottonwood is one of seven canyons that provide the Salt Lake Valley with its potable water); and, frankly, the people of Salt Lake don't want to see a lot of growth in the canyons. They want their wilderness for backcountry skiing and for summer hiking and climbing. As area manager Randy Doyle, a big, comfortable bear of a man, told me, "These mountains are actually pretty small and so close to a huge population base. There are just a lot of uses."

So Brighton is a kind of odd beast, half one thing and half another. On one hand it is a throwback, a low-key, family-oriented, historically significant locals' area. But on the other hand, the skiing/riding—the terrain, the snow conditions, the potential for personal expression and freedom—is so good that if you could somehow plunk it down in California or Colorado, you'd have a major resort on your hands. In recent years under the ownership of Boyne USA, which also owns Big Sky in Montana as well as Boyne Mountain and Boyne Highlands in Michigan and Chrystal Mountain in Washington, Brighton has undergone major upgrades toward that end: new high-speed lifts, snowmaking, a spacious new base lodge, and greatly expanded night skiing.

Little Cottonwood has the big reputation. Big Cottonwood is the people's paradise. It's been like this since before the turn of the century. Brigham Young used to gather the faithful up in the canyon for cool, summer meetings. Brighton was skiing before Alta, in part because the canyon was easier and safer to climb. Salt Lake City outing clubs—women in long skirts and men leaning on one wooden pole through their turns—rode the rope tow over by what is now the Majestic run. William Stewart Brighton built a luxury, three-story hotel (with luxury, outdoor, back-to-back six-holers) for miners and then tourists. Tenth Mountain Division troops trained here prior to World War II and before the development of legendary Camp Hale in Colorado. With the highest base in the Wasatch at 8,755 feet and some of the coldest temperatures, Brighton's snow was reliably deep and soft. The people flocked to the end of the road to try this new winter recreation.

And they're still coming, though arguably Brighton's share of the local pie has shrunk with the opening of Solitude in 1956 and, in recent decades, with the completion of the freeway up Parley's Canyon to the Canyons, Deer Valley, and Park City Mountain Resort. Perhaps the area's own promotional efforts on behalf of its excellent beginners' terrain and lessons have partially obscured the fact that this is a versatile and intriguing mountain for any level skier/rider. Brighton has become somewhat of a mecca for snowboard riders due to the exciting terrain of dips, dropoffs, natural halfpipes, and a maintained pipe and park. For whatever reasons, Brighton today is an underused ski and snowboard mountain, and that, for as long as it lasts, makes Brighton a find.

The Canyon Drive

The drive through Big Cottonwood Canyon is a treat in itself, and a crash course in the fascinating geology of the range. Quite literally a course—there is a series of information signs at key locations along the highway. It's tough to stop on the way up to a day's skiing, so plan on the way back down to stop and soak in some remarkably graphic examples of big forces at work.

You'll notice that the top half of the canyon has a broad, rolling feel, as if it's been scooped out by a giant hand. In fact, it was, by the Big Cottonwood glacier that was active up until about 30,000 years ago. Then, rather suddenly, the canyon narrows and becomes V-shaped. They call this place the Meeting of the Glaciers. The sign says that several side canyon glaciers met the main river of ice about here, and together they stopped. Big piles of ground-up rock, terminal moraines, lie like dunes on both sides of the road. Then the river dives into its canyon and the road hugs the rock walls where there is no more valley. (The Little Cottonwood Canyon glacier, by contrast, pressed all the way down to the ancient lake at the canyon mouth. That canyon has a shorter, steeper run overall and shows the characteristic glaciated U-shape from top to bottom.)

Down in the Big Cottonwood narrows there are three more signs. One points out bands of 300-million-year-old Mississippian white marble. The next describes Storm Mountain quartzites and shales, alternating yellow and brown layers that have been grotesquely folded as if they were Silly Putty and then tilted 90 degrees on end. In the curvy throat of the canyon just above the mouth, a last sign describes a wall of 700-million-year-old blue and purple shales, the bed of an ancient sea elevated by movement along the Wasatch Fault.

From an airplane or even in a car on the freeway between Provo and Salt Lake City, you can see the fault at work. It's almost a ruler line running north and south. The land to the west of the line, except for the alluvial fans of eroded mountain material and the distant Great Basin ranges, is flat as a pancake. (These days new subdivisions push up the gently tilting planes right to the canyon mouths.) To the east the mountains are thrown straight up 7,000 feet above the city.

It's as sheer a geological dichotomy as any in North America. The Rocky Mountains west of Denver, although dramatic, climb much more gradually, reaching the 12,000-foot level about 50 miles from the plains.

The Lay of the Land: How the Mountain Works

At the head of the canyon at the end of the road (Brighton's parking lot), the landscape is dominated on the south by 10,452-foot Mount Millicent, a looming pyramid with a very steep north face that is nearly always in shadow, and on the east by 10,700-foot Clayton Peak, the newest skiing at the area. Brighton's seven chairlifts climb up four different aspects of the basin, creating four distinct skiing zones. The farthest west, with its own small base facility and two chairs, is the Millicent and Evergreen area. In the center, on the mountain's north-facing flank, with three chairs, is the Mount Majestic/Crest area. The Snake Creek zone occupies the ridge between Mount Millicent and Clayton Peak to the east. The Great Western Quad, the newest and highest lift, ascends to 10,500 feet, 200 vertical feet short of the summit of Clayton Peak.

The total vertical from the top of Great Western to the base lodge is 1,745 feet. But the more meaningful numbers are those of each of the four areas: Clayton Peak, 1,745 feet; Snake Creek, 1,040 feet; Majestic/Crest, 1,207 feet; and Millicent, 1,125 feet. You can ski from one area to another via access trails, but for all practical downhill purposes, these are four separate mountains.

According to area literature there are 850 acres of skiable terrain; 1,745 feet vertical and 850 acres doesn't sound like a big area. But Brighton is what I call a Little Big Man. The numbers don't add up to a lot, but the numbers, in the end, lie. Or rather, they don't begin to tell the story. Brighton skiers like a big mountain. You want long? The combination of *Lone Star* and *Scout* mambos two miles through the woods. You want naked, oceanic bowls to lose yourself in? Try *Scree Slope* under that monster Millicent face. You want meadows? Secret trees? Exhibitionist bumps right under the chair? You want to jump off powder-coated cliffs? Brighton's got it all. With that kind of choice, does it matter whether you get your skiing in 1,000-foot chunks instead of 2,000 at the "big" areas?

To add to all this, Brighton, by any standard, is a bargain. In order to compete with the other great areas for local business, management has kept lift prices almost ridiculously low. In terms of the cost of skiing, Brighton is (ever so delightfully for us) living at least 15 years in the past.

Brighton for Beginners

Brighton's Intro-Ski programs are anything but retro. The beginner package includes full-day equipment rental, a Majestic/Explorer lift pass, and a beginner lesson, all for less than the price of a lift ticket at most areas. There is also a Works Package for all levels that includes an all-area lift ticket. Half-day and full-day Kinderski packages are available for young riders four to seven years old. Kids ten years and younger ski for free with each paying adult.

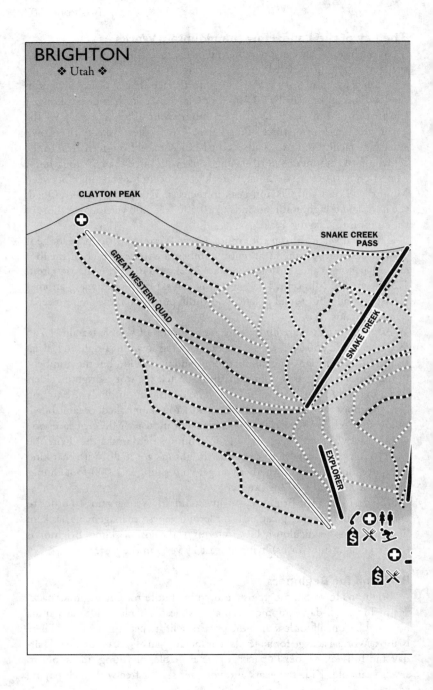

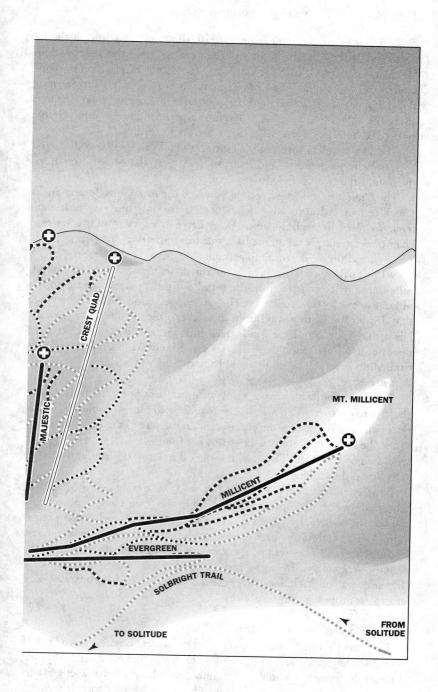

Beginner lessons are taught underneath the Explorer Triple, at the far north end of the Majestic base area. The next step up is the Majestic double chair, which, along with the longer and faster Crest quad, serves the lion's share of novice terrain. *Upper Mary* trail to lower *Majestic* is a fine learning slope, moving from the shelter of the woods out into the big, billowing rolls above the lodge. There is a lot of room to experiment here and to play the swales and hollows for the tricks they teach about turning.

The only problem with the Majestic area that I can see is crowding, and then only on weekends—and that too has largely abated with the introduction of the Crest people-mover quad.

The Crest also provides a second access to the marvelous, foresty Snake Creek terrain. Adventurous novices need brave only one easy blue trail, *Thunder Road,* to reach the green *Snake Creek Access;* or from the Majestic chair they can simply ski off the back side (off the left) to *Hawkeye* or *Snake Creek Access* into a different drainage and a different, quieter world.

While Snake Creek is primarily intermediate, there are two wonderful, mile-long novice courses from the top, both great places to rack up the mileage necessary for confidence. They start together on the northeast ridge that divides Big Cottonwood from the Heber Valley drainages to the east. Then they split. Sunshine winds deep into the woods, while Deer Park opens onto a broad shoulder with views of Mount Millicent's voluptuous timberline terrain. The single route back to Majestic is via the easy green *Hawkeye* road.

The Millicent area sports a couple of green runs as well, but it's a little tougher to get there. The *Milly Access* road is rated blue. It is narrow, and it does twist and dip with some enthusiasm on the way to the Milly base, but unless the snow conditions are unusually hard and fast, I think many novices would enjoy the ride. (Those without good braking skills might want to walk across the parking lot.)

Novices, don't ride the Millicent Lift. You'll find only intermediate and advanced runs off the top. The Evergreen Lift, Brighton's best-kept secret, is the one for novices. Evergreen is almost never crowded, and the two green runs, *Canyon* and *Main Street,* have a completely different feel from the rest of the mountain. They wander spectacularly through this area's open slopes, solitary Volkswagen-size rocks and scattered trees. *Canyon* is particularly dramatic, waltzing as it does under the mountain's steep face runs. Be aware of experts dropping in from above.

An Intermediate's Brighton

I say that Evergreen is Brighton's best-kept secret because it has a little of everything and rarely sees a lift line. The *Evergreen* trail is a delight, slipping through the forest like a hobbit path, unbulldozed, full of character and surprise. You can also get to *Perri's Bowl* off this lift, a snaky trough through treeless terrain that invites roller-coaster turns back and forth across its sides. The shapes are sometimes quite steep (though they don't stay that way for long), providing intermediates with a challenge that they are often denied at the big ballroom-type areas. Very good skiers love this terrain too. It's sensuous, flowing, and steep enough to make you think of Alberto Tomba carving big, round engraver's cuts in the snow. You can't just stand there; you have to *ski* this one.

If crowds are not a problem, and they rarely are, few intermediates bother with Evergreen because Millicent is right next door, and it's just the same only better and bigger. Millicent has almost double Evergreen's vertical and opens up many times as much terrain. Most of it is rated advanced, but there is some fine intermediate cruising on the *Backbone* ridge. This is Brighton's version of the Big Burn: soaring, high-speed stuff with the mountain falling away on both sides of the broad rib. To the left are the slumbering, white-blanketed Twin Lakes, which are part of Salt Lake City's water supply, and Twin Lakes Pass, a high saddle on the ridge separating Brighton and Alta. The Highway to Heaven, a portion of the Interconnect Trail linking the Big and Little Cottonwood Canyon areas with each other and with Park City (see the "Inside Story," The Utah Interconnect, page 325), is etched across the sheer face of Davenport Hill. To the skier's right, the rollicking, mostly ungroomed pitches of upper Millicent dance away toward *Canyon*. Some, like *Little Milly* and *Chute 2,* become transition grounds for skiers moving up into the advanced ranks. Bumps sometimes form in the gullies, but because the skiing is crafted by landforms rather than trees here, there are always mogul-less alternatives. This is the beauty of alpine terrain. In the summer these pistes are all rock. In the winter, under Brighton's 430 inches of snow, it's all white; you go wherever whim or the fall line leads you.

Snake Creek feels like a different ski area, perhaps Colorado or maybe Maine, except for the unmistakable feel of Utah snow underfoot. These runs are snipped top to bottom from dark forest cloth. Dive in and the white ribbon takes you for a ride. There are few forks in the road or choices to make. Just relax and be taken.

There are half a dozen intermediate rides here, all close to a mile long and all bouncing down a stairstep fall line to the lift base in a bright meadow. Each one suffers the odd flat spot or two, nothing so bad as a walk, but they do interrupt the flow here and there. *Thunder Head* was created when a slide cut loose on Clayton Peak and blasted through heavy timber along what was then the area's northeast boundary line. Nature's bulldozer. They are two of the best lines on the mountain. *Thor* and *Pine Martin* have a lovely, private, what-lies-around-the-next-corner feel to them.

Now, with the addition of the Great Western quad, there are two ways into *Thor.* Most Great Western terrain is black, but *Thor, Thunder Head,* and *Lone Star*—all fine blues—course the naturally gladed shapes here. Check out the breathtaking view of Timpanogas from the Snake Creek Pass and the awesome view of Snowbird's tram from the top of the Great Western Lift.

Snake Creek lacks the transition terrain that Millicent has: the small to medium-size bumps and the smooth steep of a *Perri's* or a *Christy Bowl*. The shapes go directly from long and smooth to short and nasty. To their dismay, far too many intermediates plunge into the bumps of *Doyle's Dive* and find out that it really does deserve its black diamond. But that's okay; the forest wanderers are as good, in their genre, as any in the state. Lower Pioneer and Ziggy have some manageable intermediate bumps, and most of the intermediate bump lessons are taught on Ziggy.

A final alternative for intermediates, or anyone with good basic skills, is to ski over to Solitude for part of the day. The two areas sell a combined ticket and are connected by the creatively named *Solbright Trail*.

Powderhounds and Birdmen

One of the raps against Brighton as a small area is that it lacks the big expert challenges that the major areas have. The irony of this Little Big Man misconception is that not very many expert skiers come to the top of Big Cottonwood Canyon. In fact, the expert skiing is superb, uncrowded, and suffused with a sense of adventure.

If big bumps are your measure of difficulty, however, then you will be disappointed here. The best are on Doyle's Dive, Exhibition, and a few gully shots on *Lone Pine* in Millicent Bowl, and *Rockin R* and *Desperado* off of Great Western. But it's because of lack of traffic on the steep, not because there are no steeps. Brighton excels at other aspects of the game: trees, jumps, and both backside and inbounds powder.

Powder, powder everywhere. A Brighton patrolman I know claims that the area "never gets skied out." Quite a statement, especially in light of the fact that Alta and Snowbird are substantially "skied out" the first day after a storm. But if it snows, on average, once a week through the winter, and there aren't enough strong skiers to cut up all the accessible Brighton fluff before the next storm cycle, then he's right. This is Brighton's fate and its great secret.

I experienced a graphic example of this recently. I was skiing with this same sanguine patrolman on the Snake Creek Lift in a snowstorm. He led the way into the trees next to the *Hard Coin* run. Big, red-barked Englemann spruce stood well spaced for powder turns, the alleys between their trunks extending downhill as far as I could see. The new snow was less than six inches deep, so any old tracks would have shown through. But there were none.

"There are no tracks in here," I exclaimed. "Not even any old tracks."

"Welcome to Brighton." He smiled and pushed off into the virgin quiet.

It's the same in *Saw Buck*. A short traverse to the right off the top and you are in rarely skied, powdery glades and meadows that flow all the way to *Deer Park*. Over on Millicent, the powder is more obvious; there are only a few trees, and the mountain's skin (over rocky bones) is pure white. Out in the bowl beneath the Millicent north face, two runs are identified on the map, *Lone Pine* and *Scree Slope*, but there are literally hundreds of lines. None is as monolithic a shape as, say, High Rustler at Alta, but they make up in quirky playfulness what they lack in sheer size. The ground under your skis is constantly changing. My friend the patrolman calls Millicent "a little amusement park."

One of the most popular rides in this "fun zone" pops skiers and snowboarders into the air. Boulders from 5 to 50 feet tall dot Millicent's open landscape. On a powder day, when the landings are pillow-soft, bird men and women are taking flight all around. I am not generally a jumper; I prefer to keep my skis on the ground, but Brighton does something to me. The spirit is contagious, and I find myself winging off small cliffs onto steep powder landings without missing a beat. Or screwing up the courage to jump six feet down into a chute with no other entrance, for the reward of 20 glorious powder turns below.

When the inbounds powder looks like it's mostly chopped up, strong skiers often have the option to go out of bounds, legally. (Clayton Peak used to be one of these zones. Now it is open, and the Great Western Express accesses a baker's dozen of black routes from *Clark's Roost* to *Desperado*.) The Brighton patrol maintains three gates: at the tops of Millicent and Great Western and at the entrance to what is called *Mary's Chutes*, a wild zone between Millicent and the Majestic area. When conditions are deemed safe, the gates are open, and you can use the lifts (and a little walking power) to reach some marvelous skiing.

Most popular is the back side of Millicent, where west-facing powder slopes plunge down uninterrupted to the Twin Lakes. In *Mary's Chutes* one can find perhaps the best jumping grounds in Utah. The area consists of three huge swales, like storm waves at sea, with untold slots and clefts and niches through their cliff faces. I would recommend a local guide for the first few trips in; the place is a maze. Very little shows on the map, and there are occasional booby traps. The patrol and the public have an unspoken understanding here: Skiers/riders in out-of-bounds areas will use their heads and the buddy system, and, most important, not ski in closed areas. Outside the resort boundaries, gate or no, you are on your own. Backcountry explorers should have knowledge of current avalanche conditions and must have proper rescue equipment.

Lunch

In the excitement of skiing, I completely forgot about lunch. (This happens in real life, too.) Brighton has three eateries, all at the base: Molly

Green's, a private club (in Utah parlance that means they can serve liquor), the Alpine Rose cafeteria, and the Millicent Chalet at the minuscule Milly base. The Chalet is the locals' hangout, with a sunny porch known as "the beach," good pizza, and homemade chili.

Dinner and Overnight in the Canyon

Brighton is so tiny (population about 70 during the winter) that it has just one place for dinner. Molly Green's bar and dining room is a space of joyous eclecticism: two half-scale WWI airplanes (a Sopwith Camel and a Fokker) hanging from the cathedral ceiling; giant, carved wooden elephants and cats; flowers on the tables; and cane safari chairs in front of a big fireplace.

The only place to stay right in Brighton is the 20-room Brighton Lodge Slopeside. It has a hot tub, a heated outdoor pool, continental breakfast, and a common living room. It's not chic, but it's comfortable and family-affordable. Brighton Chalet and Mount Majestic Properties rent cabins in Brighton. On Brighton Circle is Das Alpin Haus Bed and Breakfast.

Staying in the Valley

And that's about it. There are a couple of chalets for rent near the lifts and a family-style lodge down the canyon at Silver Fork, but generally, people who ski Brighton stay in the valley. Salt Lake City, Murray (at the mouth of Big Cottonwood Canyon), and Sandy (at the mouth of Little Cottonwood) together have over 50 lodging options, 10,000 rooms combined—everything from the Hilton to the Marriott to a burgeoning number of bed-and-breakfasts. The Doubletree Hotel downtown and the Comfort Inn in Sandy do a good job of catering to skiers' needs.

My pick of the bed-and-breakfasts is the Spruces on 9th East right on the way to Big Cottonwood. The house is a classic carpenter's gothic Victorian built by Norwegian Martin Gunnerson for his family in 1903. In 1915 Gunnerson transplanted 16 spruce trees from Big Cottonwood Canyon around the house. They're still there, all but hiding the place from the street. The house was remodeled to include four guest suites in 1985. The new owners were clever and careful enough to leave a big cottonwood tree growing up through the middle of the new breakfast room roof. Immediately south of the inn is the Wheeler Historic Farm, a working museum of nineteenth-century farming techniques that history buffs will love.

Staying in Salt Lake rather than up at the resorts can have its benefits. You're only 10 minutes from the airport and 45 minutes by car from any of seven resorts, an hour if you use the Utah Transit Authority ski buses. In town you're only a matter of blocks away from the Delta Center, where the NBA Jazz play basketball, or Symphony Hall, where Utah's two symphony orchestras perform. Ballet West, which summers in Aspen and winters in Salt Lake, is perhaps the finest company on this side of the continental divide. There's a planetarium, zoo, theater, galleries, and museums. Here too is Utah's number one tourist attraction, Temple Square, where you'll find programs and exhibits on the ongoing saga of Utah's original white settlers, the Mormons and their Church of Jesus Christ of Latter-day Saints. (See the "Inside Story" on the Mormons, page 342.)

Salt Lake City is more than just a regional transportation center and the capital of the Mormon state. It's grown manyfold in size and sophistication since I first visited over 30 years ago. It's become a near-perfect ski base. A visitor can sample Alta one day, Brighton the next day, and Park City another day, and return to the city in the evenings. Unlike Denver, which is a long way from its good skiing, this city really works as a staging point. If you didn't get your reservation in to the Rustler Lodge early enough this year, you can still ski Alta and then maybe take in the Jazz game that same night.

BRIGHTON DATA

Mountain Statistics

Vertical feet	1,745 feet
Base elevation	8,755 feet
Summit elevation	10,500 feet
Longest run	2 miles
Average annual snowfall	500 inches
Number of lifts	2 high-speed quads
	3 double chairs
	2 triples
Uphill capacity	11,100 skiers per hour
Skiable terrain	850 acres
Opening date	mid-November
Closing date	mid-April
Night skiing	4–9 P.M.
	Monday through Saturday
Snowboarding	Yes

Transportation

By car About 45 minutes from Salt Lake International Airport via I-80 and Wasatch Boulevard south to State 152, Big Cottonwood Canyon. Brighton is 14 miles up the road at the head of the canyon.

By bus, limo, or taxi From Salt Lake International Airport and from downtown Salt Lake City.

By plane Via major carriers to Salt Lake International Airport.

Key Phone Numbers

Ski Area Information (800) 873-5512
Snow Report (801) 533-4731 x532
Accommodations
Brighton Chalets (801) 942-8824
Das Alpin Haus (435) 649-0565
Mount Majestic Properties
   (435) 647-7063
Reservations, Brighton Lodge
   (800) 873-5512
Salt Lake Convention & Visitors
   Bureau (801) 521-2868
www.skibrighton.com
E-mail: info@skibrighton.com

Stormy-Day Strategies

Whales in the sky. The first sign of a coming storm is often those long, curving, lenticular clouds, like pods of gray whales arcing up over the mountains. Then the ceiling begins to fall, the wind spits, the sky goes white and lowers until the tips of the peaks—Superior, Patsey Marley, Clayton, and Millicent—disappear into the clouds. The first sharp snowflakes tap against your nylon shell.

For many people the day has ended. It's time for the hot-buttered comfort of the lodge. But for others, the best is yet to come. I am one of the latter, and here's why. Skiing in a storm refreshes me just as the mountain is being replenished. The snow just gets softer and softer as the day progresses. Where before my edges might have made a scraping or a rasping sound on the old snow surface, now all I hear are whispers under the scolding wind. In a storm, both sight and sound are muffled. I rely more on my sense of feel; I am in many ways closer to the mountain and its ever changing gravities.

On stormy days the fair-weather crowds are banished. Those who stay out gain an intimacy with the elements. The civilizing aspects of the sport—the lifts, the snow machines, the fashion—pale before big forces. We are puny and lucky and bold all at once. Skiing in a storm is a little like being on your own planet.

Sometimes the difference between those who enjoy stormy-day skiing and those who don't is simply a matter of equipment. Ideally, your gear should render you immune to the cold and snow, the way a diver in a dry suit can be in the sea but not get wet. Windproof jacket and pants are essential. A one-piece suit is even better; there are no chinks for cold to enter around the waist. You need good warm gloves or mittens, a hat that covers your ears, and goggles (amber or rose for low-light visibility; double lenses still beat a coated single when it comes to fogging). A high collar is nice; even nicer is a high collar plus a neck gaiter—it's more efficient than a scarf for covering up sensitive neck, cheeks, and chin.

A ski buddy of mine calls this the Inside-Inside, Outside-Outside. Inside, you are toasty and dry. Outside, the storm may rage, it may tap against the windows and doors, but it can't get in. You are encapsulated. It's a cozy, wonderful space in which to ski.

On the slopes, if the visibility is bad, ski next to or right in the trees. Their shadows give the snow surface definition. Ski on the lee side of the trees, where the wind is piling the snow up, as opposed to the exposed side, where the new snow is being carried off.

If the temperature is near freezing, bring a plastic garbage bag for sitting on wet chairlifts. The Alta ski patrol motors around on such days with heavy vinyl half skirts hanging to their knees. They flap in the wind and look generally ridiculous, but they keep bottoms dry through a day of lift riding.

If you get cold, take a break, come inside, dry out, and warm up. Have a hot drink, preferably nonalcoholic, as booze will lower your body temperature further. Eat something, fuel up, and then go out again. Ride the tram or the gondola if there is one. But keep skiing. The longer it storms, the more velvety the mountain becomes, and it's all yours.

Want to learn to ski powder? Ski in a storm. Tomorrow when the sun comes out, machines will flatten the lower-angle powder, and the hordes will descend scrambling for the rest. Today, the day before that blue-sky, flashing-colors day, you can take it where you will. Everyone else has gone home, and if you're really lucky and it's one of those beautiful Utah storms where the flakes fall fast and thick, you'll get off the lift at the top and your tracks from the last run will have disappeared.

SOLITUDE

The trail map says a lot about the way a resort perceives itself. For instance, while Deer Valley's map might feature a photograph of the elegant crystal and silver luncheon buffet at Stein's, Solitude's is more likely to feature an equally inviting shot of burgers and onion rings and chocolate chip cookies outside on a red gingham table cloth. Two of the three ski action photos on a recent season's trail map cover show families—Mom, Dad, and the two whippersnappers—playing follow the leader on crisply groomed slopes.

Solitude is still primarily a day area (although the first phase of the new Village at Solitude, including Creekside Condominiums and the Inn at Solitude, are now open). The slopes are busiest on weekends, when families, school and church groups, and racing teams drive up Big Cottonwood Canyon from the valley. Some days, in fact, the area seems given over to youth. The calendar shows numerous special events designed for children, including family fun days, children's mini-downhills, and chocolate discovery tours as well as ongoing programs like the all-day Ski Academy class. You can ski for half price on your birthday and feel like a kid no matter what your age.

The area is not just for kids, of course. Solitude is an intriguing mountain, not just for beginners but for experts and progressing intermediates as well. Compared to its glittering cousins in Little Cottonwood Canyon, this is an undiscovered powder gem. Some of the expert terrain is so remote and infrequently explored, it can hide powder caches for weeks. Much of the intermediate skiing is of the free-wheeling, treeless variety. (Big Cottonwood once had over 300 lumberjacks working to supply the wood for a growing Salt Lake City.) For the skier looking to experiment with deep snow for the first time, I can think of few pitches better than *Paradise Bowl*, as wide and unobstructed and inviting a piece of powder real estate as there is.

Finally, Solitude is currently in the throes of hard-fought, self-proscribed, major change. Beginning with a subtle but significant lift redesign in 1989, Solitude's third set of owners in a stormy 30-year history has begun revamping the area. They dismantled four of the six existing chairlifts. Two were shortened slightly to make way for the new base village. A new quad chair has been installed in the popular Inspiration area, and, most telling, a first-ever sewer system has been completed in the canyon, opening the way for resort-style accommodations here and in Brighton. This somewhat sleepy, slightly awkward (dare I say "teenage") local area is growing up.

How the Mountain Works

As it is, Solitude is a taller (2,030-foot vertical), broader (1,200 skiable acres), and more complex ski mountain than Brighton, its older neighbor at the head of the canyon. This complexity (of layout, terrain, and traffic patterns) actually causes the mountain to ski *smaller* than it is (I'll come back to this shortly).

The area occupies two side canyons on the left bank of Big Cottonwood Creek plus the broad, sloping shoulder of Eagle Ridge between them. Solitude Canyon is on the east side, a narrow and steeply cut zone of mostly expert terrain. White granite cliffs signaled silver-bearing rock to the nineteenth-century miners. There are 30 to 40 known shafts up here and a few yet to be rediscovered. Most recently a luckless ski instructor found one by skiing into it; he was unhurt.

The majority of the skiing flows off sparsely treed Eagle Ridge like a white blanket flung loosely over the mountain's spine. Two bases, Village and Moonbeam centers, rest on the blanket's lower folds.

Honeycomb Canyon runs along the backside of Eagle Ridge, a sharply gouged imprint of glaciers past. Limited access, a purposeful absence of grooming, and a long, long return road make it the least-skied part of the mountain. Honeycomb is a good example of how a mountain can ski small. There's 2,000 feet of vertical, but the really interesting skiing—and it is *really* interesting—is also quite short, plunging down either side of the canyon to the gully bottom. From there it's a long, slow, moving-sidewalk ride back around to the area low point and the Eagle Express chair.

Another example is the High Expert area served by the Summit chair. It skis like a mini-Taos—quite steep and densely treed, a 1,200-foot expert's mountain off by itself. Similarly, the mostly intermediate skiing that is served by the new Eagle Express quad can function quite independently of the rest of the area. Because the linkage between the zones is not the best, Solitude skiers tend to stay put, skiing one of the mini-mountains to the exclusion of the rest.

Solitude's Mud Slide

The addition in 1988 of the very low-angle Link Lift solved the only thorny beginners' dilemma at Solitude. Before, a skier's first mountain run pretty much had to be up the Moonbeam Lift and then down *Main Street,* which is a glorious, wide learners' avenue except for two short 15-degree pitches. For some people it was too much. The Link is a super-gentle four-degree grade.

The realigned Moonbeam II Lift opens up more of the kind of high-mileage terrain novices need to improve. It tops out at the base of *Paradise Bowl,* where there is a lot of bald, rolling, alpine-type space. *Main Street* is nice. But it has also been the main drag forever, funneling intermediate and advanced skiers down the mountain as well. New green runs called *Little Dollie, Same Street,* and *Pokey-Pine* give gentle options back to Moonbeam base.

The best option for novices who want to explore another part of the mountain is the Sunrise Lift with its two forest meanderers, *North Star* and *Deer Trail.* Care should be taken here, as *Deer Trail* is the only access to and from the Summit Lift. Fast skiers, like Mercedes on the autobahn, sometimes appear out of nowhere.

Blue Solitude

Apex, somewhat of a misnomer since it climbs but 870 feet to a frontside midpoint, is still one of the best intermediate zones on the mountain. The lift parallels the longer Powderhorn Lift and opens up some lovely, gladed slopes that used to be hard to reach. *Alta Bird* and *Stagecoach* drop invitingly from the balding top knoll.

The new quad, called Eagle Express, reaches more terrain faster than the old Inspiration double it replaced. From its high point on Eagle Ridge you can still ski *Sundancer, Hal's Hollow,* and *Rumble and Grumble,* all fine forest cruisers with character. But now you can also sample the marvelous bowl skiing up above, runs like *Rhapsody, Gravity's Rainbow,* and *Olympia,* previously out of reach. Eagle Express is 1,400 vertical feet of groomed bliss.

Former Solitude ski school director Dean Roberts loves the Honeycomb Canyon for intermediates: "If it's groomed! It can be the best thing on the

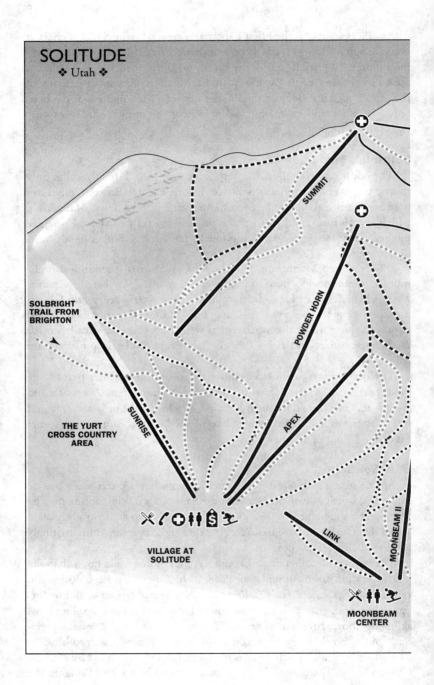

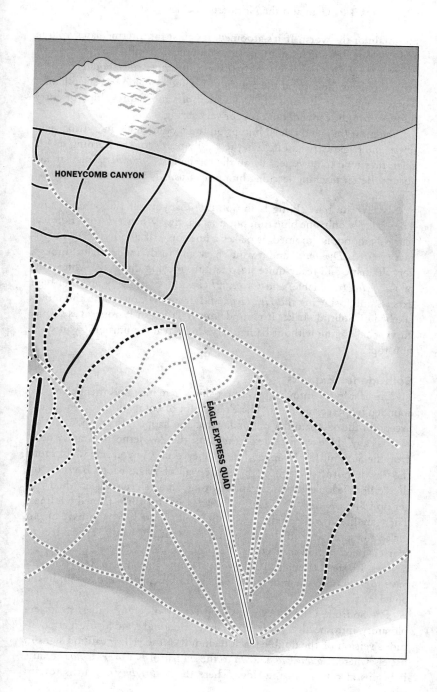

HONEYCOMB CANYON

EAGLE EXPRESS QUAD

mountain or the worst. If it's groomed, it's great for intermediates, rolling and pitching." But if it's not machine-smoothed—and it isn't always—it can be a tough slog for all but the best skiers. Intermediates should enter the canyon only at the top, off the Summit Lift, and not along its steep flanks. There are gates at the tops of the Powderhorn and Express lifts for entry midway into the canyon, but only for very strong skiers.

The most frequently skied bumps on the mountain are in a string right under the Eagle Express Lift. They're hardly pearls for the learning mogul skier; they tend to be, especially on the top half of *Inspiration,* angular and abrupt. Better teaching/learning bumps can usually be found scattered off *Eagle Ridge.*

My favorite blue skiing is in Solitude Canyon off the Summit Lift. There's really only one blue run, but it's a dandy. (When *Liberty,* a nominal black diamond, is groomed, it makes a fine top-half alternative.) The primary route is *Dynamite,* and it winds back and forth under the lift through very dramatic and really quite steep terrain: moving under the white cliffs of *Cathedral* (unskiable) and *Cathedral Cirque* (occasionally open for high experts only), skirting the *Headwall,* and dropping down onto the snowy lakebed of Solitude Lake. It reminds me of skiing in Europe; it is scenic, curvy, challenging without being scary, and a real leg-burner if you ski it nonstop.

Solitude for Experts

The heading is entirely apt. Expert skiers here may find themselves surrounded by peace and quiet. There's not a lot of competition on the steeps except for the odd Saturday or Sunday that also happens to be a powder day.

Basically, there are three expert regions: the Powderhorn/Paradise Bowl area, the Summit Lift basin, and the Honeycomb Canyon side walls. From the Powderhorn base almost the entire wall of Eagle Ridge is visible on the skyline. It looks expansive and inviting, and it's even bigger when you get up in it. *Concord, Paradise,* and *Vertigo* are just three named fall lines. There are literally hundreds, maybe thousands more here. You have but to pick your spot, peel off the ridge, and enjoy nearly 1,000 vertical feet of sparsely treed, alpine-style skiing. The pitch modulates between 20 and 30 degrees. It's steep enough to hold your attention but not so steep that you have to hold onto the mountain. This is sublime, cut-loose terrain in the powder.

The Solitude Canyon expert skiing is very different: quiet, steep, exploratory, introspective. Most of it is in the trees and rated high-expert, Solitude's version of the double black diamond or the yellow caution signs in use elsewhere. *Courageous,* known to the ski patrol as *Corner Chute* because it begins at a bend in the ridge where the *Solbright Trail* turns toward

Brighton, is a straight, shady corridor through the spruce, which, if it hasn't snowed for a while, develops some tasty bumps. Almost everything else in the *Headwall* region is wild, uncut, and unnamed. Some of the best tree runs are out the *Evergreen Traverse* (not shown on the map) from the *Courageous* corner. (Evergreen Mountain divides Solitude from Brighton and the Twin Lakes basin. Its western slope constitutes one side of Solitude Canyon.) Skiing north, each shot through the trees looks better than the last, but if you can hold out to the end, there is a special treat: a broad rockslide with room for you and 20 of your friends to match figure eights all the way to Solitude Lake.

On the map there appears to be one and only one route connecting the top of Powderhorn to the Summit area. It's called *Parachute*. The patrol calls it "Terror Chute." You might need a parachute if you are not lucky enough to be the first or second person down after a storm. This radically steep, narrow avalanche gully is rarely open, and even then rarely worth the stress on mind and equipment. There is, however, some exquisite, super-expert exploring to be had in the cliffy woods north of *Parachute*. Ski *Houli's* first, then go back up and ease your way to your right into some of the least trodden snow on the mountain. Forget about a ski route to the Summit Lift. Someday they'll have to blast one. For now, ride the Sunrise triple, an almost purely transportational lift, along with everybody else.

Honeycomb Canyon is always a dilemma: Is the skiing good enough on the short, steep upper pitches to warrant the long road back around the mountain? Do you want to end up at the Eagle Express base? In fresh snow and after the patrol has controlled the slides under the Honeycomb Cliffs to the south, the answer is often yes. When *Black Forest,* down the backside from the top of Powderhorn, is good, it is very, very good, and it is also the longest fall line in the canyon. For sheer alpine beauty, you can't beat the long traverse under the cliffs to *Crystal Point*. Dean Roberts will tell you, "It's a lot of work for 20 turns." But what an exquisite 20 turns, through sparkling steep meadows to the creek bottom!

Another time to go into Honeycomb is when there hasn't been new snow for a while. Then the long backside of Eagle Ridge provides near infinite exploring options amid twisted old limber pines. Here, in regions with names like *Here Be Dragons* and *Navarone,* you'll find an occasional jewel of a chute, a rib off the spine, untouched for weeks. Use caution throughout the area; small cliffs and rock bands abound. The fast Eagle Express chair makes round trips through Honeycomb Canyon more inviting than ever for experts.

Plans for lift improvement include the following: Moonbeam upgraded to a detachable quad, Apex upgraded to a detachable quad, Honeycomb Return Lift out of Honeycomb Canyon, Redman Lift to open more beginner terrain.

Solitude Lodging

The first phase of the new European-style Village at Solitude includes the Creekside Condominiums (18 units) and the Inn at Solitude, which houses 47 hotel rooms plus a spa and conference center. Opening in 1999–2000 will be the Powderhorn Lodge (82 units and 5,000 square feet of retail space). When the village is complete there will be 560 bedrooms along an 800-foot main walking mall. The skiers that continue to stay in the valley and commute the 30 minutes to ski will have a very unique situation when parking. The ski-in/ski-out parking lot ensures that all skiers only have to walk 100 feet (at most) to get to the slope.

SOLITUDE DATA

Mountain Statistics

Vertical feet	2,037 feet
Base elevation	7,988 feet
Summit elevation	10,035 feet
Longest run	2.5 miles
Average annual snowfall	450 inches
Number of lifts	7 chairs: 1 quad, 2 triples, 4 doubles
Uphill capacity	10,750 skiers per hour
Skiable terrain	1,200 acres
Opening date	mid-November
Closing date	mid-April
Snowboarding	Yes

Transportation

By car About 45 minutes from Salt Lake International Airport via I-80 and Wasatch Boulevard south to State 152, Big Cottonwood Canyon. Solitude is 13 miles up the road, 1 mile below Brighton.

By bus, limo, or taxi From Salt Lake International Airport and from downtown Salt Lake City.

By plane Via major carriers to Salt Lake International Airport.

Key Phone Numbers

Snow Report (801) 536-5777
Ski Area Information
    (801) 534-1400
Lodging (800) 748-4754
Salt Lake Convention & Visitors
    Bureau (801) 521-2868
www.skisolitude.com

The Utah Interconnect

So close are the big five areas on the Wasatch Front—that is, Snowbird, Alta, Solitude, Brighton, and Park City—that skiers have dreamed for years of linking them somehow to create one giant ski circus. It's been done successfully in France—Les Trois Vallées, for example, where one ticket gains you access to three interconnected valleys, numerous villages, and hundreds of lifts. In Switzerland, too, Zermatt is linked over the ridge lines with Cervinia, Italy, to the south. Wouldn't it be great, so the thinking goes, to ski from Alta to Park City, have lunch, and ski back?

One proposal has such a linkup completed with the addition of just three chairlifts. One would climb from the Alta parking lot to Twin Lakes Pass via Grizzly Gulch, thus connecting Little Cottonwood to Big Cottonwood Canyon. The return lift would tie Brighton to the same ridge line. The third lift would leave Brighton and connect with Park City in the Scotts Pass/Guardsman Pass area.

Simple, but not so simple. While the ski areas themselves are basically for the idea—assuming the details of avalanche-control work, patrolling, and jurisdictions can be ironed out—the general populace is not so sure. Some see it as a way to further promote the uniqueness of Utah skiing. There is no other place in North America where such a nexus could exist. Others see the plan as harmful and unnecessary. Backcountry skiers would mourn the loss of wilderness in canyons currently accessible only on foot. Local environmentalist groups, most notably Save Our Canyons and the Sierra Club, contend that there are already too many cars in the canyons, and that there are air and water and large-scale transportation problems to be worked out before such a linkup would be warranted. The flip side of the amazing accessibility of these mountains is that there are numerous and often competing or overlapping uses.

Happily, you can ski from area to area right now, without the lifts, via the Interconnect Adventure Tour. The five-area tour starts in Park City and passes through Brighton, Solitude, and Alta and ends in Snowbird. It runs Mondays, Wednesdays, Fridays, and Sundays and costs approximately $110. The four-area tour—Snowbird to Alta to Brighton to Solitude and back to Alta—runs Tuesdays, Thursdays, and Saturdays. Both include guides, all lift passes, and lunch at Solitude.

This is real adventure skiing in the backcountry with some walking and climbing, and, if you're lucky, some gorgeous powder turns in pristine settings. I have only skied the four-area loop tour, but I am told that compared to the longer, five-area traverse, it involves more downhill skiing.

We began with orientation and a quick clinic on the avalanche transceiver/rescue beacons we would all wear. Then it was up an early tram at Snowbird, over to Alta and up the Supreme Lift. From there we climbed and traversed for perhaps half an hour to the boundary between Big and Little Cottonwood Canyons at Catherine's Pass. From there to Brighton it was all powder, down runs like *Dog Lake Chute* and *Pillow Talk,* names only our guides knew. At Brighton we took the *Solbright Trail* around the nose of Evergreen Mountain to the Solitude base. A lunch of soup, sandwiches, and chocolate chip cookies and we were off again, up Solitude's lift system to the top of Summit. The route from there back over to Little Cottonwood Canyon follows a long and breathtaking traverse of Davenport Hill, known as the *Highway to Heaven.* For safety reasons we walked it one at a time. There was time, alone on the open slope, to take in the sweep and scale of these mountains, the porcelain bowls dropping away at your feet, the wind-sculpted crests of Patsey Marley and Wolverine peaks across the chasm. How tiny you feel inching along old avalanche paths, where, earlier in the winter, overloaded storm snow released in a monstrous whoosh down to the basin floor.

From Twin Lakes Pass, it is down Grizzly Gulch, a sinuous, shady powder run through meadows and glades to Alta's upper parking lot. Our guides, when pressed, weren't sure they favored the Interconnect lifts, even though their bosses at the Utah Ski Association are strong supporters of the plan. Who can blame them—the way it is is so much fun. I empathize, but I would like to see the Interconnect become a reality someday. The terrain practically demands it. The actual new terrain that would come under the areas' domain is quite small, and the vast new sense of choice and adventure available to the alpine skier, while in no way giving up its Utah charm, would rival the best in the Alps. For more information contact Ski Utah Interconnect at (801) 534-1907.

 # Backside Wasatch

Park City Mountain Resort It's the biggest, brawlingest, sprawlingest ski and snowboard resort in Utah. Park City doesn't get the copious snows the frontside canyons receive, but it makes up for that with snowmaking; high-speed, six-passenger chairs; fine, rambling, something-for-everyone terrain; and a real reborn mining town with excellent restaurants and clubs, and even a midwinter film festival. There is every imaginable amenity and range of lodging here, and Park City was rated as one of the top ten mountain resort towns in the United States in the February 1999 issue of *Mountain Sports & Living*.

Deer Valley Resort This ski area made its reputation on service and high-end lodging and dining. Valets help remove the skis from your car racks, there is smoked salmon for lunch at the Stein Eriksen Lodge, and a huge percentage of the trails here are buffed to corduroy perfection every night. The surprise is the hidden expert skiing in sublime aspen and evergreen glades. If you have to ask the price, you're in trouble.

The Canyons This area was bought by the American Skiing Company and by 2005 the conglomerate plans to invest $500 million to develop 7,200 acres! The Canyons, with a new name and a new future, is the closest backside area to downtown Salt Lake, located between the I-80 and Park City.

Sundance This is a secluded, idyllic forest village built by Robert Redford on the site of Provo's local ski hill. The ambience is all rough-cut timbers, down comforters, and Remington bronzes beneath the soaring white wall of Mt. Timpanogos. The skiing on two connected mountains doesn't quite live up to the tasteful elegance. The skiing is best on Back Mountain, where you just might catch a glimpse of Bob cruising on *Bearclaw*.

PARK CITY MOUNTAIN RESORT

Park City Mountain Resort (PCMR) is the anomaly among Utah ski areas—a real town, a full-on, mining-era boomtown, like Aspen or Telluride, that has been resurrected by skiing. Certainly Alta was a town, too (and it still is an incorporated municipality), but there was nothing left from its silver glory days when skiing began there in the late 1930s. Park City, on the other hand, counted about 1,000 souls living in its Victorian, gingerbread shacks in 1957 when the last of the unconsolidated mines shut down. People there still drank in the saloons and went to the movies at the Egyptian Theater even though the town was listed in a guidebook to Utah ghost towns; it was quiet but far from dead. Then in 1960 the United Park City Mines decided to develop some of its 10,000 acres of mountainous terrain west of downtown for skiing. It was a visionary move.

Today Park City is by far the largest ski resort in Utah by almost any measure: acreage, lifts, snowmaking, yearly skier visits, tourist beds in town. All that in addition to the attention the area draws for being the home of the U.S. Ski Team and for hosting big-time ski events like the America's Opening men's and women's World Cup races every November. The World Cup has never been predisposed to open its season outside Europe, so the latter is indeed a public relations coup. PCMR also hosted a World Cup snowboard event in 1999.

Another feather in the cap: Park City and neighboring Deer Valley will stage the Olympic slalom, giant slalom, freestyle, and all snowboard events in 2002. Nordic jumping and bobsled/luge will be contested a few miles out of town at the Utah Winter Sports Park. In fact, anyone can soar off the 18- and 38-meter practice jumps for a minimal cost. The price includes training by Nordic and freestyle jumpers. Check the schedule for times and days.

Park City is certainly the most international of the Utah resorts. It is a multifaceted winter and summer destination, like Aspen, with prices to match. Park City is one of the few towns in Utah not founded by Mormon settlers in the latter half of the nineteenth century. In many ways, it seems less a part of Utah than almost any other place in the state, and, in fact, its history corroborates the feeling.

Brigham Young would not allow any of his Mormon flock to prospect for or extract precious metals, so the rich veins of silver under the Wasatch Range went undiscovered until about 1863, when federal troops stationed in the valley forayed up the canyons and literally stumbled upon them. The Park City bonanza, discovered in 1872, was one of the richest ore bodies of all; $400 million in silver was extracted in less than 50 years. Mormon farm-

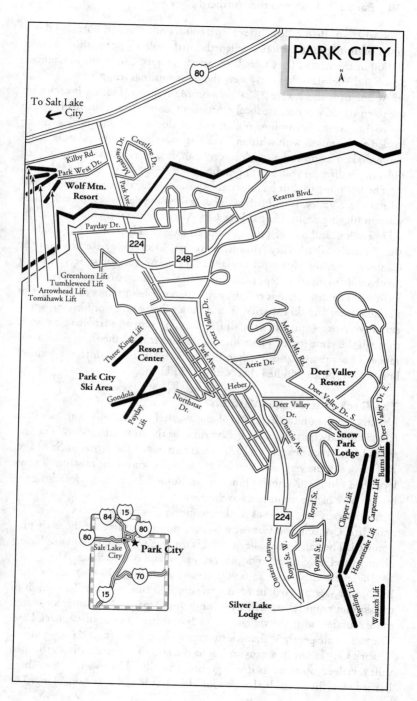

ers in what was then called Parley's Park could only watch in horror as thousands of immigrant miners swelled the little valley's population to over 10,000 by the 1890s. They were Irish, Swedes, Finns, Cornishmen, Chinese, Scots, and Yugoslavs. Very few were there for spiritual reasons.

At one time there were 27 saloons on Main Street. During Prohibition the town stayed wet because local mortician George Archer drove his hearse up to Evanston, Wyoming, pulled the shades down, and rattled home loaded to the tassels with whiskey. Park City developed as a kind of cultural and moral nonconformity in Mormon Utah. It was either an oasis or a black hole, depending on your starting point.

The last mine to shut its doors, the Ontario, near the base of the mountain at Deer Valley, is still maintained against the day when metals prices warrant digging again. United Park City Mines, while it no longer runs the ski operation, still owns all the ground. In fact, all three areas on this side of the Wasatch—Park City Mountain Resort, Deer Valley Resort, and the Canyons—are mostly on private land. This means the Forest Service is not involved in anything except plans for possible future expansion into public territory. The difference is certainly not discernible in terms of facilities or the quality of the ski experience. But Park City would not have grown as extensively or as quickly as it did if the ski company had had to wade through the same public procedures as do the areas on the front side of the range. This private-land free hand gives Park City a brashness, a kind of boomtown spirit rekindled that is unique in Utah.

The Back Side of the Wasatch

Although it's on the back side of the Wasatch Mountains from Salt Lake City, Park City is as close, in driving time, as the frontside resorts. The reason is I-80, which charges up Parley's Canyon out of the center of Salt Lake. It's freeway all the way, over the divide and down into the grassy interior valleys, then south at Kimball's Junction on Route 224, an easy lope along the eastern base of the mountains to the resorts.

You're really very close, as the Interconnect flies, to the headwaters of Big and Little Cottonwood Canyons, but the physical differences here are pronounced. The Salt Lake Valley sprawl is missing, and the mountains have a different feel, too. It has to do with elevation and orientation.

The Park City base at 6,900 feet is almost 2,000 feet lower than Brighton's. Sage and oak brush dot the dry hills east of town. Two-thirds of the ski mountain is carpeted with sun-loving aspens. Ridge lines are softer, more rounded, as if the violent Wasatch upthrust ran out of gas back here. The valleys are gently V-shaped, stream-washed rather than glacier-gouged.

Park City is not in a canyon but at the end of a narrow, flat-bottomed valley wedged up as far as it will go into the hills. The town itself is shoehorned onto the point. It's barely four blocks wide and over a mile long. The valley runs north to south, so the storefronts on one side of Main Street catch the morning sun while the businesses on the other side enjoy direct afternoon light.

The ski mountain has a similar orientation, though the main axis runs more northeast to southwest. It climbs up and away from town on one long ridge line. Ski runs drape both sides of the ridge like old lace; one side gets the morning light, the other side the late-day glow. Here and there are patches of north-facing terrain, indicated by dense evergreens, sections of dark cloth on an otherwise leafless winter quilt.

Less than a fourth of the 3,000-acre mountain is visible from the valley. Webs of lifts climb out of the monolithic Resort Center base and disappear over the ridge. The Payday, a six-passenger high-speed chair, is the fastest way out of the Resort Center. From the summit more lifts radiate in all directions, down the ridgeback and over both sides. Generally speaking, the farther back you go, the more difficult the skiing becomes, until finally the ridge peaks in the alpine zone, where four steep Alta-style bowls cap the lift-served skiing right at 10,000 feet. The mountain is much deeper than it is wide, drawing up and away from town until at the top you are probably closer to Brighton than you are to your car at the Resort Center parking lot.

Because of the lower elevation and a possible snow shadow effect, Park City measures about 100 fewer inches of the light stuff than do the front-side areas. Still, 350 inches is more than enough in most years. To guard against cover intrusions on the lower slopes, the area has developed the most extensive snowmaking system in the state. They had to have it when they began hosting World Cup and pro races in mid-November. Now they use it, as many areas around the country have learned to do, to guarantee an early opening.

There is an occasional tendency to confuse the three areas surrounding the old town: Park City, the Canyons (previously called ParkWest), and Deer Valley at Park City. While they all use the town of Park City as a hub, and visitors often ski all three areas in a single stay, they are actually three separate areas with quite separate and distinct personalities. The Canyons is four miles north of Park City and is in the process of becoming a major destination resort. Deer Valley is just east of Park City, a relatively recent, self-contained resort and real estate development with an unapologetic tilt toward the luxury end of the spectrum. Park City is in the middle of the exuberant boomtown—now a National Historic District—with an equally spirited ski and snowboard operation built on top of the diggings.

Park City for Beginners and Novices

Park City has a nicely self-contained beginner's area to the right of the Resort Center base. Two slow-moving lifts, First Time and Three Kings, glide up the sunny, east-facing slope. There is almost no incoming traffic

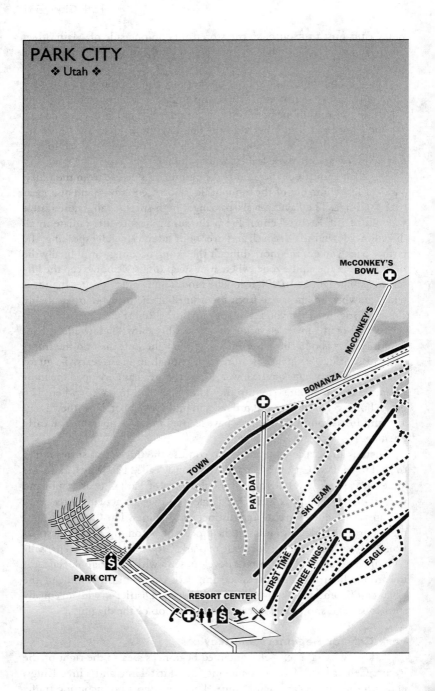

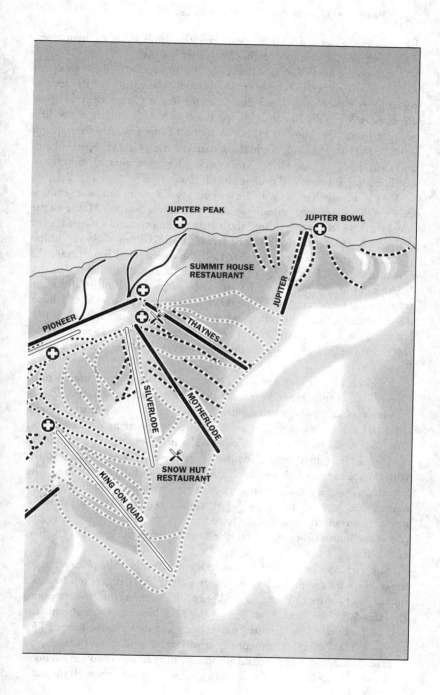

JUPITER PEAK

JUPITER BOWL

SUMMIT HOUSE
RESTAURANT

JUPITER

PIONEER

THAYNES

SILVERLODE

MOTHERLODE

SNOW HUT
RESTAURANT

KING CON QUAD

from above, so skiers just starting out have the whole thing to themselves. This is where the ski school teaches first-timer lessons.

Once you've made the transition to novice and you're ready to go up on the mountain proper, the choices multiply wonderfully. Take the Payday six-passenger (six-pack) high-speed chair from the Resort Center, then ski down *Bonanza Access* to the Bonanza Hi-Speed six-pack. Utilizing these two lifts will get you to the Summit House in about 12 minutes. Another option would be to ride the Eagle triple chair, then the King Con Hi-Speed Quad, and then the Silverlode Hi-Speed six-pack. The latter takes 17 minutes— not including ski time and time in the lift line.

Your goal, whether you ride the six-packs or the other lifts, is an exquisitely long (novices need mileage) green run from the Summit House all the way to the resort base. It's three and a half miles long, and though it's the designated "easiest way down," don't save it for the last run of the day unless you have plenty of energy left. Start off the top and ski right under the Bonanza six-pack line on *Homerun*, the Champs Elysées of the mountain. You're right on the ridgeback; it's airy and spacious, and in the afternoon your shadow precedes you weaving down the groomed promenade. Halfway down the ridge, turn right onto a switchback detour through the aspens that cut out *Silver Queen* on the steeper nose of the ridge. *Homerun* recrosses the ridge near the base of *Bonanza* and drops into the final hollow back to the Resort Center.

It's often a good idea not to ski this route all the way to the bottom. Depending on the time of year and the recent natural snow history, *Lower Homerun* is likely to be covered with man-made snow. Not the stuff people come to Utah to sink their edges into. Consequently, many novices stay on *Claimjumper* to yo-yo the Silverlode area, a north-facing zone with good cold snow and buffed runs. Ride the Silverlode six-passenger chair to the same Summit House hub and ski *Claimjumper* for its full crescent mile. The Silverlode is a good area for families or groups with differing abilities who nevertheless want to end up in the same place together. A smorgasbord of novice to advanced runs fans out from the top, then funnels back into one cup at the bottom. The Snow Hut Restaurant serves the crowd at the base of the lift.

And there can be a crowd. It's no accident that this is the place management chose for the nation's first six-seater chairlift. If it gets too bad, the novice has two options. One is to ski east, skier's right, off *Homerun* onto the *Mid-Mtn.* trail. This takes you by the Mid-Mountain Restaurant (the best on-mountain lunch; more on that later) and down to the base of Pioneer Lift. The Pioneer is infrequently crowded; it's kind of off by itself, and it serves mainly intermediate and advanced skiing so novices often overlook it. But the *Homerun/Mid-Mtn.* combination is a nice one, through the trees, strong on morning sun, shadowy in the afternoon with an easy return either to the Summit House or the base via the *Flat Iron* trail.

The other option is to ski the bottom of the mountain while everybody else is up top. This plan works basically from late morning on. The Payday six-pack serves all of the *Treasure Hollow* region, including *Homerun*. When the snow is fresh and soft, several blue runs in this domain become easier, notably *Treasure Hollow* and the signature run, *Payday*.

Park City Cruising

Everybody wants to cruise on *Payday*. It's a good run, almost 1,300 feet of vertical, wide, with a roller-coaster fall line and always plenty of snow, man-made or otherwise. This is where the snowboard half-pipe is located and where they turn the lights on for night skiing as well (4–9 P.M., seven nights a week). So it gets a lot of traffic, and traffic means scraped hard snow. For my money the really great cruising—and this is one of Park City's strengths—is on the backside in the *Silverlode* and *King Con* (short for King Consolidated Mine) region and still higher in the Thaynes Canyon realm.

The *Parleys Park* run is a classic intermediate swipe down the fall line. So wide that from one side you are barely aware of the other edge; so smooth, it's like a carpet underfoot. It starts out almost flat, tips just enough down the ridge to get you sailing, then rolls over the crown for a sustained, high-speed ride to the bottom.

More circumspect, but in some ways more interesting, is the *Hidden Splendor* route. It dips and curls along terrain changes from the *Claimjumper* ridge down a gentle sink in the center of the woods. Both drop more than 1,300 vertical feet.

There are a number of steeper groomed runs off Silverlode to the west into Thaynes Canyon. *Single Jack*, *Sunnyside*, and *Prospector* seem to dive over the edge through forests of mixed aspens and evergreens. In between, *Ford Country* and *Glory Hole* rate black diamonds. They are exactly the same pitch—not too steep for most intermediates—but their moguls are allowed to grow unimpeded. From the trough at the bottom of Thaynes Canyon, you can either ride the Motherlode triple chair and in a quick 11 minutes be back to Summit House (so much of Park City's skiing emanates like spokes from this point), or you can keep sliding down the groove another half-mile to the King Con. King Con serves an all-intermediate tract, a large area of smooth-mowed trail skiing. It's quite popular, especially now that the lift has been quadified, but I find the runs short compared to Silverlode and Thaynes, and the lower elevation can occasionally bake the snow.

The higher you get, of course, the colder and softer the snow will be. *Single Jack* takes you to the Thaynes chair, the highest, shadiest intermediate quarter on the mountain. *Keystone* carves a passage through dense spruce and fir near the head of the canyon just below Jupiter Bowl (the snow is always crisp). Or try the *Jupiter Access* trail. It's more than just access to the Jupiter Lift; it covers some delightful, lumpy-moraine terrain at the base of the *West Wall* and *Fortune Teller*. If nothing else, it's worth the peek up into this alpine zone, the cream of Park City's expert offerings.

From the Jupiter base a blue trail leads down the gulch to the Thaynes chair again. There is no groomed descent off the Jupiter ridges, so unless you are experienced in wild snow, powder, or its cut-up cousin crud, don't ride this chair. If you do, either by mistake or through misplaced machismo, *Scotts Bowl* is the lowest-angle return to civilization.

Just above the Thaynes base you'll notice a jumble of tin mine buildings. In Park City's early days skiers had the option of getting to Thaynes via the gondola (and *Single Jack*) or underground through the honeycomb of mine tunnels. They rode three miles in on a miner's train with United Park City miners at the helm. They were then lifted 1,800 feet straight up in a hoist elevator to ground level at the bottom of the Thaynes Lift. The route was abandoned 20 years ago, but now with all the talk about Interconnects and the need for traffic solutions in the canyons, the idea of using some of the hundreds of miles of tunnel under the mountains is receiving thoughtful consideration.

What to do when things back up on the Silverlode lift? Move a step uphill to the Motherlode. And when that one gets a little long? Move up another notch to Thaynes. And if Thaynes gets busy? Once again, head over the ridge to Pioneer and McConkey's six-pack. The blues are a little shorter over here, but they're almost invariably quiet. *Comstock, Red Fox,* and *Hawk Eye* are like a different world, flush with the morning sun, bright even when the sun is on the other side because they are cut through aspens and oak brush, with big views to the east at Deer Valley's double cones and south up into *Puma* and *McConkey's* bowls. Get some good north exposure skiing on *Sunrise* and *Buckeye* or test your skills in some off-trail skiing in *McConkey's Bowl*.

When it's time to go home in the afternoon, you can join the commuters on the *Homerun/Payday* hayride or you can try something a little different. Turn left off *Homerun* to the top of the Ski Team Lift and follow the wide-open ridge to the north. Your shadow should be dancing out in front all the way to the end, where you take *Gotcha Cut-off*, dodge through the aspens, and pop out on *Ladies SL,* for a final set of sweeping esses to the base. Oh, and there's one more option if your lodging is closer to the heart of Old Town than to the new stuff at the Resort Center. You can ski right down to Woodside Avenue near 8th Avenue over the old Creole mine dumps on two runs called *Creole* and *Quit'n Time.* Look for the narrow entrance off *Payday* to the right.

For townies and visitors staying in Old Town, the Town triple chair at 8th and Park Avenues makes good sense for getting up the mountain in the morning. It's strictly an access chair—you don't yo-yo it—but it'll get you to the Angle Station and you won't have to drive or ride the Park City Transit shuttle out to the Resort Center.

Park City's massive, village-unto-itself base has its advantages—namely being able to find everything around one pedestrian courtyard. The ski school is here, lift tickets, Kinderschule, Interconnect departures (for skiing to the four areas across the divide in Big and Little Cottonwood Canyons), race clinics, equipment rentals, food—fast and otherwise—and so on.

Park City for Expert Skiers

Some of the longest and cleanest expert lines on the mountain are also some of the first you see when standing at the base. The so-called *Ski Team* runs—the *Men's* and *Ladies' SL* and *GS* runs and the adjacent *Silver King* and *Shaft*—cut strong corridors through the aspen carpet. The Ski Team Lift climbs straight to the top of these runs, but there never seems to be anybody skiing them. Why? Because in Park City and the rest of Utah great snow is what you expect and merely good snow is often snubbed. The *Ski Team* runs are low on the hill and face directly east. This snow absorbs a lot of solar radiation. Then, when the sun passes overhead to the King Con side, that same snow freezes hard. If you can catch these runs soon after a snowfall they have a marvelous consistent pitch over true fall lines. Much of the time, however, they are too crunchy to compete with softer snow farther up the mountain.

Bumpers love the Thaynes/Motherlode realm. Runs like *Glory Hole, Double Jack,* and *The Hoist* (all hard-rock mining terms that are particularly expressive, it seems to me, of enthusiastic mogul mashing) provide about 1,000 vertical feet each of continuous bumping action. Closer to town the Payday Lift offers quick access to a couple of nasties called *Widowmaker* and *Nail Driver.* Neither is long, but they are steep, and the bumps, once the season is well under way, become Volkswagen size.

The best-shaped moguls, long and round, the kind made by the best skiers, are generally to be found in the *Shadow Ridge* area off Jupiter Lift. Strong mogul skiers pour down this crescent, 1,100-vertical-foot run all day long, but the bumps never get too sharp or sawed-off and unmakable.

Occasionally, there'll be small developing bumps on the *West Face* of Jupiter Peak (if it hasn't filled in with new snow for a week or so) or in the center of *Blueslip Bowl,* but generally speaking the high bowls don't see enough traffic after the powder is skied out to grow serious lumps. *Blueslip* is an interesting place. Just up Pioneer Ridge from the top of Bonanza Sixpack, it was out of bounds before the Pioneer Lift went in. Forbidden but so inviting. Bounded on one side by aspen glades and on the other by dense spruce, it plunges 500 vertical feet quite suddenly, more precipitously than anything in bounds at that time. After work ski area employees would sometimes sneak down its steep flanks. If they were caught, they were fired, given their blue slips.

Thankfully, it's now open and well served by the Pioneer chair and the McConkey's six-pack. The left side, the aspen side, gathers more sun and therefore reaps the subsequent benefits and pitfalls. On the negative side, powder sours more quickly in the direct sun, and in mid-winter the resulting crud can be nearly unskiable. In the spring, however, this is one of the first exposures to "corn up," or go through the cycle of melting and freezing that produces the marvelous, ego-boosting surface known as corn.

The right side, the evergreen side, has a totally different character. The snow stays shady and cold most of the winter. Another wonderful thing happens. Wind-driven snow from over Pioneer Ridge lands here in dense, smooth layers, like a blue-white sheet stretched over the terrain. When this happens, the right side of *Blueslip Bowl* is a winter equivalent of corn, easy-turning, easy-holding snow on an exhilaratingly steep pitch.

The crown jewels of Park City expert skiing hover regally above everything else. The summit ridge, from *Scott's Bowl* on the west to *McConkey's Bowl* on the east, with Jupiter Peak reigning in the middle, encompasses about 600 acres of bowls and chutes and steep trees, the kind of terrain that puts Park City in the same league with Alta and Snowbird. (Before the Jupiter Lift went in, in 1976, Park City was an unparalleled novice and intermediate mountain, but it lacked the high-end excitement, the real steep and deep that only happens around timberline where nature sculpts runs by means of rock slide, avalanche, and extreme weather.)

Because this is extreme terrain, not all of it will be open all of the time. The farthest out, *Puma* and *McConkey's,* open as avalanche-control work is completed. On a powder morning, locals and deep-seeking visitors will head straight for Jupiter (Payday to Bonanza to Pioneer is the fastest way); there's really no reason to stop anywhere else along the way.

The steepest runs are off to the left of the lift among the spindly trees and cliffs of *Jupiter Bowl* proper. *Six Bells* is the steepest of the steep. In the mines, six bells signaled "Look out below!" A little farther out on the ridge is the *West Face* of Jupiter Peak, where you'll find beautiful finger-thin lines with scraps of small trees in between to differentiate them. My favorite is *Om Zone*. Ski it with repetitive short turns and you'll be in a happy trance all the way to the bottom of the bowl. It's also a magic place in the afternoon, when golden light floods the face head on.

Scott's Bowl (off the chair to the right) sometimes has a sizable cornice for the air-minded. Underneath, it is the most spacious of the bowls, and the incline quickly moderates to a relatively mellow pitch. This is the place to go if you're not sure you're ready to test your skills on the hairier runs to the east.

However, if you are quite sure of your skills, then you owe yourself a trip down off the peak. It requires a walk, perhaps ten minutes from the saddle above *West Face,* but this walk earns you the most adventurous terrain on the mountain. *East Face* is broken up by rock ribs with vertical bands of snow in between. The center chute, *Hourglass,* squeezes down to about one and a half ski lengths at the throat, then opens quickly into the expanse of *Puma Bowl.* This is heart-pounding skiing, very steep but not particularly dangerous because of the open slopes below.

Chances are good the chutes will already have avalanched by the time the patrol lets you up there. They're that steep. For deeper snow on a more moderate pitch, take McConkey's six-pack and ski or board the north-facing glades of *Puma Bowl* or all the way out to the giant scoop that is *McConkey's.* Here you can weave together 50 powder turns before bumping into the *Woodside* trail and the return to Pioneer or McConkey's six-pack. Everything on the east side of the peak flows into the Pioneer drainage; everything on the west funnels back to Jupiter. Even so, a return trip to Pumaland requires only two lift rides.

Many good skiers race to the Jupiter Lift and stay there all day. It's a different world up there, separate and challenging. Sometimes the trip back down, via *Thaynes Canyon* or the Claimjumper expressway, with the maze of lifts and other skiers, is a bit of a shock. But it's a pleasant one because it underscores the specialness of the place you've been in.

Lunch on the Mountain

Steeps Cafe in the Steeps building (which will be reconstructed in 2000) serves up some pretty tasty American-inspired lunches, but my favorite on-mountain eating is at the Mid-Mountain Restaurant. The building itself is 100 years old and was built originally as a boardinghouse/dining hall for the Silver King miners. In 1987, in an astonishing feat, the ski area cut a new run in order to haul the building 4,000 feet up the mountain to its present location in the aspens near the base of the Pioneer Lift. Although it's been completely refurbished, the place retains the essence of its history. It's in the whitewashed interior, the narrow hallways, the old wainscoting and double-hung window sashes. To top it off, the walls are hung with photographic prints, some of them spectacularly sharp, of mining-era scenes. They are the kind of photos that draw you irresistibly in; the miners' faces are more like our own than the distance of history would lead us to imagine.

There's a big, sunny deck, and the food is good, too. Classic American ski resort fare: pizza, chili, stews, and sandwiches, and, of course, the locally brewed Wasatch Ale, a very respectable red bitter.

In Town: Eating, Sleeping, and Other Forms of Rejuvenation

Tough choices here. There are fine restaurants in some of the slopeside hotels, but I'm going to stick pretty much to the historic Main Street area, which you can cover on foot or by hopping the clanging little trolley in under half an hour.

Alex's is Park City's only prix fixe French restaurant; it is intimate, decorated in soft pastels with a simple, well-prepared, and reasonably priced menu. For Mexican I like Nacho Mammas, located at 1821 Sidewinder Dr., which features Mexican-style dishes combined with unique regional specialties borrowed from throughout the Southwest. For frontier-size steaks and prime rib, try the Claim Jumper, owned and operated by the same man (a former Blue Angel fighter pilot) who runs the Mid-Mountain Restaurant.

The most unusual dinner setting in the area comes aboard the Heber Creeper, a restored steam train with an elegant dining car that makes a nightly dinner loop through the Heber Valley 20 minutes southeast of Park City.

Getting a drink in Utah is not as complicated as it may seem (see the "Inside Story," Utah Liquor Laws and the Word of Wisdom, page 355). Having a drink with a meal is no difficulty. If you want to just sit in a bar and have a cocktail, you can do that, too. But there's a twist: Bars that serve wine and mixed drinks over the counter are called clubs, and you'll be asked to become a member. Two-week temporary memberships are available at all the clubs and at most hotel desks. With that one transaction out of the way, you can order a drink. The most authentic, mining-era bar on Main Street is, appropriately enough, the Club. They wouldn't take paper money until just a few years ago.

Breakfast is a key meal for skiers. For great homemade pastries, croissants, and cappuccinos, the Morning Ray on upper Main Street is the place. For an all-American, bacon-and-eggs-and-flapjacks kind of place, try the Mt. Air Cafe, a classic diner on Park Avenue near Kearns Boulevard.

The lodging list is long and the choices are multifarious. Park City has about 10,000 guest pillows. For a complete listing call the Park City Chamber Bureau, (800) 453-1360.

A few places of note: The Alpine Prospector Lodge is a genuine mining-era boardinghouse remodeled into a ski lodge with budget rates. The Old Miners' Lodge Bed and Breakfast Inn is chock-full of antiques and serves a full breakfast, and it sits next to the Town Lift. By far the least expensive lodging option is the Hidden Haven Campground, right off I-80 with hook-ups and nightly, weekly, or monthly rates for skiers who bring their lodging with them.

There are untold condominiums and condo hotels in the valley. During the 1970s building boom, some tasteless and shabby units were thrown up, but more protective and historically sensitive controls have since found favor. One of the nicest in the mid-range and within walking distance of the main base lifts is the Edelweiss Haus. Unassuming, even homely on the outside, it is very comfortable and has an outdoor pool and hot tub. The huge complex right at the base of the lifts, a kind of hulking mini-city unto itself, is the Resort Center Lodge & Inn. It's pricey, but it has everything from ice skating to shops and restaurants, and it's right at the center of the action.

One center of the action, I should say. The Resort Center and old Main Street—about half a mile apart—are twin blazes of light in the winter night air. While the Resort Center tends toward more generic, youth-oriented ski-area music and dancing, Old Town offers more rounded cultural fare.

Film lovers should plan to be in Park City in late January for the Sundance Film Festival. Created by Robert Redford's Sundance Institute as a way to encourage and promote independent filmmaking, the event has grown spectacularly since it moved to Park City in 1985. In the winter of 1989, 30,000 seats were sold for the ten-day festival. Screenings include world premiers, documentary competition, dramatic competition, a rogues' gallery of new American shorts, and special tributes and retrospectives. A scan of audience faces reveals somberly dressed and pasty-faced denizens of the New York and Los Angeles film worlds interspersed with the sun-tanned and goggle-lined visages of skier/filmophiles. For my money, it's the perfect overlap of culture and sport. At Jackson and Sun Valley they have skiing but no film. In Telluride and Aspen they have film but not during ski season. Park City, as it has for most of its nonconformist history, stands apart.

PARK CITY DATA

Mountain Statistics

Vertical feet	3,100 feet
Base elevation	6,900 feet
Summit elevation	10,000 feet
Longest run	3.5 miles
Average annual snowfall	350 inches
Number of lifts	14 lifts: 4 six-passenger chairs, 1 quad, 5 triples, 4 doubles
Uphill capacity	27,200 skiers per hour
Skiable terrain	3,300 acres
Opening date	mid-November
Closing date	mid-April
Snowboarding	Yes

Transportation

By car About 45 minutes (30 miles) from Salt Lake International Airport via I-80 east through Parley's Canyon to State 224 south. Also, Route 189/40 from Heber City and Provo to the south, about 1 hour.

By bus, limo, or taxi From Salt Lake International Airport.

By plane Via major carriers to Salt Lake International Airport.

Key Phone Numbers

Ski Area Information
  (435) 649-8111
Snow Report (435) 647-5449
Lodging Reservations
  800-222-PARK
In Utah (435) 649-0493
Utah Powderbird Guides
  (801) 649-9739
www.parkcitymountain.com

INSIDE STORY

The Mormons

The Mormons, followers of Joseph Smith and his Church of Jesus Christ of Latter-day Saints (LDS), were the first white settlers of Utah and still make up 70 percent of the state's population. Their beliefs have shaped the land and the cultural and religious fabric of the region.

Joseph Smith was born in Vermont in 1805 and grew up during a time of great foment among Protestant sects in northern New England. According to the official LDS history, Joseph inquired of God which church he should join. The Father and Son appeared to him in a vision and said, "Join none." He subsequently had a series of visits from an angel of the Lord who told him of golden plates that were buried nearby and on which was written a history of the ancient inhabitants of North America, as well as the "fulness of the Gospel." The plates were delivered, and for two years Joseph translated their hieroglyphics. The result was the Book of Mormon, first published in 1830 (Mormon being the name of the ancient prophet/historian who compiled the record). According to Smith the plates were then returned to the angel.

Joseph repudiated all other Christian denominations and soon gathered a group of followers. Disbelievers branded him a rogue and a charlatan. The formal church was organized in Fayette, New York, but by 1838 religious vigilantism had driven Joseph and his followers to Ohio, then into Missouri, and then back across the Mississippi into Illinois. Everywhere the Saints went, they alienated their neighbors with their insular ways and their insistence that they were the chosen of God, the "saints" of the latter days.

Joseph was killed by an angry mob in 1844, and Brigham Young, his right-hand man and organizational genius, decided to find a place that no one else would want, a land where the Saints could build Zion (their heavenly city) with no interference from the Gentiles. He read an account by mountain man Jim Bridger of the Great Salt Lake and the harsh valley that rimmed it. In July of 1847, after a six-month journey, Brigham glimpsed his destination from the mouth of Emigration Canyon and pronounced the famous line, "This is the place." An advance party the day before had already turned City Creek out of its banks and planted the first potatoes.

The Saints thrived. The arid, sagebrush soil turned out to be quite fertile once it was irrigated with snowmelt from the Wasatch Range. The problems of isolation and distances and arid climate only contributed to the power and coherence of the church's social organization, and it was organized. Every man, woman, and child had a place in the village, the ward, the stake, and the total church hierarchy. Everyone contributed, and in turn, everyone was cared for.

While the westward migration of the mid- to late 1800s focused almost exclusively on California and Oregon, the Saints found sanctuary in their valleys of the mountains. They were fantastically successful proselytizers. Their missionaries sent thousands of converts to Utah from northern Europe, England, and even Hawaii. They developed intensively cultivated fields of alfalfa, sugar beets, Bermuda onions, and celery. They planted orchards of cherries and apples, peaches and apricots. They built orderly towns square with the four compass directions. Thus the initially confusing but really very logical street address system in Utah's cities; to find the headquarters of the Utah Ski Association in Salt Lake City, for example, one only needs to pinpoint 307 West 200 South on the grid, and there it is.

Everywhere the Mormons went they planted "Mormon trees," Lombardy poplars, in orderly rows along irrigation ditches, streets, and farm boundaries. You can still see them in Heber City, in Logan near Beaver Mountain, in any number of small towns throughout the Wasatch. The trees were like the people, spare and straight, with their roots in the earth and branches reaching heavenward.

The Saints' days and nights were as ordered as their villages. They worked together. Some villages experimented with a very pure communism of ownership and reward. Everyone tithed 10 percent of his income to the church. They prayed, sang, and danced together. The Word of Wisdom forbade smoking or imbibing alcohol. They had as little to do with the rest of the United States as possible.

Their system was nothing like democracy. Brigham ruled through divine revelation and direct order. By his order, the Saints spread to every arable corner of the Great Basin and Colorado Plateau. Within three years of settling in Salt Lake, there were Mormon settlements in San Bernardino, California, the Carson Valley of Nevada, Oregon, Idaho, Wyoming, western Colorado, and northern Arizona. For a short time, Salt Lake City was the provisional capital of the sovereign, theocratic State of Deseret. Deseret means "honey bee" in the Book of Mormon, the symbol of social order and industriousness. Utah is known today as the Beehive State.

Actual statehood was a long time coming. The United States felt that Utah had first to clear up a number of "un-American" practices, principally the dominance of political life by the church and the sticky matter of polygamy. Only a small percentage of Mormon men took more than one wife, but the practice was openly encouraged in one of Joseph's original revelations. In the 1890s the church officially disclaimed polygamy, and in 1896 Utah was admitted to the Union as the 45th state.

The Mormon church remains a vital and potent force in Utah, though the faithful have had to accept an indefinite period of secular dominance. The rowdy, largely unwelcome Gentile miners who founded the towns of Alta and Park City are gone, but in their place is the melting pot of America, including minorities, heavy-metal rock and roll, environmental activism, and skiers. Remnants of the old days persist, such as tithing, the Temple mysteries, the Mormon trees, and the state's unusual liquor laws. But today Utah is more like the rest of the United States than it is different.

DEER VALLEY RESORT

Deer Valley is the gourmet ski resort in Utah. Writers usually talk more about the food here than the skiing. They talk about the food, the valets who whisk your skis off the roof rack when you arrive at the lodge, afternoon tea in front of the fireplace at the Stein Eriksen Lodge, the extremely low 4:1 guest-to-staff ratio, the smoked trout and caviar at the Mariposa, limited ticket sales, machine-buffed snow, padded chairlifts, chocolate cheesecake, Chateau Laffite Rothschild, and so on.

The resort doesn't mind this kind of talk; in fact, they encourage it. Deer Valley was conceived as a kind of five-star experience, from morning coffee to evening digestive. The skiing is not exactly secondary to the rest of the experience; it is an integral, highly polished part, but no more important a part than the sumptuous food or the elegant service. Deer Valley's well-heeled guests, such as Roger Penske, Sidney Poitier, Jane Fonda, Bruce Willis, and Tom Cruise, appreciate it that way.

Interestingly, while Deer Valley is one of the newest Utah ski resorts, the gentler of the area's four mountains, Bald Eagle Mountain, was the site of the first lift-served skiing on the backside of the Wasatch. In 1946 it was called Snow Park, and it was the town rope tow just a short mile east of Park City's Main Street. The development in the late 1950s of the Treasure Mountains Resort (later renamed Park City) west of town made Snow Park obsolete, but the owners of the property sensed that their time would come.

It did in 1981. After years of planning, a triumvirate including entrepreneur Edgar Stern, hotelier James Nassikas, and ski icon Stein Eriksen opened Deer Valley as their vision of an "uncommonly civilized" resort. Stern, who was at the time the largest shareholder in Sears, was the money man. Nassikas brought to the mountains the exacting standards and fanaticism for service that were his trademark at the Stanford Court Hotel in San Francisco. Stein added his considerable charm and ski experience to the project. Perhaps even more important, he lent it his bankable mystique as the very embodiment of the elegant ski lifestyle.

The opening-day $29 lift ticket (no big deal today, but a skyrocket in 1981) sent ripples through the American ski industry, but so did the ski valets. The place was an instant success, at least in terms of image. Resorts in Colorado and elsewhere around the country scrambled to imitate Deer Valley's gourmet, sit-down lunches and went to school on Deer Valley's skier services. The point was, people of means who ski (and who might be counted on to invest in slopeside real estate) won't blink at the cost of a lift ticket if they are made to feel pampered on and off the hill.

Deer Valley was, and is, by far the most expensive skiing in Utah. Locals make up but a small percentage of the on-hill traffic. It's the very opposite of Alta's corporate philosophy, which has always been aimed directly at the local skier. But this exclusivity was part of the plan from the beginning. Deer Valley set out to set itself apart and has largely succeeded. This is not skiing for Everyman; it's skiing for Privilegedman, or for anyone who wants to feel like aristocracy for a day or a holiday.

Bald Mountain, Bald Eagle, Flagstaff, and Empire Canyon: Deer Valley's Four Peaks

Deer Valley's skiing, especially the intermediate cruising, is good enough to stand on its own without the luxurious trappings. There is not as much terrain as at Park City, nothing like the expert challenge at Alta and Snowbird, and they don't get the copious snows that Brighton does, but it is still very good skiing.

Of the four mountains, Bald Mountain is the southerly and easterly peak, and at 9,400 feet, it is higher than Bald Eagle by 1,000 feet. This is where you'll find the majority of the steeper skiing. To the west is Flagstaff Mountain at 9,100 feet, featuring blue-square cruisers with one notable challenge, the funky, steep *Ontario Bowl*. The newest addition is Empire Canyon at 9,570 feet. This area is the most advanced area at Deer Valley, with eight runs, three bowls, eight chutes, and two lifts. All have a decidedly eastern feel compared to most Utah mountains. They are heavily forested round mounds, with fall-line trails cut down their flanks. Only the very top of Bald Mountain shows any sign of timberline rock and wind.

The area's total vertical, from the top of Empire Canyon to the bottom of Deer Crest, is 3,000 feet. But you can't ski it in one fell swoop. The more meaningful figures are the verticals of each peak: 1,300 feet for Empire Canyon, 1,960 feet for Bald, 1,200 feet for Bald Eagle, and 900 feet for Flagstaff Mountain. There are 18 chairlifts, 4 high-speed quads, 2 fixed-grip quads, 1 high-speed gondola, 9 triples, and 2 doubles, 10 of which access the universally well-groomed, uncrowded skiing; the other 3 are short transportation lifts linking the three peaks.

The access road from the town of Park City splits midway up the hill, leading to two Deer Valley base facilities. Snow Park Lodge at 7,200 feet at the foot of Bald Eagle is the main base. This is where the free parking, the guest service attendants, and the awesome Natural Breakfast Buffet are. The other base at Silver Lake Lodge, at 8,100 feet, snuggles into a saddle between the peaks. The parking here is limited and expensive. Silver Lake is less a base area than a chance for the hoi polloi to hang out next door to the ultra-tasteful Stein Eriksen Lodge.

More roads meander the west-facing, evergreen-and-aspen hillside between the two bases, linking a string of private homes and ski-in/ski-out lodges and condo projects, including the Stein Eriksen Lodge. One of Deer Valley's design coups is the fact that wherever you stay, you are convenient to every level of ski terrain. A novice staying high on the mountain at Stein's, for example, rides one short lift and has the entire lower mountain at his ski tips. An advanced skier at the same lodge has but to walk outside, slip into ski bindings, and slide over to the Bald Mountain lifts.

If you begin your ski day at the Snow Park base, check the big sign board outside the lodge for information. It'll tell you which lifts are open. It shows which runs were groomed the night before, which have been left unpacked, and which have moguls on them. It even indicates whether there is seating available at the various mountain restaurants. For example, if things are filling up fast at Stein's, you can call in your reservations from any of four on-mountain phones.

There's that obsession with food again creeping into every Deer Valley discussion. I'm going to resist diving into the details for now (and keep you hungry) and talk about the skiing first. We'll tuck into the cuisine a little later.

Deer Valley Cruising

This is the area's forte, its pièce de résistance. The beginner/novice terrain here is good, but the choices are limited, and the genuine advanced challenge comes up a little soft. But for sheer, burnished, high-speed, let-'em-run cruising it's tough to beat Deer Valley's combination of uninterrupted fall lines and constant machine grooming.

Look down from the top of any of the four mountains (you'd think they would have renamed either Bald Mountain or Bald Eagle in the interest of clarity), and the terrain progression is the same. The left side, the western edge, of each peak is the easiest. As you move to your right around the cone to the east, the runs become progressively more difficult.

Bald Eagle has two blue cruisers that make excellent warm-ups if you are starting your day at the Snow Park base. (Cruisers don't necessarily have to be marked blue, or intermediate. Deer Valley grooms some of its black diamonds as well, turning them into buffed autobahns. At least one green run, *Last Chance*, has the requisite combination of a flowing fall line and room to move that, for me, defines a cruiser.) *Solid Muldoon* has a concave, gully-bottom feel. *Big Stick* starts out across a gladed plateau and then drops over a big roll before merging with other trails on the beginner flats known as *Wide West*. Both descend the full 1,200-foot Bald Eagle vertical, and both are machined regularly to ensure Deer Valley's trademark corduroy texture.

Serious cruisers will head over to Bald Mountain and stay there. The vertical is bigger, and there are at least a dozen swooping dance floors on which

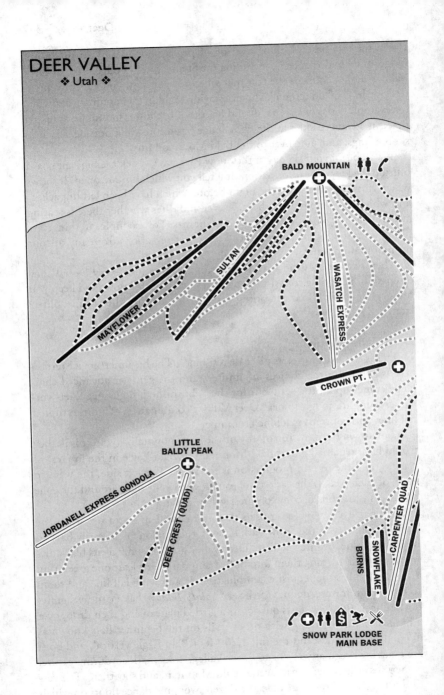

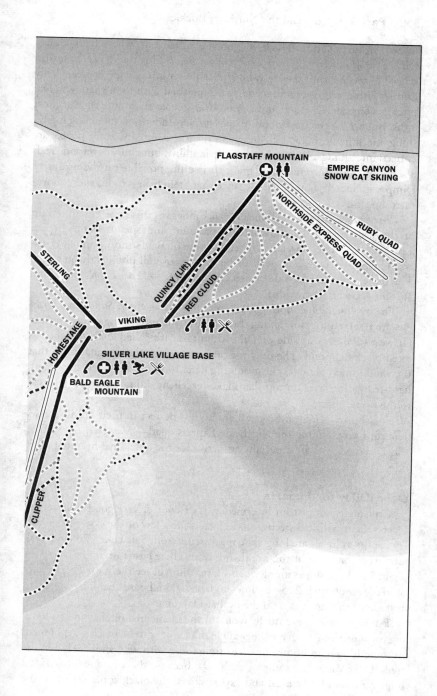

FLAGSTAFF MOUNTAIN

EMPIRE CANYON
SNOW CAT SKIING

RUBY QUAD

NORTHSIDE EXPRESS QUAD

STERLING

QUINCY (Lift)

RED CLOUD

VIKING

HOMESTAKE

SILVER LAKE VILLAGE BASE

BALD EAGLE
MOUNTAIN

CLIPPER

349

to carve your signature. The best is off the Sultan Lift, where Bald Mountain's east shoulder falls into *Perseverance Bowl*. This one has a beautiful shape. It sweeps from the steep bowl face down into a wide concave belly dotted with evergreen archipelagos and splashed with long shadows. The pitch is constant, inviting, and a good deal steeper than blue runs at most areas. But because of the smooth-carpet surface underfoot, the skiing is anything but difficult. In fact, it's deceptively, addictively easy. Some people are enticed into skiing a little too fast for their ability, but almost everyone feels a sense of fluid movement, of grace. It is quite possible on these runs to glimpse in oneself a bit of the elegance that Stein brings to his every movement on skis.

Perseverance isn't the only one. *Tycoon* toboggans this same Sultan terrain on the other side of the lift, where the predominant aspen trees tick by like a picket fence. The Wasatch Lift serves some of Bald's most popular cruisers. The busiest is *Nabob*, perhaps because its overall pitch is the gentlest. The three other side-by-side cruisers in this zone—*Keno, Legal Tender*, and *Wizard*—are rarely crowded.

The two main blue thoroughfares off the Sterling chair, *Sunset* and *Birdseye*, are reserved for slow skiing, but there is one interesting cruiser on the far west (and easiest) side of Bald Mountain. It's called *Emerald*, and it's rated black diamond. The only reason I can see for the designation is that the wind sometimes does the grooming here. It often has a wind-deposited, hard-margarine layer on top that makes excellent skiing once you get used to the ripple effect.

The shorter blues on Flagstaff are no less perfect in their fall-line ease. The runs surrounding the Northside Express quad—*Hawkeye, Lucky Star*, and *Lost Boulder*—are especially attractive for the quick five-minute return ride.

Deer Valley for Experts

Cruising is not just for intermediates, of course. Very good skiers enjoy Deer Valley's polished steeps too. In fact, quite a few of the skiers Deer Valley counts as locals are long-ski connoisseurs from Salt Lake City and Park City who come out of the woodwork when there hasn't been new snow for a while and the slopes are sleek and fast. You will see them on *Perseverance* or *Hawkeye* on their 215-centimeter giant-slalom boards banking huge arcs as if they were stock cars on the oval at Daytona.

But most experts eventually weary of the manicured pitches and go looking for something with a steeper angle than what can be machine groomed, or something with bumps on it, or something with wild snow between the trees. Deer Valley has some of each, and because the area doesn't attract a huge number of advanced and expert skiers, the black zones are often the least crowded places on the mountain.

In the past few years, Deer Valley has worked to bend its image as an adrenaline-free zone. There is a new "Experts Only" trail map highlighting some of the less obvious tree and chute skiing. Most recently, a whole new expert enclave west of the existing Flagstaff boundary, known as *Empire Canyon,* has been added. There is one high-speed quad and one fixed-grip quad, and more lifts are planned.

Bald Eagle has two black diamonds. Neither is much steeper than the surrounding terrain. They are designated as such because management allows them to grow moguls. *Know You Don't* is longer and better than *Lucky Bill,* although, due to the general caliber of skier on Bald Eagle, the bumps here tend to be small and tentative.

The best bumps are on Bald Mountain, most of them toward the east end. The left side of *Perseverance Bowl* (looking down) offers a variety of lumpy lines through gladed terrain. The map shows three named trails—*Thunderer, Blue Ledge,* and *Grizzly*—but they tend to blend together. I like them because you can pick your size: big moguls down the concave centers of the drains, smaller bumps out at the edges, or only hints of nascent mogul shapes in the open tree lines that divide the runs.

Only occasionally will you find really big bumps at Deer Valley and then only in a few, highly visible, lift-line locales like *Rattler* or *Narrow Gauge.* Even these don't come close in size and ferocity to the man-eaters on Snowbird's *Silver Fox,* for example. The place just doesn't attract skiers interested in yo-yoing the moguls.

Mayflower, at the far east end of the area, is Deer Valley's truest expert territory. It rarely gets steeper than *Perseverance Bowl,* but it has a wild feel; the grooming machines leave it alone. Near the top of *Mayflower Bowl* a lone spruce on a rocky outcrop stands as a sentinel above the steepest skiing on the mountain. A good, smooth, windblown base flows around the tree toward the gully-bottom moguls of *Morning Star* below. When there is new snow, *Morning Star* and the parallel *Fortune Teller* and *Paradise* runs are the best powder skiing on Bald Mountain. They do face the morning sun, however, so it's best to get to them before they've had a chance to absorb the rays.

The longest-lasting powder snow at any area is to be found in the trees, and Deer Valley has a wealth of underexplored trees. Once again, it seems that the lion's share of its skiers aren't out to push beyond the (very) comfortable limits of the cruising terrain. A little exploring (with the Experts Only trail map in hand) is therefore often richly rewarded.

There are two kinds of tree experiences here: aspens and evergreens. Aspens love light and hug the east-facing slopes. Occasionally you'll find them on west-facing hillsides and almost never on true north exposures. The most famous aspen patch in Deer Valley, the one where Stein is frequently photographed for brochures and articles, is the *Triangle Trees* between the Sultan and Wasatch lifts on Bald Mountain. They're easy to find. Turn left off *Tycoon* about halfway down, and you're in a maze of slim, branchless, cream-colored trunks spaced just right for powder turns. In flickering shadow and light the skiing is hypnotic and mesmerizing, a kind of metronome counterpoint to the giant leaning arcs one makes on the piste.

The evergreens are much more secretive, cooler, and darker. Skiing them is a kind of private investigation. You may spook a grouse, hooting and flapping, from his perch. You will surely see rabbit tracks and probably those of squirrels, chipmunks, and mice. You may not be able to link more than five or six turns in a row before a leafy wall closes in, but there is always the possibility you will find a hidden meadow with 10 or 12 turns that no one has skied this year.

The most accessible evergreens at Deer Valley are the ones between *Grizzly* and *Ruins of Pompeii*. They're spacious with a nice rhythm and good starter trees. (Because Deer Valley is private land, mountain crews have had a free hand in trimming limbs and shaping trees they know will see considerable traffic. Some of the results—bare trunks to eight feet above snow level—look a little like French poodles. But then, they were probably just hoping for a big snow year.)

Over on Flagstaff, *Oompa-Loompa Land* provides some of the easiest tree pitches around, with generous helpings of low-angle powder meadows. *DT's Trees,* on the other hand, are tight firs best left for the fast-twitch set.

You'll find denser, untrimmed forest on the other side of *Perseverance Bowl* between *Perseverance* and *Hawkeye.* Another good set of trees is on the west side of Bald Mountain between *Emerald* and *North Star.*

On sunny days it's a good idea to work the aspens first, before the sun can change the snow to mashed potatoes, and then slide into the deeper, darker evergreens, which may protect bowers of cold snow for days, even weeks after a storm.

One final note for Bald Mountain skiers: The upper mountain shuts down like an accordion door, east to west, in the afternoon. Mayflower closes at 3 P.M., Sultan at 3:30 P.M. Wasatch and Sterling stay open until 3:45 P.M. The Bald Eagle lifts run until 4 P.M. It's a shame, but the ski patrol has to do it this way to sweep the flock back to camp before dark.

Deer Valley for Beginners and Novices

There is some excellent green terrain here but not much of it, although the meticulous grooming means some blues are also suited to advancing novices.

Wide West underneath the Burns Lift (Snow Park base) is a super-gentle beginners' hill. Ski school pretty much takes it over in the middle of the day. The Kinderschule sets up its fun obstacle and terrain garden here as well.

After *Wide West,* ride the Carpenter Lift to the top of Bald Eagle and take the Success trail for the full ride back to the base. Success is aptly named and cleverly cut to weave the easiest route down the hill. Options off the Success route include *Little Bell, Last Chance,* and *Rosebud.* One of my favorite tours through the Bald Eagle terrain follows *Success* to *Little Bell* to *Dew Drop,* which is marked blue on the map. But it is a nonthreatening blue full of tree islands and the kinds of playful terrain that the more staid greens lack.

Adventurous novices who have done it all on Bald Eagle should make the trip up Bald Mountain to ski *Sunset,* as genial a blue as there is. It lives up to its name, curving toward the sun late in the day. When temperatures fall, the snow takes on a golden glow.

The Famous Food

Everybody needs fuel to ski, but at Deer Valley satisfying that requirement is closer to art than necessity. It's not cheap, but the value, esthetic and gastronomic, is there. Here's the way I would set up my ideal gourmet ski day.

Breakfast at the Snow Park Lodge, where they set out what they call their Natural Breakfast Buffet: fresh-squeezed juices, melons, pineapple, fruit salads, croissants, cereals, muffins, hazelnut bear claws, eggs Benedict, and omelets. Serve yourself and sit in a plush oak chair by the window. A waiter comes around to fill your coffee cup whenever it gets low or cools down.

Lunch at Stein's. You can't miss it as you fly down the *Birdseye* trail at noon; the tasteful cloth banner reads "Skiers' Buffet," with an arrow pointing into the aspens and Stein's lodge. (Stein does not actually own the lodge, but that is immaterial. He had a hand in its every design detail. His gold and silver medals from the 1952 Olympics and 1954 World Championships are proudly displayed here. His wife, Françoise, has her ultra-luxe Bjørn Stova Boutique in the lobby, and Stein prowls the restaurant and lounge every winter day that he is in town. It's quite okay to call it Stein's lodge.) The buffet spread is staggeringly opulent: creamed broccoli soup, Mediterranean lamb stew, Yucatán chili, prime rib, smoked fish and meats, salads, fresh fruits, chocolate cheesecake, apple crisp, two-tone pear pie, all in a setting of white tablecloths, silver service, stone fireplace, and carved wooden doors. You feel funny clanking around the carpet in your ski boots, but that's what everyone does.

Ski some more. Then have dinner at the Mariposa in the Silver Lake Lodge (huge laminated beams, copper fireplace covers, and flowers in the windows). Reservations are essential. Each night's menu is exquisitely fresh and artfully prepared.

For more casual dining, you could ring up the Red Banjo Pizza Parlor on Main Street in Park City. They deliver.

Lodging in Deer Valley

Staying in Deer Valley is designed, logically enough, to be commensurate with the rest of the experience. Stein's is the choice abode, for its name, its location on the slopes, the lavishly outfitted rooms and suites, the automatic doors (in case you have skis in hand), the heated sidewalks, and the fact that you can walk the halls in your lush terry-cloth robe (provided) to the windscreened, heated pool. Plus, it's downright beautiful. The tab will run anywhere from $200 to $1,500 per night.

All of the other lodging in Deer Valley is managed by Deer Valley Central Reservations and includes condominiums, private homes, and the Stag Lodge. A huge variety of lodging options and prices exists down the road in Park City.

DEER VALLEY DATA

Mountain Statistics

Vertical feet	3,000 feet
Base elevation	6,570 feet
Summit elevation	9,570 feet
Longest run	2.1 miles
Average annual snowfall	300 inches
Number of lifts	18 chairs: 4 high-speed quads, 2 fixed-grip quads, 1 high-speed gondola, 9 triples, 2 doubles
Uphill capacity	34,800+ skiers per hour
Skiable terrain	1,750 acres
Opening date	Early December
Closing date	mid-April
Snowboarding	No

Transportation

By car About 50 minutes from Salt Lake International Airport via I-80 east through Parley's Canyon to State 224 south. Into Park City and east on Deer Valley Drive for 1 mile. Also, Route 189/40 from Heber City and Provo to the south, about 1 hour.

By bus, limo, taxi, or helicopter From Salt Lake International Airport.

By plane Via major carriers to Salt Lake International Airport.

Key Phone Numbers

Ski Area Information (435) 649-1000
Snow Report (435) 649-2000

Lodging

Deer Valley Central Reservations (800) 558-3337
Stein Eriksen Lodge (800) 453-1302
www.deervalley.com

Utah Liquor Laws and the Word of Wisdom

In Brigham Young's time, the Mormon "Word of Wisdom" forbade smoking or chewing tobacco and drinking alcohol (some ascribe caffeine to the list of forbidden fruits). The body had to be kept pure for the work of building the Heavenly City.

Not all Mormons adhered strictly to the Word. Wallace Stegner tells the story, in his book *Mormon Country,* about a feisty church elder who was having breakfast with two bishops in a small-town café. After ordering, he briefly took the waitress aside, then returned to his seat. When the food came, the waitress asked, "Now, which one of you was it wanted coffee in his Postum?"

Despite popular myth, Utah never was dry and is not now. Aspects of the state's liquor laws may seem complex, even quixotic, to visitors, but it is possible to get a drink here. Once you get used to the system, in fact, it's nearly as practical as anyplace else.

Restaurants with liquor licenses may serve alcoholic beverages of any sort to your table. You used to have to purchase mini-bottles of hard liquor and a "set-up" (glass and ice), then pour it yourself, but a 1988 revision eliminated that quirk. You may also bring your own "brown bag" liquor or wine to the restaurant. They will provide glasses and charge you a "corkage" fee.

Bars in the traditional sense are called private clubs in Utah. They sell wine, beer, and mixed and blended drinks "over the bar" to members and their guests. Temporary guest memberships are available for a fee (usually $5) to visitors. You can buy them at the club or at the front desk of your lodging. In Park City and Snowbird a single "reciprocal" card is good at most if not all the clubs in town. Some bars, like the ones in the lodges in Alta, will hold your liquor bottle for you, with your name on it, and pour you a drink whenever you like.

Taverns, or beer bars, sell only beer (and 3.2 percent alcohol beer at that), but brown bagging is permitted.

Sale of packaged liquor is controlled by the state government. There is at least one State Liquor Store in each resort, sometimes in the lodges themselves. They're closed on Sundays and holidays, and they only accept cash. You can buy beer at grocery and convenience stores any day of the week.

The newest of the Utah resorts, the Canyons (formerly Wolf Mountain), has the potential to be one of America's premier ski resorts. The resort was purchased by the American Skiing Company in 1997 with plans to invest $500 million by the year 2005 and expand the skiable area to over 7,000 acres. As of February 1999 the area had already added five new chairlifts (three high-speed quads), a gondola, a mid-mountain lodge and 500 acres of terrain. The first phase of the base village will be completed for the 1999–2000 ski season. This first phase includes the 360-room Grand Summit Hotel and the 125-condominium signature Sundial Lodge. Check out www.thecanyons.com for the most recent construction update.

With the freeway, the Canyons is the closest skiing to downtown Salt Lake City, and the area has capitalized on this fact. The Canyons created an unprecedented program for their first year that gave free season passes to every Utah honor-roll student, kindergarten through high school. This program brought more than 10,000 students to the Canyons with report cards in hand. The program has since changed slightly, so if you are a student check with the ticket office for student discounts.

The Shape of the Mountain

The Canyons' ski terrain is strung out along four steep-sided ridge lines. Their parallel crowns run more or less east to west, so there is one shady cool side and one often-as-not burned-out solar side. Two of the best intermediate runs have been carved along the sharp crests of the ridges; they look like flattop haircuts. The longest runs are down the flattop ridges and along the creekbeds in the gullies at their bases. The truest fall lines spill off the sides of the ridgetops toward the gully trails which pull all the traffic, like metropolitan beltways, around the flanks and toward the base.

This base is unimposing and a little bit deceptive. From the parking lot you see only the bald, nearly treeless tip of the first ridge, probably less than 20 percent of the 2,800 skiable acres. Part of the fun here is discovering the rest, moving back and up, ever farther west until you can go no more, then filling in the blanks on your way home.

There are six discernible ski zones. The first zone is the terrain you see right outside the Day Lodge. It is like Sun Valley's Dollar Mountain: wide-open, naked, obstacle-free beginner and novice slopes. One quad chair, the Red Hawk quad, covers it thoroughly.

Next zone up and back is Lookout Peak, served by the Golden Eagle and

Raptor doubles. This has some black diamond terrain, but the lifts also provide access to the most popular intermediate zone at the resort, known as *Snow Canyon,* served by a chair of the same name. The northernmost, and longest zone (actually a separate ridge unto itself) is the Condor region: two blues, some very steep blacks, and a whole slew of double black, experts-only trails. The best of these is *Murdock Bowl,* a nice piece of timberline, walk-up turf above Condor Peak.

Intermediates who are weary from the popular Snow Canyon zone can take a cat track off the back side to the Saddleback area, 1,200 vertical feet of mostly blue glade and tree runs.

The middle zone and the heart of the Canyons is at the top of the gondola at the Red Pine Lodge area. This area is serviced by the Saddleback Express and the High-Meadow lifts. For beautiful intermediate cruising along with many north-facing black runs this is the place. The Red Pine Lodge provides a fantastic place to rest between runs and to have lunch.

Working our way north we come to the fifth zone, which we'll call the Tombstone Express Zone. Serviced by the Tombstone Express Quad, this area has a nice, long blue run, *Another World,* which is good for warming up, as well as many short south-facing black runs. Be aware of what exposure you are skiing on as the southern exposures tend to have much less snow.

The highest and southernmost zone is the Ninety Nine 90 area. This area is serviced by the Ninety Nine 90 Express lift and provides advanced black runs in a more Alpine-like setting. Much of this zone is above tree line, and you have the sense of Big or Little Cottonwood Canyon skiing.

Open Bowls for Beginners

I like the Canyon's beginner slopes. They are split into two areas: one at the bottom of the mountain, accessed by the Red Hawk lift, and the more desirable area at the top of the gondola, accessed by the High-meadow lift. The Red Hawk area runs are nice because they're a-tumble with kids and kid energy, and they're fun for anybody to ski. What I mean is that they're not simply a monolithic tilted plane, like Keystone's Checkerboard Flats. They have character: lumps and knobs and knurls, dimples and dents and hollows. It's like a throw rug (soft white shag) after the cats finish chasing each other over, under, and through. The easiest section of this ice-cream-sundae hill is on your left looking up. *Playtime* and *Sunrise* are the excellent greens on either side of the chair.

For better snow and much longer beginner runs, ride the gondola up to mid-mountain and ski *The Meadows, Showtime,* and *Enchanted Forest,* just to name a few. The Perfect Turn Ski & Board School has a meeting area next to the Red Pine Lodge at mid-mountain.

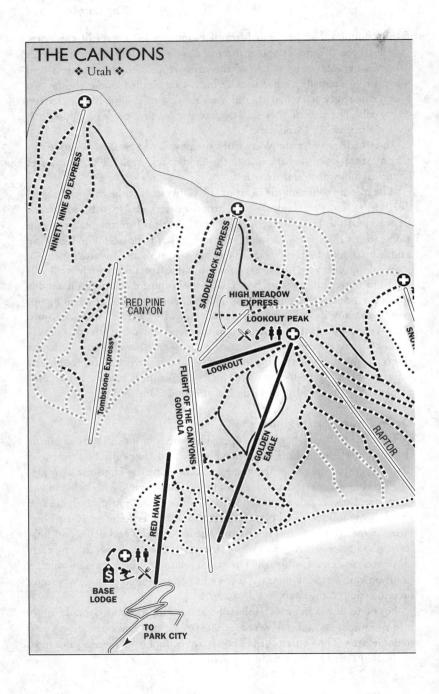

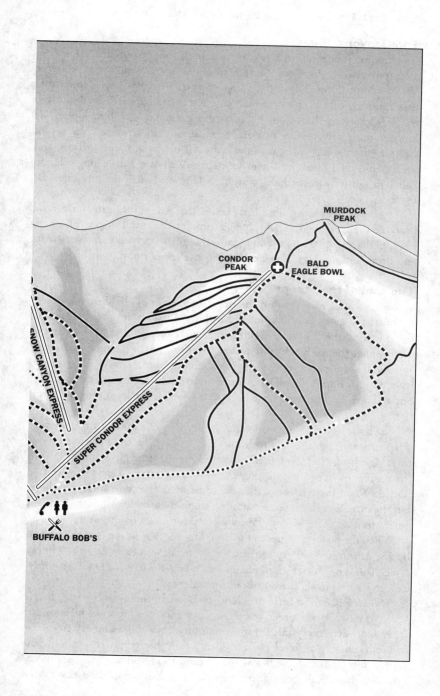

The Canyons' Blues

There are four intermediate zones where the old ego needn't suffer even a temporary jolt: the *Snow Canyon* area, the *Snow Dancer* area, *Another World,* and the long and winding *Upper Boa* trail. Snow Canyon can sometimes gum up with people on a busy day. When this happens, head south to the Saddleback or Tombstone region with its dozen or so rolling blues. The longest, most private blue run on the mountain, *Boa* rolls off the top of Condor into the elbow between the muscular biceps of Condor Ridge and the aspen-dotted forearm of Murdock Peak. Well over a mile long, the top half is delightfully pitched; the bottom half, unfortunately, falls into the cattrack category.

Upper Boa runs alongside a little ravine that, when it fills up with snow, becomes the area's second half-pipe. A completely natural shape, this one is long, perhaps a quarter-mile long, and fraught with wild surprises: twists and drops and narrows. The locals call it "the James Bond trail."

The Call of the Steeps

Because most runs flow off the ridge lines, most of the Canyons' steeps are relatively short, fall-line shots from ridge to road (with the exception of the Ninety Nine 90 area). *Kestrel,* in fact, is surrounded by similar but ungroomed (hence black) pitches on Condor's north-facing escarpment. *Aplande* is the longest. *Thrasher* has the heinous bumps. Snow Canyon also has a popular bump run off its evergreen north side. It's called *Powder Chute,* but all you'll find here are large bumps; it's used as the local mogul-contest site.

The back side, or sunny side, of Condor Ridge features a string of very steep runs through the oakbrush into *E Z Street* gully. You have to lean out from *Apex Ridge* to follow their descent. Like the little girl with the curl in the middle of her forehead, they can be very, very good, and they can be horrid. When there is snow, they are some of the steepest lines anywhere, but the extreme solar exposure and the relatively low elevation pretty much guarantee that there will not be good cover for much of the winter.

When the powder comes to the Canyons, the best skiing is in the natural bowls: *Murdock Bowl,* up at the area's western boundary, and the Ninety Nine 90 area on the far south eastern boundary. Both bowls face east-northeast, so it's best to ski them early in a powder cycle.

Murdock Bowl is a little different. It too faces the morning sun, but it keeps its powdery texture in stands of aspens and even receives infusions of fresh wind-driven crystals from time to time over the boundary ridge. To add to its charm, *Murdock Bowl* requires a short but stiff hike of about 500 vertical feet from a saddle below the Condor top terminal. You'll see snowboarders' snaky S-shaped tracks peeling off the hiking trail almost every day of the season. Two-legged skiers have the option of traversing the full breadth of the bowl to a marvelous, pure line called *Ocelot*. You can't yo-yo *Murdock Bowl*, and it stays pristine for that reason.

The view from the top of *Murdock Bowl* is one of the best on the Wasatch backside. To the east, across Parley's Park, you can see the Uinta Mountains, a rugged and largely wild range culminating in Utah's highest point, 13,528-foot Kings Peak. To the north the Wasatch rolls toward Snowbasin, Powder Mountain, and the Ogden Canyon areas. To the west, through a notch between peaks, you can catch a snippet of the Salt Lake Valley. To the south (sigh) are the softly curvaceous, timberline terrain of Red and White Pine Canyons (some of the Utah Powderbird Guides' favorite landing sites), and the country the Canyons might have been built on but wasn't quite.

Lunch on the Hill

There are four places to eat at the Canyons: one at the base, which tends to be overrun on weekends; one on Lookout Peak called Lookout Cabin, which has the big view; one new for 2000 near the bottom of the Snow Canyon Lift; and the most popular lunch spot, the Red Pine Lodge, at the top of the Flight of the Canyons gondola. I prefer the Red Pine Lodge because the food is great, it has an enormous sun deck, and you are in the middle of the resort.

Après-Ski

The Canyons' Euro-style village is under way, with the first phase to be completed by December 1999. Also, Park City is only four miles away (see the Park City section, In Town: Eating, Sleeping, and Other Forms of Rejuvenation, page 340), and there is an efficient shuttle that runs from 8:20 A.M.– 4:45 P.M.

THE CANYONS DATA

Mountain Statistics	
Vertical feet	3,190 feet
Base elevation	6,800 feet
Summit elevation	9,990 feet
Longest run	2.5 miles
Average annual snowfall	300 inches
Number of lifts	8 high-speed quads
	1 gondola
	1 double
	1 triple
Uphill capacity	24,000 skiers per hour
Skiable terrain	2,700+ acres
Opening date	late November
Closing date	end of March
Snowboarding	Yes

Transportation

By car About 40 minutes from Salt Lake International Airport via I-80 east through Parley's Canyon to State 224 south and the Canyons Drive. The Canyons is 4 miles north of Park City.

By bus, limo, or taxi From Salt Lake International Airport, and by regularly scheduled shuttle from the Park City/Deer Valley area.

By plane Via major carriers to Salt Lake International Airport.

Key Phone Numbers

Ski Area Information
  (435) 649-5400
Snow Report (435) 615-3456

Lodging Reservations

The Canyons Lodging
  (888) CANYONS (226-9667)
www.thecanyon.com

INSIDE STORY

Avalanche Hunters

When the Forest Service got involved with recreational skiing at Alta in 1938, it was an invitation for disaster. The fine skiing in Collins Gulch and the new chairlift constructed from remnants of a silver ore tram were drawing thousands of skiers into a canyon that had already seen 100 miners die in avalanches.

Turn-of-the-century boomtown Alta was battered repeatedly by slides emanating from Rustler Mountain to the south and Flagstaff and Superior to the north. At the time the situation was exacerbated by the total deforestation of these slopes for mine timbers and building lumber. The trees were making a comeback by the time skiing started, but natural slidepaths, on the ski slopes and hovering above the canyon road, still made being there on certain days a risky proposition. The Forest Service (and Alta Ski Lifts) quite properly felt a responsibility toward these new enthusiasts.

In 1941 they hired Sverre Engen, Alf's brother and fellow competitor on the professional jumping tour, to be Alta's first snow ranger. Sverre's job was to watch the accumulation of snow and determine, to the best of his judgment, when the avalanche danger warranted closing certain trails on the mountain, and ultimately closing the road from the valley. World War II interrupted Sverre's work, but immediately following the end of the war a not-so-young powder lover, Harvard man and fiction writer Montgomery Atwater, convinced the Forest Service to hire him as snow ranger.

Monty Atwater wanted to do more than just warn people when things were looking scary; he wanted to understand why snow behaved as it did, and he wanted to see if he couldn't figure out some way to *prevent* dangerous slides. Although not a trained scientist, he nevertheless had a true scientist's curiosity coupled with the physical energy of several people. For a decade, up until the mid-1950s, Atwater wore the multiple caps of father, nurturer, humorist, and one-man gang of American avalanche research.

Atwater noticed that most avalanches occur during or immediately after a storm. He therefore focused his studies on storm measurements and how they affected the snowpack at large. He'd stay up for days and nights during big storm cycles, tromping to his instruments to gauge snow depth, intensity (how fast the snow was coming down per hour), temperatures throughout the storm, crystal types and water content, wind speed and direction. He was the first to accurately describe the formation of the soft slab layers in the snowpack, that made for great powder skiing but that were also responsible for most of Alta's winter (as opposed to springtime wet-snow) avalanches.

He was the first to recognize the potential of explosives in controlling avalanches. Early in his tenure he hiked the mountain in the fall, planting a series of dynamite charges on particularly pesky, cornice-forming ridge lines. Then, in the winter, when the cornices were big enough to threaten slopes below, he blew them up, harmlessly.

But placing bombs for a one-time cleansing was impractical and inadequate. Atwater needed some way to make the slide paths run on a more or less regular basis and therefore compact and stabilize themselves. His first piece of artillery was a nineteenth-century French cannon, monstrous and unwieldy, but he convinced the Forest Service and the Utah National Guard to let him roll it up and down the highway in order to lob shells into start zones high above.

U.S. Army 75- and 105-mm Howitzers were the vogue for a while. Now Alta has a military surplus recoilless rifle permanently mounted on Wildcat Ridge. They use the gun for shooting across the highway at slides that threaten the lodges and the access to Snowbird and Alta. Within the ski area on snowy mornings, patrolmen drop hand charges in known avalanche pockets and fire an air-powered "Avalauncher," a mortarlike device Atwater commissioned in the 1950s. Avalaunchers are much cheaper but somewhat less accurate than the big military hardware. (Ski patrolmen at Snowbasin were practicing with their new Avalauncher a few years back and missed the ridge entirely, sending a projectile through the garage roof of an unlucky Ogdenite five miles away.) Today every ski area and highway department with avalanche problems uses some combination of ordnance and tactics devised by Monty Atwater at Alta.

One morning recently I woke before dawn and joined the Alta ski patrol for the firing of the big gun. It had snowed 17 inches overnight and 26 inches in the last two days. The road was closed. The tiny valley was on "interlodge" alert—that is, all guests and employees were required to stay indoors while the control work was going on.

We shoveled off the gun platform. One man went down in the concrete bunker to hand up ammunition; each shell is about three feet long and weighs 30 pounds. A second man dialed in the exact coordinates of likely start zones on Mount Superior across the way. A third man loaded the shell and locked the breech. I stood as close as possible to the barrel, where the concussive force is smallest, and held my hands over my ears.

The blast was shattering, the predawn sky briefly aflame. It was still too dark to see if our shot had done any good, but a voice over the radio, from an observer down in the valley, said we kicked off a "small" one, 3,000 vertical feet down to, but not over, the highway.

We fired a dozen shots. Gradually, the sky grew pink, then golden. Behind us on the ski trails, teams of patrolmen followed their prescribed routes. The Avalauncher team caused a small but dramatic slab to release on Sugarloaf Mountain, snow pouring over the cliffs like sugar. Another team, cutting across the High Traverse, forced sluffs in *Sunspot* and again on *West Rustler* and *Stonecrusher.* By eight o'clock the road was open, and by nine the first powderhounds were riding up the mountain, eager to ski this new snow with the impunity we have all come to take for granted.

Mysteries still abound regarding snow and snowslides. What causes late releases, for example, days and even weeks after a storm? How and why does the snow change over time deep in the snowpack, creating weaknesses and instability? Research continues here and in Europe and Japan. The Forest Service, sadly, is no longer as committed as it once was to such inquiry. Monty Atwater has moved on, leaving behind most of the avalanche terminology we use today and a wonderful book called *The Avalanche Hunters*. He is replaced by a tiny cadre of dedicated disciples.

Meanwhile, ski slopes have never been safer, and snow remains one of the least understood, most volatile solids on the planet, and one of the most romantic.

SUNDANCE

Over dinner at the Blind Miner in Brighton one evening, I eavesdropped on a telling conversation. The gentleman at the next table had ventured down to Sundance, east of Provo, for a day of skiing. His distaff companion lit up instantly. "Did you see HIM?" she asked, eyes as big as saucers.

He, of course, is Sundance's owner and guiding spirit, Robert Redford. Ole Blue Eyes actually lives here. He's been married to a Utah girl for over 35 years and a voting resident of Utah County, south of Salt Lake City, for more than 30 years. When he doesn't have to be in New York or Los Angeles, Redford the outdoorsman, family man, and skier is home in Sundance. You might just see the star of *Butch Cassidy and the Sundance Kid, Out of Africa, Downhill Racer,* and *All the President's Men* in jeans and running shoes, on his mountain bike, or on the slopes, where he has named three of the runs after his kids. Locals refer to him as Bob.

Sundance feels like a rustic, private club. Menus and guest guides are printed on heavy, textured paper. Area literature makes frequent use of the first person plural, as in "we the Sundance community" and "who we are and what we believe in." And yet the clubbish atmosphere is also welcoming: "We want to help you find those elements of the Sundance experience which will most meet *your* needs, *your* dreams."

Condominiums, called "cottages" (Redford hates the word "condominium"), dot the aspen and spruce forest just west of the ski area base. Small in scale and carefully placed for minimum impact on the landscape and their neighbors, they are constructed of rough-hewn spruce and decorated with down comforters and Indian art. They smell like a forest campsite. All facilities are elegantly spare and discreetly luxurious. The look is western, but when you write about summer theater at Sundance, you spell it "theatre."

To put Sundance in a Utah perspective: Where Deer Valley's opulence is splendid, self-conscious, and even self-congratulatory, Sundance is purposely understated and thus even more exclusive, a perfect place for one of the most recognizable faces on the planet to disappear into the rough-cut woodwork.

Exclusive though it may be, 80 percent of the ski business is local. Sundance is just 13 miles from downtown Provo. Provo is Utah's second city; it's built on the shore of giant Utah Lake, which is connected via the Jordan River to the Great Salt Lake in the north. Provo has a population of 75,000. It is the home of Brigham Young University and a major hub for mining, agriculture, and manufacturing. Provo folks have been skiing at Sundance (before it was called Sundance) since the 1940s.

At the turn of the century, a Scottish immigrant family, the Stewarts, settled this little side valley off the Provo River to raise sheep on the flanks of Mount Timpanogos. Second-generation Stewarts built a rope tow on one of their mountains in 1947. By the 1950s, it was known as Timphaven and boasted a chairlift, the original rope tow, and a burger joint named Ki-Te-Kai, Samoan for "Come and get it!" (One of the Stewarts had been called to a Mormon mission in the islands.)

Redford bought Timphaven and much of the surrounding land from the Stewarts in 1969 and named it after his most famous movie role. He began the slow process of upgrading the ski facilities and built his own house in a high, south-facing meadow across from the ski hill. In 1980 he created the Sundance Institute "to support and encourage work in independent filmmaking." There is an intimate, 200-seat screening room in the pines by the creek and a cinema workspace where Redford's own *Milagro Beanfield War* was edited. Here filmmaking labs have been hosted in the past by Paul Newman, Sydney Pollack, and Alan Alda, among others. In 1985 the institute took over sponsorship of the United States Film Festival in Park City, and the event has since grown into one of the world's premier showcases for new independent films.

In 1981 Redford initiated the project that may be closest to his soul, the Sundance Institute for Resource Management. The IRM has sponsored conferences at Sundance and elsewhere on such topics as water development in the West, the mining of uranium on Indian lands, and off-shore oil drilling in Alaska. Redford is a lover of nature and a believer in preserving natural resources (he has been called worse by Utah development interests), and the IRM, he hopes, will help resolve conflicts between use (or overuse) and preservation of America's wild riches.

If Sundance feels more like a mesquite-grill and eco-romantic hideaway than a ski resort, this is why. The cultural, artistic, and environmental concerns of "the community" have always come first. But the skiing can be exquisite as well, and it hasn't been sloughed off as a secondary amenity. Skiing (along with hiking and biking in the summer) is viewed as the physical part of a New Renaissance equation, something that Snowbird's Dick Bass has described as a rejuvenation "of body, mind, and soul." Redford loves to ski, he is good at it, and his hiring of former Demo Teamer Jerry Warren to be director of skiing is a strong sign that he is committed to improving the mountain in the future.

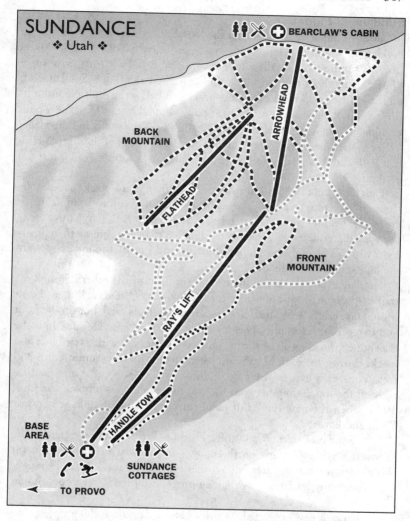

Warren is a local Springville, Utah, boy who used to stow away on the bus up to Timphaven when he was a kid. He became a protégé of Junior Bounous, a Provo native, and spent years teaching at Snowbird under Bounous, where he worked his way to eminence in the rarefied world of international ski instructor associations and demonstration teams. Warren taught Redford's kids to ski and more than once filled the boss's head with enough technical ski talk to make him completely forget the stresses of his public life. Now the two of them are working on ways to integrate some of the Sundance Institute's more idealistic concepts into ski teaching and vice versa.

Sundance's Mountain

Mount Timpanogos dominates the Wasatch skyline above Provo. It is a hulking, monolithic presence with an uninterrupted fall of nearly 8,000 feet from its summit to the valley floor. Horizontal rock bands stripe its upper slopes, giving the mountain a look similar to the Italian Alps. Sundance sits on the southeast shoulder of the big peak, well below the multiple summits (in fact out of sight of the actual high point) but high enough at the top lift terminal to gain a spectacular view of Utah Lake to the south and the Heber Valley to the north. Sharp eyes can pick out the backside of Snowbird's Hidden Peak and Alta's Baldy and Sugarloaf; Park City's Jupiter Peak is just out of sight.

Park City is about 35 minutes away, and although the creek that tumbles through Sundance's narrow valley eventually flows west into Utah Lake, the area really belongs to the Wasatch backside. As with Park City's three areas, there is a discernible snow shadow (although 325 inches is more than plenty most years). The morning sun is dominant, and late afternoons are spent in the blue shade of the divide.

Sundance has two ski mountains, one in front of the other. Though the trail map doesn't indicate names for the two peaks, locals call them Front Mountain and Back Mountain. There are three chairs total, one on the front and two on the back, plus a beginners' handle tow. Front Mountain is the easier one, providing all of the beginner/novice terrain with a few blues and blacks thrown in. Back Mountain, which claims the area summit at 8,200 feet, is primarily expert with a smattering of the most popular intermediate runs off the top. Skiing between the two mountains was problematic until 1995, when the new Ray's Lift quad solved the lack of linkage between Front and Back.

The Sundance base, at 6,000 feet, is quite low by Utah standards. The exposure is good—mostly north-facing—but the warmer temperatures at this elevation mean the area has a somewhat shorter season than its neighbors. A recently initiated snowmaking program on the lower slopes should help.

Sundance is never crowded. The record busy day was 1,400 people a couple of years ago. The parking lot simply will not hold more, and Bob Redford refuses, even if there were room in the cramped, woodsy valley bottom, to make it bigger. Nice.

The Skiing

Ray's Lift has a mid-station where you can get off. This is handy for skiers who want to yo-yo the bottom half of the mountain.

Most ski school classes are taught from this station on down. There are a couple of nice greens, *Stampede* and *Center Aisle*. The latter swoops by the summer amphitheater stage, which appears like a strange set out of *2001*. The *Maverick* run off the Ray's Lift summit station is fine, rolling blue terrain. This is also where the race courses are set up.

Above the mid-station on Ray's, the terrain jumps steeply to the Front Mountain high point. All of the skiing here is black diamond and deservedly so. Sometimes *Buntline* is groomed, transforming it into a steep but makeable plunge for intermediates.

Arrowhead, on the Back Mountain, is the best intermediate zone and also the most likely to be busy, as this lift is the only route to the summit.

Most skiers are intermediates. But as Jerry Warren and Bob Redford readily admit, there isn't quite as much intermediate cruising as they'd like to have. *Bearclaw* is just about it. Two feeder runs, *Jamie's* and *Amy's Ridge,* named for Redford children, add a little variety. But after a while you find yourself swishing down the same big humps and grooves run after run. Take a break and stop into the Warming Hut on top. The views make the walk out the back door to the outhouses doubly rewarding. There are no trees. It feels higher than it is. The awesome presence to the west is Chablis Peak, one of the false summits of Timpanogos, looming 3,000 feet above the Warming Hut. Provo Canyon drops sharply away to the south, and the rest of the Wasatch stretches to the north.

Inside the hut you'll find stills of Redford as Jedediah Smith, a nineteenth-century mountain man. A cast-iron woodstove chortles in the center of the room, and good homemade chili and chocolate chip cookies are served at the bar. On the way out the door, there's a separate trash barrel for your recyclable aluminum cans, a typically aware Sundance detail.

Experts have more options off the top than do intermediates. *Shauna's Own* (the third Redford progeny) follows the ridge line east to circumnavigate the marvelously spacious *Bishop's Bowl.* Out beyond *Shauna's,* the ridge becomes *Far East* and features a series of very steep, very interesting glade runs through mixed aspens and evergreens to the gully-bottom *Pipeline.* *Pipeline* is not much more than one snowcat wide. When it is groomed, it is fun; when it is not, it can be a trial.

The return road from *Pipeline* deposits you at the base of Flathead Lift. Strong-skiing locals and off-duty ski instructors are enamored of Flathead. You can't get to *Bishop's* or *Shauna's* from here (without also riding the Arrowhead Lift), but Flathead has *Grizzly Ridge* and *Grizzly Bowl,* along with several other semifierce black runs. (With a winch cat, a high-tech grooming vehicle that can cut moguls on steeper terrain than regular snowcats, Sundance could groom a fair percentage of *Bishop's* and *Grizzly,* thus opening up new terrain for intermediate skiers.)

The big mogul runs are off the west side of the *Amy's/Grizzly* ridge, down through evergreen corridors to *Bearclaw. Quick Draw, Hawkeye,* and *Junior's* grow some pretty big ones, though they're never in the same league with Alta's or Snowbird's; there just isn't enough skier traffic here.

When you get ready to move around to Front Mountain again, you have two options. Ride out of the hollow on Ray's Lift or ski the *Sunnyside Access* road cut around the flank of Front Mountain.

Eating and Sleeping at Sundance

I've already mentioned the cottages hidden away in the trees. There are 37 of them. With the addition of another 15 or so rental cabins, Sundance's bed base can accommodate 225 guests—not enough to create a lift line on even one of the chairlifts. (Sundance will grow, but not very much, according to Jerry Warren. "He [Bob] wants to develop, but he doesn't want to be big, to destroy the close, connected ambience.") Some Sundance skiers stay at Park City and drive over (about 35 minutes) for the day. It's not a bad hour drive from Salt Lake City either. Inevitably, Provo is the closest non-resort lodging. The Excelsior Hotel on Center Street was recommended to me by the Sundance staff. If you can swing it, though, stay in one of the cottages. They provide the ambience Redford intended for Sundance, and they are among the most charming ski accommodations you'll find anywhere.

If anything, Sundance eating is even better than Sundance sleeping. There are two restaurants in the rustic little General Store building across the creek from the lift base. The Grill serves breakfast, lunch, and dinner, while the Tree Room serves dinner only. The food is simple and delicious: linguini, tortellini, grilled chicken, fresh trout, pheasant, range-fed lamb. One evening there was a shark-and-clam soup I will not soon forget. Many of the herbs and spices are grown at Sundance. The wine selection is superior to that of most resort restaurants with the possible exception of Deer Valley's.

The Tree Room has a large, dead spruce spearing the ceiling and a nice chunk of Bob's southwest Indian art collection scattered about, including some exquisite Navajo rugs and Hopi kachinas. The Grill is more cowboy, with a big stone fireplace, saddles, and chaps and Remingtonesque bronze buckaroos.

SUNDANCE DATA

Mountain Statistics

Vertical feet	2,150 feet
Base elevation	6,100 feet
Summit elevation	8,250 feet
Longest run	2 miles
Average annual snowfall	325 inches
Number of lifts	3 chairs: 1 quad, 2 triples
Uphill capacity	5,800 skiers per hour
Skiable terrain	450 acres
Opening date	mid-December
Closing date	late March
Snowboarding	Yes

Transportation

By car Thirteen miles (20 minutes) from Provo via Highways 189 and 92, the Alpine Loop. From Park City about 35 minutes south via U.S. 40 and 189. From Salt Lake City approximately 1 hour via I-15, off at exit 275, Highway 52 to 189.

By bus, limo, or taxi From Salt Lake International Airport.

By plane Via major carriers to Salt Lake International Airport.

Key Phone Numbers

Ski Area Information
  (801) 225-4107
Snow Report (801) 225-4100
Reservations (800) 892-1600
www.sundance-utah.com

# Ogden Area

Snowbasin An undiscovered gem 90 minutes north of Salt Lake City up Ogden Canyon, Snowbasin is all skiing: no condos, no shopping, no frills. Just the terrain chosen to stage the downhills for the 2002 Winter Olympic Games. A simple lift system serves terrain that rivals Alta's for variety, surprise, and pure, unbulldozed challenge. Great beginner and intermediate shapes as well. The only problem: Ogden is no metropolis. It's best to stay in Salt Lake City and commute for the day.

Powder Mountain With the same snowfall numbers as Alta (500 inches per season) and twice the acreage (4,000 acres, all private land), Powder Mountain delivers on its name. Across Pineview Reservoir from Snowbasin, the area offers snowcat skiing and a return shuttle bus on the Backside to keep beyond-the-ropes powderhounds happy. Most of the mountain is gently rounded, great for intermediates—skiers and boarders. Very limited lodging in minuscule, bucolic Eden down the hill.

SNOWBASIN

Snowbasin is the Alta of the northern Wasatch. That is to say, you'll find steep, open terrain here, with real timberline bowls and rock peaks that justify the name "Needles." North of Snowbasin, the craggy profile of the range softens; the ridge lines are rounder and less alpine on their way to the Idaho border. So this upthrust, bolting dramatically above Ogden and the Great Salt Lake, is a kind of last hurrah for classic, Alta-like landscape.

With no lodging or resort shenanigans at the base, the skiing has to stand on its own. It compares favorably with its better-known brethren to the south. This is real Utah skiing—plenty of fine dry snow (400 inches a year), inviting, natural shapes, and not a whole lot of trees to get in the way.

Snowbasin also nearly matches Alta in longevity. In 1936 the city of Ogden turned this watershed basin over to the Forest Service for possible recreation development. In 1940 Forest Service recreation adviser (and Alta pioneer) Alf Engen visited the area and recommended that a ski area be created. They didn't wait around. On December 23 of that same year Snowbasin held its first race, hosting 75 ski racers.

This part of Utah, north of Salt Lake City and east of the lake, bills itself as the Golden Spike Empire. Representatives of the Union Pacific and Central Pacific railroads drove the final spike, a golden spike, to complete the linkup of the first transcontinental railroad at Promontory, Utah, in 1869. Ogden has been the hub of this transportation/agriculture empire since Peter Skene Ogden, a Hudson Bay Company man and trapping party leader, first camped here in the early 1800s. Now the empire has expanded to include skiing. The resorts are not nearly as well known or as busy as the central Wasatch heavies (in fact, they are little more than day areas with muscular, destination-area physiques), but that just makes them even better discoveries.

Eight miles and 1,000 vertical feet up precipitous Ogden Canyon, you pop suddenly into the open, into the broad, snowbound saucer of Ogden Valley. Pineview Reservoir fills the valley lowland. The one town in the valley, Huntsville, sits at the edge of the lake surrounded by rich farmland, soil that not so very long ago (perhaps 25,000 years ago—a mere blink in geologic time) was on the bottom of Lake Bonneville, the huge ancestor to the Great Salt Lake. The valley is ringed by mountains, ancient shorelines cutting strange, straight lines in their foundations. Imagine a teacup of a valley with a rim of peaks. Snowbasin's ski runs pour in from the southwest rim, while Powder Mountain perches squarely on the north slopes.

Snowbasin will not remain this quiet for long. The 2002 Olympics will see to that; Snowbasin will be the venue for the Downhill and the Super G. And, as part of the 2002 development, Snowbasin was granted a landswap with the Forest Service, opening the way for a destination village at the base. The area's parent company, the same folks who own Sun Valley Resort and Little America Hotels, know a thing or two about luxury destination resorts. Snowbasin foresees a bright future!

Snowbasin's Mountain

Snowbasin proper occupies the center of a free-standing, five-peak ridge. The middle rock is called the Needles. (The giant molding forces of the Wasatch Fault have turned the rock layers on end, creating vertical striations of snow and stone, ivory and ebony, like a keyboard.) To the west is Mount Ogden, at 9,572 feet the highest in the group, and to the east is DeMoisey Peak at 9,369 feet. The lift-served terrain climbs to 9,350 feet, just at tree line and just below the two alpine bowls on either side of the Needles. These

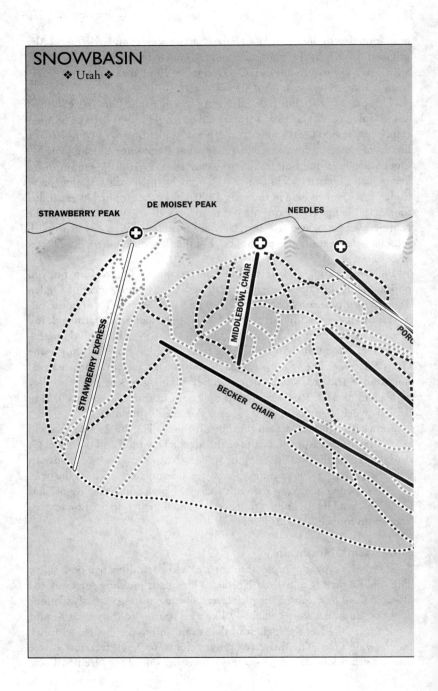

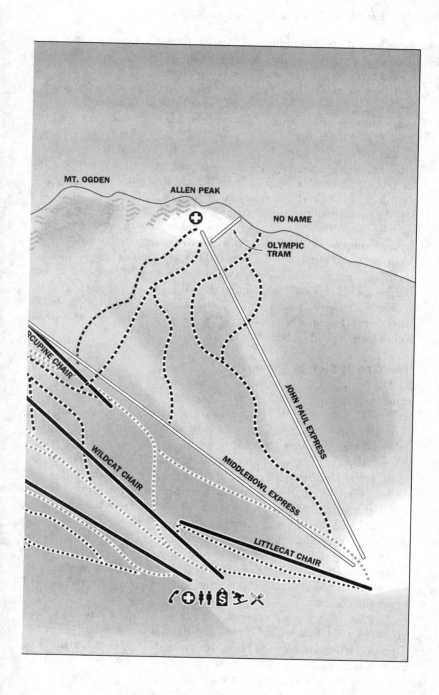

bowls have always been informal Snowbasin terrain, especially in spring, when corn conditions make for easy walking and skiing. When they have needed extra vertical for sanctioned downhill events (the base is at 6,400 feet), race organizers have set courses beginning high in Mount Ogden Bowl, giving them over 3,400 vertical feet of hair-raising descent. Swiss legend Bernard Russi has already designed the downhill race courses for the 2002 Winter Olympics.

But Snowbasin is not all hero terrain. (In fact, downhill courses more often follow high-speed intermediate cruising terrain than they do truly steep black diamonds.) There are lively intermediate pitches, particularly in *Porcupine* and *Middle* bowls. You can ski them in 1,200-foot chunks or follow the two natural drains all the way down for the full 3,400-vertical-foot ride. Beginners have a separate first-time area and a number of fine routes on the mountain as well. Experts will have to look hard for moguls (the old Utah "problem" of too much terrain and too few skiers to bump it up), but there is challenge in the timberline wild snow, in the powder glades, and on the few short steeps sprinkled around the hill.

Nine Lifts serve an efficient 3,200-acre layout. Traffic is practically nonexistent. Fall lines flow naturally, like designer clothes on a model. Alf Engen knew a good ski hill when he saw one.

The Gentle Side of Snowbasin

The Littlecat Lift off to the west of the base lodge is a fine beginners' zone. It has a gentle pitch and lots of room to roam and is safe from faster traffic. Off to the skier's left from Littlecat is a stand of trees the local children have dubbed *Garfield's* after the cartoon cat. Every year they groove some wonderful hobbit trails in there, mini–roller coasters around the trunks. It's perfect play terrain for kids. Just beware if they say, "Follow me, Dad!" I nearly lost my hat a couple of times to low-lying branches.

After the Littlecat, novices (that is, beginners who have learned to turn and stop) can ride the Wildcat Lift up the mountain. From here the *Eas-A-Long* road leads to the wonderfully concave *Bear Hollow* and to *School Hill* and *Snow Shoe,* which adds up to 1,300 vertical feet of high-mileage neophyte cruising. Off the other side, the westerly side of Wildcat, *Chicken Springs* is another option. It's marked blue on the map and is steeper in places, but it's well groomed; this is a fine route for lower intermediates and progressing novices.

Chicken Springs also provides access to the Porcupine Lift and its one green route, via *Middle Bowl Traverse* and *Board Walk,* off the top. Weather, especially wind and blowing snow, can make this upper-mountain slope more difficult for novices. But it is still possible—a rarity on mountains this big—to ski a green route top to bottom.

Snowbasin Blues

Porcupine and Middle Bowl are the two upper mountain lifts. Wildcat and Becker serve the lower mountain. Either way you choose to leave the base station, it's just two rides to the top of the mountain. I am partial to the blue skiing up high (as opposed to the lower-mountain blues) because of the fine snow quality and the billowing, ever-varying lines. *Middle Bowl* is loaded with them. *Sweet Revenge, Dan's Run,* and *Bullwinkle* all dart among the isolated trees with a playful esprit; no bulldozer has worked its homogenizing power here.

Over on Porcupine, where there are even fewer trees, *Porcupine Face* and *Race Course* both drop over a precipitous, bald knoll before settling into a cup-shaped gulch. Up here, there isn't a great deal of difference between the blues and the blacks. Some of the expert trails, like *Pork Barrel* right under the Needles and *Grizzly* off the area's easternmost ridge, do roll over steeper drops, but by and large, it's the grooming that makes the difference. The blues are kept pretty smooth; the black diamonds are left to nature's whim.

On the lower mountain Becker has the better novice terrain, while Wildcat has the two best intermediate runs in *Chicken Springs* and the glorious *Wildcat Bowl.* Seldom will you see an intermediate groove like this one gouged, as if by a giant spoon, out of the front face of the mountain. (Aspen Mountain's Spar Gulch is the only analogy that comes to mind, and it is shorter and flatter.) *Wildcat Bowl* makes a perfect Super G course for junior racers. Recreational skiers can bank off the ravine's sides at any speed and feel the rush of concave, wavelike gravities.

Advanced Snowbasin: Today and Tomorrow

Ski racers in hard turns create artificial gravities in defiance, it seems, of natural forces. Alan Miller, son of longtime Snowbasin ski school director Earl Miller, still remembers a turn the young Phil Mahre made in a race held on *Centennial* trail. Years before he would become a World Cup and Olympic champion, Mahre apparently cleaved to a line so tenuous that mere mortals would have been off into the oakbrush. But he held it, and the moment stuck in Miller's memory. Racing is a big part of Snowbasin's heritage, and the steep trails off the Wildcat ridge, like *Centennial, Bash,* and *Becks,* are perfect for slalom and giant slalom. If there have been no races for a while, these three are likely suspects if you are searching for moguls.

Snowbasin, like Alta, is a powder skier's paradise. There is so much choice, so many lines to be explored on a new-snow morning. You'll find open-slope skiing in upper *Porky's* and on either side of the *Middle Bowl* lift line. *Trail 119* is especially nice, plunging over the Roman nose at the base of the Needles. Some of the steepest powder is in the trees off *Philpot Ridge* in an area the ski patrol calls the Cirque (*Grizzly* and *Little Chicago* on the map). *Sunshine Bowl* off the east side of the Becker Lift is a real sleeper. Like an open book with north-facing evergreens on one page and sun-loving oak-brush on the other, *Sunshine* often harbors untracked snow until late in the day.

Even more tempting is the vast *Strawberry Bowl* domain east of *Philpot Ridge* and the Strawberry Express eight-passenger gondola. Here you will be greeted with 1,400 acres and 2,475 vertical feet of wide-open bowls, gullies, and ridge lines.

For now, Snowbasin remains a classic Little Big Man, that is, big-mountain skiing, just enough out of the way so that its reputation is much smaller than it deserves to be.

Lodging and Dining Options: Huntsville and Ogden

Huntsville is a sleepy little farming community in the winter, but it does offer a few après options for skiers coming down the hill. By far the most folkloric is the Shooting Star Saloon downtown, since 1879 the oldest con-tinuously serving beer bar in Utah, or so Al and Bev will tell you. Al is about six-foot-four, and Bev couldn't possibly be over five feet. Together they serve up 3.2 percent beer, chips, and wisdom underneath the jackalope nailed above the bar. According to Snowbasin employees, Al and Bev "are like Mom and Dad to us all." They're pretty nice to visitors, too.

Finding dinner up in Ogden Valley is a little tougher than finding a beer. The Jackson Fork Inn, which also has rooms available, is the place to go for chicken-steak-lobster-style hearty fare. They also do brunch, with eggs Bene-dict, huevos rancheros, and Belgian waffles. Just down the road is Chris's, a cavernous place where you can play pool, drink beer, eat homemade stew, and gander at the world's biggest goose, hanging from the ceiling in front of the fireplace.

Down at the mouth of the canyon in Ogden, I like the Greenery Restau-rant. They do soups and salads and things like turkey enchiladas and stuffed spuds for a very reasonable price.

There is almost no lodging in the valley. Besides the Jackson Fork Inn, your only option is across the lake toward Powder Mountain at the new condo development called Wolf Lodge. Originally a summer-only place, the lodge is now open for skiers, too. The units range from adequate to spartan, but there is a hot tub, sauna, and club house, and you get to wake up in the mountains.

Down in Ogden the Radisson Suite Hotel is actively courting skiers for the first time. The tallest building downtown, it is a pale-brick and high-arched, 14-story national historic site. An elegant old thing from a grander age, it has been refurbished and is very comfortable.

If you can, plan to stay at the Radisson in early January when the Hof

Festival takes over 25th Street just outside the door. It's a wonderful week of revelry as Ogden celebrates its sister city, Hof, Germany. They block off the street and turn it into a ski hill and snowboarding half-pipe. Live polka music fills the air, and good German sausages and beer abound. There's snow sculpture in the park, folk dancing and yodeling down at Union Station, ski joring (ski racers pulled by horse and rider) in the streets, and quite a few sweet people in lederhosen strolling about emitting Bavarian good vibes.

Even if you don't stay in Ogden but happen to ski Snowbasin during that week, you'll have a chance to hear the very fine Hof band (bass, tuba, accordion, trumpet, and clarinet) that entertains in the afternoons at the Snowbasin base lodge.

SNOWBASIN DATA

Mountain Statistics

Vertical feet	3,400 feet
Base elevation	5,850 feet
Summit elevation	9,250 feet
Longest run	3 miles
Average annual snowfall	400 inches
Number of lifts	2 gondolas
	1 jig-back tram
	1 high-speed quad
	4 triples
	1 double chair
Uphill capacity	13,550 skiers per hour
Skiable terrain	3,200 acres
Opening date	Thanksgiving
Closing date	early April
Snowboarding	Yes

Transportation

By car About 52 miles north of Salt Lake International Airport. Take I-15 north, exit to I-84 east to Mt. Green/Huntsville (#92), and follow the signs to Highway 167. From the north, take the 12th Street exit off of I-15, Ogden to Ogden Canyon; ski area is 17 miles east of Ogden. From Park City, take I-80 north to I-84 at Echo Junction. Continue west on I-84 to Mt. Green/Huntsville (#96) and follow the signs to Highway 167.

By plane Via major carriers to Salt Lake International Airport.

Key Phone Numbers

Ski Area Information
   (801) 399-1135
Snow Report (801) 399-0198
Ski School (801) 399-4611
www.snowbasin.com

Aspens

Ronald Reagan may or may not have said, "You've seen one tree, you've seen them all." But it is certainly not true to say, "You've skied one tree, you've skied them all." Skiing an evergreen forest—and in Utah that means mixed Engelmann spruce and alpine fir—is a totally different experience than skiing in an aspen grove. Where evergreen woods are dark and secretive, aspen woods are bright and open. Where evergreens smother sounds with millions of tiny needles, aspen glades have no leaves at all and almost no branches; the cries of powder skiers ring across space uninhibited. Skiing around aspens is almost like strolling through an abstract expressionist sculpture, an "installation" of hundreds of cool, slim, gray-green trunks and their hundreds of slim, blue, straight-line shadows.

Adding to the wonder, aspens have "eyes." Actually, they are eye-shaped scars where lower branches have been sloughed off on the tree's climb for light. Some of these eyes have even sent wrinkles into the smooth bark, like smile lines.

Aspens are members of the poplar family, along with willows and cottonwoods and the "Mormon trees," Lombardy poplars. You'll find them on every ski mountain in Utah, especially in the Park City area and on the lower slopes of Snowbasin. You'll find them in the sun, on east-, west-, and south-facing slopes. Aspens are shade intolerant, although they will occasionally invade a moist north-facing slope—the exception that proves the rule.

The aspens we see in the Rocky Mountains are known as *Populus tremuloides,* or quaking aspen, because the faintest breeze will set their heart-shaped leaves aflutter. They are deciduous, of course—bare in winter, with pale green leaves in spring and blazing gold leaves in fall. They are an important food source for deer, who nibble new buds, and beaver, who fell aspens for food and lodge-building materials. Look closely and you may find dollar bill–size cuts on some aspen trunks where elk with their great flat front teeth have gnawed their way down from the high country in the deepening fall snows. Early man found that aspen bark, chewed or brewed as a tea, was good for reducing fevers. The active compound involved, salicylic acid, became the prime ingredient in aspirin.

Aspens followed the retreating glaciers all over North America. They are aggressive pioneers, filling in newly created habitats such as burned areas or clear-cuts. In bright, open spaces their roots send up sucker shoots (all of the trees in a grove are connected underground), and the empty space is quickly filled. In one of nature's great ironies, shade-tolerant evergreens often get a toehold under the aspen canopy. Eventually the conifers, the climax species in the Rocky Mountain ecological cycle, block the aspens' light and take over completely.

So the next time you find yourself gliding through an aspen stand, think of smiling eyes, think sun, think aspirin, and watch the shadows flicker by like the frames of a silent movie.

POWDER MOUNTAIN

Powder Mountain is a pretty brave name to take in the State of Powder. But in this case, the name is justified. About half an hour from Snowbasin, across Pineview Reservoir on the northern rim of Ogden Valley, Powder Mountain receives an average 500 inches of snow per year, which ties it with Alta and Snowbird for tops in the state.

The storm track is a little different here. Powder Mountain's slopes look down on Cache Valley to the north and an uninterrupted sweep of dairy and ranchland stretching north into Idaho. Northerly storms that might not reach down into the central Wasatch dump an inordinate amount of cold, fine snow on these hills.

Then there is the commitment of Powder Mountain's people to powder skiing. There is a staggering amount of terrain set aside just for wild-snow enthusiasts. You won't find a great deal of lift-served vertical: 1,300 feet by chair and a total of 1,960 feet if you ride the backside shuttle bus. But (and this is a big but) skiable terrain now encompasses about 4,000 acres, making Powder Mountain the single biggest ski mountain in Utah; 1,600 acres are inbounds, 1,200 are in the backside "Powder Country" realm, and 1,200 are in the snowcat skiing zones beyond the northside boundaries. And, believe it or not, there is the potential to develop about 3,000 more acres. The vast majority of this terrain, all private land, is ungroomed, uncut, unfettered—wild powder country.

Not so long ago, this was all sheep country. Dr. Alvin Cobabe ("*Co* like co-op, *babe* like 'Hi, babe'"—this is a man who is comfortable helping you learn to pronounce his name) and his father ran 3,500 head of sheep and 600 head of cattle on these high ridge lines. One day in 1958 Cobabe, who was also an Ogden physician, was riding horseback on Lightning Ridge just west of where the ski area is now, when his companion said, "Boy, that would sure make a good ski run." The first two lifts, Sundown and Timberline, opened in 1972, and it's still a family-run business. Cobabe's son-in-law is president and general manager, two of his four daughters are involved

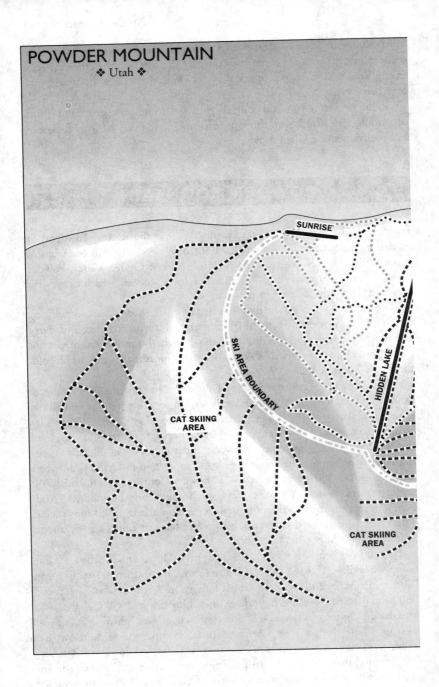

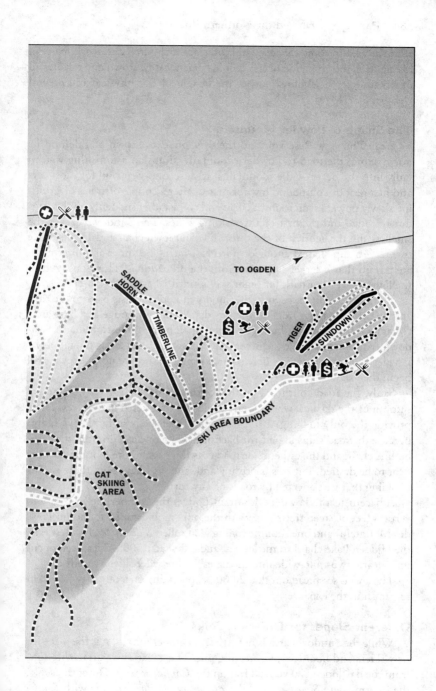

TO OGDEN

SADDLE HORN

TIMBERLINE

TIGER

SUNDOWN

SKI AREA BOUNDARY

CAT SKIING AREA

with the area in some capacity, and three grandchildren also work. Now in his eighties, the good doctor has quit his practice downtown and devotes all of his time to the ski business, to the benefit of our physical and mental well-being.

The Shape of Powder Mountain

From Pineview Reservoir and the tiny, one-store town of Eden on its north shore, the road to Powder Mountain climbs an astonishingly steep gully into the heart of the mountains. It's a second-gear pull for most cars and first gear or compound low for many. After a couple of miles of grinding slowly upward, you round a curve and come rather suddenly on the Sundown Lodge and the first of three skiing zones. The Sundown area is the smallest and the gentlest of the three. The Sundown chair and Tiger surface tow serve a cup-shaped cirque of northeast-facing beginner and intermediate terrain that is largely separate from the other zones. This is also where the lights blaze after dark for night skiing until 10 P.M.

The road continues beyond the Sundown Lodge, twists back to the east, and ascends the main ridge to the Powder Mountain Lodge and base area. (Imagined from above, the ridges form an elongated question mark: Sundown is in the curl, while the other two zones stretch out along the tail.) The Powder Mountain base is where most skiers, from novice up to expert, will begin their day.

Sadly, the road continues up the south side of the ridge to the actual summit of the ski area, where condo projects are scattered in the trees. These provide the only lodging at the area, about 300 beds so far. I say "sadly" because the road snips in half the backside skiing one can do from the Timberline chair, and the esthetics of road cuts this high in the mountains leave a lot to be desired. But this is private land, and, as I have said, there is a lot of skiing that isn't affected by roads of any sort.

Adjacent to the Powder Mountain Lodge, the Timberline zone is 900 vertical feet of steep tree shots (with the only moguls to be found on Powder Mountain) and one sublime rolling glen called *Sidewinder*. Farthest east, the Hidden Lake chairlift, the longest and tallest at 1,300 vertical feet, opens up a nearly two-mile-wide intermediates' and powder skiers' paradise.

The area is so spread out that 2,000 people skiing on a busy day just seem to vanish in the expanse.

Different Slopes for Different Folks

While the Sundown area is not strictly beginner terrain, it is the place for new skiers and boarders just starting out. The Tiger Tow surface lift runs from the day lodge 120 vertical feet up the *Confidence* run. Other trails, like the intermediate *Shot Gun* and the novice *Dead Horse*, merge with *Confi-*

dence up above, so it's not as isolated as it could be. Still, this is the gentlest teaching/learning terrain here.

Skiers ready to ride a chair will be thrilled by Sundown. Because it is a separate peak, the views from the top are spectacular. Antelope Island rises like a ghost ship out in the middle of the Great Salt Lake. Beyond the lake and the Bonneville salt flats on clear days you can see mountains in Nevada 140 miles distant. To the east a knowledgeable eye can pick out peaks in Wyoming, and up to the north the most distant horizons are part of Idaho. The novice skiing on Sundown is limited to three trails—*Confidence, Dead Horse,* and *Slow Poke*—but they are long, mileage-building descents.

Families and groups of mixed ability who nevertheless want to stay together do well on Sundown because the center of the cirque pitches steeply enough to hold four intermediate blue runs and one black diamond, and everything funnels back to the same lift base. Children under the age of five ski free with their families on Sundown.

Slow Poke stays high on Sundown's west ridge and circles the dish to provide ski access to the Powder Mountain Lodge a couple of hundred feet above the Sundown Lodge. There is one green run, *Drifter,* in the adjacent Timberline zone. It's a lovely see-forever ridge run, though it seems more blue-green than green. Way out in the Hidden Lake domain are two long, winding greens, *East 40* and the precisely named *Three Mile*. Powder Mountain is so broad that by the time most novices ski over to these trails, they will be able to call themselves intermediates.

Hidden Lake is intermediate heaven. For about three miles and the full 1,300-foot vertical, you can cruise all day on big swoopers like *Burntwood, White Pine,* and *Hidden Lake Run*. It's cold over here on the north side; the ski patrol calls this lift "Frozen Lake," but that means the snow stays silky. Don't miss the run called *Sunrise* out on the area's east edge. To get there you have to ride the little 100-foot Sunrise surface tow in the saddle. It's well worth it for the views, the late-day sun, and the long, long glade runs that never seem to get skied out. To return to the lodges from Hidden Lake, note that you must ride the Saddle Horn surface lift to the top of Timberline.

The Timberline zone is primarily black. Short, steep fall-line pitches through the trees are called *Dynamite, Exterminator,* and *Runaway*. Together they satisfy the needs of the relatively few mogul mashers here.

Expert powder seekers have been discovering Powder Mountain in increasing numbers since the opening in 1983 of what they call *Powder Country* or simply the *Backside*. It was a brilliant stroke. The best steep terrain is on the backside, plunging toward the access road from both the Sundown and Hidden Lake summits. There just weren't any lifts, and the terrain was extreme enough that lifts didn't seem practical. So Cobabe and company decided to open the skiing, when it was safe, and run a shuttle bus up and down the road every 15 minutes to pick up the grinning skiers and snowboarders.

On new-snow mornings the Sundown side, which faces the morning sun (figure that one out), is skied first. Then the hounds move around to the Hidden Lake side, which is even steeper (a good 40 degrees in some spots), more heavily treed, and west-facing. But it never gets completely skied out. There's just too much of it, about 1,200 acres with a maximum vertical of nearly 2,000 feet. I skied untracked snow on both sides of the road one winter, ten days after the last snowstorm.

New in the last few years: Powder Mountain has decided to raid another 1,200 acres of its wild-snow cache and offer cat skiing in the glades below the Hidden Lake and Timberline pads. For a fee, the cat picks you up in Cobabe Canyon or at the bottom of *Eureka* (as in, "Eureka! Fresh tracks!") and deposits you back at a lift base. It's every powder lover's dream: to float right past the boundary, past the point of no return, and on down an untracked line, knowing there is a diesel-powered conveyance waiting to bring you back up. New in 1998, the half-pipe grinder provides excellent maintenance of the half-pipe.

Eating and Sleeping

All three day lodges are open for breakfast and lunch. The Sundown Lodge stays open through the night-skiing session until 10 P.M. When it comes to après-ski food and spirits, Powder Mountain, like its Ogden Valley neighbor Snowbasin, suffers a bit from its isolation, but there are a few options. There are several new restaurants located in Eden at the bottom of Powder Mountain Road, including Eats of Edan (Italian), General Store (deli), Hungry Wolf (steak, chicken, fish, and pasta dishes) and the Cellar (casual pizza/sports bar). Scout out the three eateries in Huntsville (see the Snowbasin section, Lodging and Dining Options: Huntsville and Ogden, page 378), or, as the vast majority of skiers here do, trundle back down the canyon to Ogden. One recommendation that bears repeating is the Shooting Star Saloon in Huntsville, since 1879 the oldest beer bar in Utah. The decor is true western funk, Al and Bev are down-home hosts, and their Shooting Star Burger is a find.

There are approximately 300 rental beds right at Powder Mountain. Demand is strong, though, and short-notice vacancies are rare. For lodging information in the greater Ogden area call the Chamber Bureau at (800) 255-8824. For reservations, call Golden Spike Empire Travel Region at (800) 554-2741.

POWDER MOUNTAIN DATA

Mountain Statistics

Vertical feet	1,300 lift-served; 1,960 via shuttle bus
Base elevation	7,600 feet
Summit elevation	8,900 feet
Longest run	3 miles
Average annual snowfall	500 inches
Number of lifts	2 double chairlifts 1 triple chairlift 3 surface lifts
Uphill capacity	4,800 skiers per hour
Skiable terrain	4,000 acres 1,600 lift-served
Opening date	Thanksgiving
Closing date	Easter
Snowboarding	Yes
Night skiing	4:30 to 10 P.M.

Transportation

By car About 55 miles from Salt Lake International Airport via I-15 north; exit at 12th Street, Ogden to Ogden Canyon (State Road 39); Powder Mountain is 22 miles east of Ogden. Or via Trapper's Loop Road from Mountain Green off I-84 east of Salt Lake City.

By airport limo From Salt Lake International Airport.

By plane Via major carriers to Salt Lake International Airport.

Key Phone Numbers

Ski Area Information
  (801) 745-3772
Snow Report (801) 745-3771
Lodging Reservations
  (801) 745-3772
http:\\member.aol.com\
  powdermtn\utah.html

INSIDE STORY

Back Side

Powder Mountain assistant patrol director Dennis Perry met his wife on a rescue off the back side of the Sundown ski terrain. She was planning to ski down to the access road as other skiers had done earlier that day, but she took a wrong turn and ended up in a different drainage. It was a cold, moonlit night. Perry and the search team found her at 2 A.M. fighting through the willows halfway to the valley town of Eden. The two hit it off, and the rest is history.

Would that every backcountry rescue ended so happily. The fact is, backcountry skiing—or off-piste skiing, as the Europeans call it—is a horse of a different color compared to its on-piste, groomed, civilized cousin. The snow can be difficult, crusty, crunchy, sloppy, heavy; it can embarrass even very good skiers. Or it can be the softest, deepest, most exhilarating snow you've ever encountered. You can get cold skiing out there, very tired, or lost. A trip out of bounds might be the best run of your life, or it might be the worst.

Powder Mountain's back side is not true wilderness. There are signs to aim you the right way, and the ski patrol does sweep the terrain for stragglers at closing time. But—witness the future Mrs. Perry—you can still find trouble out there. Ditto for a sneak peak at Snowbasin's Strawberry Bowl or a trip into White Pine Canyon next to Snowbird or even a day on the Interconnect area-to-area tour. Here are a few hints to make your trip beyond the ropes safer and more enjoyable.

Always go with a partner. Four is an even better number; then if one person gets stuck, someone can stay with him while the other two go for help.

Tell somebody where you're going and when you plan to be back. Set it up so that somebody will miss you if you are late.

Pay attention to the weather. If it's cold or snowing or could get that way soon, bring the gear you'll need to stay warm and dry.

Know where you are and where you plan to end up. Nothing dampens a great powder run quite like overshooting your return traverse and having to slog uphill back to the trail.

Bring along some water and high-energy food, like dried fruits, nuts, or candies. Your friends will think you are a genius. Some backside skiers go out prepared to survive a night in the open. In a day-pack they carry an extra jacket and a space blanket to conserve body heat. It may seem ultra-cautious, silly even, until you need it.

Talk with the ski patrol about the stability of the snowpack. If there is any question in your mind about the safety of a given slope, don't ski it. *Never* ski in a closed area. Chances are the patrol has a very good reason for closing off a particular slope.

Ski within yourself. Forget looking good; off-piste is not the place for high speeds and hero turns. Ski ugly, if that's what it takes; traverse and kick turn, if that's what it takes. Develop a strong, cautious style, one that will get you down *toute neige, tout terrain,* as the French say, "any snow, any terrain."

Finally, cultivate a backcountry attitude. Respect the winter landscape, respect the steep, the cold, the vagaries of snow, rocks, and trees. The idea, after all, is to go out there, sample the wild, and come back in time for dinner.

Southern Utah

Brian Head Down in "Utah's Dixie," Brian Head attracts skiers from southern California and Nevada as well as the occasional northerner seeking sun. Two mountains, one a fine intermediate cruiser, the other a gentle learning hill, perch at the edge of the red rock canyon country. Ambience is late-model mall. Lodging consists of two full-service hotels and condos. Families are big, and side trips to Zion and Bryce National Parks (or golf in St. George) are just down the road.

BRIAN HEAD

Fact: San Diego skiers can drive to Brian Head in the same time it takes them to reach the quintessential Southern California destination, Mammoth Mountain. On a busy winter weekend it looks as if the beach crowd, minus only the sand, has been transported to the slopes. Snowboarders, those riders of the frozen wave, make up a big portion of Brian Head's business. A full 80 percent of skier days are logged by veterans of the I-15 route from the greater Los Angeles and Las Vegas metropolises.

Brian Head is the happening place down in Utah's Dixie. It's like another state. Before crossing into Arizona, the Virgin River dips to 2,700 feet in elevation. The climate is semitropical. Palm trees make green splashes against red rocks. You can play golf one day and ski the next.

The Wasatch Range, home to Utah's best-known skiing, remains out of sight to the north. Brian Head sits on the western edge of the high Colorado Plateau, where red rock highlands meet the dry, beige-colored basin-and-range country that stretches from here west all the way to the Sierras. The land is better known for its national parks than for its skiing. Zion and Bryce canyons are just minutes away. Capitol Reef, Arches, and Canyonlands national parks are all within a half-day sphere. Portions of Cedar Breaks National Monument are visible from the Dunes (Lift 7) ski terrain. Cross-country ski tours into the pink and white columns of Cedar Breaks can be arranged through the Brian Head X-C Center. Locals are fond of skiing to

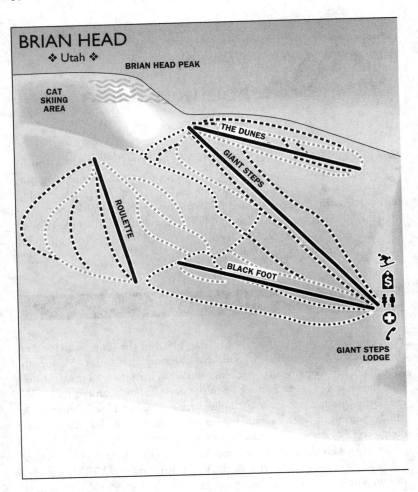

the rim of the Monument on moonlit nights, building a bonfire, and watching the night unfold on the edge of the great desert.

Brian Head is isolated, yes, but it is not small. There are 4,000 condo beds; it has the third largest uphill capacity in the state, at 11,000 skiers per hour, and more learn-to-ski and family packages than you could shake a beach towel at. The resort opened in 1965 with a used T-bar and three trailers for a base village. The growth, despite financial wobbling, has been phenomenal since then.

Brian Head is high—the base is 9,600 feet and the top is almost 11,000 feet—and the same winter jet stream that brings snow to the northern

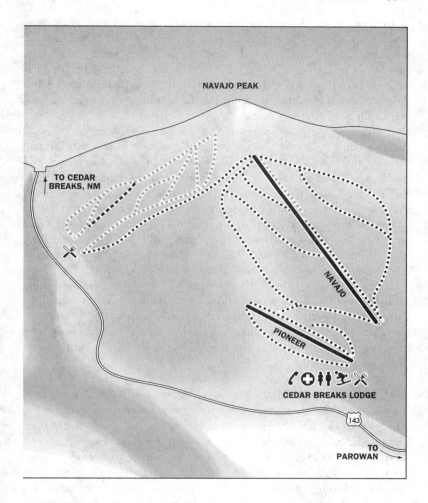

resorts deposits 425 inches a year on the forested plateaus. The terrain is not as vast or as spectacular as the glaciated Cottonwood canyons, nor is the snow as reliably cold and soft as it is in the northern Wasatch, but what skiing there is is first-rate. Five hundred thousand San Diegans can't be wrong.

Brian Head Skiing

The skiing takes place on two mountains: a gentle one to the west and a more demanding one to the east. The highway runs north and south through the narrow valley between them, leading to Cedar Breaks, Panguitch, and Bryce. There are three distinct skiing zones, two on the west mountain, one on the east. Each zone has its own base. They have to, because making the trek across the road and the parking lots from one zone to another is easier said than done. There is a free shuttle system that has recently been improved with larger shuttles and more frequent service, but longtime Brian Head hands admit that the first thing they need is a connector lift or a better way to link the two mountains.

Driving up the quite steep road from the I-15 freeway exit at Parowan, the first skiing you come to is the beginner area, with its two chairlifts and its base, the Navajo Lodge. This is the newer of the two bases, sleek and modern and well set up to accommodate new skiers, especially children. (There's a dinosaur terrain garden off to the side that looked like so much fun I had to give it a try.) The Pioneer Lift and its trio of debut runs, *First Time, You're Ready,* and *Fun Run,* are as calm a beginner zone as you'll find anywhere. It's completely isolated from faster traffic; you'll never feel a hot shot breathing down your neck. The Brian Head beginner program includes a three-hour lesson with the latest Elan Parabolic Skis for $50.

The Giant Steps Lodge is the main base area. This primarily west-facing zone has four chairs (all triples, including the namesake Giant Steps), the largest vertical at the resort (1,161 feet), and the lion's share of the intermediate and advanced terrain. Shops and services clustered at the Giant Steps base have, wittingly or not, given themselves the perfect California-away-from-home name: the Mall.

A series of mile-long, interconnecting trails weave through the Giant Steps forest. They are basically quite easy. *Hunter's Run* to *Bear Paw* to *Heavenly Daze* is the easiest, though the intersections sometimes resemble the Hollywood–Golden State freeway interchange at rush hour. *Giant Steps,* right under its namesake chair, is the most popular intermediate route and deservedly so. Skiing it is like floating down an oversize stairway in a Busby-Berkeley musical. The only genuine black diamond is called *Engens* (after the ski pioneer brothers Alf, Sverre, and Corey), and it is sometimes tamed to a steep blue when the snowcats mow the moguls down. Other challenging skiing includes Bear Paw Pitch and three fun terrain parks where you can get plenty of wall hits, air time, and 360s.

This side of Brian Head is fairly typical of the resort as a whole; it's like a ski parka ski playground. There's nothing particularly grand about the terrain, nothing scary. It's comfortable, a great place to go to learn, to feel unpressured, to feel—in the absence of serious challenge—like a hero. Past ski school director Danny Edwards, talking about powder skiing here, put it in the vernacular: "A foot of new snow is perfect. More than that, it's too flat. Let's face it. Let's get real. We need terrain."

Expert terrain, that is. There's plenty of ego-soothing stuff. There are a couple of options now for very good skiers, but they take some work. One is to climb the Peak, and depending on snow conditions that's a half-hour walk from the top of Giant Steps. (A snowcat will take you, conditions permitting, for a fee.) From the flat mesa top, ski through the gaps in the striated summit cliff bands and down the broad shoulder. Short but exciting. Snow conditions are forever changing, from icy wind crud to premium talcum powder; the Peak sticks up into a lot of weather that misses the more sheltered slopes below.

The other option for good skiers is to find your private bower in the trees. There are two fine zones: *Dark Hollow* off the north side of the Roulette Lift (big-trunk spruce with plenty of space and a rare, true north exposure), and *Sun Spot* (smaller trees leading to a pair of steeply tilted meadows) off to the skier's left of *Engens* in the Giant Steps region. The ski patrol calls these their "secret jewels." They can be exquisite, but if the snow is old or thin, they can also be nasty. Check with the patrol before you jump in, likewise when walking up to the Peak, and be sure to check out the snowcat skiing in this area.

Staying and Eating at Brian Head

The Giant Steps Lodge is a big disappointment for lunch. The cafeteria is old; it feels like a dive. Area management admits that replacing the old structure is a high priority. Much better is the cafeteria at Navajo Lodge; it's just tough to get there if you've been skiing the east mountain. If you don't want to wait for the shuttle bus, bop down to the end of the parking lot to the Mall for pizza or something sandwichy from the Bump & Grind Mountain View Cafe.

The Navajo Lodge cafeteria undergoes a marvelous transformation in the evenings to candlelight and white tablecloths and one of the best dinner menus in the region. Two other options are Pasta Luna's, a reasonably priced Italian bistro, and the Summit Dining Room in the Cedar Breaks Lodge, which is full of steaks, oak, brass, and mirrors.

Parowan, which was settled on Brigham Young's order in 1851 (the oldest Mormon community in southern Utah), provides slightly more distant lodging, 11 miles away. Cedar City, 32 miles south, is a major tourist hub with motels, inns, and cabins galore. The best reason to stay in Cedar City is its proximity to Zion and Bryce, two unusual and unsettlingly beautiful side trips to a ski adventure.

BRIAN HEAD DATA

Mountain Statistics

Vertical feet	1,200 feet
Base elevation	9,600 feet
Summit elevation	11,307 feet
Longest run	1 mile
Average annual snowfall	425 inches
Number of lifts	6 chairs: 5 triples, 1 double 3 surface lifts
Uphill capacity	11,000 skiers per hour
Skiable terrain	650 acres
Opening date	early November
Closing date	late April
Snowboarding	Yes
Terrain Parks	3

Transportation

By car Fifteen miles southeast of Parowan on State Highway 43, 32 miles from Cedar City, 3 hours from Las Vegas, 4 hours from Salt Lake City, and 8 hours from Phoenix and Los Angeles via I-15.

By chartered bus From Las Vegas and Cedar City.

By plane Via major carriers to McCarren International Airport in Las Vegas, with daily connecting flights via SkyWest Airlines to Cedar City.

Key Phone Numbers

Ski Area Information (435) 677-2035
Snow Report (435) 677-2035
Reservations (800) 272-7426
www.brianhead.com

INSIDE STORY

Side Trips

Brian Head Peak, a flattop snow and rock sandwich sitting 400 feet above the ski area's top terminal, looks out over one of the most remarkable landscapes in America. From Cedar Breaks south to the bottom of the Grand Canyon, a distance of no more than 100 miles, the earth falls away nearly 10,000 vertical feet in a geologic phenomenon called the Grand Staircase. Along the way billions of years of the earth's history are exposed.

Bristlecone pines, the planet's oldest living trees, inhabit the rim country around Cedar Breaks on the top step. They are easily reached on skis from Brian Head.

The next step down, the Paunsaugunt Plateau, is home to Bryce Canyon

National Park. Not really a canyon, Bryce is a series of natural amphitheaters peopled with thousands of goblinesque figures, columns, and pinnacles carved and weathered out of white limestone and orange sandstone.

Southwest of Bryce, the Virgin River gouged Zion Canyon out of rock that was once wind-deposited sand dunes. The Great White Throne rises straight up 2,394 feet over the grassy valley floor. Farther upriver in the Narrows section, one can touch with outstretched arms both walls of the canyon at the same time. Mountain lions still roam the canyon rims; I have yet to see one, but I have seen roadrunners, eagles, and hawks.

Down go the steps of the Grand Staircase, over the Pink Cliffs, White Cliffs, and Vermilion Cliffs to the Paria Plateau overlooking the Grand Canyon. The final step is a big one, 5,000 feet down from the North Rim to the Colorado River. There is no other geologic record like it on earth, so clearly cut are the layers of time. At the very bottom of the canyon, black metamorphic rock, known as Vishnu schist, is estimated to be four billion years old. Grand Canyon National Park is so vast and wild that there are only one or two places to scramble up out of the gorge on the 18-day raft trip from Lee's Ferry to Lake Mead.

All of these places are easy day trips from southern Utah's ski areas, and they are particularly attractive in the off-season (spring and winter) when crowds are sparse and you needn't suffer the hot summer weather.

Another park well worth visiting, though it's not on the Grand Staircase, is Capitol Reef National Park. North and east of Bryce, it was so named because its sandstone domes reminded early geologists of the capitol's architecture, and its colorful, buttressed spires reminded them of coral reefs. You'll find smooth, red rock cliffs here covered with pre-Columbian petroglyphs and a place of particular interest to Mormon history buffs called Co-Hab Canyon where polygamists once hid from crusading federal marshals.

The Northern Rockies

Jackson Hole "The Big One" has the second largest lift-served vertical in the United States (behind Big Sky) at 4,139 feet. Not just tall, Jackson Hole has huge breadth of weather, exposure, terrain variety, and challenge. More choice from the top of the famous red tram than at any other lift-served high point in the Rockies. Adventure skiing with a capital A, complete with a compact base village, the grandeur of the Tetons, and, across the still unspoiled Snake River Valley, good food and good-natured western hype in the town of Jackson.

Grand Targhee On the other side of the Tetons and facing the sunset (and the spud farms of southern Idaho), Grand Targhee complements Jackson Hole with gentle, undulating, ski-forever terrain; a cozy, self-contained, hype-free resort; and no crowding ever across 3,000 acres and 2,200 vertical feet. There's no nightlife to speak of and nothing on the hill to scare an expert skier; this is a place to dazzle yourself with your own footwork, eat well, and fall into bed. Wonderful snowcat skiing on an adjacent peak.

Big Sky Montana's only master-planned, destination luxury resort sits in the middle of a lot of wilderness within sight of Yellowstone National Park to the south. Big Sky is located on the river where they filmed *A River Runs Through It* and is surrounded by a really, really big sky. Endless low-angle cruising makes a lot of families and intermediates happy. The 1995 opening of a new tram to Lone Mountain's 11,666-foot summit gave Big Sky the vertical crown, by 41 feet, over Jackson Hole and in the process opened an abundance of steep chutes, cliffs, and above-timberline bowls.

Bridger Bowl The mid-size, nonprofit, local area for the university town of Bozeman, Bridger became famous as the schooling grounds for extreme skiers Scot Schmidt, Doug Coombs, Emily Gladstone, and Tom Jüngst. "Ridge hippies" hike to marvelously intricate steep terrain along the ridge. Mortals find excellent bumps, powder, and groomed snow on the less severe pitches below. Homey and laid-back—and a real bargain—like the old days. Rooms and eats are 25 minutes away in downtown Bozeman.

The Big Mountain The Big Mountain is a real find up in the northwest corner of Montana by Glacier National Park; it's a long drive from anywhere, but Amtrak runs right through Whitefish, and Kalispell Airport is just 19 miles away. Huge intermediate bowls, rimed "ghost" trees, one super quad, and super reasonable cat skiing off the backside together add up to big skiing. There is some lodging on the mountain; the town is funky and friendly—Aspen 30 years ago. Northern cold and a dearth of sunshine are the only things slowing the rush from Colorado.

Schweitzer Built by Sandpoint, Idaho, and Spokane, Washington, skiers who were weary of the long drive east to the Big Mountain, Schweitzer is a near twin in scale and possibility: 2,400 feet vertical, 2,400 acres, myriad lines off the ridges. It has superb intermediate bowl skiing with steeper glades virtually untouched, so few are the experts. Giant, old-growth cedars on the backside, night skiing, a secluded terrain garden for kids, and a beautiful new upscale hotel and base facilities make the journey from anywhere worthwhile.

Sun Valley The queen of Rockies resorts claims the world's first chairlift (1936) and some of the world's longest, most continuous fall-line skiing and is magnet to stars from Clark Gable to Arnold Schwarzenegger. Most lodging and dining is decidedly and unapologetically upscale, as are the crowds of well-dressed, silver-maned cruisers working their giant slalom skis over manicured steeps. Extensive snowmaking ensures skiing even in low-snow winters, though the mountain is best when new snow blankets the bowls and softens the overused boulevards. The old sheep town of Ketchum has more reasonable housing for Everyskier.

JACKSON HOLE

When the great Jean-Claude Killy came to race a giant slalom at Jackson Hole in 1967, he pronounced the ski mountain the best in America. Those are strong words, but then Killy had been everywhere. The next year he would win all three alpine gold medals—downhill, slalom, and giant slalom —at the Olympics in Grenoble, France. He won that giant slalom race in Jackson Hole too. So perhaps the glow of victory colored his bonhomie?

I think not. Killy was never shy about pronouncing his own greatness. Neither did he fail to back up his words with results. The same is true of Jackson Hole, a lusty, sprawling, avalanche-prone, weather-enriched and weather-bedeviled, wild-snow mountain that refers to itself in its own literature as "The Big One." Big Sky may now claim the total vertical title at 4,180 feet from top terminal to lowest lift base, but Jackson retains the "continuous skiing" vertical crown at 4,139 feet. Uninterrupted! Ski it without stopping if you can. It is one of those rare places that lives up to the hype and, on many days, gloriously surpasses it.

Bigness is a part of it; history is another. Jackson Hole was the center of the beaver fur trade in the early nineteenth century and the home to irascible mountain men like John Colter, Jim Bridger, and Davey Jackson. Colter, who left the Lewis and Clark expedition in 1807 on its return from the Pacific, was probably the first white man to see the area around what is now Yellowstone National Park. Back east his tales of boiling springs, spouting fountains, and sulfurous fumes were ridiculed as the work of an unbalanced mind. "Colter's Hell," they called it. But Colter also talked of great numbers of beaver in the high meadows and creeks, and with beaver-fur top hats all the rage in cities around the world, the northern Rockies were soon crawling with trappers.

South of the Yellowstone Plateau, a trapper named Davey Jackson laid claim to a spectacular valley that was almost perfectly flat and surrounded on all sides by mountains. In those days, such a valley was called a "hole." Jackson shared his with a few Flathead Indians in the summer and a lot of elk in the winter. Eventually, the valley of the upper Snake River became known as Jackson's Hole.

With the beaver almost gone by 1840, men's millinery fashion changed to silk, and Jackson Hole slumbered until the formation of Yellowstone and Grand Teton national parks. A thriving summer tourist business still left Jackson desolate for nine months of the year, until a Californian named Paul McCollister, with help from Colorado's Willy Schaeffler and Alta pioneer Alf Engen, strung the first lifts on Rendezvous Mountain. Killy arrived to race the next year, and Jackson Hole's reputation as a skiers' mecca as well as a haven for moose, bear, elk, and, yes, beaver, has grown steadily since.

Today, with an airport just minutes away and the ski area under new ownership, Jackson Hole is poised to post some big skier numbers, to join the top ranks with household names like Aspen and Vail. Growth in the 1990s has startled the old guard and sparked controversy here as it has everywhere in the trendy Rockies. But two things will probably help Jackson Hole retain its funky, western charm: the proximity of national park land never to be developed and the wild nature of the ski mountain, with its cold midwinter temperatures, its steep terrain, its occasional wind and fog, and its waist-deep snows. More than any other ski terrain in the Lower 48, Jackson Hole feels like the Alps. Killy was right—this is a *serious* mountain.

The Lay of the Land

Imagine yourself in a balloon at 10,000 feet over the Jackson Hole valley. The Snake River runs a shallow, braided course from north to south through flat ranchland. The town of Jackson wedges into the mouth of Cache Creek Canyon near the south end of the valley. Frozen Jackson Lake stretches away to the north. Everything on the ground is coated with snow.

Straight ahead to the west the Jackson Hole ski area plunges from the summit of Rendezvous Mountain to the flat valley floor. The famous Swiss-made, red aerial tram connects Teton Village at the base with the 10,552-foot peak. To the right (north), the somewhat lower summit of Après Vous Mountain (8,481 feet) is also festooned with lifts.

Lifting your gaze farther to the north, you see the sharp granite peaks of the three Tetons: South, Middle, and Grand. French trappers on the Idaho side of the range named them the Three Breasts, and indeed, from that side the resemblance makes some sense. From the Jackson side, they look like nothing so much as serrated shark's teeth. Indian tribes knew them as the Hoary-Headed Fathers and the Three Brothers. At 13,770 feet, the Grand Teton is by far the tallest rock in what is arguably the most dramatic upthrust in the Rockies. Given the number of automobile ads shot here— to give just one example—there must be few in America who have not subliminally absorbed the Tetons' stunning silhouette.

Behind the Tetons and west almost to the Idaho border sits the Grand Targhee Resort, with its major snow accumulations and views of potato-rich Teton Valley. In fact, to get there, you have to drive into Idaho and then go back east just barely across the Wyoming border on the sunset slope of the range.

Due north of your balloon the great hump of the Yellowstone Plateau spreads across 4,000 square miles, taking up the entire northwest corner of Wyoming and parts of Idaho on the west and Montana to the north. The world's first national park, Yellowstone attracts increasing numbers of winter visitors. Some come to view the bison, moose, and the elk. Others ride snow coaches or snowmobiles in to see Old Faithful. Still others cross-country ski into what remains, especially in winter, a vast, nearly roadless wilderness.

It's a 12-mile drive from the town of Jackson to the Teton Village base. Skiers stay at both places. The Village tends toward condos and upscale inns. Jackson, while it has gained tone in recent years, is still long on less-expensive motels and bed-and-breakfasts.

The ski mountain itself, for all its mega-acreage, retains a simple layout. There is just one base, out of which radiate the tram, the gondola, and two of the six chairlifts. The easiest skiing flows down from the north through

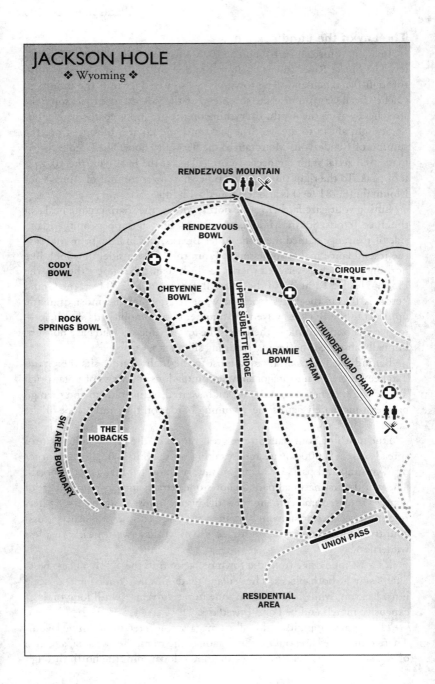

JACKSON HOLE
❖ Wyoming ❖

RENDEZVOUS MOUNTAIN

CODY BOWL

RENDEZVOUS BOWL

CIRQUE

CHEYENNE BOWL

UPPER SUBLETTE RIDGE

ROCK SPRINGS BOWL

LARAMIE BOWL

TRAM

THUNDER QUAD CHAIR

THE HOBACKS

SKI AREA BOUNDARY

UNION PASS

RESIDENTIAL AREA

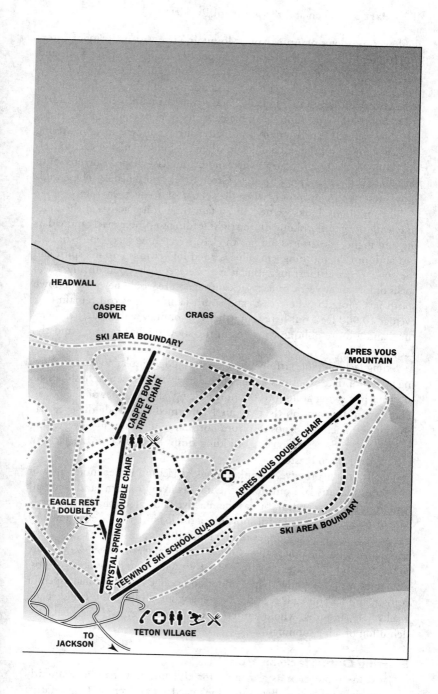

HEADWALL

CASPER BOWL

CRAGS

SKI AREA BOUNDARY

APRES VOUS MOUNTAIN

CASPER BOWL TRIPLE CHAIR

CRYSTAL SPRINGS DOUBLE CHAIR

APRES VOUS DOUBLE CHAIR

EAGLE REST DOUBLE

TEEWINOT SKI SCHOOL QUAD

SKI AREA BOUNDARY

TETON VILLAGE

TO JACKSON

the lower meadows of Après Vous Mountain. The vast majority of intermediate terrain resides above on the upper two-thirds of Après Vous and just south in the Casper Bowl region. Farther south, under the Bridger Gondola, the Gros Ventre Valley cuts a deep gouge through the gut of the mountain. Gros Ventre means "big belly," and it was the name of a local Indian tribe. South of Gros Ventre and beneath the spidery cables of the tram, Jackson's vaunted expert terrain dominates, although there are a smattering of escape routes for the less bold. And when the bold themselves get to feeling cramped inbounds, there are three more hourglass-shaped canyons south of the marked terrain: Rock Springs, Green River, and Pinedale. These wild-snow preserves are open only when the ski patrol deems them safe.

The mountain looks vaguely like a fan, three miles across at the ridge line, with the gentlest skiing on the right leading to progressively more daring and higher-elevation skiing to the left. Everything faces, more or less, east and into the morning sun. This is good for warming up the spirit and the snow on cold mornings. But it is not necessarily good during warm spells or low-snow years. In fact, Jackson's exposure would never work down south in Colorado, where east- and south-facing slopes can remain bare even at 10,000 feet. But here in northern Wyoming, with colder temperatures and a more oblique winter sun, the snow quality remains (mostly) exquisite.

Skiing Jackson Hole artfully often involves judging solar angles and moving to appropriate exposures. If the open, largely treeless southern slopes are too soft, just swing around to the north-facing, shadier sides of the bowls. There are nine major bowls, two purely intermediate, inside the everyday boundaries. Each has exposures from north around to south—everything but true west. So searching out or hiding from the sun is a puzzle Jackson Hole skiers love to master.

Finally, it is instructive, I think, to look at Jackson Hole's mountain not as a series of runs laid out down the hill, as many eastern (and western) American ski areas appear, but as the massive fault block that it is, mostly bare of trees and covered with snow like a thick white rug thrown down by the gods over the rocky bones of the land. Runs, per se, don't exist here. Some names on the trail map—*Cirque,* for example, or the *Hobacks*— are so big that they have literally hundreds of ways down and hundreds of possible lines. You follow the shapes underfoot, dodge the occasional aspen or conifer, and let your skis seek the ever-changing fall line. You could spend weeks here, months, whole winters and not know every line. That's the definition of a big mountain.

Starting Out at Jackson Hole

Jackson's reputation as a magnet for cliff jumpers may have unfairly obscured its gentler side. Beginners don't need a lot of terrain to get started on, and Jackson's Eagle's Rest and Teewinot chairs provide plenty of long, well-groomed moving sidewalks. Eagle's Rest, with its namesake run plus *Pooh Bear* and *Antelope Flats,* is the true first-time beginners' chair. It takes off near the Bridger Center, a new, family-oriented structure that houses the Kid's Ranch child-care center, ski school, lift ticket offices, and Jackson Hole Sports shop. The ski school meetingplace is right out front. You can drop skis and skiers off at the door, then return a short distance to day parking in the upper lot. (The lower parking lot, the first one you come to off Teton Village Road, makes more sense for skiers who plan to ride the tram up Rendezvous Mountain.)

First-time beginners should always take lessons. There is so much to gain by doing so and so much wasted time likely if you don't. Jackson's ski and snowboard school was run for 20-plus years by Pepi Stiegler, an outgoing Austrian who won three Olympic medals in 1960 and 1964. Now in his sixties, Pepi is the director of skiing and still exudes a youthful love of snow and graceful movement. Pepi hosts tours at 1:30 P.M. daily for those that want to learn from one of the best skiers ever.

After Eagle's Rest, the Teewinot Ski School Quad (the name is Shoshoni for "pinnacles") climbs a very gradual three-fifths of a mile up Après Vous. *Lower Werner* and *Lower Teewinot* trails shouldn't scare even the most timid novice, but they do have to accommodate occasional faster skiers coming down off *Upper Werner* and *St. Johns.* Both are equipped with snowmaking to guarantee good cover.

Wide-Open Intermediate Spaces

One piece of the (theoretically) perfect terrain progression Jackson Hole lacks is the transition zone between novices and genuine intermediates. By novices I mean second-day skiers or more timid veterans who can turn and stop on green runs but can't yet handle steeper pitches and higher speeds. Generally speaking, Jackson's slopes tend to leap directly from very gentle to exhilarating and wide-open cruising.

There is one marvelous route off the top of Après Vous Lift that is perfect for transitional intermediates. *Togwotee Pass Traverse* to *South Pass Traverse* sweeps back and forth across a big chunk of the mountain for six glorious miles. It is essentially an access road but an exquisitely long and varied one. It's a great way to give yourself the tour. The route intersects much of the intermediate terrain served by the Après Vous Lift, so you have an opportunity to check out the snow conditions, the grooming, and the look and feel of runs you may wish to try later.

Novices and low intermediates should under no circumstances attempt the skiing off the tram. That is not to say you shouldn't ride it once and then turn around and ride it back down. The trip up is an experience in itself, especially on a clear day. (On a snowy day or a big powder day, the tram packs full like a sardine can; it's tough to secure a spot by a window, and even if you do luck out, the steamy breath of all those powderhounds makes seeing anything mere wishful thinking.) The top is another story, though. With good weather, the panorama, not to mention the altitude, can be breathtaking. The Tetons leap up to the north. Cody Peak and Cody Bowl (named, of course, for Buffalo Bill) looks like a many-layered chocolate cake to the south, and to the east the valley floor, so far below, really does look like a hole.

Solid blue intermediates will find Jackson Hole a kind of heaven. The percentage of intermediate terrain may lag behind that allotted to experts (40 percent), but the length and quality of the runs compares with any of the cruising magnets, from Snowmass to Big Sky.

The easiest descents will once again be found on Après Vous. *Upper Werner, Hanna,* and *Teewinot Gully* have the wide-open, big-mountain feel that so epitomizes Jackson. Over in the Casper Bowl region, *Easy Does It* or *Timbered Island* to *Sundance Gully* provides 2,200 vertical feet of mellow, bump-free sliding, bigger than most whole mountains. To get to Casper, slide across from Après Vous on the *Togwotee Pass Traverse* or ski *Sundance* from the top of the Bridger gondola and take the *South Pass Traverse.* Casper is such a hit with intermediates that Jackson's only full-fledged, on-mountain restaurant sits near the base of Casper Lift. Another reason to ski here: At 1:30 P.M. Monday through Friday, Pepi Stiegler meets at the top of Casper to ski with the guests. How many gold, silver, and bronze medalists do you get to ski with in a lifetime?

For those who want to add a bit more pitch—and Jackson's spaciousness inspires swooping, hawklike skiing—the choices are myriad and spread across the mountain. Starting on the right again (looking at the trail map), two beautiful burners roll down the shapes of Après Vous. *Moran* to *Lower Werner* would make a super giant slalom course, pitching like mammoth ocean swells from flat to steep to flat skiing as continuous transition. *St. Johns,* over on the east side of the chair, is rated double blue, not because it's any steeper really, but for its narrower, serpentine course through sparse glades.

The runs are a little shorter over on Casper, but so is the lift ride, which is only eight minutes. Left or right at the top of the chair, everything is tilted just right for linking big turns with no fear of dropping off the edge of the world (which, as we shall see, is *not* the case on some of the black diamond stuff). North of the Casper high point, *Sleeping Indian* and *Wide Open* may grow occasional bumps—good, round intermediate ones. South of the chair most everything is groomed. *Camp Ground* and *Timbered Island* are especially nice as they meander through sheltering stands of evergreens. Beware *Sundance Gully* at rush hour, which is usually just late in the afternoon. Skiers returning to base from the Gros Ventre / Thunder lift areas spill into the gully, adding high-speed traffic to the more cautious right-laners.

Next up for intermediates is the great central gut of the mountain, the *Amphitheater,* between the Bridger gondola and the Thunder chair. This region is not exclusively blue, as the Casper primarily is, but I believe it is the finest pure intermediate terrain on the mountain, particularly for stronger intermediates. You get there by sliding the *Amphitheater Traverse* from the Casper top station or *Lupine Way* from the top of the Bridger gondola. Quite solid skiers can also get there by riding the tram, skiing the fickle *Rendezvous Bowl* to *Gros Ventre Traverse.* I say fickle because, even though Rendezvous is a black diamond on the map, depending on snow and visibility it can ski anywhere from a relatively easy blue to a nasty, white-out, wind-whipped, genuine expert trial.

Once at the top of Thunder Lift, which has just been upgraded from a rather slow double to a fixed-grip quad, the choices are European in scope. South of the ridge defined by the tram line, *Grand* plunges through fields of mostly buried tree tops. It's usually groomed and fast. *Laramie Bowl,* which used to be all expert, now sports an intermediate route right down the throat. It's an exciting trip, especially for skiers new to western, big-bowl skiing. Both *Grand* and *Laramie Bowl* drop onto *South Pass Traverse,* which leads back to Thunder base.

The choices off the north side of the ridge are even better. The snow is colder and shadier, and the main route, *Upper Amphitheater,* descends some of the most interesting, constantly changing terrain anywhere. The first north-facing drop below *Expert Chutes* offers lines from relatively easy on your right to steep and bumpy if you swing around to your left. Then the route dives through a series of big rolls and funnels perfect for banking, letting the terrain ski you. Finally, it spits you onto the giant *Amphitheater* plain, where you can turn or not turn. In fact, it's a great place to mess with terminal velocity, a surprisingly accessible and instructive reality even for intermediate skiers. Just pick a quiet moment trafficwise, stand tall and forward on your feet, like a bowsprit, and let 'em roll. On a pitch like *Amphitheater* you will stop accelerating at about 25 or 30 miles per hour. Your weight and gravity and the air pushing against you have reached equilibrium. It's a very freeing sensation. You can actually lean against the air. You will not keep accelerating forever. A caution: Try this only in uncrowded situations and only where you feel completely comfortable letting the skis run. *Lower Gros Ventre,* the main route back to the Village, is generally not the place to experiment with terminal velocity. It's a great snaking gully in which to go fast, but it can be busy and the pitch is generally too steep to eschew turning altogether.

Amphitheater and the Thunder Lift are so popular you may run into lift lines here in the heart of the day; try the Sublette quad chair for shorter lines. One final intermediate option, and it's a good one for skiers who can handle *Laramie Bowl:* At the bottom of the bowl you'll find the Sublette quad chair, another fixed-grip quad. (Detachable quads can move up to twice as fast.) From the top here, you can cut a long, exhilaratingly scenic semicircle around *Cheyenne Bowl.* The route slices beneath *Rendezvous Bowl* on *Hanging Rock* trail, then out along a high ridge to *Rendezvous Trail,* a double blue with no big surprises, just a long, consistently fine ride back to the Sublette Lift and *South Pass Traverse,* the all-important artery connecting most sections of this spread-out mountain.

Lunch on the Hill

Thunder habitués often don't want to stop skiing; they're having so much fun, but in the end they can't resist the good smells emanating from a tiny shack next to the chair. There used to be a more substantial eatery here, but a huge avalanche—a rare, 100-year phenomenon—swept it away. Now there's this little Thunder snack shack and a smattering of picnic tables in the sun. The folks inside serve up killer hot chocolate on those cold powder days. If it's nice out, I like to take my time with a melon-size bread bowl that's filled with homemade stew or soup of the day. Not to worry about the next avalanche. Improved control techniques and better patrol access to start zones on the Headwall have all but eliminated the risk.

If you're skiing Casper, the Casper Restaurant at the base of Caspar chair offers better-than-average cafeteria fare and a spacious sunny deck. Beginners are pretty much consigned to the village base, but this is no gastronomic loss. Nick Wilson's in the Clocktower building has great chili, fries, and homemade baked goods. You can find the obligatory, postprandial espresso just inside the double doors of the slopeside Village Center.

One more place to grab a quick lunch. (This mountain is so good, you'll not often be tempted to linger over a Euro-style feast.) This is in the low building hunkered onto the summit of Rendezvous Peak. It houses the ski patrol room and a small but newly remodeled eatery called Corbet's Cabin. The name resonates for Jackson aficionados as the name of the legendary mountain man and as the moniker given to Jackson's most infamous cliff jump, the airborne entrance into *Corbet's Couloir.*

The food here is minimalist; it's really just fuel to get you back out into the powder. Most is preprepared, and all of it must be shuttled up in the morning via the tram. But this is not in any way a criticism. I've had a cold drink and a monster oatmeal-raisin cookie up there that I believed at the time to be ambrosia from the gods.

Jackson for Experts

The aerial tram is the key to Jackson's expert skiing, and the tram society is the soul of the enterprise. Fifty-five people load into each of the fire engine–red cars. Some of the veterans inevitably moo as the last two or three ski patrolmen back into the crowd like human cattle prods and slide the door closed. Skis clack together, boots shuffle for room, nylon shoulders swish against other nylon shoulders, and finally the lot of you swing gently away from the dock and glide up the cable 2.4 miles and 4,139 vertical feet in ten minutes.

Steamy breath fogs the windows. The pros bring napkins from Nick Wilson's Cowboy Cafe next door and stuff them into their goggles. This way moisture from your forehead doesn't condense on the inside of the goggles. Before I learned this trick, I stepped out at the top on a cold morning and found I had the optical equivalent of shower-stall glass for goggles. It took me ten minutes inside the warming hut to chip them clear.

At the top the same 55 people trundle out and down the metal stairs to the snow. This is the great beauty of the tram. For ten minutes, until the next car reaches the summit, the world is yours. Just you and 54 buddies with all of Rendezvous Mountain at your ski tips.

You could slide down the *East Ridge* a couple hundred yards and watch the bird men and women leap into *Corbet's Couloir*. Depending on recent storm and wind conditions, it may be anywhere from a 5- to a 25-foot drop from the cornice to the first turn. About four out of five launch right out of their bindings on impact, sailing into the shady blue snow and strewing gear in what is known in the parlance as a "yard sale." One in five touches down at the right place at the right angle and survives to arc high-speed turns between the yellow rock walls and out into the sunlight at the bottom.

One of my favorite runs is down the *East Ridge* past *Corbet's* to *Tensleep Bowl*, a luscious, low-angle field dotted with rocks the size of houses at various angles of repose, giving the place the look and feel of a tumbling glacier. The powder stays untracked here longer than most other spots on the mountain.

Beyond *Tensleep*, you have the option (that's the great thing about Jackson—you always have multiple options) to drop into steep rollovers of *Expert Chutes* or circumvent them and cut to the easy throat of *Upper Amphitheater* or traverse out into the vast, treeless teacup known as the *Cirque*. The *Cirque* faces east and south, so it absorbs a lot of solar radiation, which means slush and/or ice on some days. But if you catch it early on a powder morning, what a ride! Nearly 1,000 vertical feet of uninterrupted, laundry-chute steep, falling-dream turns to the calm at the center of *Amphitheater*. Not for the faint of technique or heart. But, like a lot of Jackson's steeps, give it a couple of days and it will raise the level of your game.

You'll find Jackson's mogul meisters clustered primarily on the Thunder Lift, where north-facing shots through the trees generate big, soft, stair-step bumps. *Paint Brush, Thunder,* and *Riverton Bowl* are the main pitches. *Tower Three Chute,* when it's open—and it isn't open when the snow is thin or too hard—is a kind of litmus test of extreme mogul skiing. One slip and you're in for the full ride to the bottom.

There are more good bumps in the three bowls south of the tram: *Rendezvous, Laramie,* and *Cheyenne.* The bumps tend to develop on the north slopes, where the snow stays soft. The south-facing sides of the bowls (the skier's left) receive more sun and less traffic. There are always bump-free lines to be found in each of the bowls.

Below *Cheyenne Bowl* is a very special zone called *The Hobacks.* These are a series of three, almost treeless, 2,000-foot ridges and the gullies between them. They are saved just for powder mornings when conditions are perfect. Moguls don't have a chance to grow, so every time *The Hobacks* are open, it's a thigh-burning, powder-breathing, whipped-cream orgy: the best lift-served pure powder terrain in the Rockies.

The only thing to rival it might be the out-of-bounds country just south of Jackson Hole's southern boundary. You can see into *Cody Bowl* from the top of the tram. This is where the U.S. National Powder 8 contest is staged every March. Teams of two skiers from all around the West lay down the most rhythmic, perfectly shaped eights they can. When it's all over, 2,000 exquisitely braided turns cover the face like an early American rug.

You can walk to and ski *Cody,* as well as *Rock Springs, Green River,* and *Pinedale* bowls, in this progression to the south, but only when the patrol has deemed them safe and opened the gate near the top of *Rendezvous Bowl.* You must first stop in at the patrol room in Corbet's Cabin and sign out, tell them where you are going, and demonstrate that you do in fact know where you are going. Avalanche locators are highly recommended.

For those who may have ridden the tram with no idea whatsoever of where they'd like to go, Jackson has a very nice service called the Mountain Hosts. Every hour on the hour mountain orientation tours leave the top of the mountain. Mountain Hosts are also available at the Clocktower building at the base.

A final note on the tram. The first tram leaves the dock at 9 A.M., and the final car departs at 3:30 P.M. Be in line early if it's a powder day. New snow of eight inches or more brings the local hounds out by the hundreds.

Dining in Teton Village and the Town of Jackson

The most famous place in the Village to go for an after-ski beer is the Mangy Moose, the raucous, barnlike, longtime local hangout. The Moose has whole airplanes hanging from the ceiling and ancient skis nailed to the walls, live music, good munchies, and a surprisingly varied average-priced dinner menu. Other options for drinks and food after skiing include the Pub in the new Resort Hotel or Beaver Dicks in the Inn at Jackson.

The Alpenhof Lodge, right across from the tram building, serves continental specialties featuring veal and wild game, and the newly remodeled Resort Hotel of Jackson (formerly known as the Sojourner) serves great barbecue in the Pub downstairs and fine fare in Henessey's upstairs.

Down in the town of Jackson informal western cuisine is the norm. Bubba's Bar-B-Que Restaurant serves up such succulent ribs that there's usually a waiting line in the cramped but happy entry. Happy in part because you need to bring your own six-pack to Bubba's, and what better way to while away the time until your table is ready?

The Cadillac Grille has in recent years carved a niche with its Art Deco atmosphere, huge burgers, and salad bar.

A couple of blocks off the main square with its famous elk antler arches is the Lame Duck. They serve very credible Chinese with private tearooms and take-out orders.

A visit to Jackson would not be complete without a visit to the Million Dollar Cowboy Bar right in the Town Square. It has western dancing and saddle barstools. Most locals wouldn't be caught dead in the place. They are more likely to be down at the Americana Snow King Resort in the Shady Lady Saloon boogying to the best live music in the valley—everything from reggae to the newest alternative rock.

JACKSON HOLE DATA

Mountain Statistics

Vertical feet	4,139 feet
Base elevation	6,311 feet
Summit elevation	10,450 feet
Longest run	4.5 miles
Average annual snowfall	400 inches
Number of lifts	1 aerial tramway; 1 8-person gondola 6 chairs: 3 quads, 1 triple, 2 doubles; 1 surface lift
Uphill capacity	8,624 skiers per hour
Skiable terrain	2,500 acres
Opening date	early December
Closing date	mid-April
Snowboarding	Yes

Transportation

By car About 90 miles east of Idaho Falls, Idaho, on U.S. Highways 26 and 89, and 270 miles north of Salt Lake City, Utah, on U.S. Highway 89. The START Bus connects the town of Jackson with Teton Village from 7 A.M. to 11 P.M. $2 each way.

By plane Via American, Delta, SkyWest, Continental Express, United, and United Express from Salt Lake City and Chicago. The Jackson Hole airport is 10 minutes from both the town of Jackson and Teton Village. Airport and many lodging shuttles service all flights.

Key Phone Numbers

Ski Area Information
  (307) 733-2292
Snow Report (307) 733-2291
Jackson Hole Resort
  Lodging (800) 443-8613
Jackson Hole Central
  Reservations (800) 443-6931
www.jacksonhole.com

INSIDE STORY

Ski the Big One

Longtime Jackson Hole marketing director Harry Baxter had sought for years to find a proper vehicle to convey just how big Jackson's skiing was. He wanted to show that "dollah for dollah" (Harry is a transplanted New Englander with infectious smile lines), "you get more skiin' at Jackson Hole than any othah area in the country."

His idea: a personal achievement award called Ski the Big One, wherein anyone who racks up 100,000 vertical feet or more in a week of skiing gets a Ski the Big One pin and a certificate written in calligraphy by Harry's wife, Martha. Ski 300,000 feet or 500,000 feet or a million feet over time and you can receive bronze, silver, and gold belt buckles. Harry has 27,500 names in his computer, names of people who have made at least the first level. They've given out 340 gold belt buckles since the program started. One man, D. O. Montgomery of Redmond, Washington, is working on his fifth gold buckle; his total through the 1994 season was 4,297,000 feet. It's a privileged club, and just one more manifestation of the extended family atmosphere that, along with the less formal Tram Society, gives Jackson the comfortable feeling of reunion.

The 100,000-foot goal is really not that daunting given Jackson's ultimate uphill weapon, the 4,139-foot vertical of the tram. Harry proved it himself with an awesome 66,000-foot-vertical day on 16 tram rides a few years back. You need only average 17,000 feet per day for six days to chalk up 100,000 feet for the week. That's a leisurely two or three trams, plus a few laps on the Thunder, Après Vous, or Casper lift. The system works like this: Pick up a Ski the Big One scorecard with your lift ticket for the week, simply mark the chair rides as you ride them, and then total the vertical at the end of the day (everybody's on the honor system). Then, at the end of your stay, present your card and vertical total at the Guest Services Desk in the tram building to receive your certificate.

While you're there, take a minute to glance through the record book. Eighty-two-year-old Charlie Nebel from New Jersey made his million in 11 weeks of skiing over two years. His 79-year-old wife wrote, "He's crazy, just skis too fast for me!" Then there is Sadamitsu Tanzawa, who got his gold in 30 days. He said, "I had only two ski seasons. So I hurry to achieve." A nine-year-old Californian named Mary Wholey racked up a million feet in three seasons of skiing with her numbers-mad parents. There is a Swedish couple who managed 150,000 feet in just three days. "Those were three hard, smooth, clear days," Harry assured me. I received my certificate in February 1985, when I totaled 157,806 feet in five days at Jackson. I am especially proud of my numbers because almost every one of those turns were two feet under the snow. That week the heavens would not stop snowing. I woke up every morning to another helping of fresh powder. Since the visibility was not the best, my favorite route down *Rendezvous Bowl* to *Ten Sleep Bowl* to *Gros Ventre* was decidedly slow. I had to work hard to reach my goal, and I couldn't help it that every turn was a slow-motion powder baptism, the shimmering stuff flowing over my shoulders like white silk scarves.

Grand Targhee's address says a lot about the place: Grand Targhee Resort, Alta, Wyoming, via Driggs, Idaho. In other words, you can't get there from here without really meaning to. State borders, those clean, straight lines favored by early western mapmakers, don't mean much when it comes to a genuine identity.

Named for both the Grand Teton that looms directly to the east and a renegade chief of the Bannock tribe in the 1870s, Grand Targhee sits, technically speaking, in far-western Wyoming. But its soul (and its zip code) reside a couple miles across the border in Idaho. The quickest way to get here is from Jackson Hole on the eastern side of the Teton upthrust. Just drive over 8,431-foot Teton Pass, beneath the awesome sweep of Glory Bowl (a very large avalanche path that doubles as a springtime hike-and-ski mecca for local hard cores), and then down through Victor, Idaho (population 292), and north into the Teton Valley. From Driggs, with its square, western storefronts and woodsmoke haze, drive back east onto the western slope of the Tetons to tiny Alta, Wyoming. It's simple, and it takes about an hour to drive in good weather. Access from Idaho Falls to the south and from Bozeman, Montana, up north will take much, much longer.

The trip is worth every minute. Targhee is one of the last unpolished jewels of American skiing. It is a beautiful, spacious, well-designed, modestly priced, family-oriented ski mountain that just happens to get more powder than any other resort in the Rockies except Alta, Utah. (Something magic in that name?) The average is just over 500 inches per season. They don't have any snowmaking because they don't need it. Their motto is "Snow from heaven, not hoses."

On my first trip I skied around taking care not to nip the branches of the little evergreens that dot the slopes like toy soldiers on white bed sheets. Then somebody told me they were actually the tops of mature, 20-foot trees. So prodigious are the snowfalls that fully half of Targhee's mountain (1,500 acres) is reserved for snowcat powder skiing. On the other 1,500 acres—1,200 of which are designated ungroomed powder reserves—you can ski 9 A.M. to 4 P.M. off trail and never cross your own tracks and never even see your skis under the crystalline surface.

But Targhee is no Jackson Hole; it is no magnet for the cornice-jumping, extreme-skiing Doug Coombses of the world. Most of the terrain is tilted a few degrees shy of scary. Seventy percent of the map is rated intermediate, and the area has developed a reputation as a near-perfect place to *learn* to ski powder, to touch a tentative toe onto the off-piste.

The village is designed around skiing families, conservative Idahoans for the most part, but it is developing a growing destination clientele from elsewhere. Everything is clustered in one woody meadow: three lodges with room for a total of 300 guests, four restaurants, one bar (the Teton Valley and indeed most of eastern Idaho tends to be staunchly Mormon), one outdoor pool, two hot tubs, rental and retail shops, a video arcade, a general store, the children's center and . . . and that's it. Eat, sleep, play games, and ski powder. What else do you need?

The Big Picture

Back when mountain men combed the Tetons for beaver, the Teton Valley was known as Pierre's Hole. Trappers from French Canada were the first in the region, and it was they who named the granite peaks cresting the range les Trois Tetons, the three breasts. On this western side the spiky, pink granite fins dominate far more dramatically than they do on the Jackson side of the crest. When late afternoon sun pours across the valley, turning snow the color of cherry blossoms, and the Tetons become a rich apricot color, it's easy to agree with past Targhee ski school director Gene Palmer, who calls this "the *Grand* side of the Tetons."

Palmer was typical of the genuine western ambience that pervades Targhee. (Everybody here wore cowboy hats before Billy the Kidd dreamed of donning his.) Palmer lived down the road in Rexburg, Idaho, and was a spud farmer in the off season. He was so country he was embarrassed a few years ago to drive down the streets of his hometown with those new, pink K2 skis tied to his station wagon roof.

Palmer's domain was known as Fred's Mountain, which has the lift-served skiing. Next to it is the snowcat preserve of Peaked Mountain. Both are part of the same, uniformly tilted fault block. The front side (west side) is perfectly angled for skiing. The back side is closed, a jagged layer cake of cliff bands plunging into South Leigh Creek Canyon. Adding to the front side's skiability is an ancient burn that sheared most of the trees. So what you have now are long, near-naked ridges—more like wrinkles, really—scoring the full 2,200-foot vertical with shallow, inviting bowls and the gullies between. Names on the trail map sometimes refer to whole drainages where a skier might scribe any of a hundred lines. Big chunks of real estate have no names at all. Most of the terrain is wide open, fluid, sculptural the way a Michelangelo marble is devoid of straight lines.

There are but three chairlifts. Three chairs for 1,500 acres. A supremely simple and efficient layout. Everything flows back to the center of the compact village. Until recently, there were not enough skiers to result in a lift line here. Due to increasing notoriety, the number one chair, the base-to-summit Bannock double, sometimes used to back up. Now the high-speed detachable Dreamcatcher quad has taken care of any lines.

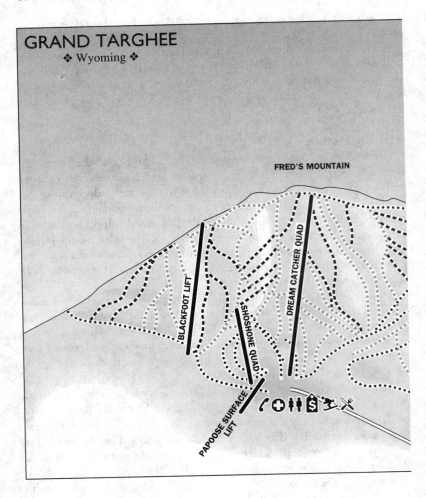

Beginners: A Separate Place

Few areas of any size can match the quality and safety of Targhee's beginner terrain. A gentle Mitey Mite surface tow serves a short run right outside the Kid's Club cabin at the edge of the village. This is where they teach the first-timers gliding maneuvers, turns, and stops.

A few steps away the Shoshone quad chair climbs 1,800 feet through sunny aspen glades to the main learning runs. *Big Horn, Little Big Horn,* and *The Meadows* are completely free of faster traffic as they arc back to the base, while *Big Scout* ventures into the zone around the base of the Dreamcatcher

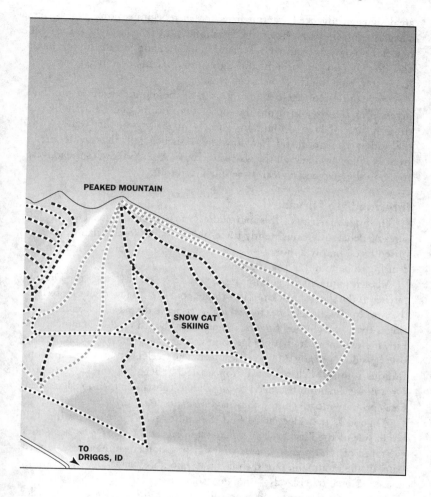

quad and thus intersects intermediate routes off the upper mountain. Big Scout in particular serves as a return thoroughfare for skiers coming down off the popular *Sitting Bull* ridge. But true beginners and novices who stay north of the Shoshone chair will never feel the swoosh of speeding commuters.

Interestingly enough, the wide-open glades below *South Street* are marked "Intermediate Powder Area" on the trail map. I've never seen this anywhere else. Powder Reserves with no trails or names per se, these are places that never feel the weight of a grooming machine. Depending on the pitch, they are designated advanced, intermediate, and even beginner powder areas. Yes, a beginner powder area! It's off the Shoshone Lift to the far right as the skier descends. No turns required. Just stand in balance and feel the ski tips bend and float as you run straight through snow that hisses and sparkles and leaves soft, blue trenches where you pass.

A final option for novices seeking a top-of-the-mountain adventure: The *Teton Vista Traverse* runs from the top of the Dreamcatcher Lift along the summit ridge of Fred's Mountain, with the huge views of the Grand, Middle, and South Tetons, and then down the V-shaped gully that divides Fred's from Peaked Mountain all the way to the base. At 2.8 miles, it's the longest route on the map and a great, sweeping green tour.

Intermediate Nirvana

The huge majority of this mountain is rated intermediate. That's 1,000 acres of deliciously, consistently tilted blue terrain. No cliff bands, no surprised faces, hardly a mogul in sight. Just some of the best, big-mountain cruising to be found in the West.

All of it pours off the summit ridge and is accessed by either the Dreamcatcher or the shorter Blackfoot Lift to the north. With few trees to interfere, the runs follow the fall lines in two major concave drains and atop the three ridges that, like chubby fingers, define them. South of the Dreamcatcher Lift, the two most dramatic ridge routes, *Crazy Horse* and *Wild Willie,* dive side-by-side for nearly 2,000 vertical feet. The treeless expanse and the continuous rolling pitch have a European feel. The other big ridge off the Dreamcatcher summit is called *Sitting Bull.* It runs along the top edge of the area's primary mogul chutes, the *Good Medicine/Bad Medicine* area.

As good as the ridges are, I find the gullies even more interesting. Off either side of the Blackfoot Lift, *Blackfoot Bowl* and *Chief Joseph Bowl* offer the rarest of intermediate treats: wide-open, groomed skiing in the cupped palm of the mountain, plus the playful terrain idiosyncrasies—banks, rolls, and occasional tree islands—that give shape to a descent.

In between the groomed blue runs are miles of intermediate powder reserves. Try one whipped-cream turn off the packed trails or, if you can, spend a month sleuthing the soft areas; these are probably the most accessible and the most reliable and least threatening powder zones in the Rockies. The biggest is the vast *Sunnyside Bowl* under the Dreamcatcher Lift. But, as the name implies, this exposure receives a lot of solar during clear periods and may not have the best snow quality. Wind, as area personnel will readily admit, is also a factor. Targhee faces straight into the oncoming weather; there are no buffer ranges. Thus the extraordinary snowfalls. But it also means some storms roar through with winds that ripple the snow surface into a variety of slabs and crusts, some more forgiving than others. The exposed ridge lines are generally hardest hit. The best snow usually settles on the lee shoulders and in the trees. In fact, the returning forests cluster almost exclusively in northside lee pockets.

That's where intermediates should look for the most forgiving powder. The *Lost Squaw* and *North Boundary* areas to the skier's far right off the Blackfoot Lift protect bowers of deep snow in the lee of aspens and evergreens. In a windy period, the lower-elevation slopes offer the best protection. The Powder Reserve below *South Street*, for example, stays relatively sheltered.

Strong intermediates who particularly want to master, or at least grow comfortable in, powder should consider a day or two on Peaked Mountain riding one of the area's three snowcats to uncut stashes (see "Inside Story," Snowcat Skiing, page 420). A recent revolution in powder skis has made floating in the deep stuff much more accessible to nonheroes. The skis are affectionately known as "fat boys," and their greater surface area, nearly twice that of regular alpine skis, floats you up high in the snow, reducing resistance and greasing the turns. Targhee's ski shop has fat boys to rent.

The preponderance of terrain on Peaked Mountain is intermediate as well, and there are more trees here than on Fred's. Snow quality improves with shade, and the definition provided by the trees helps visibility during storm or fog episodes. Sign up for half- or full days with the cats. Expect eight to ten runs for approximately 10,000 to 20,000 vertical feet. Full days include a guide, snack, and lunch. Special half-day powder lessons are also available. Targhee encourages snowboarders and telemarkers to ride with the cats too.

Targhee for Good Skiers

For several years Targhee has hosted advanced ski clinics with the Northface Extreme Team, comprising two sets of extreme-skiing, film-starring brothers, the Des Lauriers and the Egans. One of the four kicked off a terrifying cornice avalanche on a permanently closed section of Peaked Mountain for the film cameras a couple of years back. But other than this piece of genuine hazard, I'm hard pressed to think of where the brothers could go on this mountain to teach steep technique. Powder, yes, of course. But really steep? I'm not sure.

There are two semiprecipitous zones on Fred's Mountain where most of the black diamonds are clustered. One drops from the *Sitting Bull* ridge into the area's only true north-facing hillside. The trees are relatively thick here, and the snow is cold and soft. The *Headwall, Good Medicine, Bad Medicine,* and *The Ugly* fall straight and steep into *Chief Joseph Bowl.* The last two, *Bad Medicine* and *The Ugly,* grow the biggest moguls on the mountain.

The other expert zone hugs the south border of Fred's, where gentle, south-facing snow fields nose over into the Teton Vista Traverse. Here you'll find a series of short, steep shots through tree fingers known as *Lost Groomers Chute, Patrol Chute, Instructor's Chute,* and so on. The term "chute" may be a teensy bit misleading, especially if you are familiar with Alta Chutes at Jackson Hole, for example. These are nowhere near the elevator-shaft category, but they do roll over nicely and can be a real challenge in hard or wind-blown conditions.

In any event, the goal at Targhee is not the search for base-baring steeps. Good skiers are rewarded the same way intermediates are, with hundreds of acres of wild-snow terrain, an abundance of terrain that practically guarantees a new sense of freedom and expression.

The North Boundary glades hide many days worth of powder lines. On the other side of Blackfoot Lift *Steam Vent* and *Fallen Timber* offer myriad lines through random, maverick trees. The biggest expanse is off to the south of Dreamcatcher, where empty, oceanic shapes almost never get completely tracked out. There is no name on the trail map, but the ski school calls this area Instructor's after the many powder lessons taught there.

Good skiers who do not link up with the snowcats for at least one day are missing a rare opportunity. While Peaked's terrain never reaches the steepness of the Monashees, the alchemy of so many linked turns on a virgin canvas will change you and bring on random cries of delight.

There are those for whom even the semiwilderness of the snowcat preserve is not enough. For these intrepid solitude seekers and backcountry powder skiers, Targhee is a fine base from which to explore the west side of the Tetons. For a little (or a lot) of guidance, contact Carole Lowe and Glenn Vitucci at Rendezvous Ski Tours in Victor, Idaho at (208) 787-2906. They know the landscape better than anyone, and they maintain three cozy yurts in the high country for overnight tours to exquisite free-heel terrain.

Targhee Dining

All five eating establishments at Grand Targhee are located in the Rendezvous Base Lodge, where they've successfully included a little something for everyone. At the top of the heap, Skadi's Steakhouse (named for the original avalanche transceiver worn by ski patrolmen) is the fine-dining restaurant. A notch down in price and panache, the Wizard of Za serves pizza and sandwiches. Snorkels is the popular stop for latte lovers, cappuccino cravers, and espresso addicts. The chef is in at 4 A.M. every day baking pastries and starting the soup of the day. Finally, there's Wild Bill's Grill for quick breakfasts, express grille, salad bar, and so on.

The Trap Bar ("It's so much fun, you get trapped") has moved upstairs, where a new deck lords over the base and offers glorious views of the mountain.

Down the road in Alta, the Teton Teepee offers a nice dinner alternative. The Teepee is a family lodge with guest rooms in a circle around a soaring central fireplace and living/dining room. The Melehes family accepts reservations from nonguests for dinner. The camaraderie is a throwback to the days when everyone stayed at full-board lodges. The hearty food is served family-style: great steaming bowls of soup, platters of meat, baskets of rolls, all passed hand-to-hand along with introductions and tales of the day.

In Driggs, the locals' favorite is the Royal Wolf, a pub and dining room with a delightfully incongruous menu, including a couple of very good Thai dishes.

GRAND TARGHEE DATA

Mountain Data

Vertical feet	2,200 feet (lift-served), 2,800 feet (cat skiing)
Base elevation	8,000 feet
Summit elevation	10,200 feet
Longest run	2.8 miles
Average annual snowfall	500 inches
Number of lifts	1 high-speed detachable quad
	1 fixed-grip quad
	1 double chair
	1 Mighty Mite
	3 snowcats
Uphill capacity	3,600 skiers per hour
	10 skiers plus guide per snowcat
Skiable terrain	1,500 acres (lift-served), 1,500 acres (cat skiing)
Opening date	mid-November
Closing date	late April
Snowboarding	Yes

Transportation

By car About 1 hour northwest of Jackson, Wyoming, over Teton Pass, via Highways 22 and 33. About 2 hours northeast of Idaho Falls, via U.S. Highways 26, 31, and 33.

By plane Via major carriers to Jackson, Pocatello, or Idaho Falls.

Key Phone Numbers

Ski Area Information
   (800) TARGHEE
Snow Report (800) TARGHEE
Lodging Information
   (800) TARGHEE
www.grandtarghee.com

Snowcat Skiing

If heli-skiers drink Dom Perignon, then snowcat skiers settle for garden-variety champagne. They don't imbibe as many vertical feet each day, and they don't thrill to the power of flight.

But snowcat skiers do enjoy a number of advantages over their airborne brethren. First, they never fall out of the sky, and second, they never get weathered out. Storms that ground the flyboys just make skiing better for the cat skiers, and you can cat ski for a fraction of the cost of heli-skiing: under $225 a day on Targhee's Peaked Mountain, including a snack and lunch. A day at Great Divide Snow Tours in Monarch, Colorado, costs only $80. By contrast, a typical heli-ski day will run $450–550.

Snowcat skiing is often more accessible than heli-sliding. Many U.S. operations work the backsides of some pretty decent lift-served terrain. Targhee is one. Aspen is another where cats ply the untrammeled Little Annie region behind Aspen Mountain. Big Mountain, Montana, is another. They've got a special deep-snow tree preserve on the north side of the mountain open only to cat skiers.

The cats, of course, are those growling, diesel-powered grooming machines retrofitted with comfy cabins on the back for carrying up to a dozen skiers. The Targhee cats can accommodate ten skiers plus the guide; Big Mountain's cat has a used six-person gondola welded onto the back. A cat-skiing day feels very much like a heli-skiing day, only slower. Guides comb the backcountry for the best-quality snow. You clamber out, click in bindings, and drop into that creamy place where your skis never really touch bottom, where gravity lowers you like a gentle hand and cold crystals fill every wrinkle in your grin.

On the way back up steamy breath fogs the cabin windows and there's nothing to see, so you chat up new friends. The cat lurches to a stop, everyone trundles out, and you do it all again, never once crossing another skier's track. Depending on the terrain and the skill level of the group, cat skiers can make up to 15 runs a day. Eight to ten is the average; by then most people are ready for the hot tub.

If the weather is good, lunch is served on the snow: hot soup, tea, sandwiches, chocolate, fruit. Targhee's guides lay out a sumptuous spread inside a high-altitude yurt, which is a circular cloth tent that serves as a warming hut midway down Peaked's slopes. The food tastes like ambrosia in the sharp, high-elevation air. It is also essential fuel. Powder skiing all day will leave you limp of leg and emotionally spent. It is time so well spent you may be back for more. The powder skiing high is among the most addictive in the known world, and the snowcat is the surest route—short of your own foot power—for reaching the heights.

BIG SKY

Big Sky is about to hit the big time. Twenty-five years after sliding their first chairlift under their first fanny, this tiny enclave in an otherwise empty corner of southwest Montana is poised to join the ranks of household names, alongside Alta and Aspen and Park City.

A lot of people recognize the name. Perhaps it's because the developers went out on a bold marketing limb and took the name of the "big sky" state. And a lot of skiers remember that Big Sky was the brainchild of former NBC anchorman Chet Huntley. But Huntley passed away in 1974, less than four months after the resort opened. Ownership changed. The ski mountain and its attendant facilities grew slowly, albeit steadily, while visitor numbers remained tiny. But now, almost like a child who has blossomed suddenly into adulthood, Big Sky has quietly become the biggest, classiest, brassiest and best-known ski destination in the northern Rockies. The reasons have to do with location, vision, and the most exciting new lift in America, the Lone Peak Tram.

Vision first. In the sixties, Huntley, a Montana native, set out in search of a major recreational property. He found it on the West Fork of the Gallatin River north of Yellowstone National Park and south of Bozeman, a sleepy agricultural center and home to Montana State University. He and his corporate partners, which included General Electric, Chrysler, Continental Oil, Burlington Northern, and Northwest Airlines, bought 11,000 spectacular, empty acres on and around Lone Mountain. The first three chairlifts and a gondola opened for business in 1973. Then in 1974, just a few days before the grand opening of the luxurious Huntley Lodge, Huntley succumbed to lung cancer at the age of 62. Lacking Huntley's vision, the other investors decided to sell. The new owner was, and still is, Boyne USA, the family-owned, Michigan-based corporation that also owns Boyne Mountain and Boyne Highlands in Michigan, Brighton Ski Resort in Utah, and Crystal Mountain in Washington.

These folks have serious visions of their own, because today Big Sky opens over 3,500 acres of varied terrain. The lift system has expanded to include the Lone Peak Tram, four quad chairs (three high-speed), one gondola, three triples, three doubles, three other surface lifts, and the kids' Mitey Mite. What was once correctly knocked as white-bread terrain—from an expert's point of view—has been jazzed up with the addition of some of the West's most dramatic chute skiing, the A-Z Chutes off the Challenger chair. So dramatic, in fact, that movie-star extreme skiers Scot Schmidt and Tom Jüngst switched allegiance from Bridger Bowl north of Bozeman, a place of legendary steeps, to test their skills here.

Most significant, in 1996 Big Sky installed the Lone Peak Tram, a 15-passenger, single-stage, European-style lift that rises just 16 feet short of the top of Lone Mountain (11,166 feet).

The total vertical claim, I must say, illustrates the power of marketing over substance. True, Big Sky's "total" vertical is now one of the biggest in the nation, but that number involves a math trick. Jackson's vertical is all one piece, top-to-bottom; ski it without stopping if you can. To experience Big Sky's total vertical, you have to ski from the peak to the village—a substantial 3,650 vertical feet—then ride up onto adjacent Andesite Mountain and ski to its lowest point. Think of it as continuous skiable vertical versus total vertical feet.

The hot, new expert terrain complements already huge chunks of novice and intermediate cruising. There are now 1,500 hotel and condo units in the valley capable of accommodating 9,000 guests. Three airlines, Northwest, Delta, and Horizon fly full-size jets into Bozeman airport, 43 miles away.

Big Sky's location turns out to be a fortuitous blend of isolation and accessibility, wilderness and notoriety. When you are on the mountain, or in the base village during certain times of light, there is a palpable sense of seclusion. It's almost islandlike. It's as if the cold and the quiet and the arc of the sky were indeed bigger than other places you've been.

And in fact, Big Sky is surrounded by impressive sweeps of legal wilderness, millions of acres' worth, protected forever. But the place also resonates a certain romantic chic that is growing more and more recognizable as western Montana is discovered by the outside world. Ted Turner and Jane Fonda's place is just to the north. And Peter Fonda's ranch sits just out of sight to the east. Californians by the Lexus-load fall in love with the landscape and scramble to purchase a piece of it. The cat is out of the bag. What writer William Kittredge called "the last best place" is fast becoming the best-known place in a big, formerly empty but rapidly changing state.

The Last, Best, Famous, Still Mostly Empty Place

All is not lost to tabloid America. I shared my first gondola ride up the mountain at Big Sky with a family of wheat farmers from North Dakota. The kids were really sweet and polite and excited, and Mom allowed as how

Big Sky was their favorite place to ski and "only" 12 hours from their home on the eastern plains. "Well, that's if you're speeding," she said, blushing, "which we were."

More out-of-state visitors come to Big Sky from North Dakota than from any other state. The cosmopolitan glitz of Aspen and the freeway urbanity of Vail are both still a long way off, and may, in fact, never reach the high valleys of the Madison and Gallatin ranges. The land itself may take care of that.

Three world-famous trout streams flow north off the Yellowstone Plateau toward Bozeman and Interstate 90. From east to west they are the Yellowstone, the Gallatin, and the Madison rivers. Big Sky is just off the Gallatin, the stream they used to film *A River Runs Through It*. The Madison Range, which divides the Gallatin from the Madison drainages, is Big Sky's backyard. In the center of the chain, Lone Mountain rears its volcanic-looking cone to 11,166 feet, easily the highest summit around. With treeline at about 9,000 feet, most of the vertical looms starkly white except where it is broken by cliff bands. Now lifts climb right to the summit on the big mountain, and to 8,800 feet on neighboring Andesite Mountain.

Lodging and all services are clustered in three locations along the West Gallatin. Most of the hotel and condominium beds are in the Mountain Village at the base of the lifts. The Meadow Village a few miles downvalley has some condo and private home rentals. And down at the river confluence in the Gallatin Canyon, are a number of motels and guest ranches. The Lone Mountain Ranch, one of the premier cross-country skiing destinations in the country, sits high on the valley's shoulder, overlooking the Meadow Village.

From the top of Lone Mountain on a clear day, you can see the Grand Teton 100 miles to the south, if you know which serrated bump you are looking for. The nearer views are far more spectacular. The Spanish Peaks cut a rugged, white-crested swath across the northern skyline. And off to the south, the Taylor Hilgard Wilderness peaks skyward between Big Sky and the massive vault of the Yellowstone Plateau just 18 crow-miles away. Down to the west, a long way down, you can see winter-golden fields bordering the Madison River with the Tobacco Root Mountains behind. The only signs of man's presence, besides the ski trappings, are the occasional clear-cut blocks snipped out of the forest carpet.

Much of the valley land, including Lone Mountain, is private, courtesy of railroad land grants in the last century. This is a double-edged sword for Big Sky's developers. On one hand, private land on the ski mountain means building new lifts and trails when needed without having to wade through the red tape of the public-lands approval process. Thus the quick implementation of the tram, the likes of which we will not see on public-lands

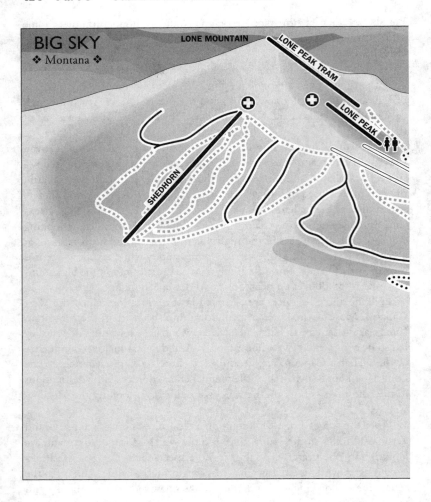

ski areas. Similarly, the Iron Horse quad and attendant trails have been carved out of the private, 25,000-acre Moonlight Basin Ranch. Easy.

On the other hand, the possibility remains that there will be more clear-cutting or other development inappropriate to the scenic values of wilderness. And more and more of the surrounding land is becoming legal wilderness. An activist environmental community has seen to that, in addition to negotiating conservation agreements with many of the region's landowners. The signs are good that Big Sky will always be a strikingly pristine place, one that reminds you over and over that skiers are privileged interlopers in an uncivilized realm.

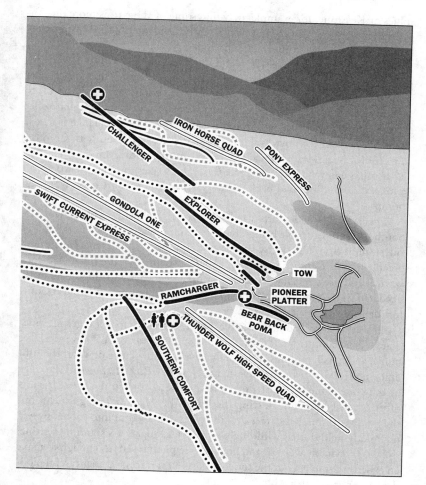

Big-Time Intermediate Skiing

The addition of new expert terrain has not detracted from Big Sky's reputation as a super intermediate mountain. Two intermediate mountains, in fact. Let's take Andesite Mountain first, the smaller but by no means lesser of the two.

This is the quickest access to intermediate terrain, thanks to the Ram-Charger high-speed quad out of the base and, on the backside, the Thunder Wolf high-speed quad. Even an expert can run his legs to rubber yoying these two burners. The skiing is long, smooth, and deliciously pitched for giant slalom cranking. In fact, intermediates familiar with the sedate blues of Keystone, for example, may find some of these runs more precipitous than they are used to. But not to worry; they are beautifully prepared, and one soon grows to appreciate the added gravity.

On the front side, *Silver Knife* and the broad *Ambush* run under the lift are guaranteed coverage thanks to snowmaking. Ambush Meadows also has a new half-pipe and terrain park. A couple of very interesting blues off to the west side of the lift, the spacious *Hangman's* and the looping roller coaster known as *Africa,* need more natural cover to open. There is a very nice escape route for novices skiing the gentler backside Southern Comfort area (or for beginners who really didn't mean to be riding up on Andesite). That run is eponymously called *Pacifier,* and it snakes through the woods on a long and winding road back to safety. *Africa* offers some good frontside bumps.

The backside divides into two distinct zones, each with its own chair. The Southern Comfort triple brings lower-level intermediates back to the Andesite summit from a perfectly sequestered, uniformly tilted, sun-worshiping green zone. *El Dorado, Sacajawea,* and *Deep South* run the full 1,250-foot vertical and provide a lot of mileage at the stage when learning skiers really need it. The 12-minute ride back up is a long one, but most Southern Comfort denizens appreciate the recovery time.

The other zone is one of Big Sky's best, especially for stronger intermediates. The Thunder Wolf quad, built in 1993, races over 1,700 vertical feet in five and a half minutes. You barely have time to glance down at the sublime, mostly wide-open terrain sailing below. *Elk Park Meadows* off the ridge of the same name is one of the ten best cruising runs in the West. It starts off innocently enough, skirting the lip of the *Mad Wolf* mogul field, but then it dives through the trees over three big rolls and out into a long, sweeping, giddy field dotted with huge, maverick Douglas firs standing sentinel over the inevitable whoops and hollers. The pitch is serious enough to make an expert want to get out the super G skis, but not so steep that careful plodders won't enjoy the rush.

Skier's left on the *Elk Park* is always kept smooth. Out in the expanse to the right, various gullies and sidehills and rollicking natural shapes are left wild. This makes for some superb powder dancing for intermediates and an increasing number of slumming experts who are hip to the warm exposure, the protection from wind, and the huge number of reps you can do on the quad.

Opposite *Elk Park Ridge* is the *Big Horn* run, skier's right facing down the lift line. This one's a classic of a different sort: a long, easy ride between forest walls that suddenly turns 90 degrees and drops into a shady, north-facing bowl and gully system, complete with high banks like Aspen's Spar Gulch, for banking big, lazy, high-speed turns back to the bottom of Thunder Wolf.

The best intermediate bumps at Big Sky grow on the lower two-thirds of *Mad Wolf,* which is rated black diamond but, except for the topmost pitch, drops gently enough to keep the moguls round. And there are a myriad ways in and out of the bumps from *Elk Park* on the left side.

A final note: Outside the Dug Out Snack Shop atop Andesite Mountain, where the three lifts converge, is a wooden bench for sitting. This has become common with the advent of snowboarders and their need to sit and click in bindings to start each run. But this bench comes equipped with screwdrivers and pliers for use by anybody who would adjust a DIN setting or fix a boot buckle or alter the stance on a freestyle board. It's a courtesy you used to see everywhere before the days of lawsuit madness. Here it's a welcome anomaly, an indication that Big Sky would be a real skier's mountain.

Blue square offerings on Lone Mountain have a very different flavor. Dropping through the trees on either side of the gondola, *Crazy Horse, Lobo,* and *Calamity Jane* belie their names and have a decidedly eastern feel: They are relatively narrow, wavy, fall-line cruisers with the occasional bump run cut a little more steeply between them. Note: One of the two original gondolas remains to serve this terrain. But the four-passenger bubble is essentially rendered obsolete by the parallel and much faster Swift Current quad chair.

Most intriguing for intermediates is the terrain off the Lone Peak triple in the huge, Euro-style, above-timber bowl just below Lone Mountain's summit cliffs and couloirs. This is genuine big-mountain skiing, with all its attendant beauties and vagaries: high winds, deep snow, shapes created by the rocks below and not by any tree cutter's hand. Two routes off the top, *Never Sweat* and *Upper Morning Star,* are cut with the cats to guarantee a packed way down. But in the right conditions, the whole 180-degree bowl can be good skiing. I've seen it when high winds smoothed and packed the whole thing, creating unlimited lines around twisted, dwarfed lodgepole pines. And when the powder falls unmolested by retreating tempests, *The Bowl* surely is one of the sweetest, easiest intermediate fall lines in the Rockies. In the spring, there are few sensations finer than banking the serpentine corn-snow walls of *Never Sweat,* like skateboarding the inside of a mammoth, porcelain bathtub.

Big Sky's longest continuous descent is from the top of the tram via Liberty Bowl to Middle Road down to the base area—six miles top to bottom. This pretty much signifies Lone Peak's excellent intermediate combo: relatively demanding and similarly rewarding high-elevation stuff and the easy, sheltered cruising of the lower mountain.

Expert Zones from A to Z

As you ride the Lone Peak triple through the gut of *The Bowl,* your eye can't help but wander the string of chutes, like claw marks on the south-facing ridge above. These are the *A-Z Chutes;* there are indeed 26 of them, more or less depending on how snow fills in between the rocks. Years before the tram they were the reason hot skiers from Bozeman, including a few extreme stars, regularly made the drive down to Big Sky. And they're still there, of course; they've just been superseded by the extreme riches offered up by the tram.

You have to work to reach the A-Z Chutes. Nobody gets there by accident. From the top of the Challenger chair, it's a hike of a few hundred feet to the ridge itself and then a ridge-line balancing act of up to a quarter-mile to the chosen snow slot. The most popular are the closest in (before reaching the *A-Z Chutes* proper), known as *The Pinnacles* for the rust-colored outcroppings that frame the descent like crumbling fortifications. All of the chutes, from *The Pinnacles* up through *Z Chute,* face south around to east, so variable snow conditions, including sun and wind crusts, should be expected.

You don't have to go hiking to find wonderful advanced and expert skiing in the Challenger Lift zone. With a vertical of over 1,700 feet and a plethora of true steeps, this is an experts' playground, the prime fallback when wind shuts down the summit tram. There are three zones to explore, each a different aspect off this northern prow of Lone Mountain. Drop off the ridge to the east right from the top of the chair, and you are in the *Little Tree* basin, which begins as a near-featureless porcelain hip and then funnels into a series of slots through the trees, scraggly, white-bark pines, many gnarled by the wind or left silvery barkless by beetle infestations. The biggest openings are skier's left on the descent. The farther right you go, the tighter and steeper the lines. Finish by taking the intermediate *Bert Road* back to Challenger base.

The middle aspect, facing northeast underneath the chair, is aptly named the *Rock Tongue.* The snow here is shaped underneath by pure rock that cuts like a glacier from the ridge well into the forest below, leaving a swath of open, undulating skiing. *Kurt's Glade* is the most accessible drop from the ridge. It's steep enough that a fall on hard snow will result in a long slide to the basin below. *Little Rock Tongue* and *Big Rock Tongue* drop through shallow rock fins and are not always themselves filled sufficiently for skiing from the top. The lower half of the lolling "tongue" offers some super, treeless powder and crud skiing.

The third aspect, to the right of the chair riding up, is the *Moonlight Basin* region. The slopes face true north, and the snow is some of the softest and best protected on the mountain. The sun doesn't reach in here much in midwinter; when it does, it comes from directly behind you, so you ski with your own shadow projected 100 feet or more down the slope ahead. *Moonlight Highway* off the top takes a fair amount of wind, as do all the treeline ridges, but the effect can be exquisite: smooth, granular snow that carves like soap and rarely develops into moguls. Lower down in the trees, bumps do form in the soft snow, but because they are shaped by good skiers, the net effect is rhythmic and playful.

You can exit *Moonlight* back to the Challenger chair via *Fast Lane* or continue, due to the addition of the Iron Horse Lift, downslope on *Bad Dog, Powder River,* or *Snake Bite.*

The Lure of the Tram

Good skiers will be forgiven if they never even give Challenger a second look. Such is the allure of the tram and the awesome terrain it serves. From the top, where you feel as if you've been thrust up on the tip of the world, you will have four options: Descend the sprawling, treeless *South Face;* work your way down the east ridge to one of the six *Gullies;* tackle the real test pieces, the serpentine *Big Couloir* twists through the cliffs off the mountain's northwest ridge; or, if discretion becomes the better part of valor, ride the tram back down. There is no disgrace in this.

If you decide to ski, the *South Face* is the place to start. *Liberty Bowl* slides off at the gentlest pitch, although it is ungroomed and far from gentle. The center line usually fills with whitecap bumps. Off to the sides, cut-up powder turns to crud in the sun. Move east across the face, and the going gets steeper and steeper. *Thunder* and *Lightning, The Wave,* and *Dictator Chutes* plummet a good 1,000 feet before moderating at treeline. Try *Castro's Shoulder* at the far south end of *Dictator Chutes.* At 50 degrees, it is reputed to be the steepest named pitch on the mountain.

South Face skiers have the option to take *Duck Walk* road around the peak's burly shoulder to the front side, to the Lone Peak triple and another tram ride. Or they can continue downhill into groomed, blue woods for an additional 1,400-foot vertical to the Shedhorn chair base. Shedhorn's trees provide good stormy-day cover and yet another cruising zone for intermediates with a bit of wanderlust. At the end of the day, everyone on the back side must exit via *Duck Walk* road to the Village side of the mountain.

The *Gullies* (one through six) and the couloir really mean business. Few public-lease ski areas in this litigious land would even consider opening such serious steeps. Just to get to the top of Big Couloir you have to check in with the ski patrol, have a partner, and carry avalanche rescue gear. Many of the local hot shots wear helmets; a slide into the rocks on either side is not an option. Stumble when the snow is hard, and you're in for a long, scary slide. But ski these intoxicating drops well, with care and respect, and they will raise the level of your game. Everything else—the black diamonds at other ski areas—will seem like child's play.

Big Sky for Beginners

Big Sky is making a big push to lure families. Kids ages ten and under ski and stay free. There are fine Playcare and Ski Day Camp programs. And the learning terrain is excellent and sufficiently segregated from faster traffic.

I'm a believer in surface lifts for beginners—you get twice the mileage of a chairlift, skiing uphill as well as down. And the Mighty Mite surface tow provides that mileage. Next to it is the Explorer double chair with its brace of low-angle greens, *Lone Wolf* and *White Wing.* A third green run branches off the top of Explorer and merges with *Mr. K,* the excellent novice route off the top of the gondola. At rush hours—noon and late afternoon—watch over your shoulder as commuters race the corduroy ribbon on their way down from the upper mountain.

Most of the time there is no traffic to speak of. Big Sky has consistently ranked in the top three nationally in ski magazine polls for least crowded conditions. There is just so much terrain and so few skiers.

Moving up from the Explorer chair, novices have just one option on Lone Mountain, and that is the aforementioned *Morning Star/Mr. K.* It's a heck of an option, though. You get to ride the gondola right up to treeline and then slide down over 1,500 vertical feet and nearly two miles over wide, beautifully prepared boulevards that go on and on and on. The longest continuous descent on the mountain is a full six miles and quite doable by novice and lower-intermediate skiers. The top mile off the Lone Peak triple chair is rated intermediate, but with good snow and weather conditions, the route should pose no problems even for snowplowers.

A final note for snowboarders. One of the most playful natural half-pipes anywhere runs down the right side of *Lower Morning Star,* where a shady gully provides endless banks and lips and spines to play on. *Ambush* also has a new terrain park and half-pipe maintained by a pipe-dragon grooming machine.

Dining Big Sky

There isn't much on the mountain. In fact, the Dug Out Snack Shop atop Andesite Mountain is the *only* food right on the slopes: Polish dogs and picnic-table dining indoors or out. But they really don't need high-altitude restaurants because all the skiing funnels back directly to the Mountain Village. At the gondola base, the Mountain Mall contains nine eating establishments plus retail and rental shops. It is a bit odd to clunk along in ski boots with scores of mall rats. But the indoor ambience is a big plus in cold and stormy weather, and the whole thing has a relaxed feel. Besides, it allows for a choice of smaller eateries under one roof.

In nice weather the big metal deck outside the Lone Peak Cafe is the happening place. You can bring food out from any of the shops inside or order burgers, etc., from the cafeteria. Mountain Top Pizza (by the slice) is one of the locals' favorites. The Bing Lee family serves up authentic Chinese at their Twin Pandas restaurant. Dante's Inferno is the place for live music, beers, and munchies after skiing. Or try Scissorbills, with its vintage telemark decor and killer margaritas.

Two or three walking minutes away from the mall, the Huntley Lodge offers more elegant dining (breakfast and dinner only) in an expansive room with tall windows out to the slopes. Adjacent Chet's Bar has nightly entertainment and live poker games. (Yes, low-stakes gambling is legal in Montana. You even see it at gas stations and truck stops.) The bar itself, a hand-carved, 100-year-old, solid oak beauty, was discovered by Huntley in Anaconda, Montana.

One night you owe it to yourself to travel downvalley to the Lone Mountain Ranch for dinner. (The breakfast buffet is also sublime.) In a gorgeous log cabin, fine seafood, beef, and wild game entrees are prepared by a gourmet Dutch flyfisherman chef. (See "Inside Story" following this chapter.)

BIG SKY DATA

Mountain Statistics

Vertical feet	4,180 feet
Base elevation (village)	7,500 feet
Base elevation (Thunder Wolf)	6,970 feet
Summit elevation	11,150 feet
Longest run	6 miles
Average annual snowfall	400 inches
Number of lifts	1 fifteen-passenger tram, 1 four-passenger gondola, 4 quad chairs, 3 triples, 3 doubles, and 4 surface tows
Uphill capacity per hour	18,000 skiers
Skiable terrain	3,500 acres
Opening date	Thanksgiving
Closing date	mid-April
Snowboarding	Yes

Transportation

By car One hour south of Bozeman, Montana, via Highway 191; 3 hours north and west of Jackson Hole via West Yellowstone on Highways 22, 33, 32, and 191; 6 hours north of Salt Lake City via Interstate 15 to Highway 191.

By plane About 43 miles from Bozeman airport, which is served by Delta, Northwest, Horizon (full-size jets), and SkyWest airlines. Taxi and van service from the airport.

Key Phone Numbers

Area Information
   (800) 548-4486
Lodging Info (800) 548-4486
Snow Conditions
   (406) 995-5900
Lone Mountain Ranch
   (406) 995-4644
www.bigskyresort.com

Lone Mountain Ranch

Cross-country skiing consistently ranks first on all those exercise charts of calories burned per hour of exercise. And it's true, the whole body is involved in the diagonal striding/poling, kick-and-glide of classical track skiing—the real-world antecedent of the Nordic Track indoor exercise machine.

Sometimes this reputation for serious aerobic demand keeps alpine skiers and others away from the sport. As if it is somehow not really skiing after all, not really the same graceful gliding over snow that lift-assisted skiing is. Nothing could be further from the truth. Cross-country is everything alpine is: sliding, schussing, turning, skidding, carving, floating, laughing, eating, hot-tubbing, and storytelling over hill and dale in the pristine winter air. And it is more. Because you provide your own propulsion, you get to eat more of that good food without guilt, you get to wear fewer and sexier clothes, you enjoy a quieter, wilder piece of the mountains where moose and ermine stare at you through the trees, and you get to enjoy the Puritan notion that you earned every inch of giddy descent through your own uphill efforts.

At the Lone Mountain Ranch, a few short miles down the hill from Big Sky's Mountain Village, the cross-country art has been honed to perfection. Fifty-five guests stay in 23 log cabins, some dating back to the ranch's founding in 1915. They all eat together in the soaring glass-and-log dining room. And they all come to ski the 75 kilometers of groomed trail that radiate into the surrounding national forest. The trails are the key. Bob and Vivian Schaap are convivial hosts, the food is superb, and the staff is genuinely friendly and involved, but it is the trails—like magic carpets—that bring 80 percent of the guests back year after year.

Start from the back door of the ski shop, with its busy waxing bench and its warm, not altogether incongruous smell of blueberry muffins and melted blue wax. Take your skating skis. The track is set up so you can run (or walk) along in the preset grooves—which is called diagonal striding or "classical technique" skiing—or skate on the wide, smooth skating lane, like a corduroy sidewalk, to the side.

Skating on skis goes back thousands of years to nomadic Norwegian hunters, but it has only recently become a widely popular skiing subsport. Skaters use shorter skis, as short as 147 centimeters. (One ski manufacturer's magazine ad matches their short ski up, centimeter for centimeter, with a certain vertically challenged French emperor.) The short skis are easy to han-dle, light and quick, and glide almost as effortlessly as a traditional skinny ski of 200 or 205 centimeters. Like an ice skater or an urban, in-line roller skater, you push to the side off the edge of one ski and onto the other, leav-ing long, herringbone tracks on the snow.

After a short climb in the woods, you burst out on a great bald ridge, like a white whale back with split-rail fences and the meadows of the West Gal-latin valley below. On the flats, your skis glide 30 feet with each push. The snow makes soft hissing noises under you as the trail loops playfully into hollows and around island stands of white-bark aspens.

On a well-waxed, slippery skating ski, you can even glide uphill. You shorten your stride to an easy jog, open your stance so the skis don't slip backwards, and lean forward into the hill. With a little practice you slide right up as if riding an escalator. After a while it becomes pure rhythm, a moving meditation of legs and arms and heart and lungs. No worries. There is no possibility of getting lost; the track winds into the distance and inevitably back to the lodge. Your only choices are whether or not to stop here for a drink of water or stop up in those aspen trees or stop up ahead where the view of Lone Mountain and the Madisons spreads out like a movie backdrop or a mural in blues and whites. Kilometers fly by beneath your skis, 5, 10, 20 K's like creek water. On the final downhill plunge to the lodge, you step into the machined track along the right-hand edge of the trail and let the twin grooves turn you. It is a final letting go. Like bumper cars between curbs or a toboggan in its chute, the skis turn as the trail turns. You just stand there and ride it, hanging on, skis humming with speed, shadow and light flicking by like strobes. And then you skid to a halt back at the ski shop, your legs rubbery and your whole body thrumming a well-used, well-filled vibration. Hot tub time. Dinner beneath the elk chande-liers. Fall in under the quilts. Dream of caressing the hills with your feet.

BRIDGER BOWL

A small ad in the ski magazines a couple of years back featured the requisite, red-clad powder skier in mid-float. The text caught my attention. It read: "Don't Let Our $25 Lift Ticket Fool You! We're Bridger Bowl, a nonprofit ski area in Bozeman, Montana. We have no owners to pay. Experience ski-ing like it used to be . . . a big mountain with over 2,000 feet of vertical for $25/day."

Nonprofit? Big mountain skiing for $25 a day? Here's another take on Bridger's unique position in American skiing. Marketing Director Doug

Wales, a graduate of Montana State University and a longtime Bridger Bowl skier, says this whole place "is kind of like a '57 Chevy." He means it's a classic, unchanging, a little long in the tooth but still possessing in abundance the virtues that made skiing great in the first place: superb terrain; good natural snow; plenty of programs for kids and students; a homegrown management that is relaxed, friendly, and frankly uninterested in real estate sales; and finally, a mystique surrounding its exceptional extreme terrain, known as the Ridge, and the movie-star, extreme-skiing champions who developed their craft there, including Scot Schmidt, Doug Coombs, Emily Gladstone, and Tom Jüngst.

The mystique grew slowly but steadily through the 1970s and 1980s as self-professed "Ridge hippies" rode the aging Bridger Lift and hiked the final 400 vertical feet to chutes with names like *Sometimes A Great Notion* and *The O's* (short for the Orgasms). Some of them lived whole winters on one month's salary from fishing in Alaska. Some rode their bikes to the mountain every morning with skis on their backs. They developed a skiing style that because of the walking and the narrow snow-choked hallways between the rocks was more efficient than flashy; it was all about grace and nonchalance, no wasted movement, and continuous turns where no panicking or seizing up is allowed. Don't waste your energy in one burst; use it over a whole day. It's a way of skiing that most people are too hurried and impatient to learn.

Throughout the West, serious skiers knew Bridger to be a last mecca for a dying breed of hard-core, committed, first-chair-to-last, 130-days-per-season ski bums.

But that's not all it is. Bridger is the quintessential locals' mountain. Locals started the ski hill over 40 years ago, and locals still run it in the form of the nonprofit Bridger Bowl Ski Area, Inc. To be a member, you must be a Montana resident and pay a $25 initiation fee and a $1-per-year membership fee. And with that you are a voting member of the association, eligible to election on the nine-member board of directors. The nonprofit status allows the area to keep prices down to nearly 1957 levels—thus the $25 daily ticket and an adult full-season pass of only $360 in 1994. A remarkable 3,600 locals hold season passes, a big number in a university town of 25,000.

Montana State University offers physical education credits in skiing up at the bowl. Local high schools run recreational programs and field ski teams. Bridger Bowl is kind of like the town's wintertime backyard; it's a little unkempt, perhaps, and in need of some work, but it's a place that beckons every weekend and never fails to deliver.

"We have a very demanding audience," says Wales, sipping a Spanish Peaks Ale ("the beer of choice here") at the base lodge and sitting under a classic early photo of a grizzled Jim Bridger, the nineteenth-century mountain man for whom the area was named. A demanding audience and a very knowledgeable one. For example, the Bridger telephone snow report lists temperature and wind speed at both the base and top of the mountain in addition to the snow depths. That way Ridge skiers will know which exposures are filling in and which are losing snow to a scouring wind. And the information is updated every hour. Down in Bozeman, a blue beacon atop the venerable Baxter Hotel lights up whenever there is an accumulation of one or more inches of new snow. "Just to let 'em know," says Wales, grinning.

When skiers come up the quick 16 miles from town to the mountain, they are rewarded with some of the best skiing and certainly some of the best value this side of Alta, Utah, which happens to be another unpretentious, debt-free, community-based ski area with a penchant for keeping the price down.

How long can it last in this era of condo bondage and real estate–driven expansion? Film star Michael Keaton has already built a home in the Canyon. Then there is Big Sky to the south, with shiny big dreams and neighbors like Ted Turner and Jane Fonda. Newcomers are discovering Bozeman's charms by the hundreds each month. (The smart ones change their license plates in a hurry to avoid the wrath of those who feel invaded.) Bridger Bowl may be in for major changes in the not too distant future. An out-of-state developer has purchased a big chunk of private land near the base with plans to build on-slope lodging and new lifts to connect with the existing terrain. Will "skiing like it used to be" and the $25 dollar lift ticket survive?

The Lay of the Land

The Bridger Range pokes a long, narrow finger across the horizon north of Bozeman and I-90. By Colorado standards, these are small peaks, with summits below 9,000 feet. But the view from the Ridge is huge in all directions. The wonderfully named Crazy Mountains shine to the east; the Tobacco Roots blaze bright white to the west; the Spanish Peaks hide Big Sky to the south; and the Absaroka and Bear Tooth mountains loom to the southeast on the border of Yellowstone National Park. With inversion clouds covering the valleys (a common phenomenon on cold, high-pressure days), the wild, 360-degree sweep feels like Montana pre–Lewis and Clark.

The ski area sits on the back side of the range near the head of Bridger Creek, which tumbles the 16 miles through Bridger Canyon to Bozeman's broad valley. The area layout couldn't be simpler: one base, six chairs, and one spanking-new mid-mountain restaurant. The terrain sweeps up in a natural progression from the easiest in the meadows and trees near the lodge and gradually pitches to more difficult up near treeline to the steepest terrain in the rocks and avalanche gullies at the top. From a bird's-eye view

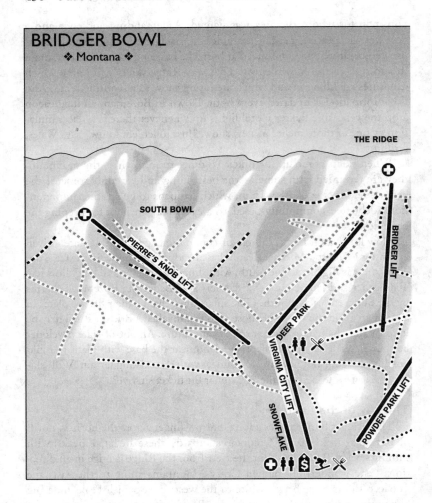

above the Jim Bridger Lodge at the base, the whole thing spreads out like an oriental fan, with the 50 or so named runs pouring down the fall lines to a central point. No hidden zones, no back sides, and nothing you can't see at a glance.

From ground level, though, a first-time Bridger skier might need some orientation. Which lifts go to what sort of terrain? The answer isn't obvious, thanks to the abundant forest. Take out the trail map and consider the mountain in terms of its four major regions. The Virginia City and Powder Park lifts leave from the base and serve the lion's share of beginner/

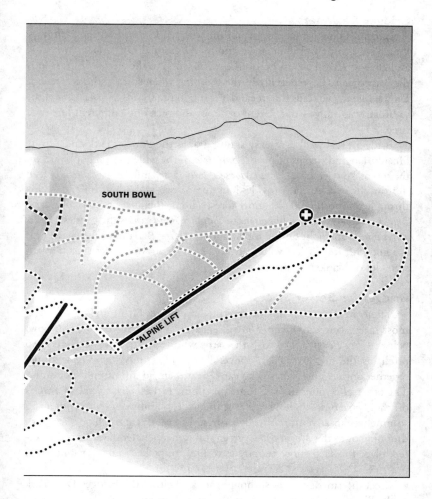

novice terrain. To the right (north) and higher up is the Alpine Lift, with its
mix of long novice and intermediate trails. The Pierre's Knob/South Bowl
area climbs the mostly intermediate south flank. Right in the center and
pushing up the black diamond ridge are the Bridger and Deer Park lifts.

Traveling from one zone to another is relatively straightforward, thanks
to a network of cat tracks, but because the area is much wider than it is high
and because the lifts are quite long and relatively slow, most skiers stake out
a region and stay there a while. The 1996 addition of the Alpine Quad has
greatly improved access to the popular upper-mountain runs.

Bridger Beginners

Learning skiers should start out on Virginia City. From the off-ramp, they have a bunch of choices, including *Missouri Breaks, Moose Meadows,* and *Bridger Run.* The last is also the main access to the Bridger Lift, so it is the least preferable, especially in the morning when skier traffic is heaviest. Unlike the novice trails that meander through the woods, *Moose Meadows* is so broad you can yo-yo it dozens of times and pick out a different line each time.

Bridger's real wealth of easy skiing drapes the Powder Park and Alpine lifts like languid strings of pearls. *Sunnyside* is the wide central boulevard off the top of Powder Park. *Mogul Mouse, Mully Road,* and *Lower Limestone* feed in from the side. Alpine provides long (up to two-and-a-half-mile) descents through the muffled, cold-snow forests along the area's north boundary. *North Meadows Road* to *Limestone* to *Summer Road* carries the gentlest grade. *Porcupine* loops right off the top and joins *Alpine Run* under the chair. This is a good lift for novices who want to stay high above the occasional inversion clouds blanketing the valley.

Bridger for Better Skiers

There are a number of fine intermediate routes off Alpine as well. The most interesting are in the *Three Bears* area, a generous open-palm bowl below *Three Bears Chutes* with the same wild feel (but not the same steep pitch) as the hike-to terrain above. *Three Bears* and *Alpine Face* funnel together onto *Alpine Run,* so you can repeat them ad infinitum if you want. The other nifty intermediate route on Alpine is the *Powder Park* area that's off the *Three Bears Traverse* south of the lift top terminal. This is not a run so much as an adventure through timberline glades and a big, open park dropping onto the *Mogul Mouse* green run. On a powder day, this is the perfect place for deep-snow neophytes to find untracked snow for unhurried practice.

Most intermediate skiers, though, stick to either the Bridger/Deer Park or the Pierre's Knob lifts. The big draw off the top of the Bridger is the spacious *North Bowl.* This is the real thing: treeless, naked, go-anywhere-you-want-to-point-'em skiing. There is even a route in the bowl called *Freedom. North Bowl* grows some of the best intermediate bumps on the mountain, though you always have a choice; there's so much room, you can always opt for bumps or no bumps.

Off to the south of Bridger Lift, the Deer Park Lift serves an interesting variety of rolling timberline terrain and snaky shots through the trees. To the skier's left (looking down from the top), *Deer Park Face, Hanton's Hollow, Powder Horn,* and *Boothill* are rated blue and are usually groomed. On the skier's right from the top are *Sluice Box* and *Ptarmigan;* these two tend to develop sizable bumps and are thus rated black diamond. They are not always intimidating to stronger intermediates, however, and you can check them out with impunity by traversing out and back on *Deer Park Road.*

The far south end of the ski area is called Pierre's Knob, with a lift of the same name emanating from the Deer Park confluence. (Deer Park base, Pierre's Knob base, and the Virginia City top terminal all meet beside the Deer Park Chalet restaurant.) Pierre's gives you access to the invitingly pitched *South Bowl.* The middle of the bowl is often kept mogul free with a smooth swath down the gut, as is *Emile's Mile* just to the right. These two, along with *Missouri Breaks* to *White Lightning,* provide some of the longest and best cruising at Bridger. Though not of the same scale as Park City cruising, for example, they are perhaps superior when it comes to intriguing micro-terrain, the little dips and rolls that give a descent playfulness and flavor.

Like *North Bowl, South Bowl* is allowed to develop bumps in the hollows where they form naturally. The pitch is never so steep that the moguls become scary. These are good learning grounds, and you can always bail out to something smooth next door. For bumps with a little more tilt, try *Coulter's Crawl* and *Psychopath,* skier's left of *South Bowl.* These are outruns for steeper chutes off the Ridge, and the bumps are usually well formed by good skiers.

Intermediates should, under no circumstances, attempt the hike to the Ridge. There are no easy ways down, only very steep, rocky, and tricky drops with nothing remotely like an escape route. Everything qualifies as the "no fall zone." Not to worry, though, you can't get up there by accident. The ski patrol has a pretty fool-proof screening procedure that requires you to have a working avalanche transceiver, which is verified by an electronic sensor. In addition, you must carry a shovel (to dig out a buried companion) and go with someone who has been there before. This is serious business.

Expert Bridger

Not all experts feel comfortable on the elevator-shaft steepness of most Ridge lines. The 400-vertical-foot hike, known as the *Stairway to Heaven,* discourages many who may not have the breath or the quads. I'll talk in detail about the Ridge in the "Inside Story" on page 441. For the moment, let's look at lift-served expert options below the Ridge.

The pitches are not particularly long, but the bumps on *Bronco* and *Ptarmigan* south of the Bridger Lift pose as good a fast-twitch challenge as any in the Rockies. And farther south, *Avalanche Gulch* and *The Nose* are even more like gale-tossed seas. I mentioned the traverse out *Deer Park Road.* That'll take you to the mid-point on these monsters. To get even higher, take the *High Traverse* off the top of Bridger Lift. Up here *Avalanche*

Gulch plunges like a drain pipe with Volkswagen-size stair steps on which to set an edge. Beyond *Avalanche,* the trail shrivels to a darting path through twisted survivor trees. Roots and rocks require dancing feet until you come to any of a dozen chutes known collectively as *The Nose.* They're not on the trail map, but they've all got names like *Deviated Septum* and *Nasal Cavity.* Return via *South Bowl Run* to the Deer Park Lift.

Many experts like to yo-yo the Bridger Lift, repeating runs on *Bronco, Ptarmigan, Out-Of-Site,* or *Easy Money,* which is easier now that the Powder Park chair is in place. Bridger was shortened (from the bottom), allowing for the installation of more chairs and a subsequent upping of capacity to the area's high point.

If Bridger Lift is too busy, chances are Deer Park or Pierre's Knob are not. *Lower Avalanche Gulch* and *Devil's Dive* offer some good, steep bumps south of the Deer Park Lift. Over on Pierre's, there is some sweet glade skiing on *South Boundary* and a rash of genuinely gnarly treelines on *Flipper's* and the north-facing pitches below the chair.

Good Eats

Bridger's Ridge hippies are famous for eating on chairlift rides — the better to squeeze in one more trip to the Ridge. If you want to stop moving for a while and unbuckle your boots, stop at the mid-mountain Deer Park Chalet and the multipurpose Jim Bridger Lodge at the base.

The original 1957 Deer Park Lodge was replaced in 1996 by a handsome new chalet with more than twice the seating and the same soups, stews, and homemade breads.

Jim Bridger Lodge, built in 1988, houses a ski school, rentals and retail ski shops, day care, reservations, and a very serviceable cafeteria with high ceilings and big windows looking onto *Moose Meadows.* Comfy yet utilitarian and befitting a nonprofit community. If you'd like a more intimate lunch, Jimmy B's bar serves excellent hot sandwiches and beer upstairs by the fireplace.

For après-ski activities most locals and visitors head downvalley to the myriad offerings of town. (There are a few beds in Bridger Canyon in private cabins and lodges, but most visitors stay in Bozeman in the score of moderately priced motels and inns.) The Hofbrau, known as the Hof, is the locals' bar. The Bacchus Pub is a classic old place serving brews, salads, soups, and burgers. For a white-tablecloth dinner try O'Brien's on Main Street. The Spanish Peaks serves microbrewed beers and mounds of good Italian food. The Leaf and Bean and the Rockie Mountain Roasting Company are the places to go for gourmet coffees.

BRIDGER BOWL DATA

Mountain Statistics

Vertical feet	2,000 feet lift-served, 400 to 600 feet more on the Ridge
Base elevation	6,100 feet
Summit elevation	8,100 feet
Longest run	2.5 miles
Average annual snowfall	350 inches
Number of lifts	1 quad and 5 doubles
Uphill capacity	7,300 skiers per hour
Skiable terrain	1,200 acres
Opening date	early December
Closing date	early April
Snowboarding	Yes

Transportation

By car 16 miles (20 minutes) up Bridger Canyon, State Highway 86, from Bozeman, Montana. Bozeman is just off I-90 between Billings and Missoula, and 1½ hours north of West Yellowstone via Highway 191.

By plane Via major carriers, including Delta, Northwest, Horizon Air, and SkyWest to Bozeman's Gallatin Field. Connections from Salt Lake City, Minneapolis, Denver, and Seattle.

By bus Many lodgings in Bozeman provide ski-area shuttle service.

Key Phone Numbers

Ski Area Information
  406) 587-2111
Snow Report (406) 586-2389
Reservations (800) 223-9609
www.bridgerbowl.com

INSIDE STORY

Joining the Ridge Hippies

Bridger Bowl's creaky old lifts got a boost with the addition of a new fixed-grip quad, the mostly green Powder Park Lift. But area managers promise that no quad will ever breast the Ridge, which is the cliff- and chute-strewn curtain that hangs above the lift-served skiing here. "The quads that take you there," says Bozeman writer and photographer Gordon Wiltsie, "will have to be your own." Anyone without a decent set of quadriceps, and lungs to match, need not attempt the walk, which begins near the top of Bridger chair at 8,100 feet. The route follows an old rope tow the ski patrol rigged up long ago but seldom uses. It's hard to imagine anyone holding on for the ride; the heavy yellow rope drapes limply down an impossibly steep gash in the woods. Look closely and you'll see the line of steps cut by countless ski boots heading to the powder. This is the Stairway to Heaven, the one and only way up.

Before starting, however, you must pass the ski patrol shack and an odd-looking appendage, like a microphone, outside. Pull the electric sensor to your chest, and if you have an avalanche transceiver and it is working, a buzzer and red light signals the OK to proceed. If you don't also have a shovel in your pack and a partner who knows the terrain above, then you are asked to stay on the lifts. While the patrol does indeed shoot the obvious slide paths before opening the Ridge, most of the drops are so steep that the potential for slides always exists. Everyone takes the dangers very seriously, and, consequently, no one has been seriously hurt on the Ridge for years.

Once through the electronic gate, you begin to climb. No switchbacks, no fooling around with moderate grades; this sucker only goes straight up. If you are carrying your skis over a shoulder, your tips will brush the snow in front; that's how steep it is. And that's why most of the Ridge hippies wear small shovel packs to which they can also affix their skis.

Moving now through the Pearly Gates, a narrowing of the track through rock walls, each step is a big pull up. These stairs would never meet code. Chances are they were formed early in the season by locals in a hurry. You have no choice but to follow in their footsteps. To venture off to the side would be to wallow in waist-deep fluff.

The speed record for the 400 vertical feet straight up is under 10 minutes. If you do it in 20 you are doing well. Even then—and even on the coldest days—you are sweating by the top. It's a good idea to wear moisture-wicking (hydrophobic) underwear and to layer your outerwear so you can peel off as you go and then add more at the top.

At the top of the Stair Chair, the Ridge stretches north and south for a mile in either direction. To the north, it snakes its corniced way to a high point of 8,700 feet. There you can drop into *Hidden Gully,* which is no more than 12 feet wide through its rock-walled top section only to fan out onto the spacious *Apron* above the Alpine Lift.

To the south, the Ridge wanders by *Patrolman's,* the shortest walk and the quickest way back to the Bridger Lift, and then up and over *The Nose* and out to the area's south boundary, where parallel shafts called *The Fingers* and *The Three Virtues* plummet into *South Bowl.*

Gordon Wiltsie took me to two of the easiest and most accessible routes off the Ridge. First north by hiking a little more on skis up the cornice that's like a lip overhanging the rocky chin to our right. Then down one of the so-called *Bridger Chutes,* full of twisted, gnomish, survivor trees, and on to *Three Bears Bowl* and a face full of deep, soft, wind-blown snow called *The O's* that stands, appropriately enough, for orgasms. Back across *North Bowl* to the Bridger Lift and up again to the Stair Chair.

Bridger was having one of its frequent temperature inversions: warm, clear air up on the Ridge; colder, foggy air partway down the mountain. This time as we walked, we emerged from the cloud into a feeble sun, a cottonball sea of mist below us.

Gordon led the way to *The Nose.* The first pitch, called *Test Face,* started off deceptively mellow and rolled gradually steeper and steeper until we couldn't see but 40 feet ahead. The trees on the sides appeared to be stepping off the edge of the world. The deep snow—knee-deep and better—held us on the pitch. We had to force ourselves to reach down the hill with our poles. Each turn was like jumping off the roof. Ultimately *Test Face* plunges over a cliff, but Gordon peeled left into *Exit Chute,* where we bounced through a narrow drain and out into the moguls and the relative civility of *Avalanche Chute.*

Some Ridge hippies pump a dozen runs a day on the Ridge, eating out of their anorak pouches on chairlifts, stopping only to shed a sweater or share a water bottle. You can do the Ridge that way, or you can treat it as a backcountry tour, an adventure, and a change to the inbounds routine. For me, on that particular day, two was enough. After the Ridge, riding through the fog on the lower trails was like flying; it was so easy and natural that it seemed we were somehow cheating gravity.

THE BIG MOUNTAIN

There is some understandable confusion surrounding the name of this up-and-coming destination in Montana's far northwest corner. Is it Big Mountain, Montana, or The Big Mountain, Montana? It certainly is big. At 3,000 skiable acres with another 1,040 acres in the permit, it is indisputably Montana's biggest ski area. But the name?

Most of the official literature refers to the place as The Big Mountain. One real estate rag sports the headline "Big is our middle name." The official address is: The Big Mountain Ski and Summer Resort, Whitefish, Montana. Still, the added article sounds awkward to the American ear. We're not like the French, who regularly use the definite article with their ski areas, as in *le* Brévent; *les* Grands Montets; *les* Menuires. *The* Big Mountain. "Yeah, it sounds weird," says area communications manager Lisa Jones. "We thought of changing it to Whitefish or just Big Mountain. But this is what the locals have called it from the beginning, and it does help to distinguish us from Big Sky. So I guess we're stuck with it."

Actually, the community members who sold shares and volunteered their labor to put up the first T-bar in 1947 wanted to call it Hell Roaring Ski Area after the name of the creek drainage where the first skiing was done on the back side of the current development in the 1930s. But propriety and a marketing logic that said people might not flock to a place called Hell Roaring prevailed, and so we have the Big Mountain.

The Big Mountain rises to a rounded, balding 7,000-foot summit between bucolic Whitefish Lake and the railroad/timber/summer-vacation town of Whitefish on the west and the higher, sharper peaks of Glacier National Park to the east. This mountain has a great location at the north end of the burgeoning Flathead Valley, with great snow, sublime natural terrain, and weather so atrocious that until recently nobody save the denizens of the 49th parallel knew about the place. Cold and fog combine to turn the trees in the big summit bowls to rimed phantasmagoric creatures in a white-on-white ballroom. More often than not, you just don't see them. Blue sky days are as rare as lift lines.

The mountain's natural gifts were readily apparent to the postwar Whitefish Chamber of Commerce; they wanted to expand business past the fall hunting season and into winter. Those attributes were fine enough to attract a ski hero the caliber of Toni Matt, who came up from Sun Valley to run the ski school and cut some of the first trails. Matt was the Austrian super skier who was the first (and still the only) person to schuss the 1,000-foot Headwall at Tuckerman Ravine on New Hampshire's Mount Washington. That he did it in full flight during the infamous Inferno downhill race cast him as an instant and enduring legend.

Matt arrived, as do about 25 percent of today's skiers, on the train. Whitefish, population 4,000, is a major stop on the Burlington Northern Empire Builder line. Amtrak passenger trains from Seattle and Minneapolis come through each day. Seattle skiers have figured a way to save two nights' lodging on a trip to the Big Mountain by taking the night train that arrives in Whitefish, only eight miles from the mountain, at 6:30 A.M., and returning home on the 9:30 P.M. train, snoozing on the way, to save another night. Maximize the skiing, minimize the expense. This is not to say that the Big Mountain is pricey to begin with. Both the mountain and the town have a downhome, mid-American kind of freshness. U.S. gold medalist downhiller Tommy Moe grew up here before moving to Alaska and the Ski Team. There's a signed poster of Moe in the Hell Roaring Saloon at the base of the high-speed quad chair. It bears the inscription, "To my friends at The Big Mountain, where I learned to ski FAST." That he did. The whole town went fairly crazy when Moe won his gold and silver at Lillehammer in February

1994. His mother and stepfather still live here. His stepfather drives a snow-cat on the mountain and just about jumped out of his cab, so proud was he to tell me about his boy.

The Hell Roaring Saloon is housed in the Chalet, the original lodge on the mountain and now the area's administrative offices. In the 1950s, you had a room, all your meals, and a lift ticket for one price. Skiers were a brother- and sisterhood then. Everyone was in this new snow-sliding adventure together, and that's pretty much the feeling you still get at the Big Mountain. The Hell Roaring Saloon bristles with great old wooden skis and sepia photographs. If you buy one of their baseball caps, you get one free beer per day for the rest of your life. The brotherhood.

In Whitefish, the Glacier Grand Bar offers free appetizers from 5 to 6 P.M. every night (that's dinner for some of the local ski bums). The Glacier Grand also has live entertainment. Look for guitarist/raconteur Leo Kottke, for example, rather than John Denver. The Moguls Bar & Grille slopeside opens a free keg every Monday after skiing hosted by the ski school. The Bierstube, the ski patrol's favorite bar, is right across the parking lot and maintains a Wednesday tradition that is not to be missed, the presentation of the weekly Frabert Award for the clutziest move of the week. Frabert is a toy monkey encased in plaster casts and slings that hangs over the bar. The night I was there, the award went to a lift operator who slipped, fell, and accidentally bit a girl's nose. Some weeks the recipient is not an employee at all but a visitor who has somehow—wittingly or not—stumbled into the brotherhood.

There are only 300 lodging units, about 1,500 pillows, up at the mountain. But Whitefish is growing fast. An excellent local transit system called WART—Whitefish Area Rapid Transit—makes town-mountain connections simple. The million acres of Glacier National Park right next door, the exponential growth around Flathead Lake and nearby Kalispell, and the word leaking out about the Big Mountain's hero terrain and its quick quad to the summit would all seem to spell bigger numbers for the future. Some long-time locals already complain about the Aspenization of Whitefish. That seems a little extreme.

From here, about the only place less crowded to move to would be Alaska.

Bottom line: The thing that will probably save the Big Mountain from overcrowding will be that old northern Rockies weather. It is no accident that local patrolman Kerry Critendon has invented (and is now marketing) a foam and nylon ski accessory called Butt Flaps, designed to be worn like an apron in reverse, for keeping the posterior dry in cold, wet conditions. Perfect for riding chairs all day in the fog, chill, and dumping storms of the Big Mountain. Those are the conditions, after all, that make the stuff under your skis so silky soft and silent.

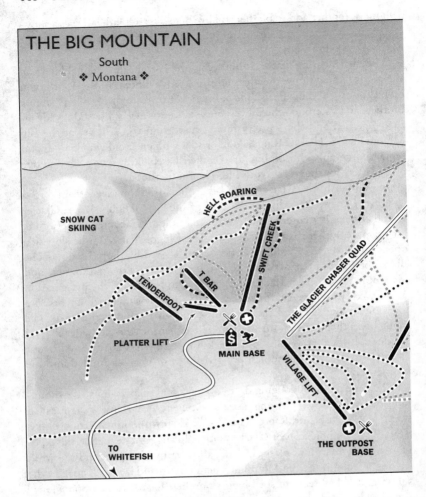

The Big Layout

The base situation here is a little confusing at first, due perhaps to the way the skiing evolved adjacent to the original Chalet. Now the Chalet is part of a horseshoe-shaped ring of eclectic buildings, including ski school and rental shops and restaurants and condos, that all but surround the number one parking lot. Ski lifts take off in three directions from the outside of the ring. If you get there early enough to park in this inner lot, you have but a short walk to everything in the village. If you are a little late, you may have

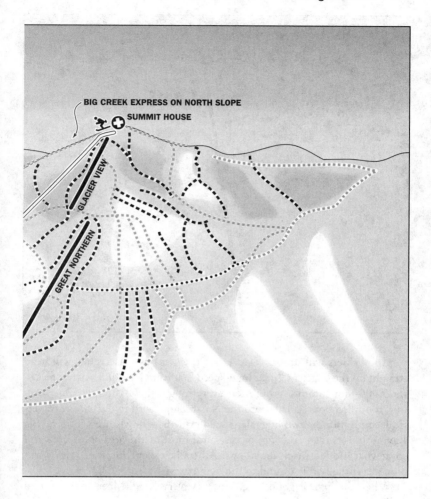

to park in a series of terraced lots outside the ring, each a little farther away from the action.

That's the old base. There is now a second base to the south known as the Outpost at the bottom of Chair 6, the Village Lift. The Outpost includes a new restaurant, sun deck, ticket windows, ski school desk, patrol room, lockers, and its own parking. The Village Lift serves all beginner terrain and takes pressure off the more congested beginner and intermediate lifts above the old base.

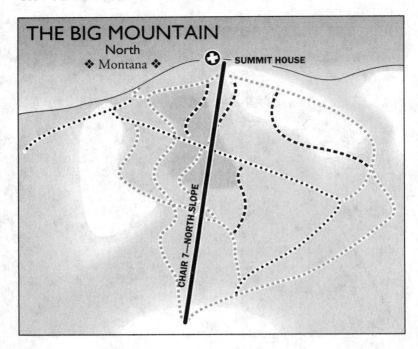

Good skiers will probably never see the Outpost base. They will head straight up the Glacier Chaser high-speed quad and its 2,088 vertical feet to the 7,000-foot summit. From there everything is down. Simple. One summit, four directions: north onto the North Slope with its 1,200 feet of vertical; south into the two huge, largely intermediate bowls; west into the Big Ravine and its long cruising; or east onto most of the area's protected and somewhat hidden black diamonds. All trails, except those on the North Slope, eventually roll around to the twin bases.

When the light is good here, it is very, very good. Most of the terrain spills south and west from the summit. These exposures would likely not be skiable down south in Colorado, for example. But here, with the lower sun angle and the generally colder temperatures, there is little problem. The winter sun beams unobstructed, and that means the afternoon light paints a golden magic.

One way to remain in that light longer is to return after skiing to the Summit House. A big, glassy, functional building on the peak with little to recommend itself on the outside, Summit House has from the inside one of the most brilliant sunset views in the north country. The cafeteria is open for breakfast, lunch, and cocktails and for a special Bavarian Buffet on selected Wednesday nights and every Saturday night during the season. They remove a few chairs from the Glacier quad and replace them with gondola cars, so you ride up and down in style.

When you come down, there's still skiing. A cluster of trails on the area's west end around Chairs 2 and 3 and the T-bar are lit for night skiing Wednesday through Sunday. An all-day lift ticket is good under the lights until 6 p.m. Eight dollars extends to closing at 10 p.m. Holders of multiday tickets ski all night with no additional charge. True to its community roots, the Big Mountain hosts three different night race leagues for alpine skiers, telemarkers, and snowboarders.

Beginners Ski Free

The Village Lift and the Platter Lift are free all the time for everybody. The hook, of course, is to get you hooked and then entice you into lessons and lifts up the mountain. For about $20 you can ride the Tenderfoot Lift (Chair 3) with its one blue and two green runs, and they throw in a group lesson. These folks know how to get people started.

Lessons are always a good idea for first-timers. With the new runs to the Outpost base and the accompanying Village Lift, there is ample room for any number of first-timers. *Beargrass, Huckleberry Patch,* and *Chipmunk* are rated double green, the easiest of all. Tenderfoot is the next step up in the terrain progression, with its slightly steeper greens of *Alpinglow Alley* and *Question Mark.*

Grandest of all for novices (beginners who have rudimentary turning and stopping skills), there is a green route right from the mountain's summit. It's called *Easy Street,* and it straddles the Big Mountain's east ridge for a mile and then turns back toward the village for another mile and a half on a gentle cat track. At two and a half miles, it's the longest descent on the hill.

Big Cruising

There's another long, gentle run off in the opposite direction, down the west ridge, that the locals call *Around the World.* Parts of it are rated blue, but it is always groomed, broad, and easy enough to be a good transition route for novices and low-level intermediates. It starts on the timberline boulevard called *The Big Ravine,* continues down the green-circle *Interstate,* and finishes blue again on *Hibernation,* one of the runs cut for the original 1947 T-bar. Spectacular views, lots of mileage, that top-of-the-world sensation, and the opportunity to ride the quad add up to a near perfect low-angle cruiser.

Flat-out, let-it-roll, high-speed cruising is one of the Big Mountain's big strengths. *Toni Matt, Ptarmigan Bowl, Inspiration,* and *North Bowl* are all groomed every night, creating top-to-bottom roller coasters to die for. *Toni Matt* is particularly sweet as it dives off *The Big Ravine* and onto a broad, convex ridge that serpentines right to the base of the Glacier quad. To the skier's right is *Good Medicine,* one of the most spacious, low-angle glades anywhere. It is rated black diamond, but solid intermediates will love it in powder or spring conditions. To the left is *Ptarmigan Bowl,* also rated black, but the groomed swath down the center means there are tasty, smooth giant slalom turns for intermediates as well.

The same is true for *Inspiration* and *North Bowl* farther east around the front side of the mountain. Inspiration plunges for the greatest vertical on the mountain, the full 2,300 feet, which puts you at the Outpost base. That's an extra 3.5 minute ride on the Village Lift to get back to the quad, or you can cut it short at *Easy Street* and beeline straight for the return trip to the top.

The quad has changed traffic patterns forever. Though there is rarely a lift line, you may, if you are looking for less crowded slopes, venture back to the older lifts that serve primarily intermediate terrain, Chairs 2, 4, and 5. Numbers 4 and 5 especially are little used now that the quad covers the same distance to the peak in half the time. But the skiing off Chair 4 from *Langley* (part of the National Championship downhill cut by Toni Matt in 1948) to *Corkscrew* to the glades of *Powder Trap* is superb, and there's nobody there.

A word about the term "glade." Back east, a glade is any wooded area with room enough to squeeze a pair of skis through. In Colorado, glades are often created by cutting down whole forests and leaving a few clusters of trees here and there for ambience. At the Big Mountain the entire upper half of the mountain is peppered with small, rime-encrusted trees with enough room between them to make a mistake, recover, and choose a new path without fear of smacking into anything. It's a liberating kind of tree skiing for both intermediates and experts.

Bumps? Hmmm. This mountain is so big and there are so few skiers that bumps just don't happen consistently. The best intermediate bumps will be on *Lower Mully's* off Chair 2. *Heap Steep* and *Powder Trap,* two relatively short open glades off Chair 4, also grow shaggy most winters and the groomers leave them be. For my money, say Hallelujah that there's a mountain where you don't *have* to ski bumps!

The Big Mountain's Hidden Steeps

First, let me say that big-time cruising should not be reserved for intermediates. With the quick return speed of the Glacier quad, experts will certainly want to rip off a few laps on the *Bowls, Toni Matt,* and *The Big Ravine.* The rush of speed and the wide-open, undulating shapes are the closest most of us will ever get to free flight. This is hero stuff, Tommy Moe stuff, and everybody likes to feel like a hero.

The steep stuff is mostly concentrated at the east end between *Easy Street* and *Inspiration* flowing into the *North Bowl* drain from the two ridge lines. This is by no means a small pocket; the dozen named black diamonds harbor countless lines between them, enough for many months of concentrated exploring.

The steepest shots are the double diamonds called *East Rim* and *Haskill Slide*. *East Rim* features a couple of launchable rock outcroppings on what is otherwise a baby-smooth, cliff-free mountain. *Haskill* is genuinely jump-turn steep; air beneath your bases. The rest are steep but not scary openings through the tree fabric. My favorites start off *Inspiration* with a mellow rollover into *Fault 1* or *Fault 2*. The snow stays cold and deep in the shade here. Then, after a brief traverse, it's down again into the funky mixed woods of *Movieland* or *Elk-weed*. At the bottom, as I plump down onto *Easy Street,* I always feel like a musician who has been only partially successful in weaving a continuous melody down the hill. There were measures, even whole pages of fluid sound, but here and there interrupted by cacophonous encounters with snow-laden evergreens or pesky willows. A good challenge.

As noted before, bumps are not a big part of the ski experience here. But if you really want to find some, try the back side of the mountain, where *Marmot, Black Bear,* and *Bighorn* cut narrow swaths through trees and grow substantial moguls. *Bighorn* in particular funnels skiers down a frighteningly steep tree chute that feels more like one of Stowe's Front Four than a western powder mountain; except for the snow, that is, which on this shady side of the peak stays cold and dry and untracked long after a storm. The reason? Not many skiers of any stripe—green, blue, or black—venture back here because of the 13-minute lift ride back to the top. The terrain is super and the snow may be the best quality on the mountain, but everybody's spoiled by the frontside quad, with its bigger vertical and 7.6-minute ride time.

One of the coolest things for advanced and expert skiers to do at the Big Mountain is hire the snowcat for half a day. It's a phenomenal bargain compared to the pricey ride at many snowcat operations and, if the snow is good, it's the perfect way to ski untracked. They can do it so cheaply because the cat actually makes a very short loop, ferrying you from near the top of the mountain out beyond *Easy Street* to a place called Flower Point. You ski down some of their future expansion terrain to a spot near the base of the North Slope chair, ride the chair back up, ski to the cat, which has returned to *Easy Street,* and rumble on.

The cat itself is a flash from the past. It's a 1958 vintage Tucker with the four independent tracks, and high up on the back they've bolted on a six-person gondola car. It's a lurching, steamy ride, as all cat rides are, but when you get out, the fluff beneath your feet banishes everything but anticipation.

The day I lucked into the cat scene at the Big Mountain, nine new inches blanketed the base area at opening time. Then, throughout the day, it kept coming, deeper and softer and colder with each hour. Over two feet total, up to the middle of your thigh standing still. Our tracks on the steep benches of the Flower Point runs filled in and disappeared from one run to the next.

I skied, by chance, with five fellows from all over the country who went to Dartmouth together. Once a winter they gather somewhere snowy for a reunion and a bit of cat skiing. One man brought his father, who had skied the Big Mountain in the 1950s with the Old Goats ski club. They had stayed in the Chalet and skied the T-bar, which shut down, he remembered, for lunch. He went to Dartmouth, too, a classmate of skiing legend Dick Durrance.

I'll never forget an image from the last run of that day. I stopped at the first bench and turned to watch one of my companions, David, on the pitch behind me. David wore goggles with fluorescent pink rims. As he approached through the maelstrom of his own powder cloud, all I could see was a faint pink glow where his head would be. That was it—no skis, no poles, no hands, no nothing. Just this eerie pink glow from within a wave of snow.

Eating at the Big Mountain

Here's a list of recommended restaurants in the resort area:

Moguls Bar & Grille. Slopeside espresso bar, free keg Monday après-ski courtesy of the ski school.

Summit House. Breakfast, lunch, cocktails, and a special German Bavarian Buffet dinner on select Wednesdays and every Saturday night on top of the mountain.

Cafe Kandahar and Snug Bar. Finest dining in the area in the Kandahar Lodge near the mountain. Reservations recommended.

Hell Roaring Saloon. Burgers, beer, nachos, and ski memorabilia in the historic Chalet building.

The 'Stube. Home of the Wednesday night Frabert "Clod of the Week" Award, sandwiches, videos, great beer and ale selection, live entertainment.

The Glacier Grand. Downtown Whitefish; free appetizers from 5 to 6 P.M., live music.

The Great Northern. In Whitefish; good, inexpensive Tex-Mex.

THE BIG MOUNTAIN DATA

Mountain Statistics

Vertical feet	2,300 feet
Base elevation	4,700 feet
Summit elevation	7,000 feet
Longest run	2.5 miles (Easy Street)
Average annual snowfall	300 inches
Number of lifts	8 chairs, including 1 high-speed quad, 1 fixed-grip quad, 5 triples, and 1 double, plus 1 platter lift and 1 T-bar
Uphill capacity	13,000 skiers per hour
Skiable terrain	3,000 acres, plus 1,000 acres of snowcat terrain
Opening date	Thanksgiving
Closing date	early April
Snowboarding	Yes

Transportation

By car About 126 miles north of Missoula and I-90 via Highway 93 to Whitefish. The Big Mountain is 8 miles northeast of Whitefish.

By train Via Amtrak, which serves Whitefish twice daily (once each direction) on its western Empire Builder Route from Chicago and Minneapolis to Seattle and Portland.

By plane Delta and Horizon Air fly into Glacier Park International Airport in Kalispell, 19 miles from the resort.

By bus From the Whitefish Amtrak station and from Glacier Park Airport.

Key Phone Numbers

Ski Area Information (406) 862-1900
Snow Report (406) 862-7669
Reservations (800) 858-5439
Flathead Convention & Visitor Association (800) 543-3105
www.bigmtn.com

INSIDE STORY

Dealing with Cold

The fanciful "snow ghosts" that populate the upper reaches of the Big Mountain wouldn't last in a warmer clime. In fact, they'd probably never be created in the first place. Rime is water or cloud moisture supercooled to below its freezing point that somehow survives in liquid form until it bumps into something like a tree on a summit ridge. Then it sticks as solid ice and adds to the white-on-white sculpture garden through which we ski on the Big Mountain and on ridge lines at Bridger Bowl, for example, and Schweitzer Mountain in Idaho's northern panhandle. Rime usually forms as a storm is leaving the area, when colder, high-pressure air sweeps in to replace the low-pressure storm front.

So what strategies can you bring to the mountain to deal effectively with cold temperatures? Three things: generate heat, keep it in, and know when to bail.

First, give your body all the fuel it needs to generate its own heat. Eat a hearty breakfast loaded with complex carbohydrates—cereals, whole grain toast, and muffins—and fats. Yes, fats. Butter, milk and yogurt, cream cheese on your bagel, bacon, sausage. Fats give your body quick energy and generate lots of warmth. High-altitude climbers and Arctic explorers eat butter by the stick. Don't worry, you'll be burning it off and then some.

Second, keep moving on the hill. Ski on runs that make you work rather than just stand and ride. Ski some bumps. Whatever it takes to keep the heart rate up and the blood flowing.

What you wear to keep the heat in is extremely important. (Battery-powered boot warmers have to be considered another form of energy consumption, but they work. If you have chronically cold toes, give them a try.) First, keep your core well insulated. That means layers of polypropylene, silk, wool, or down around your trunk, where your mass is. If your hands and feet feel cold, chances are your core is not warm enough. Frostbite occurs when your body automatically reduces blood flow to the extremities in an effort to keep the central core warm.

After your mid-section, pay attention to your head. We lose up to 40 percent of our body warmth through the head and neck. All those brain cells firing at once, I guess. A good wool or pile hat and—most underestimated of all ski accessories—a fuzzy, warm neck gaiter or scarf will keep you feeling impervious in the nastiest cold. Oh, yes, goggles are much warmer than glasses.

A wind-resistant outer shell will cut the wind-chill factor out of the equation. Most of the new waterproof/breathable fabrics and coatings like Gore-tex and Ultrex do a super job of boxing out wind. Denim doesn't do it. Wool by itself won't either. You need an outer layer from neck to ankle with a tight enough weave to stop the wind. Perversely, a truly waterproof garment, like a rain suit, will keep the wind at bay, but you will end up colder in the end. Your perspiration—and you will sweat even on the coldest days—cannot exit the impermeable fabric and will leave you clammy and colder on the inside. That's the beauty of breathable outerwear and hydrophobic (water-hating) fabrics next to your skin. Perspiration water vapor is transported outward layer to layer, eventually to the atmosphere, while your skin feels dry and therefore warmer.

Finally, hands and feet. Mittens are warmer than gloves, though a bit more awkward. Those little hand-warmer packets filled with powdered pepper really do work. Placed on a palm inside a glove, they'll keep your hands warm for hours. As for the feet, adding more socks or thicker socks is usually counterproductive. One thin wool sock that allows room for toes to move and blood to flow is usually warmer than a thicker sock that may restrict capillary flow.

When you're out skiing on a cold day, have your buddies check any exposed skin—like the tips of noses and cheeks—for frostbite. They will show a spot of pure white, like the snow. Take off your mitten and hold a bare palm against the spot. Don't rub; the skin really is frozen. In a few seconds the color should come back. Watch each other carefully, and go inside if the nipped spots reappear.

That's the final thing. Go inside. Have a hot drink, though nothing alcoholic; that'll just lower your core body temperature further. Fuel up with a Power Bar or something sweet. Stand next to the fire. Warm up from the outside in and the inside out. Nobody's paying us to suffer out there. Skiing is supposed to be fun. If you're prepared, even when it's well below zero, you can defy the elements and slip through the cold like a hot knife. But if it gets too bad, in spite of your best polar bear imitation, just bag it. Head for the hot tub. Read a book. The sun will be out tomorrow.

SCHWEITZER

Idaho's Schweitzer Basin, or Schweitzer Mountain Resort as it is now called, is an almost spooky physical twin to the Big Mountain, its neighbor four hours east in Montana. It is also a big mountain. Big, as in 2,350 inbound acres, the most in Idaho, even more than Sun Valley. Big, as in 2,400 feet of vertical, big snow numbers and a long season (there is a little snowmaking, but nobody's quite sure if it's ever been used). And big, as in wide-open, primarily intermediate pitches with rime-encrusted "snow ghosts" in the summit bowls.

Even Schweitzer's birth is linked to the Big Mountain. Jack Fowler, a local dentist, was returning from a rather wet and foggy ski weekend in Montana in 1960 when he pulled over in Hope, Idaho, to stare in wonder at the then-inaccessible, snowy ridge-line bowls above Schweitzer Creek. Three years later Fowler and partners cranked up the first lifts.

Both mountains rise above newly trendy, reawakened timber towns;

Schweitzer's is Sandpoint on the west shore of Lake Pend Oreille. To get to both mountains, you have to ascend long, switchbacking roads that go through rugged country. The road to Schweitzer is even longer and steeper than the Big Mountain's, snaking 11 miles from the lakeshore to the base lodge. Both mountains have much more skiing than they have skiers. Until recently, Schweitzer was almost completely unknown outside the Pacific Northwest.

Just get a load of these ski area marketing slogans (I am not making these up): "Fish the big hole, ski the big bowl," or "Ski the big potato," and "Ski Schhhhweitzer."

Well, that last one just might come back in favor someday, because Schweitzer, like the Big Mountain, is about to explode onto the national scene. The secret is out. Here's why: In 1990 the resort launched a ten-year, $100 million expansion plan. First, they pushed a new high-speed quad chair dubbed the Great Escape from the base up to the ridge where Schweitzer's two huge bowls come together. Next, they replaced the rickety, original day lodge with a shiny, 40,000-square-foot skiers' center complete with cafeteria, shops, kinder care, and five-minute massages. (Habitués of the original lodge, designed in 1963 by one of Schweitzer's early boosters, remember that when the band really got going on the top-floor Bierstube, pitchers of beer would bounce right off the tables.) Next door to the day lodge is an 82-room, luxury hotel called Green Gables that gave the mountain instant "destination" panache.

The resort was able to do all this so quickly because the area is all private land—no public-land agencies to petition or battles to fight. Future terrain expansion, condo construction, and so on will also take place on private ground, so the pace will be set by project economics. The lobby of Green Gables looks like a comfy, upper-middle-class living room: cartoons on the TV, checkerboards on the tables, kids lounging on couches waiting for Mom and Dad to hurry up and get ready to ski. Kids under the age of 12 on packages with their families stay and ski for free. *The Enchanted Forest* terrain garden is one of the best children's learning zones anywhere. There are video arcades and movies for the off-hours, and kids seem to be the prime beneficiaries of the Friday and Saturday night skiing. The service is friendly and informal everywhere you go, kind of like cousins.

Accessibility is still the big factor in keeping the numbers low. Recent yearly totals of about 180,000 skier days would amount to a big week at Vail. The nearest airport is in Spokane, Washington, which is 80 miles away. The nearest population centers are Seattle, Washington, and Calgary, Alberta, both about seven hours away. So for now Schweitzer is pretty much yours to share with the Sandpoint locals. But, like other beautiful areas previously deemed inaccessible—Telluride, Colorado, comes to mind—watch out. Spontaneous discovery may be just around the corner.

Room with a View

From the Green Gables Lodge, and indeed from just about everywhere on the mountain's front side, which is known as South Bowl, there is an unobstructed view of Lake Pend Oreille, Idaho's biggest lake. It is 43 miles long and 1,000 feet deep in some places, but it is just a remnant of a much bigger ice-age lake that stretched all the way to Missoula, Montana, 10,000 years ago. Because of the lake's depth, the U.S. Navy built a training center here during World War II, for, believe it or not, testing submarines.

This big, east-sweeping view is down Schweitzer Gulch, named for a demented Swiss trapper who lived in a cabin here around the turn of the century. Always formal and polite, he was nevertheless discovered to have trapped a number of Sandpoint's pet cats and turned them into cat stew. He twice appeared out of the fog at night and without a word took the reins from a young woman on horseback and led her home from work. Soon after, he was led away to an asylum. But the name lives on.

From up on the *Sky Edge* trail at 6,400 feet, a more complete panorama unfolds. You are in the southern folds of the Selkirk Range, one of the famous north-south trending heli-skiing ranges of British Columbia. To the east the Cabinet Mountains define the border with Montana. Far to the south, you can see pieces of the Bitterroot Wilderness. The Pack River flows into Lake Pend Oreille from the north. The Clark Fork River (a gorgeous drive on State Highway 200 to Missoula) feeds the lake from the east. Pend Oreille River drains the lake to the west on its way to meet the Columbia River.

The mountain layout is one of the simplest you'll find. There are two bowls, Schweitzer (South Bowl) and Colburn (North Bowl), the latter named for the little jewel of a lake at the base of the steeps. The village is in South Bowl, with 1,700 vertical feet above the lodge and 592 vertical feet below in the Chair 2 beginners' area. The 2,400-feet maximum vertical is measured in North Bowl from the summit ridge to the Outback warming hut in the bottom of the drain.

Of the four chairlifts in South Bowl, two climb to the Great Divide and access North Bowl. The two North Bowl lifts, Chairs 5 and 6, will both bring you back over the top and home. There is no way to ski from the Outback warming hut back around to the front.

The uniform cup shape of both bowls makes trail designation simple: The easiest pitches are in the bottom, the intermediate tilts reside in the middle elevations, and almost all the black diamonds drop from the ridges —short but oh so sweet.

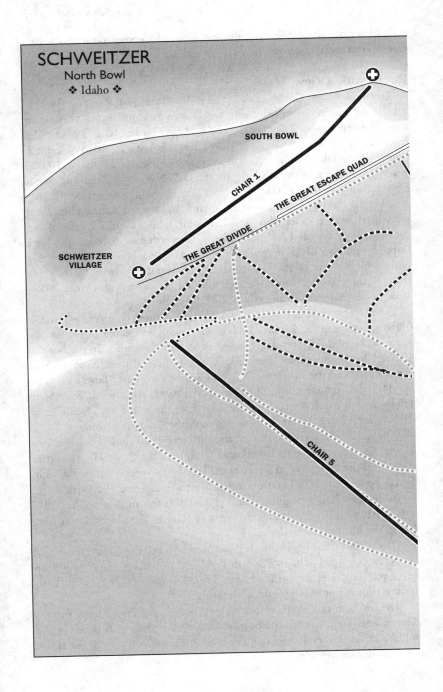

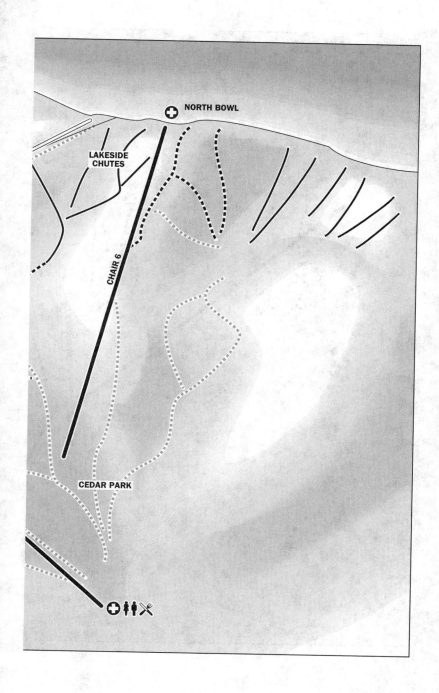

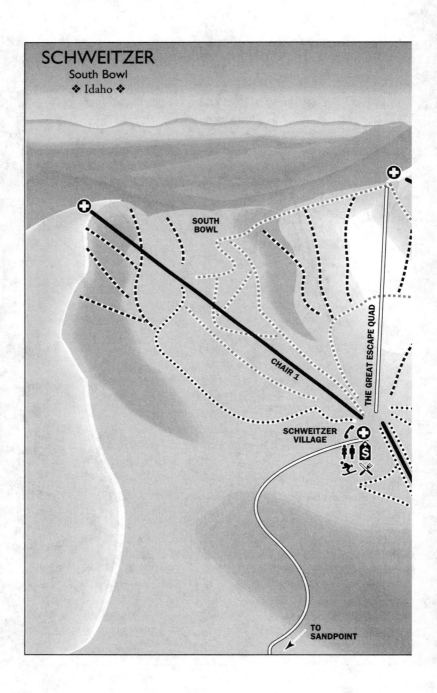

SCHWEITZER
South Bowl
❖ Idaho ❖

SOUTH
BOWL

CHAIR 1

THE GREAT ESCAPE QUAD

SCHWEITZER
VILLAGE

TO
SANDPOINT

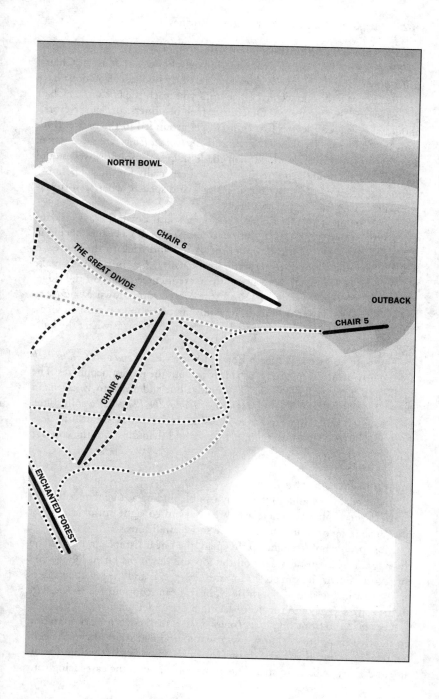

461

Happy Trails to Beginners

The Chair 2 beginners' area, affectionately known as Musical Chairs, drifts down the gully below the Headquarters Day Lodge, so you don't have to ride any over-the-snow conveyance until you reach the bottom of Chair 2. Just strap 'em on and go. Of course, true beginners, or "never-evers," should always take a lesson first thing to get grounded in the basics. Both runs served by the chair, *Happy Trails* and *Enchanted Forest*, are rated green. *Enchanted Forest* features added man-made shapes—mounds, waves, and darting routes through the trees—designed especially for kids. There is a remnant pocket of old-growth cedars, dark and special, where resort personnel teach environmental awareness.

Above the day lodge, in the immensity of South Bowl, there is just one green trail, and that is *Gypsy* to *Crystal* to *Jam Session*. It's a beauty, slicing in a big semicircle through the timberline glades and back to the center. It starts at the midway unloading station on Chair 1. Beginners, don't make the mistake of riding all the way up; there are no green runs off the ridge. Although, if you do forget to get off, the escape route down *Sky Edge* to upper *Gypsy*, while rated blue, is certainly manageable for most novices. You'll notice *Jam Session* packed with snowboarders. This is where the half-pipe is built.

There are no greens in North Bowl, although *Vagabond* and *Cedar Park* are exquisite, wide, scenic runs suitable for all but the newest neophytes. The problem is getting off the Great Divide ridge line and down to *Vagabond* in the belly of the basin. The easiest route, *Down the Hatch*, is a solid blue. Here's a good transition run for progressing novices: Ride Chair 4 to *Teakettle Trail*, which traverses the upper glades and then dips into the concave fun of *Lower Stiles*.

Intermediates in the Zone

Intermediates should not have any trouble finding a zone that combines comfort and challenge. There are three ways to go right out of the ticket line, depending on your whim and the snow conditions.

Most people bolt straight up the quad, the Great Escape, and decide on the way up. You can turn right off the top and down the Great Divide and into North Bowl. You can go left toward *Upper Stiles* and the big open spaces on the east-facing side of South Bowl, or you can scoot out *North Sky Edge* all the way to *Gypsy* and the north-facing blues under Chair 1.

Let's take the front side first. *Upper Stiles* is marked as a black diamond on the trail map, but it almost always has a groomed swath down the center, turning it into that rarest of birds, a steep, smooth run that intermediates and experts alike can soar. The only problem with the east-facing runs on either side of the quad is their tendency to soak up the solar, when it is out, and go crunchy overnight. For that reason, I prefer the blues around to the left (looking up the mountain): the big boulevard of *Ridge Run,* the steady sweep of *Sparkle,* and the always interesting, intertwining glade routes of *Sam's Alley.* These guys are in shade most of the day, and the snow is soft and cold and therefore forgiving. You can reach them either from the quad or from the midway unload on Chair 1.

The longest intermediate routes are in the Chair 5 region on the backside. These are the cruisers: *Vagabond, Cathedral Aisle, G3,* and *Zip Down.* Fifteen hundred and fifty vertical feet per lap. Soft, north-facing snow. Big trees. Big fun. There's another blue zone in the North Bowl along the area's west boundary. It's designated as a Family Skiing Zone. You get there by riding Chair 6, getting off at the midway and skiing *Snow Ghost* to *Cedar Park* to the Outback Restaurant. While in *Cedar Park,* you've got to stop and kiss one of the immense, old-growth trees dotting the bottom of the gully like 100-foot chess pieces. Legend has it that if you kiss one of these ancient trees, you will surely be back again one day. If you don't want to kiss it, just stand for a minute under the canopy and imagine being 500 years old.

There are more big trees on *Zip Down,* which is another must for its spacious, groomed, roller-coaster spirit. As long as we're on musts and since we're in Idaho, you really owe it to yourself to have a baked spud with all the trimmings—from sour cream to chili to chutney—at the Outback. The indoor picnic tables might be jammed and the windows steamy, but, especially here, there's nothing quite as tasteful as a tater.

The easiest way out of North Bowl is *Cat Track* to *Village* from the top of Chair 5, a green waltz all the way.

With the exception of a few genuinely precipitous chutes cutting north and south, there is not a lot of terrain in these ski-anywhere bowls that strong intermediates cannot handle in the right snow conditions. That caveat is key, however. *Upper Sam's Alley,* for example, may be intermediate heaven with a light frosting of new snow on a firm base, or it might be a full-on death struggle in deep, crusty, or windblown snow. Use good sense and don't hesitate to venture into inviting-looking glades, which are about as user-friendly here as any trees in the land.

Expert Ridges

Like Bridger Bowl, Schweitzer's steeps are concentrated almost exclusively on the top 400 to 500 vertical feet. Unlike at Bridger, you don't have to walk for any of it. With Chairs 1 and 6 and the quad rising to strategic high points along the ridges, you can shuffle off and immediately down the best fall lines on the mountain. The very best are the chutes strung out like the folds of a curtain along the far side, the north-facing side of South Bowl. There are no rocks or cliff bands to speak of, just smooth, straight-ahead drops through gnomish survivor trees that are often unrecognizable under their coats of wind-driven ice. *A Chute* starts just left of Chair 1 at the top. Then comes *B Chute, C Chute,* and so on, all the way out the alphabet. There is so much skiing on this face alone that explorers will find untracked snow for days or weeks after a storm.

One thing you won't find is moguls. Oh, there are a few here and there, on *The Face,* for example, and maybe *White Lightning,* and a few short pitches in the North Bowl. But by and large, they just don't have a chance to form—too much terrain and too few skiers.

One of the finest runs in new powder conditions is the *Lakeside* area of North Bowl. I say Lakeside area because the scale is too huge to call this a single run. Hundreds of skiers could lay down tracks side by side and never cross each other's lines. A hundred turns high above Colburn Lake, *Lakeside* is like the *Big Burn* at Snowmass with occasional dead snags and clusters of tiny trees standing like toy soldiers here and there, except *Lakeside* is bigger and steeper than the *Big Burn.* I don't know if it was logged at one time or burned, but for good skiers looking to heli-ski for the price of a lift ticket, this is the place.

If and when you tire of *Lakeside,* try exploring either side of this massive opening, particularly the north-facing runs that peel off the Great Divide. Between *Whiplash, Chute the Moon,* and *Debbie Sue,* there's a whole week's worth of poking around in the powder. Nothing scary: no cliffs, little avalanche danger, no inescapable drains or slogging back to civilization. Everything leads back, eventually, to Chairs 5 or 6. Be sure to check out *Glade-iator* and *Kathy's Yardsale* off the back side of Chair 5 for some exciting high-level glade skiing on north facing slopes.

Everything depends, of course, on snow conditions, how the wind blows, what the sun influence has been, where the white carpet is forgiving, and where it turns harsh. When conditions are right, some of my favorite expert skiing happens on the mellower, sunny exposures of *Sundance* and *Upper* and *Lower J.R.* They're rated black diamond because the snow you find is always a roll of the dice.

A breakable sun crust can be hell to bash through, but a solid sun crust (or wind crust), one dense enough to support your weight, can provide the smoothest imaginable platform. The trees in the quad region are gnarled and well spaced. To dance a reactive, ever-changing line between them—on any consistent surface, and without having to worry about your brakes—is a gift. The kind of gift that is generously forthcoming at Schweitzer.

Eating at Schweitzer

Here's a list of recommended restaurants in the resort area:

On the Mountain

The Outback Inn has great and huge Idaho spuds, baked and stuffed with anything and everything.

Jean's Northwest Bar & Grill, located in the Green Gables Lodge, serves breakfast, lunch, and dinner, and features indigenous northwestern wines and food.

Headquarters Cafe is the cafeteria in the day lodge. It is open for night skiing.

St. Bernard is within walking distance down the road. It has informal, family-style dining downstairs, and a club upstairs that serves cocktails and various entertainments such as comedy, jazz, and mystery dinner theater.

In Sandpoint

Java Adagio, a great coffee fix, is located near the Cedar St. Bridge, a covered bridge market.

Jalapeños is the call if you are looking for Mexican food.

Spud's, located next to Starbucks, has great chicken and salads.

SCHWEITZER DATA

Mountain Statistics

Vertical feet	2,400 feet
Base elevation	4,700 feet at Village; 4,000 feet at Outback
Summit elevation	6,400 feet
Longest run	2.7 miles, the Great Divide
Average annual snowfall	300 inches
Number of lifts	1 high-speed quad 5 double chairs
Uphill capacity	7,092 skiers per hour
Skiable terrain	2,350 acres
Opening date	Thanksgiving
Closing date	early April
Snowboarding	Yes

Transportation

By car Eleven miles from Sandpoint on Schweitzer Basin Road; 80 miles (90 minutes) from Spokane, Washington, via I-90 to Highway 95 North; 7 hours from Seattle via I-90, and 7 hours from Calgary, Alberta, via Highway 95 South.

By plane To Spokane International Airport, which is served by Horizon, Morris Air, Northwest, Delta, United, and Continental airlines. Coeur d'Alene Airport, 45 miles south of Sandpoint, is served by Empire Airlines.

By train Via Amtrak daily east-west service through Sandpoint. Schweitzer will arrange transfers from airports and Amtrak station with advance notice.

Key Phone Numbers

Ski Area Information
  (208) 263-9555
Snow Report (208) 263-9562
Reservations (800) 831-8810
www.schweitzer.com
E-mail ski@schweitzer.com

INSIDE STORY

Fog

On a sunny day you may not notice the poles with their Day-Glo circles set at regular intervals along the *North Sky Edge* and along the sides of other easiest routes at Schweitzer. On a foggy day, though, they may save your life.

Perhaps it's the ski area's proximity to Lake Pend Oreille, but Schweitzer, along with its spiritual and geographic cousin the Big Mountain on the shores of Whitefish Lake in Montana, suffers an occasional day when the clouds roll in so thick and soupy, you may not see the next snow ghost or your friend two turns ahead of you.

And thus the poles, set just far enough apart so that you can see the next one glowing faintly through the gloom. Follow them and you will not fall off any unexpected precipices. Slalom your way faithfully with your fellows—who appear and vanish and reappear like gray ghosts out of the periphery—and you will eventually bump into civilization.

If, on the other hand, you know perfectly well where you are—on the groomed headwall of *Upper Stiles,* for example—and you choose to leave the security of the disks, you may open yourself to a skiing epiphany. With no visual cues, no horizon to play off, you will have a hard time pinpointing the fall line. Sometimes your skis fall away easily into a turn, and sometimes they hang up stubbornly as if pushing against an unseen bank. Are you moving across the hill or glancing more directly toward the center of the earth? Gravity becomes a wider, vaguer tug than you remember. Speed is just the wind peppering your cheeks, and without eyes you must depend on your sense of feel instead.

Your skis are, in fact, your best source of information. Trust their messages: Lighter means they are falling off; heavier means they are climbing slightly. If they are riding flat to the snow, the pitch is gentle; if they are up on a thin edge, the slope is dropping away. Even without the advance warning of sight, this information is enough; it is instant and true. You can begin to concentrate on just riding your skis, staying in trim aboard them. That's your job—to stay more or less vertical, fore-and-aft and side-to-side, above your own sliding, hungry feet.

I say hungry because they will soon be ravenous for sensation. The other senses are shut out. You smell nothing but the clean, mid-cloud dankness. The wind and the billions of water droplets muffle even the sound your skis make on the snow. Your collar grows stiff with frozen breath. You snuggle your chin down in your neck gaiter and tune in as best you can to the stimuli from the ground. You let go of the vision thing.

After a while it is like a falling dream. Only you are in control. Falling through the cloud, suspended, making no discernible progress toward the valley. Just falling, and carving the air. Balancing, hanging as if by a string. Turn after turn, untouched by distance or time.

When it's done and you finally bump into the lodge or the base of a lift, or other skiers pierce your reverie with their forms and shouts, you feel relief, but you also feel cheated. You realize you don't need to see to ski. Your feet are smarter than you thought, and that pure visceral touch is as rich as the brightest blue-sky view.

Sun Valley started it all. It is the beginning point for every Rockies ski story and indeed a keystone in the story of modern skiing around the world.

In 1935, there were no ski resorts in the United States. There were a few ski tows, mainly rope tows, driven by old Ford and Dodge motors and looped around rear-drive axles to drag intrepid skiers up New England pastures and Canadian sugarbushes and even a few timberline passes out West. Even the Alps were not much more sophisticated. Yes, the Brits did play in the snow, skating and sleighing at elegant hotels in St. Moritz and Gstaad, and Hemingway did ride the cog trains up Swiss passes only to swoop back down on skis to the village and the inevitable wine lunch. But downhill skiing, and ski resorts as we know them, didn't yet exist.

Enter a young Averell Harriman, chairman of the board of Union Pacific Railroad and an avid skier. Harriman very much wanted to increase passenger traffic to the West and decided that a European-style winter destination resort would be just the ticket. So he hired an Austrian count, Felix Schaffgotsch, to scour the mountains for the perfect location, with the caveat that it be accessible by rail.

Count Schaffgotsch spent the winter of 1935–36 on tour with his knickers and six pairs of hickory skis. He rejected Washington's Mount Rainier because all the surrounding land was publicly owned. He nixed Oregon's Mount Hood as too wet. Aspen flunked because its base elevation at 8,000 feet was considered too high for strenuous alpine exercise. Jackson Hole was deemed inaccessible.

The good count was about to return a failure when a Union Pacific representative in Idaho wired him to take a look at the area around Ketchum, an isolated sheep and cattle ranching town at 6,000 feet elevation with a dwindling population of 270 souls. Schaffgotsch arrived on a new-snow day with the sun dazzling the rounded, nearly treeless slopes of the Pioneer Range. Very little wind found its way through the protective rings of peaks. Due to the nearness of the desert and the long, dry route storms took in getting there, the snow Schaffgotsch found was too dry to make good snowballs; it was mostly air, the better to float down on skis.

The location was perfect, and Harriman wasted no time implementing his plan. By New Year's Eve 1936, the luxurious Sun Valley Lodge had already hosted champagne banquets for the likes of Sam Goldwyn, Errol Flynn, and Claudette Colbert. Guests stepped off the train and twirled around the glorious ice rink or swam in a glass-enclosed, circular pool under the stars. Even more amazing for skiers, Harriman had built the world's first chairlift, engineered by a designer of conveyor systems for loading banana boats in Central America. Replace the banana hook with a single chair, add a safety bar and a blanket for your lap, and up the mountain you go.

Sun Valley changed skiing forever, making it glamorous. Hemingway moved into room 206 in the Lodge to finish *For Whom the Bell Tolls*. A carefully orchestrated marketing program brought the most glamorous Hollywood stars of the day to ski and be seen: Clark Gable, Ingrid Bergman, Gary Cooper, Sonja Henie, Jimmy Stewart, Marilyn Monroe. They even made movies there. Henie and John Payne starred in the 1941 romance *Sun Valley Serenade,* which still screens three times a week in the rooms of the Lodge and the Inn and at the Opera House, a short walk from the Lodge. A former mistress of gangster Bugsy Seigel named Virginia Hill had shoe boxes full of cash delivered to the Lodge by limousine each month. She later fell in love and ran off with one of Sun Valley's handsomest ski instructors, Austrian Hans Hauser.

In those days most ski teachers in America were Austrians, disciples of the great Hannes Schneider, founder of the Arlberg School in St. Anton, Austria. When I first visited Sun Valley in 1963 (on the overnight train from Los Angeles), I wanted nothing more than to ski like ski school director Sigi Engl, who coursed the mountain with effortless élan. Every turn was the same, beginning with a crisp edge check and then a hop of the tails up off the snow and across the fall line, his wool gabardine slacks creased to perfection, feet and knees so tight together it was as if they were sewn in place.

More than the social swirl, the long, long uninterrupted trails of Bald Mountain dictated that the great skiers of several eras put in their time at Sun Valley: Norwegian super skier and founder of Alta, Utah, Alf Engen; America's first ski Olympian, Dick Durrance; master teacher and filmmaker Otto Lang; Aspen pioneer Freidl Pfeifer; Toni Matt; Stein Eriksen . . . the list goes on and on. More recent shining stars have included Christin Cooper, GS silver medalist in the 1984 Olympics, and Picabo Street, silver medalist in downhill at the 1994 Lillehammer Games, gold medalist in Super G at the 1998 Nagano Games, and World Cup downhill champion for 1995 and 1996.

The Austrian connection still runs strong. When Arnold Schwarzenegger goes skiing, it is to Sun Valley. Last time I skied on Baldy, I met Adi Erber, Arnold's private instructor when the muscled one is in town. Adi is Austrian, with a movie-star cleft chin, bright smile, and the requisite romantic accent. "Mr. Schmooth," Arnold calls him.

Gone are the boiled wool jackets and jaunty Tyrolean caps, but the spirit of gemütlichkeit still pervades the valley. The Ram Bar is still the place to hoist a beer and carve your initials in the thick wooden tables. There is still jazz every night in the elegant Duchin Room at the Lodge. There is elegant

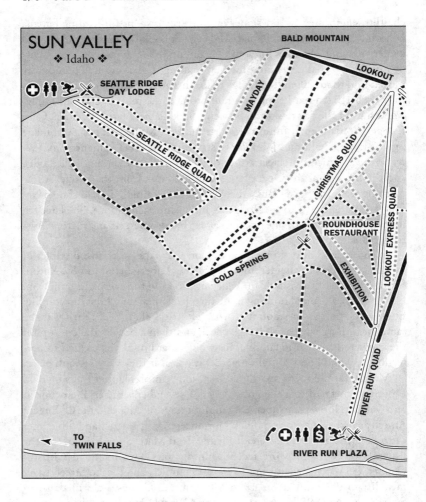

dining on the mountain and off and a pace and an ambience that owes more to its European predecessors than to its western, sheep-town roots.

In recent years, the skiing has undergone a greater change than any other aspect of life along the Big Wood River. Bald Mountain has always been recognized as one of the finest natural ski hills in the West, with 3,400 feet of lift-served vertical (3,260 feet of it continuous skiing) and a plethora of unobstructed, rock-free, sinuous fall lines in three directions off the summit. But Sun Valley, some years, has a problem with snow. The name says it all: Sun Valley averages 280 days of sunshine per year. Eighty percent of the

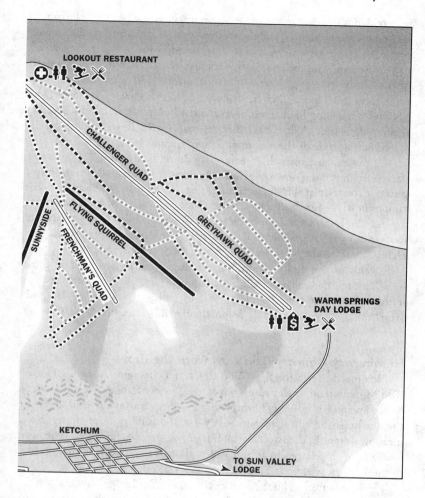

days in ski season are sunny. The sagebrush-covered hills immediately south and west of Baldy tell the tale another way: Sagebrush cannot live in a climate much wetter than 16 inches of rain per year. This is the edge of the Great Basin, 210,000 square miles of desert, including most of Nevada, Utah, eastern Oregon, and southern Idaho. Sun Valley—unlike Alta or Grand Targhee—doesn't advertise its average annual snowfall totals. (It receives 220 inches, versus 500 for Alta and Grand Targhee.)

This was a problem neither Harriman nor Schaffgotsch had counted on, and it contributed to a slow decline for the grande dame of American ski resorts. Union Pacific never made any money on the project; Harriman's interest turned to politics, and the area was sold. Neglect tarnished the glamour until current owner Earl Holding decided to do something about nature. Beginning in the late 1980s, Holding invested $18 million in a state-of-the-art snowmaking system—top-to-bottom, 630 acres, covering runs up to three miles long. Then he made access to that guaranteed snow twice as easy by installing high-speed quad chairs all over the mountain, seven of them to date. One chair, the Challenger, roars up 3,144 vertical feet on the Warm Springs side of the mountain in ten minutes.

You can exhaust yourself in half a day skiing Baldy now. A good many people try, bombing down the Warm Springs and Seattle Ridge groomed pistes on long, quiet skis designed to go fast. When it snows, jump into the famous bowls—*Christmas Bowl, Easter Bowl, Sigi's Bowl, Mayday Bowl*—or try out the bumps on *Exhibition* where Warren Miller shot his first ski footage in the 1950s. When it doesn't snow, join Arnold, Bruce Willis, and Demi Moore on the baby-bottom-smooth, perfect runs under the sun.

Royalty, of the Hollywood kind, the European ski-god kind, and the New York railroad magnate kind, made Sun Valley. Now it almost feels as if the reverse were true: People go to Sun Valley in hopes the place will somehow bestow a special grace on them, and more often than not, it does.

Hemingway Country: The View from the Top

Papa loved to fish the Big Wood River that cuts right along the base of Bald Mountain on its way south out of the Pioneer Range. The old town of Ketchum sprawls at Baldy's foot, while a half-mile away up Trail Creek to the northeast the village of Sun Valley just about fills a once-empty sheep meadow. In truth, the two have all but grown together in recent years; the whole resort is referred to as Sun Valley, though the folks in Ketchum like to think of themselves as a crustier western zip code.

The utterly treeless knob south of the Sun Valley Lodge is Dollar Mountain, the original ski hill and the place where that first chairlift groaned into being. Dollar is still a key component in the overall ski scene; it's the primary teaching hill for the Sun Valley Ski & Snowboard School, with a private beginner's area. Four chairs ply the 638 vertical feet to the summit at 6,638 feet. But next to Baldy across the valley, it is just a bump.

Baldy rises from the river, at an elevation of 5,750 feet, to 9,150 feet in a single, steep, mostly forested mound with naked bowls capping the ridges facing south and east. From the sumptuous log and glass Seattle Ridge Lodge near the summit, you can see most of southern Idaho—from the sagebrush plains around Twin Falls to the south to the Pioneer and Boulder Peaks east of Sun Valley, Galena Summit to the north, and endless rows of the jagged Sawtooth Range to the north and west.

The skiing divides into four major zones: the shady northwoods of Warm Springs; the sharp V of the River Run drainage on the east; the bowls; and the mellow avenues of Seattle Ridge farthest south. It's hard to get lost on this mountain; there are only two ways on and two ways off. Fourteen lifts spread the crowds out (an average day is 3,500 people) over the 2,000 acres of skiable terrain.

River Run is the original base, and it now sports a huge new base lodge and skier services plaza to go along with the parking and high-speed quads. The other base is at Warm Springs, where another new day lodge (opened in 1992 with oak-paneled ski lockers and computerized boot-drying service) presides at the foot of the Challenger quad. Warm Springs feels like an exclusive European hunting lodge with gourmet food and prices to match. But don't despair. Irving's Red Hots, Chicago-style wieners, inhabit that little shack across the street. There is no parking at the Warm Springs base, but a good local shuttle hustles skiers from the big park-and-ride lot at the corner of Warms Springs Road and Saddle Road. The bus service is excellent throughout the valley. Yellow Sun Valley buses run continuously between the Village, Baldy, and Dollar Mountain. Blue municipal KART buses connect Ketchum, Sun Valley Village, the Baldy and Dollar bases, and most major hotels.

Although there are a dozen or so green-circle designated runs on the Baldy trail map, this is not a mountain for true beginners. The standard designations have been ratcheted up a notch. The Seattle Ridge greens, for example, while perfectly smooth, would still rate blue on most other mountains. And the blues in the bowls—*Christmas, Mayday, Lefty's*—would no doubt be black diamonds elsewhere. So, beginners beware, start out on Dollar Mountain, and when you can cruise *Graduation* with impunity, you are ready to move up to the big hill.

Suits Cruising

With the coming of the quads and the man-made snow, Sun Valley has earned a reputation as a quintessential cruising mountain. It was always pretty good for rolling fast over the shapes until your own quads were screaming. But now, thanks to the fast chairs, you can double or triple your vertical in a day, and the fastidious snow farming means that bothersome interruptions like bare spots and moguls never enter the picture.

Warm Springs run remains the gold standard for western cruising: three miles long, over 3,000 vertical feet with nary a break—no flats, no roads, no divergence from its pure, fall-line charge to the river. It's so long that they divide it into three sections on the map, *Warm Springs Face, Mid Warm Springs,* and *Lower Warm Springs.* Most of it is rated blue and the bottom is green, but it's all relative. Elsewhere, this kind of persistent pitch would warrant a black diamond. But because it's kept smooth, intermediates thrill to big gravity and experts rip the high-speed shapes. One of the traditions sadly no longer in effect is the awarding of the Sun Valley Two-Star pin for skiing *Warm Springs,* top to bottom, without stopping and without falling.

On a busy day in the 1990s, it seems thousands are trying to accomplish that very thing all at once, all of them wearing the latest one-piece suits and riding expensive, vibration-absorbing skis. You might spy silver-maned Bobby Burns, inventor of The Ski, a popular ski brand in the 1970s, and a man who has a heli-ski lodge named after him in the Canadian Rockies. You might spot Clint Eastwood arcing turns through the gully. You see, the stars never really abandoned the place; they were just hiding out until the skiing became irresistibly good.

If *Warm Springs* gets a little hectic, try *Limelight,* which plunges even more steeply over a series of stairsteps before joining *Warm Springs* halfway down. Or smooth your way out on *Upper College,* the more gently pitched ridge to the east, and then hard down *Flying Squirrel* again to meet the *Warm Springs* funnel to the base. The last section of *Warm Springs* is hash-marked on the map, meaning it's a slow skiing area, and they really mean it. Traffic from a half-dozen major thoroughfares converges here, and you need to go slow and watch your back.

Much less crowded than *Warm Springs* is the *River Run* gully bounded by *College* on the north and the *Round House Ridge* on the south. The cruising is not as long, and it takes two chairs, River Run and the Lookout Express, to reach the top, but the payoff comes in relatively quiet trips down blue-square runs like *Canyon* and *Blue Grouse* and the *River Run* itself, which is a wonderful, deep-throat, bank-sided gulch reminiscent of Aspen's Spar Gulch.

This is also the zone where novices moving up to intermediate skiing on Baldy should start. The floor of the drain under River Run Lift is a good place to start. Then climb higher and follow *Upper* and *Lower College* to the *Lilly Marlane* cat track and back into the gut of the zone for a really long, varied descent. On the other side, take the Exhibition Lift up the steep north-facing pitch to *Round House Slope* and *Olympic Lane,* a twisting forest route back to the gully. (Some of Sun Valley's best bump skiers spend time here, and you can watch them—without having to negotiate the same terrain—bopping under the lifts on *Exhibition* and *Holiday.)* Or continue south from the top of Exhibition on *Gun Tower Lane* across the vast lower bowls to the Seattle Ridge Lift and its huge novice/intermediate area.

The newest intermediate terrain on Baldy was opened up in the winter of 1994–95 between *Warm Springs* and *River Run.* It's called *Frenchman's Gulch.* It has its own high-speed quad and five new blue-square runs through the trees between *Lower College* and *Flying Squirrel.* The northeast exposure should be perfect for holding cold, crisp snow; and the location is sure to siphon off a bit of the *Warm Springs* crowd. Take note: There is no egress from the bottom of *Frenchman's;* you have to ride to the top and exit either into the *Warm Springs* or *River Run* basins.

The reason Seattle Ridge has become such a popular addition to the mountain—besides the gourmet pastas and the heated, glassed-in deck of the Seattle Ridge restaurant—is the miles and miles of easy-swinging, groomed terrain served by the Seattle Ridge quad. *Broadway, Christin's Silver, Southern Comfort,* and *Gretchen's Gold* (named for Sun Valley's 1948 Olympic gold medalist Gretchen Fraser) are all covered by the new snow-making system and buffed to talcum by the big machines. Many intermediates just stay here all day. To get home, you take *Lower Broadway* to the old Cold Springs double chair, which lifts you up and out, back into *River Run.*

Looming above the boulevards of Seattle Ridge, the bowls and their myriad possibilities may or may not beckon intermediates. Due to their sunny exposures, you can't count on snow cover, except on *Christmas Ridge,* where the snow guns have poached out into the semiwild. When the natural cover is good, groomed swaths down *Christmas* and *Mayday* and *Broadway Face* make this terrain a real treat for intermediates. At other times and conditions, the bowls' rugged, unshaved nature is best left to very good skiers with wild-snow experience. If at the top you change your mind, you can always ski the summit ridge line back to Seattle Ridge.

Expert Exhibition

I've already mentioned the kick experts get screaming down the ultra-smooth groomers in the *Warm Springs* area. There's nothing like it anywhere. But after a while, good skiers want some variety, and Baldy has it in spades.

The bowls are the best, when the snow is there. They flow at a delicious pitch, steep but not too steep, finger after nude finger, gully after treeless gully across a mile of ridge. *Christmas* is the longest, dropping from the Lookout Restaurant all the way to the base of the Cold Springs Lift. *Lookout* and *Easter bowls* are the steepest. Connoisseurs yo-yo the Mayday chair's 1,600-foot vertical and work the lines on either side—powder if the snow is new, bumps if the snowpack is old and deep, north-trending snow ribbons between the sage if the sun has been doing its thing.

The moguls on the north-facing hillside of *River Run* gulch are classics, the biggest and best-formed on the mountain. *Exhibition* is aptly named; generations of bump meisters have showed off underneath the chairlift of the same name. *Holiday* sports some of the steepest bumps on the mountain. (The official, steepest bumps at Sun Valley cascade down *Inhibition* in the *Lower Christmas Bowl* region, but they suffer the fickle snow-cover syndrome over on the sunny side.) The most interesting mogul shapes, to my mind, are those on *Upper River Run,* where the trail drops over the mountain's prow like a frozen river at spring break-up, tumbling through a shady tree alley.

But interestingly enough, Sun Valley is not really a bumper's mountain in the sense that Telluride and Aspen are. In big snow years, sure. When the bowls are full and creamy, and the moguls have a chance to build and shape from storm to storm. It takes a lot of natural snowfall to carve a good mogul field, and the processes involved in making and grooming artificial snow pretty much preclude turning those runs over to bumps. Besides, the majority of Sun Valley's customers are not looking for mogul madness; they're after the big smooth, and that's what they're getting.

Dollar for Your Thoughts

Some areas have segregated beginner zones off to the side. Sun Valley has a whole beginner's mountain practically right outside the Lodge door. Dollar is the original ski mountain in the valley, and it's got enough variety and challenge to keep many an intermediate happy as well. The only reason more good skiers don't ski on Dollar is the outstanding big hill across the way. In fact, if Dollar Mountain were transposed to the Midwest somewhere, it would be a major resort.

Part of the fun of Dollar is knowing who has schussed this hallowed terrain before you. There's a marvelous black-and-white photo in the Lodge hallway—a must for any history buff—of Clark Gable and Gary Cooper straight running in the spring powder on Dollar, wearing identical brimmed caps and pressed white jackets. The Lodge corridor also boasts wonderful shots of Lucille Ball, Marilyn Monroe, Ricky Nelson, Jackie O., a slim Liz Taylor; the hit parade goes on.

All made tracks on the Quarter Dollar, Half Dollar, or Dollar chairlifts and took the sun on the deck out front of the Dollar Cabin at the base. The terrain is perfect: treeless, north-facing, with infinite microterrain choices from the *Cabin Practice Slope* to meandering *Hidden Valley* to slightly steeper and blue-rated *Face of Dollar.*

The huge majority of skiers you will see here are participating in ski school. But there are other very good reasons to come and ski Dollar. Families with children can ski together here with no worries about high-speed interlopers and no chance to get separated or lost. The pace is more old-fashioned; the chairs are all leisurely old doubles and triples. One more reason to check Dollar out: When there is new powder blanketing the valley, you can bet all the hot shots are ripping it up on the big mountain, but on Dollar the snow lies sparkling, intact, and waiting for the few skiers who will claim their Dollar's worth of uncontested fresh tracks in *Sheepherder* and *Sepp's Bowl* and the other historic lines.

Eating at Sun Valley

Here's a list of recommended restaurants in the resort area:

On the Mountain

Warm Springs Lodge. Elegant cafeteria-style dining with an outdoor BBQ, weather permitting.

Irving's Red Hots. Chicago-style wieners and sodas across the street from Warm Springs Lodge. It's a favorite of local race brats, snowboarders, and anyone in a hurry.

Roundhouse. The original, tiny, deck-encircled restaurant on the mountain at the top of Exhibition and Cold Springs lifts. It has a cafeteria and a cozy fireplace.

Seattle Ridge Lodge. Huge logs, pink granite bathrooms, silent carpet, heated decks, and a surprisingly reasonable mesquite grill, fresh pastas, and salads, all with the spectacular views from the summit ridge.

Lookout Restaurant. Highest food on the mountain at the top of the Challenger, Christmas, and Lookout quads, with a friendly, utilitarian cafeteria.

Dollar Cabin. Cafeteria at the base of Dollar Mountain, with the ghosts of Gary Cooper and Marilyn Monroe.

In the Village

The Lodge Dining Room. You still see couples in evening dress here (though it is not required); continental cuisine.

The Ram Bar. In the old Challenger Inn (now called the Sun Valley Inn), good Austrian gemütlichkeit, beer, and accordion music.

Trail Creek Cabin. Hemingway drank here. The quality of the food varies, but the ambience is killer. Ride the sleigh from Sun Valley Lodge, but not on a night that's −5 degrees.

Bald Mtn. Pizza & Pasta. Great for family dining, complete with game room.

In Ketchum

The Pioneer. An old Ketchum watering hole on Main Street with classic western fare, steaks, trout, etc.

Michel's Cristiania. New glitz in town with continental cuisine, game specialties.

SUN VALLEY DATA

Mountain Statistics

Vertical feet	3,400 feet
Base elevation	5,750 feet
Summit elevation	9,150 feet
Longest run	3 miles
Average annual snowfall	220 inches
Number of lifts	On Baldy: 13 chairlifts, including 7 high-speed quads, 4 triples, 2 doubles; 1 surface lift on Dollar Mountain: 3 doubles and 1 triple chair; 1 surface lift
Uphill capacity per hour	26,380 skiers
Skiable terrain	2,000 acres
Opening date	late November
Closing date	mid-April
Snowboarding	Yes

Transportation

By car About 300 miles north of Salt Lake City via I-15 and I-84 to Twin Falls, then north on Highway 75 through Hailey to Ketchum; 150 miles from Boise, via Highways 20 and 75. From the north through Salmon and Stanley on Highways 93 and 20.

By plane Via Horizon Air and SkyWest to Hailey's Friedman Memorial Airport, 17 miles from the resort. Gateway cities for major carriers include Boise, Idaho Falls, and Twin Falls, Idaho, and Salt Lake City, Utah.

By bus Via available charter from gateway cities; complimentary pickup for Sun Valley Company guests at Hailey Airport. Ski company and municipal bus service around the resort village and Ketchum.

Key Phone Numbers

Ski Area Information
  (208) 622-4111
Snow Report (800) 635-4150
Reservations (800) 786-8259
www.sunvalley.com
Sun Valley Express
  (800) 634-6539
www.sunvalex.com

Ski Schools

The strong Austrian flavor to the Sun Valley ski school is no accident, and it isn't just because Averell Harriman's scout in the resort's formative years was Austrian count Felix Schaffgotsch. In the 1930s, almost every ski school in America owed at least some fealty to the great Hannes Schneider, who had developed the first real systematic ski-teaching method at his school in St. Anton. It was called the Arlberg method, and for nearly 30 years it was almost universal.

Schneider sent protégés to start ski schools around the world—Sepp Ruschp to Mount Mansfield at Stowe, Vermont; Sig Buchmayr to Peckett's-on-Sugar Hill, New Hampshire; Hans Hauser and Friedl Pfeifer to Sun Valley. Otto Lang became a kind of filmmaker/roving ambassador for the Arlberg method.

Back then skis were wooden, long, stiff, and heavy, and the boots were leather, soft, and imprecisely clamped to the skis. Turning technique required that you drive the skis through a turn with a powerful rotating of the upper body and arms, like a bus driver twisting a three-foot steering wheel. Then you needed to unweight, often hopping the tails completely off the snow, to begin a direction change. The skis worked as one, feet and knees clamped tight together. The finished product, which everyone in ski school in those days hoped fervently to imitate, was stylish, elegant, and fiendishly difficult to master.

As ski equipment got better, so too was there room for new and divergent teaching theory. In the 1960s the French National School rose to prominence on the theories of George Joubert and the race results of Jean-Claude Killy. Boots had buckles instead of laces, though they were still made of leather, and skis were built of much more responsive metal laminates. The French showed how to direct the skis with the lower body while keeping the upper body quiet. Several ski schools in the United States still show strong French influence, including Squaw Valley, California, and Loveland in Colorado.

In the 1970s, the Italians became fashionable following the successes of Gustavo Thoeni. Riding on even better fiberglass skis and in stiffer boots, Thoeni and the Italian School demonstrated how a wide, balanced stance and strong edging by the outside knee resulted in superior turns.

Also in the 1970s, the national schools of all the alpine nations—Switzerland, Austria, France, Italy, Germany, plus the United States and

Japan—got together every couple of years to show off their newest teaching theories. Precision ski demonstration teams in matching uniforms competed informally but with great pageantry for bragging rights to the newest and most innovative methodologies.

In 1974, to the surprise and chagrin of the traditional powers, the U.S. team of PSIA (Professional Ski Instructors of America) demonstrators stole the show with their unveiling of the American Teaching Method. This was the first teaching system that was totally student-oriented, completely learning-based; and, most shocking of all to the Europeans who had invested decades in competing national styles, ATM subjugated form to pure function.

Gone was the need to imitate a particular style, or affect a look. ATM focused instead on the key skiing skills—balance, gliding, edging, and pressuring the ski—that *all* effective skiing embodies. ATM rocked the Europeans and became the standard at virtually every ski school in America.

So now when you go take a lesson at Sun Valley, for example, your instructor may be from Austria (he might even be Arnold's instructor), and he may have an elegant, feet-together Austrian style when he free skis, but the lesson he gives you will be pure American Teaching Method, with an emphasis not on what you look like but on the core skills you need to make skiing easier and more fun—to develop basic skills to the point that your own personal style shines through.

PART 4

California and the Pacific Northwest

SETH MASIA

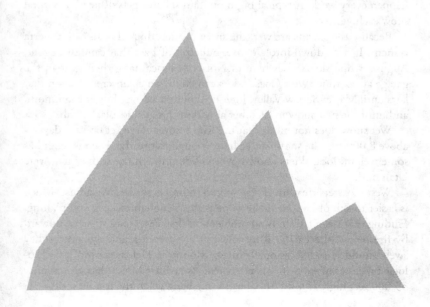

Hot Rocks and
Cold Water

Fʀᴏᴍ the San Bernardino range east of Los Angeles to the Alaska Range, the skiable bits of the North American Pacific Rim stretch out over 2,000 miles. It's a procession of volcanos, some lively, some dormant, most extinct. Fly up the West Coast, and on a clear day you can count the cones: Mount San Gorgonio, Mount Whitney, Mount Humphreys, Mount Ritter, Freel Peak, Mount Rose, Lassen Peak, Mount Shasta, Mount Scott, Three Sisters, Mount Hood, Mount Adams, Mount St. Helens, Mount Rainier, Mount Baker, Mount Garibaldi. They continue on north into the vast wilderness of British Columbia and Alaska. Rising 10,000 to 14,000 feet, these mountains force the moist Pacific winds high into the cold upper atmosphere, pulling huge falls of snow out of the air.

When a winter storm boils over from the Gulf of Alaska, a five-day blizzard can drop 10 feet of snow on sunny California and 15 feet on the wet forests above Seattle and Vancouver. In a good snow year, two-day storms happen every week. A typical big-mountain ski area gets 40 feet of natural snow each winter.

Because the storms are wet, the snow is often thick. Locals call it Sierra cement. It beds down into a dense, bulletproof base that can last beyond August; while skiers elsewhere in North America hang their gear in the garage at tax time, West Coast skiers can count on a sunscreen season that lasts until May at Squaw Valley, June at Alpine Meadows, July at Mammoth, and until the first snow in October at Mount Hood and Blackcomb.

Wet snow does not mean that the Rim resorts never get powder days—above 8,000 feet the snow can be light enough to breathe. Even when it has some weight, local skiers know how to glide through the stuff as if it were Utah fluff.

West Coasters treat muck the way Vermonters ski ice: We adjust. Muck is easier to ski, of course, if the slope is steep enough to keep you planing. Finding that steep terrain is no problem on the West Coast. Pushed upward by fire below, the Pacific Rim volcanos are growing and dynamic. They swell, shudder, and occasionally burst (Mount St. Helens is proof that geologic processes move swiftly here). Scientists say that Mount Lassen was once 35,000 feet high; it must have been some bang when the top blew off.

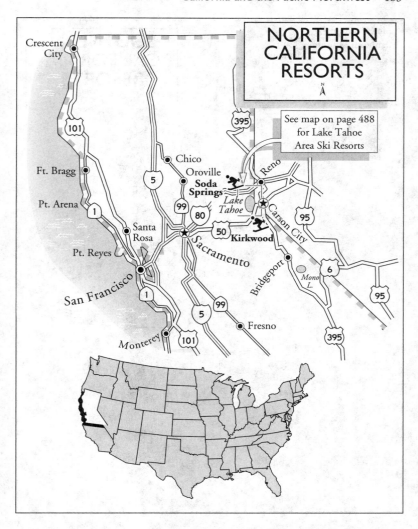

NORTHERN
CALIFORNIA
RESORTS

See map on page 488
for Lake Tahoe
Area Ski Resorts

Hyperactive geology can create scenery of vast verticality—think of Yosemite Valley, Shasta, Rainier. It also builds rugged, high-relief ski terrain, an incredible variety of it. And that's what this section is about. Why ski on the West Coast? The terrain is why.

First of all, you can't have a broad variety without establishing that the expert terrain is truly difficult. At West Coast areas, the standard is high. The black diamond runs are usually natural couloirs or cliff faces. Farther east (with the exception of a couple of hairball places like Jackson Hole and Snowbird), this kind of terrain would be labeled double black, or simply

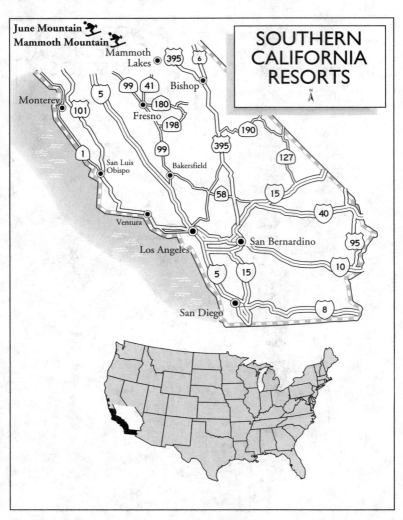

closed. The stem christie skier can get down most Rocky Mountain black diamonds; on the left coast, the same skier is likely to arrive at the bottom of Headwall or Cornice Bowl sliding on nylon instead of on skis.

The steepest terrain here is simply steeper, and the reason is our geology. The Rocky Mountain ranges are older, more weathered; ski areas there tend to top out on nicely rounded summit snowfields (think of Vail, Aspen, Snowmass, Sun Valley). West Coast areas invariably build their lifts to narrow ridge lines, so a powder run out here often starts with a big first step into thin air (think of Whistler, Crystal, Squaw, Sugar Bowl, Kirkwood,

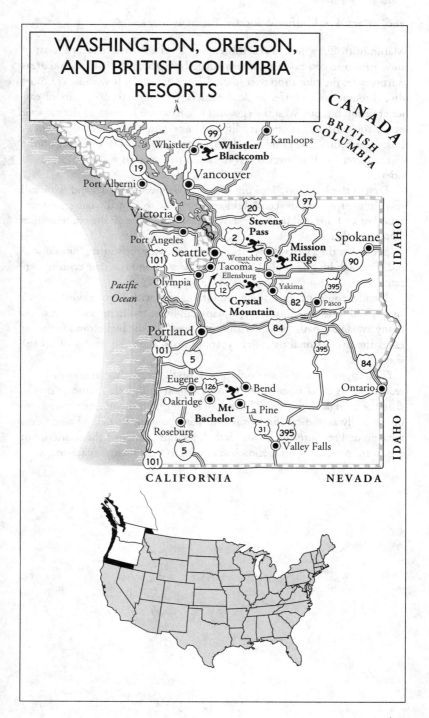

WASHINGTON, OREGON, AND BRITISH COLUMBIA RESORTS

CANADA
BRITISH COLUMBIA

Whistler • 🎿 **Whistler/ Blackcomb** Kamloops

(99)

(19)

Vancouver

Port Alberni •

Victoria

Port Angeles

(101)

Seattle •

Tacoma •

Olympia

Pacific Ocean

(2)

Stevens Pass 🎿

Wenatchee

Ellensburg

(12)

🎿 **Crystal Mountain**

(20)

(97)

Mission Ridge 🎿

Spokane

(90)

Yakima

(82)

(395)

Pasco

IDAHO

Portland •

(101)

(5)

Eugene •

(126)

🎿

Oakridge •

Mt. Bachelor

Roseburg •

(5)

(101)

(84)

(395)

Ontario •

(84)

• Bend

La Pine

(31)

(395)

• Valley Falls

IDAHO

CALIFORNIA   **NEVADA**

485

Mammoth). Elsewhere in the United States ski areas try to sculpt most of their runs into ego-boosting intermediate boulevards. West Coast ski areas normally let the runs drop over natural contours, and where those contours dive through rocky chutes, so do the skiers. Of course there's plenty of easier cruising, but out West the ego stuff begins at the bottom of the summit bowl. You can't always hop on a lift and be certain you'll find an easy (or at least intermediate) way down; it doesn't work that way. The only way off the top may very well be over the cornice. So this section is for two kinds of skiers.

First is the hardbody looking for gravity-powered thrills and who will revel in the freedom the coastal ski areas provide to ski truly dangerous terrain. For each lift and peak, I'll show you how to squeeze the contour lines closer together.

Second is the skier who wants to have fun without scaring himself stupid. For each lift and peak, I'll show you how to find the sane cruising terrain.

Finally, you can't learn these mountains well with a casual visit; there's simply too much to absorb—too many fall lines, too many exposures, too many avalanche paths masquerading as "lines." At the biggest mountains it takes the professional patrollers years to learn even the names of all the shots.

To a large extent, this section depends on the accumulated knowledge of real locals. A local is someone who has spent a lifetime memorizing the shape of a single mountain. The real local can get off the summit in a whiteout as easily as you can find your own bathroom in the dark. These skiers have guided me into their own secret lines and explained the subtleties of the storm patterns. This section owes much to their mental space-maps.

The Sierras and Tahoe

Mammoth Mountain This is the soul center of southern California skiing. The highest lift-served ski mountain on the West Coast, Mammoth gets the deepest snow—and the biggest crowds. It is vast and varied, with precipitous summit bowls and easy cruising down low. Mammoth's boisterous nightlife is a kind of snowy Mardi Gras.

June Mountain Mammoth's sister area, a half an hour north, is the reverse of the coin: It is serene and secluded, with miles of easy terrain on the upper slopes and good expert steeps below. It's a romantic and private destination for honeymoon skiers.

Kirkwood Lift-served adventure skiing an hour south of Tahoe, Kirkwood is a remote high valley with limited lodging and no nightlife, but good snow and dozens of steep chutes off the two-mile ridge line.

Sierra-at-Tahoe Two ski areas in one: classic, steep Sierra tree skiing at one end and broad open Colorado-type cruising at the other, all served by modern high-speed quads. No lodging and no village here, but it's a great day-skier destination for Sacramentans and Tahoe-area visitors.

Heavenly Head in the clouds, feet in the Tahoe casinos, Heavenly boasts California's biggest vertical, with intermediate cruising and big bump runs on the California side and steep bowls and tree skiing on the Nevada side. An awkward lift layout guarantees long lines on weekends. Cheap lodging and great nightlife in Stateline casinos.

Alpine Meadows A friendly, family-oriented area backed up to the Sierra Crest. There is an excellent variety of terrain on two peaks, with a low-pressure atmosphere. There's no nightlife and little lodging at the base area—Alpine skiers stay in Tahoe City, six miles south. Snowboarding verboten.

Squaw Valley The steepest, most macho mountain on the West Coast, with a fast, efficient lift system to keep lift lines minimal even when the trails are

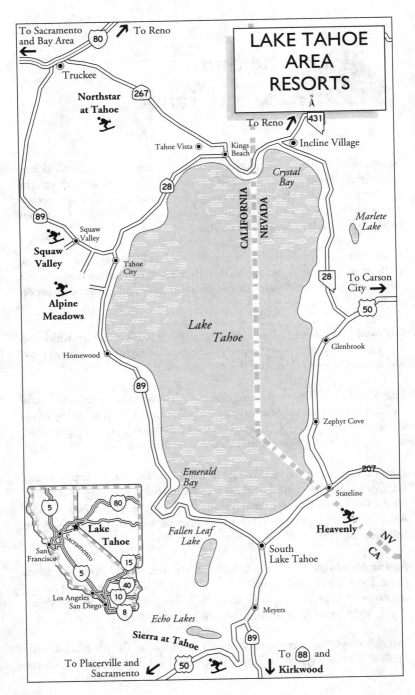

crowded. The relatively short but very steep terrain provides spectacular challenge in good weather, but it is nearly unskiable on storm days, thanks to high winds and avalanche danger. Squaw attracts athletes, and the go-for-it attitude is reflected in an overheated bar scene.

Northstar-at-Tahoe   This is a comfortable condo community built around a lovely family ski area. Northstar's front side is ideal for beginners and intermediates, while the backside cruisers give advanced skiers a workout. There's good dining on site and in nearby Truckee.

Sugar Bowl   Perched on Donner Pass, Sugar Bowl is the oldest major ski area in California and a favorite powder stash for knowledgeable locals who take advantage of the area's proximity to Sacramento and make the dash up the hill when conditions are prime. Limited on-site lodging in the atmospheric Sugar Bowl Lodge.

MAMMOTH MOUNTAIN

The psychological center of California skiing, Mammoth Mountain is a sort of high-altitude extension of the SoCal beach scene. Six hours from the city along Highway 395, the town of Mammoth Lakes fills up every weekend with tanned, athletic Los Angelenos. They overflow the base lodges, clog the lifts, and party through the night at dozens of bars and restaurants around town.

It's actually an easy six hours. Highway 395 arrows across the Mojave Desert and then climbs gradually up the Owens Valley. That's 300 miles of dry, straight road with no stoplights. Beyond Bishop—a good place for a late snack on a Friday night—the road climbs steeply to 7,000 feet, and drivers brave snowpacked roads only for the last 30 miles into Mammoth Lakes.

If coming by air, plan to catch a charter flight from Long Beach to the Mammoth Lakes Airport, or fly to Reno for a three-hour drive down Highway 395 from the north (in mid-winter much of this drive can be on snowpacked roads).

At 11,053 feet, Mammoth is the highest lift-served peak on the West Coast, and most years it gets the best, the driest, and the deepest snow. With about 3,500 acres of skiable terrain, 150 named trails, and 29 lifts sprawling over 3,100 vertical feet, it's also among the largest single ski mountains in the United States. The top of the ridge line, stretching for a couple of miles west of town, consists of precipitous bowls and steep, narrow chutes; it's paradise for an expert but no place for the timid. Down low, sheltered in forests of huge ponderosa pines, are long, rolling intermediate and beginner trails. In between you'll find every kind of open glade, buffed-out cruiser, or mogul field a skier could ask for.

There are four ways to get onto the mountain: at the rambling old Main Lodge (drive up Minaret Road, or take the Red Shuttle); at the Stump Alley Express (on Minaret, a mile closer to town); at the more modern Canyon Lodge (take Canyon Boulevard or the Blue Shuttle); or take the Eagle Express gondola from the Eagle Lodge Area (at the head of Meridian Boulevard, served by the Yellow and Green Shuttle routes).

There's plenty of free parking near both base lodges, and Mammoth does a creditable job of keeping the roads clear. I like to get up early, park close in, and have breakfast at the base lodge while waiting for the lifts to open at 8:30 A.M. (8 A.M. on weekends). Driving up Minaret Road at 7:30 A.M., I've often seen coyotes trotting home after a night-long feast in the base lodge dumpster.

The town lifts serve the east end of the Mammoth complex, consisting of long, gentle beginner-intermediate cruisers like *Bridges, Christmas Tree, Manzanita,* and *Holiday.* (Bridges is also the name of a condo complex alongside the trail; it's the only true ski-in/ski-out lodging on the mountain.) From the top of 15 and 24, ski down to Chair 9 for the long ride up into the high bowls below Dragon's Back Ridge, where experts find uncrowded skiing for days after a storm. You can jump on Chair 25 to the top of Mount Lincoln; there's one easy way down from Lincoln, appropriately labeled *Relief.* The rest of the peak is steepish, consisting of chutes, mogul faces, and expert-level tree skiing.

Canyon Lodge is a massive three-story building with locker rooms, cafeterias, retail and rental shops, and ski patrol and ski school offices. Four lifts fan out from the hut. Chair 7 serves a secluded network of beginner trails that are removed from the main flow of high-speed traffic. Chair 8 can put you into some short intermediate terrain or return you to the town chair complex. Chair 17 goes to some easy intermediate cruisers. Ride Chair 16, a high-speed quad, for transport out of the Canyon complex toward the summit or Chair 2 area.

From Chairs 8, 16, or 17 you can reach Chair 22, the most popular route to the top of Mount Lincoln. Chair 22 goes straight up Lincoln's steepest face, and on a powder day, you'll find the best tree skiers in town yo-yoing this chair.

Four lifts branch out from the Chair 2 area. Chairs 10 and 21 serve some nice long intermediate cruisers sheltered in the woods on the lower flanks of the mountain—this is a great place to ski on a storm day. Chairs 2 and 18 go to the open slopes above the Mid-Chalet; ride these lifts to access the summit or the Main Lodge.

The Main Lodge—four stories of shops, offices, and restaurants, all spreading out from the Panorama gondola base station—is the jumping-off point for most people who want to ski the summit. From here the gondola

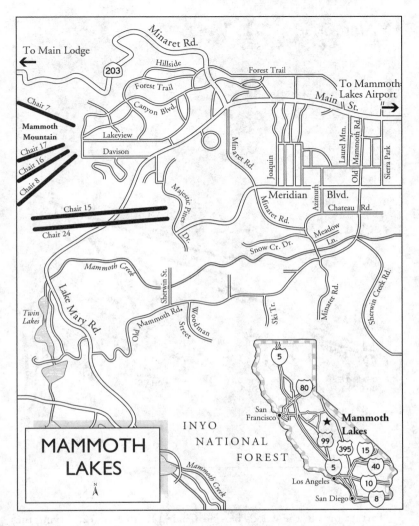

rises 2,140 feet to the top; get off at mid-station if you don't want to ski the expert-level summit chutes.

Five more lifts move traffic away from the Main Lodge. Chair 6 and the high-speed Discovery quad are for beginners. Chair 1, a high-speed quad, and the T-bar access *Broadway* (the main route back to the lodge for most intermediate skiers) and a variety of steeper, expert-rated cruising trails.

Another route to the summit is via Chair 19 (serving the lower half of the mountain) to Chair 23, which is engineered to climb through the cornice to the summit.

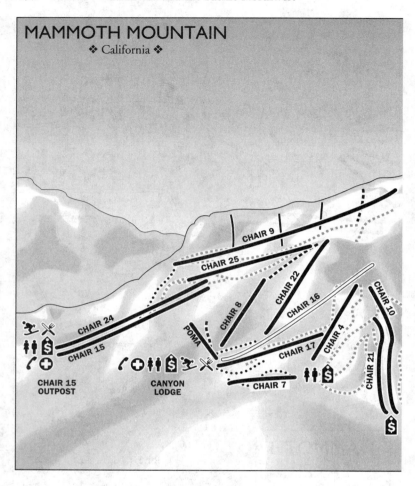

MAMMOTH MOUNTAIN
❖ California ❖

CHAIR 9

CHAIR 25

CHAIR 22

CHAIR 16

CHAIR 24

CHAIR 8

CHAIR 10

POMA

CHAIR 15

CHAIR 4

CHAIR 17

CHAIR 21

CHAIR 15 OUTPOST

CANYON LODGE

CHAIR 7

Farther out, in the woods beyond Chair 11, is Chair 12, serving the intermediate terrain of White Bark Ridge. Ride 12 to reach the distant Chair 14 Outpost at the far western end of the complex.

About the Weather

Like any California ski area, in a big snow year Mammoth is occasionally prey to the monster three-day blizzard. The powerful winds accompanying these storms can close the upper lifts, but there's plenty of uncrowded skiing lower down (most Mammoth skiers are fair-weather folks). Another tactic on storm days is to head up the road to June Mountain, where trees shelter the lifts right to the summit.

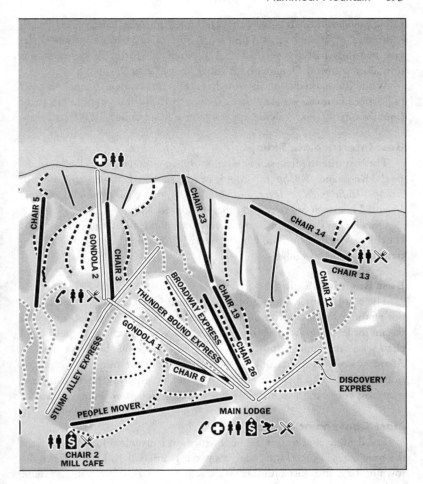

Best Expert Skiing

The best expert skiing is on Mammoth's summit. The summit rises 1,000 feet above the treeline and provides some of the hairiest chutes in North America. There's one way down for intermediates: *Road Runner* follows the ridge line to the west, eventually descending toward Chair 14. From *Road Runner,* experts can peel off down the reasonably wide (and normally bumped-up) *Cornice Bowl,* or through the narrow shots called *Climax, Hangman's Hollow, Dropout, Wipeout,* and *Philippe's Couloir.* From the top of the gondola, traverse east to reach the popular *Dave's Run* (named for Mammoth founder Dave McCoy) or the scary *Huevos Grande.*

On storm days, when the summit is closed due to high winds, you'll find prime powder in the relatively sheltered tree runs off Chair 22 on Lincoln Mountain, or, closer to the Main Lodge, off Chairs 26 and 19 (these chairs give you only half the vertical of 22). After the storm, savvy locals find untracked snow off Dragon's Back Ridge above Chair 9.

While it's marked as an intermediate trail, *St. Anton* is one of the great high-speed cruisers—a long easy groomer perfect for arcing big GS turns from the top of Chair 3 all the way back to the Main Lodge, 1,700 feet below.

Best Intermediate Skiing

The best intermediate skiing is on *St. Anton,* of course, as well as on *Lost-in-the-Woods* and *Wall Street,* a couple of tree-sheltered cruisers off Chair 10. *Bridges, Holiday, Manzanita,* and *Juniper,* the long trails paralleling Chairs 15 and 24, stretch out over two miles of relaxed skiing.

On a storm day, if you want to stay out of the wind and near the hot chocolate, the best bets are Chairs 8 and 17, serving the short but rolling trails near Canyon Lodge.

Best Beginner Skiing

The best beginner skiing is off Chair 7 near Canyon Lodge; the runs are out of the main flow of traffic; its main trails, *Hansel* and *Gretel,* are prime terrain for learning. At the Main Lodge, the new Discovery high-speed quad chair serves the same purpose. Use *Jill's Trail.* There's one beginner trail, *St. Moritz,* that winds down from the Mid-Chalet so adventurous newcomers can ride the gondola up there for lunch. Be aware that expert skiers, moving fast, may cross your path as *St. Moritz* zigs across trails like *Mambo* and *Patrolman.*

Most Convenient Lodging

The Bridges condo complex offers the most convenient lodging, and it is the only true ski-in/ski-out lodging since it is situated 100 yards above the town lift base area. Just a minute's walk across the parking lot from the Main Lodge sits the Mammoth Mountain Inn, with 200 hotel rooms. A dozen different condo developments spread out within walking distance of the Warming Hut II parking lot; check with central reservations (phone (800) 367-6572) for availability. Motels are abundant around the intersection of Canyon Boulevard and Minaret Road, just a short drive from either the Main Lodge or Warming Hut II. When a storm is brewing, I often check into the Travelodge simply because it has covered parking.

Best Eats

On-mountain food service is strictly cafeteria-style, but you can get a real sit-down lunch at the Mountainside Grill in the Mammoth Mountain Inn. Mammoth Lakes offers dozens of restaurants, ranging from pedestrian pizza joints and Mexican restaurants to rather deluxe dining. The most romantic spot in town is Skadi (phone (760) 934-3902, $15 and up), occupying the old site of the Cask and Cleaver in Sherwin Plaza II. Skadi serves Continental and American cuisine and offers great views of the mountain. A locals' favorite is Whiskey Creek (phone (760) 934-2555, $18 and up), serving prime rib, pasta, and so on. Whiskey Creek has a dance floor and the best wine list in town. Ocean Harvest (phone (760) 934-8539, $16 and up) is famous for very fresh fish. My favorite place for family dining is Angel's (phone (760) 934-7427, $6 and up), a warm and friendly spot serving everything from barbecue to chicken pot pie. For the best breakfast in town, it's the Matterhorn (phone (615) 934-3369).

MAMMOTH MOUNTAIN DATA

Mountain Statistics

Vertical feet	3,100 feet
Base elevation	7,953 feet
Summit elevation	11,053 feet
Longest run	3 miles
Average annual snowfall	353 inches
Number of lifts	25, including 8 high-speed lifts
Uphill capacity	56,600 skiers per hour
Skiable terrain	3,500 acres
Opening date	mid-November
Closing date	June/July
Snowboarding	Yes

Mammoth shares its lift ticket with June Mountain.

Transportation

By car From Los Angeles, 6 hours via U.S. 395. From Reno, 3 hours via U.S. 395.

By air Commuter airlines to Mammoth Lakes Airport, 7 miles away.

Key Phone Numbers

Ski Area Information
(888) 4MAMMOTH or
(760) 934-2571

Snow Report (760) 934-6166

Reservations (800) 228-4947 or
(760) 934-2581

www.mammoth-mtn.com

LITO'S TECH TIP

Avalanche Danger, How to Avoid It

Avalanches are the dark side of winter. How can such beautiful landscapes—snow-draped peaks, shadowed cornices, sparkling alpine bowls—be so dangerous? How is it possible that an innocent excursion outside the ski area's boundary ropes to enjoy an afternoon of untracked powder can be a form of Russian roulette? For as long as people have lived in mountains, avalanches have been a problem, and avalanche danger has been something to try to understand, predict, and avoid. At ski areas, thankfully, the problem has been solved. Avalanches and avalanche awareness are the responsibility of the ski patrol, not of the individual skier. And these patrollers have paid their dues. They attend special avalanche courses. They study the weather, carefully plotting each winter's worth of wind, temperature, humidity, and snowfall on comparative charts. They spend hours digging snow pits, studying different snow strata under a glass. They are constantly studying, testing, learning . . . and setting off avalanches, before they can trap skiers. American skiers are safe from avalanches, period. That is, as long as they stay within the ski boundaries and obey all the warning signs the patrol has put up.

But some skiers are particularly attentive to the siren call of adventure beyond the ropes. Ski areas occupy only a fraction of the skiable terrain in the West. And every season hundreds—no, thousands—of skiers succumb to the temptation of untracked slopes outside the ski areas. How to do this and stay safe? How to make sure you won't become an avalanche victim?

I'm going to share a few tips, rules of thumb that have kept me out of avalanche trouble in almost 30 years of mountaineering, skiing, and backcountry skiing. But first a caveat. Safety in the mountains, especially in avalanche country, is a matter of knowledge and judgment, not ignorance and luck. If you are interested in skiing away from ski areas into untracked, untamed, wild snow, then you too should start studying. Read a serious manual like the Forest Service *Avalanche Handbook*. Take an avalanche safety course that offers hands-on practice digging snow pits to analyze snow stability. (Such courses are offered in many mountain ski-resort communities; they don't cost much, and they can save your life.) Spend a few extra dollars to purchase the essential, minimal avalanche safety gear: transceiver radio beacons (or "beepers") for each skier, for the quick location of someone swept away in an avalanche; plus shovels and ski poles that double as probe poles. Learn how to use them, and don't leave them at home when you head off for an out-of-area ski adventure. In a word, don't rely on my advice or anyone else's when it comes to avalanche danger. Take the subject seriously, learn all you can, and develop your own backcountry judgment.

What I can tell you is this: Avalanche hazard is generally much higher in the dry, cold climate of the Rockies than it is in the damper, warmer climate of coastal ranges. A high hazard from brittle, ready-to-fracture slabs of snow can persist for weeks in the backcountry of Colorado or Wyoming. But in California's High Sierra, and in the ranges of the Pacific Northwest, acute avalanche danger is highest for 24 hours after a storm; it declines rapidly thereafter. Ski a few days after a storm and the odds, at least, are with you.

Perhaps the first rule of backcountry skiing is this: Don't ski it alone.

Three skiers represent a minimum safe party. If you have doubts about a slope, ski it one at a time, with the rest of the group watching from a safe location. But if a slope really makes you nervous, trust your gut instincts; don't ski it. Hike back out, if you must, rather than ski a suspect slope when that little voice inside you is crying out: *Don't do it!*

Slopes 30 degrees or steeper are always suspect, but luckily there's an enormous amount of great skiing (most skiing, in fact) on slopes less than 30 degrees in pitch. Different ski areas have different policies about your using their lifts to get high on the mountain and then taking off for the backcountry; some facilitate it, some forbid it. Nowadays, for example, many Colorado ski areas have specially marked gates for skiers who want to exit the area and access the untracked, but also unpatrolled, national forest slopes beyond. If your thoughts are pulling you in that direction, I suggest you talk to a ski patroller first. Ask who is responsible for avalanche control at the area, and ask those patrollers about the backcountry conditions and snow stability. They'll know, and they'll tell you.

In winter, the greatest danger is from slab avalanches: consolidated sheets of snow that slide as a block on a weak underlayer. In spring, loose slides of wet, soggy snow from a point source are more common. In spring, too, the assessment of a slope's safety or risk is much easier. If the snow is firm enough for good skiing, it is probably safe from avalanches. When it gets soggy and unpleasant to ski in the afternoon—watch out!

JUNE MOUNTAIN

It happens every Friday night from October to June, and it's terrifying; the Mojave Desert is transformed into an extension of the Los Angeles freeway system. The usually desolate Route 395 is packed solid with cars rushing north in bumper-locked precision, all carrying skiers bound for the little town of Mammoth Lakes. There, skiers jam onto Mammoth's lifts and pour like lemmings down its slopes. They turn Mammoth, the second largest ski mountain in the United States, into an anthill. At day's end, Angelenos convert the whole area into a disco—neon spandex, sunglasses in the dark, haircuts that defy gravity.

If this is not your scene, you need to drive 20 miles farther north to the High Sierra valley of June Lake. Here, June Mountain's slopes cascade down a classic glacial profile. The mountain is a reasonably flat plateau on top, steepening sharply into a precipice down low.

The hamlet of June Lake is popular with fishermen and hikers in the summer, so it offers a surprising variety of lodging in the form of condos,

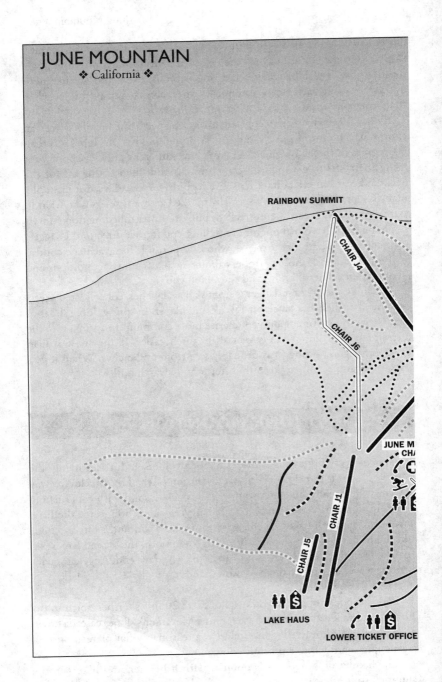

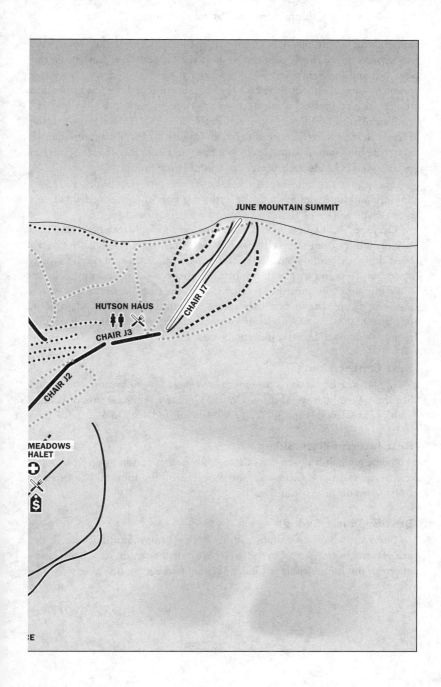

motels, and cabins, all within a mile of the lifts via shuttle bus (there's no ski-in/ski-out lodging). Best dining is at the Carson Peak Inn (steak and seafood) and the Fern Creek Grill (traditional American). Traffic is rarely a problem—on the roads or trails—in this beautiful little valley. Quiet and romantic, it's a perfect couples' getaway, with or without kids.

June offers 2,600 feet of vertical, but the lowest 1,100 feet, known as the Face, is so steep as to be unskiable by nonexperts. Ride the tram or Chair J1 up to the mid-station June Meadows Chalet and examine what the Face has to offer—it is heady deep powder or intimidating bumps.

The upper runs are much friendlier. There are two peaks, Rainbow Summit and June Mountain. Most of the beginner and intermediate terrain rolls down the face of Rainbow, served by Chairs J6 and J4.

On June Mountain (Chair J7) the runs are decidedly tougher. Drop into any of half a dozen steep chutes (the best is called, aptly, *Powder Chute*), blast down the wide-open slopes of *Matterhorn,* or take on *Sunset,* which starts out steep and then rolls out into a blanket of skiable bumps.

While June's summit rises to 10,135 feet, the trees go all the way to the top. This means that when winter storms close the upper half of Mammoth, pushing 20,000 crazed Angelenos together on the lower slopes, most of June remains sheltered, skiable, and uncrowded.

Best Expert Skiing

My favorite high-speed cruiser is *Schatzi,* a classic giant slalom course that begs for linked high-speed turns. Go fast. Go faster. After a storm, of course, grab your widest skis and hit *The Face, Carson,* and *Gull Ridge.*

Best Intermediate Skiing

There are half a dozen runs that qualify as sweet, don't-stop-now cruisers: *Bodie, Comstock, Gunsmoke,* and *Rosa Mae* on Rainbow and *Sunrise* and *Matterhorn* on June Mountain.

Best Beginner Skiing

Silverado, winding a couple of miles from Rainbow Summit, may be the longest true beginner trail in the West. Most of the terrain off Chair J2, rising from the June Meadows Chalet, is easily handled by new skiers.

JUNE MOUNTAIN DATA

Mountain Statistics

Vertical feet	2,590 feet
Base elevation	7,545 feet
Summit elevation	10,135 feet
Longest run	2.5 miles
Average annual snowfall	250 inches
Number of lifts	8
Uphill capacity	10,000 skiers per hour
Skiable terrain	500+ acres
Opening date	December
Closing date	April
Snowboarding	Yes

June Mountain shares its lift ticket with Mammoth Mountain; the June Mountain ticket is valid at Mammoth with an upgrade charge.

Transportation

By car From Los Angeles, 6½ hours via U.S. Highway 395; from Reno, 3 hours via U.S. Highway 395.

By air Reno's Cannon International Airport or commuter airlines to Mammoth Lakes (25 miles).

Key Phone Numbers

Ski Area Information (888) JUNEMTN or (760) 648-7733
Snow Report (760) 934-2224
Reservations (760) 648-7584
www.junemtn.com

KIRKWOOD

Journalists who write about California love to point out that if the state were an independent nation, it would have the seventh largest economy in the world; the Golden State ranks right up there in industrial strength with Germany and France. Reading this, you'd think the state were paved with high-tech factories and industrial-strength farms. In fact, as you travel eastward in from the coast, the state quickly grows emptier and wider and becomes more nineteenth century in its atmosphere. In the Sierra foothills, the economy is based not on silicon chips and stealth bombers but on winemaking, gold panning, and river rafting. In the high mountains, the economy vanishes altogether, except for a few ski resorts tucked up in isolated valleys.

None is more isolated than Kirkwood, 100 miles east and 7,800 feet up from Stockton and Sacramento, 30 miles south of Lake Tahoe, and 100 years back in time. Kirkwood is named for Zachary Kirkwood, a cattle rancher who opened, in 1864, a way station on the lonely road over the

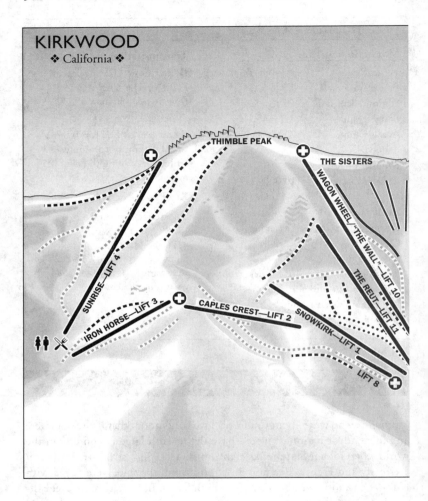

mountains between Carson City and Stockton. The legend is that the inn was situated where El Dorado, Amador, and Alpine counties meet, and the bar itself wasn't nailed to the floor. That way, whenever a county tax collector showed up, the liquor business could be skidded across the room into another jurisdiction.

In 1972 when the first ski lifts were built at Kirkwood, Pacific Gas and Electric declined to pay for power lines into the valley. So, while Kirkwood lies in the most populous state in the Union, it is an anomaly—the high valley too remote for rural electrification. The ski area built, and still runs, its own diesel-fired generating station.

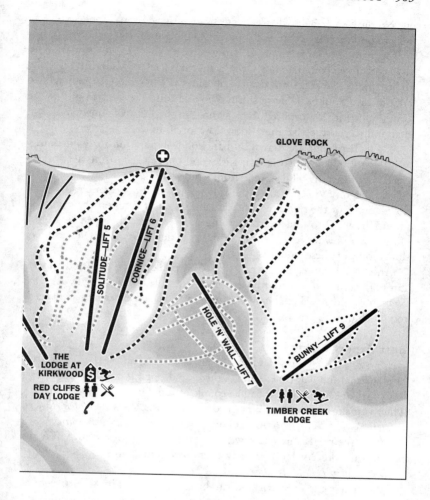

Because of the elevation, Kirkwood snow does seem lighter and drier than what you get at most Tahoe areas. With a higher base—about 1,700 feet above the surface of the lake—Kirkwood is one of the first places to count on for good powder when the storms come through.

While Kirkwood now boasts about 220 condominium units (about 100 of them are available for rent to visiting skiers) plus a couple of nice restaurants with their own bars, the nightlife is not what you'd call rip-roaring. In fact, there's no real town here—no blocks of retail stores, clubs, and lodges. The ski shop is part of the main day lodge. There's a deli/mini-mart to serve the rambling collection of condo buildings, and up the road a little way is the Nordic Center. This will all change soon—the resort has applied for permits to build a village that will triple the lodging capacity.

Meanwhile, people come to Kirkwood to ski, pure and simple. The weekend crowd comes mainly from California's Central Valley, and it tends to be families and kids from small local colleges. While most vacationers stay at South Lake Tahoe, a Sierra storm is a good reason to sleep in one of the condo units; it's a lot more fun to be first on the lift on a snowy morning than it is to get stuck behind a snowplow for 30 miles.

The college kids are drawn by Kirkwood's reputation for wild skiing. With just 2,000 feet of vertical, Kirkwood offers a surprising network of steep, exciting trails, all dropping from a mile-long ridge. Ride Cornice Lift (6) or Wagon Wheel (10) to the ridgetop, and choose your route back down: Some of the runs are wide, easy cruising, but you don't have to look far at Kirkwood to find heart-stopping narrow chutes between ridge-line cliffs. On a powder day, you can drop weightlessly for 1,500 vertical feet down some of these couloirs.

Around the corner, on the east side of Thimble Peak, you'll find Sunrise Lift (4), serving the broad, rolling cruiser run called, misleadingly, *Elevator Shaft*, plus a huge, wide-open bowl apparently labeled expert because there's too much of it to groom.

Best Expert Skiing

One of my favorite descents in all of California is *The Drain*, an immense natural half-pipe. You get there by dropping through (or traversing under) the Sisters, a cliff band a couple of hundred yards west of Lift 10. Then you ski one of the six marked chutes—*All the Way, Notch, Sisters, Schaeffer's, Saddle,* or *Cliff.* All six point more or less into *The Drain.*

When the ridge runs get crowded, it's time to hike west from Lift 6 out toward Palisades Bowl. On the way, peer down into another series of chutes —*Jim's, Sentinel, Rabbit, Chamoix,* and *Fireball.*

The final group of steep shots can be reached from Lift 4. Turn right at the top, traverse over to *Larry's Lip,* and, snow conditions permitting, peel off into *Thunder, Two-Man, One-Man,* or *Bogie's.*

On storm days, the ridge lifts may close due to high winds. Ride the Reut (pronounced "root," named for trailbuilder Dick Reuter) and ski the short, steep runs below Norm's Nose.

Best Intermediate Skiing

The Sunrise runs—*Elevator Shaft* and *Happiness*—offer great, wide-open cruising. Solitude Lift (5) serves the lower, easier sections of half a dozen long trails cascading off the ridge line.

Hole-in-Wall Lift (7), rising from the Timber Creek Lodge at the west parking lot, serves mostly easy, sheltered intermediate terrain.

Best Beginner Skiing

Stick to Bunny Lift (9), serving four out-of-the-way learner runs west of Timber Creek, home of Kirkwood's learn-to-ski program.

Convenient Lodging

The condos. That's all there is for now. They're comfortable and within walking distance of the lift. On a storm day, staying here means you make first tracks all morning instead of crawling along Route 88 behind a snowplow.

Additionally, completion of the Mountain Club is slated for winter 1999–2000. It will be located in the heart of the new mountain village, just steps away from six major lifts. Amenities will include a health club, an outdoor spa, lounges and restaurants, and underground parking.

Best Eats

For Old West atmosphere and a wildly eclectic menu—featuring hamburgers, ribs, pasta, lamb, and seafood—go to the old Kirkwood Inn; for charm and a nicely varied menu, try Caples Lake Resort. Within the ski area complex there's Snowshoe Thompson's at the Timber Creek Lodge for pizza and pasta, family style, and the Whiskey Run Restaurant (lunch only). The Cornice Cafe, in the Sun Meadows complex across the road from Chairs 5 and 6, serves lunch and dinner and offers a full wine list and bar.

KIRKWOOD DATA

Mountain Statistics

Vertical feet	2,000 feet
Base elevation	7,800 feet
Summit elevation	9,800 feet
Longest run	2.5 miles
Average annual snowfall	500 inches
Number of lifts	12
Uphill capacity	16,300 skiers per hour
Skiable terrain	2,300 acres
Opening date	mid-November
Closing date	mid-May
Snowboarding	Yes

Transportation

By car From Reno, 90 minutes via U.S. Highway 395 to Route 88; from South Lake Tahoe, 35 minutes via U.S. Highway 50 to Meyers, then Routes 89 and 88; from Stockton, 2 hours via Route 88.

Key Phone Numbers

Ski Area Information (209) 258-6000
Snow Report (209) 258-3000
Reservations (800) 967-7500 or www.skikirkwood.com

Tahoe area locals—and this includes savvy Sacramento skiers—have a couple of deep secrets, places they like to sneak off to for uncrowded powder skiing. At the north end of the lake, off I-70, it's Sugar Bowl; at the south end, on Echo Summit off U.S. Highway 50, it's Sierra-at-Tahoe.

A generation of skiers found their way up the twisting two-lane highway from Placerville to ski at the family-owned Sierra Ski Ranch. The place was a low-key joy—no lodging, no bars, no hoopla, just 2,000 acres of wide-open cruising on West Bowl and hair-raising steeps and tree skiing on the face of Huckleberry Mountain. In 1993 the area was purchased by Fibreboard, the parent company of Northstar-at-Tahoe. Fibreboard changed the area's name and installed a bar (the Sierra Pub) but didn't touch the nearly perfect skiing.

Vern Sprock, who founded the place, designed the trail system with taste and intelligence. Beginners have their own area with three lifts and half a dozen trails just above the base lodge. There's even a short beginner trail down the backside. Intermediates and advanced skiers get eight immense rolling cruiser trails served by a couple of mile-long lifts in West Bowl. If skiers want to check out the view from Huckleberry, they can ride to the top and descend safely via a neat network of easy trails on the backside, served by two short lifts. Experts get a vast area of steep tree skiing, laced with three precipitous trails and served by two more mile-long lifts. There's something exciting for everyone.

There's nothing wishy-washy about Sierra's trail markings: The beginner terrain is very easy; the intermediate terrain is truly broad and inspiring; the expert terrain, like that at Squaw Valley, should be attempted only by skiers with good technical skills and mucho self-confidence.

Cruising skiers should head directly down *Marmot,* west of the base lodge, to pick up the Slingshot high-speed quad lift. From the top, Powderhorn trails cascade away, dividing as they fall into a network of wide-open trails—*Dogwood, Bashful, Pyramid,* and *Beaver*—that invite easy, relaxed skiing or lose-your-hat speed, about 1,500 vertical feet of it.

Steep skiers should slide east of the base lodge to ride the Grand View Express quad. Here you'll find 1,600 feet of vertical on three very steep trails—*Castle, Preacher's Passion,* and *Dynamite*—plus a lot of very hairy skiing among the pines.

Beginners can ride to the top of Huckleberry, too. There's a rambling, easy way down along the ridge line that is appropriately labeled *Sugar'n*

Spice. But beginners will also find a nice variety of trails off the Nob Hill and Rock Garden lifts and off the gentle Easy Rider Express quad.

The best place for lunch on the mountain is at the Grand View Bar and Grille at the summit of Huckleberry. It feels remote because it is. In nice weather the entire Tahoe Basin is visible from the Grand View Bar and Grille. Below the restaurant a warren of intermediate trails descends through the scrub pine and manzanita to Eldorado Lift (it takes you back to the summit) or to Short Stuff Lift (it goes to the top of Nob Hill, located in the saddle between Huckleberry and West Bowl).

Beginners can descend the backside, too, via the gentle *Wagon Trail.* It's a scenic treat for folks usually confined to a couple of acres of ski school terrain.

Best Beginner Skiing

First-timers stick to Easy Rider Express and the *Broadway* trail. Ambitious, athletic newcomers have come to the right place: Sierra offers more skiable variety, off the Nob Hill and Eldorado lifts and along *Sugar'n Spice*, than almost any other mountain.

Best Intermediate Skiing

For speed, try *Dogwood* and *Beaver,* or *Powderhorn* and *Bashful* in West Bowl. For relaxed skiing, try *Powderhorn* and *Pyramid.* For scenery, try *Smokey* and *Coyote* on the backside.

Best Expert Skiing

For raw speed, there's *Clipper* and *Horsetail* in West Bowl. For adrenaline, it's *Preacher's Passion* and *Dynamite.* For out-of-your-skull deep powder, there are the trees on either side of *Preacher's Passion.*

Getting There

U.S. Highway 50, from Placerville heading west, or heading east from South Lake Tahoe, is the only way in. Expect traffic to move slowly when the road is snowpacked, and remember to carry snow chains.

Convenient Lodging and the Best Eats

There is no lodging—no base village, no condos, no hotels. For now, Sierra-at-Tahoe is for day skiing. Strawberry Lodge sits in splendid isolation on Highway 50, five miles west of the ski area. Most overnight visitors lodge in South Lake Tahoe, which is about 25 minutes east over Echo Summit. There's free shuttle service.

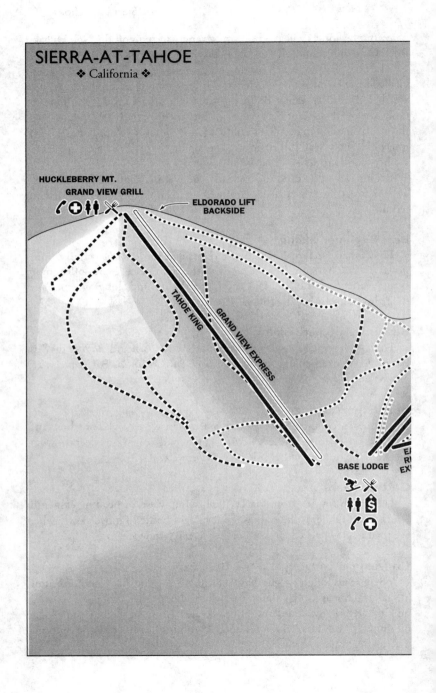

SIERRA-AT-TAHOE
❖ California ❖

HUCKLEBERRY MT.
GRAND VIEW GRILL

ELDORADO LIFT
BACKSIDE

TAHOE KING

GRAND VIEW EXPRESS

BASE LODGE

EA
RI
EXP

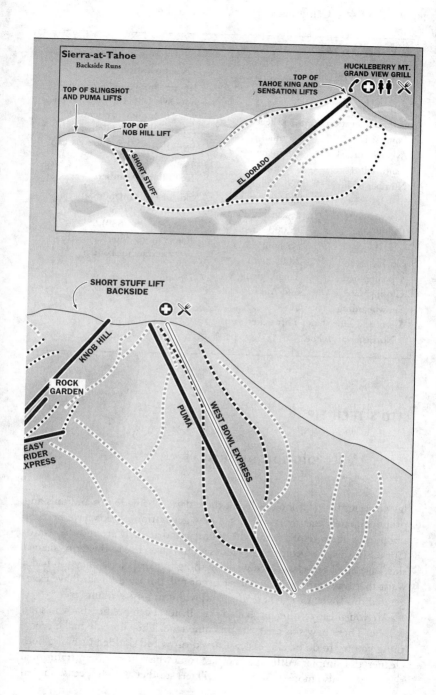

SIERRA-AT-TAHOE DATA

Mountain Statistics

Vertical feet	2,212 feet
Base elevation	6,640 feet
Summit elevation	8,852 feet
Longest run	3.5 miles
Average annual snowfall	475 inches
Number of lifts	9, including 3 high-speed detachable quads
Uphill capacity	15,000 skiers per hour
Skiable terrain	2,000 acres
Opening date	Thanksgiving
Closing date	mid-April
Snowboarding	Yes

Sierra-at-Tahoe shares a lift ticket with Northstar-at-Tahoe.

Transportation

By car From San Francisco, 4 hours via I-80, then U.S. Highway 50; from Sacramento, 90 minutes via U.S. Highway 50; from Reno, 90 minutes via U.S. Highway 50.

Key Phone Numbers

Ski Area Information (530) 659-7453
Snow Report (530) 659-7475
Reservations (800) 288-2463
www.sierratahoe.com

LITO'S TECH TIP

A Revolution in Skis

It's no secret that skis look different these days. The wide tips and tails and proportionately narrower waist of a new generation of skis have become ubiquitous at ski resorts across the country, and actually around the world. Curiously, this new geometry in ski design has given rise to the term "shaped skis," although our classic skis were anything but shapeless. They too had a waist that was narrower than either tip or tail; but modern skis have exaggerated this shape to a great degree, and with impressive results.

Are you already skiing on shaped skis? If not, I can predict that you soon will be. These new skis are a dream come true. They literally make everything you try to do on skis easier. Carved turns and skidded turns are both cleaner and simpler. Although they are somewhat shorter than traditional skis, they are also more stable, so you will feel steadier at high speeds. Shaped skis can actually make you a better skier. They'll expand your horizons, your technique, and the limits of your performance on snow. How? Why?

It's simple. The sidecut or side curve of skis has always been what made them arc graceful turns across the snow. The wide tip bites deeper into the snow than the rest of the ski and pulls you into the start of your turn. At the same time, the narrow waist is pressed out into the snow by the skier's weight so that the ski itself becomes bent into an arc—that's why skilled skiers always make such an effort to transfer their weight to the outside ski of each turn: to bend the ski. Then, instead of tracking forward in a straight line, your ski wants to track in an arc, following its own curved shape. Voilà, a carved turn.

Carved turns have always been an expression of polished, expert skiing. Carved turns look great, and they feel even better. By carving the end of each turn you can control your speed without skidding and without fatiguing your legs. Yet until recently, skiers had to ski very fast to create enough energy to bend their skis and carve.

Today, on shaped or super-sidecut skis, skiers discover that their skis will bend into smooth arcs at much slower speeds, at any speed really, because most of that arc is already present in the deep curve of the ski's edge. Shaped skis have put carving within reach of virtually every skier. And if you are already an expert, if you already know how to carve turns, you will soon discover that your carving skills are amplified and refined by these new skis. Mine certainly have been.

What's the downside of this extreme shaped-ski geometry? I've been skiing on super-sidecut skis for three seasons now and I have yet to find any disadvantages. Their wide tips offer greater flotation on powder. Their deep sidecuts make your turns through moguls quicker and more secure. Above all, you can carve perfect arcs on the snow that you never thought possible. These skis are not a fad; they are here to stay. World Cup racers are winning international races on shaped skis. Instructors are having more fun than ever before on shaped skis. And I'm betting that you will too. Remember, these new skis don't work differently than classic skis, they just work better!

Naturally, there are a host of small, easy to master tricks for getting the most from your new shaped skis (subtle techniques like "phantom edging"). I've condensed my experience teaching hundreds of skiers on these stunning new tools into a one-hour videotape, *Breakthrough on Skis III, The New Skis* (available from Western Eye, (800) 333-5178). But even without specialized instruction, I know you will feel the difference. Shaped skis will change your life as a skier—for the better. That's a promise.

HEAVENLY

Heavenly, boasting a skiable vertical of 3,500 feet, offers the highest lifts in the Tahoe region. Heavenly keeps its feet in the roaring casino towns at the south end of the lake and its head in the thin air at over 10,000 feet. The mountain claims 4,800 acres of terrain (nonsense—that would make the place bigger than Vail, Mammoth, Whistler, or Blackcomb, and it ain't). Heavenly is pretty sizable, sprawling as it does across the state line—there are base lodges on the Nevada and the California side, and you traverse sovereignties by riding to the summit.

There's no "resort village" per se. The ski lifts were built from the launching pad of what already looked like, in the mid-1960s, runaway development based on casino and summer resort business. The twin cities of Stateline, Nevada, and South Lake Tahoe, California, are pretty garish by ski area standards—at night you can read a newspaper anywhere along the main drag by the light of the neon signs. The Nevada side, supported by casinos, has gone in for massive high-rise hotels. The California side runs to sprawling two-story resort motels. The whole effect is of busy suburbia.

Heavenly's trail system can be as confusing to the initiate as the Los Angeles freeway system. Like a freeway system, Heavenly's trails center on a few critical interchanges, where skiers have to ride lifts up out of gulleys. On a busy weekend, skiers sometimes gridlock at these junctions, standing bumper to bumper even to get on the new high-speed quads. Cannily, management has placed on-mountain restaurants at each of these high-traffic areas, so you can get a burger and beer, sit on the boardwalk, and watch the parade go by.

Heavenly's huge snowmaking system now extends from the California and Nevada base lodges all the way to the summit, providing the full skiable vertical on both sides even in California's drought years.

In a good snow year, Heavenly offers some of the best tree skiing in the world, and on the Nevada side Mott and Killebrew canyons are as steep as anything at Squaw Valley or Kirkwood.

This said, Heavenly's real strength is its endless intermediate cruisers. You can roll for miles along rhythmic classics like *Olympic Downhill, Ridge Run, Big Dipper,* and *Canyon.*

Heavenly can also be an inexpensive place to vacation. The big casino hotels often provide cheap rooms and meals (subsidized by the gamblers), and there's always free shuttle service to the mountain.

Heavenly has three base lodges: the main lodge on the California side, at the head of Ski Run Boulevard, and the Boulder and Stagecoach lodges on the Nevada side near the summit of Kingsbury Grade (Nevada Route 207).

Coming from Reno on a weekday (80 minutes), the quickest way to Heavenly is via U.S. Highway 50. But when weekend traffic snarls the roads in Stateline (and the weather is good), it's quicker to follow Highway 395 south to Routes 206 and 207, and use the Boulder or Stagecoach parking lot.

There are three mid-mountain lodges: Top of the Tram above the California base lodge and Sky Deck and East Peak Lodge in the sheltered hollows halfway up the California and Nevada sides.

There's no fast way to the summit. From the California side, you'll ride three lifts to get to the top of Sky Express, and from the Nevada side three or four, depending on where you start. Beginners should enter from the California side or go to Nevada's Boulder Lodge; there's no marked beginner terrain at Stagecoach. You'll find a teaching area at Boulder, and another off to the south side of the California parking lot.

The three lifts rising from the California base lodge serve some pretty severe expert terrain. The Tram and Gunbarrel lifts all go to Monument Peak; World Cup Lift goes halfway up and serves the World Cup race trail. The trails descending from Monument are long, steep, and often heavy with moguls. Intermediates may want to bypass *The Face, Gunbarrel, East Bowl,* and *Pistol* in favor of cruising the easy *Roundabout* cat track.

Use Waterfall or Powderbowl lifts to ride out of the gulley below Monument. Beginners will find easy cruising here on *Mombo Meadows, Maggie's Run,* and *Swing Trail.* Intermediates and experts should turn left and follow the signs toward Sky Deck.

On the way, you'll pass the loading stations for Ridge and Canyon lifts, both of which go to *Ridge Run,* with its unsurpassed views of the Tahoe Basin. Also accessible from here is a network of rolling and interesting intermediate trails cut through the scrub pine and manzanita—*Liz's, Rusutsu, Betty's, Canyon,* and *Steamboat.*

If you pass up Ridge and Canyon lifts, you'll come to Sky Express, the high-speed route to the summit. From here, cruise *Ridge* or *Liz's,* or take *Ellie's,* a delightful high-speed roller coaster. When the snow is deep, there's great tree skiing on either side of *Ellie's;* at this elevation, nearly 10,000 feet, the woods are naturally thin. To get to the Nevada side, ride Sky Express and turn left onto *Skyline Trail.*

Skyline Trail exits near the top of Nevada's Dipper Express. You can turn left down *Dipper Knob* and partake of the wide cruising terrain above the East Peak Lodge or turn right into the expert terrain in Milky Way Bowl, leading down to the truly severe chutes in Killebrew and Mott Canyons.

From these upper slopes of the Nevada side, Heavenly provides one of the grandest views in all of skiing. You look 6,000 feet down into the Carson Valley and can see halfway across Nevada.

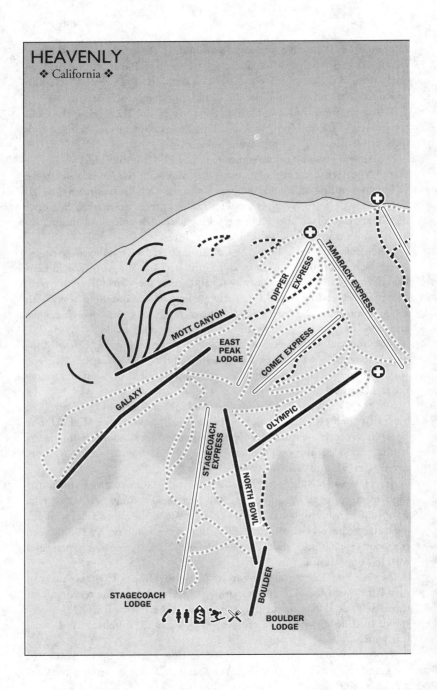

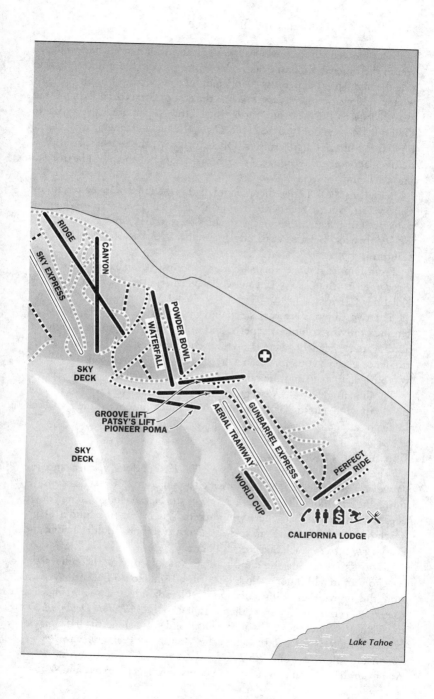

Enter Heavenly from the Nevada lodges, and your first lift rides will take you to the ridge above East Peak Lodge. Here you can scoot down *Pepi's* to ride the high-speed upper lifts (Dipper and Comet Express) or hit the truly wonderful lower cruisers, *Stagecoach* to the east of Stagecoach Express, and *North Bowl* to the west of North Bowl Lift. North Bowl takes you to Olympic Lift, the only way to get to *Olympic Downhill,* one of my favorite high-speed intermediate cruisers. On a storm day, the nicely spaced ponderosa glades on either side of *Olympic* make some of the prettiest tree skiing you'll find anywhere.

Below East Peak Lodge there's more of this sheltered cruising terrain off Galaxy Lift, but to get there, or anywhere, you'll have to ride *Dipper* or *Comet* out of the gulley. From the top of *Comet,* cruise *Jack's, Comet,* or *Little Dipper* back to East Peak Lodge or follow *49er* back to Sky Deck and California.

From Dipper Express, there are more options: *Orion* back to East Peak, *Big Dipper* to the Galaxy Lift network, or *Milky Way* down to Mott and Killebrew Canyons.

The two canyons are very steep and often unstable and should be attempted only by confident experts, and only through the nine designated access gates. Avalanche safety is a serious consideration here; crossing a control fence may get you more than a dressing down by the patrol—it may get you buried. To exit from the canyons, traverse left to Mott Canyon Lift.

For lunching, Sky Deck is a great picnic site in nice weather, but it's outdoors. In wind, clouds, or snow, plan to do lunch indoors at the East Peak Lodge or at Top of the Tram.

Exiting the Mountain

Tired legs often turn rubbery on *The Face* and *Gunbarrel,* and the *Roundabout* cat track can be very crowded after about 2:30 P.M., so consider riding the tram down. If you park at one of the Nevada lodges, skiing down is easier, but remember where you parked: When you cross under Stagecoach or North Bowl lifts, make every *left* turn to find Boulder Lodge and every *right* turn to reach Stagecoach Lodge.

Many skiers leaving the mountain get stuck in one of the gulleys and have to wait in a lift line to climb out. It is possible to ski the entire vertical from the top without riding a lift. On the Nevada side, follow the ridge line (*Sand Dunes* trail) to *Crossover,* then turn left to find *Olympic Downhill.* On the California side, turn right at Sky Deck and skate along the flat *Maggie's* cat track, then cross far to the left at the Monument Peak gulley to *Roundabout,* and follow it around to *Pistol* and *Gunbarrel.* You can also ski *Ridge Run* from the summit and stay left to cruise down *Powderbowl* and *Mombo* to *Roundabout.*

Best Beginner Skiing

The beginner slopes at Boulder Lodge are generally less crowded and more relaxing than the California scene, but there's more variety and challenge on the Mombo Meadows complex off Powderbowl Lift. Plan to ride the tram down at the end of the day; to get there, you'll have to ride the short Patsy's or Groove lifts.

Best Intermediate Skiing

My favorite cruising is *Olympic Downhill,* which is accessed by a new high-speed quad, Stagecoach Express. To maximize skiing time, use the *Dipper/Orion* trail network off Dipper Express (Nevada side) or *Liz's* and *Canyon* off Sky Express (California side).

Best Expert Skiing

For raw challenge, try *Mott* and *Killebrew canyons.* For powder in the trees, it's alongside *Olympic Downhill* (on a storm day) or *Ellie's* (after the storm). For high-speed cruising, take *Olympic Downhill* or *Ellie's.* For bumps, take *The Face* into *Gunbarrel* and *East Bowl.*

Convenient Lodging

Heavenly offers some of the cheapest good lodging in North American ski resort areas, because rooms in the big casino hotels (Harrah's, Caesar's, Harveys, the Horizon) are to some extent subsidized by gambling. The hundreds of smaller motels in the area, many with their own casinos, have to compete on room rates. None of the hotels provides much in the way of traditional ski-lodge ambience, but they're comfortable and efficient, with free shuttle service to the mountain so you can avoid traffic and parking hassles. The big hotels also offer good restaurants and Vegas-style shows with Hollywood headliners, so there are plenty of ways to spend the money you saved on the room.

But if you come to Heavenly simply to ski hard and enjoy the mountain scenery, a couple of lodges are situated within walking distance of the lifts: Ridge Tahoe and Eagle's Nest Inn near the Stagecoach Lodge and Tahoe Seasons Resort near the California tram building.

Best Eats

There are literally dozens of good restaurants in town. My own picks are the Christiana, across the street from the California parking lot, which serves continental cuisine (this is the closest place for a good meal if you stay at the Tahoe Seasons); the Charthouse on Kingsbury Grade (steak/seafood); Chevy's and the Cantina Bar & Grill for Tex-Mex and southwestern cuisine; the Edgewood (at the golf course); Fresh Ketch at Tahoe Keys, a marina-style restaurant (guess what they serve); and, at the tops of the big casino hotels, with great views of the mountains and lake, Harrah's Summit and Harvey's Llewellyns.

HEAVENLY DATA

Mountain Statistics	
Vertical feet	3,500 feet
Base elevation	6,540 feet
Summit elevation	10,400 feet
Longest run	5.5 miles
Average annual snowfall	300 inches
Number of lifts	26, including 3 high-speed quads, 1 high-speed six-pack
Uphill capacity	33,000 skiers per hour
Skiable terrain	4,800 acres (patrolled)
Opening date	Thanksgiving
Closing date	late April, early May
Snowboarding	Yes

Transportation

By car One hour from Reno via U.S. Highway 50; 2½ hours from Sacramento via U.S. Highway 50; 4½ hours from San Francisco via I-80 to Sacramento, then U.S. Highway 50.

By bus Free shuttle bus from most Lake Tahoe hotels. Tahoe Casino Express from Reno-Tahoe airport—$17 one way.

By air Major carriers to Reno-Tahoe International Airport (70 miles, frequent bus service).

Key Phone Numbers

Ski Area Information (775) 586-7000
Snow Report (530) 541-7544
Reservations (800) 243-2836
www.skiheavenly.com

ALPINE MEADOWS

Alpine Meadows, a friendly and unpretentious medium-size area, sits in the canyon just south of Squaw Valley, backed up to the Sierra Crest. Alpine offers the same snow, the same precipitous summit bowls, and the same gentle plateau runs as its neighboring Tahoe resorts. But it's not as overbuilt as most, and it has managed to retain an intimate atmosphere. While the upper bowls and steep tree runs provide some of the most exciting skiing in the region, Alpine tends to play down its expert terrain in favor of its lovely, rolling intermediate cruisers. Management loves to cater to families; it maintains one of the friendliest ski schools in California and even grooms special training runs for young bump skiers.

Alpine's permit area covers about 2,000 acres spread across two peaks—Ward Peak (8,637 feet) and Scott Peak (8,289 feet). The resort also offers two separate base areas. The main lodge (6,840 feet), complete with cafeteria, bar, ski shop, and locker rooms, sits at the head of Alpine Meadows Road off Highway 89, 12 miles south of Truckee and 6 miles north of Tahoe City. The Sherwood base area offers limited parking and a snack bar, but it functions as a convenient back-door entrance for folks lodging on the west shore of the lake. You can reach it from Highway 89 south of Tahoe City.

Because Route 89 is a winding two-lane highway subject to blockage by both avalanche and traffic accident, it clogs with traffic each morning and evening, especially on weekends. The absolute worst time to travel is Sunday evening, when the entire sporting population of northern California tries to funnel through the two-lane railroad bridge at Truckee and onto I-80 for the slow trip over Donner Pass. If it's snowing, plan to have a leisurely dinner before joining the exodus.

The best way to avoid traffic hassles is to stay over in Tahoe City for the night and travel on Monday morning. This means making a right turn out of the Alpine Meadows road for a short, easy trip back to the hotel and a nice dinner at Jake's on the Lake (steak and seafood) or Wolfdale's (French and Japanese fusion) or River Ranch (game and steak) right at the base of the Alpine Meadows Road.

While Alpine's total vertical from the main lodge to the summit is modest—less than 1,800 feet—the lofty base elevation, combined with a sizable snowmaking capacity, means that Alpine can count on good coverage from mid-November right through to early June. In fact, the area has been open on snowmaking trails on Halloween, and a July 4 ski race is not unheard of. A big snow season means summer skiing, but it also means the risk of the Monster Sierra Storm, which can close the area for two or three days at a time. When a storm hunkers down over the lake, the roads close too. Bring a good book and your powder skis because when the weather lifts, you'll have the ski area all to yourself until Highway 50 and I-80 reopen.

Eight of the twelve lifts load near the base lodge. Beginners have an area all to themselves, served by Subway and Meadow chairs and Tiegel Poma. Intermediates can cruise any marked run off Roundhouse, Kangaroo, or Hot Wheels chairs. Most advanced skiers can hop right onto the high-speed Summit Six for the six-minute trip to the top of Alpine Bowl.

The Chalet Restaurant is another jumping-off point on the front of the mountain. Located alongside *Weasel Run* in the sheltered gulley between Ward and Scott Peaks, the Chalet sits near the loading stations for Yellow chair (serving intermediate terrain) and Scott chair (now a triple chair, offering access to the intermediate Lakeview and Back Bowl areas and to the steep *Scott Chute* and *Promised Land*).

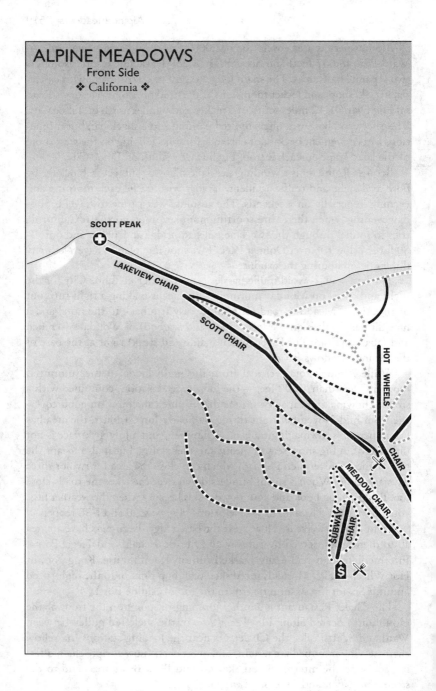

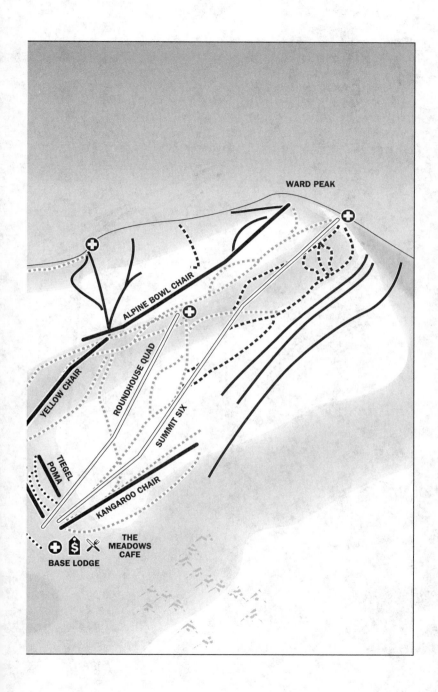

WARD PEAK

ALPINE BOWL CHAIR

YELLOW CHAIR

ROUNDHOUSE QUAD

SUMMIT SIX

TIEGEL POMA

KANGAROO CHAIR

THE MEADOWS CAFE

BASE LODGE

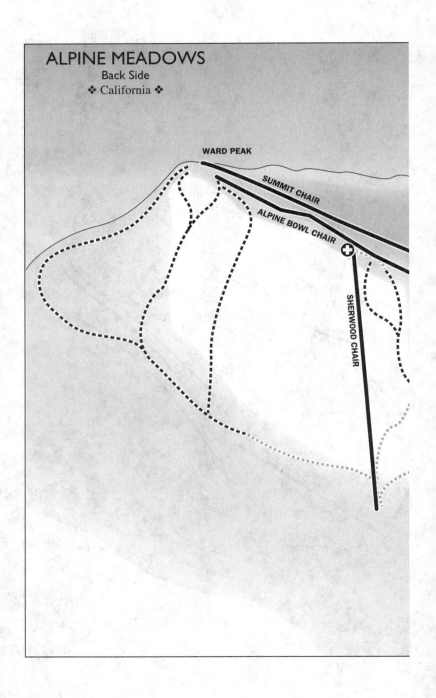

ALPINE MEADOWS
Back Side
❖ California ❖

WARD PEAK

SUMMIT CHAIR

ALPINE BOWL CHAIR

SHERWOOD CHAIR

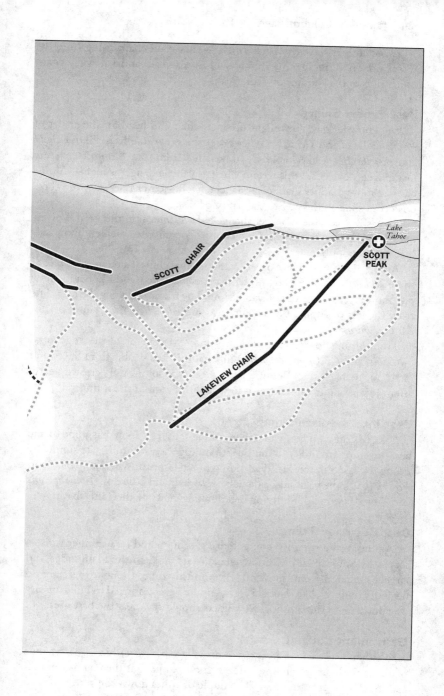

Two chairlifts serve the Back Bowls—Sherwood chair, rising from the West Shore parking lot to a shoulder of Ward Peak, and Lakeview chair, which rises to the summit of Scott Peak.

Best Expert Skiing

On a powder day, go straight up Scott chair and head for the glades of *Promised Land* and *Gentian Gulley.* After the snow stabilizes, *Beaver Bowl* and *Estelle Bowl,* reachable by traversing from the Summit Six, are magnificent. Never ski this terrain when avalanche danger is high—Alpine has had more than its share of avalanche fatalities over the years, and these bowls can slide all the way to the parking lot.

An easily accessible expert challenge is *D-8 Chute* into the steep Wolverine Bowl, then down *Waterfall,* which usually comprises the best bump skiing on the mountain.

Alpine also offers plenty of steep and narrow chutes. The most public of these is *Scott Chute,* directly under Scott chair, where local hotshots show off. Shorter yet steeper terrain can be found by traversing along the ridge line from the top of Alpine Bowl chair, into *Keyhole, High Yellow,* and, best of all, *Our Father.*

From Alpine Bowl chair you can also pop over the top of the ridge to ski *Sun Bowl* and *CB Chute;* the adjoining *South Face* is skiable from Sherwood chair on the back side. Because these areas face south, they crust up early after the sun comes out and turn to wonderful corn in the spring.

Best Intermediate Skiing

Like to cruise on big, wide-open rolling terrain? Alpine has some of the best nonstops around. You can pile up mileage at a stunning rate simply by riding the fast Summit Six, descending in big GS turns via *Alpine Bowl* and *Red Trail.* On the back side, ride Lakeview chair and cruise on *Twilight Zone* and *Outer Limits,* both offering breathtaking views of the Tahoe basin.

Best Beginner Skiing

Alpine runs a friendly, competent ski school, and its beginner runs—served by Subway and Meadow chairs—are close to the main lodge and largely sheltered from the wind. Beyond this zone, though, there are no beginner trails. Unlike most ski areas, Alpine never bothered to build an easy way down from the summit. New skiers should stay near the base area.

Convenient Lodging

Neither of these base areas is a resort village per se; within a quarter-mile of the main lodge you'll find a dozen condo units, but there's no commercial development until you roll a couple of miles down the access road to

Highway 89. Here, nestled around the bridge that crosses the Truckee River, are a ski shop, a deli, some more condos, and the atmospheric old River Ranch, with its bar, restaurant, and hotel rooms. For weekend skiing, the River Ranch should be the first choice for comfortable, convenient lodging and meals. Most Alpine Meadows skiers stay in Truckee or Tahoe City motels (a good bet is Granlibakken Resort in Tahoe City or Sunnyside Resort in Sunnyside), or they travel around the lake from one of the big resort hotels on the Nevada side, either at Incline Village (half an hour by road) or Southshore (an hour). All these lodges are served by the Tahoe Area Rapid Transit (TART), which connects with the Alpine Meadows shuttle bus. Hours of bus operation can vary with weather and road conditions, so call ahead for details.

ALPINE MEADOWS DATA

Mountain Statistics

Vertical feet	1,800 feet
Base elevation	6,840 feet
Summit elevation	8,637 feet
Longest run	2.5 miles
Average annual snowfall	425 inches
Number of lifts	12, including 2 high-speed lifts
Uphill capacity	16,000 skiers per hour
Skiable terrain	2,000 acres
Opening date	mid-November
Closing date	after Memorial Day
Snowboarding	Yes

Transportation

By car Four hours from San Francisco; 2 hours from Sacramento; 1 hour from Reno via I-80 to Truckee, then south on Route 89. Turn right at Alpine Meadows access road. From Lake Tahoe locations, to Tahoe City via Routes 89 or 28, then continue north on Route 89. Turn left at Alpine Meadows access road.

By bus TART and shuttle bus.

By plane Via most major airlines to Reno-Tahoe International Airport.

Key Phone Numbers

Ski Area Information (530) 583-4232
Snow Report (530) 581-8374
Reservations (800) 499-3296
www.skialpine.com

To Wax or Not to Wax?

That is the question. To wax or not to wax? And there is only one answer: a resounding yes. I know that a lot of skiers aren't thrilled by speed, have no desire to ski faster than they already do, and believe that waxing skis is only for racers or experts in search of ever more speed. Even if you are the calmest skier on the hill, I'd like to encourage you to wax your skis (or have your local ski shop do it), and then keep them well waxed. Why?

Waxing doesn't automatically make you ski faster. Paradoxically, one can ski much slower on a well-waxed pair of skis than on skis that aren't waxed. That's because waxing merely makes skis slippery; it reduces the friction between skis and snow. And that in turn means that it takes less force, less muscle power, and also less speed to make a waxed ski turn. It's true. A well-waxed pair of skis responds to the slightest twisting action of your feet like a well-trained horse to a slight touch of the rein. Even if you've never been lured by the thrill of speed, every mountain has a few boring flat spots you have to get across—gliding or walking—and waxed skis will let you slide across these flats while your friends are pushing with their poles, and skating or shuffling to keep moving.

How often should you wax your skis? Spring snow is more granular and wears wax off the bases of your skis more quickly than cold winter snow; but if you possibly can, I'd recommend getting your skis waxed every few skiing days. For most skiers that means every weekend. Whatever level skier you are, you will be amazed at the difference in your skiing performance.

I mentioned having your ski shop do it. Why not just buy some wax and put it on yourself? Ideally, wax should be melted and ironed onto the bases of your skis—"hot waxing," in ski jargon. This can be done with an old second-hand iron, or with any number of high-tech gizmos that ski shops keep around to melt and apply wax. The hot wax penetrates the pores of your plastic ski bases and lasts a lot longer than wax that is just rubbed on. Once the hot wax is melted into the bases of your skis, it should then be scraped down to a very, very thin layer. And finally, depending on the type of snow, it can be "structured." That's a strange expression for scratching tiny micro-grooves into the ski's base with a very fine wire or plastic bristle brush. The purpose of this "structure" (this almost invisible texture of tiny grooves) is to break up the suction due to water in the snow, suction that can slow your skis considerably. Water in the snow? Indeed. We used to think that water in the snow was only a factor in late spring, when the snowpack begins to melt. Not so. Research has shown that the pressure a skier puts on the snow can momentarily melt a minuscule layer of water, just under the ski's bases. And "structuring" or texturing the running surface of your skis will eliminate the drag of this tiny film of water.

So you can see that a good wax job is more complex than one might think. And we haven't discussed the problem of selecting the perfect wax for today's conditions. You're probably better off to take your skis to a shop at first (ask a ski instructor for the name of the best shop in your area). Later, if you decide to get serious about waxing your own skis, my advice is to pick one of the main brands of wax and stick to it for at least a season, discovering through trial and error just what colors and blends of that wax produce the smoothest-running skis.

Of course, waxed skis will run much faster than unwaxed boards, if you're looking for speed. But waxed skis just plain ski better too. Getting your skis waxed and keeping them waxed may do more for your technique than a private lesson.

SQUAW VALLEY

Squaw Valley has a reputation—the ultimate macho, bad-boy mountain. The steep walls of KT-22, Cornice II, Palisades, Siberia, Granite Chief, and Tram Bowl have trained several generations of racers and extreme skiers. Olympic medalists Jimmie Heuga and Tamara McKinney grew up at Squaw, as did dozens of other U.S. Ski Team members.

Television and the movies have contributed to Squaw's image. Site of the 1960 Winter Olympics (the first televised winter games), Squaw was also the training ground for Warren Miller, who shot his early films here. Cliff-leaping stuntman Rick Sylvester, who occasionally skis in James Bond films, lives and trains at Squaw. No modern ski film is finished until it includes footage of Scot Schmidt, Glen Plake, Kevin Anderson, Robby Huntoon, Mike Slattery, or Tom or Lizzy Day dropping through the rocks of Palisades.

This rowdy history rankles Squaw's management. Alex Cushing, who, with Wayne Poulsen, founded the place in 1949, would much rather attract a crowd of civilized, reasonably disciplined citizens. In recent years he's rebuilt all the lifts and restaurants, knocking off the rough edges in favor of friendly efficiency. Much is made of the fancy skating rink and swimming pool at High Camp, hovering 2,000 feet above the base lodges. A helpful fact is that Squaw's 30 lifts now constitute the fastest single-mountain lift system in North America (only the combination of Whistler and Black-comb can move more people upward in an hour).

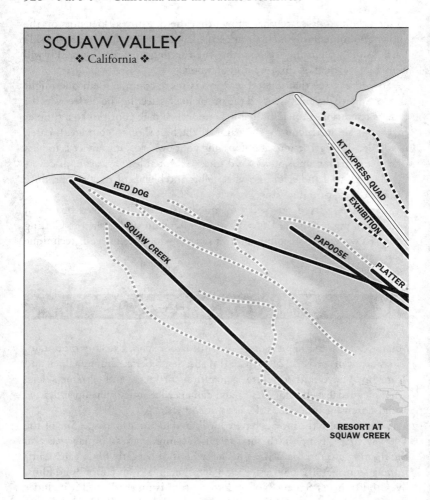

Squaw is growing. Intrawest, the large Canadian company that owns Whistler/Blackcomb, Panorama, Mammoth, and Copper Mountain (plus a number of ski resorts in the East), has begun construction on a new village with underground parking, 640 residential units, and about 80 shops and restaurants. The construction zone occupies half of the vast paved parking lot, and it remains to be seen how Squaw will handle parking and traffic during the 1999–2000 ski season.

Traffic shouldn't be a problem up on the mountain: the lift system has been augmented again. The new Funitel (replacing the old gondola) makes

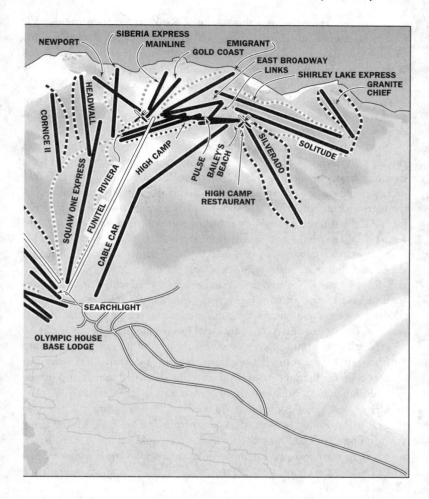

the two-mile trip from the base area to the Gold Coast in eight minutes—and the 15-passenger cars hang from two cables, so the wind won't swing them much. In theory, the Funitel can operate in winds up to 75 mph, so transport to and from the upper mountain will be possible even in those notorious Sierra blizzards. Beginners and nonskiers can transfer between the Gold Coast and High Camp restaurants on the Pulse Funitel.

None of this is the reason Squaw regulars return year after year after year. The real reason is Squaw's huge extent of genuinely steep terrain. The mountain now claims about 4,000 acres of skiing, which may or may not be true; a few years ago they claimed 6,000 acres, then backed off. I have no way of measuring the actual acreage, but it's probably a bit smaller than Mammoth, which claims 3,500, and on the same scale (or larger) than Heavenly, which claims 4,800. The important thing is that Squaw is vast enough that it takes an expert skier at least a couple of hours to ski from one end of the complex to the other; ski patrolmen take two solid seasons to learn the mountain well enough to be considered useful employees.

Squaw can be intimidating to the new arrival. From the parking lot, you can see only about 10 percent of the skiable terrain, including some of the steepest parts of Snow King, KT-22, Cornice II, and Headwall. Plus the theoretically unskiable cliffs under the Cable Car (Rick Sylvester skied one of the narrow chutes there in 1968, dropping like a waxed rock for the first 500 feet). All the intermediate skiing is out of sight on the broad plateaus and gentle bowls above the two mid-station restaurants.

Squaw does a lousy job of trail marking; trail names aren't even listed on the official trail map, and if you ask a local for directions you may get several different names for any given trail because the ski school and ski patrol tend to have their own naming systems. Instead of naming trails, Squaw tends to name various areas of the mountain after the peak or the lift that serves it. Lifts, rather than trails, are given green-blue-black designations, so it's especially important to keep your wits about you. It's easy to cruise onto a lift and then find yourself on terrain you didn't expect. That's why this chapter is longer than the others in this section; I've tried to make up for the general vagueness of Squaw's own nomenclature.

Driving to Squaw is easy in good weather, via I-80 from the Bay Area (3.5 hours) or Reno (1 hour), then south from Truckee for 12 miles along the winding two-lane Route 89, following the banks of the Truckee River, with a right turn onto the Olympic Valley access road. In stormy weather, when Donner Pass may close, the trip from Sacramento and San Francisco can take all night.

I like to get there early (before 8 A.M.), park close in, and have breakfast at Dave's Deli or Mother Barclay's (both in the Olympic House base complex); there's also a coffee shop in the Cable Car building, where you can get a croissant and latte while waiting to load on the lift. Locals avoid morning lift lines by parking near Children's World (the day care facility at the southeast corner of the parking lot behind the movie theater) and riding Papoose chair to get into the trail network. There's no ticket window at this site, so if you want to use this option, buy multiday tickets in advance. This route is wonderfully convenient for parents—drop the kids at Children's World and scoot straight up Papoose.

Squaw has two base areas and two mid-mountain lodges. At the base (elevation 6,200 feet) are the Resort at Squaw Creek, with its Squaw Creek chair (you will not be allowed to park here unless you are registered at the resort), and the Olympic House complex, served by the Cable Car (also called the tram by locals), the new Funitel, Red Dog, Exhibition, KT-22, and Squaw One Express. Papoose chair and the beginner lifts—the pony tows and Exhibition/Searchlight—also originate here.

At mid-mountain (elevation 8,200 feet) you'll find Gold Coast Lodge at the top of the Funitel and High Camp Bath & Tennis Club (the good-weather home of the ski school) at the top of the Cable Car.

Here are Squaw's major "neighborhoods," working from east to west:

The Resort Runs are served by Squaw Creek chair. The area is named for the Resort at Squaw Creek, the plush 500-room hotel at the bottom of the Squaw Creek Lift. There's mostly intermediate cruising terrain here, but if you drop off the ridge line to the north, you'll find very steep tree skiing and bump runs. There are no beginner runs here.

Snow King Mountain, also called Red Dog, is served by the Red Dog and Papoose chairs. Mostly steep, race-course terrain (this was the site of the women's Olympic GS courses), Snow King has intermediate trails winding across the bottom of Olympic Lady to emerge above the Olympic House base lodge. It's the normal transfer route from the Resort at Squaw Creek to the main lift network. The last 300 yards of this trail are steep, so it's not recommended to beginners, who, instead, should ride the shuttle bus.

Olympic Lady is the very steep mountain hidden between Snow King and KT-22. Because the lift loads in the secluded gulley above the base area and because the Olympic Lady terrain is never groomed, this area remains a secret hideaway for Squaw's local experts. There's fantastic bump skiing, tree skiing, and powder here. Intermediate skiers shouldn't bother—there's no safe way down. Olympic Lady was the site of the Olympic women's downhill in 1960.

Exhibition serves a steepish and very public bump run overlooking the main lodge and provides access to the steeper Schimmelpfennig Bowl. The bowl was the men's slalom stadium during the Olympics but now serves as a bump run and exit route for skiers descending the Nose of KT-22. Advanced intermediates will be comfortable here when the face of Exhibition has been groomed. Exhibition offers no beginner terrain.

KT-22 (named for the 22 kick turns executed by Sandy Poulsen when her husband, Squaw Valley pioneer Wayne Poulsen, first hauled her up there) is world famous for its magnificent steep terrain. The runs are rarely groomed. Get off the lift and turn left into *GS Bowl;* it's very steep but also very broad, so there's plenty of room to recover when you get in trouble. Follow the ridge line back under the lift line (a hazardous route at best) to reach the Nose and the Fingers cliffs. Turn right off the lift and drop off the edge into *Chute 75*, a long exhilarating couloir of perfectly consistent pitch. One relatively easy trail follows the ridge line to the west toward *Saddle* (this is the exit route for intermediate skiers). Drop off the ridge to the north to find exhilarating steeps in the appropriately named *Rock Garden* and *Dead Tree*.

Squaw normally grooms an intermediate escape route down *Saddle*, reachable via the ridge lines from KT-22 and Cornice II lifts. Just to the west of *Saddle's* low point is an irregular bowl called *Enchanted Forest*, usually my first destination on a good powder morning.

The western descents from KT-22 and the *Saddle* trails descend to *Mountain Run*, the main route off the upper mountain. Situated just below the *Mountain Run* road cut is Cornice II chair. Cornice II serves some of the steepest face skiing at Squaw. The intermediate exit route from the top of the lift is to turn left and follow the ridge line east toward *Saddle;* experts can drop off the ridge into the *Horse Trails* area, descend the *Classic* and *Hourglass* chutes, or simply ski the steepish *Cornice II* face (one of the great lines on a powder day is directly under the Cornice II lift line). From the top of Cornice II local nutcases can climb a few yards and jump into *Light Tower* (also called *Bell Tower*), reputed to be the steepest lift-served chute on the hill. Experts and advanced skiers only on Cornice II.

Headwall chair goes over the northern shoulder of Cornice to the saddle at the east end of Squaw Peak. Turn left here onto the broad, smooth *Sunbowl*, a wonderful intermediate cruiser that's best on powder days and in spring corn. *Sunbowl* exits onto *Horse Trails* or *Saddle*. The other intermediate exit from Headwall chair is straight ahead, onto *Chicken Bowl*, the wide landing field for bodies falling off the Squaw Peak Palisades. Most skiers getting off Headwall chair make a 180-degree turn and follow the cat track 100 yards east to *North Bowl, The Nose,* or *Headwall. North Bowl* starts as a very steep face, usually bumped out, and flattens out to merely steep; it all overlooks the Gold Coast Restaurant, so make your best turns. The *Headwall* is quite steep and, since it lies under the lift, also very public. Both faces are left ungroomed. My favorite run off *Headwall* is *The Nose*, the convex spine that separates *Headwall* from *North Bowl*. The bumps are longer and more rhythmic, and it leads straight down to the high-speed Siberia quad.

Because it overlooks the great Gold Coast/Mainline plateau (cruising ground for Squaw's intermediate skiers), *Siberia Bowl* attracts a lot of ambitious advanced skiers. The bowl is groomed frequently, but because it's steep and fast, it bumps out quickly. The escape route is to the north, along the ridge line to the *Mainline* and *Gold Coast* runs. The ungroomed portions of *Siberia Bowl* are strictly expert. Newport chair serves Siberia's lower, gentler slopes.

Mainline and Gold Coast serve the rolling intermediate runs above Gold

Coast Restaurant. Most of these trails are wide and gentle, with easily visible dropoffs, but beware the heavy cross-traffic near the restaurant.

Emigrant chair goes, of course, to the summit of Emigrant Peak. Intermediates have two choices here: Turn left and ski back toward *Gold Coast* or go straight ahead and follow the cat track around to the right to *Attic,* a steep but wide and smooth trail leading toward the high-speed Shirley Lake quad. Experts can duck back under the Emigrant lift line and pound down the very steep *Funnel* (beware the rock band hidden under the snow in the middle) or follow the road toward *Attic* and peel off to the left to descend the tree runs on the backside of Emigrant. There's no beginner terrain off Emigrant Peak.

The easiest terrain at Gold Coast consists of a couple of wide, gentle, and consistent runs served by the East Broadway chair. These are pleasant low-intermediate runs, used for ski school classes and practice. Somewhat more varied and challenging intermediate terrain can be found at High Camp Lift, which starts alongside *Mountain Run* a few hundred feet downhill from the Gold Coast Restaurant.

The best beginner terrain at Squaw is on the three ski school lifts clustered on the High Camp plateau: *Bailey's Beach, Links,* and *Belmont.* Because of the high elevation (8,200 feet), High Camp gets dependable snow. You reach this area via the Cable Car; beginners should plan to ride the Cable Car back down at the end of the day.

North of the High Camp plateau are two lifts suitable for intermediates —Shirley Lake and Solitude—and two for experts, Granite Chief and Silverado.

When the wind is from the west, as is usually the case, Shirley Lake and Solitude are sheltered. Shirley, a high-speed quad, serves the lower slopes of Emigrant's north side and five tree runs that are really wide boulevards separated by thin stands of ponderosa and silver fir. Solitude's trails loop far to the east to give lower intermediates an easy way down and feature one advanced-to-expert bump bowl directly under the lift. *Solitude Bowl* itself, near the top of the lift, makes a good introduction to steep skiing because it rounds out nicely to a flat runout.

Beyond the bottom of Shirley Lake lies Granite Chief chair. All the terrain off the top is quite steep. Turn left and follow the ridge line until one of the many lines down the bowl looks appealing, or turn right and peel off down *Secret Bowl.* After a storm, this is the last terrain secured by the avalanche patrol, and powder skiers find untracked lines in the trees by traversing farther and farther across the flanks of Granite Chief Peak.

Just east of High Camp Bath & Tennis Club, the terrain plunges away in the precipitous *Tram Bowl.* Experts drop through the cliff band, and advanced skiers can cruise the bowl by skirting below the Bailey's Beach tennis courts to the Broken Arrow saddle and then turning left. This is all delicious powder skiing after a storm, and it opens whenever Silverado chair is running.

The final lift is Broken Arrow, which loads near the bottom of Siberia Express alongside *Mountain Run* and takes you to the top of *Broken Arrow Bowl.* Never groomed, *Broken Arrow* is a magnificently long, rolling expanse of expert chutes, glades, and ridges, facing mostly east and south. It's hidden from the general run of traffic on *Mountain Run,* so it's rarely crowded. But the southern exposure means the powder turns crusty and heavy within a few days after a storm; only strong powder skiers should go there.

Tricks of the Trade

On a crowded day, the fastest way up the mountain will be to bypass the lines at the Funitel and Cable Car and ride Squaw One Express to Siberia Express. If you have a season pass or multiday pass, avoid traffic jams by parking behind the Squaw Valley theater, and ride Papoose chair into the trail network.

At the end of the day, skiers elbow their way down *Mountain Run*—it's an ugly mob scene. Intermediates can skirt the worst of it by skiing down *Sunnyside,* on the north side of the valley. Experts have more fun: From High Camp, traverse around Broken Arrow Peak to ski *Sundance* (locals still call it *Tower 16*) under the Funitel, or go straight to Broken Arrow and follow the ridges and gullies all the way back to the base lodge bars.

Best Expert Skiing

My favorite runs in powder and corn are the glades on either side of the Granite Chief lift line, the hidden shot off the north side of Emigrant Peak called *McGoo's Madness, Broken Arrow,* and the two *Noses* on *Headwall* and KT-22. On a storm day, the best skiing is *Poulsen's Gulley* (under Red Dog chair) and the forests on either side.

Best Intermediate Skiing

When it's uncrowded, *Mountain Run* is a wonderful cruiser (it was the men's downhill course in 1960). Otherwise, the Shirley Lake tree runs give you the most challenge and the most skiing per hour, thanks to the high-speed lift.

Best Beginner Skiing

In good weather, the High Camp plateau can't be beat. In bad weather, go to Alpine Meadows, because the limited beginner terrain on Exhibition/Searchlight chair is intolerably crowded.

Convenient Lodging

Until the new village complex opens, Squaw still has only five hotels, of which the most comfortable are the Squaw Valley Lodge, the Resort at Squaw Creek, and the Olympic Village Inn. The lodge is a big modern condo/hotel complex complete with covered parking, pools, and exercise and weight rooms. It sits just behind the Olympic House base area and offers ski-in/ski-out convenience. The Resort at Squaw Creek is a plush 500-room hotel with its own shopping mall, three good restaurants, a ski shop, and a skating rink. The Resort, too, is a ski-in/ski-out lodge, with its own base area and lift, though beginner skiers will have to ride the shuttle bus over to the main base area because all the linking ski runs are intermediate or higher. The Olympic Village Inn is a short walk from the main base area (or you can ride their shuttle); built as athlete housing for the 1960 Olympics, the place was thoroughly renovated in the early 1980s and is now a picturesque, rambling condotel with a very good dining room.

Most Squaw Valley skiers stay in Truckee or Tahoe City, but weekend traffic jams on the access road and Route 89 are so appallingly bad that if you can afford to stay in the valley, you should.

Best Eats

On the mountain there are good cafeterias at High Camp (with a spectacular panoramic view to the north, east, and south), Gold Coast, and Olympic houses. You can have good sit-down lunches at Alexander's (High Camp), Salsa (Olympic House), and Bullwhacker's (Resort at Squaw Creek).

Several good restaurants have set up recently within the valley. I like Glissande (continental) and Montagne (Italian) at the Resort at Squaw Creek, the dining room at the Olympic Village Inn, and Graham Rock's (eclectic haute cuisine) in the old Poulsen House at the northeast corner of the parking lot. For cheap eats, nothing beats pizza at the Chamois, the traditional après-ski hangout for ski instructors and patrolpersons.

On a snowy evening, the better part of valor lies in dining in the valley, rather than fighting the standstill traffic clotted all the way into Truckee. Traffic thins out after 8 P.M., so choose a designated driver and relax.

SQUAW VALLEY DATA

Mountain Statistics	
Vertical feet	2,850 feet
Base elevation	6,200 feet
Summit elevation	9,050 feet
Longest run	3 miles
Average annual snowfall	450 inches
Number of lifts	30, including 6 high-speed lifts
Uphill capacity	49,100 skiers per hour
Skiable terrain	4,000 acres (claimed)
Opening date	mid-November
Closing date	Memorial Day or later
Snowboarding	Yes

Transportation

By car From Reno, 1 hour via I-80 to Truckee, then Route 89; from San Francisco, 4 hours via I-80 to Truckee, then Route 89; from Sacramento, 2 hours via I-80 to Truckee, then Route 89; from Lake Tahoe area, Route 28 or 89 to Tahoe City, then Route 89 north.

By bus Shuttle bus from most Lake Tahoe and Reno hotels.

By air Major carriers to Reno-Tahoe International Airport (40 miles).

Key Phone Numbers

Ski Area Information
(530) 583-6985 or
(800) 545-4350
Snow Report (530) 583-6955
Reservations (800) 545-4350 or
(888) SNOW-321
www.squaw.com

INSIDE STORY

Sierra Cement

Sierra Cement. It doesn't sound very inviting, that term for the heavy, wet, maritime snow that sometimes falls not only in California's High Sierra, but also up and down the West Coast ranges. I suppose it isn't very inviting, especially compared to fluffy Utah powder.

But skilled Far-West skiers develop a kind of affection for the stuff—nothing improves your skiing more than responding to challenging conditions, and Sierra Cement is a major challenge.

After learning to ski in western Switzerland, I began my ski-teaching life in this country at Squaw Valley, and I was soon wrestling with Sierra Cement. The result was an unexpected plus: Having made my peace with this awkward, heavy snow, I then discovered that I could ski untracked snow anywhere else in the world, easily. It was a tough apprenticeship, but one that worked. I should say too, to dispel a baseless rumor, that Sierra Cement is far from the only kind of snow that falls on these West Coast ranges. It's merely one end of the full spectrum of snow (the heavy, wet end) that West Coast skiers can encounter in the course of a season. And it's only really a challenge in its unpacked state; once it has been packed and groomed, it's just, well, snow.

But you'd like to ski this stuff, or to ski it better. You wake up in the morning and look at a mountain covered with three feet of snow overnight, and you feel thrilled until you go out on the porch and discover you can squeeze water out of a snowball—ugh! Sierra Cement. Let's give it a go. Are you ready?

Naturally you want to approach this wet western snow like powder, with your weight evenly distributed over both skis. The next thing you need is a steeper-than-normal slope. This heavy wet snow will slow you down—so much so that if you aren't on a steep slope, you may wind up having to walk downhill through it. So steepness becomes an additional part of the challenge. In the Rocky Mountains you can ski powder on very gentle pitches (true powder is so light that it doesn't slow you down much), but not out here, not on Sierra Cement. So let me suggest a couple of confidence-building exercises before you attack a steep slope of Sierra Cement directly. Begin with a few uphill turns, to get used to the extra resistance of the snow. Traverse down and across that steep slope; flex your legs deeply; and make a turn to a stop by extending your legs down and away from you. That's right, an uphill christie by extending your legs and pushing out the tails of your skis. This is a powerful move. It would be out of place, excessive, on a packed slope; but in two feet of untracked Sierra Cement it works great. Now practice a few more of these special uphill christies from steeper and steeper traverses, until finally you can turn out to a stop from a run straight down the fall line, straight down the hill.

Now we're ready to tackle the start or launch phase of our turns in this heavy snow. My suggestions: Use a little more speed than normal; make a very powerful up movement or lift at the start of the turn (to break your skis loose from the grip of this heavy snow); and finally, bank your whole body in the direction you want to turn. Banking is curious. It's often a mistake, a problem, in modern skiing since it tends to put too much weight on the inside ski. But here, in heavy deep snow, it works wonders. As you bank your body in the direction of your turn (the way a bicyclist or motorcyclist leans into a turn), you also bank your skis against the snow. And the resistance of this heavy snow against the tilted or banked bases of your skis will actually push you around, into the turn.

In short, the recipe for success in skiing untracked Sierra Cement is three-fold. Exaggerated (powerful but smooth) movements, a little more speed than normal, and a steeper slope. It will take time before you can relax in this heavy wet snow, but the first step is simply to turn in it, no matter how crudely. Then with increasing success, increasing confidence, you will be able to smooth out and refine your movements. You'll find out just how much power you need, just how far to bank into the turn. And you'll also discover that skiing hard conditions, easily, is one of the great thrills of our sport. Sierra Cement provides that thrill.

NORTHSTAR-AT-TAHOE

Northstar, created in 1972 on logging company land, for years built its reputation on family skiing. The huge, gladed bowl above the Lodge at Big Springs was perfect for turning the kids loose in: all traffic coming off its gentle cruising runs had to pass the lodge, so a watchful parent had no trouble rounding up the herd at the end of the day.

Well, those kids grew up and wanted more challenging skiing. Northstar obliged by opening a high-speed quad lift to serve a dozen backside trails of leg-burning length and pitch. Between these trails lies some of the sweetest tree skiing at the lake. Mom and Dad can no longer depend on the kids to cycle past the lunch deck every half hour; it's too tempting to get lost in the woods. Future plans call for additional lifts that will open new terrain rolling down toward the existing Schaeffer's Camp cross-country trail.

For now, the lift layout is still pretty simple: From Northstar Village, ride the gondola up to the Lodge at Big Springs or take the Echo Lift to the same destination. The base village (it has a mini-mall with shops and services alongside the short walk from parking lot to gondola entrance) is simple and woodsy; it's a pleasantly low-key entrée, thanks in large measure to the fact that pedestrian traffic all moves in one direction: toward the gondola in the morning and toward the parking in the afternoon.

From the Lodge at Big Springs, at the top of the gondola, the real skiing begins. Beginners have a choice of three short lifts (Bear Paw, plus Bear Cub and Chipmunk, which are reserved for the ski school), all isolated behind the Lodge at Big Springs. Intermediates and experts can hop on the Vista high-speed quad (it goes up the east side of the bowl), Lookout Lift (up the west side), or Arrow Express (right up the middle). All three lifts serve a mix of intermediate and advanced slopes; none is too scary for gutsy kids.

To get to the summit (and the backside), ride to the summit of Mount Pluto via Arrow Express and Comstock Express (serving the upper half of the front bowl).

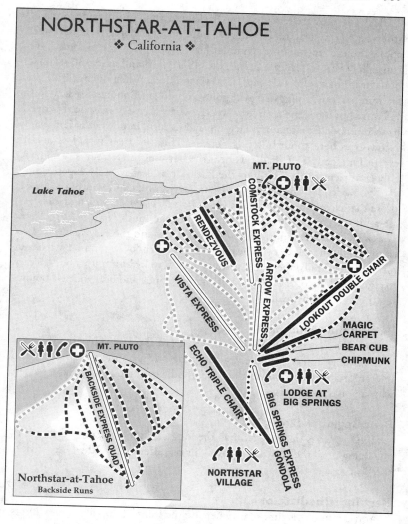

The runs off the East Ridge, served by Comstock and the shorter Rendezvous triple chair, are marked as expert terrain, but they're just steep enough to keep your skis sliding easily in powder. These trails—*Grouse, Flume, Crosscut, Tonini's, Chute, Dutchman,* and *Delight*—are about perfect for learning to ski powder, and experts will enjoy popping off the trails into the glades.

The West Ridge runs—*Corridor, Plunge, Ax Handle, Stump Alley, Luggi's, Jibboom,* and *Flying Squirrel*—are a bit steeper for a short upper section, then flatten out into easy intermediate cruising.

Backside runs are served by the Backside Express Lift (some locals may still refer to this area as Schaeffer's Camp, but that name is more properly applied to the cross-country complex farther down). When groomed, these runs allow you to set up a consistent GS rhythm and crank 30-mile-per-hour turns for a solid mile and 1,860 vertical feet. When the Backside trails are bumped out, youngsters will pound on down. Boomers stick with the GS turns but move them into the woods, where the trees are spaced perfectly to accommodate that natural medium-radius turn, in powder or corn snow. No worries here about bursting between close-set trees to fall off a cliff; except for a couple of road cuts near the bottom, the terrain is of remarkably consistent pitch. Think of the Backside as user-friendly expert skiing.

The Backside runs are generally similar in pitch and width; of course, those that closely parallel the lift (*Iron Horse, Polaris, Rapids,* and *Burnout*) are a bit steeper than the trails that loop to the south (*Rail Splitter, Sierra Grande, Challenger*) and north (*Promised Land* and the easy *Lookout Road* cat track). Don't relax as you near the bottom: While the terrain flattens out on the return trails, the traffic is heavy here so they bump up a bit. It's easy to come honking off *Iron Horse* going mach schnell and find yourself bouncing through a minefield.

Exiting the Mountain

Village Run gets very crowded at the end of the day. While the terrain is very easy, beginners should consider riding down on the gondola—it's an uncomfortable sensation to fall in the middle of the trail with expert skiers whizzing past both ears.

Best Beginner Skiing

Village Run is that rare animal: the long beginner cruiser; and it's pleasant skiing until the crowds get rowdy in late afternoon. Otherwise, stick to the Bear Paw terrain.

Best Intermediate Skiing

You can find this almost anywhere on the front. If you like long cruisers, take *West Ridge* to *Luggi's* to *Lumberjack* to *Main Street*—that drops you 1,800 vertical feet back to the bottom of Arrow Express. The longest trail on the mountain—roughly two miles and 2,200 vertical feet—is *East Ridge* to *Logger's Loop* to the *Woods*. Just turn left at the top of *Comstock* and then make every right turn all the way down.

Best Expert Skiing

This can be found in Backside's trees in powder or corn. The trees, generously spaced, can soak up dozens of powder freaks after a storm.

Convenient Lodging

Northstar provides the best assortment of ski-in/ski-out lodging in California, with 262 condo units at slopeside or within walking distance of the gondola. A friendly shuttle service cycles past all the Northstar condos, making it easy for families to cut the teens loose to find their way out and back, morning and evening. The advantage to staying right in Northstar, rather than at a Truckee or Tahoe City lodge, is that you avoid Tahoe's spectacular weather-caused traffic snarls. Getting to and from Northstar from Reno or Sacramento involves creeping through Truckee via Highway 267, a tense experience when the roads are slick and impossible when Donner Pass closes. Getting there from the lake means driving Highway 267 over Brockway Summit (7,200 feet), which can be impossible without four-wheel-drive or chains. When weather threatens, allow extra travel time.

Best Eats

Timbercreek seems to be the favorite at Northstar, featuring honey-barbecued salmon and rack of Sonoma lamb. In Truckee, I like Cottonwood (phone (916) 587-5711) for nouvelle cuisine in a rambling old roadhouse setting, the Left Bank for French specialties, and Jordan's Pacific Crest.

NORTHSTAR-AT-TAHOE DATA

Mountain Statistics

Vertical feet	2,280 feet
Base elevation	6,400 feet
Summit elevation	8,610 feet
Longest run	2.9 miles
Average annual snowfall	350 inches
Number of lifts	12, including 4 high-speed lifts
Uphill capacity	19,400 skiers per hour
Skiable terrain	2,420 acres
Opening date	mid-November
Closing date	mid-April
Snowboarding	Yes

Transportation

By car From Reno, 45 min. via I-80 to Truckee, then Route 267; from Lake Tahoe area, via Route 28 to Tahoe Vista, then Route 267 over Brockway Summit (7,200 feet); from Sacramento, 2 hours via I-80 to Truckee, then Route 267; from San Francisco, 4 hours via I-80 and Route 267.

By air Major carriers to Reno-Tahoe International Airport (33 miles).

Key Phone Numbers

Ski Area Information
   (530) 562-1010
Snow Report (530) 562-1330
Reservations (800) 466-6784
www.skinorthstar.com

SUGAR BOWL

Sugar Bowl is a trip back in time. Built in 1939 by an alliance of San Francisco socialites and Walt Disney, the Sugar Bowl Lodge remains a picturesque warren of dark, narrow corridors and stairwells, with warm, luxuriously appointed rooms and lounges, and, of course, a formal dining room. If I still entertained any hope of impressing my wife with my old-time courtly sophistication, I'd burrow in here for a few second honeymoon nights.

Part of the charm of the place is how you reach it. Sugar Bowl is the closest major ski area to Sacramento and the Bay Area (it's about three hours from the Bay Bridge), but you can't, strictly speaking, "drive in." Instead, you turn off I-80 at Soda Springs, cruise three miles up Old Highway 40, and pull into the parking structure on the right. Unload the car and climb on the old Magic Carpet gondola for a ride across the Union Pacific railroad tracks to the ski area.

Until 1994, this was the only way to enter Sugar Bowl. Now, with the opening of the Mount Judah expansion, a new access road lets you park right at the bottom of the Jerome Hill Lift and Mount Judah Express Quad.

Sugar Bowl is relatively small (1,000 acres, 1,500 vertical feet) but contains a nice variety of terrain for beginners and experts. The great attraction for most Sugar Bowl skiers is the quality of the snow. The whole Tahoe region is famous for monumental dumps and 40-foot snowpack, but Sugar Bowl gets more. Royal Gorge, a chasm 4,000 feet deep carved by the American River, points straight at the backside of the ski area and funnels Pacific storms so that the clouds spill right over the top of Mount Lincoln, Sugar Bowl's summit. The result is average snowfall of about 500 inches, or 41 feet. As you drive up Old Highway 40, look at the old houses along the roadside; they're all built with a second entrance on the upper floor or with a long wooden tunnel out to the road. The National Forest Service maintains its national snow research laboratory in town.

So Sugar Bowl is a good bet for powder skiing and a relatively easy drive during a moderate Sierra storm; coming from the Bay Area, you don't have to cross Donner Pass. If the road is open to Soda Springs, it's open to Sugar Bowl.

Sugar Bowl now has two separate base areas: Mount Judah and the Lodge. The Mount Judah side is simple: The Jerome Hill high-speed quad, named for the railroad heir who built the Magic Carpet gondola, and the Mount Judah Express quad serve 900 vertical feet of mostly intermediate cruising terrain (when groomed, these trails can tempt experts to maintain high-speed GS turns all the way down). To reach the main lift complex, turn right when getting off the lift and follow the easy *Pioneer Trail* to *Christmas Tree Lane;* this will put you at the Mid-Mountain Day Lodge, with access to Christmas Tree and Silver Belt lifts.

From the Lodge, most skiers ride the short Nob Hill fixed-quad lift; from there, turn right and descend to the Mount Disney or Crow's Nest lifts, both serving the 7,900-foot ridge of Mount Disney, or turn left and follow the cat track to the Mid-Mountain Day Lodge and Silver Belt Lift, a fixed-quad to the summit of Mount Lincoln (8,383 feet). Also accessible here is Christmas Tree Lift, serving mostly beginner and intermediate terrain.

To return to the Mount Judah base area, ride Christmas Tree Lift and follow *Harriet's Hollow* or *Jerome Bound* back to *Pioneer Trail.* From the top of Mount Lincoln, take *Bill Klein's Schuss* into *Harriet's Hollow.*

When the weather is good, I head straight up Silver Belt, named for the traditional ski race that used to descend through the *Silver Belt Chute* just under the summit and then dived down *Steilhung* (I raced in the very last Silver Belt race, held in 1989 during a classic Sierra blizzard, with no very distinguished result). The summit chutes *Fuller's Folly* and *The '58s* (named for the big avalanche of 1958) are short but genuinely hair-raising. The groomed runs off Mount Lincoln (*Shute One* and *Two, Crowley's,* and *Lake View*) are rolling, rhythmic intermediate challenges. Beginners should *not* go to the summit because there is no easy way down.

Christmas Tree Lift serves most intermediate cruising runs, with a couple of long easy beginner trails (*Sleigh Ride* and *Cat Walk*). Especially on *Cat Walk,* be careful of expert skiers exiting at high speed from the Mount Lincoln runs.

On a storm day, I head up Mount Disney Lift. From here you can turn left and ski the long steep East Face runs (*Sugar Bowl, East Face, Bacon's Gully,* and *Market Street*), all of which exit above the Mid-Mountain Day Lodge. Turn right and cruise the bowls and tree runs toward Crow's Nest Lift (*Disney's Nose, Avalanche, Eagle, Donald Duck, Pony Express*). Riding Crow's Nest on a powder day, you can find first tracks all day on *Montgomery* and *MacTavish* and in the woods alongside *Mad Dog* and *Overland.*

Best Beginner Skiing

If you're on the Village side, Nob Hill has the ski school and best practice terrain. On the Mount Judah side, the resort is adding a new beginner chair and expanding the learning area for the winter of 1999–2000. The nice thing about the lift network is that there are easy ways to get around the mountain between the two base areas and Mid-Mountain Day Lodge by using the Nob Hill, Christmas Tree, and Jerome Hill lifts.

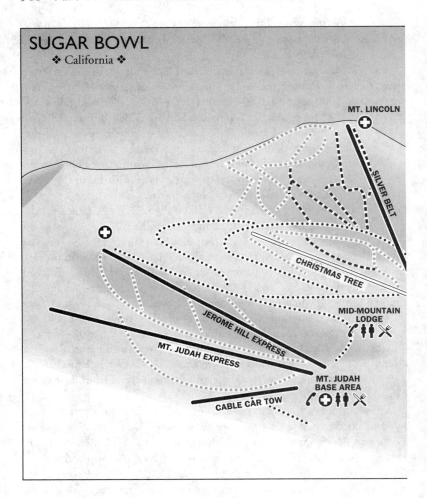

Best Intermediate Skiing

For challenge, try the eastern trails on Mount Lincoln (*Shute One* and beyond). For cruising, ski the Mount Judah runs.

Best Expert Skiing

For challenge, ski *Silver Belt* and *Fuller's Folly* on Mount Lincoln. For bumps, it's *Bacon's Gully*. For trees, go over to the glades alongside *Donald Duck* and *Crow's Face*.

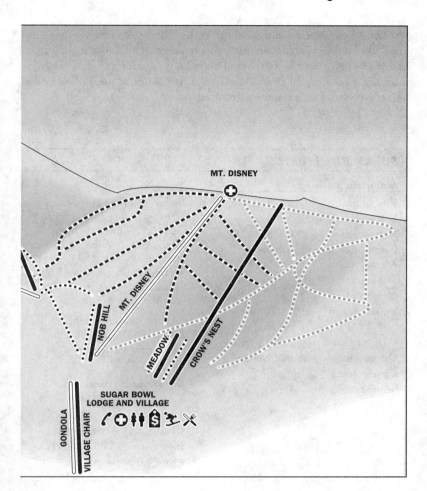

Convenient Lodging

Stay at the Sugar Bowl Lodge if you can possibly get in. Otherwise, stay in Soda Springs or Truckee (15 minutes east over Donner Pass; note that Old Highway 40 occasionally closes during the winter, so you might have to backtrack through Soda Springs and pick up I-80).

Best Eats

The only choice for dinner is the Lodge Dining Room, where gentlemen still wear jackets (ties are no longer required). You'll find standard ski-resort lunches, cafeteria-style, at the Main Lodge at Mount Judah, the Mid-Mountain Lodge, and the Village Lodge. Java Juice at the Village Lodge serves espresso, fruit smoothies, and fresh baked goods.

SUGAR BOWL DATA

Mountain Statistics

Vertical feet	1,500 feet
Base elevation	6,883 feet
Summit elevation	8,383 feet
Longest run	3 miles
Average annual snowfall	500 inches
Number of lifts	13
Uphill capacity	14,030 skiers per hour
Skiable terrain	1,500 acres
Opening date	mid-November
Closing date	April 30
Snowboarding	Yes

Transportation

By car From San Francisco, 3 hours via I-80 to Soda Springs, then Old Highway 40; from Sacramento, 1½ hours via I-80 to Soda Springs, then Old Highway 40; from Reno, 1 hour via I-80 to Soda Springs, then Old Highway 40.

By air Major carriers to Reno-Tahoe International or Sacramento Metropolitan Airport.

Key Phone Numbers

Ski Area Information
   (530) 426-9000
Ski school (530) 426-6770
Snow Report (530) 426-1111
www.sugarbowl.com

The Pacific Northwest

Mount Bachelor A big volcano with interesting, rhythmic skiing in nearly all directions from the summit, Bachelor has a swift, efficient lift system and snow that lasts until July. There's no base village; skiers stay in the lovely, relaxing town of Bend.

Crystal Mountain The great secret of Washington skiing—a big, wild mountain in the shadow of Mount Rainier, 90 minutes from Seattle. Crystal's steeps and tree skiing are world-class, the snow reliably deep but Northwest-sloppy. There is intimate rustic lodging but a limited nightlife.

Stevens Pass There is dependably exciting day skiing at Stevens Pass with easy fun cruising on the front side and a vast natural bowl out back to soak up the adventurous. There is no base village and no lodging accommodations.

Mission Ridge On the east side of the Cascades, Mission Ridge gets the lightest, driest snow in the Northwest. The area is rarely crowded, but the lift system is crude. Happily, it serves some classic terrain, with plenty of long cruisers and good, steepish chutes and tree skiing.

Whistler/Blackcomb The best for last—North America's biggest ski complex, in every way: extent and variety of terrain, vertical feet, and lift capacity. A modern, cosmopolitan village bustles all day and all night. Whistler Village, two hours north of Vancouver, rivals the great European resorts for sophistication and scenic grandeur. The mountains surpass everything else on this continent for sheer leg-burning scale and challenge.

MOUNT BACHELOR

Mount Bachelor ranks among the top ten resorts in the United States for skier visits, even without a lot of "destination" skiing by easterners. This fact may startle folks from back East, but it's a tribute to the fanaticism of Ore-

547

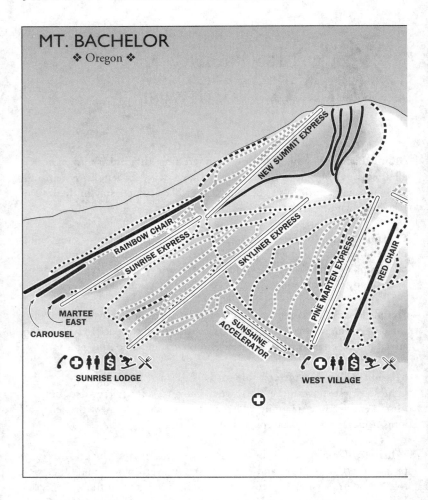

gon's hardbody locals, who can "Just Do It" until the mountain finally closes after the July Fourth weekend.

Not that destination skiing would be a bad idea. While Bachelor has no proper base area village, the tidy little city of Bend, 20 miles down the road, makes about as hospitable a vacation getaway as anyone might ask for. You can get to Bend via Highway 26 and 97 from Portland, via Highway 20 from the west or east, or Highway 97 from the south. From Bend, follow Century Drive Highway west and south out of town to the ski area. None of these roads develops any special traffic problem. Parking is free and close to the lodges. There's a free shuttle bus from the park-and-ride lot in town.

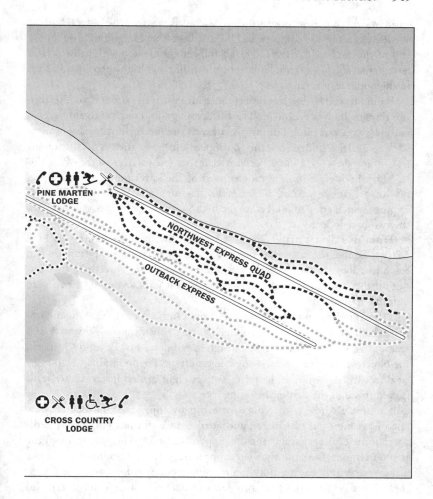

A dormant volcano whose forested, gully-etched lower slopes collect snow in six-foot drifts, Bachelor is one of a group of dramatic peaks (Mount Jefferson, Three Sisters, Mount Bailey) that makes central Oregon such a startlingly beautiful landscape. The upper slopes provide a geology lesson, bristling with cinder cones, plugs, and half-pipes that once roared with lava flows. Over half of the 3,365 vertical feet lies above timberline, and those broad slopes are a testing ground for high-speed skiing—every turn begs you to bank your skis against some lunar-landscape protuberance.

Bachelor is big—3,686 honest acres, with 13 lifts including 7 high-speed quads. The lifts fan out from the summit, making a full skirt around the entire northern perimeter of the cone. Access is via two base lodges, Sunrise at the east end of the complex and West Village Day Lodge a mile out at the end of the auto road. Each lodge is a full-service facility, with its own cafeteria, rental shop, ski school office, beginner lift, and high-speed quad access to the upper mountain.

From Sunrise Lodge, the fastest route into the trail system is via the Sunrise Express high-speed quad. The lift takes you 800 feet up to timberline, and here you can catch Summit Express to the top or hit the easy cruisers back to Sunrise Lodge. Another option would be to turn right off the lift and follow the *West Village Getback* road that crosses over to the West Village Day Lodge; en route it crosses most of the lower mountain runs; peel off down *Cliffhanger, Pat's Way, Chipper, Dentist,* or *DSQ* to reach Skyliner Express, which goes 1,600 feet up the hill to serve most of the trails between the two base lodges.

From the West Village Day Lodge, ride Pine Marten Express to Pine Marten Lodge, the large mid-mountain cafeteria. From this point you can reach just about any trail on the lower mountain, either directly or by turning off the *Summit Crossover* catwalk (Summit Crossover goes straight to Summit Express Lift).

Pine Marten also provides access to the Outback complex, which comprises half a dozen very long, rolling cruising runs dropping almost 1,800 feet and is served by the Outback high-speed quad lift. Beyond Outback, the Northwest Express quad—the longest lift on the mountain at 2,400 vertical feet (it's 1.7 miles in length)—serves eight gladed intermediate trails carved through the dense, sheltering forest.

Summit Express takes you to the top to enjoy the 360-degree view encompassing most of Oregon and northern California. Three intermediate fall-line cruisers parallel the lift. Experts can pick their way through the lava outcrops at the summit, then drop through the chutes into the *Cirque,* a vast steep amphitheater full of entertaining cones, ridges, and rills.

Storm days present fewer problems at Bachelor than at most exposed West Coast mountains. Because the six lower mountain express chairs end at timberline, they're sheltered from the wind. Roughly half the mountain's vertical and about two-thirds of its skiable acreage can be skied through all but the most severe storms. I've spent days messing up the powder drifted alongside the trees on the Pine Marten and Outback runs, and warming up every hour or so at the Pine Marten Lodge.

On busy days, Red Chair (paralleling Pine Marten) and Rainbow Chair (paralleling Sunrise Express) provide relief from crowds on the high-speed quads.

Best Beginner Skiing

Sunshine Accelerator is a high-speed quad exclusively serving easy learner terrain. Carrousel Lift, at Sunrise Lodge, is the other beginner lift. *Skyliner* and *Marshmallow* are long easy cruisers designed for beginners.

Best Intermediate Skiing

For the longest cruise, pick up *Healy Heights* or *Beverly Hills* from the summit and continue into *Carnival* or *Flying Dutchman* below timberline—the combination gives you well over two miles of nonstop skiing. Similar terrain can be found on *Cliffhanger, Chipper, DSQ, Kangaroo,* and *Ed's Garden*.

Best Expert Skiing

For challenge, try the steep and narrow *Summit Chutes* and (on the backside of the summit) *Cow's Face*. The *Cirque* is endlessly entertaining, steep, and narrow. For moguls, check out *Downunder West*. On a powder day *Boomerang* provides good pitch and deep drifts sheltered between the Outback forests. Those woods offer spectacular, deep powder on storm days.

Convenient Lodging

Your best bets are the Inn at the Seventh Mountain and Sunriver Lodge, both about 15 miles down the road. Sunriver has its own airstrip, a handy item if you happen to fly your own plane. Best Western Entrada sits halfway between the inn and the town of Bend.

Best Eats

On the mountain, all three lodges have good cafeterias. In town, my favorites include Cafe Paradiso (great continental cuisine), Honkers, serving American fare (watch the geese on the Deschutes River), the Deschutes Brewery (burgers and microbrew), and the picturesque Pine Tavern (traditional American).

MOUNT BACHELOR DATA

Mountain Statistics

Vertical feet	3,365 feet
Base elevation	5,700 feet
Summit elevation	9,065 feet
Longest run	2 miles
Average annual snowfall	325 inches
Number of lifts	13, including 7 high-speed detachable quads
Uphill capacity	Approximately 23,000 skiers per hour
Skiable terrain	3,686 acres
Opening date	mid-November
Closing date	July 4
Snowboarding	Yes

Transportation

By car From Eugene, 2½ hours via Route 126, then east on U.S. Highway 20; 3½ hours from Portland via U.S. Highway 26, then south on U.S. Highway 97; 6 hours from Seattle/Tacoma via I-5, then U.S. Highways 26 and 97; from northern California via I-5 to Weed, then north on U.S. Highway 97.

By plane Major airlines to Portland or United Express to Redmond, Oregon.

By bus Free shuttle bus from Bend.

Key Phone Numbers

Ski Area Information
  (800) 829-2442 or
  (541) 382-2442
Snow Report (541) 382-7888
Reservations (800) 829-2442
www.mtbachelor.com

CRYSTAL MOUNTAIN

Crystal Mountain is a 7,000-foot peak just east and a little north of Mount Rainier, literally in the volcano's evening shadow. Crystal shares Rainier's weather, pulling copious snow out of storms tracking in from the Gulf of Alaska. While Crystal's powder often falls al dente, the mountain provides plenty of pitch to keep expert skiers moving through it.

Crystal is also the best-kept secret in American skiing. Who would believe that you could take an area with 2,300 acres of skiable terrain, 3,100 feet of steep vertical, 10 lifts, and 30 feet of snowfall in an average year and hide it in such a way that folks in the Midwest and California have never heard of it? Crystal owes some of its obscurity to the fact that there are smaller Crystal Mountains in Michigan (375 vertical feet) and in British Columbia (600 vertical feet). Outside the lucky state of Washington, skiers may simply be confused.

Getting to the big Crystal means a 90-minute drive from either Seattle or Tacoma. To navigate from Enumclaw, pick up Route 410 to the east and climb this two-lane forest track along the Greenwater and White rivers until the road ends. Turn left and drive six miles up the ski area access road. During the winter months, Crystal is the only destination on this route, and the only traffic will be skier traffic. Carry chains for use on the steep access road. You can also ride the weekend bus from Seattle, Bellevue, Tacoma, Renton, and Enumclaw (call (800) 665-2122 for reservations).

The ski area sits below a ridge line that crests at four different places, making for lots of subsidiary ridges and intervening bowls to catch and shelter the powder. While the mountain is wild, with a potentially confusing diversity of bowls and chutes, the lifts are laid out intelligently. Most lower lifts—especially Discovery and Quicksilver at the head of the valley (to your left as you look up from the base lodge) are of a gentle to moderate pitch and are appropriate for beginners and low intermediates. The third lift here, Gold Hills, serves a broad intermediate slope designed for setting slalom and GS courses. The upper lifts, those going to the ridge line, serve mostly advanced and expert terrain, with a few long, rolling cruisers, but nothing appropriate for new skiers or even for hesitant intermediates. Two huge backcountry areas provide plenty of natural snow challenge for experts.

If Crystal has a drawback, it's the weather. When the weather is nice, the grooming crews turn the cruising runs into smooth carpets, and the views of Rainier and the surrounding Cascade ridges are superb. But when a three-day Gulf of Alaska storm rolls in, visibility in the bowls drops to nil in snow and fog. Experts revel in steep powder chutes and glades, but intermediates bog down in heavy Cascade concrete. You don't get 350 inches of snow in an average year without enduring storm cycles. I've talked with Seattle-area skiers who complain that in their years of skiing Crystal they've never seen the sun, and then there are others who swear the weather's always fine. The trick is to live in the Seattle-Tacoma area and to go skiing on the day after the storm breaks.

Parking is plentiful and free, but early arrivals get to park close in at the upper lot. The lower lots stretch away half a mile down the road, which means a ride on a shuttle or a long uphill trudge to the lifts. The base lodge climbs the hill, too—buy your lift ticket at the bottom of the steps before heading up toward the cafeteria and lifts, or you'll just have to cycle back later and start the climb over again.

The fastest way up the mountain is via the Chinook Express six-person chair, to the Rainier Express high-speed quad. This route puts you at Sum-

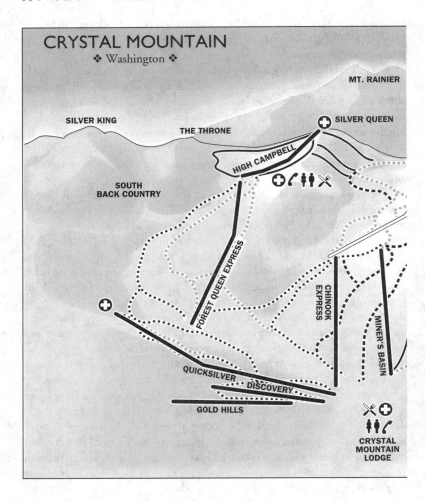

CRYSTAL MOUNTAIN
❖ Washington ❖

MT. RAINIER

SILVER KING

THE THRONE

SILVER QUEEN

HIGH CAMPBELL

SOUTH
BACK COUNTRY

FOREST QUEEN EXPRESS

CHINOOK
EXPRESS

MINER'S
BASIN

QUICKSILVER

DISCOVERY

GOLD HILLS

CRYSTAL
MOUNTAIN
LODGE

mit House, the mountaintop restaurant. Ski straight ahead into Green Valley, a big rolling bowl stitched with two groomed intermediate cruisers. Turn
right and follow the fast *Iceberg Ridge* into steep *Iceberg Gulch* (this shady,
sheltered gulley is often icy) or the long, steep plunges back to the base area
called *Bull Run* and *Exterminator*. The southeast face of the peak, on either
side of Rainier Express, is a broad collection of glades and bowls called *Last
Scream* (south of the lift) and *Sunnyside* (north of the lift, leading toward
Iceberg Gulch). There is a relatively easy intermediate run looping back to the
base of Rainier Express—the popular *Lucky Shot*. You can get there by turn-

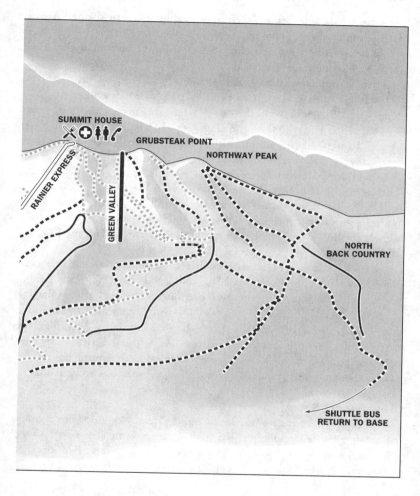

ing right when you get off the lift, following the ridge line about 100 yards, and cutting right to follow the cat track back under the lift. *Lucky Shot* meanders out into a broad bowl, then steepens briefly before the trees close in to funnel everyone back toward Rex. Watch for cross traffic just above the lift station.

The Green Valley runs collect at the bottom of Green Valley Lift, serving both *Green Valley* and the more secluded (and steeper) Snorting Elk Bowl. *Northway Ridge,* a cruiser, follows the area's northern boundary back to Green Valley Lift; as you ski it, check out the views into the North Back

Country bowls and ridges. Intermediates should return to the lift base; experts can continue down the ridge as it turns into the very steep *Right Angle*. Intermediates can exit Green Valley from the bottom of the lift via the long, looping *Kelly's Gap* road.

From the top of Chinook Express, take a left and follow the signs back to the Forest Queen. From here, three long intermediate cruisers (*CMAC, Magoo,* and *Downhill*), and the easy 3.5-mile *Queens* descend to the base arc. Above the Forest Queen, the *High Campbell* double lift goes to Silver Queen, Crystal's highest summit (7,002 feet), with truly steep expert shots into *Campbell Basin* (to the south of Grizzly Ridge) and onto the north face (north of Grizzly Ridge). When the snow is stable, experts can hike over the Throne into *Avalanche Basin* and *South Back Country.*

The Back Country areas are neither patrolled nor controlled. Don't bother going into either area unless you're confidently expert in natural snow, tight chutes, and trees; never go in unless avalanche danger is low, and never ski alone.

South Back Country terrain generally requires hiking to reach Avalanche Basin, Silver Basin, or the flanks of Silver King and Three Way Peak. Exiting the area means skiing the steep woods overlooking the head of the valley.

North Back Country is more accessible — just drop off Northway Ridge into Paradise Bowl, or make the short walk over Northway Peak to ski the farther bowl lines or the treelines below *Brand X.* You get back to the base area along the I-5 cat track or ski *Lower Northway* to the shuttle bus pickup that is about a mile down the access road. Buses run about every half-hour.

Best Expert Skiing

For high adventure, it's the Back Country areas. Hook up with a group of locals for expert guidance. For high-speed cruising, try *Green Valley, Downhill,* and (when groomed) *Iceberg Ridge* and *Gulch,* and *Bull Run.* For bumps, ski *Exterminator* and *Sunnyside.* For tree skiing, try the K2 Face.

Best Intermediate Skiing

The best of Crystal's intermediate skiing comprises *Green Valley, Lucky Shot,* and *Downhill.*

Best Beginner Skiing

New skiers train on *Discovery.* Novices can cruise *Quicksilver* and *Tinkerbell* on the Quicksilver Lift and *Queens* on Forest Queen. *Broadway* and *Skid Road* are easy ways down from Chinook Express and Miner's Basin lifts, but mind the fast traffic exiting the upper mountain, especially at lunch and closing hours.

Convenient Lodging

Crystal Village has only three hotels plus two small condo complexes. All are situated within walking distance of the lifts. For hotel reservations call (888) 754-6400; for condominium reservations, call (888) 668-4368. At the base of Crystal Mountain is Alta Crystal, offering chalet-style accommodations. For reservations, call (800) 277-6475.

Best Eats

At the base, there's the Silver Creek lodge cafeteria for breakfast or lunch, or for table service lunches, there's Sourdough Sal's on the top floor of the lodge. On the mountain, the Summit House (at the top of Rainier Express) serves pizza and pasta. For sit-down dining, there are restaurants at the Alpine Inn (continental, steak, and seafood).

CRYSTAL MOUNTAIN DATA

Mountain Statistics

Vertical feet	3,100 feet
Base elevation	4,000 feet
Summit elevation	7,012 feet
Longest run	3.5 miles
Average annual snowfall	340 inches
Number of lifts	10, including 1 high-speed detachable quad and 2 high-speed detachable six-person lifts
Uphill capacity	17,310 skiers per hour
Skiable terrain	2,300 acres
Opening date	mid-November
Closing date	mid-April
Snowboarding	Yes

Transportation

By car From Seattle or Tacoma, 90 minutes via Route 167 to the Puyallup area, then Route 410 east.

By bus Daily service from Kent, Auburn, and Enumclaw. Call the ski area for schedule.

By air Major carriers to Sea-Tac Airport.

Key Phone Numbers

Ski Area Information (360) 663-2265
Snow Report (888) 754-6199
www.skicrystal.com

When the Great Northern Railroad built its tortuous switchbacks up the Wenatchee River, over the pass, and down the Skyhomish, the deep snow made it nearly impossible to keep the tracks open in winter. In 1910, a nine-day blizzard triggered avalanches that swept two stalled trains into the river, killing 100 travelers. It still snows like that on Stevens Pass. January 1990, for instance, yielded 242 inches (20 feet!) in 31 days. In the course of that winter, the highway department cleared 191 avalanches off the road. In an average year, the place gets 415 inches of snow.

The ski area has been popular with Seattle day skiers since its first rope tows were strung after World War II. In the late 1980s, Stevens opened the vast Mill Valley area on its back side and transformed itself from a little intermediate hill into a major site for adventure skiing.

Stevens Pass now boasts 1,125 skiable acres and 11 lifts—major-league stuff for a day area with no lodging. Driving up U.S. Highway 2 from the Seattle-Everett area (about 90 minutes from Seattle), you get a queasy Twilight Zone sense that you've made a 3,000-mile wrong turn and wound up in New England. The town of Startup (where you start up the pass, of course) even has a white church and steeple. The misty weather, clapboard houses, and twisty two-lane roads are vintage Vermont. But look closer and the trees are unmistakably bigger, the rivers wilder, the verticals more profound than anything in the East.

At the ski area, a short hike from the parking lot takes you past a brand-new day lodge, completed in the summer of 1999. It features a food pavilion, a bar and lounge, guest services, and ticketing. The modern steel-and-glass, four-story base lodge is also up-to-the-minute, with spotless lounge areas and a first-class cafeteria featuring an unlimited variety of deli sandwiches.

The terrain is equally varied. The older lifts seem to have been placed haphazardly (you'll do a little climbing to reach one of the base stations), but it's nice that each lift serves a specific type of terrain. Three of the older lifts have been completely converted and redesigned; two have been converted into high-speed quads, and the Tye-Mill Lift has been changed to a triple chair with a redesigned loading area. Beginners will be happy on Daisy Lift, intermediates on the long Skyline and Brooks lifts, and experts on Big Chief and Hogsback chairs.

The front side of Stevens, with its eight lifts, is pretty good for mainstream skiing, with a nice mix of cut trails and some small glades. But the Mill Valley backside is a huge, wonderful bowl, cleared years ago of most of

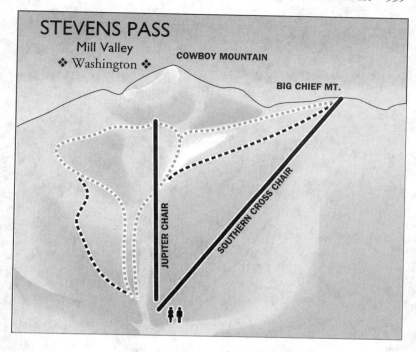

its hemlock and silver fir by a lightning-strike fire. Like Vail's backside, the bowl is roughly subdivided into drainages—*Corona Bowl, Pegasus,* and *Polaris*—with long hogback ridges between them.

My own favorite shots are along the perimeters. On the right side going down, the power-line cut called *Borealis* has exactly the same pitch as the wonderful clear-cuts you stumble across in Canada's Cariboos. On the left, the ski-area boundary follows Polaris Creek, a narrow gully into which the snow drifts deeply with each storm. The creek forms a perfect half-pipe. Bank off the sides or jump the right-hand edge onto Andromeda Face.

The backside is served by two long lifts, Jupiter and Southern Cross. Southern Cross is actually an extension of the frontside Double Diamond Lift. The cable runs from one terminal up over the summit and down to the other terminal. Everyone gets off at the top, regardless of which direction you're riding. Stevens Pass simply got two lifts for the price of one motor.

Best Expert Skiing

For challenge, ski the short, steep chutes off Seventh Heaven Lift, and several more off Double Diamond. For high-speed cruising, it's *I-5* and *Aquarius,* on the backside. For powder, it's all of Mill Valley after a storm.

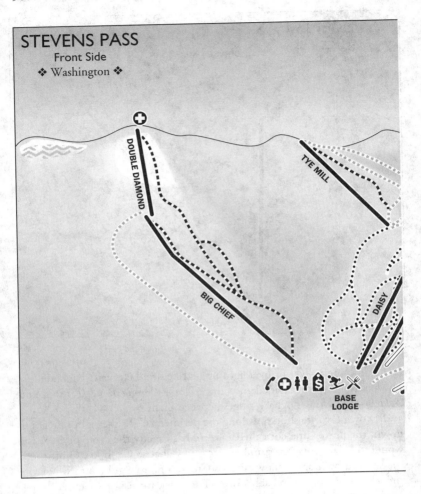

Best Intermediate Skiing

For long groomed cruising, try *Aquarius* in Mill Valley and the easy rolling trails along Barrier and Brooks lifts.

Best Beginner Skiing

You can find this on anything off Daisy Lift.

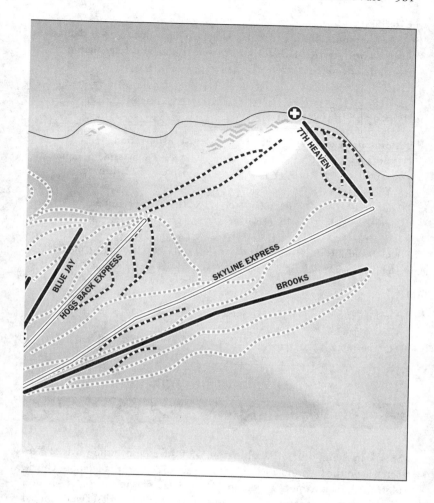

Convenient Lodging

There is none, but Leavenworth, a resort town with plenty of motels and some good restaurants, lies 34 miles to the east—the wrong direction for Seattle skiers. For folks from the city, it's usually easier to head home on Saturday night.

If you do opt for Leavenworth, try the Bayern Village Motor Inn, Der Ritterhof, or Obertal. The German names are not accidental—Leavenworth does its level best to look like a Bavarian village.

Best Eats

At the mountain, the new day lodge cafeteria does a great deli act. In Leavenworth, try Kristall's for family-style dining and Katzenjammer's for steak and seafood.

STEVENS PASS DATA

Mountain Statistics		Transportation
Vertical feet	1,800 feet	**By car** From Seattle, 90 minutes via Route 522, then west on U.S. Highway 2.
Base elevation	4,000 feet	
Summit elevation	5,800 feet	
Longest run	1.5 miles	**Key Phone Numbers**
Average annual snowfall	415 inches	Ski Area Information (360) 973-2441
Number of lifts	10	Snow Report (206) 634-1645
Uphill capacity	15,210 skiers per hour	www.stevenspass.com
Skiable terrain	1,125 acres	
Opening date	mid-November	
Closing date	mid-April	
Snowboarding	Yes	

MISSION RIDGE

Smack in the middle of Washington, 6,000 feet above the town of Wenatchee on the Columbia River, lies a horseshoe canyon called Squilchuck. Not much of a name. The ski area at the head of the canyon is Mission Ridge (nearby Mission Peak was named for the French priests who worked among the local Indians in the 1860s).

Bowls and glades cascade down both sides of the canyon from the 6,770-foot summit. Skiable vertical is a modest 2,200 feet, but the full vertical is skiable in a single, long, giddy run from most points along the three-mile circumference of the horseshoe. This means that the number of lines is nearly unlimited.

You can cruise the groomed trails that loop and bank up the lower walls of the canyon or traverse along the ridge and drop into broad, steep powder fields like *Bowl Four* or through the chutes of *Bomber Cliffs*.

Mission Ridge has only four chairlifts, but they fan out around the canyon to serve the entire 2,000 acres of terrain. Almost anything with snow on it is skiable here, a circumstance that tends to breed hard-core skiers. Scot Kauf, a former mogul pro champ, mastered his craft at Mission Ridge, and Bill Johnson, the first American to win a World Cup downhill, trained here en route to the U.S. Ski Team.

It's a 12-mile climb from Wenatchee and a three-hour drive from Seattle. The remote location puts Mission Ridge out of reach of all but those smart skiers who are determined to find good snow and uncrowded lifts. A typical Saturday draws about 2,500 skiers, and since the lifts haul 4,300 skiers per hour, the crowd can count on half a dozen runs before lunch.

Bomber Bowl is not named for Bill Johnson but for the Army Air Force B-24 Liberator that crashed here in rain and fog back in 1944. A hunk of the plane's wing is mounted on posts in Bomber Bowl.

A rollicking roller coaster, *Bomber Bowl* run skirts the base of Bomber Cliffs. If you know the terrain well enough to anticipate the landings off the numerous blind jumps, you can let your skis run. You can also turn right off *Bomber Bowl* and plunge down *Bomber Chutes* or *Ka-Wham,* all labeled as double diamonds. Locals consider *Nertz*—to the right of *Bomber Bowl*—one of the prime bump runs. The pitch—about 30 degrees—is just right, and it sits in full view of Lift 2 so that a knee-proud young *Nertz*-pounder will always have an audience.

On the east side of the canyon the big cruising runs are *Skookum, Toketie, Kiwa,* and *Tillikum.* They flow more or less parallel to Lift 3. These are the first runs to be groomed after a storm, so the ungroomed shots between them are the first target for powder moles. Most of the lower runs are flatter and easier cruisers or beginner terrain.

The Castle Face cliffs off Lift 4—and the area above Lift 4—offer some of the mountain's best skiing. Follow the ridge line eastward from the summit to *Bowl 4* and peel off the rim rock for the long, consistent blast to join up with the *Chak Chak* and *Sitkum* cruisers. But be aware that *Bowl 4* is technically out-of-bounds and is not patrolled. Check with the ski patrol before heading there.

The canyon gets an average of about 12 feet of natural snow each winter. That's only half of what they get at Crystal Mountain, which is some 70 miles by air to the west at the same elevation. But because Mission Ridge is on the eastern, desert-facing slope of the Cascades, the natural snow here is considerably drier and lighter than on the ocean-facing slope. It averages 10 percent density—closer in quality to Rocky Mountain fluff (6 to 8 percent) than to Cascade concrete (up to 15 percent). Powder heaven in Pacific terms.

Best Expert Skiing

For challenge, try *Bomber Cliffs, Chutes,* and *Ka-Wham* and the trees in *Central Park* and *Castle Peak Face.* For powder, ski *Bowl 4.* For bumps, it's

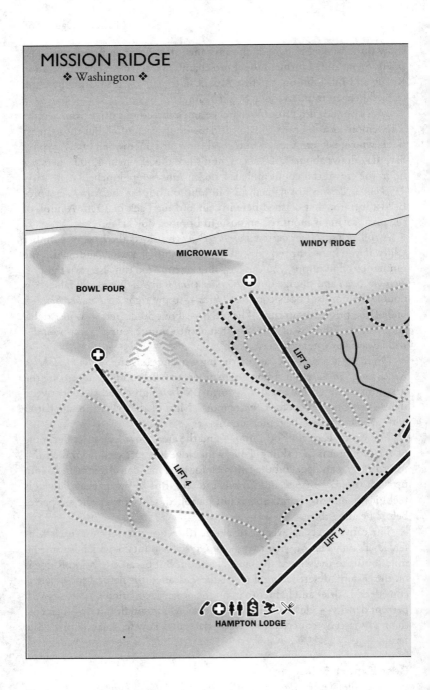

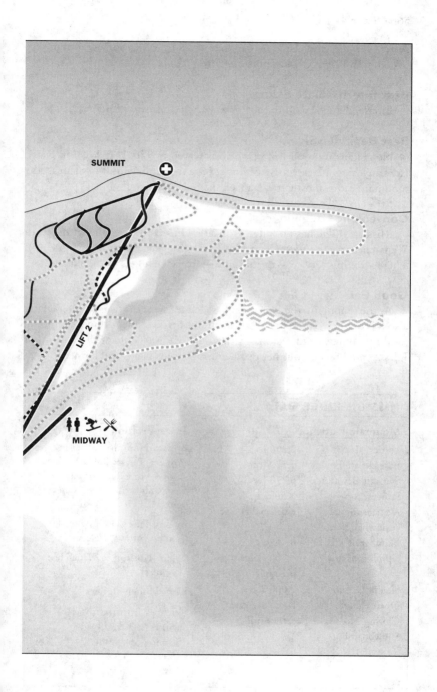

Nertz, Lemolo, and *Lip Lip.* For fast cruising on groomed terrain, try *Tillikum* and *Bomber Bowl* plus *Elip* into *Sitkum.*

Best Intermediate Skiing

Intermediates should try out *Bomber Bowl, Skookum,* and *Toketie.*

Best Beginner Skiing

New skiers train on *Mimi,* which is served by Lift 1. If Mission Ridge lacks anything, it's expansive beginner terrain—unlike most local areas, the mountain caters mostly to advanced skiers.

Convenient Lodging

Mission Ridge has no lodging on site. Out-of-towners stay at hotels in Wenatchee (try the West Coast Hotel, Travelodge, Cedars Inn, Rivers Inn). There's free bus service—the SkiLink—from the hotels to the ski area.

Good Eats

At the mountain, the Hampton base lodge serves the usual cafeteria fare; also located here is the Chair 5 Restaurant for sit-down dining, including local microbrews and regional wines. The Midway Cafe at the bottom of Lifts 2 and 3 serves gourmet pizza and soup, plus salads and barbecue.

MISSION RIDGE DATA

Mountain Statistics

Vertical feet	2,200 feet
Base elevation	4,570 feet
Summit elevation	6,770 feet
Longest run	5 miles
Average annual snowfall	estimated at 136 inches
Number of lifts	6
Uphill capacity	4,300 skiers per hour
Skiable terrain	2,000 acres
Opening date	late November
Closing date	early April
Snowboarding	Yes

Transportation

By car   From the Seattle/Everett area, 2½ hours via U.S. Highway 2 or I-90 to U.S. Highway 97, then Route 2; from Spokane, 3 hours via U.S. Highway 2.

By bus   Free weekend bus service from downtown Wenatchee.

By air   Horizon to Wenatchee (18 miles).

Key Phone Numbers

Ski Area Information
   (509) 663-6543
Snow Report   (800) 374-1693 or
   (509) 663-3200
www.missionridge.com

Stand between the base stations of the Whistler Village gondola and Black-comb's Excalibur gondola; they're only a few yards apart, and between them they can take you to more contiguous lift-served terrain than you'll find anywhere else in the Western Hemisphere.

Between them, Whistler and Blackcomb mountains, located two hours north of Vancouver, provide 7,000 acres of skiing; an even mile (5,280 feet) of vertical, a third of it above timberline; 32 lifts, half of them high-speed chairs and gondolas; four glaciers, with runs up to 11 miles long. Most of the lower mountain trails are laid out as endless intermediate cruisers; up top experts can find everything from hairball chutes and cliff bands to broad, gentle powder bowls. The complex is simply bigger than anything outside of Europe, and like the European resorts, it attracts a cosmopolitan crowd; on the lunch deck you'll hear French, Japanese, German, Italian, Chinese, and Korean, and, of course, English. The ski terrain is so vast that even a very good skier isn't going to see all of it in a week. The descriptions for these two ski areas are broken out into separate sections that follow this combined introduction.

Whistler Resort (the term includes Blackcomb Mountain) is also clearly one of the cleanest, most efficient, most pleasant places to ski on the planet. Part of the appeal is that Whistler Resort is new. The first lifts went in at Whistler Mountain in 1966, but construction really got rolling in 1980, when Blackcomb opened. By 1997 the village boasted over 102 hotel/condominium lodges, small pensions, and B&Bs, as well as over 96 restaurants and a dozen discos.

Most skiers get to Whistler by driving up Canada's Highway 99, the Sea-to-Sky Highway, from Vancouver. It's a 75-mile, two-hour trip (about five hours from Seattle counting traffic delays at the border), on good broad pavement with no mountain passes to cross. In good weather, the wonderful views across Georgia Strait toward Vancouver Island are distracting. Try to keep your eyes on the winding road. In bad weather, the road will be wet and possibly snowpacked, and, as everywhere in the Northwest, invisibly treacherous black ice is a possibility in spite of road salting. Mind your speed or the Mounties will. Canada posts speed limits in kilometers, and for some reason this baffles a lot of Murricans. Eighty kph is 50 mph.

Whistler gets daily train service from Vancouver, and there's hourly bus service from the Vancouver Airport.

Whistler Village sits at 2,000 feet above sea level, which is great for folks who haven't been doing their aerobic exercises. It means you sleep drenched in oxygen: none of those sleepless nights that distress sea-level lungs at 8,000 and 9,000 feet in the Rockies. By the same token, winter storms often bring rain to the village. Don't panic; this usually means snow a few hundred feet up the mountain. The summits get about 350 inches of snow a year—good, dense Gulf of Alaska snow that lasts through May. At this latitude (52 degrees north) winter days are short, so the lifts close at 3:30 P.M. Your legs will have given up by then.

As in a narrow Alpine valley, most of the Village lodges are within walking and skiing distance of the lifts. There's also lots of free parking within a couple of hundred yards of the base areas, but on busy days the lots can clot with traffic. My preference is to park the car at the lodge and rely on the shuttle buses, if only because there are too many bars between the trail's end and the parking lot at the end of the day.

Convenient Lodging

There is ski-in/ski-out lodging at Woodrun, Greystone, Chateau Whistler (Blackcomb), Delta Whistler, Powder's Edge, and Westbrook (Whistler Village).

Best Eats

Among the dozens of good restaurants, I've had great meals at La Rua (continental), Thai One On (Thai), and Monk's Grill (steak and seafood).

Whistler Mountain

Whistler Mountain has two base areas, each a village in its own right. The mountain shares Whistler Village with Blackcomb Mountain, and it has Whistler Creekside all to itself about four miles south down Canadian Highway 99 toward Vancouver. Day skiers from the city can avoid village traffic hassles by parking at Creekside.

From Whistler Village, the only route onto Whistler Mountain is via the Whistler Village Gondola, rising 3,800 feet to Roundhouse Lodge, a new 50,000-square-foot lodge with gourmet food and more than 1,700 seats (6,000 feet). The gondola is the second tallest lift in North America (only the Jackson Hole tram in Wyoming serves more vertical), and it goes only to the timberline, which is about two-thirds of the way up the hill.

You can reach Roundhouse Lodge from Whistler Creekside by riding the Creekside gondola to Mid-Station (about 4,300 feet) and then the Big Red Express.

The best bet for a newcomer to Whistler is to join one of the guided tours offered every day at 10:30 A.M. and 1 P.M. They meet at the Guest Satisfaction Centre at the Alpine lightboard.

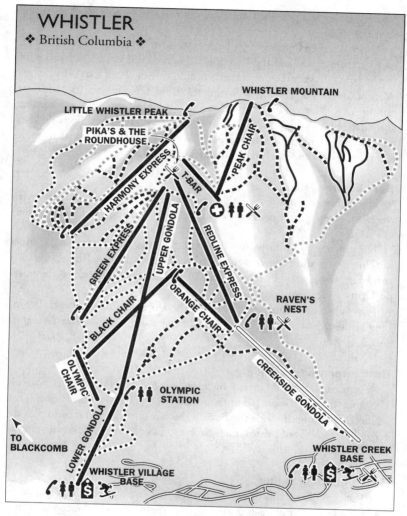

WHISTLER
❖ British Columbia ❖

WHISTLER MOUNTAIN

LITTLE WHISTLER PEAK

PIKA'S & THE
ROUNDHOUSE

PEAK CHAIR

HARMONY EXPRESS

T-BAR

GREEN EXPRESS

UPPER GONDOLA

REDLINE EXPRESS

BLACK CHAIR

ORANGE CHAIR

RAVEN'S
NEST

OLYMPIC
CHAIR

CREEKSIDE GONDOLA

OLYMPIC
STATION

TO
BLACKCOMB

LOWER GONDOLA

WHISTLER CREEK
BASE

WHISTLER VILLAGE
BASE

Most of the terrain below Roundhouse Lodge consists of broad, rolling intermediate cruising trails. You might expect to find wonderful tree skiing in this part of the world, but in fact it's a temperate rain forest—below timberline the trees grow so close together as to make the woods impenetrable.

A favorite high-speed cruiser for strong locals is *Franz's,* usually groomed like an undulating superslab for over three miles back to Whistler Creekside. Less ambitious skiers head for *Jolly Green Giant,* half as long, and cycle back to the top via the Emerald Express. There are even a couple of impossibly long beginner trails from Roundhouse Lodge—the easiest way down is via

Upper Whiskey Jack past the Green Express to *Olympic Run*—all the way to Whistler Village.

Above lies the High Alpine, a huge expanse of terrain served by the Harmony Express quad and the Peak quad. High Alpine consists of seven immense bowls. In general, only experts should ride the Peak into Whistler and West bowls. In good weather, Symphony Bowl offers plenty of gentle terrain for new skiers and is easily accessible off Harmony Express. Harmony and Glacier bowls supply a good mix of intermediate piste skiing and spectacularly varied natural-snow steeps. This part of the world contains many cliff bands, so ski with a level-headed friend.

Best Expert Skiing

For challenge, explore the couloirs at the top of Glacier and West bowls, the short steep chutes on *Harmony Horseshoes* and (especially in powder) *Waterfall.*

For powder and bumps, ski the sheltered *Boomer Bowl,* a huge funnel necking down into the trees; you get there from Harmony Ridge. *Seppo's,* a consistent fall-line shot under Black Chair, is nicely sheltered, so the powder drifts in deep for good storm skiing.

For high-speed cruising, blast down the aforementioned *Franz's.* Beginning at the top of Orange and Black chairs, cruise *Dave Murray Downhill* and *Bear Paw.*

Best Intermediate Skiing

Intermediates can ski up top on *Harmony Ridge* and the *Glades,* both off Harmony Express; below Roundhouse Lodge, try *Bear Paw* and *Franz's.* For an incredibly long run, ride the Peak to the summit (7,160 feet) and pick up *Highway 86.* It's about three miles back to *Franz's,* and then another couple to Creekside or the village.

Best Beginner Skiing

Most new skiers will train on Olympic Chair near the village gondola's Olympic station. But easy trails wind all the way from the top of Little Whistler Peak (6,900 feet), off Harmony Express. In good weather an athletic novice should be able to make the seven-mile run from the top via *Burnt Stew* and *Sidewinder*—it's an adventure. Beginners can also descend from Roundhouse Lodge via *Ego Bowl, Whiskey Jack,* or *Pony Trail.*

Best Eats

If you're driving up from Vancouver in the morning, grab breakfast on the mountain at Creekside. You can have lunch at Roundhouse Lodge, at the Raven's Nest Restaurant located at the top of the Creekside gondola, or at the Garibaldi Lift Company Bar & Grill at the village gondola base. For early birds, Fresh Tracks breakfast is served at dawn each day at the Roundhouse Lodge—you ride up the Whistler Village Gondola in the dark, pound down the all-you-can-eat breakfast, and hit the groomed trails ahead of the crowd.

Blackcomb Mountain

Newer and a bit taller than Whistler, Blackcomb Mountain offers a trail layout that lies more consistently in the fall line. The fastest way up the mountain is from Blackcomb Base—take the Wizard Express to Solar Coaster Express. Between them, the two chairs lift you 3,900 feet to Rendezvous at the timberline.

The other gateways to the mountains are at Whistler Village. Here, the Excalibur gondola rises only 1,600 vertical feet to the bottom of Excelerator chair. The new Village and Garbanzo lifts will also take you to the top. From the top of Excelerator, ski rolling cruisers down to *Solar Coaster,* but mind the high-speed traffic merging from *Black Magic* and *Sorcerer.*

From the top of *Solar Coaster,* you'll find some of the best rolling cruiser trails in the world. Appropriately, one of the finest is named *Cruiser;* it drops off the Rendezvous ridge and pours the full 3,900 vertical feet (about three miles) back to the base lodge. Another niftily rhythmic groomer is *Choker;* exit to *Slingshot* or *Gear Jammer* for the rush back to base, or rest while riding back to Rendezvous aboard Catskinner triple chair.

On sunny days, follow the *Expressway* or *7th Avenue* cat track around to the base of Blackcomb peak, where 7th Heaven Express chair serves a broad powderfield leading into half a dozen broad swaths through the thin woods at timberline. The skiing here is deluxe in springtime corn.

At the top of 7th Heaven, Horstman Hut perches on the spine of the mountain overlooking Horstman Glacier. Descend to the glacier via *Blueline.* The upper half of Horstman, served by two T-bars, is of consistently intermediate pitch, and it presents no special challenge except in flat light, when it's easy to become disoriented. Below Horstman T-bar, though, the routes down grow narrow and steep; you'll ski to one side or the other of the impressive cliff band called the Great Pyramid, then dive between the trees at timberline and pound bumps down to Glacier Creek. From here, pick up Glacier Express Lift and ride 2,000 vertical feet back to the glacier or ride Jersey Cream Express back to Rendezvous. You can also ride Crystal chair into a secluded network of half a dozen intermediate and advanced runs below the Crystal Hut restaurant.

The longest run on the mountain—some seven miles long—is *Blackcomb Glacier.* To get there, ride the Showcase T-bar at the head of Horstman

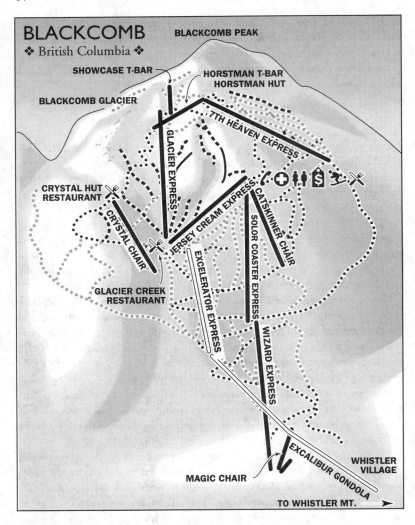

Glacier and pop over the back. *Blackcomb Glacier* beckons, half a mile wide. You'll descend a couple of thousand feet of easy intermediate skiing, then a short bit of steeper stuff at the foot of the glacier. At timberline, all the lines converge into an endless easy run-out through the woods, looping for miles back to Excelerator Express and the base.

Best Expert Skiing

For challenge, Blackcomb has its share of hairball experts-only terrain. Most famous is the *Couloir Extreme,* better known to locals by its original designation, the *Saudan Couloir.* The couloir starts at an honest 50-degree pitch and "flattens" after 50 meters to a more rational 40 to 45 degrees. You'll drop about 1,000 feet before the terrain rounds out at the bottom of *Jersey Cream Bowl.* Between storms, the couloir bumps out nicely with round long-ski moguls. To get to the couloir, follow the ridgetop down from Horstman Hut; the couloir will open on your left. Can't miss it.

If you skip the couloir and follow the right side of the ridge farther, it will bring you to Secret Bowl, ending in the chutes called *Pakalolo;* this is terrain for experts who leave their brains at home.

Here's some more terrain your mother warned you about: At the top of Horstman Glacier, you can traverse below the cliffs overhanging Glacier Express Lift and cross the ridge line via *Spanky's Ladder* into *Garnet, Diamond,* and *Ruby Bowls*—steep routes funneling among the cliff bands, about 1,500 feet of exhilarating descent to *Blackcomb Glacier.*

For high-speed cruising, try anything groomed along *7th Heaven, Catskinner,* or *Solar Coaster,* right down to the village.

For bumps and powder, ski the broad stretch below Horstman Glacier and the Heavenly Basin.

Best Intermediate Skiing

You can find the best intermediate skiing on the dozen long, rolling groomers alongside Solar Coaster, Excelerator, and Wizard chairs; or *Southern Comfort, Panorama,* and *Cloud Nine* on *7th Heaven;* or *Blackcomb Glacier.*

Best Beginner Skiing

New skiers train on Magic chair at the Blackcomb Base and can graduate to *Green Line* off Catskinner chair (*Green Line* is actually an easy cat track winding all the way from Horstman Hut to the bottom of the mountain).

Special Traffic Precaution

At the end of the day, everyone exits via *Lower Merlin's* (to Blackcomb Base) or *Village Run* (to Whistler Village). If you're nervous about being rear-ended, consider downloading on Wizard Express or Excalibur.

Best Eats

For on-the-mountain eats, there's the Wizard Grill in the Blackcomb Day Lodge. There are cafeterias at Glacier Creek and Rendezvous (Rendezvous also has a nice sit-down restaurant called Christine's), and good, hot soups are served at Horstman. Crystal Hut serves a 1950s-style menu including wood-oven-roasted vegetables, meat loaf, salmon or trout fillets, and fresh-baked fruit pies.

WHISTLER/BLACKCOMB DATA

Blackcomb Statistics

Vertical feet	5,280 feet
Base elevation	2,140 feet
Summit elevation	7,494 feet
Longest run	8.5 miles
Average annual snowfall	360 inches
Number of lifts	19
Uphill capacity	35,000
Skiable terrain	3,344 acres
Opening date	mid-November
Closing date	August
Snowboarding	Yes

Whistler Statistics

Vertical feet	5,020 feet
Base elevation	2,140 feet
Summit elevation	7,160 feet
Longest run	7 miles
Average annual snowfall	360 inches
Number of lifts	15
Uphill capacity	23,495
Skiable terrain	3,657 acres
Opening date	mid-November
Closing date	mid-June
Snowboarding	Yes

Whistler and Blackcomb lift tickets are a combined ticket, giving skiers dual-mountain access.

Transportation

By car From Vancouver, 2 hours north via Highway 99; from Seattle, 4 hours via I-5 to Highway 99.

By rail BC Rail from Vancouver daily.

By bus Maverick Coach Lines several times daily. Perimeter Bus service to Whistler Village hourly.

By air Major carriers to Vancouver International Airport.

Key Phone Numbers

Guest Relations (604) 932-3434
Administration (604) 932-3141
Snow Report (604) 932-4211
Reservations (800) 777-0185
www.whistler-blackcomb.com

Ski Tuning without Tears

Ski tuning is a little like going on a diet or getting more exercise. A lot of skiers know they should do it but somehow don't get around to it. I'm hoping that this simple explanation will do the trick, push you over the brink, and encourage you to get your skis tuned, then keep them in perfect, or near perfect, shape. Why bother? For the simplest of reasons. You'll ski better, much better, on well-tuned skis. Often, when I noticed that one of my ski-school students wore about the same size boot as I did, I would suggest that we trade skis for a run or two, just out of curiosity. Half the time I could barely make a turn on these skis which, at Vail, were often very expensive models, the latest Rossignols, K2s, and other top-of-the-line skis that I knew should ski wonderfully. The problem was always tuning, or rather lack of it.

Here's what happens to skis that makes tuning vital. Early in the season, alas, there are always rocks showing somewhere, poking through the snow cover like mines ready to grab your skis and gouge them. A few scratches and gouges aren't that bad, but often you'll get a scratch right alongside the edge of your ski. This makes that edge dig deeper into the snow. So the ski, at least when turning in one direction, tends to "rail in" and virtually refuses to turn. A lot of skiers simply adjust to this frustrating situation, hopping their skis a little, or generally "horsing" their skis around with a lot of extra body English. Those same early-season rocks can also bash the metal edges of your skis, creating big jagged burrs that catch in the snow and interfere with the smooth sliding and gliding of your skis. A burr on the inside edge of either ski can be enough to block or break the smooth sliding action of the ski in a turn.

And then there's the damage done by just plain skiing, continuous skiing, weekend after weekend, all season long. What happens is that the base of your skis wears down more in the center than it does near the edges. This happens all season long, but especially in granular spring snow conditions. The base then becomes concave or hollow. A ski in this condition is sometimes called a "railed" ski. This too causes the edges to grip excessively, hanging up the turn. What can you do?

The early-season state of your skis' bases is easy to monitor. Just run your fingers along the edges of your skis every time you take them off. They should be silky smooth to the touch. If you feel any jagged burrs, the remedy is dead simple. Just whip a small sharpening stone out of the pocket of your ski suit and rub it over the damaged edge (first parallel to the base, then parallel to the side of the ski). I'm not kidding. I always carry one of those little $2.50 Carborundum stones in my pocket until the snow gets deep and the rocks disappear in January or February. (By the way, an ordinary file won't take these burrs off your ski edge. The burr is "case hardened" from the heat of its contact with the rock, followed by the quenching effect of the cold snow. Only a sharpening stone can smooth out the torn edge.)

Long-term wearing down of the skis' bases (or the presence of a scratch or groove right next to an edge) demands more draconian measures. Take your skis in to the best tuning shop you can find (ask an instructor for a recommendation) and have them redo the bases completely. That means grinding the bases off smooth and flat with a high-tech base grinder (most likely made in Switzerland), and then touching up the job with a hand file to make sure the machine hasn't introduced any small burrs of its own. Unlike waxing, you only need to have your skis tuned a couple of times a season, not every week.

Is it worth it? You bet! A good ski tune-up by a real pro is probably the best bargain in skiing. I love to tune my skis by hand, and after years of practice I'm pretty good at it. But I can't do as good a job as one of the Montana base grinding machines that are now standard at most well-equipped shops. These machines can also put a so-called bevel on your ski edges. What's that? Beveling means that instead of the base being perfectly flat, it is filed to be a tiny bit convex—the opposite of the hollow or railed bases that you need to correct. The theory is that a slight bevel (1 degree or 1½ degrees) is enough to make the skis initiate or start turns more easily. And it works on most, if not all, skis. If beveling your skis is an option, ask the shop for a 1-degree bevel. Don't overdo it.

Of course, the shop will also wax your skis after tuning them. And you will feel like a new skier.

Index

1999–2000 Unofficial Guide Reader Survey

If you would like to express an opinion about your ski trip or this guidebook, complete the following survey and mail it to:

Unofficial Guide Reader Survey
P.O. Box 43673
Birmingham, AL 35243

Inclusive dates of your visit: _____

Where did you ski? Rate each ski area on a scale of 1 to 10.

_____   _____

_____   _____

How did you travel to the mountains? ❑ Air ❑ Car ❑ Train

Did you rent a car during your stay? ❑ Yes ❑ No
If yes, which rental agency did you use? _____
Rate the agency on a scale of 1 to 10 with 10 being the best: _____

Where did you stay on your most recent visit? _____

Concerning your accommodations, on a scale with 100 the best and 0 the worst, how would you rate:

The quality of your room: _____
The value for the money: _____
Staff helpfulness: _____
How long did you wait to check in? _____ Check out? _____

Please list any restaurants that you enjoyed and would like to recommend to our readers.

_____

_____

Hometown: _____ State: _____
Number of adults: _____ Minors: _____
Your age: _____ and Gender: M   F

Your skill level: beginner   intermediate   advanced   expert

Other comments about your ski vacation? _____

_____

_____

_____

_____